MICROECONOMICS

MICROECONOMICS

Second Edition

DOMINICK SALVATORE
FORDHAM UNIVERSITY

HarperCollins*CollegePublishers*

Executive Editor: John Greenman
Developmental Editor: Rebecca Kohn
Project Coordination, Text and Cover Design: York Production Services
Cover Art: Giacoma Balla. *Screen (with speed lines).* 1917. Oil on canvas. 151 × 126 cm.
  From the Beatrice B. Davis Collection, Kansas City, MO.
Production: Jeffrey Taub
Compositor: York Production Services
Printer and Binder: R. R. Donnelley & Sons Company
Cover Printer: The Lehigh Press, Inc.

MICROECONOMICS, Second Edition
Copyright © 1994 by HarperCollins College Publishers

Library of Congress Cataloging-in-Publication Data

Salvatore, Dominick.
    Microeconomics / Dominick Salvatore.—2nd ed.
      p.   cm.
    Includes index.
    ISBN 0-06-501377-8
    1. Microeconomics.   I. Title.
  HB172.S139   1994
  338.5—dc20   93-16020
                                                                      CIP

    94 95 96 9 8 7 6 5 4 3 2

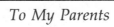

To My Parents

BRIEF CONTENTS

*Core Chapter

DETAILED CONTENTS

LIST OF EXAMPLES

PREFACE

I had three principal aims in writing this text: to present a judicial blend of the standard topics of traditional microeconomic theory and the many exciting recent developments in the field; to bring important but neglected international aspects into the course; and to devise a number of fresh, realistic, and truly useful examples that could vividly demonstrate modern microeconomic theory at work.

This is a text for modern undergraduate courses in intermediate microeconomics in economics and business programs. A prior course in principles of economics is required, and only simple geometry is used. There is an optional mathematical appendix at the end of the text for students who have had calculus.

The Modern Approach to Microeconomics

A unique feature of this text is that it presents not only the standard topics of traditional microeconomic theory but also the many exciting recent developments in the field. Most other texts either stress the traditional at the expense of the new and exciting or overstress the new at the expense of the traditional. The former texts sound old and tired and are backward rather than foreword looking. The latter texts, in their attempt to be new and trendy, throw away too much of what is traditional and useful. This text seeks to overcome both problems by presenting a judicial blend of all the useful, traditional topics as well as the most exciting recent developments in the field.

Some of the exciting new developments covered in this text are the learning curve, new pricing practices, contestable markets, experimental economics, new advances in game theory, financial microeconomics, the theory of public choice, industrial policies and firm competitiveness, the economics of information, and the efficiency wage theory.

International Dimension of Microeconomics

Another unique feature of this text is the introduction of an international dimension into microeconomics to reflect the globalization of production and distribution in today's world. Other microeconomics texts approach microeconomics as if the international economy did not exist. However, many of the commodities we consume are imported, and firms today purchase many inputs abroad and sell an increasing share of their outputs overseas. Even more importantly, domestic firms face more and more competition from foreign producers. None of these issues are reflected in current microeconomic texts, and I feel it is time to rectify such deficiencies by incorporating international ramifications throughout the intermediate course.

Modern microeconomics should deal with the effect of imports on domestic prices, the international convergence of tastes, technological progress and international competitiveness, minimizing costs internationally, the new economies of scale, dumping, immigration and domestic wages, domestic production and strategic trade policies, and other such topics.

Putting the Theory to Work

To introduce more current realism than most other microeconomics texts offer, this text includes three to five demarked examples in each chapter—not the usual tired examples but truly relevant and modern ones. These examples (75 in all) show how theory can be used to analyze and yield possible solutions to important present-day economic problems. My intention is to demonstrate that only by "putting theory to work" does theory truly come alive. Examples deepen understanding of the theory and enhance motivation by displaying the usefulness of theory in specific modern contexts.

Some of the exciting new examples are Gillette Introduces the Sensor Razor—A Truly Global Product; What Is an "American" Car?; General Motors Decides Smaller Is Better; How Xerox Lost and Regained International Competitiveness; The Market-Sharing Ivy Cartel; Wal-Mart's Preemptive Marketing Strategy; and An "Information Superhighway"? .

Other Innovative Features of This Book

I have tried to balance traditional topics with contemporary concerns in these ways:

- A new chapter discusses *game theory* (Chapter 11). This chapter is a clear introduction to advances that have been made in this field, and it provides significant insights into modern business behavior in oligopolistic markets. There is a discussion of the prisoners' dilemma, price and nonprice competition, threats, commitments, credibility, entry deterrence, repeated games, and strategic moves.
- A chapter on *market structure, efficiency, and regulation* (Chapter 12) examines the efficiency implications of monopoly, monopolistic competition, and oligopoly. It also evaluates the case for deregulation of economic activities.
- A complete chapter concentrates on *financial microeconomics* (Chapter 15). Financial microeconomics, in general, and the cost of capital, in particular, are of growing importance in today's world, but they are not covered in most other microeconomics texts.
- *The economics of information* (Chapter 18)—another important, modern topic—

is covered by a full-length chapter. The chapter deals with the economics of search, asymmetric information and adverse selection, moral hazard, market signaling, the principal-agent problem, the efficiency wage theory, and other topics.

- *Other important topics covered are:* the concept of the margin as the key unifying theme in all of microeconomics, the characteristics approach to consumer demand theory, the learning curve, the new economies of scale, two-part tariff, tying, bundling, limit pricing, cost-plus pricing, contestable markets, experimental economics, the theory of public choice, and effluent fees for optimal pollution control.
- *More advanced optional topics are covered (in chapter appendices):* consumer choices under uncertainty, index numbers and changes in consumer welfare, demand estimation and forecasting, Cobb-Douglas production function, extensions and uses of production and cost analysis, the Cournot and Stackelberg models, and others.

New to the Second Edition

- A new chapter on game theory (Chapter 11)
- A revised, single chapter on general equilibrium and welfare economics (Chapter 16)
- New or extensively revised examples (more than half; all other examples are updated)
- A new section on technological progress and international competitiveness (section 6.6)
- A new section on dynamic changes in costs—the learning curve (section 7.6)
- A new section on minimizing costs internationally (section 7.7)
- A new appendix to Chapter 7 on extensions and uses of production and cost analysis
- A new section on two-part tariff, tying, and bundling (section 9.7)
- A new appendix to Chapter 10: The Cournot and Stackelberg Models
- An extensively revised section (16.4) on perfect competition, economic efficiency, and equity, including a discussion of the first and second theorems of welfare economics
- A new section on the efficiency wage theory (section 18.7)
- Expanded mathematical appendix at the end of the text for students who have had calculus (mathematical footnotes are removed from the text in this edition)

Organization of the Text

The text is organized into six parts:

- *Part One* (Chapters 1–2) introduces microeconomic theory and reviews some principles of economics. This part shows clearly the importance and relevance of the international dimension in microeconomic theory and how it will be integrated into this text.

- *Part Two* (Chapters 3–5) presents the theory of consumer behavior and demand. It examines how consumers maximize utility and how an individual's and the market's demand curves are derived. It also shows the measurement and usefulness of the various demand elasticities.
- *Part Three* (Chapters 6–8) examines the theory of production, cost, and pricing in competitive markets. The international aspects of domestic production are shown throughout.
- *Part Four* (Chapters 9–12) focuses on the theory of the firm in imperfectly competitive markets. It brings together the theory of consumer behavior and demand (from Part Two) and the theory of production and costs (from Part Three) to analyze how price and output are determined under various types of imperfectly competitive markets.
- *Part Five* (Chapters 13–15) examines the theory of input pricing and employment (i.e., how input prices and the level of their employment are determined in the market). As in previous parts of the text, the presentation of the theory is reinforced with many real-world examples and important modern applications.
- *Part Six* (Chapters 16–18) presents the theory of general equilibrium and welfare economics, examines the role of the government in the economy, and deals with the economics of information. This part interrelates material covered in all the previous parts of the text.

   The nine core chapters are 1, 3–9, and 13. Additional chapters and topics may be emphasized at the discretion of the instructor.

Pedagogical Features

This text has been carefully planned to facilitate student learning using the following pedagogical features:

- The main sections of each chapter are numbered for easy reference, and longer sections are broken into two or more subsections.
- All of the graphs and diagrams are carefully explained in the text and then summarized briefly in the captions.
- Diagrams are generally drawn on numerical scales with background grids to allow the reading of answers in actual numbers rather than simply as distances. Consistent, judicious use of color and shading in the illustrations aid student understanding.
- No calculus is used in the text but an extensive (and optional) Mathematical Appendix is given at the end of the book.
- A glossary of important terms is given at the end of the text.

Each chapter also contains the following teaching aids:

- Key terms are boldfaced when they are first introduced and are listed at the end of each chapter; definitions, arranged alphabetically, are provided in the Glossary at the end of the text.

- A Summary reviews the main points covered in the chapter.
- Twelve Review Questions help the student remember the material covered in the chapter.
- Twelve Problems ask students to actually apply and put to use what they learned from the chapter. Answers to selected problems, marked by an asterisk (*), are provided at the end of the book for the type of quick feedback that is so essential to effective learning.

Accompanying Supplements

The following ancillaries are available for use with this book:

1. A substantial *Instructor's Manual*, written by the text author, is available. It includes chapter objectives, lecture suggestions, detailed answers to all end-of-chapter questions and problems, a set of 25 multiple-choice questions and answers for each chapter that I personally feel cover the most important ideas in each chapter. The *Manual* also includes *additional examples and problems* (with answers) for class discussions and/or examinations. Finally, there is an annotated list of *Supplementary Readings* with references on the various topics covered in each chapter. The *Manual* was prepared with as much care as the text itself.
2. A separate *Test Bank*, prepared by Professor Michael Morgan of the College of Charleston, contains nearly 1,000 multiple-choice questions with answers and is available to adopters of the text. This comprehensive *Test Bank*, more extensive than that of any competing text, is also available in computerized form for custom test-making on IBM PCs, the Macintosh, and compatibles.
3. Key figures and tables in the text—92 of them—are reproduced as *Transparency Acetates* and are available to adopters. In addition, *all other* figures and tables in the text are available as *Transparency Masters*.
4. A *Study Guide*, prepared by Professor James Pinto of Northern Arizona University, is available from HarperCollins to assist students in text content review and practice. It provides, for each text chapter, an annotated chapter outline, 30 or more multiple-choice questions with answers, 3 solved demonstration problems, and 10 problems to be worked out by students with answers.
5. A *Problem-Solving Software Program*, created by Professor Brooker of Gannon University, allows student practice with particular microeconomics problems, many with graphs. The software program also lists all problems in the text itself that can be worked using the software diskette.

Acknowledgments

This text grew out of the undergraduate and graduate courses in microeconomics that I have been teaching at Fordham University during the past 20 years. I was very fortunate to have had many excellent students who, with their questions and comments, have contributed much to the clarity of exposition of this text.

I owe a great intellectual debt to my brilliant former teachers: William Baumol (New York and Princeton Universities), Victor Fuchs (Stanford University and National Bureau of Economic Research), Jack Johnston (University of California), and Lawrence Klein (University of Pennsylvania and Wharton School of Business). It is incredible how many of the insights that one gains as a superb economist's student live on for the rest of one's life.

Many of my colleagues in the Department of Economics at Fordham University made numerous comments that significantly improved the final product. Professors Joseph Cammarosano and Lee Redding in particular read through the entire manuscript and made invaluable notes for improvements. Many valuable suggestions were also made by Clive Daniel, Edward Dowling, James Heilbrun, William Hogan, and David Horning. My former colleague, Frank Fabozzi, now a visiting professor at the Sloan School of Management at MIT, also made valuable suggestions.

The following professors reviewed the second edition of this text and made many valuable suggestions for improvements:

Richard Ballman
Augustana College

Joseph Barr
Framingham State College

William Beaty
Tarelton State University

William Buchanan
University of Texas-Permian Basin

John Cochran
Metropolitan State College

G. R. Ghorashi
Stockton State College

Ralph O. Gunderson
University of Wisconsin-Oshkosh

John D. Harford
Cleveland State University

Andy Harvey
St. Mary's University

Paul M. Hayashi
The University of Texas-Arlington

Thomas R. Ireland
University of Missouri-St. Louis

H. A. Jafri
Tarleton State University

Janet Koscianski
Shippensburg University

Vani Kotcherlakota
University of Nebraska-Kerney

Jessica McGraw
University of Texas at Arlington

Kathryn Nantz
Fairfield University

Edward O'Relley
North Dakota State University

Paul Okello
University of Texas at Arlington

Ray Pepin
Stonehill College

Martin Richardson
Georgetown University

Timothy P. Roth
University of Texas-El Paso

Anne E. Winkler
University of Missouri-St. Louis

H. A. Zavareei
West Virginia Institute of Technology

The following professors reviewed the first edition and this book and their numerous and excellent comments that resulted in a much improved text:

Mary Acker
Iona College

Taeho Bark
Georgetown University

Gordon Bennett
University of Southern Florida

Charles Berry
University of Cincinnati

Joseph Brada
Arizona State University

Charles Breeden
Marquette University

Robert Brooker
Gannon University

Elizabeth Erikson
University of Akron

Reza Ghorashi
Stockton College of New Jersey

James Giordano
Villanova University

Paulette Graziano
University of Illinois

Ralph Gunderson
University of Wisconsin-Oshkosh

Simon Hakim
Temple University

Mehdi Haririan
Bloomsburgh University of Pennsylvania

Roy Hensley
University of Miami

Joseph Jadlow
Oklahoma State University

Joseph Kiernin
Fairleigh Dickinson University

W. E. Kuhn
University of Alabama

Louis Lopilato
Mercy College

Mike Magura
University of Toledo

Larry Mielnicki
New York University

Stephen Miller
University of Connecticut

Thomas Mitchell
Southern Illinois University-Carbodale

Peter Murrell
University of Maryland

Felix Ndukwe
Lafayette College

Patricia Nichol
Texas Tech University

Lee Norman
Idaho State University

Patrick O'Sullivan
State University of New York-Old Westbury

Donal Owen
Texas Tech University

Howard Ross
Baruch College

Timothy P. Roth
University of Texas at El Paso

Siamack Shojai
Manhattan College

Philip Sorensen
Florida State University

Charles Stuart
University of California-Santa Barbara

Michael Szenberg
Pace University

Allen Wilkins
University of Wisconsin-Madison

Greg Winczewski
Saint Peter's College

Finally, I would like to express my gratitude to Rebecca Kohn for her outstanding development effort and to the entire staff of HarperCollins, especially John Greenman, for his truly expert assistance throughout this project. My thanks also go to Angela Bates and Marie Sundberg (the department secretaries at Fordham University) for their efficiency and cheerful dispositions.

Dominick Salvatore

About the Author

Dominick Salvatore is Professor of Economics at Fordham University, where he was Department Chairman from 1982 to 1988. He is Co-Chairman of the New York Academy of Sciences, Chairman of the Society for Policy Modeling, and consultant to the Economy Policy Institute in Washington, the United Nations, and the World Bank.

Professor Salvatore is the author of more than 30 books, among which are *Managerial Economics in a Global Economy*, 2nd edition (1993) and *International Economics*, 4th edition (1993). He has also written the Schaum's Outline in *Microeconomics*, 3rd edition (1992), which was translated in ten languages and sold more than one-half million copies.

Professor Salvatore is the editor of the *Handbook Series in Economics* for the Greenwood Press. He is Co-Editor of the *Journal of Policy Modeling* and *Open Economies Review*, and Associate Editor of the *American Economist* (the Journal of the International Honor Society in Economics). His research has been published in more than 80 articles in leading scholarly journals and presented at numerous national and international conferences.

INTRODUCTION TO MICROECONOMICS

Part One (Chapters 1 and 2) presents an introduction to microeconomic theory and a review of some basic tools of economics. Chapter 1 deals with scarcity as the fundamental economic fact facing every society and examines the function and purpose of microeconomic theory and its methodology. Chapter 1 also introduces the concept of the margin as the central unifying theme in microeconomics and examines the importance of introducing an international dimension in microeconomic analysis. Chapter 2 is a brief review of the concepts of demand, supply, equilibrium, and elasticities. In addition, the chapter examines the benefits and costs resulting from the growing interdependence of the United States in the world economy.

1

INTRODUCTION

Microeconomic theory is perhaps the most important course in all economics and business programs. Microeconomic theory can help us answer such questions as why there is a trade-off between spending on defense and spending on social programs; why the price of housing has risen sharply in recent years; why the price of beef is higher than the price of chicken; why the price of gasoline rose sharply during the 1970s and declined in the 1980s; why textiles are produced with much machinery and few workers in the United States but with many workers and a small amount of machinery in India; why there are only a handful of automakers but many wheat farmers in the United States; why the courts ordered the breakup of AT&T in 1982; why physicians earn more than cab drivers and college professors; why raising the minimum wage leads to increased youth unemployment; why environmental pollution arises and how it can be regulated; why the government provides some goods and services such as national defense. Microeconomic theory provides the tools for understanding how the U.S. economy and most other economies operate.

Microeconomic theory is also the basis for most "applied" fields of economics such as industrial economics, labor economics, natural resources and environmental economics, agricultural economics, regional economics, public finance, development economics, and international economics.

In this introductory chapter, we define the subject matter and the methodology of microeconomics. We begin by examining the meaning of scarcity as the fundamental economic fact facing every society. We then discuss the basic economic functions that all economic systems must somehow perform and the way they are performed in a free-enterprise economic system such as our own. We also examine why the concept of the margin is the central unifying theme in microeconomics and the importance of introducing an international dimension into microeconomic analysis. Subsequently, we examine the role of theory or models in microeconomics, discuss the basic methodology of economics, and distinguish between positive and normative economics.

1.1 WANTS AND SCARCITY

According to the usual definition, **economics** deals with the allocation of scarce resources among alternative uses to satisfy human wants. The essence of this definition rests on the meaning of human wants and resources and on the scarcity of economic resources in relation to insatiable human wants.

Can Human Wants Ever Be Fully Satisfied?

Human wants refer to all the goods, services, and conditions of life that individuals desire. These wants vary among different people, over different periods of time, and in different locations. However, human wants always seem to be greater than the goods and services available to satisfy them. Although we may be able to get all we desire of hamburgers, beer, pencils, and magazines, there are always more and better things that we are unable to obtain. In short, the sum total of all human wants can never be fully satisfied.

    Economic resources are the inputs, the factors, or the means of producing the goods and services we want. They can be classified broadly into *land* (or natural resources), *labor* (or human resources), and *capital*. These are the resources that firms must pay to hire. Land refers to the fertility of the soil, the climate, the forests, and the mineral deposits present in the soil. Labor refers to all human effort, both physical and mental, that can be directed toward producing desired goods and services. It includes entrepreneurial talent that combines other labor, capital, and natural resources to produce new, better, or cheaper products. Finally, capital refers to the machinery, factories, equipment, tools, inventories, irrigation, and transportation and communications networks. All of these "produced" resources greatly facilitate the production of other goods and services. In the economist's sense, money is not capital because it does not produce anything. Money simply facilitates the exchange of goods and services.

Scarcity: The Pervasive Economic Problem

Resources have alternative uses. For example, a particular piece of land could be used for a factory, housing, roads, or a park. A laborer could provide cleaning services, be a porter, construct bridges, or provide other manual services. A student could be trained to become an accountant, a lawyer, or an economist. A tractor could be used to construct a road or a dam. Steel could be used to build a car or a bridge. Because economic resources are limited, they command a price. While air may be unlimited and free for the purpose of operating an internal-combustion engine, *clean* air to breathe is not free if it requires the installation and operation of antipollution equipment.

    Because resources are generally limited, the amount of goods and services that any society can produce is also limited. Thus, it must choose which commodities to produce and which to sacrifice. In short, society can only satisfy some of its wants. If human wants were limited or resources unlimited, there would be no scarcity and there would be no need to study economics.

Over time, the size and skills of the labor force rise, new resources are discovered and new uses are found for available land and natural resources, the nation's stock of capital is increased, and technology improves. Through these advances, the nation's ability to produce goods and services increases. But human wants always seem to move well ahead of society's ability to satisfy them. Thus, scarcity remains. Scarcity is the fundamental economic fact of every society (see Example 1).

Example 1

Fewer Guns Could Mean a Lot More Butter

With the collapse of communism in the former Soviet Union and its virtual removal as a military threat, the United States could reap a sizable "peace dividend"; that is, U.S. military expenditures (which in 1990 were 26% of the government's total budget) could be reduced sharply and be redirected toward the private sector and other forms of government spending to stimulate growth. Over a decade, the savings from military expenditures could amount to as much as $150 billion per year. Growth would also be stimulated by gradually redeploying toward civilian uses the 30% of all scientists and engineers now employed in defense-related research and production.

There are already many conflicting claims on such a potential peace dividend. Some want to use the money to help the Eastern European countries and the former Soviet republics restructure their economies to promote democracy. Others want to use it to improve health, education, and infrastructure in this country. Still others want to use it to reduce the immense federal deficit; this would reduce public borrowing, lower interest rates, and stimulate housing and other private investments.

Some think use of the peace dividend to improve health, education, and infrastructure would increase long-term national growth considerably. For example, a billion dollars could provide comprehensive prenatal care to an additional 1.5 million poor pregnant women or add 400,000 children to the Head Start program. It has been estimated that each dollar spent on Head Start saves almost $5 in welfare, remedial education, and other costs later. Improving infrastructure would also be productive. According to the Federal Transportation Department, urban areas waste 2 billion hours a year on highway delays. Flight delays at 21 primary airports amount to 20,000 hours per year. The peace dividend could be used to overcome these bottlenecks and promote long-term national growth.

Source: "$150 Billion a Year—How to Spend It," *New York Times,* March 9, 1990, p. 34; "The Defense Whizzes Making It in Civvies," *Business Week,* September 7, 1992, pp. 88–90; and "The Peace Dividend's Collateral Damage," *New York Times,* September 13, 1992, p. E1.

1.2 FUNCTIONS OF AN ECONOMIC SYSTEM

Faced with the pervasiveness of scarcity, all societies, from the most primitive to the most advanced, must somehow determine (1) what to produce, (2) how to produce, (3) for whom to produce, (4) how to provide for the growth of the system, and (5) how to ration a given quantity of a commodity over time. Let us see how the **price system** performs each of these functions under a free-enterprise system (such as our own). In a **free-enterprise system** individuals own property and individuals and firms make private economic decisions.

What to produce refers to which goods and services to produce and in what quantities to produce them. No society can produce all the goods and services it wants, so it must choose which to produce and which to forgo. Over time, only those goods and services for which consumers are willing and able to pay a price sufficiently high to cover at least the costs of production will generally be produced. Automobile manufacturers will not produce cars costing $1 million if no one is there to purchase them. Consumers can generally induce firms to produce more of a commodity by paying a higher price for it. On the other hand, a reduction in the price that consumers are willing to pay for a commodity will usually result in a decline in the output of the commodity. For example, an increase in the price of milk and a reduction in the price of eggs are signals to farmers to raise more cows and fewer chickens.

How to produce refers to the way in which resources or inputs are organized to produce the goods and services that consumers want. Should textiles be produced with a great deal of labor and little capital or, alternatively, with little labor and a great deal of capital? Since the prices of resources reflect their relative scarcity, firms will combine them in such a way as to minimize costs of production. By doing so, they will use resources in the most efficient and productive way to produce those commodities that society wants and values the most. When the price of a resource rises, firms will attempt to economize on the use of that resource and substitute cheaper resources so as to minimize their production costs. For example, a rise in the minimum wage leads firms to substitute machinery for some unskilled labor.

For whom to produce deals with the way that the output is distributed among the members of society. Those individuals who possess the most valued skills or own a greater amount of other resources will receive higher incomes and will be able to pay and coax firms to produce more of the commodities they want. Their greater monetary "votes" enable them to satisfy more of their wants. For example, society produces more goods and services for the average physician than for the average clerk because the former has a much greater income than the latter.

In all but the most primitive societies there is still another function that the economic system must perform: it must provide for the growth of the nation over time. Although governments can affect the rate of **economic growth** with tax incentives, and with incentives for research, education, and training, the price system is also important. For example, interest payments provide the savers an incentive to postpone present consumption, thereby releasing resources to increase society's stock of capital goods. Capital accumulation and technological improvements are stimulated by the expectations of profits. Similarly, the incentive of higher wages (the price of labor services) induces people to acquire more training and education, which increases their productivity. Through capital accumulation, technological improvements, and increases in the quantity and quality (productivity) of labor, a nation grows over time.

Finally, an economic system must allocate a given quantity of a commodity over time. **Rationing over time** is also accomplished by the price system. For example, the price of wheat is not so low immediately after harvest that all the wheat is consumed very quickly, thus leaving no wheat for the rest of the year. Instead, some people (speculators) will buy some wheat soon after harvest (when the price is low) and sell it later (before the next harvest) when the price is higher; the available wheat is thus rationed throughout the year.

1.3 MICROECONOMIC THEORY AND THE PRICE SYSTEM

In this section, we define the subject matter of microeconomic theory, briefly examine the determination and function of prices in a system of free enterprise, and show how governments affect the operation of the economic system.

The Circular Flow of Economic Activity

Microeconomic theory studies the economic behavior of *individual* decision-making units such as individual consumers, resource owners, and business firms and the operation of individual markets in a free-enterprise economy. This contrasts with **macroeconomic theory,** which studies the total or *aggregate* level of output and national income and the level of national employment, consumption, investment, and prices for the economy *viewed as a whole*. Both microeconomics and macroeconomics provide useful tools of analysis, and both are important. While macroeconomics often makes the headlines, microeconomics attempts to explain some of the most important economic and social problems of the day. These range from environmental pollution, welfare programs, rent control, minimum wages, safety regulations, rising medical costs, monopoly, discrimination, and labor unions to wages and leisure, crime and punishment, taxation and subsidies, and so on. Microeconomics focuses attention on two categories of economic units: households and business firms. And it examines the operation of two types of markets: the market for goods and services and the market for economic resources.

The interaction of households and business firms in the markets for goods and services and in the markets for economic resources represents the core of the free-enterprise economic system. Specifically, households own the labor, the capital, the land, and the natural resources that business firms require to produce the goods and services households want. Business firms pay households wages, salaries, interest, rents, and so on for the services and resources that households provide. Households then use the income that they receive from business firms to purchase the goods and services produced by business firms. The incomes of households are the production costs of business firms. The expenditures of households are the receipts of business firms. The **circular flow of economic activity** is complete.

Determination and Function of Prices

The prices of goods and services are determined in the markets for goods and services, whereas the prices of resources and their services are determined in the markets for resources. If households want to purchase more of a commodity than is placed on the market by business firms, the price of the commodity will be bid up until the *shortage* of the commodity is eliminated. This occurs because at a higher price households will want to *purchase less* of the commodity while business firms will want to *produce more* of the commodity. For example, if automobile prices rise, consumers will want to purchase fewer automobiles while automakers will want to produce more automobiles. Automakers can produce more automobiles at higher prices because they are able to bid resources (labor, capital, and land) away from other uses.

On the other hand, if households want to purchase less of a commodity than business firms place on the market, the price of the commodity will fall until the *surplus* of the commodity disappears. This occurs because at a lower price households will want to *purchase more* of the commodity while business firms will want to *produce less* of the commodity. For example, if consumers want to purchase less beef than farmers send to market, the price of beef will fall until the quantity demanded of beef matches the quantity supplied. In the process, farmers will hire fewer resources, so that some resources will be freed to produce more of other commodities that consumers value more highly. Thus, it is the system of commodity prices that determines which commodities are produced and in what quantities (the "what to produce" question of the previous section) and how resources are used.

Turning to factor markets, or the market for economic resources, if households provide less of a resource or service than business firms want to hire at a given price, the price of the resource will be bid up until the shortage of the resource is eliminated. This occurs because at higher resource prices, households usually provide more of a resource or service while business will try to use less of it to minimize production costs. For example, if hospitals want to hire more nurses than are available, nurses' salaries rise. This results in more people entering nursing schools and in hospitals finding less expensive substitutes for nurses, such as orderlies or nurses' aides, until the adjustment (i.e., the shortage of nurses) is eliminated.[1]

---

[1]The shortage of nurses may last many years if the demand for hospital care and for nurses outstrips the increasing number of nurses being trained or if market imperfections and government licensing restrictions prevent wages from rising to the equilibrium level. This is what seems to have happened, in fact, in many areas of the United States.

On the other hand, if too much of a resource is made available at a given price, the price falls until the surplus is eliminated. This occurs because at lower resource prices households usually provide less of the resource or service, while business firms will substitute the cheaper resource for the more expensive one. Thus, in a free-enterprise economy, the system or resource prices determines how production is organized and establishes the income of resource owners (the "how to produce" and the "from whom to produce" questions of the previous section).

Microeconomic theory is often referred to as **price theory** because of the crucial function of prices in determining what goods are produced and in what quantities, how production is organized, and how income and output are distributed.[2]

What Role for the Government?

So far our discussion has deliberately excluded government. Bringing government into the picture will modify somewhat the operation of the system, but it will not, in a free-enterprise system such as our own, replace the operation of markets. Governments affect the circular flow of economic activity by purchasing goods and services for public consumption (education, defense, police, and so on) that compete with privately consumed goods and services. Governments may themselves produce some goods and services, thereby leaving fewer resources for business firms to use. Most importantly, governments, through taxes and subsidies, usually redistribute income from the rich to the poor. By doing so, they can greatly affect the circular flow of economic activity. Governments also use taxes to discourage the consumption of certain commodities such as alcohol and tobacco and provide incentives for the consumption of others such as housing and education. Thus, ours is a **mixed economy** comprising private enterprise and government actions and policies.

Although government policies certainly affect the circular flow of economic activity in a free-enterprise system, they do not replace the price system.[3] This is to be contrasted with a centrally planned economy such as that of the former Soviet Union where most economic decisions were made almost exclusively by government officials or planning committees. In this type of economy, the government rather than the markets set prices. The result is usually persistent shortages of certain commodities and excess production of others. Thus, central planning is usually less efficient than a free-enterprise system.

---

[2]We shall see in later chapters that the price system does not always function as the ideal discussed here.

[3]Government sometimes does replace the price system in some markets by imposing price controls such as rent ceilings and minimum wages. In general, however, in a free-enterprise economy such as our own, government works through the market (with taxes and subsidies) rather than supplanting it.

In the United States and other free-enterprise or mixed economies, the price system operates so smoothly that people are not even aware of it. Only on rare occasions (usually as a result of government interference), do we become aware that something is wrong. The long lines at most gas stations in 1979 were the result of the U.S. government's attempt to keep gasoline prices below the market or equilibrium level. When price controls were eliminated and the price of gasoline was allowed to rise to the market level, gasoline lines disappeared. When bad weather sharply reduced the output of Florida oranges in 1977 and 1981, and that of fresh fruits and vegetables in 1984, no waiting lines were seen outside food stores in the United States. The prices of oranges and vegetables simply rose, and this rationed available supplies to match the amounts that consumers wanted to purchase at the higher prices.

Example 2
Drought in Kansas Sends Wheat Prices Soaring

During 1988 and 1989, Kansas suffered the worst drought since the "dust bowl" days of the early 1930s. Kansas normally produces more than one-third of the nation's crop of hard red winter wheat (the wheat used for making bread), and with about 40% of this crop destroyed by the drought, wheat prices shot up from about $2.50 per bushel in 1987 to over $4.25 in spring 1989. American wheat stocks were heavily depleted, and American wheat exports fell sharply. The drought in the United States also encouraged Canada, Argentina, and Australia to plant more wheat and replace U.S. wheat exports to other nations such as the Soviet Union. The wheat market is actually one big global market.

Consumer prices in the United States did not increase very much, however, because a $1 loaf of bread contains only 4 cents' worth of wheat (the rest reflects manufacturing and marketing costs) and because food prices represent only one-sixth of the consumer price index. Most wheat farmers' income also increased because wheat prices rose proportionately more than the reduction in crops and because the U.S. government provided a subsidy ranging from $3.17 to $3.80 for each bushel of wheat lost to drought. Millions of acres of wheat lands, however, were permanently destroyed by drought and wind erosion. A persistence of drought conditions could have lead to much higher grain prices in the future and a further loss in U.S. agricultural exports, and it could have had a significant impact on domestic inflation. The rains came back in 1990, however, and wheat output increased and wheat prices declined. This example vividly portrays the workings of the price system, the effect of government intervention, and the interdependence in the world economy.

Sources: T. Tregarthen, "Drought Sends Farm Prices Soaring," *The Margin*, January/February 1989, pp. 22–23, and "Farmers Are Back in the Green," *Business Week*, June 11, 1990, pp. 18–19.

1.4 THE MARGIN: THE KEY UNIFYING CONCEPT IN MICROECONOMICS

In this section, we provide an overview of the crucial importance of the margin as the central unifying theme in all of microeconomics and examine some clarifications on its use.

The Crucial Importance of the Concept of the Margin

Because of scarcity, all economic activities give rise to some benefits but involve some costs. The aim of economic decisions is to maximize net benefits. Net benefits increase as long as the marginal or extra benefit from an action exceeds the marginal or extra cost resulting from the action. Net benefits are maximized when the **marginal benefit** is equal to the **marginal cost.** This concept applies to all economic decisions and market transactions. It applies to consumers in spending their income, to firms in organizing production, to workers in choosing how many hours to work, to students in deciding how much to study each subject and how many hours to work after classes, and to individuals in determining how much to save out of their income. It also applies in deciding how much pollution society should allow, in choosing the optimal amount of information to gather, in choosing the optimal amount of government regulation of the economy, and so on. Indeed, the **concept of the margin** and **marginal analysis** represent the key unifying concepts in all of microeconomics.

Specifically, the aim of consumers is to maximize the satisfaction or net benefit that they receive from spending their limited income. The net benefit or satisfaction of a consumer increases as long as the marginal or extra benefit that he or she receives from consuming one additional unit of a commodity exceeds the marginal or opportunity cost of forgoing or giving up the consumption of another commodity. A consumer maximizes satisfaction when the marginal benefit that he or she receives per dollar spent on every commodity is equal. More concretely, if the satisfaction or benefit that an individual gets from consuming one extra hamburger with a price of $2 is more than twice as large as the satisfaction of consuming a hot dog with a price of $1, then the individual would increase net benefits or satisfaction by consuming more hamburgers and fewer hot dogs. As the individual does this, the marginal benefit of consuming each additional hamburger declines, while the marginal loss in giving up each additional hot dog increases. The individual maximizes net benefits when the marginal benefit per dollar spent on each becomes equal. This central unifying theme of the margin in consumer behavior and demand is examined in Part Two (Chapters 3–5) of the text.

Similarly, it pays for a firm to expand output as long as the marginal or extra revenue that it receives from selling each additional unit of the commodity exceeds the marginal or extra cost of producing it. But as the firm produces and sells more units of the commodity, the marginal revenue may decline while its marginal cost rises. The firm maximizes total profits when the marginal revenue is equal to the marginal cost. The application of the marginal concept in firms' production decisions is examined in detail in Part Three (Chapters 6–8) of the text. The same general concept applies to an individual's decision on how many hours to work. The individual will maximize welfare when the marginal benefit he or she receives from the wages of an extra hour of work just matches the marginal cost in terms of the leisure or earnings and consumption forgone by not working the extra hour. The optimal amount of savings by an individual is the one at which the marginal benefit from the interest earned from saving an extra dollar just matches the marginal cost of postponing spending the dollar on present consumption. These applications of marginal analysis are examined in Part Five (Chapters 13–15).

To a stout conservationist any amount of pollution is probably too much, but a little reflection will convince us that this position does not make much sense, because some pollution is the inevitable result of production or consumption. The concept of the margin leads us to conclude that the optimal amount of pollution is the one at which the marginal benefit of pollution (in the form of avoiding more costly methods of waste disposal) equals the marginal cost of pollution (in terms of higher cleaning bills, more respiratory illnesses, and so on). Similarly, the optimal amount of government regulation of the economic system is the one at which the marginal benefit of such intervention just matches its marginal cost. The same concept applies to the gathering of information. Gathering information provides some benefits but involves some costs. Thus, the optimal amount of information gathering is the one at which the marginal benefit equals the marginal cost. These uses of the marginal concept are examined in Part Six (Chapters 16–18) of the text.

Some Clarifications on the Use of the Margin

Several clarifications are in order on the application of the concept of the margin and marginal analysis in microeconomics. First, the maximization of net benefits by marginal analysis does not imply that individuals are entirely selfish and does not preclude a certain degree of altruistic behavior. A more selfish person will maximize satisfaction in terms of material goods and services that the individual himself or herself consumes. A less selfish person will maximize satisfaction by using part of his or her income or resources in helping others. Similarly, a firm may contribute part of its profits to some "worthy causes" or choose to maximize sales rather than profits. Second, individuals, firms, and governments seldom have all the information required to maximize net benefits at the margin precisely. The concept of optimization at the margin is, nevertheless, an invaluable tool of analysis because it provides the motivation or driving force for most economic actions. Even when individuals and firms are not explicitly trying to maximize net benefits, they often behave as if they are. In fact, the assumption has very good predictive power. Third, marginal analysis leads to the maximization of individual benefits but not to the maximization of the welfare of society as a whole when private benefits and costs differ from social benefits and costs. One situation that leads to this arises in the presence of imperfect competition and justifies government intervention in the economic system to overcome the problem, or at least to minimize its harmful impact. Indeed, whenever some individuals in society can be made better off without making someone else worse off, there is a case for government intervention at the margin to improve society's welfare. When production and consumption can no longer be reorganized so as to improve the welfare of some without at the same time reducing the welfare of others, society is said to be at **Pareto optimum.** These applications of marginal analysis are examined in Part Four (Chapters 9–12) and Part Six (Chapters 16–18) of the text.

Despite these clarifications and qualifications, we can clearly see that the concept of the margin and marginal analysis provide the central unifying theme in all of microeconomics.

1.5 INTERNATIONAL FRAMEWORK OF MICROECONOMICS

As consumers, we purchase Japanese Toyotas and German Mercedes, Italian handbags and French perfumes, Hong Kong clothes and Taiwanese calculators, Scotch whiskey and Swiss chocolates, Canadian fish and Mexican tomatoes, Costa Rican bananas and Brazilian coffee. Often, we are not even aware that the products we consume, or parts of them, are in fact made abroad. For example, imported cloth is used in American-made suits, many American brand-name shoes are entirely manufactured abroad, and a great deal of the orange juice that we drink is imported. American multinational corporations produce and import many parts and components from abroad and export an increasing share of their output. Most of the parts and components of the IBM PC are in fact manufactured abroad (see Example 3), and more than one-third of IBM revenues and profits are generated abroad. The strongest competition and challenge faced by IBM today is not from the American Digital Equipment Corporation (DEC) but from Japanese Mitsubishi and Hitachi. General Motors, Ford, and Chrysler face increasing competition from Toyota, Nissan, and Honda. Many U.S. steel companies almost collapsed during the 1980s as a result of rising steel imports; the U.S. government came to their rescue, however, by negotiating export restraints with the major exporting nations.

In view of the **internationalization of economic activity** and the international repercussions of domestic competitiveness policies, we cannot study microeconomics in an international vacuum. The large and growing degree of interdependence of the United States in the world economy today makes a closed-economy approach to the study of microeconomics unrealistic. This text will explicitly introduce and integrate the international dimension into the body of traditional microeconomics to reflect the globalization of most economic activities in the world today.

Example 3

Even the IBM PC Is Not All American!

Table 1–1 shows that of the total manufacturing cost of $860 for the IBM PC in 1985, $625 was for parts and components made abroad (of which, $230 was from U.S.-owned plants). Even though all the parts made overseas could be manufactured domestically, they would have cost more and would have led to higher PC prices in the United States (and reduced competitiveness of IBM PCs in international markets). Today, even a larger proportion of parts and components going into the IBM PC are made abroad. Indeed, IBM manufactured the PS/55 PC entirely in Japan in 1991.

TABLE 1–1 Distribution of Manufacturing Costs for the IBM PC in the United States and Abroad

Total manufacturing cost:					$860
Portion made abroad:				$625	
in U.S.-owned plants			$230		
in foreign-owned plants			$395		
Distribution of manufacturing costs:					
Monochrome monitor	(Korea)	$ 85			
Semiconductors	(Japan)	105			
Semiconductors	(U.S.)	105			
Power supply	(Japan)	60			
Graphics printer	(Japan)	160			
Floppy disk drives	(Singapore)	165			
Assembly of disk drives	(U.S.)	25			
Keyboard	(Japan)	50			
Case and final assembly	(U.S.)	105			
		$860			

Sources: "America's High-Tech Crisis," *Business Week,* March 11, 1985, pp. 56–67, and "Selling Now in Tokyo: The Thinnest IBM Portable," *The New York Times,* April 11, 1991, p. D1.

1.6 MODELS, METHODOLOGY, AND VALUE JUDGMENTS

We now discuss the meaning and function of theory or models, examine the methodology of economics, and distinguish between value-free positive economics and normative economics.

Models and Methodology

In microeconomic theory, we seek to predict and explain the economic behavior of individual consumers, resource owners, and business firms and the operation of individual markets. For this purpose we use models. A **model** abstracts from the many details surrounding an event and identifies a few of the most important determinants of the event. For example, the amount of a commodity that an individual demands over a given period of time depends on the price of the commodity, the individual's income, and the price of related commodities (i.e., substitute and complementary commodities). It also depends on the individuals' age, sex, education, background, whether the individual is single or married, whether he or she owns a house or rents, the amount of money he or she has in the bank, the stocks the individual owns, the individual's expectations of future income and prices, geographic location, climate, and many other considerations.

However, given the consumer's tastes and preferences, demand theory identifies the price of the commodity, the individual's income, and the price of related commodities as the most important determinants of the amount of a commodity demanded by an individual. Although it may be *unrealistic* to focus only on these three considerations, demand theory postulates that these are generally capable of predicting accurately and explaining consumer behavior and demand. One could, of course, include additional considerations or variables to gain a fuller or more complete explanation of consumer demand, but that would defeat the main purpose of the theory or model, which is to simplify and generalize.

A theory or model usually results from casual observation of the real world. For example, we may observe that consumers, in general, purchase less of a commodity when its price rises. Before such a theory of demand can be accepted, however, we must go back to the real world to test it. We must make sure that individuals in different places and over different periods of time do indeed, as a group, purchase less of a commodity when its price rises. Only after many such successful tests and the absence of contradictory results can we accept the theory and make use of it in subsequent analysis to predict and explain consumer behavior. If, on the other hand, test results contradict the model, then the model must be discarded and a new one formulated.

To summarize, a theory or model is usually developed by casual observation of the real world, but we must then go back to the real world to determine whether the implications or predictions of the theory are indeed correct. Only then can we accept the theory or model. According to the Nobel Laureate economist Milton Friedman, a model is not tested by the realism or lack of realism of its assumptions, but rather by its ability to predict accurately and explain. The assumptions of the model are usually unrealistic in that they must necessarily represent a simplification and generalization of reality. However, if the model predicts accurately and explains the event, it is tentatively accepted. For example, demand theory, as originally developed, was based on the assumption that utility (i.e., the satisfaction that a consumer receives from the consumption of a commodity) is cardinally measurable (i.e., we can attach specific numerical values to it). This assumption is clearly unrealistic. Nevertheless, we accept the theory of demand because it leads to the correct prediction that a consumer will purchase less of a commodity when its price rises (other things, such as the consumer's income and the price of related commodites, remaining equal).

While most assumptions represent simplifications of reality, and to that extent are unrealistic, most economists take a broader position. According to them, the appropriate **methodology of economics** (and science in general) is to test a theory not only by its ability to predict accurately, but also by whether the predictions follow logically from the assumptions and by the internal consistency of those assumptions. For example, the theory of perfect competition postulates that the economy operates most efficiently when consumers and producers are too small individually to affect prices and output. But this theory cannot be tested for the economy as a whole. It can only be tested by tracing the loss of welfare of individual consumers when the atomistic assumptions of the theory do not hold. Thus, an adequate test of the theory requires not only confirming that the predictions are accurate but also showing how the outcome follows logically or results directly from the assumptions.

Throughout this text we will look at many economic theories or models that seek to predict and explain the economic behavior of consumers, resource owners, and business firms as they interact in the markets for goods, services, and resources. The models presented are generally those that have already been successfully tested. In a microeconomic theory course, we are not concerned with the actual testing of these theories or models, but rather with their presentation, usefulness, and applications.

Positive and Normative Economics

An important distinction made in economics is that between positive economics (or analysis) and normative economics.

Positive economics or analysis studies what *is*. It is concerned with how the economic system performs the basic economic functions of what to produce, how to produce, for whom to produce, how it provides for growth, and how it rations the available supply of a good over time. In other words, how is the price of a commodity, service, or resource actually determined in the market? How do producers combine resources to minimize costs of production? How does the number of firms in a market and the type of product they produce affect the determination of the price and quantity sold of the commodity? How does the number and type of owners and users of a resource affect the price and quantity of the resource placed on the market? How do specific taxes and subsidies affect the production and consumption of various commodities and the use of various resources? What are the effects of minimum wages on employment and incomes? the level of real wages on work and leisure? rent control on the availability of housing? deregulation of gas on gas prices and consumption? How does the economic system provide for the growth of the nation? How does it ration the available supply of a commodity over time? All of these and many more topics fall within the realm of positive economics. Positive economics is entirely statistical in nature and is devoid of ethical or value judgments.

Normative economics, on the other hand, studies what *ought* to be. It is concerned with how the basic economic functions *should* be performed. Normative economics is thus based on value judgments and, as such, is subjective and controversial. Whereas positive economics is independent of normative economics, normative economics is based on positive economics and the value judgments of society. Controversies in positive economics can be (and are) usually resolved by the collection of more or better market data. On the other hand, controversies in normative economics usually are not, and cannot, be resolved. Take for example, the case of providing national health insurance. Many people favor it, but others are opposed, and no amount of economic analysis can resolve the controversy. Economists can provide an analysis of the *economic* costs and benefits of national health insurance. Such an analysis can be useful in clarifying the economic issues involved, but it not likely to lead to general agreement on the proposition that national health insurance should or should not be provided. The economists' tools of analysis and logic can be applied to determine the economic benefits and costs of normative questions, but they leave for society as a whole (through elected representatives) the task of making normative decisions.

It is extremely important in economics to specify exactly when we are leaving the real world of positive economics and entering that of normative economics, that is, when disagreements can be resolved by the collection of more or better data (facts) and when ethical or value judgments are involved. This book is primarily concerned with positive economics. A statement such as "national health insurance should be established" is a proposition of normative economics because it is based on value judgments. Normative economics will be discussed in Chapters 16 and 17.

 Example 4

Do Economists Ever Agree on Anything?

You have probably heard some of the many jokes about economists disagreeing on almost everything. "How many opinions on the same subject do you expect to find in a room with three economists?" Answer: "four." In response to an economist's answer framed as "on the one hand . . . and on the other hand . . .," President Truman is supposed to have snapped: "Give me a one-hand economist." Such jokes do not seem justified according to the results of a recent study.

Table 1–2 reports the responses to 10 of 40 propositions from 464 respondents to a questionnaire sent to a random sample of 1,350 economists in 1990. These responses can help us determine which of the propositions belong to positive economics and which to normative economics. For example, the first three propositions in Table 1–2 can be taken to be propositions of positive economics because they elicit general agreement. As you can see, the vast majority of economists agreed that a ceiling on rents reduces the quantity and quality of housing, tariffs and import quotas usually reduce general economic welfare, and fiscal policy has a significant stimulative effect on a less than fully employed economy. But the last two propositions in the table are normative and gave rise to wide disagreement among economists. In general, there was much more agreement on questions of microeconomics (which are overrepresented in the propositions reported in Table 1–2) than on questions of macroeconomics.

TABLE 1–2   Responses of Economists to Various Propositions

Proposition	Percentage of Respondents Who Agreed	Disagreed*
1. A ceiling on rents reduces the quantity and quality of housing available.	92.9	6.5
2. Tariffs and import quotas usually reduce general economic welfare.	92.6	6.5
3. Fiscal policy (e.g., tax cuts and/or expenditure increase) has a significant stimulative impact on a less than fully employed economy.	89.9	9.1
4. Cash payments increase the welfare of recipients to a greater degree than do transfers-in-kind of equal cash value.	83.9	15.1
5. A large federal budget deficit has an adverse effect on the economy.	82.7	15.7
6. The reduction of income distribution within the U.S. is a legitimate role for government.	81.9	16.8
7. A minimum wage increases unemployment among young and unskilled workers.	78.9	20.5
8. Antitrust laws should be enforced vigorously to reduce monopoly power from its current level.	71.8	27.6
9. Reducing the regulatory power of the Environmental Protection Agency (EPA) would improve the efficiency of the U.S. economy.	36.0	62.3
10. The U.S. government should retaliate against (foreign) dumping and subsidies in international trade.	50.2	47.6

*The sum of the percentages of those who agree and disagree does not add to 100 because of nonrespondents to the particular question.
Source: R. M. Alston, J. R. Kearl, and M. B. Vaughn, "Is There a Consensus Among Economists in the 1990's?" *American Economic Review*, Vol. 82, No. 2 (May 1992), pp. 203–209.

SUMMARY

1. Economics deals with the allocation of scarce resources among alternative uses to satisfy human wants. Scarcity of resources and commodities is the fundamental economic fact of every society.

2. All societies must decide what to produce, how to produce, for whom to produce, how to provide for the growth of the system, and how to ration a given amount of a commodity over time. Under a free-enterprise or mixed economic system such as our own, it is the price system that performs these functions, for the most part.

3. Microeconomic theory studies the economic behavior of individual decision-making units such as individual consumers, resource owners, and business firms and the operation of individual markets in a free-enterprise economy. This is contrasted with macroeconomic theory, which studies the economy viewed as a whole. Microeconomic theory focuses attention on households and business firms as they interact in the markets for goods and services and resources.

4. Because of scarcity, all economic activities give rise to some benefits but involve some costs. The aim of economic decisions is to maximize net benefits. Net benefits increase as long as the marginal or extra benefit from an action exceeds the marginal or extra cost resulting from the action. Net benefits are maximized when the marginal benefit is equal to the marginal cost. This concept applies to all economic decisions and market transactions. It applies as much to the consumption decision of individuals as to the production decisions of firms, the supply choices of input owners, and government decisions. Indeed, the concepts of the margin and marginal analysis represent the key unifying concepts in all of microeconomics.

5. Many of the commodities we consume today are imported, and American firms purchase many inputs abroad, sell an increasing share of their products to other nations, and face increasing competition from foreign firms in the U.S. market and around the world. The international flow of capital, technology, and skilled labor has also reached unprecedented dimensions. Furthermore, a nation must constantly consider the repercussions of its domestic policies on other nations. In view of such internationalization of economic activity in the world today, it is essential to introduce an international dimension into the body of traditional microeconomics.

6. Theories make use of models. A model abstracts from the details surrounding an event and seeks to identify a few of the most important determinants of an event. A model is tested by its predictive ability, the consistency of its assumptions, and the logic with which the predictions follow from the assumptions.

KEY TERMS

Economics
Human Wants
Economic Resources
Price System
Free-Enterprise system
What to Produce

How to Produce
For Whom to Produce
Economic Growth
Rationing over Time
Microeconomic Theory
Macroeconomic Theory

Circular Flow of Economic
  Activity
Price Theory
Mixed Economy
Marginal Benefit
Marginal Cost

Concept of the Margin
Marginal Analysis
Pareto Optimum

Internationalization of
    Economic Activity
Model

Methodology of Economics
Positive Economics
Normative Economics

REVIEW QUESTIONS

1. Will the problem of scarcity disappear over time as standards of living increase?
2. Distinguish between the real and the financial flows that link product and factor markets.
3. Explain in terms of the circular flow of economic activity why some individuals are richer while others are poorer.
4. Explain why some football players earn more than others. Why would a team sign a superstar for millions of dollars when it could sign a good player for much less?
5. Does a firm maximize its total revenue when it maximizes its total profits?
6. It has been proven that a speed limit of 55 MPH, rather than 65 MPH, on the nation's highways saves lives and fuel. Is there any cost in keeping the speed limit at 55 MPH?
7. Why is it that imports and exports as a percentage of gross national product (GNP) are much smaller in the United States than in Switzerland?
8. What is the relationship between import prices and domestic prices?
9. What happens to the dollar price of Japanese exports to the United States and to the yen price of U.S. exports to Japan if the Japanese yen increases in value with respect to the U.S. dollar?
10. Two models predict equally well, but one is based on a larger number of assumptions and the logic with which the predictions follow from the assumptions is more intricate than for another model. Why is the second model better?
11. A model using three variables explains 85% of an event (say, a price increase), while another model, using ten variables, explains 95% of the event. Which of the two models is better? Why?
12. The government should pass more stringent pollution control laws. Do you agree? What can economists contribute to the discussion?

PROBLEMS

*1. Why do we study microeconomics?
2. Explain why the "peace dividend" in the United States does not eliminate the scarcity problem even temporarily.
3. Briefly explain how the sharp increase in petroleum prices since the fall of 1973 affected driving habits and the production of cars in the United States during the 1970s and early 1980s.
4. Explain why India produces textiles with much more labor relative to capital than the United States.
5. Explain how the introduction of government affects the circular flow of economic activity.
*6. Explain the effect of government setting the price of a commodity

a. below that which would prevail without the price ceiling;
b. above that which would prevail without the price floor.
7. How does the concept of the margin provide a key unifying concept in microeconomics?
*8. Using some data obtained from a publication such as *The Survey of Current Business, The U.S. Statistical Abstract,* or *International Financial Statistics,* available in your library, show that the interdependence of the U.S. economy with the rest of the world has increased sharply during the past 20 years or so.

_____

* = Answer provided at end of book.

9. a. If two models predict equally well but one is more complicated than the other, indicate which one you would use and why.

  b. Indicate how you would determine which of the two models is more complex.

10. a. Explain how you would go about constructing a model to predict total sales of American-made cars in the United States next year.

  b. Indicate how you would test your model.

11. Economists often disagree on economic matters, so economics is not a science. True or false? Explain.

*12. Briefly indicate which aspects of the redistribution of income from higher- to lower-income people involve
  a. positive economics;
  b. normative economics.

2

BASIC DEMAND
AND SUPPLY
ANALYSIS

H ave you ever stopped to think about how the price of a commodity (say, the price of your favorite music cassette) is determined and why it often changes over time? In this chapter we seek to answer these questions by providing an overview of the functioning of markets. We begin by defining the concept of a market. Next we discuss the meaning of demand, a change in demand, and the price elasticity of demand. After reviewing supply, we examine how the interaction of the forces of market demand and supply determine the equilibrium price and quantity of a commodity. Then we examine how the equilibrium price and quantity of a commodity are affected by changes in demand and supply and by imports. Finally, we examine the effect of modifications and interferences in the operation of markets. So widespread is the applicability of the market model, that one could safely start answering any question of microeconomics by saying that it depends on demand and supply.

2.1 MARKET ANALYSIS

Most of microeconomic analysis is devoted to the study of how individual markets operate. A **market** is the network of communications between individuals and firms for the purpose of buying and selling goods and services. Markets provide the framework for the analysis of the forces of demand and supply that, together, determine commodity and resource prices. As explained in Chapter 1, prices play the central role in microeconomic analysis.

A market can, but need not, be a specific place or location where buyers and sellers actually come face to face for the purpose of transacting their business. For example, the New York Stock Exchange is located in a building at 11 Wall Street in New York City. On the other hand, the market for college professors has no specific location; rather, it refers to all the formal and informal information networks on teaching opportunities throughout the nation. There is a market for each good, service, or resource bought and sold in the economy. Some of these markets are local, some are regional, and others are national or international in character.

Throughout this chapter, we assume that markets are perfectly competitive. A **perfectly competitive market** is one in which no buyer or seller can affect the price of the product, all units of the product are homogeneous or identical, resources are mobile, and knowledge of the market is perfect. For the purpose of the present chapter, this definition of a perfectly competitive market suffices. A more detailed definition and analysis of this and other types of markets is given in Chapter 8 and in Part Four of the text, respectively.

2.2 MARKET DEMAND

The concept of demand is one of the most crucial in microeconomic theory and in all of economics. In this section, we review the concepts of the market demand schedule and the market demand curve, examine the meaning of a change in demand, and review the measure of price elasticity of demand.

Demand Schedule and Demand Curve

A **market demand schedule** is a table showing the quantity of a commodity that consumers are willing and able to purchase over a given period of time at each price of the commodity, while holding constant all other relevant economic variables on which demands depends (the *ceteris paribus* assumption). The variables held constant are consumers' incomes, their tastes, the prices of related commodities (substitutes and complements), and the number of consumers in the market.

For example, Table 2–1 provides a hypothetical daily demand schedule for hamburgers in a large market (say, New York City, Chicago, or Los Angeles). At the price of $2.00 per hamburger, the quantity demanded is 2 million hamburgers per day. At the lower price of $1.50, the quantity demanded is 4 million hamburgers per day. At the price of $1.00, the quantity demanded is 6 million hamburgers, and at the prices of $0.75 and $0.50, the quantity demanded is 7 and 8 million hamburgers, respectively.

TABLE 2–1   Market Demand Schedule for Hamburgers

Price per Hamburger	Quantity Demanded per Day (million hamburgers)
$2.00	2
1.50	4
1.00	6
0.75	7
0.50	8

FIGURE 2–1   Market Demand Curve for Hamburgers

Market demand curve *D* shows that at lower hamburger prices, greater quantities are demanded. This is reflected in the negative slope of the demand curve and is referred to as the "law of demand."

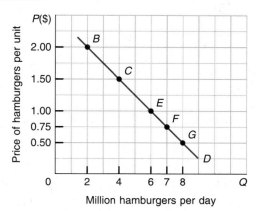

Million hamburgers per day

At lower prices, greater quantities of hamburgers are demanded. Each additional hamburger consumed per day provides declining marginal or extra benefit, and so consumers would only purchase greater quantities at lower prices. This is true for most commodities. Lower commodity prices will also bring more consumers into the market. The inverse price-quantity relationship (indicating that a greater quantity of the commodity is demanded at lower prices and a smaller quantity at higher prices) is called the **law of demand.**

By plotting on a graph the various price-quantity combinations given by the market demand schedule, we obtain the **market demand curve** for the commodity. The price per unit of the commodity is usually measured along the vertical axis, while the quantity demanded of the commodity per unit of time is measured along the horizontal axis. For example, Figure 2–1 shows the market demand curve for hamburgers corresponding to the market demand schedule of Table 2–1. The demand curve has a *negative slope*; that is, it slopes downward to the right. This is a reflection of the law of demand or inverse price-quantity relationship.

The various points on the demand curve represent *alternative* price-quantity combinations. For example, at the price of $2.00 per hamburger, the quantity demanded is 2 million hamburgers (point *B* in Figure 2–1). If the price is $1.50, the quantity demanded is 4 million hamburgers (point *C*), and so on. A demand curve also shows the maximum price consumers are willing to pay to purchase each quantity of a commodity per unit of time. For example, the demand curve of Figure 2–1 shows that for 2 million hamburgers, consumers are willing to pay the maximum price of $2.00 per hamburger (point *B*); for 4 million hamburgers, consumers are willing to pay the maximum price of $1.50 (point *C*), and so on. Finally, a particular demand curve refers to a specific period of time. The demand curve of Figure 2–1 is for one day. The demand curve for hamburgers for a month is correspondingly larger.[1]

Changes in Demand

A demand curve can shift so that more or less of the commodity would be demanded at any commodity price. The entire demand curve for a commodity would shift with a change in (1) consumers' incomes, (2) their tastes, (3) the price of related commodities, or (4) the number of consumers in the market (the variables held constant in drawing a market demand curve). For example, with a rise in consumer income the demand curve for most commodities (normal goods) shifts to the right, because consumers can then afford to purchase more of each commodity at each price. The same is true if consumers' tastes change so that they demand more of the commodity at each price, or if the number of consumers in the market increases.

A demand curve also shifts to the right if the price of a substitute commodity rises or if the price of a complementary commodity falls. For example, if the price of hot dogs (a substitute for hamburgers) rises, people will switch some of their purchases away from hots dogs and demand more hamburgers at each and every price of hamburgers (a rightward shift in the demand for hamburgers). Similarly, if the price of the bun (a complement of hamburgers) *falls*, the demand for hamburgers also shifts to the right (since the price of a hamburger *with the bun* is then lower).

On the other hand, the demand curve for a commodity usually shifts to the left (so that less of it is demanded at each price) with a decline in consumer income, the price of substitute commodities, or the number of consumers in the market. The demand curve also shifts to the left if the price of complementary commodities rises or if consumer tastes change so that they demand less of the commodity at each price.

Figure 2–2 shows D, the original demand curve for hamburgers (from Figure 2–1) and D', a higher demand curve for hamburgers. With D', consumers demand more hamburgers at each price. For example, at the price of $1.00, consumers demand 12 million hamburgers per day (point E') as compared with 6 million demanded (point E) on curve D. The shift from D to D' leads consumers to demand 6 million *additional* hamburgers per day at each price.

A shift in demand is referred to as a *change in demand* and must be clearly distinguished from a *change in the quantity demanded*, which refers instead to a movement along a given demand curve as a result of a change in the commodity price. Thus, the shift in demand from D to D' is an increase in demand, while the movement along D, say, from point E to point F, is a change in the quantity demanded. The change in demand is caused by the

---

[1]The demand curve in Figure 2–1 is drawn on a light background grid to facilitate the reading of the various price-quantity alternatives on the curve. The grid is used as a visual aid in most figures in the text. A demand curve could be drawn and the analysis could be conducted more generally without numerical values and without the grid.

FIGURE 2–2   Change in Demand for Hamburgers

Consumers demand more hamburgers at each price when the demand curve shifts to the right from D to D'. Thus, at $P = \$1.00$, consumers purchase 12 million hamburgers with D' instead of only 6 million with D.

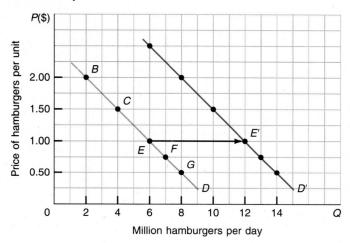

change in the economic variables that are held constant in drawing a given demand curve (the *ceteris paribus* assumption), whereas a change in the quantity demanded is a movement along a given demand curve as a result of a change in the price of the commodity (with all the other economic variables on which demand depends remaining constant).

Price Elasticity of Demand

The responsiveness in the quantity demanded of a commodity to a change in its price is important to consumers and producers alike. For example, when the price of gasoline rose sharply in the fall of 1973, consumers reduced their purchases of gasoline, but they ended up spending much more on gasoline because they could not quickly and easily replace their gas guzzlers with more fuel-efficient compact cars, and because they could not easily find alternative means of transportation. Similarly, a producer may consider lowering the price of a commodity if the increase in the quantity demanded increases his or her total revenue (price times quantity), but not if he or she expects the total revenue from the sale of the commodity to decline.

The responsiveness in the quantity demanded of a commodity to a change in its price could be measured by the inverse of the slope of the demand curve (i.e., by $\Delta Q/\Delta P$).[2] The disadvantage is that the inverse of the slope is

_____

[2]Since the turn of the century, the convention in economics (started by Alfred Marshall) is to plot price on the vertical axis and quantity on the horizontal axis. Therefore, the quantity response to a change in price could be measured by $\Delta Q/\Delta P$, which is the inverse of the slope of the demand curve.

expressed in terms of the units of measurement. A change of 100,000 units in the quantity demanded of a commodity is very large if the commodity is new housing units, but it is not very large if the commodity is hamburgers. Similarly, a price change of one dollar is insignificant for houses, but very large for hamburgers. Thus, measuring the responsiveness in the quantity demanded of a commodity to a change in price by the inverse of the slope of the demand curve is not very useful. Furthermore, comparison of changes in quantity to changes in price across commodities is meaningless. These problems can be resolved by using percentage rather than absolute changes in quantity and prices.

In order to have a measure of the responsiveness in the quantity demanded of a commodity to a change in its price that is independent of the units of measurement, Alfred Marshall, the great English economist of the turn of the century, refined and popularized the concept of the price elasticity of demand. This is defined in terms of *relative* or *percentage* changes in quantity demanded and price. As such, price elasticity of demand is a pure number (i.e., it has no units attached to it), and its value is not affected by changes in the units of measurement. As shown in the following example, this also allows meaningful comparisons in the price elasticity of demand of different commodities.

The **price elasticity of demand** is given by the percentage change in the quantity demanded of a commodity divided by the percentage change in its price. Letting η (the Greek letter eta) stand for the coefficient of price elasticity of demand, ΔQ for the change in quantity demanded, and ΔP for the change in price, we have the formula for the price elasticity of demand:

$$\eta = -\frac{\Delta Q/Q}{\Delta P/P} = -\frac{\Delta Q}{\Delta P} \cdot \frac{P}{Q} \qquad \text{[2–1]}$$

Since quantity and price move in opposite directions, we use (as a convention) the negative sign in the formula (i.e., we multiply by -1) to make the value of η positive. Note that the inverse of the slope of the demand curve (i.e., $\Delta Q/\Delta P$) is a component, but only a component, of the elasticity formula.

Formula [2–1] measures **point elasticity of demand** or the elasticity at a particular point on the demand curve.[3] More frequently, we are interested in the price elasticity between two points on the demand curve. We then calculate the **arc elasticity of demand.** If we used formula [2–1] to measure arc elasticity, however, we would get different results depending on whether the price rises or falls.[4] To avoid this, we use the *average* of the two prices and the *average* of the two quantities in the calculations. Letting P_1 refer to the higher of the two prices (with Q_1 the quantity at P_1) and P_2 refer to the lower of the two

---

[3]For a discussion of the price elasticity of demand using calculus, see section A.5 of the Mathematical Appendix at the end of the book.

[4]As we will see below, this results because a different base is used in calculating percentage changes for a price increase than for a price decrease.

prices (with Q_2 the corresponding quantity), we have the formula for arc elasticity of demand:[5]

$$\eta = -\frac{\Delta Q}{\Delta P} \cdot \frac{(P_1 + P_2)/2}{(Q_1 + Q_2)/2} = -\frac{\Delta Q}{\Delta P} \cdot \frac{(P_1 + P_2)}{(Q_1 + Q_2)} \qquad [2\text{-}2]$$

Using formula [2–1] to measure elasticity for a *price decline* from point C to point E on the demand curve of Figure 2–1, we get

$$\eta = \left(-\frac{2}{-0.50}\right)\left(\frac{1.50}{4}\right) = \frac{3}{2} = 1.5$$

On the other hand, measuring elasticity for a *price increase* from point E to point C on the same demand curve, we get

$$\eta = \left(-\frac{-2}{0.50}\right)\left(\frac{1}{6}\right) = \frac{2}{3} = 0.67$$

Using instead formula [2–2] for arc elasticity, we get

$$\eta = -\left(-\frac{2}{0.50}\right)\frac{(1.50 + 1.00)/2}{(4 + 6)/2} = \frac{2.5}{2.5} = 1$$

Different Goods, Different Price Elasticities of Demand

Price elasticity of demand is usually different at and between different points on the demand curve, and it can range anywhere from zero to very large or infinite. Demand is said to be *elastic* if η is larger than 1, *unitary elastic* if η equals 1, and *inelastic* if η is smaller than 1. In general, the closer and the greater are the number of substitutes available for a commodity, the larger is the price elasticity of demand. The reason for this is that an increase in the price of a commodity that has many close substitutes results in a very large decline in the quantity purchased of that commodity. For example, as the price of hamburgers rises, people will purchase more hot dogs, a close substitute. So, the price elasticity of hamburgers is large. Similarly, as the period of time allowed for the adjustment to a given price change increases, so does the quantity, and thus the price elasticity of demand. For example, the price elasticity of demand for gasoline was found to be much larger when measured over several years than when measured over several months, because people had more time to adjust to the price change.

The price elasticity of demand can also differ widely for different commodities and services. For example, the price elasticity of demand was found to be 3.6 for motion pictures, 1.9 for electricity, and 1.8 for foreign travel, but only

---

[5]For the second ratio in the formula, we could use $\overline{P}/\overline{Q}$, where the bar on P and Q refers to their average value.

0.3 for potatoes and sugar (when sufficient time was allowed for consumers to adjust fully to price changes).[6] The price elasticity of demand of 3.6 for motion pictures means that a 1% reduction in the price of movie tickets increases the quantity demanded by 3.6%, so that total expenditures (price times quantity) on motion pictures increases. The demand for motion pictures, electricity, and foreign travel is elastic (i.e., $\eta > 1$).

If a 1% reduction in price increases the quantity demanded by 1%, total expenditures remain unchanged, and demand is said to be unitary elastic (i.e., $\eta = 1$). Finally, if a 1% reduction in price increases the quantity demanded by less than 1%, so that total expenditures on the commodity declines, demand is said to be inelastic (i.e., $\eta < 1$). For example, a 1% reduction in the price of sugar increases the quantity of sugar demanded by only 0.3%, so that total expenditures on sugar declines. The same is true for potatoes. In this case, $\eta < 1$ and demand is then said to be inelastic.

Why is the price elasticity of demand for motion pictures so large while that for sugar is so low? The answer is that good substitutes are available for motion pictures (such as watching cable TV at home) but not for sugar (saccharin and honey being poor substitutes).[7]

2.3 MARKET SUPPLY

We have examined the market demand, now it is time to turn to the supply side.

Supply Schedule and Supply Curve

A **market supply schedule** is a table showing the quantity supplied of a commodity at each price for a given period of time. It assures that technology, resource prices, and, for agricultural commodities, weather conditions are held constant (the *ceteris paribus* assumption). Table 2–2 gives a hypothetical daily supply schedule for hamburgers. Starting at the bottom, the table shows that at the price of $0.50 per hamburger, the quantity supplied is 2 million hamburgers per day. At the higher price of $0.75 per hamburger, the quantity supplied is 4 million hamburgers per day. At the price of $1.00, the quantity supplied is 6 million hamburgers per day, and so on. Higher hamburger prices allow producers to bid resources away from other uses and supply greater quantities of hamburgers.

The various price-quantity combinations of a supply schedule can be plotted

---

[6]See, H. Houthakker and L. D. Taylor, *Consumer Demand in the United States: Analyses and Projections* (Cambridge, Mass.: Harvard University Press, 1970), and H. Schultz, *The Theory and Measurement of Demand* (Chicago: University of Chicago Press, 1951).

[7]A more extensive discussion of the price elasticity of demand is found in section 5.2.

TABLE 2–2   Market Supply Schedule for Hamburgers

Price per Hamburger	Quantity Supplied per Day (million hamburgers)
$2.00	14
1.50	10
1.00	6
0.75	4
0.50	2

on a graph to obtain the **market supply curve** for the commodity. For example, Figure 2–3 shows the market supply curve for hamburgers corresponding to the market supply schedule of Table 2–2. The *positive slope* of the supply curve (i.e., its upward-to-the-right inclination) reflects the fact that higher prices must be paid to producers to cover rising marginal, or extra, costs and thus induce them to supply greater quantities of the commodity.

As with the demand curve, the various points on the supply curve represent *alternative* price-quantity combinations. For example, at the price of $0.50 per hamburger, the quantity supplied is 2 million hamburgers per day (point *R* in Figure 2–3). If instead the price is $0.75, the quantity supplied is 4 million hamburgers (point *N*), and so on. A supply curve also shows the *minimum* price that producers must receive to cover their rising marginal costs and supply each quantity of the commodity. For example, the supply curve of Figure 2–3 shows that suppliers must receive the minimum price of $0.50 per hamburger in order to supply 2 million hamburgers per day (point *R*); produc-

FIGURE 2–3   Market Supply Curve for Hamburgers

Market supply curve *S* shows that higher hamburger prices induce producers to supply greater quantities.

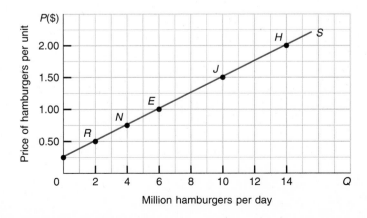

ers must receive the minimum price of $0.75 per hamburger to supply 4 million hamburgers (point N), and so on. A particular supply curve is drawn for a specific period of time. The supply curve of Figure 2–3 is for one day. The supply curve of hamburgers for a month is correspondingly larger or farther out.

Changes in Supply

An improvement in technology, a reduction in the price of resources used in the production of the commodity, and, for agricultural commodities, more favorable weather conditions (i.e., a change in the *ceteris paribus* assumptions) would cause the entire supply curve of the commodity to shift to the right. Producers would then supply more of the commodity at each price. For example, Figure 2–4 shows that at the price of $1.00, producers supply 12 million hamburgers per day (point E') with S' as opposed to only 6 million hamburgers with S.

The shift to the right from S to S' is referred to as *an increase in supply*. This must be clearly distinguished from *an increase in the quantity supplied*, which is instead a movement on a given supply curve in the upward direction (as, for example, from point E to point J, in Figure 2–4) resulting from an increase in the commodity price (from $1.00 to $1.50). On the other hand, a decrease in supply refers to a leftward shift in the supply curve and must be clearly distinguished from a decrease in the quantity supplied of the commodity (which is a movement down a supply curve and results from a decline in the commodity price).

FIGURE 2–4   **Change in the Supply of Hamburgers**

When the supply curve shifts to the right from S to S', producers supply more hamburgers at each price. Thus, at P = $1.00, producers supply 12 million hamburgers with S' instead of only 6 million with S.

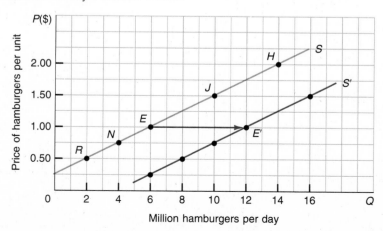

Price Elasticity of Supply

The **price elasticity of supply** measures the responsiveness or sensitivity in the quantity supplied of a commodity to a change in its price. We calculate price elasticity of supply by dividing the percentage change in quantity supplied by the percentage change in price. Because it is expressed in terms of relative percentage changes, the price elasticity of supply is a pure number (i.e., it has no units attached to it), and its value does not change when the units of measurement are changed. This allows meaningful comparisons in the price elasticity of supply of different commodities.[8]

Letting ϵ (the Greek letter epsilon) stand for the coefficient of price elasticity of supply, ΔQ for the change in the quantity *supplied*, and ΔP for the change in price, we can measure **point elasticity of supply** by the following formula:

$$\epsilon = \frac{\Delta Q/Q}{\Delta P/P} = \frac{\Delta Q}{\Delta P} \cdot \frac{P}{Q} \qquad [2\text{–}3]$$

Note that the inverse of the slope of the supply curve is a component, but only a component, of the formula for the price elasticity of supply. Since quantity and price move in the same direction (i.e., the supply curve is usually positively sloped), ϵ is positive.

Formula [2–3] measures point elasticity of supply or the elasticity at a particular point on the supply curve.[9] More frequently, we measure **arc elasticity of supply** between two points on the supply curve. If we used formula [2–3] to measure arc elasticity, we would get different results depending on whether the price rises or falls. To avoid this, we use the average of the two prices and the average of the two quantities (as was done in measuring arc elasticity of demand). Letting P_1 now refer to the lower of the two prices (with Q_1 the quantity at P_1) and P_2 to the higher of the two prices (with Q_2 the corresponding quantity), we can measure arc elasticity of supply by

$$\epsilon = \frac{\Delta Q}{\Delta P} \cdot \frac{(P_1 + P_2)/2}{(Q_1 + Q_2)/2} = \frac{\Delta Q}{\Delta P} \cdot \frac{(P_1 + P_2)}{(Q_1 + Q_2)} \qquad [2\text{–}4]$$

For example, using formula [2–4] to measure arc elasticity between points E and J on the supply curve of Figure 2–4, we get

$$\epsilon = \frac{4}{0.50} \cdot \frac{(1.00 + 1.50)/2}{(6 + 10)/2} = \frac{5}{4} = 1.25$$

The price elasticity of supply increases over time because it takes time for producers to respond to price changes. The supply curve is said to be *elastic*

---

[8]The discussion in section 2.2 on the advantages of using the price elasticity of demand rather than the inverse of the slope of the demand curve as a measure of the responsiveness in the quantity demanded of a commodity to a change in its price also applies here.

[9]For a discussion of price elasticity of supply using calculus, see section A.5 of the Mathematical Appendix at the end of the book.

if ϵ is larger than 1, *unitary elastic* if ϵ equals 1, and *inelastic* if ϵ is smaller than 1. A straight-line supply curve is elastic throughout if (as S in Figure 2–4) it crosses the price axis; it is unitary elastic if it crosses the origin (as S in problem 3a); and inelastic if (as S' in Figure 2–4) it crosses the quantity axis. The reason is that the relative change in the quantity supplied is greater than, equal to, or smaller than the relative change in price depending on whether the straight-line supply curve crosses the price axis, the origin, or the quantity axis, respectively.[10]

The price elasticity of supply for different products can vary greatly. For example, the long-run price elasticity of supply was estimated to be 0.26 for green peppers and 4.70 for spinach.[11] The type of land and other resources used in the production of spinach is much less specialized and can be transferred much more easily in the long run to and from other uses than the resources used in the production of green peppers. Thus, a given change in the price of spinach leads to a proportionately much greater production response than for green peppers (i.e., the price elasticity of supply for spinach than for peppers).[12]

2.4 WHEN IS A MARKET IN EQUILIBRIUM?

We now examine how the interaction of the forces of demand and supply determines the equilibrium price and quantity of a commodity in a perfectly competitive market. The **equilibrium price** of a commodity is the price at which the quantity demanded of the commodity equals the quantity supplied and the market clears. The process by which equilibrium is reached in the marketplace can be shown with a table and illustrated graphically.

Table 2–3 brings together the market demand and supply schedules for hamburgers from Tables 2–1 and 2–2. From Table 2–3, we see that only at P = \$1.00 is the quantity supplied of hamburgers equal to the quantity demanded and the market clears. Thus, P = \$1.00 is the equilibrium price and Q = 6 million hamburgers per day is the equilibrium quantity.

At prices above the equilibrium price, the quantity supplied exceeds the quantity demanded and there is a **surplus** of the commodity, which drives the price down. For example, at P = \$2.00, the quantity supplied (QS) is 14 million hamburgers, the quantity demanded (QD) is 2 million hamburgers,

---

[10]You can convince yourself of this by drawing on graph paper three straight-line supply curves: one crossing the price axis, one going through the origin, and the other crossing the quantity axis. Then calculate arc elasticity between any two points on each supply curve.

[11]See, M. Nerlove and W. Addison, "Statistical Estimation of Long-run Elasticities of Supply and Demand," *Journal of Farm Economics* (now *Journal of Agricultural Economics*), Vol. 40, November 1958, pp. 861–880.

[12]More will be said on the price elasticity of supply in Chapter 8.

so that there is a surplus of 12 million hamburgers per day (see the first line of Table 2–3). Sellers must reduce prices to get rid of their unwanted inventory accumulations of hamburgers. At lower prices, producers supply smaller quantities and consumers demand larger quantities until the equilibrium price of $1.00 is reached, at which the quantity supplied of 6 million hamburgers per day equals the quantity demanded and the market clears.

On the other hand, at prices below the equilibrium price, the quantity supplied falls short of the quantity demanded and there is a **shortage** of the commodity, which drives the price up. For example, at $P = \$0.50$, $QS = 2$ million hamburgers while $QD = 8$ million hamburgers, so that there is a shortage of 6 million hamburgers per day (see the last line of Table 2–3). The price of hamburgers is then bid up by consumers who want more hamburgers than are available at the low price of $0.50. As the price of hamburgers is bid up, producers supply greater quantities while consumers demand smaller quantities until the equilibrium price of $P = \$1.00$ is reached, at which $QS = QD = 6$ million hamburgers per day and the market clears. Thus, bidding drives price and quantity to their equilibrium level.

The determination of the equilibrium price can also be shown graphically by bringing together on the same graph the market demand curve of Figure 2–1 and the market supply curve of Figure 2–3. In Figure 2–5 the intersection of the market demand curve and the market supply curve of hamburgers at point E defines the equilibrium price of $1.00 per hamburger and the equilibrium quantity of 6 million hamburgers per day.

At higher prices, there is an excess supply or surplus of the commodity (the top shaded area in Figure 2–5). Suppliers then lower prices to sell their excess supplies. The surplus is eliminated only when suppliers have lowered their price to the equilibrium level. On the other hand, at below equilibrium prices, the excess demand or shortage (the bottom shaded area in the figure) drives the price up to the equilibrium level. This results because consumers are unable to purchase all of the commodity they want at below-equilibrium prices and they bid up the price. The shortage is eliminated only when consumers have bid up the price to the equilibrium level, that is, only at $P = \$1.00$,

TABLE 2–3 Market Supply Schedule, Market Demand Schedule, and Equilibrium

Price per Hamburger	Quantity Supplied per Day (million hamburgers)	Quantity Demanded per Day (million hamburgers)	Suplus (+) or Shortage (−)	Pressure on Price
$2.00	14	2	12	Downward
1.50	10	4	6	Downward
1.00	6	6	0	Equilibrium
0.75	4	7	−3	Upward
0.50	2	8	−6	Upward

FIGURE 2–5   Demand, Supply, and Equilibrium

The intersection of D and S at point E defines the equilibrium price of $1.00 per hamburger and the equilibrium quantity of 6 million hamburgers per day. At P larger than $1.00, the resulting surplus will drive P down toward equilibrium. At P smaller than $1.00, the resulting shortage will drive P up toward equilibrium.

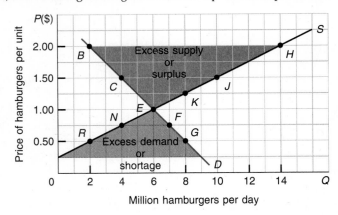

$QS = QD = 6$ million hamburgers per day, and the market is in equilibrium (clears). So, both demand and supply play a role in determining price.[13]

Equilibrium is the condition which, once achieved, tends to persist in time. That is, as long as D and S do not change, the equilibrium point remains the same.

At a particular point in time, the observed price may or may not be the equilibrium price. However, we know that market forces always push the market price toward the equilibrium. This may occur very rapidly or slowly. Before the market price reaches a particular equilibrium price, demand and supply may change (shift) defining a new equilibrium price. For now we will assume that, in the absence of price controls, the market price *is* the equilibrium price.

2.5 ADJUSTMENT TO CHANGES IN DEMAND AND SUPPLY: COMPARATIVE STATIC ANALYSIS

What is the effect of a change in demand and supply on the equilibrium price and quantity of a commodity? Because the demand and supply curves of a commodity often shift over time, it is important to analyze how these shifts affect equilibrium. This is called **comparative static analysis**.

---

[13]For a mathematical presentation of how equilibrium is determined using algebra, see section A.11 of the Mathematical Appendix at the end of the book.

FIGURE 2–6   Adjustment to an Increase in Demand

D and S are the original demand and supply curves (as in Figure 2–5). The shift from D to D' results in a temporary shortage of hamburgers, which drives the price up to $P=\$1.50$ at which $QS=QD=10$ million hamburgers.

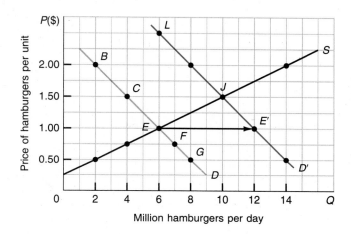

Adjustment to Changes in Demand

We have seen that the market demand curve for a commodity shifts as a result of a change in consumers' income, their tastes, the price of substitutes and complements, and the number of consumers in the market (i.e., a change in the *ceteris paribus* assumption). Given the market supply curve of a commodity, an increase in demand (a rightward shift of the entire demand curve) results both in a higher equilibrium price and a higher equilibrium quantity. A reduction in demand has the opposite effect.

Figure 2–6 shows a shift from D to D' resulting, for example, from an increase in consumer income. The shift results in a temporary shortage of 6 million hamburgers (EE' in the figure) at the original equilibrium price of $P = \$1.00$ (point E). As a result, the price of hamburgers is bid up to $P=\$1.50$ at which $QS=QD=10$ million hamburgers. As the price of hamburgers rises to $P = \$1.50$, the quantity demanded declines (from point E' to point J along D') while the quantity supplied increases (from point E to point J along S) until the new equilibrium point J is reached. At the new equilibrium point J, both P and Q are higher than at the old equilibrium point E and the market, once again, clears.

Adjustment to Changes in Supply

The market supply curve of a commodity can shift as a result of a change in technology, resource prices, or weather conditions (for agricultural commodities). Given the market demand curve for the commodity, an increase in supply (a rightward shift of the entire supply curve) results in a lower equilib-

FIGURE 2–7   Adjustment to an Increase in Supply

D and *S* are the original demand and supply curves. The shift from *S* to *S'* results in a temporary surplus of hamburgers, which drives the price down to *P* = $0.50 at which *QS* = *QD* = 8 million hamburgers.

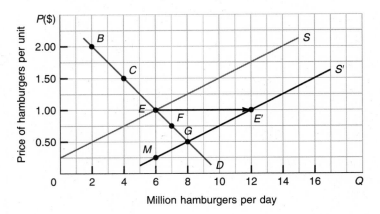

Million hamburgers per day

rium price but a larger equilibrium quantity. A reduction in supply has the opposite effect.

Figure 2–7 shows a shift from *S* to *S'* resulting, for example, from a reduction in the price of beef. The shift results in a temporary surplus of 6 million hamburgers (*EE'* in the figure) at the original equilibrium price of *P* = $1.00 (point *E*). To get rid of their surplus, sellers reduce their price to *P* = $0.50, at which *QS* = *QD* = 8 million hamburgers. As the price of hamburgers falls to *P* = $0.50, the quantity demanded increases (from point *E* to point *G* along *D*) while the quantity supplied decreases (from point *E'* to point *G* along *S'*) until the new equilibrium point *G* is reached. At new equilibrium point *G*, *P* is lower and *Q* is higher than at old equilibrium point *E* and the market, once again, clears.

Starting from Figure 2–5, you should be able to show what happens to the equilibrium price and quantity if both the demand and supply of hamburgers increase, if both decrease, or if one increases and the other decreases. We can similarly examine the effect of changes in demand and supply on the equilibrium price and quantity of any other commodity or service. For example, we can determine that the price of gold declined in 1992 because its demand decreased and its supply increased. On the other hand, the cost (price) of adopting a child has increased sharply in the United States during the past decade because of an increase in demand in the face of a decrease in supply.[14] Example 1 analyzes the effect of the sharp increase in petroleum prices on the U.S. automobile market during the 1970s and the decline since the mid-1980s.

---

[14]See, "Gold Still Isn't Much of a Prospect," *Business Week*, April 6, 1992, p. 79, and "Adoption Market: Big Demand, Tight Supply," *The New York Times*, April 5, 1987, p. 1.

Example 1

Petroleum Prices and Toyota's Gains Over General Motors

The sharp increase in petroleum prices between the fall of 1973 and 1974, which resulted from the Arab oil embargo, caught American automakers completely off guard. They had preferred making large gas guzzlers rather than small, fuel-efficient automobiles because profits were much higher on the former than on the latter. American automakers thus left the small-car market practically to imports. When petroleum prices shot up in fall 1973, however, the demand for large automobiles suddenly collapsed, while the demand for small, fuel-efficient cars increased sharply. As a result, the price of small automobiles increased relative to the price of large automobiles, and since it takes several years to retool for the production of small automobiles, most of the increased demand for small automobiles in the United States was satisfied by imports. Indeed, without the large increase in automobile imports in the mid-1970s, the price of small automobiles in the United States would have increased much more.

Over the years, U.S. automakers shifted production from large to small automobiles and increased average fuel efficiency for newly produced cars from 14.2 miles per gallon in 1974 to 28.5 miles per gallon in 1986. Since the collapse of petroleum prices in 1986, however, there has hardly been any improvement in gasoline efficiency, and today the American love affair with large, powerful automobiles seems to be reemerging. This analysis shows how the shift in tastes from large to small automobiles increased the demand for small automobiles and how, over time, American producers responded (until 1986) by expanding their production (supply) of small automobiles in relation to large ones. By that time, however, one-quarter of the U.S. auto market had been permanently taken by imports (mostly Japanese). Indeed, by 1992, the Japanese had captured about one-third of the U.S. market if we include the production by Japanese-owned plants in the United States (transplants). Toyota had become more than half the size of General Motors—up from less than a quarter in 1980.

Sources: "What Lies Ahead Down Small Car Lane," *Fortune*, July 1974, pp. 80–83; "U.S. Progress in Fuel Efficiency is Halting," *The New York Times*, February 27, 1989, p. 1; and "How American Industry Stacks," *Fortune*, March 9, 1992, pp. 30–46.

2.6 DOMESTIC DEMAND AND SUPPLY, IMPORTS, AND PRICES

When the domestic price of a commodity is higher than the commodity price abroad, the nation will import the commodity until domestic and foreign prices are equalized, in the absence of trade restrictions and assuming no transportation costs. This is shown in Figure 2–8. Curves D_T and S_T in Panels

FIGURE 2–8   Equilibrium Commodity Price with Trade

The U.S. demand for textile imports (D) in Panel B is derived from the excess demand at below-equilibrium prices in the absence of trade in Panel A. On the other hand, the foreign supply of textile exports to the United States (S) in Panel B is derived from the foreign excess supply at above-equilibrium prices in the absence of trade in Panel C. The D and S curves intersect at point E★ in Panel B, establishing the equilibrium price of $2 per yard and the equilibrium quantity of textiles traded of 300 million yards.

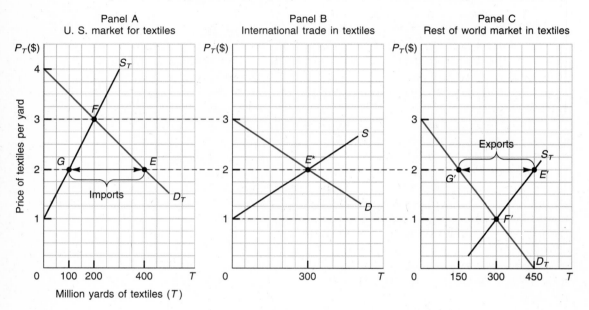

A and C refer to the demand and supply curves for textiles in the United States and in the rest of the world per year, respectively. Panel A shows that in the absence of trade, the United States produces and consumes 200 million yards of textiles at the price of $3 per yard (point F). Panel C shows that the rest of the world produces and consumes 300 million yards at the price of $1 per yard (point F'). With free trade in textiles, and assuming (for simplicity) zero transportation costs, the price of textiles will be $2 per yard both in the United States and abroad. The United States will import 300 million yards of textiles (EG in Panel A), which is equal to the textile exports of the rest of the world (E'G' in Panel C). This result, which is easily visualized by examining Panels A and C only, is formally derived in Panel B.

Panel B shows the U.S. demand for textile imports (D) and the foreign supply curve of textile exports (S). The U.S. demand for textile imports in Panel B is derived from the U.S. **excess demand** for textiles at each price below the U.S. equilibrium price in Panel A. Specifically, at the equilibrium price of $3 per yard, the United States produces and consumes 200 million yards of textiles (point F in Panel A). This corresponds to the vertical intercept of the U.S. demand curve for textile imports (D) in Panel B. At $P_T = \$2$, the United

States produces 100 million yards domestically (point G in Panel A), consumes 400 million yards (point E in Panel A), and thus imports 300 million yards (EG in Panel A). This corresponds to point E^* on the U.S. demand curve for textile imports (D) in Panel B.

The foreign supply curve of textile exports to the United States (S in Panel B) is derived from the **excess supply** of textiles in the rest of the world at prices above the equilibrium price in Panel C. Specifically, at the equilibrium price of $1 per yard, the rest of the world produces and consumes 300 million yards of textiles (point F' in Panel C). This corresponds to the vertical intercept of the supply curve of textile exports of the rest of the world (S) in Panel B. At $P_T = \$2$, the rest of the world produces 450 million yards (point E' in Panel C), consumes 150 million yards (point G' in Panel C), and exports 300 million yards ($E'G'$ in Panel C). This corresponds to point E^* on the supply curve of textile exports of the rest of the world (S) in Panel B.

The U.S. demand curve for textile imports (D in Panel B) intersects the foreign supply curve of textile exports from the rest of the world (S in Panel B) at point E^*, resulting in the equilibrium quantity of textiles traded of 300 million yards at the equilibrium price of $2 per yard. Just as for any other commodity, the equilibrium price and quantity of textiles traded is given at the intersection of the demand and supply curves. Note that in the absence of any obstruction to trade in textiles and assuming no transportation costs, the price of textiles is equal in the United States and abroad. Thus, the price of textiles with trade is lower in the United States and higher in the rest of the world than in the absence of trade. With transportation costs, the price of textiles in the United States would exceed the price of textiles in the rest of the world by the cost of transportation.

This analysis clearly shows that in today's interdependent world, the tendency for the domestic price of a commodity to rise is moderated by the inflow of imports of the commodity. For example, the price of small, fuel-efficient automobiles rose by much less than it would have in the absence of imports after the price of petroleum shot up in the fall of 1973. As pointed out in Example 1, however, the sharp increase in automobile imports replaced less-fuel-efficient U.S.-made cars and led to huge losses of American automotive jobs. Import restrictions to save American jobs during the first half of the 1980s only led to higher automobile prices for U.S. consumers and the threat of retaliation by other nations against U.S. exports. Example 2 examines the large U.S. automotive trade deficit and the major U.S. commodity imports and exports in 1991.

Example 2
The Large U.S. Automotive Trade Deficit

Table 2–4 shows that even though automotive products (vehicles, parts, and engines) were by far the largest class of both imports and exports of the United States, the United States had an automotive trade deficit of $45 billion

TABLE 2–4   Major U.S. Commodity Imports and Exports in 1991 (billions of dollars)

Imports		Exports	
Product	**Value**	**Product**	**Value**
Automotive vehicles, parts, and engines	$85	Automotive vehicles, parts, and engines	$40
Petroleum	51	Civilian aircraft, engines, and parts	36
Computers, peripherals and parts	26	Foods and beverages	36
Foods and beverages	26	of which grains	13
Chemicals, excluding medicinals	15	Chemicals, excluding medicinals	31
Semiconductors	13	Computers, peripherals and parts	27
Electrical generating machinery	13	Semiconductors	14
Nonferrous metals	13	Electrical generating machinery	14
Civilian aircraft, engines, and parts	12	Energy products	14
Telecommunications equipment	10	Nonferrous metals	11
Iron and steel products	10	Telecommunications equipment	10
Paper	8	Oil drilling, mining, and construction machinery	10

Source: U.S. Department of Commerce, *Survey of Current Business* (Washington, D.C.: U.S. Government Printing Office, June 1992), pp. 92–95.

in 1991. This represented nearly half of the total U.S. trade deficit for that year. Table 2–4 also shows that the other major U.S. imports were petroleum products, computers, and foods and beverages, and the other major U.S. exports were aircraft, foods and beverages, chemicals, and computers.

▲

2.7 SUPPLANTING VERSUS WORKING THROUGH THE MARKET

In the analysis presented so far in this chapter, we have implicitly assumed that the market is allowed to operate without government or other interferences. In that case demand and supply determine the equilibrium price and quantity for each commodity or service. If, on the other hand, the government imposed effective price controls (say, in the form of rent control or an agricultural price-support program), the market would be *supplanted or replaced* (i.e., the market would not be allowed to operate) and a persistent shortage or surplus of the commodity or service would result. Contrast this situation with *working through or within the market* (as, for example, with the imposition of an excise tax). Working through the market would result in a shift in demand or supply, but the equilibrium price and quantity of the commodity or service would still be determined by demand and supply, and no persistent shortage or surplus would arise.

Current, real-world examples can illustrate the differences. Example 3 shows the detrimental effect of rent control in New York City. Example 4 shows the waste that results from U.S. agricultural price-support programs. On the other hand, Example 5 examines the economic effects of working through the market with the imposition of an excise tax.

Example 3
Rent Control—The Best Way to Destroy New York City

"There is probably nothing that distorts a city worse than rent regulation. It accelerates the abandonment of marginal buildings, deters the improvement of good ones and creates wondrous windfalls for the middle class—all the while harming those it was meant to help, the poor."[15] Indeed, rent control has been described as the best way to destroy New York City! More than 90% of economists would agree (see Table 1–2).

Rent control was adopted in New York City as an emergency measure during World War II, but it has been kept ever since. Although rent control is most stringent in New York City, today more than 200 cities (including Boston, Los Angeles, and San Francisco) have some form of rent control. More than 10% of rental housing in the United States is under rent control.[16]

Rent controls are **price ceilings** or maximum rents set below equilibrium rents. Although designed to keep housing affordable, the effect has been just the opposite–a shortage of apartments. For example, Figure 2–9 might refer to the market for apartment rentals in New York City. Without rent control, the equilibrium rent is $500 and the equilibrium number of apartments rented is 2.4 million. At the controlled rent of $300 per month, 3 million apartments could be rented. Only 1.8 million apartments are available at that rent, so there is a shortage of 1.2 million apartments. Indeed, apartment seekers would be willing to pay a rent of $700 per month rather than go without an apartment when only 1.8 million apartments are available.[17]

Rent control introduces many predictable distortions into the housing market. First, as we have seen, rent control results in a shortage of apartments for rent. This is evidenced by the great difficulty and time required to find a vacant, rent-controlled apartment to rent. Second, owners of rent-controlled apartments usually cut maintenance and repairs to reduce costs, and so the quality of housing deteriorates. Because of the shortages to which rent control gives rise, apartments vacated as a result of inadequate maintenance can be filled easily and quickly. Third, rent control reduces the return on investment

---

[15]"End Rent Control," *New York Times*, May 12, 1987, p. 30.

[16]"A Model for Destroying a City," *Wall Street Journal*, March 12, 1993, p. A8.

[17]A price ceiling at or above the equilibrium price has no effect. For example, rent is $500 and the number of apartments rented is equal to 2.4 million in Figure 2–9 regardless of whether a rent ceiling of $500 or higher is imposed. Only if rent control or the maximum rent allowed by law is below the equilibrium rent of $500 does a shortage of apartments for rent result.

FIGURE 2–9 Rent Control

At the controlled rent of $300 per month, 3 million apartments could be rented. Only 1.8 million apartments are available at that rent, so there is a shortage of 1.2 million apartments. Apartment seekers would be willing to pay a rent of $700 per month when only 1.8 million apartments are available.

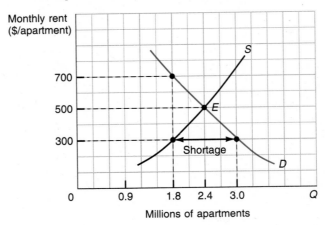

in rental housing, and so fewer rental apartments will be constructed.[18] Fourth, rent control encourages conversion into cooperatives (since their *price* is not controlled), which further reduces the supply of rent-controlled apartments.[19] Finally, with rent control, there must be a substitute for market price allocation; that is, nonprice rationing is likely to take place as landlords favor families with few or no children or pets and families with higher incomes.

In summary, we can predict that rent control leads to (1) a shortage of rental housing, (2) lower maintenance, (3) inadequate allocation of resources to the construction of new rental housing, (4) reduction in the stock of rental housing through conversion into cooperatives and condominiums, and (5) nonprice rationing of apartments for rent. One study revealed that the vacancy rate of rent-controlled apartments in New York City was less than 1%, expenditures on repairs were only about half as much as on noncontrolled apartments, and the shortage of new rental housing construction amounted to over $3 billion.[20] One way to eliminate the housing shortage and other distortions introduced by rent control, and at the same time protect tenants in residence from sudden sharp rent increases, is to decontrol apartments only as they become vacant.

Similar distortions result from the imposition of price ceilings on other commodities. For example, it was estimated that the price ceiling on gasoline

---

[18]To overcome this, rent control laws usually exempt new apartments.

[19]Many localities have passed laws restricting this practice.

[20]"A Model for Destroying a City," *Wall Street Journal*, March 12, 1993, p. A8.

in the United States in the summer of 1979 resulted in $200 million in lost time and 100 million gallons of gas wasted per month from waiting in long lines to obtain gasoline. Black markets also sprung up as some consumers were willing to pay a higher price for gasoline rather than stand in lines, and some suppliers were willing to accommodate them at higher prices. When price control was abolished, gasoline prices rose to the equilibrium level and long lines at the pumps and other market distortions soon disappeared.

Example 4

American Consumers Get Milked . . . Again—The Saga of U.S. Farm Support

"The federal government is heading for the grocery store this spring with a simple shopping list. It's going to buy cheese, butter, and nonfat dry milk. A *lot* of cheese, butter, and nonfat dry milk. . . . The problem is that Congress thinks milk prices are too low. It's ordered the Agriculture Department's Commodity Credit Corporation to go out and buy more dairy products to get the price up.[21] For more than 50 years American agriculture has been the nation's largest recipient of political intervention and economic aid. In fact, "Federal agricultural spending—more than $25 billion this year—is the equivalent of giving every full-time subsidized farmer two new $30,000 Mercedes-Benz automobiles."[22] Why such insanity? Again, demand and supply can help us analyze and evaluate the various U.S. farm-support programs.

The federal government has used the following three basic methods to prop up farm incomes. (1) From the 1930s until 1973, the federal government operated a price-support program (i.e., it established a **price floor** or a minimum price above the equilibrium price) for several agricultural commodities to increase farm incomes. This resulted in a surplus of agricultural commodities, which was purchased by the government. The government then used part of the surplus to assist low-income people, to subsidize school lunch programs, and for foreign aid. But a great deal of the surplus had to be stored and some spoiled. (2) From the early 1960s, the government also provided incentives for farmers to keep part of their land idle to avoid ever-increasing surpluses. (3) Starting in 1973, the government gave farmers a direct subsidy if the market price of certain commodities fell below a target price.

---

[21]T. Tregarthen, "American Consumers Get Milked . . . Again," *The Margin*, January/February 1989, pp. 18–19.

[22]"Farm Subsidies Stifle Agriculture," *New York Times*, May 29, 1988, p. F3.

FIGURE 2–10   Agricultural Support Programs

At the price floor of $4 per bushel, farmers supply 2.2 billion bushels, consumers purchase 1.8 billion bushels, and the government purchases the surplus of 0.4 billion bushels at a total cost of $1.6 billion.

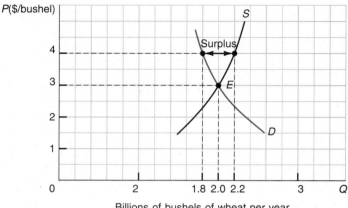

Billions of bushels of wheat per year

We can analyze the effect of these three farm-support programs with the aid of Figure 2–10, which refers to the wheat market. In the absence of any support program, wheat farmers produce the equilibrium quantity of 2 billion bushels per year, sell it at the equilibrium price of $3 per bushel, and realize a total income of $6 billion. If the government establishes a price floor of $4 per bushel for wheat, farmers supply 2.2 billion bushels per year, consumers purchase only 1.8 billion bushels, and the government must purchase the surplus of 0.4 billion bushels at the support price of $4 per bushel, for a total cost of $1.6 billion. This does not include the cost of storing the surplus. The price floor has no effect if the market price rises above it.

If, through acreage restriction, output falls from 2.2 to 2.1 billion bushels at the supported price of $4 per bushel, the surplus declines to 0.3 billion bushels, and the cost of the price-support program falls to $1.2 billion. With direct subsidies, farmers sell the equilibrium quantity of 2 billion bushels at the equilibrium price of $3 per bushel, and the government then provides farmers a direct subsidy of $1 per bushel at a total cost of $2 billion (if the government sets the target price for wheat at $4 per bushel). With a direct subsidy, however, there is no storage problem, and consumers obtain wheat at the lower market price of $3 per bushel.

Although the government has the responsibility to smooth structural adjustments as fewer and fewer farmers are needed to feed the nation and even export a large surplus, and to reduce farmers' hardships, the farm-support program has been extremely wasteful. Most of the benefits seem to have gone to owners of large farms rather than to small, poor farmers, and the program has impeded the long-run adjustment required by changing tastes and technology. What is worse is that there seems to be little political will to find a long-run solution to the problem. Waste is even greater in Europe, and because European-subsidized agricultural exports take away foreign markets from American farmers, there have been serious trade disputes.[23]

▲

By interfering with the working of markets, rent control, ceilings on gasoline, and agricultural price-support programs create huge waste and inefficiencies in the economy. These result because markets communicate crucial information to consumers about the relative availability of goods and services, and to suppliers about the relative value that consumers place on various goods and services. Without the free flow of information transmitted through market prices, persistent shortages and surpluses—and waste—arise. Working through the market (see Example 5) leads to different results.

Example 5
Working Through the Market with an Excise Tax

An **excise tax** is a tax on each unit of a commodity.[24] If collected from sellers, the tax causes the supply curve to shift up by the amount of the tax, because sellers require that much more per unit to supply each amount of the commodity. The result is that consumers purchase a smaller quantity at a higher price, while sellers receive a smaller *net* price after payment of the tax. Thus consumers and producers share the burden or **incidence of a tax**.

We can analyze the effect of an excise tax collected from sellers through the use of Figure 2–11. In the figure, D and S are the demand and supply curves of hamburgers with the equilibrium defined at point E (at which $P = \$1.00$ and $Q = 6$ million hamburgers, as in Figure 2–5). If a tax of $0.75 per hamburger is collected from sellers, S shifts up by the amount of the tax to S'', since sellers now require a price $0.75 higher than before to realize the same net after-tax price. Now D and S'' define equilibrium point C with $Q = 4$ million hamburgers and $P = \$1.50$, or $0.50 higher than before the imposition of the tax. Thus, at the new equilibrium point, consumers purchase a smaller quantity and pay a higher price. Sellers also receive the smaller net price of $0.75 (the price of $1.50 paid by consumers minus the $0.75 collected by the government on each hamburger sold).

---

[23]"Life Can Be Sweet on Europe's Subsidized Farms," *New York Times*, April 12, 1992, p. E3.

[24]An excise tax can be of a given dollar amount *per unit* of the commodity or of a given percentage of the price of the commodity (ad valorem). If all units of the commodity are of equal quality and price (as we assume here), the per-unit and the ad valorem excise tax are equal and the distinction is unnecessary.

FIGURE 2–11   Effect of an Excise Tax

With D and S, $P = \$1.00$ and $Q = 6$ million hamburgers (point E), as in Figure 2–5. If the tax of \$0.75 per hamburger is collected from sellers, S shifts up by \$0.75 to S''. With D and S'', $Q = 4$ million hamburgers and $P = \$1.50$ for consumers (point C), but sellers receive a net price of only \$0.75 after paying the \$0.75 tax per unit.

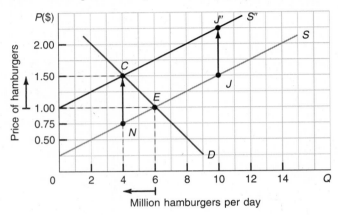

Million hamburgers per day

In the case shown in Figure 2–11, two-thirds of the burden of the tax falls on consumers and one-third on sellers. That is, consumers pay \$0.50 more and sellers receive a net price that is \$0.25 less than before the imposition of the excise tax. Thus, even though the tax is collected from sellers, the forces of demand and supply are such that sellers are able to pass on or shift part of the burden of the tax to consumers in the form of a higher price for hamburgers. Given the supply of a commodity, the less sensitive the quantity demanded is to price (i.e., the steeper and less elastic is the demand curve), the greater is the share of the tax paid by consumers in the form of higher prices. On the other hand, given the demand for a commodity, the less sensitive the quantity supplied is to price (i.e., the steeper and less elastic is the supply curve), the smaller is the share of the tax paid by consumers and the larger is the share left to be paid by sellers (see Problem 12).

If the government collected the tax of \$0.75 per hamburger from buyers or consumers rather than from sellers, D would shift down by \$0.75 to D'' (pencil D'' in Figure 2–11 through point N, parallel to D). With D'' and S, $Q = 4$ million hamburgers, $P = \$0.75$ (that buyers pay to sellers) and then buyers have to pay the tax of \$0.75 per hamburger to the government. Again, consumers pay \$1.50, which is \$0.50 more than the previous equilibrium price, and sellers receive \$0.25 less. Therefore, the net result is the same whether the tax is collected from sellers or from buyers.

One type of excise tax is the **import tariff**. This is nothing other than a tax on each unit of the imported commodity. As such, it has both a production and a consumption effect; these, as well as the welfare effects of a per-unit tax and an import tariff, are analyzed in section 8.8.

SUMMARY

1. Most of microeconomic analysis is devoted to the study of how individual markets operate. A market is the network of communications between individuals and firms for the purpose of buying and selling goods, services, and resources. Markets provide the framework for the analysis of the forces of demand and supply that determines commodity and resource prices. A market can, but need not, be a specific place or location. A perfectly competitive market is a market in which no buyer or seller can affect the price of the product, all units of the products are homogeneous, resources are mobile, and knowledge is perfect.

2. A market demand schedule is a table showing the quantity demanded of a commodity at each price over a given time period while holding constant all other relevant economic variables on which demand depends. The market demand curve is the graphic representation of the demand schedule. It is negatively sloped, which reflects the inverse price-quantity relationship or the law of demand. A change in consumers' incomes, tastes for the commodity, the number of consumers in the market, or the price of substitutes or complements shift the demand curve. The price elasticity of demand is measured by the percentage change in quantity demanded divided by the percentage change in price.

3. A market supply schedule is a table showing the quantity supplied of a commodity at each price over a given time period. The market supply curve is the graphic representation of the supply schedule. Because of rising marginal costs, the supply curve is usually positively sloped, which indicates that producers supply more of the commodity at higher prices. A change in technology, resource prices, and, for agricultural commodities, weather condi-

tions, shifts the supply curve. The price elasticity of supply is measured by the percentage change in the quantity supplied divided by the percentage change in price.

4. The equilibrium price and quantity of a commodity are defined at the intersection of the market demand and supply curves of the commodity. At higher than equilibrium prices, there is a surplus of the commodity, which leads sellers to lower their prices to the equilibrium level. At lower than equilibrium prices, there is a shortage of the commodity, which leads consumers to bid prices up to the equilibrium level. Equilibrium is the condition that, once achieved, tends to persist.

5. An increase in demand (a rightward shift in the demand curve) results in an increase in both the equilibrium price and quantity of the commodity. A decrease in demand has the opposite effect. On the other hand, an increase in supply (a rightward shift in the supply curve) results in a lower equilibrium price but a higher equilibrium quantity. A decrease in supply has the opposite effect.

6. A nation's demand for imports is derived from the nation's excess demand for the importable commodity at below-equilibrium prices in the absence of trade. On the other hand, the foreign supply of exports of the commodity is derived from the foreign excess supply of the commodity at above-equilibrium prices in the absence of trade. The equilibrium price and quantity of the traded commodity are given at the intersection of the demand and supply curves of imports of the commodity. In today's interdependent world, the tendency for the domestic price of a commodity to rise is moderated by the inflow of imports of the commodity.

7. A price ceiling below the equilibrium price (such as rent control) leads to a shortage of the commodity and possibly black mar-

kets. A price floor above the equilibrium price (as for some agricultural commodities) leads to a surplus of the commodity. Given the supply of a commodity, the steeper or the less elastic is the demand for the commodity, the greater is the burden or incidence of a per-unit tax on consumers.

KEY TERMS

Market
Perfectly Competitive Market
Market Demand Schedule
Law of Demand
Market Demand Curve
Price Elasticity of Demand (η)
Point Elasticity of Demand
Arc Elasticity of Demand
Market Supply Schedule

Market Supply Curve
Price Elasticity of Supply
Point Elasticity of Supply (ϵ)
Arc Elasticity of Supply
Equilibrium Price
Surplus
Shortage
Equilibrium
Comparative Static Analysis

Excess Demand
Excess Supply
Price Ceiling
Price Floor
Excise Tax
Incidence of a Tax
Import Tariff

REVIEW QUESTIONS

1. Which of the following cause demand to increase? An increase in consumers' income, an increase in the price of substitutes, an increase in the price of complements, an increase in the number of consumers in the market.

2. Will the supply curve shift to the right or to the left if (a) technology improves or (b) input prices increase? (c) What happens if both (a) and (b) occur?

3. In the text, the statement was made that one could begin answering any question in economics by saying, "It depends on demand and supply." What about the statement, "It depends on elasticities."?

4. Explain why $Q=4$ is not the equilibrium quantity in Figure 2–5 and how equilibrium is reached.

5. Explain why $Q=8$ is not the equilibrium quantity in Figure 2–5 and how equilibrium is reached.

6. Using comparative static analysis, explain how a wheat shortage was avoided in the United States after the drought in Kansas in 1988 and 1989 that was described in Example 2 in Chapter 1.

7. Is the increase in the demand for large automobiles in the United States since the collapse of petroleum prices in 1986 rational? Do you foresee any difficulty for the United States if this trend continues?

8. Why is the textile price of $1.50 in Figure 2–8 not the equilibrium price?

9. What would be the difference in textile prices between the United States and the rest of the world if textiles were freely traded but the cost of transporting each yard of textiles between the United States and the rest of the world was $1? What would be the quantity of textiles traded?

10. a. When is the price ceiling or price floor ineffective?
    b. What is an example of an effective price ceiling? What is its effect?
    c. What is an example of an effective price floor? What is its effect?

11. a. Does it make any difference whether an excise tax is collected from sellers or from buyers? Why?
    b. If the market demand curve for a commodity is more elastic than the market supply curve, is the burden of an excise tax greater on buyers or sellers?

12. Determine the minimum size of a prohibitive tariff in Figure 2–8 in the absence of transportation costs.

PROBLEMS

1. Given the following demand schedule of a commodity

P($)	6	5	4	3	2	1	0
QD	0	10	20	30	40	50	60

show that by substituting the prices given in the table into the following demand equation or function, you obtain the corresponding quantities demanded given in the table:

$$QD = 60 - 10P$$

*2. a. Derive the demand schedule from the following demand function:

$$QD' = 80 - 10P$$

   b. On the same graph, plot the demand schedule of problem 1 and label it D and the demand curve of part (a) of this problem and label it D'.
   c. Does D' represent an increase in demand or an increase in the quantity demanded? Why?

3. a. Derive the supply schedule from the following supply function:

$$QS = 10P$$

   b. Derive the supply schedule from the following supply function:

$$QS' = 20 + 10P$$

   c. On the same graph, plot the supply schedule of part (a) and label it S and the supply curve of part (b) and label it S'.
   d. What may have caused S to shift to S'?

4. a. Find the price elasticity of demand curve D of problem 1 for a price decline from $P = \$5$ to $P = \$4$ and for a price increase from $P = \$4$ to $P = \$5$; then find the arc elasticity between the two points.
   b. Find the price elasticity of supply curve S of problem 3a for a price increase from $P = \$4$ to $P = \$5$ and for a price decrease from $P = \$5$ to $P = \$4$; then find the arc elasticity between the two points.

*5. a. Construct a table similar to Table 2–3 giving the supply schedule of problem 3a and the demand schedule of problem 1. In the same table identify the equilibrium price and quantity of the commodity, the surplus or shortage at prices other than the equilibrium price, and the pressure on price with a surplus or a shortage.
   b. Show your results of part (a) graphically.

6. a. Repeat the procedure in problem 5a for the supply schedule of problem 3b and the demand schedule of problem 2a.
   b. Show your results of part (a) graphically.
   c. On the same graph, draw D and S from problem 5b and D' and S' from problem 6b. What general conclusion can you reach as to the effect of an increase in the demand and supply of a commodity on the equilibrium price and quantity of the commodity?

7. On separate sets of axes, show that
   a. a decrease in demand reduces the equilibrium price and quantity of the commodity.
   b. a decrease in supply increases price but reduces quantity.
   c. a decrease in both demand and supply will reduce quantity but may increase, reduce, or leave price unchanged.

8. On separate sets of axes, show that
   a. an increase in both demand and supply will increase quantity and may increase, reduce, or leave price unchanged.
   b. a decrease in demand and an increase in supply will reduce price but may increase, decrease, or leave quantity unchanged.
   c. an increase in demand and a decrease in supply will increase price but may increase, decrease, or leave quantity unchanged.

*9. Indicate what happens in the market for hamburgers if
   a. the price of hot dogs increases.
   b. a disease develops that kills a large proportion of cattle.
   c. a new breed of cattle is developed with much faster growth.
   d. medical research proves that this new breed results in hamburgers with less cholesterol.

_____

* = Answer provided at end of book.

e. a direct subsidy on each head of cattle is given to farmers raising cattle.

10. Using Panels A and C of Figure 2–8, show the price of textiles in the United States and in the rest of the world. Also show the quantity of textiles traded if the cost of transportation for each yard of cloth is $1 and if this cost falls equally on the United States and the rest of the world.

11. With reference to your answer to problem 5a, indicate the effect of the government imposing on the commodity a
    a. price ceiling of $P = \$2$.
    b. price ceiling of $P = \$3$.
    c. price ceiling higher than $P = \$3$.
    d. price floor of $P = \$5$.

e. price floor of $P = \$4$.

f. price floor equal to or smaller than $P = \$3$.

*12. Draw a figure showing that
    a. given the supply of a commodity, the less sensitive the quantity demanded is to price (i.e., the steeper is the demand curve), the greater is the share of the tax paid by consumers in the form of higher prices.
    b. given the demand for a commodity, the less sensitive the quantity supplied is to price (i.e., the steeper is the supply curve), the smaller is the share of the tax paid by consumers and the larger is the share paid by sellers.

PART TWO

THEORY OF CONSUMER BEHAVIOR AND DEMAND

P art Two (Chapters 3–5) presents the theory of consumer behavior and demand. Chapter 3 examines the tastes of the consumer and how the consumer maximizes utility or satisfaction in spending his or her income. These concepts are used and extended in Chapter 4 to derive the consumer's demand curve for a commodity. Chapter 5 shows how, by aggregating or summing up individual consumers' demand curves, we get the market demand curve for the commodity. Chapter 5 also examines in detail the measurement and usefulness of various demand elasticities. Each chapter in Part Two has an optional appendix presenting some more advanced topics in consumer demand theory. As in other parts of this text, the presentation of the theory is reinforced throughout with real-world examples and important applications.

3

CONSUMER PREFERENCES AND CHOICE

In this chapter, we begin the formal study of microeconomics by examining the economic behavior of the consumer. A consumer is an individual or a household composed of one or more individuals. The consumer is the basic economic unit that determines which commodities are purchased and in what quantities. Millions of such decisions are made each day on the more than $6 trillion worth of goods and services produced by the American economy each year.

What guides these individual consumer decisions? Why do consumers purchase some commodities and not others? How do they decide how much to purchase of each commodity? What is the aim of a rational consumer in spending income? These are but a few of the important questions to which we seek answers in this chapter. The theory of consumer behavior and choice is the first step in the derivation of the market demand curve, the importance of which was clearly demonstrated in Chapter 2.

We begin the study of the economic behavior of the consumer by examining tastes. Consumers' tastes can be related to utility concepts or indifference curves. These are discussed in the first two sections of the chapter. In section 3.3, we examine the convergence of tastes internationally. We then introduce the budget line, which gives the constraints or limitations faced by the consumer in purchasing goods and services. Constraints arise because the commodities that the consumer wants command a price in the marketplace (i.e., they are not free) and the consumer has limited income. Thus, the budget line reflects the familiar and pervasive economic fact of scarcity as it pertains to the individual consumer.

Because the consumer's wants are unlimited or, in any event, exceed his or her ability to satisfy them all, it is important that he or she spend income so as to maximize satisfaction. Thus, a model is provided to illustrate and predict how a rational consumer maximizes satisfaction, given his or her tastes (indifference curves) and the constraints he or she faces (the budget line).

The several real-world examples and important applications presented in the chapter demonstrate the relevance and usefulness of the theory of consumer behavior and choice. In the optional appendix, we examine consumer choices under uncertainty and apply this theory to the choice of a portfolio.

3.1 UTILITY ANALYSIS

In this section, we discuss the meaning of utility, distinguish between total utility and marginal utility, and examine the important difference between cardinal and ordinal utility. The concept of utility is used here to introduce the consumer's tastes. The analysis of consumer tastes is a crucial step in determining how a consumer maximizes satisfaction in spending income.

Total and Marginal Utility

Goods are desired because of their ability to satisfy human wants. The property of a good that enables it to satisfy human wants is called **utility**. As an individual consumes more of a good per time period, his **total utility (TU)** or satisfaction increases, but his marginal utility diminishes. **Marginal utility (MU)** is the extra utility received from consuming one additional unit of the good per unit of time while holding constant the quantity consumed of all other commodities.

For example, Table 3–1 indicates that one hamburger per day (or, more generally, one unit of good X per period of time) gives the consumer a total utility (TU) of 10 utils, where a **util** is an arbitrary unit of utility. Total utility increases with each additional hamburger consumed until the fifth one, which leaves total utility unchanged. This is the *saturation point*. Consuming the sixth hamburger then leads to a decline in total utility because of storage or disposal problems.[1] The third column of Table 3–1 gives the extra or marginal

TABLE 3–1 Total and Marginal Utility

Q_x	TU_x	MU_x
0	0	. . .
1	10	10
2	16	6
3	20	4
4	22	2
5	22	0
6	20	−2

---

[1]That is, some effort (disutility), no matter how small, is required to get rid of the sixth hamburger. Assuming that the individual cannot sell the sixth hamburger, he or she would not want it even for free.

utility resulting from the consumption of each *additional* hamburger. Marginal utility is positive but declines until the fifth hamburger, for which it is zero, and becomes negative for the sixth hamburger.

Plotting the values given in Table 3–1, we obtain Figure 3–1, with the top panel showing total utility and the bottom panel showing marginal utility. The total and marginal utility curves are obtained by joining the midpoints of the bars measuring *TU* and *MU* at each level of consumption. Note that the *TU* rises by smaller and smaller amounts (the shaded areas) and so the *MU* declines. The consumer reaches saturation after consuming the fourth hamburger. Thus, *TU* remains unchanged with the consumption of the fifth hamburger and *MU* is zero. After the fifth hamburger, *TU* declines and so *MU* is negative. The negative slope or downward-to-the-right inclination of the *MU* curve reflects the **law of diminishing marginal utility**.

FIGURE 3–1   Total and Marginal Utility

In the top panel, total utility *(TU)* increases by smaller and smaller amounts (the shaded areas) and so the marginal utility *(MU)* in the bottom panel declines. *TU* remains unchanged with the consumption of the fifth hamburger, and so *MU* is zero. After the fifth hamburger per day, *TU* declines and *MU* is negative.

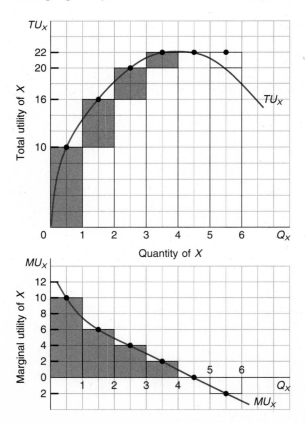

Utility schedules refer to the tastes of a particular individual; that is, they are unique to the individual and reflect his or her own particular subjective preferences and perceptions. Different individuals may have different tastes and different utility schedules. Utility schedules remain unchanged so long as the individual's tastes remain the same.

Cardinal or Ordinal Utility?

The concept of utility discussed in the previous section was introduced at about the same time, in the early 1870s, by William Stanley Jevons of Great Britain, Carl Menger of Austria, and Léon Walras of France. They believed that the utility an individual receives from consuming each quantity of a good or basket of goods could be measured cardinally just like weight, height, or temperature.[2]

Cardinal utility means that an individual can attach specific values or numbers of utils from consuming each quantity of a good or basket of goods. In Table 3–1 we saw that the individual received 10 utils from consuming one hamburger. He received 16 utils, or 6 additional utils, from consuming two hamburgers. The consumption of the third hamburger gave this individual 4 extra utils, or two-thirds as many extra utils, as the second hamburger. Thus, Table 3–1 and Figure 3–1 reflect cardinal utility. They actually provide an index of satisfaction for the individual.

In contrast, **ordinal utility** only *ranks* the utility received from consuming various amounts of a good or baskets of goods. Ordinal utility specifies that consuming two hamburgers gives the individual more utility than he receives from consuming one hamburger, but it does not specify exactly how much additional utility the second hamburger provides. Similarly, ordinal utility would say only that three hamburgers give this individual more utility than two hamburgers, but *not* how many more utils.[3]

Ordinal utility is a much weaker notion than cardinal utility because it only requires that the consumer be able to rank baskets of goods in the order of his or her preference. That is, when presented with a choice between any two baskets of goods, ordinal utility requires only that the individual indicate if he or she prefers the first basket, the second basket, or is indifferent between the two. It does not require that the individual specify how many more utils he or she receives from the preferred basket. *In short, ordinal utility only ranks*

---

[2]A market basket of goods can be defined as containing specific quantities of various goods and services. For example, one basket may contain one hamburger, one soft drink, and a ticket to a ball game, while another basket may contain two soft drinks and two movie tickets.

[3]To be sure, numerical values could be attached to the utility received by the individual from consuming various hamburgers, even with ordinal utility. However, with ordinal utility, higher utility values only indicate higher rankings of utility, and no importance can be attached to actual numerical differences in utility. For example, 20 utils can only be interpreted as giving more utility than 10 utils, but not twice as much. Thus, to indicate rising utility rankings, numbers such as 5,10, 20; 8, 15, 17; or I (lowest), II, and III are equivalent.

various consumption bundles, whereas cardinal utility provides an actual index or measure of satisfaction.

The distinction between cardinal and ordinal utility is important because a theory of consumer behavior can be developed on the weaker assumption of ordinal utility without the need for a cardinal measure. And a theory that reaches the same conclusion as another on weaker assumptions is a superior theory.[4] Utility theory provides a convenient introduction to the analysis of consumer tastes and to the more rigorous indifference curve approach. It is also useful for the analysis of consumer choices in the face of risk, which is presented in the appendix to this chapter.

3.2 CONSUMER'S TASTES: INDIFFERENCE CURVES

In this section, we define indifference curves and examine their characteristics. Indifference curves were first introduced by the English economist F. Y. Edgeworth in the 1880s. The concept was refined and used extensively by the Italian economist V. Pareto in the early 1900s. Indifference curves were popularized and greatly extended in application in the 1930s by two other English economists: R. G. D. Allen and J. R. Hicks. They are a crucial tool of analysis because they are used to represent an ordinal measure of the tastes and preferences of the consumer and to show how the consumer maximizes utility in spending income.

Indifference Curves—What Do They Show?

Consumers' tastes can be examined with ordinal utility. An ordinal measure of utility is based on three assumptions. First, we assume that when faced with any two baskets of goods, the consumer can determine whether he or she prefers basket *A* to basket *B*, *B* to *A*, or whether he or she is indifferent between the two. Second, we assume that the tastes of the consumer are *consistent* or *transitive.*. That is, if the consumer states that he prefers basket *A* to basket *B* and also that he prefers basket *B* to basket *C*, then he will prefer *A* to *C*. Third, we assume that more of a commodity is preferred to less; that is, we assume that the commodity is a **good** rather than a **bad**, and the consumer is never satiated with the commodity.[5] The three assumptions can be used to represent an individual's tastes with indifference curves. In order to conduct the analysis by plane geometry, we will assume throughout that there are only two goods, *X* and *Y*.

An **indifference curve** shows the various combinations of two goods that give the consumer equal utility or satisfaction. A higher indifference curve

---

[4]This is like producing a given output with fewer or cheaper inputs, or achieving the same medical result (such as control of high blood pressure) with less or weaker medication.

[5]Examples of bads are pollution, garbage, and disease, of which less is preferred to more.

TABLE 3–2 **Indifference Schedule**

Hamburgers (X)	Soft Drinks (Y)	Combination
1	10	A
2	6	B
4	3	C
7	1	F

refers to a higher level of satisfaction, and a lower indifference curve refers to less satisfaction. However, we have no indication as to how much additional satisfaction or utility a higher indifference curve indicates. That is, different indifference curves simply provide an ordering or ranking of the individual's preference.

For example, Table 3–2 gives an indifference schedule showing the various combinations of hamburgers (good X) and soft drinks (good Y) that give the consumer equal satisfaction. This information is plotted as indifference curve U_1 in the left panel of Figure 3–2. The right panel repeats indifference curve U_1 along with a higher indifference curve (U_2) and a lower one (U_0).

Indifference curve U_1 shows that one hamburger and ten soft drinks per unit of time (combination A) give the consumer the same level of satisfaction

FIGURE 3–2 **Indifference Curves**

The individual is indifferent among combinations A, B, C, and F since they all lie on indifference curve U_1. U_1 refers to a higher level of satisfaction than U_0, but to a lower level than U_2.

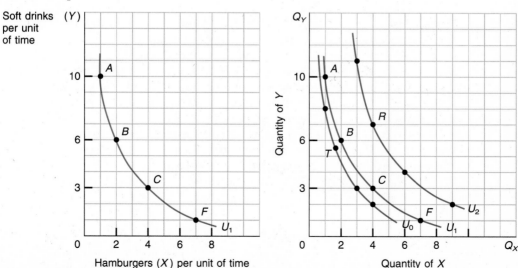

as two hamburgers and six soft drinks (combination B), four hamburgers and three soft drinks (combination C), or seven hamburgers and one soft drink (combination F). On the other hand, combination R (4 hamburgers and 7 soft drinks) has both more hamburgers and more soft drinks than combination B (see the right panel of Figure 3–2), and so it refers to a higher level of satisfaction. Thus, combination R and all the other combinations that give the same level of satisfaction as combination R define higher indifference curve U_2. Finally, all combinations on U_0 give the same satisfaction as combination T, and combination T refers to both fewer hamburgers and fewer soft drinks than (and therefore is inferior to) combination B on U_1.

Although in Figure 3–2 we have drawn only three indifference curves, there is an indifference curve going through each point in the XY plane (i.e., referring to each possible combination of good X and good Y). Another way of saying this is that between any two indifference curves, an additional one can always be drawn. The entire set of indifference curves is called an **indifference map** and reflects the entire set of tastes and preferences of the consumer.

Characteristics of Indifference Curves

Indifference curves are usually negatively sloped, cannot intersect, and are convex to the origin (see Figure 3–2). Indifference curves are negatively sloped because if one basket of goods X and Y contains more of X, it will have to contain less of Y than another basket in order for the two baskets to give the same level of satisfaction and be on the same indifference curve. For example, since basket B on indifference curve U_1 in Figure 3–2 contains more hamburgers (good X) than basket A, basket B must contain fewer soft drinks (good Y) for the consumer to be on indifference curve U_1.

A positively sloped curve would indicate that one basket containing more of both commodities gives the same utility or satisfaction to the consumer as another basket containing less of both commodities (and no other commodity). Because we are dealing with goods rather than bads, such a curve could not possibly be an indifference curve. For example, in the left panel of Figure 3–3, combination B' contains more of X and more of Y than combination A', and so the positively sloped curve on which B' and A' lie cannot be an indifference curve. That is, B' must be on a higher indifference curve than A' if X and Y are both goods.[6]

Indifference curves also cannot intersect. Intersecting curves are inconsistent with the definition of indifference curves. For example, if curve 1 and curve 2 in the right panel of Figure 3–3 were indifference curves, they would indicate that basket A^* is equivalent to basket C^* since both A^* and C^* are on

---

[6] Only if either X or Y were a bad would the indifference curve be positively sloped as in the left panel of Figure 3–3.

FIGURE 3–3   Indifference Curves Cannot Be Positively Sloped or Intersect

In the left panel, the positively sloped curve cannot be an indifference curve because it shows that combination B', which contains more of X and Y than combination A', gives equal satisfaction to the consumer as A'. In the right panel, since C^* is on curves 1 and 2, it should give the same satisfaction as A^* and B^*, but this is impossible because B^* has more of X and Y than A^*. Thus, indifference curves cannot intersect.

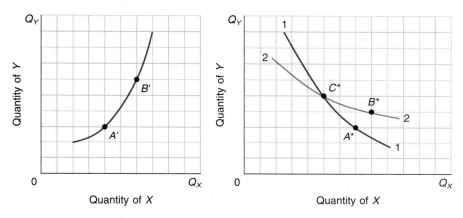

curve 1, and also that basket B^* is equivalent to basket C^* since both B^* and C^* are on curve 2. By transitivity, B^* should then be equivalent to A^*. However, this is impossible because basket B^* contains more of both good X and good Y than basket A^*. Thus, indifference curves cannot intersect.

Indifference curves are usually convex to the origin; that is, they lie above any tangent to the curve. Convexity results from or is a reflection of a decreasing marginal rate of substitution, which is discussed next.

The Marginal Rate of Substitution

The **marginal rate of substitution (MRS)** refers to the amount of one good that an individual is willing to give up for an additional unit of another good while maintaining the same level of satisfaction or remaining on the same indifference curve. For example, the marginal rate of substitution of good X for good Y (MRS_{XY}) refers to the amount of Y that the individual is willing to exchange per unit of X and maintain the same level of satisfaction. Note that MRS_{XY} measures the downward vertical distance (the amount of Y that the individual is willing to give up) per unit of horizontal distance (i.e., per additional unit of X required) to remain on the same indifference curve. That is, $MRS_{XY} = -\Delta Y/\Delta X$. Because of the reduction in Y, MRS_{XY} is negative. However, we multiply by -1 and express MRS_{XY} as a positive value.

For example, starting at point A on U_1 in Figure 3–4, the individual is willing to give up four units of Y for one additional unit of X and reach point B on U_1. Thus, $MRS_{XY} = -(-4/1) = 4$. This is the absolute (or positive value

FIGURE 3–4   Marginal Rate of Substitution (MRS)

Starting at point A, the individual is willing to give up 4 units of Y for one additional unit of X and reach point B on U_1. Thus, $MRS_{XY} = 4$ (the absolute slope of chord AB). Between points B and C, $MRS_{XY} = 3/2$. Between C and F, $MRS_{XY} = 2/3$. MRS_{XY} declines as the individual moves down the indifference curve.

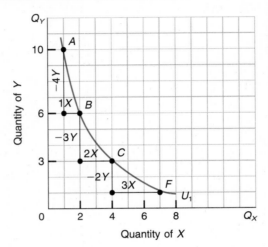

of the) slope of the chord from point A to point B on U_1. Between point B and point C on U_1, $MRS_{XY} = 3/2 = 1.5$ (the absolute slope of chord BC). Between points C and F, $MRS_{XY} = 2/3 = 0.67$. At a particular point on the indifference curve, MRS_{XY} is given by the absolute slope of the tangent to the indifference curve at that point. Different individuals usually have different indifference curves and different MRS_{XY} (at points where their indifference curves have different slopes).

We can relate indifference curves to the preceding utility analysis by pointing out that all combinations of goods X and Y on a given indifference curve refer to the same level of total utility for the individual. Thus, for a movement down a given indifference curve, the gain in utility in consuming more of good X must be equal to the loss in utility in consuming less of good Y. Specifically, the increase in consumption of good X (ΔX) times the marginal utility that the individual receives from consuming each additional unit of X (MU_X) must be equal to the reduction in Y ($-\Delta Y$) times the marginal utility of Y (MU_Y). That is,

$$(\Delta X)(MU_X) = -(\Delta Y)(MU_Y) \qquad \text{[3–1]}$$

so that

$$MU_X/MU_Y = -\Delta Y/\Delta X = MRS_{XY} \qquad \text{[3–2]}$$

Thus, MRS_{XY} is equal to the absolute slope of the indifference curve and to the ratio of the marginal utilities.[7]

Note that MRS_{XY} (i.e., the absolute slope of the indifference curve) declines as we move down the indifference curve. This follows from, or is a reflection of, the convexity of the indifference curve. That is, as the individual moves down an indifference curve and is left with less and less Y (say, soft drinks) and more and more X (say, hamburgers), each remaining unit of Y becomes more valuable to him and each additional unit of X becomes less valuable. Thus, he is willing to give up less and less of Y to obtain each additional unit of X. It is this property that makes MRS_{XY} diminish and indifference curves convex to the origin. We will see in section 3.5 the crucial role that convexity plays in consumer utility maximization.[8]

Some Special Types of Indifference Curves

Although indifference curves are usually negatively sloped and convex to the origin, they may sometimes assume other shapes, as shown in Figure 3–5. Horizontal indifference curves, as in the top left panel of Figure 3–5, would indicate that commodity X is a **neuter**; that is, the consumer is indifferent between having more or less of the commodity. Vertical indifference curves (not shown in the figure) would indicate that commodity Y is a neuter.

The top right panel shows indifference curves that are negatively sloped straight lines. Here, MRS_{XY} or the absolute slope of the indifference curves is constant. This means that an individual is always willing to give up the same amount of good Y (say, two cups of tea) for each additional unit of good X (one cup of coffee). Therefore, good X and two units of good Y are *perfect substitutes* for this individual.

The bottom left panel shows indifference curves that are L-shaped. These show goods that are *perfect complements* for the individual. This means that having more of one good without having more of the other also does not increase the individual's satisfaction. Another way of saying this is that the MRS between the two goods is zero. An example of this is right and left shoes.

Finally, the bottom right panel shows indifference curves that are concave rather than convex to the origin. This means that the individual is willing to give up more and more units of good Y for each additional unit of X (i.e., MRS_{XY} increases). For example, between points A and B on U_1, $MRS_{XY} = 2/2 = 1$; between B and C, $MRS_{XY} = 3/1 = 3$; and between C and F, $MRS_{XY} = 3/0.5 = 6$. In section 3.5, we will see that in this unusual case, the individual would end up consuming only good X or only good Y.

---

[7]For a mathematical presentation of indifference curves and their characteristics using rudimentary calculus, see section A.1 of the Mathematical Appendix at the end of the book.

[8]A movement along an indifference curve in the *upward* direction measures MRS_{YX}, which also diminishes.

FIGURE 3–5   Some Unusual Indifference Curves

Horizontal indifference curves, as in the top left panel, indicate that X is a neuter; that is, the consumer is indifferent between having more or less of it. Indifference curves that are negatively sloped straight lines, as in the top right panel, indicate that MRS_{XY} is constant, and so X and Y are perfect substitutes for the individual. The bottom left panel shows L-shaped indifference curves for perfect complements. The bottom right panel shows indifference curves that are concave to the origin (i.e., MRS_{XY} increases).

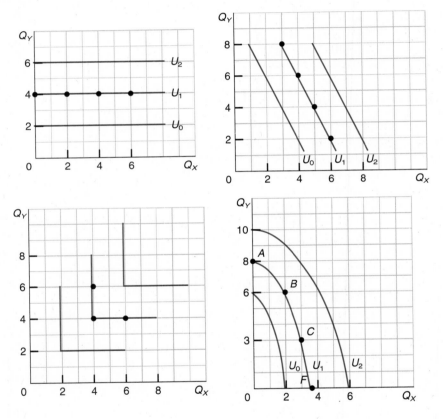

Even though indifference curves can assume any of the shapes shown in Figure 3–5, they are usually negatively sloped, nonintersecting, and convex to the origin. These characteristics have been confirmed experimentally.[9] Because it is difficult to derive indifference curves experimentally, however, firms try to determine consumers' preferences by marketing studies, as explained in Example 1.

---

[9]See, for example, K. R. MacCrimmon and M. Toda, "The Experimental Determination of Indifference Curves," *Review of Economic Studies*, October 1969.

Example 1
How Ford Decided on the Characteristics of Its Taurus

Although indifference curves are an extremely important theoretical construct, it is very difficult to actually derive them experimentally in the real world. Firms, however, can learn about consumers' preferences by conducting or commissioning marketing studies without deriving consumers' indifference curves. The firm can identify the most important characteristics of a product, say styling and performance for automobiles, and conduct a marketing study to determine how much more consumers would be willing to pay to have more of each attribute, or how they would trade off more of one attribute for less of another. This approach to consumer demand theory, which focuses on the characteristics or attributes of goods and on their worth or *hedonic prices* rather than on the goods themselves, was pioneered by Kelvin Lancaster. This is in fact how the Ford Motor Company decided on the characteristics of its 1986 Taurus, which duplicated the great auto-market success of its 1964 Ford Mustang. Specifically, Ford determined by marketing research that the two most important characteristics of an automobile for the majority of consumers were styling (i.e., design and interior features) and performance (i.e., acceleration and handling) and then produced a car (the Mustang that made its debut in 1964 and the Taurus in 1986) that incorporated those characteristics. The rest is history.

Market studies can also be used to determine how consumers' tastes have changed over time. In terms of indifference curves, a reduction in the consumer's taste for commodity X (hamburgers) in relation to commodity Y (soft drinks) would be reflected in a flattening of the indifference curve of Figure 3–4, indicating that the consumer would now be willing to give up less of Y for each additional unit of X. The different tastes of different consumers are also reflected in the shapes of their indifference curves. The consumer who prefers soft drinks to hamburgers will have a flatter indifference curve than a consumer that does not.

Sometimes, however, marketing studies can go wrong—as the Coca-Cola Company learned. The company replaced its traditional drink with the New Coke in 1985 and was subsequently forced, by nothing short of a consumers' revolt, to reintroduce it as Coca-Cola Classic. Ford, on the other hand, did not make that mistake in restyling its Taurus and in 1992 regained its status as having the best-selling car in America—a position that it had lost to Honda (Accord) in 1989.

Sources: Kelvin Lancaster, *Consumer Demand: A New Approach* (New York: Columbia University Press, 1971); "Ford Puts Its Future on the Line," *New York Times Magazine,* December 4, 1985, pp. 94–110; " 'Old' Coke Coming Back After Outcry by Faithful," *New York Times,* July 11, 1985, p. 13; "How to Steal the Best Ideas Around," *Fortune,* October 19, 1992, pp. 102–106; and "Top of the Car Lots," *The Economist,* January 16, 1993, p. 67.

▲

3.3 INTERNATIONAL CONVERGENCE OF TASTES

A rapid convergence of tastes is taking place in the world today. Tastes in the United States affect tastes around the world and tastes abroad strongly influence tastes in the United States. Coca-Cola and jeans are only two of the most obvious U.S. products that have become household items around the world. One can see Adidas sneakers and Walkman personal stereos on joggers from Central Park in New York City to Tivoli Gardens in Copenhagen. You can eat Big Macs from Piazza di Spagna in Rome to Pushkin Square in Moscow. Pizza become such a common food item in the United States that many people even deny its foreign origin. We find Japanese cars and VCRs in New York and in New Delhi, French perfumes in Paris and in Cairo, and Perrier in practically every major (and not so major) city around the world. Texas Instruments and Canon calculators, Zenith and Hitachi portable PCs, and Xerox and Minolta copiers are found in offices and homes more or less everywhere. With more rapid communications and more frequent travel, the world-wide convergence of tastes has even accelerated. Bananas were considered an exotic specialty in the 1950s and it took a decade for them to become a household fruit. Few in the United States had even heard of kiwi a few years ago; now most U.S. supermarkets carry this fruit. Such a worldwide convergence of tastes is important to us as consumers for the greatly expanded range of consumption choices that we enjoy. It is even more important for producers who must think in terms of global production and marketing to remain competitive in today's rapidly shrinking world.

In his 1983 article "The Globalization of Markets" in the *Harvard Business Review*, Theodore Levitt asserted that consumers from New York to Frankfurt to Tokyo want similar products and that success for producers in the future would require more and more standardized products and pricing around the world. In fact, in country after country, we are seeing the emergence of a middle-class consumer life-style based on a taste for comfort, convenience, and speed. In the food business, this means packaged, fast-to-prepare, and ready-to-eat products. Market researchers have discovered that similarities in living styles among middle-class people all over the world are much greater than we once thought and are growing with rising incomes and education levels. With the tremendous improvement in telecommunications, transportation, and travel, the cross-fertilization of cultures and convergence of tastes can only be expected to accelerate, and such change has important implications for consumers, producers, and sellers of an increasing number and types of products and services.

Example 2

Gillette Introduces the Sensor Razor—A Truly Global Product

As tastes become global, firms are responding more and more with truly global products. Such products are introduced more or less simultaneously in most countries of the world with little or no local variation. This is leading to what has been aptly called the "global supermarket."

Consider these examples. In 1990 Gillette introduced its new Sensor Razor at the same time in most nations of the world and advertised it with virtually the same TV spots (advertisements) in 19 countries in Europe and North America. By 1992, Gillette had sold more than 50 million of the razors and more than 1 billion twin-blade cartridges. Gillette is now planning to exploit its leading position in razors and blades to introduce a new global brand of grooming products for men. The Coca-Cola Company and Nestlé S.A. have entered into a joint venture to produce and market globally ready-to-drink coffees and teas. The list of global products is likely to grow rapidly in the future. After all, some people had predicted that the French would never eat McDonald's hamburgers. Now they eat them just as Americans do (even though the sauce is less sugary and has a more mustard taste in France than in the United States).

The trend toward the global supermarket is spreading rapidly in Europe as borders fade. A growing number of companies are creating "Eurobrands"— single products for most countries of Europe—and advertising them with "Euroads," which are identical or nearly identical across countries, except for language. Many national differences in taste will, of course, remain; for example, Nestlé markets more than 200 blends of Nescafé to cater to differences in tastes in different markets. Nevertheless, international differences in tastes are likely to become less and less important in the future. An increasing number of products are likely to be introduced at the same time in many countries as competition becomes increasingly global. This is true not only for foods and inexpensive consumer products but also for automobiles, tires, portable computers, phones, and many other durable products.

Sources: "Building the Global Supermarket," *New York Times*, November 18, 1988, p. D1; "Selling in Europe: Borders Fade," *New York Times*, May 31, 1990, p. D1; "Global Lather," *Forbes*, February 5, 1990, p. 146–148; "Coke and Nestlé Launch First Coffee Drink," *Wall Street Journal*, October 1, 1991, p. B1; and "The Cutting Edge," *Wall Street Journal*, April 6, 1992, p. R6.

▲

3.4 **THE CONSUMER'S INCOME AND PRICE CONSTRAINTS: THE BUDGET LINE**

In this section, we introduce the constraints or limitations faced by a consumer in satisfying his or her wants. In order to conduct the analysis by plane geometry, we assume that the consumer spends all of his or her income on only two goods, X and Y. We will see that the constraints of the consumer can then be represented by a line called the budget line. The position of the budget line and changes in it can best be understood by looking at its endpoints.

Definition of the Budget Line

In section 3.2, we saw that we can represent a consumer's tastes with an indifference map. We now introduce the constraints or limitations that a consumer faces in attempting to satisfy his or her wants. The amount of goods that a consumer can purchase over a given period of time is limited by the consumer's income and by the prices of the goods that he or she must pay. In what follows we assume (realistically) that the consumer cannot affect the price of the goods he or she purchases. In economics jargon, we say that the consumer faces a **budget constraint** due to his or her limited income and the given prices of goods.

By assuming that a consumer spends all of his or her income on good X (hamburgers) and on good Y (soft drinks), we can express the budget constraint as

$$P_X Q_X + P_Y Q_Y = I \qquad\qquad \text{[3–3]}$$

where P_X is the price of good X, Q_X is the quantity of good X, P_Y is the price of good Y, Q_Y is the quantity of good Y, and I is the consumer's money income. Equation [3–3] postulates that the price of X times the quantity of X plus the price of Y times the quantity of Y equals the consumer's money income. That is, the amount of money spent on X plus the amount spent on Y equals the consumer's income.[10]

Suppose that $P_X = \$2$, $P_Y = \$1$, and $I = \$10$ per unit of time. This could, for example, be the situation of a student who has $10 per day to spend on snacks of hamburgers (good X) priced at $2 each and on soft drinks (good Y) priced at $1 each. By spending all income on Y, the consumer could purchase $10Y$ and $0X$. This defines endpoint J on the vertical axis of Figure 3–6. Alternatively, by spending all income on X, the consumer could purchase $5X$ and $0Y$. This defines endpoint K on the horizontal axis. By joining endpoints J and K with a straight line we get the consumer's **budget line**. This shows the various combinations of X and Y that the consumer can purchase by spending all income at the given prices of the two goods. For example, starting at endpoint J, the consumer could give up two units of Y and use the $2 not spent on Y to purchase the first unit of X and reach point L. By giving up another $2Y$, he or she could purchase the second unit of X. The slope of -2 of budget line JK shows that for each $2Y$ the consumer gives up, he or she can purchase $1X$ more.

By rearranging equation [3–3], we can express the consumer's budget constraint in a different and more useful form, as follows. By subtracting the term $P_X Q_X$ from both sides of equation [3–3] we get

$$P_Y Q_Y = I - P_X Q_X \qquad\qquad \text{[3–3A]}$$

----

[10]Equation [3–3] could be generalized to deal with any number of goods. However, as pointed out, we deal with only two goods for purposes of diagrammatic analysis.

FIGURE 3–6   **The Budget Line**

With an income of $I = \$10$, and $P_Y = \$1$ and $P_X = \$2$, we get budget line JK. This shows that the consumer can purchase $10Y$ and $0X$ (endpoint J), $8Y$ and $1X$ (point L), $6Y$ and $2X$ (point B), . . . , or $0Y$ and $5X$ (endpoint K). $I/P_Y = \$10/\$1 = 10 = Q_Y$ is the vertical or Y-intercept of the budget line and $-P_X/P_Y = -\$2/\$1 = -2$ is the slope.

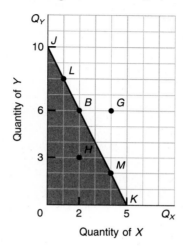

By then dividing both sides of equation [3–3A] by P_Y, we isolate Q_Y on the left-hand side and define equation [3–4]:

$$Q_Y = I/P_Y - (P_X/P_Y)Q_X \qquad\qquad \textbf{[3–4]}$$

The first term on the right-hand side of equation [3–4] is the vertical or Y-intercept of the budget line and $-P_X/P_Y$ is the slope of the budget line. For example, continuing to use $P_X = \$2$, $P_Y = \$1$, and $I = \$10$, we get $I/P_Y = Q_Y = 10$ for the Y-intercept (endpoint J in Figure 3–6) and $-P_X/P_Y = -2$ for the slope of the budget line. The slope of the budget line refers to the rate at which the two goods can be exchanged for one another in the market (i.e., $2Y$ for $1X$).

The consumer can purchase any combination of X and Y on the budget line or in the shaded area below the budget line (called *budget space*). For example, at point B the individual would spend $\$4$ to purchase $2X$ and the remaining $\$6$ to purchase $6Y$. At point M, he or she would spend $\$8$ to purchase $4X$ and the remaining $\$2$ to purchase $2Y$. On the other hand, at a point such as H in the shaded area below the budget line (i.e., in the budget space), the individual would spend $\$4$ to purchase $2X$ and $\$3$ to purchase $3Y$ and be left with $\$3$ of unspent income. In what follows, we assume that the consumer *does* spend all of his or her income and is on the budget line. Because of the income and price constraints, the consumer cannot reach combinations of X and Y above the budget line. For example, the individual cannot purchase combination G ($4X$, $6Y$) because it requires an expenditure of $\$14$ ($\$8$ to purchase $4X$ plus $\$6$ to purchase $6Y$).

Changes in Income and Prices and the Budget Line

A particular budget line refers to a specific level of the consumer's income and prices of the two goods. If the consumer's income and/or the price of good X or good Y change, the budget line will also change. When only the consumer's income changes, the budget line will shift up if income (I) rises and down if I falls, but the slope of the budget line remains unchanged. For example, the left panel of Figure 3–7 shows budget line JK (the same as in Figure 3–6 with $I = \$10$), higher budget line $J'K'$ with $I = \$15$, and still higher budget line $J''K''$ with $I = \$20$ per day. P_X and P_Y do not change, so the three budget lines are parallel and their slopes are equal. If the consumer's income falls, the budget line shifts down but remains parallel.

If only the price of good X changes, the vertical or Y-intercept remains unchanged, and the budget line rotates upward or counterclockwise if P_X falls and downward or clockwise if P_X rises. For example, the right panel of Figure 3–7 shows budget line JK (the same as in Figure 3–6 at $P_X = \$2$), budget line JK'' with $P_X = \$1$, and budget line JN' with $P_X = \$0.50$. The vertical intercept (endpoint J) remains the same because I and P_Y do not change. The slope of budget line JK'' is $-P_X/P_Y = -\$1/\$1 = -1$. The slope of budget line JN' is

FIGURE 3–7   **Changes in the Budget Line**

The left panel shows budget line JK (the same as in Figure 3–6 with $I = \$10$), higher budget line $J'K'$ with $I = \$15$, and still higher budget line $J''K''$ with $I = \$20$ per day. P_X and P_Y do not change, so the three budget lines are parallel and their slopes are equal. The right panel shows budget line JK with $P_X = \$2$, budget line JK'' with $P_X = \$1$, and budget line JN' with $P_X = \$0.50$. The vertical or Y-intercept (endpoint J) remains the same because income and P_Y do not change. The slope of budget line JK'' is $-P_X/P_Y = -\$1/\$1 = -1$, while the slope of budget line JN' is $-\frac{1}{2}$.

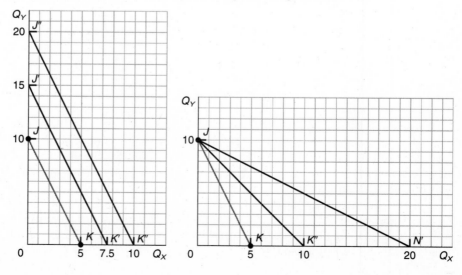

$-\frac{1}{2}$. With an increase in P_X, the budget line rotates clockwise and becomes steeper.

On the other hand, if only the price of Y changes, the horizontal or X-intercept will be the same, but the budget line will rotate upward if P_Y falls and downward if P_Y rises. For example, with $I = \$10$, $P_X = \$2$, and $P_Y = \$0.50$ (rather than $P_Y = \$1$), the new vertical or Y-intercept is $Q_Y = 20$ and the slope of the new budget line is $-P_X/P_Y = -4$. With $P_Y = \$2$, the new Y-intercept is $Q_Y = 5$ and $-P_X/P_Y = -1$ (you should be able to sketch these lines). Finally, with a proportionate reduction in P_X and P_Y and constant I, there will be a parallel upward shift in the budget line; with a proportionate increase in P_X and P_Y and constant I, there will be a parallel downward shift in the budget line.

3.5 CONSUMER'S CHOICE

We will now bring together the tastes and preferences of the consumer (given by his or her indifference map) and the income and price constraints faced by the consumer (given by his or her budget line) to examine how the consumer determines which goods to purchase and in what quantities to maximize utility or satisfaction. As we will see in the next chapter, utility maximization is essential for the derivation of the consumer's demand curve for a commodity (which is a major objective of this part of the text).

Utility Maximization

Given the tastes of the consumer (reflected in his or her indifference map), the **rational consumer** seeks to maximize the utility or satisfaction received in spending his or her income. A rational consumer maximizes utility by trying to attain the highest indifference curve possible, given his or her budget line. This occurs where an indifference curve is tangent to the budget line so that the slope of the indifference curve (the MRS_{XY}) is equal to the slope of the budget line (P_X/P_Y). Thus, the condition for **constrained utility maximization, consumer optimization,** or **consumer equilibrium** occurs where the consumer spends all income (i.e., he or she is on the budget line) and

$$MRS_{XY} = P_X/P_Y \qquad\qquad [3-5]$$

Figure 3–8 brings together on the same set of axes the consumer indifference curves of Figure 3–2 and the budget line of Figure 3–6 to determine the point of utility maximization. Figure 3–8 shows that the consumer maximizes utility at point B where indifference curve U_1 is tangent to budget line JK. At point B, the consumer is on the budget line and $MRS_{XY} = P_X/P_Y = 2$. Indifference curve U_1 is the highest that the consumer can reach with his or her budget line. Thus, to maximize utility the consumer should spend \$4 to purchase $2X$ and the remaining \$6 to purchase $6Y$. Any other combination of goods X and

FIGURE 3–8   Constrained Utility Maximization

The consumer maximizes utility at point B, where indifference curve U_1 is tangent to budget line JK. At point B, $MRS_{XY} = P_X/P_Y = 2$. Indifference curve U_1 is the highest that the consumer can reach with his or her budget line. Thus, the consumer should purchase $2X$ and $6Y$.

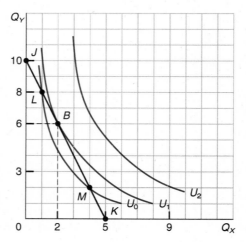

Y that the consumer could purchase (those on or below the budget line) provides less utility. For example, the consumer could spend all income to purchase combination L, but this would be on lower indifference curve U_0.

At point L the consumer is willing to give up more of Y than he or she has to in the market to obtain one additional unit of X. That is, MRS_{XY} (the absolute slope of indifference curve U_0 at point L) exceeds the value of P_X/P_Y (the absolute slope of budget line JK). Thus, starting from point L, the consumer can increase his or her satisfaction by purchasing less of Y and more of X until he or she reaches point B on U_1, where the slopes of U_1 and the budget line are equal (i.e., $MRS_{XY} = P_X/P_Y = 2$). On the other hand, starting from point M, where $MRS_{XY} < P_X/P_Y$, the consumer can increase his or her satisfaction by purchasing less of X and more of Y until he or she reaches point B on U_1, where $MRS_{XY} = P_X/P_Y$. One tangency point such as B is assured by the fact that there is an indifference curve going through each point in the XY commodity space. The consumer cannot reach indifference curve U_2 with the present income and the given prices of goods X and Y.[11]

Utility maximization is more prevalent (as a general aim of individuals) than it may seem at first. It is observed not only in consumers as they attempt

---

[11]For a mathematical presentation of utility maximization using rudimentary calculus, see section A.2 of the Mathematical Appendix.

to maximize utility in spending income but also in many other individuals— including criminals. For example, a study found that the rate of robberies and burglaries was positively related to the gains and inversely related to the costs of (i.e., punishment for) criminal activity.[12] Utility maximization can also be used to analyze the effect of government warnings on consumption, as Example 3 shows.

Example 3

 ## Utility Maximization and Government Warnings on the Consumption of Diet Sodas

Suppose that in Figure 3–9, good X refers to regular soda and good Y to diet soda, $P_X = \$1$, $P_Y = \$1$, and the consumer spends his or her entire weekly allowance of \$10 on sodas. Suppose also that the consumer maximizes utility by spending \$3 to purchase three regular sodas and \$7 to purchase seven diet sodas (point B on indifference curve U_1) before any government warning on the possible danger of cancer from diet sodas. After the warning, the consumer's tastes may change away from diet and toward regular sodas.[13] This can be shown with dashed indifference curves U_0' and U_1'. Not that U_0' is steeper than U_1 at the original optimization point B, indicating that after the warning the individual is willing to give up more diet sodas for an additional regular soda (i.e., MRS_{XY} is higher for U_0' than for U_1 at point B). Now U_0' can intersect U_1 because of the change in tastes. Note also that U_0' involves less utility than U_1 at point B because the seven diet sodas (and the three regular sodas) provide less utility after the warning. After the warning, the consumer maximizes utility by consuming six regular sodas and only four diet sodas (point B', where U_1' is tangent to the budget line).

The above analysis clearly shows how indifference curve analysis can be used to examine the effect of any government warning on consumption patterns.[14] Indeed, we can analyze the effect on consumption of any new information by examining the effect it has on the consumer's indifference map. Similarly, indifference curve analysis can be used to analyze the effect

---

[12]See, I. Ehrlich, "Participation in Illegitimate Activities: A Theoretical and Empirical Investigation," *Journal of Political Economy*, May/June 1973, and W. T. Dickens, "Crime and Punishment Again: The Economic Approach with a Psychological Twist," National Bureau of Economic Research, *Working Paper No. 1884*, April 1986.

[13]It may be argued that government warnings change the information available to consumers rather than tastes. That is, the warning affects consumers' perception as to the ability of various goods to satisfy their wants. See, M. Shodell, "Risky Business," *Science*, October 1985.

[14]Another example of a government warning is provided by the 1965 law requiring manufacturers to print on each pack of cigarettes the warning that cigarette smoking is dangerous to health.

FIGURE 3–9   Effect of Government Warnings

The consumer maximizes utility by purchasing 3X and 7Y (point B on indifference curve U_1) before the government warning on the consumption of Y. After the warning, the consumer's tastes change and are shown by dashed indifference curves U_0' and U_1'. The consumer now maximizes utility by purchasing 6X and only 4Y (point B', where U_1' is tangent to the budget line).

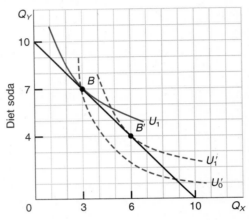

on consumer purchases of any regulation such as the one requiring drivers in many states to wear seat belts.

▲

Corner Solutions

If indifference curves are everywhere either flatter or steeper than the budget line, or if they are concave rather than convex to the origin, then the consumer maximizes utility by spending all income on either good Y or good X. These are called **corner solutions.**

In the left panel of Figure 3–10, indifference curves U_0, U_1, and U_2 are everywhere flatter than budget line JK, and U_1 is the highest indifference curve that the consumer can reach by purchasing 10Y and 0X (endpoint J). Point J is closest to the tangency point, which cannot be achieved. The individual could purchase 2X and 6Y and reach point B, but point B is on lower indifference curve U_0. Since point J is on the Y-axis (and involves the consumer spending all his or her income on good Y), it is called a corner solution.

The middle panel shows indifference curves that are everywhere steeper than the budget line, and U_1 is the highest indifference curve that the consumer can reach by spending all income to purchase 5X and 0Y (endpoint K). The individual could purchase 1X and 8Y at point L, but this is on lower indifference

FIGURE 3–10   **Corner Solutions**

In the left panel, indifference curves are everywhere flatter than the budget line, and U_1 is the highest indifference curve that the consumer can reach by purchasing 10Y only (point J). The middle panel shows indifference curves everywhere steeper than the budget line, and U_1 is the highest indifference curve that the consumer can reach by spending all income to purchase 5X (point K). In the right panel, concave indifference curve U_1 is tangent to the budget line at point B, but this is not the optimum point because the consumer can reach higher indifference curve U_2 by consuming only good Y (point J).

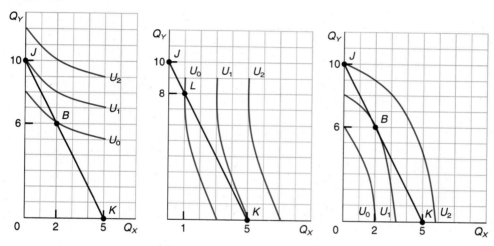

curve U_0. Point K is on the horizontal axis and involves the consumer spending all his or her income on good X, so point K is also a corner solution.

In the right panel, *concave* indifference curve U_1 is tangent to the budget line at point B, but this is not optimum because the consumer can reach higher indifference curve U_2 by spending all income to purchase 10Y and 0X (endpoint J). This is also a corner solution. Thus, the condition that an indifference curve must be tangent to the budget line for optimization is true only when indifference curves assume their usual convex shape and are neither everywhere flatter nor steeper than the budget line.

Finally, although a consumer in the real world does not spend all of his or her income on one or a few goods, there are many more goods that he or she does not purchase because they are too expensive for the utility they provide. For example, few people purchase a $2,000 watch because the utility that most people get from the watch does not justify its $2,000 price. The nonconsumption of many goods in the real world can be explained by indifference curves which, though convex to the origin, are everywhere either flatter or steeper than the budget line, yielding corner rather than interior solutions. Corner solutions can also arise with rationing, as Example 4 shows.

Example 4

Water Rationing: A Recurring Problem in the West and Northeast

Because goods are scarce, some method of allocating them among individuals is required. In a free-enterprise economy such as our own, the price system accomplishes this for the most part. Sometimes, however, the government rations goods, such as water in the West and the Northeast of the United States (as a result of recurrent droughts) and gasoline in 1974 and 1979 (at the height of the petroleum crisis). If the maximum amount of the good that the government allows is less than the individual would have purchased or used, the **rationing** will reduce the individual's level of satisfaction.

The effect of rationing on utility maximization and consumption can be examined with Figure 3–11. In the absence of rationing, the individual maximizes satisfaction at point B, where indifference curve U_1 is tangent to budget line JK, by consuming $2X$ and $6Y$ (as in Figure 3–8). Good X could refer to hours per week of lawn watering, while good Y could refer to hours per week of TV viewing. If the government did not allow the individual to use more than $1X$ per week, the budget line becomes JLK', with a kink at point L. Thus, rationing changes the constraints under which utility maximization occurs. The highest indifference curve that the individual can reach with budget line JLK' is now U_0 at point L, by consuming $1X$ and $8Y$.

FIGURE 3–11   Rationing

In the absence of rationing, the individual maximizes satisfaction at point B, where indifference curve U_1 is tangent to budget line JK, and consumes $2X$ and $6Y$ (as in Figure 3–8). If the government did not allow the individual to purchase more than $1X$ per week, the budget line becomes JLK', with a kink at point L. The highest indifference curve that the individual can reach with budget line JLK' is now U_0 at point L, by consuming $1X$ and $8Y$.

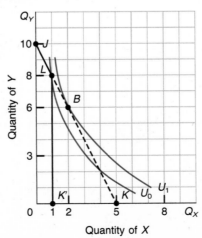

In our water rationing case, this refers to one hour of lawn watering and eight hours of TV viewing per week. With water rationing, the incentive arises to illegally water lawns at night under the cover of darkness. On the other hand, gasoline rationing during 1974 and 1979 led to long lines at the gas pump and to black markets where gasoline could be purchased illegally at a higher price without waiting. Thus, rationing leads to price distortions and inefficiencies.

If rations were $2X$ or more per week, the rationing system would not affect this consumer since he or she maximizes utility by purchasing $2X$ and $6Y$ (point B in the figure). Rationing is more likely to be binding or restrictive on high-income people than on low-income people (who may not have sufficient income to purchase even the allowed quantity of the rationed commodity). Thus, our model predicts that high-income people are more likely to make black-market purchases than low-income people. Effective rationing leads not only to black markets but also to "spill over" of consumer purchases on other goods not subject to rationing (or into savings). Both occurred in the U.S. during the 1974 and 1979 gasoline rationing periods.

▲

Marginal Utility Approach to Utility Maximization

If utility were cardinally measurable, then the condition for constrained utility maximization would be for the consumer to spend all income on X and Y in such a way that

$$\frac{MU_X}{P_X} = \frac{MU_Y}{P_Y} \qquad [3\text{--}6]$$

Expression [3–6] reads, the marginal utility of good X divided by the price of good X equals the marginal utility of good Y divided by the price of good Y. MU_X/P_X is the extra or marginal utility per dollar spent on X. Likewise, MU_Y/P_Y is the marginal utility per dollar spent on Y. Thus, for constrained utility maximization or optimization, the marginal utility of the last dollar spent on X and Y should be the same.[15]

For example, Table 3–3 shows a portion of the declining marginal utility schedule for good X (from Table 3–1) and good Y, on the assumption that MU_X is independent of MU_Y (i.e., that MU_X is not affected by how much Y the individual consumes, and MU_Y is not affected by Q_X consumed). If the consumer's income is $I = \$10$, and $P_X = \$2$ and $P_Y = \$1$, the consumer should spend \$4 to purchase $2X$ and the remaining \$6 to purchase $6Y$ so that condition [3–6] is satisfied. That is,

$$\frac{6 \text{ utils}}{\$2} = \frac{3 \text{ utils}}{\$1} \qquad [3\text{--}6A]$$

---

[15]We will see in footnote 16 that condition [3–6] also holds for the indifference curve approach.

TABLE 3–3   Marginal Utility of X and Y

Q_X	MU_X	Q_Y	MU_Y
1	10	4	5
2	6	5	4
3	4	6	3
4	2	7	2
5	0	8	1

If the consumer spent only $2 to purchase 1X and the remaining $8 to purchase 8Y, $MU_X/P_X = 10/2 = 5$ and $MU_Y/P_Y = 1/1 = 1$. The last (second) dollar spent on X thus gives the consumer five times as much utility as the last (eighth) dollar spent on Y and the consumer would not be maximizing utility. To be at an optimum, the consumer should purchase more of X (MU_X falls) and less of Y (MU_Y rises) until he or she purchases 2X and 6Y, where condition [3–6] is satisfied.[16] This is the same result obtained with the indifference curve approach in section 3.5. Note that even when the consumer purchases 1X and 4Y condition [3–6] is satisfied ($MU_X/P_X = 10/2 = MU_Y/P_Y = 5/1$), but the consumer would not be at an optimum because he or she would be spending only $6 of the $10 income.

The fact that the marginal utility approach gives the same result as the indifference curve approach (i.e., 2X and 6Y) should not be surprising. In fact, we can easily show why this is so. By cross multiplication in equation [3–6], we get

$$\frac{MU_X}{MU_Y} = \frac{P_X}{P_Y} \qquad \text{[3–7]}$$

But we have shown in section 3.2 that $MRS_{XY} = MU_X/MU_Y$ (see equation [3–2]) and in section 3.5 that $MRS_{XY} = P_X/P_Y$ when the consumer maximizes utility (see equation [3–5]). Therefore, bringing together equations [3–2], [3–5], and [3–7], we can express the condition for consumer utility maximization as

$$MRS_{XY} = \frac{MU_X}{MU_Y} = \frac{P_X}{P_Y} \qquad \text{[3–8]}$$

Thus, the condition for consumer utility maximization with the marginal utility approach (i.e., equation [3–6]) is equivalent to that with the indifference curve approach (equation [3–5]), except for corner solutions. With both approaches, the value of equation [3–8] is 2.

---

[16]By giving up the eighth and the seventh units of Y, the individual loses 3 utils. By using the $2 not spent on Y to purchase the second unit of X, the individual receives 6 utils, for a net gain of 3 utils. Once the individual consumes 6Y and 2X, equation [3–6] holds and he or she maximizes utility.

SUMMARY

1. The want-satisfying quality of a good is called utility. More units of a good increases total utility (*TU*) but the extra or marginal utility (*MU*) declines. The saturation point is reached when *TU* is maximum and *MU* is zero. Afterwards, *TU* declines and *MU* is negative. The decline in *MU* is known as the law of diminishing marginal utility. Cardinal utility actually provides an index of satisfaction for a consumer, whereas ordinal utility only ranks various consumption bundles.

2. The tastes of a consumer can be represented by indifference curves. These are based on the assumptions that the consumer can rank baskets of goods according to his or her preferences, tastes are consistent and transitive, and he or she prefers more of a good to less. An indifference curve shows the various combinations of two goods that give the consumer equal satisfaction. Higher indifference curves refer to more satisfaction and lower indifference curves to less. Indifference curves are negatively sloped, cannot intersect, and are convex to the origin. The marginal rate of substitution (*MRS*) measures how much of a good the consumer is willing to give up for one additional unit of the other good and remain on the same indifference curve. Indifference curves also generally exhibit diminishing *MRS*.

3. A rapid convergence of tastes is taking place in the world today. Tastes in the United States affect tastes around the world, and tastes abroad strongly influence tastes in the United States. With the tremendous improvement in telecommunications, transportation, and travel, the convergence of tastes can only be expected to accelerate–with important implications for us as consumers, for firms as producers, and for the study of microeconomics.

4. The budget line shows the various combinations of two goods (say X and Y) that a consumer can purchase by spending all income (I) on the two goods at the given prices (P_X and P_Y). The vertical or Y-intercept of the budget line is given by I/P_Y and $-P_X/P_Y$ is the slope. The budget line shifts up if I increases and down if I decreases, but the slope remains unchanged. The budget line rotates upward if P_X falls and downward if P_X rises.

5. A rational consumer maximizes utility when reaching the highest indifference curve possible with the budget line. This occurs where an indifference curve is tangent to the budget line so that their slopes are equal (i.e., $MRS_{XY} = P_X/P_Y$). Government warnings or new information may change the shape and location of a consumer's indifference curves and the consumption pattern. If indifference curves are everywhere either flatter or steeper than the budget line or if they are concave, utility maximization requires the consumer to spend all income on either good Y or good X only. These are called corner solutions. Corner solutions can also arise with rationing. The marginal utility approach postulates that the consumer maximizes utility when he or she spends all income and the marginal utility of the last dollar spent on X and Y are the same. Since $MRS_{XY} = MU_X/MU_Y = P_X/P_Y$, the marginal utility and the indifference curve approaches are equivalent.

KEY TERMS

Utility	Marginal Utility (*MU*)	Law of Diminishing Marginal
Total Utility (*TU*)	Util	Utility

Cardinal Utility
Ordinal Utility
Good
Bad
Indifference Curve
Indifference Map
Marginal Rate of Substitution
  (MRS)

Neuter
Budget Constraint
Budget Line
Rational Consumer
Constrained Utility
  Maximization

Consumer Optimization
Consumer Equilibrium
Corner Solution
Rationing
Expected Income ($\bar{I}$)

REVIEW QUESTIONS

1. What is the aim of a rational consumer in spending income?
2. The utility approach to consumer demand theory is based on the assumption of ordinal utility, while the indifference curve approach is based on ordinal utility. Which approach is better? Why?
3. If Alan is indifferent between Coke and Pepsi, what would Alan's indifference curves look like?
4. The indifference curve between a good and garbage is positively sloped. True or false? Explain.
5. What is the relationship between two goods if the marginal rate of substitution between them is zero or infinite? Explain.
6. What is the marginal rate of substitution between two complementary goods?

7. Are indifference curves useless because it is difficult to derive them experimentally?
8. Why is there a convergence of tastes internationally?
9. If John's budget line has intercepts 20X and 30Y and $P_Y = \$10$, what is John's income? What is P_X? What is the slope of the budget line?
10. Must a consumer purchase some quantity of each commodity to be in equilibrium?
11. Janice spends her entire weekly food allowance of $42 on hamburgers and soft drinks. The price of a hamburger is $2, and the price of a soft drink is $1. Janice purchases 12 hamburgers and 18 soft drinks, and her marginal rate of substitution between hamburgers and soft drinks is 1. Is Janice in equilibrium? Explain.
12. Why is a consumer likely to be worse off when a product that he or she consumes is rationed?

PROBLEMS

1. From the following total utility schedule

Q_X	0	1	2	3	4	5	6	7
TU_X	0	4	14	20	24	26	26	24

a. derive the marginal utility schedule.

b. plot the total and the marginal utility schedules.
c. Where does the law of diminishing marginal utility begin to operate?
d. Where is the saturation point?

2. The following table gives four indifference schedules of an individual.

	U_1		U_2		U_3		U_4	
Combination	Q_X	Q_Y	Q_X	Q_Y	Q_X	Q_Y	Q_X	Q_Y
A	3	12	6	12	8	15	10	13
B	4	7	7	9	9	12	12	10
C	6	4	9	6	11	9	14	8
F	9	2	12	4	15	6	18	6.4
G	14	1	15	3	19	5	20	6

a. Using graph paper, plot the four indifference curves on the same set of axes.
b. Calculate the marginal rate of substitution of X for Y between the various points on U_1.
c. What is MRS_{XY} at point C on U_1?
d. Can we tell how much better off the individual is on U_2 than on U_1?

*3. a. Starting with a given *equal* endowment of good X and good Y by individual A and individual B, draw A's and B's indifference curves on the same set of axes, showing that individual A has a preference for good X over good Y with respect to individual B.
b. Explain the reason for drawing as you did individual A's and individual B's indifference curves in problem 3a.

4. Draw an indifference curve for an individual showing that
a. good X and good Y are perfect complements.
b. item X becomes a bad after 4 units.
c. item Y becomes a bad after 3 units.
d. MRS is increasing for both X and Y.

5. Suppose an individual has an income of $15 per time period, the price of good X is $1 and the price of good Y is also $1. That is, $I = 15, $P_X = 1, and $P_Y = 1.
a. Write the equation of the budget line of this individual in the form that indicates that the amount spent on good X plus the amount spent on good Y equals the individual's income.
b. Write the equation of the budget line in the form that you can read off directly the vertical intercept and the slope of the line.
c. Plot the budget line.

6. This problem involves drawing three graphs, one for each part of the problem. On the same set of axes, draw the the budget line of problem 5 (label it 2) and two other budget lines:
a. One with $I = 10 (call it 1), and another with $I = 20 (label it 3), and with prices unchanged at $P_X = P_Y = 1.
b. One with $P_X = 0.50, $P_Y = 1, and $I = 15 (label it 2A), and another with $P_X = 2 and the same P_Y and I (label it 2B).
c. One with $P_Y = 2, $P_X = 1, and $I = 15 (label it 2C), and another with $P_X = P_Y = 2 and $I = 15 (label it 2F).

*7. a. On the same set of axes, draw the indifference curves of problem 2 and the budget line of problem 5c.
b. Where is the individual maximizing utility? How much of X and Y should he or she purchase to be at optimum? What is the general condition for constrained utility maximization?
c. Why is the individual not maximizing utility at point A? At point G?
d. Why can't the individual reach U_3 or U_4?

8. On the same set of axes (on graph paper), draw the indifference curves of problem 2 and budget lines
a. 1, 2, and 3 from problem 6a; label the points at which the individual maximizes utility with the various alternative budget lines.
b. 2 and 2A from problem 6b; label the points at which the individual maximizes utility on the various alternative budget lines:

*9. Given the following marginal utility schedule for good X and good Y for the individual, and given that the price of X and the price of Y are both $1, and that the individual spends all income of $7 on X and Y,

Q	1	2	3	4	5	6	7
MU_X	15	11	9	6	4	3	1
MU_Y	12	9	6	5	3	2	1

a. indicate how much of X and Y the individual should purchase to maximize utility.
b. show that the condition for constrained utility maximization is satisfied when the individual is at his or her optimum.
c. How much total utility does the individual receive when he or she maximizes utility? How much utility would the individual get if he or she spent all income on X or Y ?

10. Show on the same figure the effect of (1) an increase in cigarette prices, (2) an increase in consumers' incomes, and (3) a government warning that cigarette smoking is dangerous to health, all in such a way that the net effect of all three forces together leads to a net decline in cigarette smoking.

11. a. Draw a figure showing indifference curve,

U_2 tangent to the budget line at point B (8X), and a lower indifference curve (U_1) intersecting the budget line at point A (4X) and at point G (12X).

b. What happens if the government rations good X and allows the individual to purchase no more than 4X? No more than 8X? No more than 12X?

c. What would happen if the government in-

stead mandated (as in the case of requiring auto insurance, seat belts, and so on) that the individual purchase at least 4X? 8X? 12X?

*12. Show by indifference curve analysis the choice of one couple not to have children and of another couple, with the same income and facing the same costs of having and raising children, to have one child.

APPENDIX   CONSUMER CHOICES UNDER UNCERTAINTY

Traditional demand theory implicitly assumes a riskless world. It assumes that consumers face complete certainty as to the results of the choices they make. Clearly, this is not the case in most instances. For example, when we purchase an automobile we cannot be certain as to how good it will turn out and how long it will last. Similarly, when we choose an occupation, we cannot be exactly certain as to how rewarding it will be in relation to alternative occupations. Thus, the applicability of traditional economic theory is limited by the fact that it is based on the assumption of a riskless world, while most economic decisions are made in the face of risk.

Traditional economic theory could not deal with choices subject to risk or uncertainty because of its strict adherence to the principle of diminishing marginal utility of money (MU). This explains why an individual would not accept a fair (i.e., a 50–50) bet of winning or losing a given sum of money, say, $1,000. That is, because of diminishing MU, the individual's loss of utility in losing $1,000 exceeds his or her gain in utility in winning $1,000. Thus, an individual would not accept a fair bet and certainly would not accept an unfair one (i.e., one where the odds of winning are less than 50%).

By postulating a total utility of money function (as in Figure 3–12) that first increases at a decreasing rate (MU declines) and then increases at an increasing rate (MU increases), Milton Friedman and L. J. Savage[17] could explain or at least rationalize why a family would purchase insurance against the small chance of a large loss (say, through a fire), and also purchase a lottery ticket offering a small chance of a large win (i.e., gamble). Such seemingly contradictory behavior was left entirely unexplained by traditional economic theory.

Figure 3–12 gives a total utility curve which first faces down and then faces up when plotted against income. Suppose that the family's income is OA with utility AA' without a fire, and OB with utility BB' with a fire. If the probability of *no* fire is p (so that the probability of a fire is $1 - p$), the **expected income** of the family is

$$\bar{I} = (p)(OA) + (1 - p)(OB) \qquad [3-9]$$

For example, suppose a family owns a small business that generates a daily income of $OA = \$200$ without a fire and $OB = \$20$ after a fire, and the probability of *no* fire is $p = 0.9$, so that $1 - p = 0.1$ Then $\bar{I} = (0.9)(\$200) + (0.1)(\$20) = \$182$. The income of $182 is not actually available to the family. That is, the family faces only two alternatives:

---

[17]See, M. Friedman and L.J. Savage, "The Utility Analysis of Choices Involving Risk," *Journal of Political Economy*, August 1948.

FIGURE 3–12   Insurance and Gambling

With a family's income of OA with probability p of no fire, and OB with probability
$1 - p$ of a fire, the family's expected income $\bar{I} = (p)(OA) + (1 - p)(OB)$. If $\bar{I} = OC$,
the family should purchase insurance at cost AD because DD' (the utility of insured
income OD) exceeds CC' (the utility of expected income OC without insurance).
Furthermore, if a lottery ticket costs AD with probability $1 - p'$ of winning and thereby
raises the family's income to OF, the expected income would be $\bar{I}' = (p')(OD) + (1 - p')(OF)$. If $\bar{I}' = OC$, the family would also purchase the ticket because CC'' exceeds
AA'.

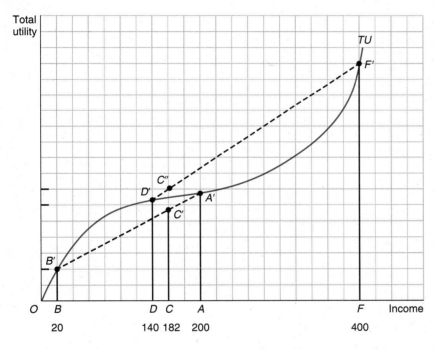

(1) an income of $200 with probability of 90% and (2) an income of $20 with probability
of 10%. The expected income of $182 is a weighted average of these two alternatives
using the probabilities as weights. However, the family would never actually have
the income of $182. Different probabilities of occurrence attached to incomes $OA = \$200$
and $OB = \$20$ result in a different expected income. For example, if $p = 0.8$, $\bar{I} = (0.8)(\$200) + (0.2)(\$20) = \$164$.

The utility of the expected income is given by the height of dashed line $B'A'$ at the
point directly above the level of the expected income. For example, the utility of
expected income $OC = \$182$ is CC', with endpoint C' on the straight dashed line $B'A'$
(see Figure 3–12). This convenient geometric property results directly from the definition of the expected income (i.e., as the weighted average of the two alternative
incomes using objective probabilities as the weights). The utility of the expected income
does not fall on the total utility curve because the expected income is not an income
that the family can actually achieve (such as OA or OB).

Now suppose that in fact $\bar{I} = OC = \$182$ with utility CC'. If the cost of insurance
is $AD = \$60$ (see the figure), the family's actual daily income after the purchase of

the insurance is $OD = \$140$ (given by $OA - AD$). The utility of assured income $OD = \$140$ is DD' on the total utility curve (because income OD is actually achieved by the family with the purchase of the insurance). Since the utility associated with income OD with insurance (i.e., DD') exceeds the utility of the expected income of OC without insurance (i.e., CC') the family would purchase the insurance. That is, since the family receives the utility of DD' with the secure (insured) income of OD as compared with the lower utility of CC' with the uninsured expected income of OC (made up of income OA with probability p or income OB with probability $1 - p$), the family would be better off by purchasing the insurance.

Next we turn to the analysis of gambling. Starting again with income OA, the family will also contemplate purchasing a lottery ticket costing $AD = \$60$.[18] With the lottery ticket, the family's income will be $OD = \$140$ (from $OA - AD$) with utility DD' without winning, and $OF = \$400$ with utility FF' by winning (see the figure). If the probability of *not* winning is p', the expected income $(\bar{I}')$ is

$$\bar{I}' = (p')(OD) + (1 - p')(OF) \qquad \text{[3–9A]}$$

If $\bar{I}' = OC$ with utility CC'', with endpoint C'' on dashed line $D'F'$, the family would purchase the lottery ticket because CC'' exceeds AA' (the utility of income OA without purchasing the ticket).[19]

Thus, the family buys insurance and also gambles—a seemingly contradictory behavior that traditional theory could not explain. By postulating a total utility function that first rises at a decreasing rate (so that the marginal utility declines) and then increases at an increasing rate (so that marginal utility rises) as shown in Figure 3–12, Friedman and Savage were able to rationalize a great deal of market behavior involving risk that traditional economic theory could not deal with. Note that in choices subject to risk, the consumer maximizes *expected* utility rather than utility. Even though the above theory faces many shortcomings,[20] it does provide at least an indication of the factors to consider in the analysis of decisions involving risk. This is clearly shown in Example 5, which deals with the choice of a portfolio of stocks and bonds.

Example 5
Balancing Risks and Returns in Choosing a Portfolio

An important application of the economic theory of choices involving risk is in the selection of a portfolio (stocks and bonds) in which to invest part of

---

[18]To keep Figure 3–12 simple, we assume that the cost of the lottery ticket is the same as the cost of the previous insurance premium for the family, but the two analyses are independent.

[19]Point CC'' is on straight dashed line $D'F'$ and gives the utility of the family's expected income with the purchase of the lottery ticket. Since CC'' exceeds AA' (the utility of income OA without the purchase of the ticket), it pays for the family to purchase the lottery ticket. Note that point C on the horizontal axis is much closer to point D than to point F because the probability of winning is very small.

[20]One of the shortcomings is that the theory *rationalizes* more than *explains* economic behavior in the face of risk. Arrow has also found that many people do not take out flood insurance even at favorable government-subsidized rates, whereas flight insurance and lotteries offer examples of people accepting extremely unfavorable odds. See, K. Arrow, "Risk Perception in Psychology and Economics," *Economic Inquiry*, January, 1982.

one's wealth. Each portfolio has an expected rate of return and an expected rate of risk (usually measured by the variability of the return). These are measured on the vertical and horizontal axes, respectively, of Figure 3–13. Since investors, on the average, are risk averse, they will hold a more risky portfolio only if it provides a higher return. For example, the additional risk (a bad) that the individual faces at point E than at point C on indifference curve U_1 is just balanced by the higher return that he or she receives at point E. Thus, indifference curves are here positively sloped as indicated in the figure. Indifference curve U_1 represents more utility than U_0 because it involves either a higher return for a given risk or a smaller risk for a given return.

Suppose for simplicity that there exist only two assets, with return and risk given by points A and B, respectively. If the risk of assets A and B are independent, the investor can choose any mixed portfolio of assets A and B shown on curve AEB. To understand the shape of curve AEB, note that the investor has available mixed portfolios with a return anywhere between that of asset A and asset B alone, depending on the particular combination of assets A and B in the portfolio. As far as risk is concerned, there are portfolios on frontier AEB that have lower risks than those which are comprised

FIGURE 3–13   Choosing a Portfolio

Indifference curves U_0, U_1, and U_2 show various levels of satisfaction, with $U_2 > U_1 > U_0$. Points on a given indifference curve (such as C and E on U_1) show the various combinations of return and risk that assure the investor equal satisfaction. On the other hand, frontier AEB represents those combinations of return and risk that are obtainable with a mixed portfolio of asset A and asset B with independent risk. The optimum portfolio for the investor is represented by point E, where U_1 is tangent to the frontier AEB. A more risk-averse investor would have steeper indifference curves and choose a mixed portfolio such as F with a lower risk and return than E.

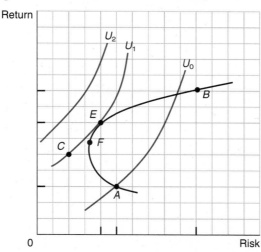

exclusively of either asset A or asset B.[21] That is, by diversifying his or her investment, the investor can reduce overall risks. This accords with the old saying "don't put all your eggs in one basket."[22]

The optimum portfolio for the investor in Figure 3–13 is the mixed portfolio indicated by point E, where indifference curve U_1 is tangent to frontier AEB. A more risk-averse investor would have steeper indifference curves and would choose a less risky (but a lower-return) portfolio on AEB (as indicated, for example, by point F).

When faced with uncertainty in the marketplace, consumers often attempt to reduce it by searching for more information. They may do so by purchasing published information, by visiting more stores or dealers to get a better deal (for example, in purchasing a new car), or by hiring consultants. Such a search would end when the marginal return from the search has fallen to the level of the marginal or extra cost of additional searching. (See Chapter 18, which deals with the economics of information.)

▲

---

[21]For example, suppose that the probability of a low return is ¼ on asset A and ½ on asset B and that we now take the probability of a low return as the measure of risk. If these probabilities are independent, the probability of a low return on both A and B at the same time is $(½)(¼) = ⅛$ or smaller than for either A or B separately.

[22]If the return of asset A were inversely correlated with that of asset B, so that when the return of one asset is high, the return of the other asset is low, curve AEB would be even more bowed out than it is.

CONSUMER BEHAVIOR AND INDIVIDUAL DEMAND

In Chapter 3 we saw how a consumer maximized utility by reaching the highest possible indifference curve with the given budget line. In this chapter, we examine how the consumer responds to changes in income and prices while holding tastes constant. Incomes and prices change frequently in the real world, so it is important to examine their individual effects on consumer behavior.

We begin by examining how the consumer responds to changes in his or her income when prices and tastes remain constant. This will allow us to derive a so-called Engel curve and to distinguish between normal and inferior goods. Then we examine the consumer's response to a change in the price of the good and derive the individual's demand curve for the good. This is the basic building block for the marked demand curve of the good (to be derived in Chapter 5), the importance of which was outlined in Chapter 2.

After deriving an individual's demand curve, we discuss how to separate the substitution from the income effect of a price change for normal and inferior goods. The ability to separate graphically the income from the substitution effect of a price change is one of the most powerful tools of analysis of microeconomic theory. It has wide applicability in the evaluation of many important issues, and it is used to examine the possible but rare exception to the law of negatively sloped demand. Subsequently, we examine the degree by which domestic and foreign goods and services are substitutable and the great relevance of this in the study of microeconomics. Finally, we consider some important applications of the theory presented in the chapter. These applications, together with the real-world examples included in the theory sections, highlight the importance of the theory of consumer behavior and demand. The optional appendix to this chapter deals with index numbers and how to measure changes in consumer welfare.

4.1 CHANGES IN INCOME

A change in the consumer's income shifts his or her budget line, and this affects consumer purchases. In this section we examine how a consumer reaches a new optimum position when his or her income changes but prices and tastes do not change.

Income-Consumption Curve and Engel Curve

By changing the consumer's money income while holding constant prices and tastes, we can derive the consumer's income-consumption curve. The **income-consumption curve** is the locus (i.e., joins) consumer optimum points resulting when only the consumer's income varies. From the income-consumption curve we can then derive the consumer's Engel curve.

For example, the top panel of Figure 4–1 shows that with budget line JK the consumer maximizes utility or is at an optimum at point B, where indifference curve U_1 is tangent to budget line JK and the consumer purchases $2X$ and $6Y$ (the same as in Figure 3–8). That is (continuing with the example of Chapter 3), the best way for the student to spend his or her daily income allowance of $10 on snacks of hamburgers (good X) and soft drinks (good Y) is to purchase two hamburgers and six soft drinks per day. If the prices of hamburgers and soft drinks remain unchanged at $P_X = \$2$ and $P_Y = \$1$ but the daily income allowance rises from $10 to $15 and then to $20, budget line JK shifts up to $J'K'$ and then to $J''K''$ (the same as in the left panel of Figure 3–7). The three budget lines are parallel because the prices of X and Y do not change.

With an income of $15 and budget line $J'K'$, the consumer maximizes utility at point R, where indifference curve U_2 is tangent to budget line $J'K'$ and the consumer purchases $4X$ and $7Y$ (see the top panel of Figure 4–1). Indifference curve U_2 is the same as in the right panel of Figure 3–2 because tastes have not changed. Finally, with an income of $20 and budget line $J''K''$, the consumer maximizes utility or is at an optimum at point S on U_3 by purchasing $5X$ and $10Y$ per unit of time (per day). By joining optimum points B, R, and S we get (a portion of) the income-consumption curve for this consumer (student). Thus, the income-consumption curve is the locus of consumer optimum points resulting when only the consumer's income varies.[1]

From the income-consumption curve in the top panel of Figure 4–1, we can derive the Engel curve in the bottom panel. The **Engel curve** shows the amount of a good that the consumer would purchase per unit of time at various income levels. To derive the Engel curve we keep the same horizontal scale as in the top panel but measure money income on the vertical axis.

---

[1] At each point along the income-consumption curve the value of the MRS_{XY} is the same. This is so because $-P_X/P_Y$ is the same for each of the budget lines (i.e., parallel lines have identical slopes).

FIGURE 4–1 Income-Consumption Curve and Engel Curve

With budget lines JK, $J'K'$, $J''K''$ and indifference curves U_1, U_2, and U_3 in the top panel, the individual maximizes utility at points B, R, and S, respectively. By joining optimum points B, R, and S we get the income-consumption curve (top panel). By then plotting income on the vertical axis and the various optimum quantities purchased of good X along the horizontal axis, we can derive the corresponding Engel curve $B'R'S'$ in the bottom panel.

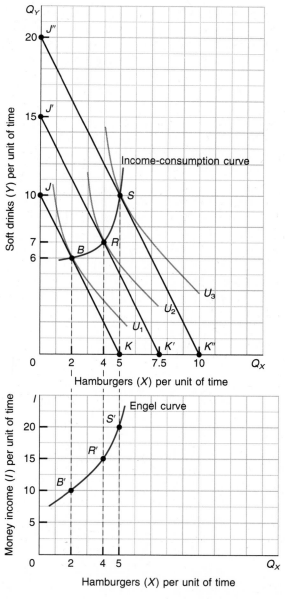

The derivation of the Engel curve proceeds as follows. With a daily income allowance of $10, the student maximizes utility by purchasing two hamburgers per day (point B) in the top panel. This gives point B' (directly below point B) in the bottom panel. With an income allowance of $15, the student is at an optimum by purchasing four hamburgers (point R) in the top panel. This gives point R' in the bottom panel. Finally, with a daily income allowance of $20 the student maximizes utility by purchasing five hamburgers (point S in the top panel and S' in the bottom panel). By joining points B', R', and S' we get (a portion of) the Engel curve in the bottom panel. Thus, the Engel curve is derived from the income-consumption curve and shows the quantity of hamburgers per day (Q_X) that the student would purchase at various income levels (i.e., with various income allowances). Since the Engel curve is derived from points of consumer (student) utility maximization, $MRS_{XY} = P_X/P_Y$ at every point on it.

Engel curves are named after Ernst Engel, the German statistician of the second half of the 19th century who pioneered studies of family budgets and expenditure patterns. Sometimes Engel curves show the relationship between income and *expenditures* on various goods rather than the *quantity* purchased of various goods. However, because prices are held constant, we get the same result (i.e., the same Engel curve).

For some goods, the Engel curve may rise only gently. This indicates that a given increase in income leads to a proportionately larger increase in the quantity purchased of the good. These goods are sometimes referred to as "luxuries." Examples of these may be education, recreation, and steaks and lobsters (for some people). On the other hand, the Engel curve for other goods rises rather rapidly, indicating that a given increase in income leads to a proportionately smaller increase in the quantity purchased of these goods. These are called "necessities." Basic foodstuffs are usually regarded as necessities. A more precise definition of luxuries and necessities is given in Chapter 5.

Example 1
Engel's Law After a Century

Table 4–1 gives the percentages of total consumption expenditures on various items for U.S. families in selected income classes in 1991. The table shows that higher–income families spend a smaller percentage of their income than lower–income families on food, housing, and health care, but a larger percentage on entertainment.

The decline in the proportion of total expenditures on food as income rises has been found to be true not only for the United States in the period of the survey, but also at other times and in other nations. Thus, food in general is a necessity rather than a luxury. This regularity is sometimes referred to as "Engel's law." Indeed, the higher the proportion of income spent on food in a nation, the poorer the nation is taken to be. For example, in India more than 50% of income is spent on food on the average. Less regularity has been found in the proportion of expenditures on other goods.

TABLE 4–1 **Percentage of Total Consumption by Income Class for U.S. Families in 1991**

Consumption Item	Annual Income		
	$10,000–$19,999	$20,000–$29,999	$30,000–$39,999
Food	17.5%	15.3%	14.7%
Housing	32.4	30.8	29.9
Apparel and services	5.9	5.3	6.0
Transportation	17.0	18.8	18.1
Health care	7.3	6.2	5.0
Entertainment	3.9	4.5	5.3
Other	16.0	19.1	21.0
Total	100.0	100.0	100.0

Source: U.S. Department of Labor, Bureau of Labor Statistics, *Consumer Expenditure in 1991, Report 835* (Washington D.C.: December 1992), Table 2.

▲

Normal and Inferior Goods

A **normal good** is one of which the consumer purchases more with an increase in income. An **inferior good** is one of which the consumer purchases less with an increase in income. Good X in Figure 4–1 is a normal good because the consumer purchases more of it with an increase in income. For example, an increase in the student's income allowance from $10 to $15 leads to an increase in his or her purchase of hamburgers from two to four per day. Thus, for a normal good, the income-consumption curve and the Engel curve are both positively sloped, as in Figure 4–1.

Figure 4–2 shows the income-consumption curve and the Engel curve for an inferior good. This results from supposing that the student, instead of spending his or her daily income allowance on soft drinks (good Y) and hamburgers (good X), spends it on soft drinks and candy bars (good Z), and he or she views candy bars as an inferior good.[2] With the price of soft drinks at $1 and the price of candy bars also at $1, the budget line of the student is JK' with a daily income allowance of $10 and J'N with an income of $15 (see the top panel of Figure 4–2).

---

[2]Other commodities that are, perhaps, even more readily recognized as inferior goods in the United States today are bologna, and cheaper cuts of meats.

FIGURE 4–2 Income-Consumption Curve and Engel Curve for an Inferior Good

With budget lines JK' and $J'N$ and indifference curves U_1' and U_2' in the top panel, the individual maximizes utility at points V and W, respectively. By joining points V and W we get the income-consumption curve (top panel). By then plotting income on the vertical axis and the optimum quantities purchased of good Z along the horizontal axis, we derive corresponding Engel curve $V'W'$ in the bottom panel. Since the income-consumption curve and Engel curve are negatively sloped, good Z is an inferior good.

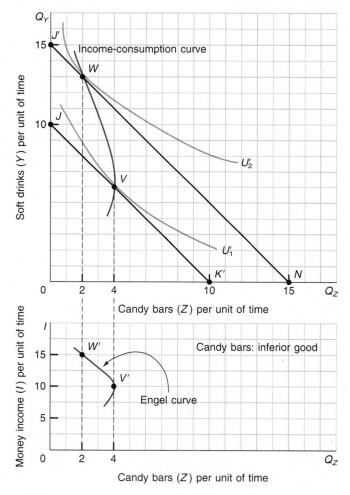

If indifference curves between soft drinks and candy bars are U_1' and U_2', the student maximizes satisfaction at point V, where indifference curve U_1' is tangent to budget line JK' with a daily income allowance of \$10, and he or she maximizes utility at point W, where indifference curve U_2' is tangent to budget line $J'N$ with an income of \$15 (see the top panel of Figure 4–2). Thus, the consumer purchases four candy bars with an income of \$10 and only two candy bars with an income of $15. Candy bars are, therefore, inferior goods for this student. The income-consumption curve for candy bars (VW in the top panel of Figure 4–2) and the corresponding Engel curve ($V'W'$ in the bottom panel) are both negatively sloped, indicating that the student purchases fewer candy bars as his or her income allowance increases.

The classification of a good into normal or inferior depends only on how a specific consumer views the particular good. Thus, the same candy bar can be regarded as a normal good by another student. Furthermore, a good can be regarded as a normal good by a consumer at a particular level of income and as an inferior good by the same consumer at a higher level of income. For example, with an allowance of $40 dollars per day, the student in the previous section may begin to regard hamburgers as an inferior good, because he or she now can afford steaks and lobsters. Also note that an inferior good is not a "bad" because more is preferred to less, and indifference curves remain negatively sloped (refer back to section 3.2).

In the real world, most broadly defined goods such as food, clothing, housing, health care, education, and recreation are normal goods. Inferior goods are usually narrowly defined cheap goods, such as bologna, for which good substitutes are available. As pointed out earlier, a normal good can be further classified as a luxury or a necessity, depending on whether the quantity purchased increases proportionately more or less than the increase in income.

4.2 CHANGES IN PRICE

Commodity prices frequently change in the real world, and it is important to examine their effect on consumer behavior. A change in commodity prices changes the consumer budget line, and this affects his or her purchases. In this section we examine how the consumer reaches a new optimum position when the price of a good changes but the price of the other good, income, and tastes remain unchanged.

Price-Consumption Curve and Individual Demand Curve

By changing the price of good X while holding constant the price of good Y, income, and tastes, we can derive the consumer's price-consumption curve for good X. The **price-consumption curve** for good X is the locus of (i.e., joins) consumer optimum points resulting when only the price of good X varies. From the price-consumption curve we can then derive the consumer's demand curve for good X.

For example, the top panel of Figure 4–3 shows once again that with budget line JK, the consumer maximizes utility or is at an optimum at point B, where indifference curve U_1 is tangent to budget line JK and the consumer purchases $2X$ and $6Y$ (the same as in Figure 3–8). Suppose that the consumer's income (i.e., the student allowance) remains unchanged at $I = \$10$ per day and the price of good Y (soft drinks) also remains constant at $P_Y = \$1$. A reduction

FIGURE 4–3   Price-Consumption Curve and the Individual's Demand Curve

The top panel shows that with $I = \$10$ and $P_Y = \$1$, the consumer is at an optimum at point B by purchasing $2X$ with $P_X = \$2$, at point E by purchasing $6X$ with $P_X = \$1$, and at point G by purchasing $10X$ with $P_X = \$0.50$. By joining points BEG, we get the price-consumption curve for good X. In the bottom panel, by plotting the optimum quantities of good X on the horizontal axis and the corresponding prices of good X on the vertical axis, we derive the individual's negatively sloped demand curve for good X, d_X.

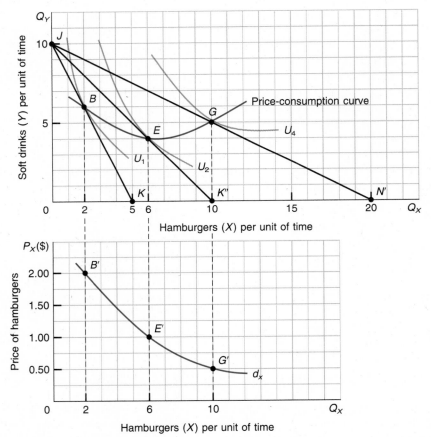

in the price of good X (hamburgers) from $P_X = \$2$ to $P_X = \$1$ and then to $P_X = \$0.50$ would cause the consumer's budget line to become flatter or to rotate counterclockwise from JK to JK'' and then to JN' (the same as in the right panel of Figure 3–7).[3]

---

[3]Remember that the X-intercepts of the budget lines are obtained by I/P_X. Thus, with $I = \$10$ and $P_X = \$2$, we get endpoint K and budget line JK. With $P_X = \$1$, we get endpoint K'' and budget line JK'', and with $P_X = \$0.50$, we get endpoint N' and budget line JN'.

With $P_X = \$1$ and budget line JK'', the consumer maximizes utility at point E, where indifference curve U_2 is tangent to budget line JK'' and the consumer purchases $6X$ and $4Y$ (see the top panel of Figure 4–3). Indifference curve U_2 is the same as in the right panel of Figure 3–2 because tastes have not changed. Finally, with $P_X = \$0.50$ and budget line JN', the consumer maximizes utility or is at an optimum at point G on U_4 by purchasing $10X$ and $5Y$ per unit of time (per day). By joining optimum points B, E, and G we get (a portion of) the price-consumption curve for this consumer (student). Thus, the price-consumption curve for good X is the locus of consumer optimum points resulting when only the price of X changes.[4]

From the price-consumption curve in the top panel of Figure 4–3, we can derive the individual consumer's (student's) demand curve for good X in the bottom panel. The **individual's demand curve** for good X shows the amount of good X that the consumer would purchase per unit of time at various alternative prices of good X while holding everything else constant. It is derived by keeping the same horizontal scale as in the top panel but measuring the price of good X on the vertical axis.

The derivation of the individual's demand curve proceeds as follows. With $I = \$10$, $P_Y = \$1$, $P_X = \$2$, the student maximizes utility by purchasing $2X$ (two hamburgers) per day (point B) in the top panel. This gives point B' (directly below point B) in the bottom panel. With $P_X = \$1$, the consumer is at optimum by purchasing $6X$ (point E) in the top panel. This gives point E' in the bottom panel. Finally, with $P_X = \$0.50$, the consumer maximizes utility by purchasing $10X$ (point G in the top panel and G' in the bottom panel). Other points could be obtained similarly. By joining points B', E', and G' we get the individual consumer's demand curve for good X, d_X, in the bottom panel. Thus, the demand curve is derived from the price-consumption curve and shows the quantity of the good that the consumer would purchase per unit of time at various alternative prices of the good while holding everything else constant (the *ceteris paribus* assumption).

We will see in Chapter 5 that the marked demand curve for a good (our ultimate aim in Part Two of the text) is obtained from the addition or the horizontal summation of all individual consumers' demand curves for the good. Note that the individual consumer's demand curve for a good (d_X in the bottom panel of Figure 4–3) is negatively sloped. This reflects the *law of demand*, which postulates that the quantity purchased of a good per unit of time is inversely related to its price. Thus, the individual purchases more hamburgers per unit of time when their price falls and less of them when their price rises. Also note that an individual consumer's demand curve for a good is derived by holding constant the individual's tastes, his or her income, and the prices of other goods. If any of these change, the entire demand

---

[4]At each point along the price-consumption curve, $MRS_{XY} = P_X/P_Y$. However, unlike the case of the income-consumption curve, these ratios will vary because the budget lines are no longer parallel.

curve will shift. This is referred to as a change in demand as opposed to a change in the quantity demanded, which refers instead to a movement along a given demand curve as a result of a change in the price of the good while holding everything else constant (refer back to section 2.2).

Price-Consumption Curve and Price Elasticity of Demand

We can determine whether an individual's demand curve for a commodity is elastic, unitary elastic, or inelastic directly from the slope of the price-consumption curve. From section 2.2 we know that the price elasticity of demand (η) is given by the percentage change in the quantity demanded of a good divided by the percentage change in its price. Demand is said to be elastic, unitary elastic, or inelastic depending on whether η exceeds 1, is equal to 1, or is smaller than 1, respectively. This can be determined directly from the shape of the price-consumption curve. That is, the demand curve is elastic, unitary elastic, or inelastic depending on whether the price-consumption curve falls, is horizontal, or rises.

We can show this with Figure 4–4. The horizontal axis in each of the three panels measures the quantity of good X purchased per unit of time (as before). Instead of measuring the quantity of good Y along the vertical axes, we now measure *money spent on all goods other than X*. With money income of $I = \$10$ and $P_X = \$2$, we get budget line JK in each panel. That is, if the consumer spent all money for other goods and purchased no X, he or she would be at vertical intercept or endpoint J of budget line JK. However, by spending all income on good X, the individual can purchase 5X (endpoint K in each panel). Joining endpoints J and K we get budget line JK in each panel. On the other hand, with $P_X = \$1$, we would get budget line JK'' in each panel.

Each indifference curve in the three panels would then show the various combinations of money for all other goods and the quantity of X purchased that give the individual the same level of utility. As a starting point, each panel shows that with budget line JK, the individual maximizes utility at point B by purchasing 2X and spending $6 (0R) on all other goods. Thus, $JR = \$4$ is the amount spent on X. That is, with $I = \$10$ (0J) and $6 (0R) spent on all other goods, $4 ($JR$) is the remaining amount spent on X. The distance from the vertical intercept of the budget line down to the point directly across from the point of consumer utility maximization always measures the amount of money spent on good X in this type of figure.

With $P_X = \$1$ and budget line JK'' in each panel, we now have three alternative situations. With indifference curve U_2 in the top panel, the individual is at optimum at point E by purchasing 6X and spending $6 ($JS$) on X. Since the amount of money income spent on X increases (from $JR = \$4$ to $JS = \$6$) when P_X falls, the percentage increase in the quantity purchased of X (the numerator of the elasticity formula) must be greater than the percentage decline in the price of X (the denominator of the elasticity formula), and so the demand curve is price elastic over this range. This is reflected in the

FIGURE 4–4   Price-Consumption Curve and the Price Elasticity of Demand

The top panel shows that as P_X falls, the money spent on X increases from JR to JS. This gives a price-consumption curve (PCC) that slopes downward, and the demand for X is price elastic. In the middle panel, a reduction in P_X leaves expenditures on X constant. Thus, the PCC is horizontal and demand is unitary elastic. In the bottom panel, the PCC slopes upward and demand is inelastic.

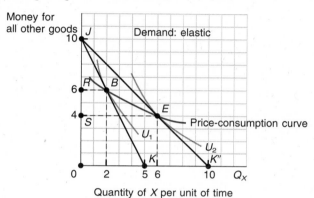

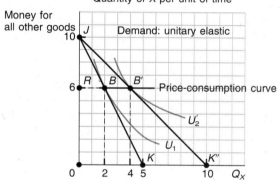

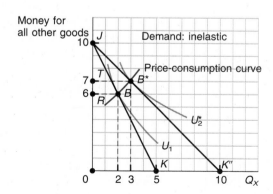

negatively sloped price-consumption curve in the top panel. Thus, whenever total expenditures on a good increase when its price falls, the price-consumption curve is negatively sloped and the demand for the good is price elastic.

The middle and the bottom panels show that with *alternative* indifference curves U_2' and U_2^*, we get a different situation. With budget line JK'' and indifference curve U_2' in the middle panel, the consumer maximizes utility at point B' by purchasing $4X$ and spending $JR = \$4$ on X. Since the amount of money income spent on X is the same ($JR = \$4$) when $P_X = \$1$ as when $P_X = \$2$, the increase in Q_X must be proportionately equal to the decline in P_X, and so d_X is unitary elastic over this range. This is reflected in the horizontal (zero sloped) price-consumption curve in the middle panel. Thus, whenever the price-consumption curve is horizontal, a change in the price of the good will leave total expenditures on the good unchanged, and the demand curve has a price elasticity of 1.

Finally, with budget line JK'' and indifference curve U_2^* in the bottom panel, the consumer is at optimum at point B^* by purchasing $3X$ and spending only $JT = \$3$ on X (down from $JR = \$4$). This means that the percentage increase in Q_X must be smaller than the percentage decline in P_X, so that d_X is inelastic over this range. This is reflected in a positively sloped price-consumption curve in the bottom panel of Figure 4–4. Thus, whenever total expenditures on a good decrease when its price falls, the price-consumption curve is positively sloped, and the demand for the good is price inelastic.

Summarizing, we can say that the demand curve for a commodity is price elastic, unitary elastic, or inelastic if the price-consumption curve is negatively, zero, or positively sloped, respectively. This can be confirmed by using formula [2–2] for measuring arc elasticity (see section 2.2). By doing so, the student would find that $\eta = 6/4 = 1.5$ over the range of the demand curve that could be derived from the top panel of Figure 4–4, $\eta = 1$ for the middle panel, and $\eta = 0.6$ for the bottom panel.

As pointed out in Chapter 2, the price elasticity of demand usually changes at different points on the demand curve. Thus, d_X in the bottom panel of Figure 4–3 is price elastic over range $B'E'$ (because the price-consumption curve falls over range BE) and is inelastic over the $E'G'$ range (because the price-consumption curve rises over the EG range). At point E the slope of the price-consumption curve is zero, and so d_X has unitary price elasticity at point E'. More will be said on this in Chapter 5, where we return to the topic of elasticities in greater detail.

4.3 SUBSTITUTION AND INCOME EFFECTS

In this section, we separate the substitution effect from the income effect of a price change for both normal and inferior goods. This will give us an important analytical tool with wide applicability and will also allow us to examine the exception to the law of downward sloping demand.

How Are the Substitution and Income Effects Separated?

We have seen in the previous section that when the price of a good falls the consumer buys more of it. This is the combined result of two separate forces at work called the substitution effect and the income effect. We now want to separate the total effect of a price change into these two components. We begin by first reviewing how the total effect of a price change (discussed in section 4.2) operates.

In Figure 4–5, $I = \$10$ and $P_Y = \$1$ and these remain constant. With $P_X = \$2$, we have budget line JK and the consumer maximizes utility at point B on indifference curve U_1 by purchasing $2X$. When the price of good X falls to $P_X = \$1$, the budget line becomes JK'' and the consumer maximizes utility at point E on indifference curve U_2 by purchasing $6X$ (so far this is the same as in Figure 4–3). The increase in the quantity purchased from $2X$ to $6X$ is the total effect or the sum of the substitution and income effects. We are now ready to separate this total effect into these two components.

First, consider the **substitution effect.** In Figure 4–5, we see that when the price of X falls from $P_X = \$2$ to $P_X = \$1$, the individual moves from point B

FIGURE 4–5   Income and Substitution Effects for a Normal Good

Starting from optimum point B (as in the top panel of Figure 4–3), we can isolate the substitution effect by drawing imaginary budget line to U_1 at T. The movement along U_1 from point B to point T is the substitution effect and results from the relative reduction in P_X only (with real income constant). The shift from point T on U_1 to point E on U_2 is then the income effect. The total effect ($BE = 4X$) equals the substitution effect ($BT = 2X$) plus the income effect ($TE = 2X$).

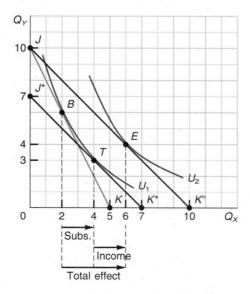

on U_1 to point E on U_2 so that his or her level of satisfaction increases. Suppose that as P_X falls we could reduce the individual's money income sufficiently to keep him or her on original indifference curve U_1. We can show this by drawing hypothetical or imaginary budget line J^*K^* in Figure 4–5. Imaginary budget line J^*K^* is parallel to budget line JK'' so as to reflect the *new* set of relative prices (i.e., $P_X/P_Y = \$1/\$1 = 1$) and is below budget line JK'' in order to keep the individual at the original level of satisfaction (i.e., on indifference curve U_1).[5] The individual would then maximize satisfaction at point T, where indifference curve U_1 is tangent to imaginary budget line J^*K^* (so that $MRS_{XY} = P_X/P_Y = \$1/\$1 = 1$).

The movement along indifference curve U_1 from original point B to imaginary point T measures the substitution effect only (since the individual remains on the same indifference curve or level of satisfaction). From Figure 4–5, we see that the substitution effect, by itself, leads the individual to increase the quantity purchased of good X from two to four units when P_X falls from \$2 to \$1. That is, the individual substitutes hamburgers for, say, hot dogs and purchases two additional hamburgers and fewer hot dogs per unit of time. The substitution effect results exclusively from the reduction in the **relative price** of X (from $P_X/P_Y = \$2/\$1 = 2$ to $P_X/P_Y = \$1/\$1 = 1$) with the level of satisfaction held constant. Because indifference curves are convex, the substitution effect always involves an increase in the quantity demanded of a good when its price falls.

Next, consider the **income effect**. The shift from the imaginary point T on U_1 to the actual new point E on U_2 can be taken as a measure of the income effect. The shift from point T to point E does not involve any price change. That is, since the imaginary budget line J^*K^* and the actual new budget line JK'' are parallel, relative prices are the same (i.e., $P_X/P_Y = 1$ in both). The shift from indifference curve U_1 to U_2 can thus be taken as a measure of the increase in the individual's real income or purchasing power.[6] Because good X is a normal good, an increase in the consumer's purchasing power or real income leads him or her to purchase more of X (and other normal goods). In Figure 4–5, the income effect, by itself, leads the consumer to purchase two additional hamburgers (i.e., to go from $4X$ to $6X$).[7]

Thus, the total effect of the reduction in P_X ($BE = 4X$) equals the substitution effect ($BT = 2X$) plus the income effect ($TE = 2X$). The substitution effect reflects the increase in Q_X resulting only from the reduction in P_X and is independent of any change in the consumer's level of satisfaction or real

---

[5] Budget line J^*K^* is imaginary in the sense that we do not actually observe it, unless the reduction in P_X is in fact accompanied by a lump-sum tax that removes \$3 ($JJ^* = K''K^*$) from the money income of the individual.

[6] The shift from point T to point E could be observed by giving back to the consumer the hypothetical lump-sum tax of \$3 collected earlier. Only with such an increase in real income or purchasing power can the consumer move from point T on U_1 to point E on U_2.

[7] It also leads the individual to purchase one additional soft drink (i.e., to go from $3Y$ to $4Y$). See the figure.

income. On the other hand, the income effect reflects the increase in Q_X resulting only from the increase in satisfaction or real income. Only the total effect of the price change is actually observable in the real world, but we have been able, at least conceptually or experimentally, to separate this total effect into a substitution effect and an income effect.

In Figure 4–5 the substitution effect and the income effect are of equal size. In the real world, the substitution effect is likely to be much larger than the income effect. The reason is that most goods have suitable substitutes, and when the price of a good falls, the quantity of the good purchased is likely to increase very much as consumers substitute the now-cheaper good for others. On the other hand, with the consumer purchasing many goods and spending only a small fraction of his or her income on any one good, the income effect of a price decline of any one good is likely to be small. There are, however, exceptional cases in which the income effect exceeds the substitution effect.[8] Also note that although the substitution effect of a price reduction is always positive (i.e., it always leads to an increase in the quantity demanded of a good), the income effect can be positive if the good is normal or negative if the good is inferior.[9]

Example 2

 ## Substitution and Income Effects and the Gasoline Tax Rebate Proposal

One of the biggest political battles likely to be fought in Congress in the 1990s is over an energy policy in general and the size of the federal gasoline tax in particular. The federal gasoline tax now stands at 14.1 cents per gallon in the United States, as compared with more than $2 per gallon in Europe and Japan. Ever since the first petroleum crisis in 1973–1974, many in Congress have sought a gasoline tax of as much as 50 cents per gallon. The tax would increase gasoline prices for American motorists and lead to a reduction in gasoline consumption and American dependence on foreign oil (which now stands at more than 40%, up from 35% in 1973). To avoid the deflationary impact (i.e., the reduction in purchasing power) of the tax on the economy, it is proposed either to return to consumers the amount of the tax collected on gasoline in the form of a *general* tax rebate unrelated to gasoline consumption or to reduce other taxes.

---

[8]The separation of the substitution effect from the income effect of a price change using rudimentary calculus is shown in section A.4 of the Mathematical Appendix at the end of the book.

[9]We could derive a demand curve along which real, rather than nominal, income is kept constant (i.e., showing or reflecting only the substitution effect). Such a demand curve would be steeper or less elastic than the usual demand curve (which shows both the substitution and the income effects) if the good is normal (because in that case the income effect reinforces the substitution) and flatter or more elastic than the usual demand curve if the good is inferior (because in that case part of the substitution effect would be neutralized by the opposite income effect).

All of the proposals rely on the distinction between the substitution effect and the income effect of an increase in gasoline prices. The substitution effect would result as people switch to cheaper means of transportation (trains, buses, subways), car pools, and more fuel-efficient cars and economize on the use of automobiles in general. The general income subsidy would then neutralize the reduction in real income associated with the increase in the price of gasoline. Thus, while the reduction in purchasing power would be neutralized by the general income subsidy, the increase in the gasoline price would reduce its consumption. Despite strong opposition to gasoline tax rebate proposals from road builders, tourist interests, farm groups, the oil industry, and truckers, a large increase in the gasoline tax seems likely.

Sources: "Fight over a Gasoline Tax Rise," *New York Times*, December 30, 1988, p. D1; "A Nickel More for Gasoline as U.S. Raises Its Fuel Tax," *New York Times*, December 1, 1990, p. 11; "50-Cents-a-Gallon Tax Could Buy a Whole Lot," *New York Times*, October 18, 1992, p. F5; and "Coming Soon, to a Station Near You," *The Economist*, January 9, 1993, p. 24.

▲

Substitution and Income Effects for Inferior Goods

For a normal good, the substitution and the income effects of a price decline are both positive and reinforce each other in leading to a greater quantity purchased of the good. On the other hand, when the good is inferior, the income effect moves in the opposite direction from the substitution effect. That is, when the price of an inferior good falls, the substitution effect continues to operate as before to *increase* the quantity purchased of the good. This results from the convex shape of indifference curves. However, the increase in purchasing power or real income resulting from the price decline leads the consumer to purchase *less* of an inferior good. But, because the substitution effect is usually larger than the income effect, the quantity demanded of the inferior good increases when its price falls and the demand curve is still negatively sloped.

We can separate the substitution effect from the income effect of a price decline for an inferior good by returning to the candy bar (inferior good Z) example of the previous section. In the top panel of Figure 4–6, the consumer is originally at optimum at point V, where indifference curve U_1' is tangent to budget line JK' and the consumer purchases four candy bars (as in the top panel of Figure 4–2). If now the price of candy bars declines from $P_Z = \$1$ to $P_Z = \$0.50$, the consumer moves to optimum point S, where indifference curve U_2' is tangent to budget line JN' and the consumer purchases 6Z. The movement from point V to point S (+2Z) is the sum or net effect of the substitution and income effects.

To separate the substitution effect from the income effect, we now draw the imaginary budget line J^*N^*, which is lower than, but parallel to, budget line JN' and tangent to U_1' at point T. The movement along U_1' from the original point V to imaginary point T is the *substitution effect*. It results exclusively

FIGURE 4–6   Income and Substitution Effects for Inferior Goods

Starting from optimum point V in the top panel, we can isolate the substitution effect by drawing J^*N^* parallel to JN' and tangent to U'_1 at point T. The movement along U'_1 from point V to point T is the substitution effect. The movement from point T on U'_1 to point S on U'_2 is the income effect. Since the income effect is negative, good Z is inferior. However, since the positive substitution effect exceeds the negative income effect, Q_Z increases when P_Z falls. In the bottom panel, the positive substitution effect $(VT = 4Z)$ is smaller than the negative income effect $(TS^* = -6Z)$, so that Q_Z declines by $2Z$ when P_Z falls. Good Z is then a Giffen good.

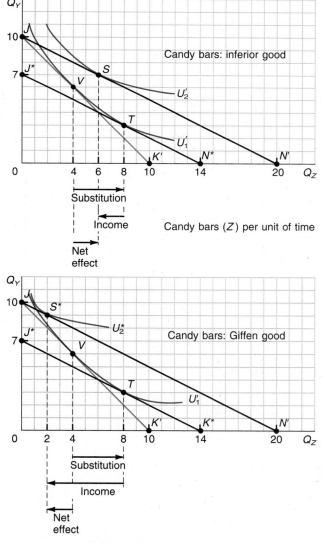

Candy bars (Z) per unit of time

from the reduction in P_Z relative to P_Y and is independent of any increase in real income. Thus, the substitution effect, by itself, leads the individual to purchase four additional units of good Z per unit of time (from 4Z to 8Z).

On the other hand, the movement from imaginary point T on U_1' to the new point S on U_2' can be taken as a measure of the *income effect*. It results exclusively from the increase in the level of satisfaction of the consumer with relative prices constant ($P_Z/P_Y = \$0.50/\$1 = \frac{1}{2}$ for imaginary budget line J^*N^* and for new budget line JN'). The income effect, by itself, leads the consumer to purchase two *fewer* units of good Z per unit of time (from 8Z to 6Z) because good Z is an inferior good.

Thus, the total effect ($VS = 2Z$ given by the movement from point V on U_1' to point S on U_2') equals the positive substitution effect ($VT = 4Z$ given by the movement from point V to T on U_1') plus the negative income effect ($TS = -2Z$ given by the movement from point T on U_1' to point S on U_2'). However, since the positive substitution effect exceeds the negative income effect, the consumer purchases two additional units of good Z when its price declines. Thus, the demand curve for good Z is negatively sloped, even though good Z is an inferior good. That is, the consumer purchases 4Z at $P_Z = \$1$ and 6Z at $P_Z = \$0.50$.

On the other hand, if the positive substitution effect is smaller than the negative income effect when the price of an inferior good falls, then the demand curve for the inferior good is positively sloped. This very rarely, if ever, occurs in the real world, and is referred to as the **Giffen good,** after the 19th century English economist, Robert Giffen, who supposedly first discussed it. Note that a Giffen good is an inferior good, but not all inferior goods are Giffen goods. If it existed, a Giffen good would lead to a positively sloped demand curve for the individual and would represent an exception to the law of negatively sloped demand.[10]

The bottom panel of Figure 4–6 is drawn on the assumption that good Z is now a Giffen good. There, the consumer is originally at optimum point V and hypothetically moves to point T because of the substitution effect (as in the top panel). However, with *alternative* indifference curve U_2' in the bottom panel (as opposed to U_2' in the top panel), the income effect is given by the movement from point T to point S^*. Point S^* is to the left of point T because good Z is an inferior good, so that an increase in real income leads to less of it being purchased. The total effect is now VS^* ($-2Z$) and is equal to substitution effect VT (4Z) plus income effect TS^* ($-6Z$). Because the positive substitution effect is smaller than the negative income effect, the quantity demanded of good Z *declines* when its price falls, and d_Z would be positively sloped over this range. That is, the individual would purchase 4Z at $P_Z = \$1$ but only 2Z at $P_Z = \$0.50$.

---

[10]If we kept real rather than nominal income constant in deriving the demand curve (i.e., if the demand curve showed or reflected only the substitution effect), there would be no Giffen exception to the law of negatively sloped demand.

Although theoretically interesting, the Giffin paradox rarely, if ever, occurs in the real world. The reason is that inferior goods are usually narrowly defined goods for which suitable substitutes are available (so that the substitution effect usually exceeds the opposite income effect). Giffen thought that potatoes in 19th century Ireland provided an example of the paradox, but subsequent research did not lead credence to his belief. The separation of the substitution effect from the income effect (and all of the analysis in this chapter) could easily be shown for a price increase rather than for a price decline. These alternatives are assigned as end-of-chapter problems.

4.4 SUBSTITUTION BETWEEN DOMESTIC AND FOREIGN GOODS

The substitution between domestic and foreign goods and services has reached an all-time high in the world today and is expected to continue to increase sharply in the future. This has been the result of (1) transportation costs having fallen to very low levels for most products, (2) increased knowledge of foreign products due to an international information revolution, (3) global advertising campaigns by multinational corporations, (4) the explosion of international travel, and (5) the rapid convergence of tastes internationally. For homogeneous products such as a particular grade of wheat or steel, and for many industrial products with precise specifications such as computer chips, fiber optics, and specialized machinery, substitutability between domestic and foreign products is almost perfect. Here, a small price difference can lead quickly to large shifts in sales from domestic to foreign sources and vice versa. Indeed, so fluid is the market for such products that governments often step in to protect these industries from foreign competition.

Even for differentiated products, such as automobiles and motorcycles, computers and copiers, watches and cameras, TV films and TV programs, soft drinks and cigarettes, soaps and detergents, commercial and military aircraft, and most other products that are similar but not identical, substitutability between domestic and foreign products is very high and rising. Despite the quality problems of the past, U.S.-made automobiles today are highly substitutable for Japanese and European automobiles, and so are most other products. Indeed, intraindustry trade in such differentiated products now represents over 60% of total U.S. trade and an even larger percentage of the trade of most other industrial countries.[11] With many parts and components imported from many nations, and with production facilities and sales around the world often exceeding sales at home, even the distinction between domestic and foreign products is fast becoming obsolete.

---

[11]See, D. Salvatore, *International Economics,* 4th ed. (New York: Macmillan, 1993), Section 6.4.

Example 3
What Is an "American" Car?

A "buy American" movement is sweeping the country. For example, Detroit's *Free Press* reported that in a nationwide poll 51% of those polled said that they will consider buying only an American car the next time they purchase an automobile, and 45% answered that they will consider either an American or a foreign car. Only 4% said that they will consider only a foreign car. Furthermore, more and more companies are offering their employees bonuses to buy American cars. This buy American movement is the result of the increased desire on the part of the American public to help U.S. producers and stimulate the U.S. economy. In the case of automobiles, the increased desire to buy American has also been stimulated by the dramatic improvement in the quality of American cars since 1986.

The problem is that it has become exceedingly difficult to determine which car is an American car. Should a Honda Accord produced in Ohio be considered American? What about a Chrysler minivan produced in Canada? Is a Kentucky Toyota or Mazda that uses nearly 50% of imported Japanese parts American? It is clearly becoming more and more difficult to define what's American, and opinions differ widely. For some, any vehicle assembled in North America (the United States, Canada, and Mexico) should be considered American because these vehicles use U.S.-made parts. But the United Auto Workers union views cars built in Canada and Mexico as taking away U.S. jobs. Some regard automobiles produced by Japanese-owned plants in the United States as American because they provide jobs for Americans. Others regard production by these Japanese "transplants" as foreign, because the jobs they create were taken from the U.S. automakers, because they use nearly 50% of imported Japanese parts, and because they remit profits to Japan. What if Japanese transplants increased their use of American parts to 75% or 90%? Is the Ford Probe, built for Ford by Mazda in Mazda's Michigan plant, American? Yes, it is difficult to decide exactly what is an American car! One could even ask if this question is important—is it relevant in a world growing more and more interdependent and globalized.

Sources: "Growing Movement to 'Buy American' Debates the Term," *Wall Street Journal,* January 24, 1992, p. 1, and "Honda's Nationality Proves Troublesome for Free-Trade Pact," *New York Times,* October 9, 1992, p. 1.

4.5 SOME APPLICATIONS OF INDIFFERENCE CURVE ANALYSIS

We now can apply the tools developed in this chapter to analyze the economics of the food stamp program, consumer surplus, and exchange. These applications deal only with the demand for goods and services, but the tools developed in this chapter have many other applications (examined in other parts of the text). For example, the distinction between the substitution and income effects is useful in analyzing the effect of overtime pay on the number of hours worked and on leisure time. Because this topic deals with the supply of labor, however, it is appropriately postponed until Chapter 13, which deals with input price and employment. Indifference curve analysis is also useful in analyzing the choice between borrowing or lending from present income (examined in Chapter 15), in general equilibrium and welfare economics (examined in Chapter 16), and in the analysis of time as an economic good (discussed in Chapter 18).

Is a Cash Subsidy Better Than Food Stamps?

Under the federal **food stamp program,** low-income families receive free food stamps, which they can use only to purchase food. In 1988, more than 4.8 million eligible low-income families received free food stamps at a cost of $12.4 billion to the federal government. The important question is whether it would have been better (i.e., provided more satisfaction) to have given an equal amount of subsidy in cash to poor families.

We can examine this question with Figure 4–7. Suppose that, initially, a

FIGURE 4–7   Food Stamps Versus Cash Aid

A poor family's budget line, *AC*, becomes *AB'C'* with $50 worth of free food stamps per week, and *A'C'* with a $50 cash subsidy instead. The family maximizes utility at point *B* on U_1 without any aid, at point *B'* on U_2 with food stamps, and at point *B"* on U_3 with the cash subsidy. However, another family with the same original income and budget line *AC* but with a stronger preference for food may go instead from point *F* on U'_1 to point *F'* on U'_3 either with the cash subsidy or with food stamps.

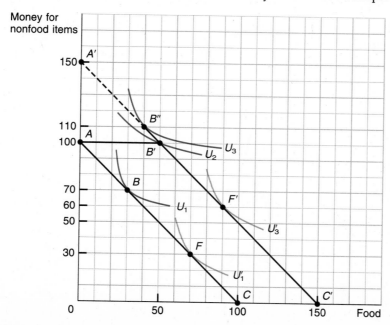

typical poor family has a weekly income of $100. If the poor family spent its entire weekly income on nonfood items, it could purchase $100 worth of nonfood items per week (point A on the vertical axis). On the other hand, if the poor family spent the entire $100 on food, it could purchase 100 units of food per week if the unit price of food is $1 (point C on the horizontal axis). The initial budget line of the family is then AC.

With free food stamps that allow the family to purchase $50 worth of food per week, the budget line of the family becomes $AB'C'$, where $AB' = CC' = 50$. Combinations on dashed segment $A'B'$ are not available with the food stamp program because the family would have to spend more than its $100 money income on nonfood items and less than the $50 of food stamps on food (and this is not possible if it cannot sell its food stamps). Were the government to provide $50 in cash rather than in food stamps, the budget line would then be $A'C'$. Thus, we have three alternative budget lines for the family: budget line AC without any aid, budget line $AB'C'$ with $50 in food stamps, and budget line $A'C'$ with $50 cash aid instead.

If the family's indifference curves are U_1, U_2, and U_3, the family maximizes utility at point B where U_1 is tangent to AC before receiving any aid, at point B' on U_2 with food stamps, and at point B'' (preferred to B') on U_3 with the cash subsidy. In this case, the cash subsidy allows the family to reach a higher indifference curve than food stamps.[12] However, *another family* with the same initial income of $100 (and budget line AC) but stronger preference for food and facing indifference curves U_1' and U_3' will move instead from point F on U_1' to point F' on U_3', either with the cash subsidy or with food stamps. Thus, depending on the family's tastes, *a cash subsidy will not be worse than food stamps and may be better* (i.e., provide more satisfaction). Why then does the federal government continue to use food stamps? One reason is to improve nutrition.

The same type of analysis can be used to show that an unrestricted trust fund will not be worse than an equal college trust fund (which can be used only to cover college expenses) and may be better (i.e., provide more satisfaction to the recipient). College trust funds are, nevertheless, popular because they allow parents or other donors to ensure that the funds are used in a way that the donor believes to be in the best long-term interest of the children or recipient.

Consumer Surplus Measures Unpaid Benefits

Consumer surplus is the difference between what a consumer is willing to pay for a good and what he or she actually pays. It results because the consumer pays for *all* units of the good only as much as he or she is willing to pay for the *last* unit of the good (which gives less utility than earlier units). We can see how consumer surplus arises and how it can be measured with the aid of Figure 4–8.

---

[12]Both cost the government $50.

The figure shows that $5 is the maximum amount that the consumer is willing to pay for the first unit of good X (say, hamburgers) rather than go without it. Thus, the area of the first rectangle (with height of $5 and width of 1) measures the marginal value or benefit that the consumer gets from the first hamburger. After all, by being willing to purchase the first hamburger for $5, the consumer indicates that he or she prefers paying $5 for the first hamburger rather than keeping the $5 in cash or spending the $5 on other goods. The second unit of good X (hamburger) gives the consumer less utility than the first, and the consumer would be willing to pay $4 for it rather than go without it. Thus, $4 (the area of the second rectangle) can be taken as a measure of the marginal value or benefit of the second hamburger to the consumer. The third hamburger gives the consumer less utility than either the first or the second and so the consumer is willing to pay only $3 for it. Thus, the marginal value or benefit of the third hamburger is $3 and is given by the area of the third rectangle. For the fourth hamburger, the consumer would be willing to pay $2 (the area of the fourth rectangle), and this is a measure of the marginal value or benefit of the fourth hamburger, and so on.

To summarize, the consumer would be willing to pay $5 for the first hamburger, $4 for the second, $3 for the third, and $2 for the fourth, for a total of $14 for all four hamburgers. Thus, $14 is the total benefit that the consumer receives from purchasing four hamburgers. However, if the market price is

FIGURE 4–8   Consumer Surplus
The difference between what the consumer is willing to pay for $4X$ ($5 + $4 + $3 + $2 = $14) and what he or she actually pays ($8) is the consumer surplus (the shaded area that equals $6). If good X could be purchased in infinitesimally small units, the consumer surplus would equal the area under d_X and above $P_X = $2 (area $AEB = $8).

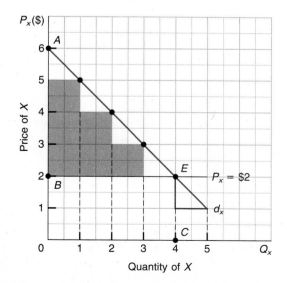

$2 per hamburger, the consumer can purchase all four hamburgers at a total cost of (i.e., by actually spending) only $8. Because the consumer would be willing to pay $14 for the first four hamburgers rather than go entirely without them, but actually pays only $8, he or she enjoys a net benefit or *consumer surplus* equal to the difference ($6).

To put it another way, the consumer is willing to pay $5 for the first hamburger, but since he or she can purchase it for only $2, he or she receives a surplus of $3 for the first hamburger. Since he or she is willing to pay $4 for the second hamburger but pays only $2, there is a surplus of $2 on the second hamburger. For the third hamburger, the consumer is willing to pay $3, but since he or she pays only $2, the surplus is $1. For the fourth hamburger, the consumer is willing to pay $2, and since he or she has to pay $2 for it, there is no surplus on the fourth hamburger. The consumer would not purchase the fifth hamburger because he or she is not willing to pay the $2 market price for it.

By adding the consumer surplus of $3 on the first hamburger, $2 on the second, $1 on the third, and $0 on the fourth, we get the consumer surplus of $6 obtained earlier. This is given by the sum of the shaded areas in the figure. The same result would have been obtained if the consumer had been asked for the maximum amount of money that he or she would have been willing to pay for four hamburgers rather than do entirely without them—*all or nothing.*

If hamburgers could have been purchased in smaller and smaller fractions of a whole hamburger, then the consumer surplus would have been given by the entire area under demand curve d_X above the market price of $2. That is, the consumer surplus would have been the area of triangle AEB, which is $\frac{1}{2}(4)(4) = \$8$. This exceeds the consumer surplus of $6 that we have found by adding only the shaded areas in the figure. Specifically, the consumer would have been willing to pay $16 (the area of $OAEC$) for four hamburgers. Note that $OAEC$ is composed of triangle AEB plus rectangle $OBEC$. Since the consumer only pays $8 ($OBEC$), the consumer surplus is $8 ($AEB$). If P_X fell to $1, the consumer would purchase five hamburgers and the consumer's surplus would be $12.50 (the area under d_X and above $P_X = \$1$ in the figure) if hamburgers could be purchased by infinitely small fractions of a whole hamburger.[13]

The concept of the consumer surplus was first used by Dupuit in 1844 and was subsequently refined and popularized by Alfred Marshall. The concept helped resolve the so-called **water-diamond paradox,** which plagued classical economists until 1870. Why is water, which is essential for life, so cheap,

---

[13]Measuring consumer surplus by the area under the demand curve and above the prevailing market price is only an approximation (it is based on the assumption that a consumer's indifference curves are parallel), but for most purposes it is sufficiently accurate to be a useful tool of analysis. See, R. D. Willig, "Consumer Surplus without Apology," *American Economic Review*, September 1976.

while diamonds, which are not essential, so expensive? The explanation is that because water is so plentiful (relatively cheap) and we use so much of it, the utility of the last unit is very little (washing the car), and we pay as little for all units of water as we are willing to pay for the last *nonessential* unit of it. On the other hand, diamonds are scarce in relation to demand, and because we use very little of them, the utility and price of the *last unit* are very great. The *total* utility and the consumer surplus from all the water used are far greater than the total utility and the consumer surplus from all the diamonds purchased. However, demand depends on marginal utility, not on total utility. In a desert, the first glass of water would be worth much more than any glassful of diamonds.

The above analysis referred to an individual's demand curve, but a similar analysis would also apply to a market demand curve. In subsequent chapters we will use the concept of consumer surplus to measure the benefits and costs of excise taxes, import tariffs, pollution control, government projects, and other microeconomic policies, as well as to measure the benefits and costs of alternative market structures.

Benefits from Exchange

Suppose that two individuals, A and B, have a given amount of good X and good Y and decide to trade some of these goods with each other. If the exchange is voluntary, the strong presumption is that both individuals gain from the exchange (otherwise, the individual who loses would simply refuse to trade). We can examine the process of voluntary exchange by indifference curve analysis.

Suppose that individual A's tastes and preferences for good X and good Y are shown by indifference curves U_1, U_2, and U_3 in the top left panel of Figure 4–9. On the other hand, individual B's tastes and preferences are given by indifference curves U_1', U_2', and U_3' (with origin O') in the top right panel. Initially, individual A has an allocation of $3X$ and $6Y$ (point C in the top left panel) and individual B has $7X$ and $2Y$ (point C' in the top right panel).

We now rotate individual B's indifference diagram by 180 degrees (so that origin O' appears in the top right corner) and superimpose it on individual A's indifference diagram in such a way that the axes of the two diagrams form the so-called **Edgeworth box diagram,** shown in the bottom panel of Figure 4–9. The length of the box ($10X$) measures the combined amount of X initially owned by individual A ($3X$) and individual B ($7X$). The height of the box ($8Y$) measures the amount of Y initially owned by individual A ($6Y$) and individual B ($2Y$). A's indifference curves are convex to origin O (as usual), while B's indifference curves are convex to origin O'.

Any point inside the box indicates how the total amount of X and Y may be distributed between the two individuals. For example, the initial distribution of X and Y given by point C indicates that individual A has $3X$ and $6Y$ (viewed from origin O) and individual B has the remainder of $7X$ and $2Y$ (when viewed

FIGURE 4–9   Edgeworth Box Diagram

The top left panel shows individual A's indifference curves and the top right panel shows B's indifference curves. The box in the bottom panel is obtained by rotating by 180 degrees B's indifference map diagram and superimposing it on A's diagram in such a way that the dimension of the box equals the initial combined amount of goods X and Y owned by A and B. Any point in the box refers to a particular distribution of X and Y between A and B. At point C, MRS_{XY} for the two individuals differs (U_1 and U_1' cross) and there is a basis for mutually beneficial exchange until a point between D and F on curve DEF is reached (where MRS_{XY} for A and B are equal).

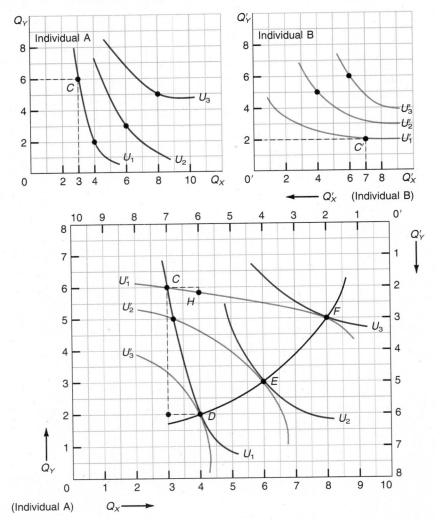

from origin O') for a total of $10X$ and $8Y$ (the dimensions of the box). Individual A is on indifference curve U_1 and individual B is on indifference curve U_1'.

Since at point C (where U_1 and U_1' intersect), the marginal rate of substitution of good X for good Y (MRS_{XY}) for individual A exceeds MRS_{XY} for individual B, there is a basis for mutually beneficial exchange between the two individuals. Starting at point C, individual A would be willing to give up $4Y$ to get one additional unit of X (and move to point D on U_1'). On the other hand, individual B would be willing to give up about $0.2Y$ for one additional unit of X (and move to point H on U_1'). Because A is willing to give up more of Y than necessary to induce B to give up $1X$, there is a basis for trade in which individual A gives up some of Y in exchange for some of X from individual B.

Whenever the MRS_{XY} for the two individuals differ at the initial distribution of X and Y, either or both may gain from exchange. For example, starting from point C, if individual A exchanges $4Y$ for $1X$ with individual B, A would move from point C to point D along indifference curve U_1, while B would move from point C to U_1' to point D on U_3'. By moving from indifference curve U_1' to indifference curve U_3', individual B receives all of the gains from the exchange while individual A gains or loses nothing (since A remains on U_1). At point D, U_1 and U_3' are tangent, and so their slopes (MRS_{XY}) are equal. Thus, there is no basis for further exchange (at point D, the amount of Y that A is willing to give up for $1X$ is exactly equal to what B requires to give up $1X$). Any further exchange would make either one or both individuals worse off than they are at point D.

Alternatively, if individual A exchanged $1Y$ for $5X$ with individual B, individual A would move from point C on U_1 to point F on U_3, while individual B would move from point C to point F along U_1'. Then, A would reap all the benefits from exchange while B would neither gain nor lose. At point F, MRS_{XY} for A equals MRS_{XY} for B and there is no further basis for exchange. Finally, starting again from point C on U_1 and U_1', if A exchanges $3Y$ for $3X$ with B and gets to point E, both individuals gain from the exchange since point E is on U_2 and U_2'.

Starting from any point within $CDEF$ but not on curve DEF, both individuals can gain from exchange by moving to a point on curve DEF between points D and F. The closer individual A gets to point F (i.e., the more shrewd A is as a bargainer), the greater is the proportion of the total gain from the exchange accruing to A and the less is left for B. The Edgeworth box is named after the English economist F. Y. Edgeworth, who in 1881 first outlined its construction. (We will return to exchange in greater detail in Chapter 16.)

SUMMARY

1. The income-consumption curve joins consumer optimum points resulting when only the consumer's income is varied. The Engel curve is derived from the income-consumption curve and shows the amount of a good that the consumer would purchase per unit of time at various income levels. A normal good is one of which the

consumer purchases more with an increase in income. An inferior good is one of which the consumer purchases less with an increase in income. The income-consumption curve and the Engel curve are positively sloped for normal goods and negatively sloped for inferior goods.

2. The price-consumption curve for a good joins consumer optimum points resulting when only the price of the good varies. This shows the amount of the good that the consumer would purchase per unit of time at various prices of the good while holding everything else constant. The individual consumer's demand curve for a good is negatively sloped, reflecting the law of demand. Demand is elastic, unitary elastic, or inelastic depending on whether the price-consumption curve is negatively sloped, horizontal, or positively sloped.

3. When the price of a good falls, consumers substitute this for other goods and their real income rises. If the good is normal, the income effect reinforces the substitution effect in increasing the quantity purchased of the good. If the good is inferior, the substitution effect tends to increase while the income effect tends to reduce the quantity demanded of the good. Because the former usually exceeds the latter, the quantity demanded of the good increases and the demand curve is negatively sloped. Only if the income effect overwhelms the opposite substitution effect for an inferior good will the quantity demanded of the good decrease when its price falls, and the demand curve will slope upward. This is the Giffen good, but it has never really been observed in the real world.

4. With the substitutability between domestic and foreign goods and services having reached an all-time high in the world today, and with the expectation that it will rise even more in the future, the need to introduce an important international dimension in the study of microeconomics becomes even clearer.

5. A cash subsidy leads to an equal or greater increase in utility than a subsidy in kind (such as the food stamp program) that costs the same. The consumer surplus is given by the difference between what the consumer is willing to pay for a good and what the consumer actually pays for it. Its value can be approximated by the area under the demand curve and above the market price of the good. An Edgeworth box diagram is constructed by rotating by 180 degrees an individual's indifference map diagram and superimposing it on another's, so that the dimensions of the box equal the combined initial distribution of the two goods between the two individuals. It can be used to analyze voluntary exchange.

KEY TERMS

Income-Consumption Curve
Engel Curve
Normal Good
Inferior Good
Price-Consumption Curve
Individual's Demand Curve

Substitution Effect
Relative Price
Income Effect
Giffen Good
Food Stamp Program
Consumer Surplus

Water-Diamond Paradox
Edgeworth Box Diagram
Income or Expenditure Index
 (E)
Laspeyres Price Index (L)
Paasche Price Index (P)

REVIEW QUESTIONS

1. A consumer buys a Toyota for $14,000 instead of an Oldsmobile for $16,000. Does that mean that the consumer prefers the Toyota to the Oldsmobile?

2. How would indifference curves between money and automobiles differ between two individuals with the same money income but with one having a stronger preference for automobiles than the other?

3. Why would the use of gasoline decline if its price rose as a result of a gasoline tax but the effect of the price rise was compensated by a tax rebate?

4. The income effect of a 20% increase in housing rents is larger than a 20% increase in the price of salt. True or false? Explain.

5. A demand curve showing only the substitution effect can never be positively sloped, not even theoretically. True or false? Explain.

6. Is a demand curve showing both the substitution and income effects flatter or steeper than the demand curve showing only the substitution effect? Explain.

7. Will a consumer purchase more or less of an inferior good when its price declines? Explain.

8. Can all goods purchased by a consumer be inferior?

9. In 1991, the Men's Hair Company increased the price of its shampoo and sold more than in 1990. Is the demand curve for this company's shampoo positively sloped? Explain.

10. Why is the gift of any good likely to provide less satisfaction to the recipient than an equal cash gift?

11. When would the gift of a good provide the recipient as much satisfaction as an equal cash gift?

12. How can a black market in food stamps be explained?

PROBLEMS

1. a. Derive the income-consumption curve and Engel curve from the indifference curves of problem 2 in Chapter 3 and the budget lines from problem 6a in Chapter 3. Is good X a normal or an inferior good? Why?

   b. Derive the Engel curve for good Y. Is good Y a normal or an inferior good? Why?

2. a. For the budget lines of problem 6a in Chapter 3, draw indifference curves that show that good X is inferior; derive the income-consumption curve and the Engel curve for good X.

   b. Draw the Engel curve for good Y. Must good Y be normal?

*3. a. Derive the price-consumption curve and demand curve for good X from the indifference curves of problem 2 in Chapter 3 and the budget lines from problem 6b in Chapter 3 when the price of X falls from P_X = $2 to P_X = $1 and then to P_X = $0.50.

   b. Use the figure for your answer to 3a to explain how you would derive the price-consumption curve and demand curve for good X when the price of X rises from P_X = $0.50 to P_X = $1 and then to P_X = $2.

4. a. Is the demand curve for good X (d_X) that you derived in problem 3 elastic, unitary elastic, or inelastic? Why?

   b. Use the formula for arc elasticity to measure the price elasticity of d_X between points B' and E' and between points E' and G'.

5. Using the indifference curves of problem 2 in Chapter 3 and the budget lines of problem 6b in Chapter 3, separate the substitution effect from the income effect when the price of X falls from P_X = $2 to P_X = $1 and then from P_X = $1 to P_X = $0.50.

*6. Separate the substitution effect from the income effect for an *increase* in the price of an inferior good.

7. Separate the substitution effect from the income effect for an increase in price of a Giffen good.

*8. It is sometimes asserted that rice in very poor Asian countries might be an inferior good. Even though there is no evidence that this is indeed the case, explain the reasoning behind the assertion.

9. The average number of children per family has declined in the face of rapidly rising family incomes, so children must be an inferior good. True or false? Explain.

———————

* = Answer provided at end of book.

*10. Show with indifference curve analysis that a poor family can be made to reach a given higher indifference curve with a smaller cash subsidy than with a subsidy in kind (such as, for example, by the government paying half of the market price of food for the family). Why might the government still prefer a subsidy in kind?

11. With reference to Figure 4–8 in the text, indicate the size of the consumer surplus when $P_X = \$3$ if

a. good X can only be purchased in whole units.
b. good X can be purchased in infinitesimally small fractional units.

12. With reference to Figure 4–9 in the text, indicate how exchange could take place starting from the initial distribution of good X and good Y between individual A and individual B given by the intersection of U_1 and U'_2.

APPENDIX INDEX NUMBERS AND CHANGES IN CONSUMER WELFARE

In this appendix, we discuss index numbers and their use in measuring changes in standards of living or welfare, especially during inflationary periods. For example, workers and their unions are keen to know if money wages are keeping up with rising prices. Cost-of-living indices are often used for inflation adjustment in wage contracts, for pensions and welfare payments and, since 1984, even for tax payments. In this appendix, we will define three indices and, by comparing the values of these indices in two different time periods, determine if the standard of living has increased, decreased, or remained unchanged. For simplicity, we will assume that the consumer spends all income on only two commodities, X and Y.

Expenditure, Laspeyres, and Paasche Indices

To measure changes in the standard of living or welfare from one time period to another, we begin by defining three indices: the income or expenditure index, the Laspeyres price index, and the Paasche price index.

The **income or expenditure index** (E) is the ratio of period 1 to base period money income or expenditures. That is,

$$E = \frac{x_1 P_{x1} + y_1 P_{y1}}{x_0 P_{x0} + y_0 P_{y0}} \qquad [4–1]$$

where x and y refer to the quantities of commodities X and Y purchased, respectively; P refers to price, and the subscripts "1" and "0" refer to period 1 and the base period, respectively.

Thus, the income and expenditure index is the sum of the product of period 1 quantities and their respective period 1 prices divided by the sum of the product of base period quantities and their respective base period prices. In short, E measures the ratio of the consumer's period 1 expenditures or income to the base period expenditures or income. If E is greater than 1, the individual's *money* income or expenditures have increased from the base period to period 1. However, since prices usually also rise, we cannot determine simply from the value of E whether the individual's *real* income or standard of living has also increased. To do that, we need to define the

Laspeyres and the Paasche price indices and compare their value with that of the income or expenditure index.

The **Laspeyres price index (L)** is the ratio of the cost of *base period quantities* at period 1 prices relative to base period prices. That is,

$$L = \frac{x_0 P_{x1} + y_0 P_{y1}}{x_0 P_{x0} + y_0 P_{y0}} \qquad\qquad \text{[4–2]}$$

In the Laspeyres price index, we use the base period quantities as the weights and measure the cost of purchasing these base period quantities at period 1 prices relative to base period prices.

The **Paasche price index (P)** is the ratio of the cost of *period 1 quantities* at period 1 prices relative to base period prices. That is,

$$P = \frac{x_1 P_{x1} + y_1 P_{y1}}{x_1 P_{x0} + y_1 P_{y0}} \qquad\qquad \text{[4–3]}$$

In the Paasche price index, we use period 1 quantities as the weights and measure the cost of purchasing period 1 quantities at period 1 prices relative to base period prices. Thus, the difference between the Laspeyres and the Paasche price indices is that the former uses the base period quantities as the weights while the latter uses the period 1 quantities.

For example, using the hypothetical data in Table 4–2, we can calculate

$$E = \frac{x_1 P_{x1} + y_1 P_{y1}}{x_0 P_{x0} + y_0 P_{y0}} = \frac{(3)(\$2) + (6)(\$1)}{(4)(\$1) + (3)(\$2)} = \frac{\$12}{\$10} = 1.2 \text{ or } 120\%$$

$$L = \frac{x_0 P_{x1} + y_0 P_{y1}}{x_0 P_{x0} + y_0 P_{y0}} = \frac{(4)(\$2) + (3)(\$1)}{\$10} = \frac{\$11}{\$10} = 1.1 \text{ or } 110\%$$

$$P = \frac{x_1 P_{x1} + y_1 P_{y1}}{x_1 P_{x0} + y_1 P_{y0}} = \frac{\$12}{(3)(\$1) + (6)(\$2)} = \frac{\$12}{\$15} = 0.8 \text{ or } 80\%$$

How Are Changes in Consumer Welfare Measured?

Because some quantities and prices rise over time and others fall, it is often impossible to determine by simple inspection of the quantity-price data whether an individual's standard of living or welfare has increased, decreased, or remained unchanged from one time period to the next. To measure changes in the standard of living, we compare the value of the income or expenditure index to the value of the Laspeyres and the Paasche price indices.

An individual's standard of living is higher in period 1 than in the base period if E is greater than L. That is, the individual is better off in period 1 than in the base period if the

TABLE 4–2   Hypothetical Quantity-Price Data in a Base Period and in Period 1

Period	x	P_x	y	P_y
0 (base)	4	$1	3	$2
1	3	2	6	1

increase in his or her money income (E) exceeds the increase in the cost of living using base-period quantities as weights (L). For example, since we calculated from Table 4-2 that $E = 1.2$ or 120% while $L = 1.1$ or 110%, the individual's standard of living increased from the base period to period 1 because his or her income has risen more than his or her costs or prices.

On the other hand, *the individual's standard of living is higher in the base period than in period 1 if E is smaller than P.* That is, the individual is better off in the base period than in period 1 if the increase in his or her money income (E) is smaller than the increase in the cost of living using period 1 quantities as the weights (P). If E is not smaller than P, the individual's standard of living is not higher in the base period. For example, since $E = 120\%$ and $P = 80\%$ from Table 4-2, the individual is not better off in the base period than in period 1. Thus, with E greater than L and E not smaller than P, the individual of the above numerical example is definitely better off in period 1 than in the base period.

Figure 4-10 presents a graphic interpretation of the numerical example of Table 4-2. In the figure, I_0I_0 is the individual's budget line in the base period. That is, with $X = 4$, $P_X = \$1$, $Y = 3$, and $P_Y = \$2$, the individual's total income (I) and expenditure in the base period is $10 (obtained from $4X$ times $1 plus $3Y$ times $2). If the individual had spent the entire base-period income of $10 on commodity X, he or she could have purchased $10X$. If instead the individual had spent his or her entire base-period income of $10 on commodity Y, he or she could have purchased $5Y$. This defines I_0I_0 as the individual's budget line in the base period. The individual's purchase of $4X$ and $3Y$ in the base period (see the first row of Table 4-2) is indicated by point B_0 on budget line I_0I_0. We can similarly determine from the second row of Table 4-2 that in period

FIGURE 4-10   Changes in Consumer Welfare

An individual is better off at B_1 in period 1 that at B_0 in the base period because B_0 was available in period 1 (i.e., B_0 is below period 1 budget line, I_1I_1) but was not chosen. Had the individual been at point A in the base period, we would need the individual's indifference curves to determine if B_1 is superior, inferior, or equal to A.

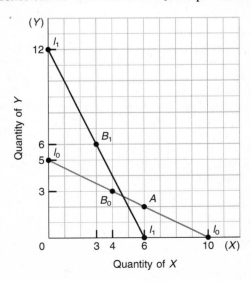

Quantity of X

1 the individual's income is $12 (obtained from $3X$ times $2 plus $6Y$ times $1), so that his or her budget line is I_1I_1. The individual's purchase of $3X$ and $6Y$ in period 1 is indicated by point B_1 on budget line I_1I_1.

From Figure 4–10 we can conclude that since point B_0 is below budget line I_1I_1, the individual must be better off in period 1 than in the base period. That is, since B_0 was available to the individual in period 1 but was not chosen, the individual must be better off in period 1. Specifically, in period 1 the individual could have purchased the base period bundle (B_0) at period 1 prices by spending only $11 ($4X$ times $2 plus $3Y$ times $1) of his or her period 1 income of $12. On the other hand, in the base period the individual could not have purchased period 1 quantities at base period prices since that would have required an expenditure of $15 ($3X$ times $1 plus $6Y$ times $2), which would have exceeded his or her base period income of $10. Thus, the individual must be better off with B_1 in period 1 than with B_0 in the base period.

Had the individual been at a point such as A rather than at point B_0 on budget line I_0I_0 in the base period (see Figure 4–10), we could no longer determine without the individual's indifference curves whether the individual was better off in period 1, in the base period, or was equally well off in period 1 as in the base period. This would depend on whether point B_1 was on a higher, lower, or the same indifference curve as point A, respectively. You should be able to calculate from comparing point A on I_0I_0 in the base period to point B_1 on I_1I_1 in period 1 that $E = 120\%$, $L = 140\%$, and $P = 80\%$. Since E is not larger than L (so that the individual is not necessarily better off in period 1) but E is not smaller than P (so that the individual is not necessarily better off in the base period), we have conflicting results and we cannot tell whether the standard of living is higher, lower, or equal in period 1 as compared with the base period. This confirms the inconclusive results of the graphic analysis (in the absence of the individual's indifference curves) in Figure 4–10.

Because the Laspeyres price index (L) uses base period quantities as the weights, L becomes available sooner than the Paasche price index (P).[14] The most common of the price indices is the Consumer Price Index (CPI), which has been published monthly by the Bureau of Labor Statistics for more than 60 years. This is a Laspeyres index for a "typical" urban family of four. It is the weighted average of the price of 400 goods and services purchased by consumers in the United States. The weights of the various commodities in the basket are periodically changed to reflect variations in consumption patterns. Other important (Laspeyres) price indices are the wholesale price index (WPI) and the GNP deflator. The latter is used to calculate GNP in real terms.

One application of index numbers is measuring changes in real earnings and standards of living over time. According to the Bureau of Labor Statistics, total private nonagricultural weekly money earnings in the United States was $235.10 in 1980 and $354.66 in 1991. The CPI rose from 100 in 1980 to 165.3 in 1991. Dividing the weekly money earnings by the corresponding CPI, we find that weekly *real* earnings declined from $235.10 in 1980 to $214.56 in 1991. Thus, weekly real earnings declined by an average of 9.1% between 1980 and 1991 in the United States. Since the CPI is known to have an upward bias, the true decline in real earnings may in fact have been somewhat smaller.

---

[14]The Laspeyres price index also uses period 1 prices. However, period 1 prices become available much sooner than period 1 quantities.

MARKET DEMAND AND ELASTICITIES

In this chapter, we first see how the *market* demand curve for a commodity is obtained by summing up the individuals' demand curves for the commodity. As shown in Chapter 2, we are interested in the market demand curve for a commodity because it (together with the market supply curve) determines the equilibrium price of the commodity and is used in most other economic analyses. After deriving the market demand curve for a commodity, we discuss the various elasticities of demand, including price and income elasticities in international trade. An important dose of realism is introduced into the discussion by several examples and applications that present real-world estimates of the various elasticities for many commodities and examine their usefulness in the analysis of current economic issues.

Finally, since consumers' expenditures on a commodity represent the revenues of the producers or sellers of the commodity, we consider the producer's side of the market. This is done by examining total and marginal revenues from the sale of the commodity and their relationship to the price elasticity of demand. The optional appendix to this chapter deals with the important but more advanced topic of demand estimation and forecasting.

5.1 THE MARKET DEMAND FOR A COMMODITY

In this section, we examine how the market demand curve for a commodity is derived from the individuals' demand curves. The **market demand curve** for a commodity is simply the *horizontal summation* of the demand curves of all the consumers in the market. Thus, the market quantity demanded at each price is the sum of the individual quantities demanded at that price. For example, in the top of Figure 5–1, the market demand curve for hamburgers (commodity X) is obtained by the horizontal summation of the demand curve of individual 1 (d_1) and individual 2 (d_2), on the assumption that they are the only two consumers in the market. Thus, at the price of $1, the market quantity demanded of 10 hamburgers is the sum of the 6 hamburgers demanded by individual 1 and the 4 hamburgers demanded by individual 2.

If instead there were 1 million individuals in the market, each with demand curve d_X, the market demand curve for hamburgers would be D_X (see the bottom part of Figure 5–1). Both D_X and d_X have the same shape, but the horizontal scale for D_X refers to millions of hamburgers. Note that d_X is the individual's demand curve for hamburgers derived in Chapter 4 (see Figure 4–3).

FIGURE 5–1   From Individual to Market Demand

The top part of the figure shows that the market demand curve for hamburgers, D, is obtained from the horizontal summation of the demand curve for hamburgers of individual 1 (d_1) and individual 2 (d_2). The bottom part of the figure shows an individual's demand curve, d_X, and the market demand curve, D_X, on the assumption that there are 1 million individuals in the market with demand curves for hamburgers identical to d_X.

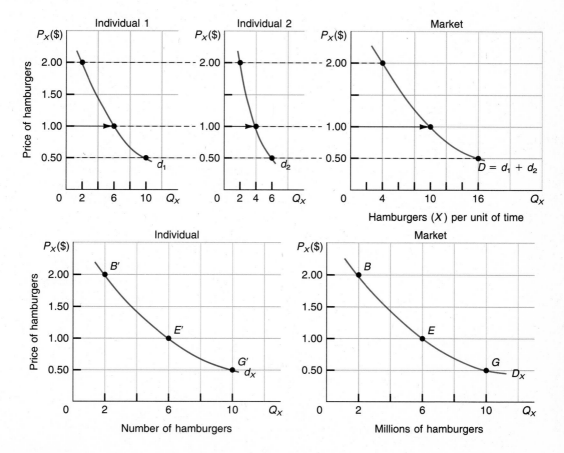

The market demand curve for a commodity shows the various quantities of the commodity demanded in the market per unit of time at various alternative prices of the commodity while holding everything else constant. The market demand curve for a commodity (just as an individual's demand curve) is negatively sloped, indicating that price and quantity are inversely related. That is, the quantity demanded of the commodity increases when its price falls and decreases when price rises. The things held constant in drawing the market demand curve for a commodity are incomes, the prices of substitute and complementary commodities, tastes, and the number of consumers in the market. A change in any of these will cause the market demand curve for the commodity to shift (see section 2.2).[1]

Finally, it must be pointed out that a market demand curve is simply the horizontal summation of the individual demand curves *only if* the consumption decisions of individual consumers are independent. This is not always the case. For example, people sometimes demand a commodity because others are purchasing it and to be "fashionable." The result is a **bandwagon effect** to "keep up with the Joneses." That is, sometimes, the greater is the number of people purchasing a commodity as its price falls, the more people join in purchasing it in order to be fashionable and not feel left out. This results in the market demand curve for the commodity being flatter or more elastic than otherwise.

At other times, the opposite or **snob effect** occurs as many consumers seek to be different and exclusive by demanding less of a commodity as more people consume it. That is, as the price of a commodity falls and more people purchase the commodity, some people will stop buying it in order to stand out and be different. This tends to make the market demand curve steeper or less elastic than otherwise. There are then some individuals who, to impress people, demand more of certain commodities (such as diamonds, mink coats, Rolls Royces, etc.) the more expensive these goods are. This form of "conspicuous consumption" is called the **Veblen effect** (after Thorstein Veblen, who introduced it). For example, some high-income people may be less willing to purchase a $4,000 mink coat than a $10,000 one when the latter clearly looks much more expensive. This also results in a steeper or less elastic market demand curve for the commodity than otherwise.[2]

In what follows, we assume that the bandwagon, snob, and Veblen effects are not significant, so that the market demand curve for the commodity can be obtained simply by the horizontal summation of the individual demand

---

[1]A change in expectations about the future price of the commodity will also affect its demand curve. For example, the expectation that the price of the commodity will be lower in the future will shift the market demand curve to the left (so that less is demanded at each price in the current period) as consumers postpone some of their purchases of the commodity in anticipation of a lower price in the future.

[2]Conceivably, in some cases, the snob and Veblen effects could even make the market demand curve for the commodity positively sloped, though no such case has yet been found in the real world.

curves. Example 1 examines the market demand for Big Macs, and Example 5 in the appendix to this chapter discusses the actual estimation and forecast of the demand for electricity in the United States.

 ## Example 1

The Growth of Demand for Big Macs Is Slowing Down

The growth of demand for fast food in general for Big Macs in particular is slowing at McDonald's. After three decades of double-digit gains, domestic sales have been growing slowly since 1986. With nearly 8,800 restaurants nationwide and 3,700 outlets overseas, McDonald's remains by far the largest fast-food restaurant in the United States and the world. McDonald's holds approximately a 30% share of the $65 billion U.S. restaurant business and 46% of its $2.6 billion burger business. It serves more than 22 million customers a day and, with sales of $18.8 billion in 1991, dwarfs its competitors. (Sales at the other top five fast-food chains in 1991 were $6.1 billion at Burger King, $5.8 billion at Kentucky Fried Chicken, $4.9 billion at Pizza Hut, $3.2 billion at Hardee's, and $3.1 billion at Wendy's.)

The slowing down in sales growth at McDonald's in the United States reflects higher prices, changing tastes, slow growth of the domestic economy, demographic changes, increased competition from other fast-food chains, and other forms of delivering fast foods. Price increases at McDonald's exceeded inflation in each year since 1986 and in 9 of the past 17 years. The average check at McDonald's is now $4—a far cry from the 15-cent hamburger on which McDonald's got rich—and sent customers streaming to lower-pricing competitors. Concern over cholesterol, fat, and calories, as well as a slowing down of growth of the economy and personal incomes, has also reduced growth. Another important reason for reduced growth in the demand for Big Macs is that the proportion of the 15- to 29-year-olds (the primary fast-food customers) in the total population has shrunk from 27.5% to 22.5% during the past decade. Increased competition from other fast-food chains, other fast-food options (pizza, chicken, tacos, and so on), frozen fast foods, mobile units, and vending machines has also slowed down the growth of demand for Big Macs.

McDonald's has not sat idle; it has tried to meet its challenges head on. To meet the competition from lower-pricing competitors, McDonald's introduced a "value menu" in 1990 with small hamburgers that sell for as little as 49 cents (down from 89 cents) and a combination of burger, French fries, and soft drink for as much as half off. In response to increased public concern about cholesterol, fat, and calories, McDonald's began publicizing the nutritional content of its menu offerings, substituted vegetable oils for beef tallow in frying its french fries, replaced ice cream with low-fat yogurt, and introduced bran muffins and cereals to its breakfast menu. It also introduced the McLean DeLuxe—a reduced-fat quarter-pound hamburger made of leaner beef, water, carrageenan (a seaweed), and beef flavor that contains 9 grams of fat and 320 calories (as compared with 20.7 grams of fat and 410 calories for the regular Quarter Pounder) and for which McDonald's spent from $50 to $70 million to develop and promote. Sales of the McLean Deluxe do not seem strong yet. People may "talk healthy" but they simply do not seem to be willing to trade taste for lower cholesterol and fat and fewer calories. McDonald's, however, insists that extensive tests show that the McLean DeLuxe tastes as good as the real thing. In the meantime, McDonald's fast-food competitors were quick to attack the new entry as a water-and-seaweed burger and renamed it the "McFake." Nevertheless, they are carefully monitoring sales and are getting ready to imitate it if customers develop a strong liking for McLean. In that case, we are likely to see a new burger war—this time over nutrition.

Furthermore, in response to increased competition from frozen fast foods, mobile units, and vending machines, an increasing number of McDonald's franchises have drive-throughs, from which they now generate almost half their business.

McDonald's is also expanding rapidly abroad where the company faces much less competition and where there is much more room for growth. In fact, in 1991 McDonald's was already in 60 countries, and in 1992 it planned to open 450 restaurants abroad as compared with 250 in the United States. The 10 top McDonald's restaurants in sales and profits are now outside the United States. In April 1992, the world's largest McDonald's restaurant opened in Beijing (with sitting capacity of 700 and 29 cash registers). On its first day, it made 13,214 transactions and served about 40,000 customers! This replaced Moscow's McDonald's, which had opened its doors in January 1990, as the world's largest.

Sources: "An American Icon Wrestles with a Troubled Future," *New York Times*, May 12, 1991, Section 3, p. 1; "Fast Food Lightens Up But Sales are Often Thin," *New York Times*, March 19, 1991, p. D1; "Overseas Sizzle for McDonald's," *New York Times*, April 17, 1992, p. D1; and "Billions Served (and That Was Without China)," *New York Times*, April 24, 1992, p. 4.

▲

5.2 PRICE ELASTICITY OF MARKET DEMAND

In this section, we show how we can measure graphically the price elasticity at any point on a demand curve. We also examine the important relationship between the price elasticity of demand and the total expenditures of consumers on the commodity. That is, when the price of a commodity changes, will consumers' expenditures on the commodity increase, decrease, or remain unchanged? Finally, we examine the determinants or the factors that affect the size of the price elasticity of demand.

Price Elasticity Graphically

In section 2.2 we defined the price elasticity of demand, η, as -1 times the percentage change in the quantity demanded of the commodity divided by

FIGURE 5–2   Measurement of Price Elasticity of Demand Graphically

In the left panel, the price elasticity at point E on D_X is measured by drawing tangent AEH to point E on D_X and dropping perpendicular EJ to the horizontal axis. At point E, $\eta = JH/OJ = 6/6 = 1$. In the right panel, $\eta = 1$ at point E (the midpoint of D'_X), $\eta > 1$ above the midpoint, and $\eta < 1$ below the midpoint.

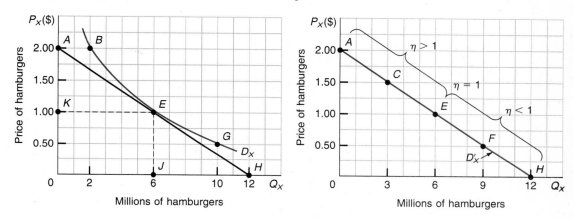

the percentage change in its price.[3] We now show how to measure graphically price elasticity at any point on a linear or nonlinear demand curve.

To measure the price elasticity at point E on D_X in the left panel of Figure 5–2, we proceed as follows. We draw tangent AEH to point E on D_X, and drop perpendicular EJ to the quantity axis. Minus 1 times the slope of tangent line AEH is constant throughout and can be measured by

$$ -\frac{\Delta P}{\Delta Q} = \frac{JE}{JH} $$

The first component of the price elasticity formula is given by -1 times the inverse of the slope of the demand curve or

$$ -\frac{\Delta Q}{\Delta P} = \frac{JH}{JE} $$

The second component of the price elasticity formula is

$$ \frac{P}{Q} = \frac{JE}{OJ} $$

Reassembling the two components of the elasticity formula, we have

$$ \eta = -\frac{\Delta Q}{\Delta P} \cdot \frac{P}{Q} = \frac{JH}{JE} \cdot \frac{JE}{OJ} = \frac{JH}{OJ} = \frac{6}{6} = 1 $$

That is, the price elasticity of D_X at point E in the left panel of Figure 5–2 is

---

[3]For a discussion of the price elasticity of demand using calculus, see section A.5 of the Mathematical Appendix at the end of the book.

equal to 1. Since *EJH, AKE,* and *AOH* are similar triangles (see the left panel of Figure 5–2), the price elasticity of D_X at point E can be measured by any of the following ratios of distances:

$$\eta = \frac{JH}{OJ} = \frac{KO}{AK} = \frac{EH}{AE} \qquad\qquad [5\text{–}1]$$

The price elasticity of demand at any other point on D_X can be found in a similar way by drawing a tangent to D_X at that point and then proceeding as indicated above (see problem 1). This provides a convenient and easy way to measure the price elasticity of demand at any point on a nonlinear demand curve.

The same procedure can be used to measure the price elasticity at any point on a straight-line demand curve. For example, by inspecting the right panel of Figure 5–2, we can find that $\eta = 9/3 = 3$ at point C on D'_X, $\eta = \frac{3}{6} = \frac{1}{2}$ at point F, and $\eta = \frac{6}{6} = 1$ at point E (the midpoint of D'_X). Furthermore, $\eta \to \infty$ (infinity) at point A and $\eta = 0$ at point H (see problem 2). Thus, while the slope of a straight-line demand curve is constant throughout, its price elasticity varies between each point on (and declines as we move down) the demand curve. As a general rule, a straight-line demand curve is unitary elastic at its geometric midpoint, price elastic above its midpoint, and inelastic below the midpoint (see the right panel of Figure 5–2).

Two other simple rules are useful in considering the price elasticity of demand. The first is that of two parallel demand curves (linear or nonlinear), the one further to the right has a smaller price elasticity at each price (see problem 3a, with answer at the end of the text). Second, when two demand curves intersect, the flatter of the two is more price elastic at the point of intersection (see problem 3b, with the answer also provided at the end of the text).

Price Elasticity and Total Expenditures

An important relationship exists between the price elasticity of demand and the total expenditures of consumers on the commodity. This relationship is often used in economics. It postulates that a decline in the commodity price results in an increase in total expenditures if demand is elastic, leaves total expenditures unchanged if demand is unitary elastic, and results in a decline in total expenditures if demand is inelastic.

Specifically, when the price of a commodity falls, total expenditures (price times quantity) increase if demand is elastic because the percentage increase in quantity (which by itself tends to increase total expenditures) exceeds the percentage decline in price (which by itself tends to reduce total expenditures). Total expenditures are maximum when $\eta = 1$ and decline thereafter. That is, when $\eta < 1$, a reduction in the commodity price leads to a percentage increase in the quantity demanded of the commodity that is smaller than the

TABLE 5–1 Total Expenditures and Price Elasticity of Demand

Point	P_x ($)	Q_x (million units)	Total Expenditures (million $)	η
A	2.00	0	0	∞
C	1.50	3	4.5	3
E	1.00	6	6.0	1
F	0.50	9	4.5	⅓
H	0	12	0	0

percentage reduction in price, and so total expenditures on the commodity decline. This is shown in Table 5–1, which refers to D'_x in Figure 5–2.

From Table 5–1 we see that between points A and E, $\eta > 1$ and total expenditures on the commodity increase as the commodity price declines. The opposite is true between points E and F over which $\eta < 1$. Total expenditures are maximum at point E (the geometric midpoint of D'_x in Figure 5–2). The general rule summarizing the relationship among total expenditures, price, and the price elasticity of demand is that *total expenditures and price move in opposite directions if demand is elastic and in the same direction if demand is inelastic* (see Table 5–1).

Figure 5–3 shows a demand curve that is unitary elastic throughout. Thus, $\eta = JH/JO = 6/6 = 1$ at point E on D^*, $\eta = LJ/OL = 3/3 = 1$ at point B′, and $\eta = HN/OH = 12/12 = 1$ at point G′. Note that total expenditures (price times quantity) are constant ($6 million) at every point on $D^\star$. This type of demand curve is a *rectangular hyperbola*. Its general equation is

$$Q = \frac{C}{P} \qquad\qquad \text{[5–2]}$$

where Q is the quantity demanded, P is its price, and C is a constant (total expenditures). Thus, $P \cdot Q = C$. For example, at point B′, $(P)(Q) = (\$2)(3) = \$6$. At point E, $(\$1)(6) = \$6$, and at point G′, $(\$0.50)(12) = \$6$ also.

What Determines Price Elasticity?

Because the price elasticity of demand is so useful (i.e., it tells us, among other things, what happens to the level of total expenditures on the commodity when its price changes), it is important to identify the forces that determine its value. The size of the price elasticity of demand depends primarily on two factors. First and foremost, *the price elasticity of demand for a commodity is larger the closer and the greater are the number of available substitutes*. For example, the demand for coffee is more elastic than the demand for salt because coffee has

FIGURE 5–3   Unitary Elastic Demand Curve

Demand curve D^* has unitary elasticity throughout. Thus, $\eta = JH/OJ = 6/6 = 1$ at point E, $\eta = LJ/OL = 3/3 = 1$ at point B', and $\eta = HN/OH = 12/12 = 1$ at point G'. Total expenditures ($P \cdot Q$) are the same ($6 million) at every point on D^*. This demand curve is a rectangular hyperbola.

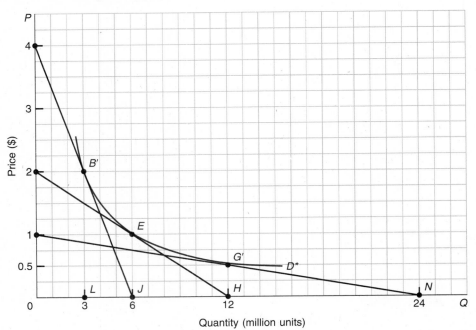

Quantity (million units)

better and more substitutes (tea and cocoa) than salt. Thus, the same percentage increase in the price of coffee and salt elicits a larger percentage reduction in the quantity demanded of coffee than of salt.

In general, a commodity has closer substitutes and thus a higher price elasticity of demand the more narrowly the commodity is defined. For example, the price elasticity for Marlboro cigarettes is much larger than for cigarettes in general, and still larger than for all tobacco products. If a commodity is defined so that it has perfect substitutes, its price elasticity of demand is infinite. For example, if a wheat farmer attempted to increase his or her price above the market price, he or she would lose all sales as buyers switch all their wheat purchases to other farmers (who produce identical wheat).

Second, *price elasticity is larger, the longer is the period of time allowed for consumers to adjust to a change in the commodity price.* The reason for this is that it usually takes time for consumers to learn of a price change and to fully respond or adjust their purchases to it. For example, consumers may not be able to reduce much the quantity demanded of electricity soon after they learn of an increase in the price of electricity. Over a period of several years, however, households can replace electric heaters with gas heaters, purchase appliances that consume less electricity, and so on. Thus, for a given price change, the quantity response *per unit of time* is usually much greater in the long run than in the short run, and so η is larger in the former than in the latter time period. This is clearly shown in Example 2.[4]

Example 2

▽ ## Price Elasticity of Demand for Radio and TV Repairs Increases with Time

The first row of Table 5–2 shows that the price elasticity of demand for radio and TV repairs in the United States is only 0.47 in the short run but becomes 3.84 in the long run. This means that a 1% increase in price leads to a reduction in the quantity demanded of radio and TV repairs of only 0.47% in the short run but rises to 3.84% in the long run. Evidently, people get frustrated by

TABLE 5–2   Selected Price Elasticities of Demand

Commodity	Short Run	Long Run
Radio and TV repairs	0.47	3.84
Motion pictures	0.87	3.67
China and glassware	1.54	2.55
Household natural gas*	1.40	2.10
Tobacco products	0.46	1.89
Electricity (household)	0.13	1.89
Foreign travel	0.14	1.77
Bus transportation (local)	0.20	1.20
Medical insurance	0.31	0.92
Jewelry and watches	0.41	0.67
Gasoline†	0.20	0.60
Stationery	0.47	0.56

Sources: H. S. Houthakker and L. S. Taylor, *Consumer Demand in the United States: Analyses and Projections* (Cambridge, Mass.: Harvard University Press, 1970).
*G.R. Lakshmanan and W. Anderson, "Residential Energy Demand in the United States," *Regional Science and Urban Economics,* August 1980.
†J. L. Sweeney, "The Response of Energy Demand to Higher Prices? What Have We Learned?" *American Economic Review,* May 1984.

---

[4]Sometimes it is stated that the price elasticity of demand is larger the greater is the number of uses of the commodity. However, no satisfactory reason has been advanced as to why this should be so. It is also sometimes said that price elasticity is lower the smaller is the importance of the commodity in consumers' budgets (i.e., the smaller is the proportion of the consumers' incomes spent on the commodity). However, empirical estimates often contradict this.

rising radio and TV repair prices and purchase new radios and TV sets in the long run, rather than have their old sets repaired.

On the other hand, the price elasticity of demand for stationery (the last row of Table 5–2) rises from 0.47 in the short run to only 0.56 in the long run. It seems that people cannot find suitable substitutes for stationery even in the long run. The table also shows the short-run and long-run price elasticities of demand for a selected list of other commodities. The estimated price elasticity of demand for any commodity is likely to vary (sometimes widely) depending on the nation under consideration, the time period examined, and the estimation technique used. Thus, estimated price elasticity values should be used with caution.

Many economic policies (such as reducing American dependence on imported petroleum) rely crucially on price elasticities. For example, with the price of gasoline of about $1.50 per gallon and a short-run price elasticity of 0.2 (see Table 5–2), a $0.50 tax per gallon would increase the price of gasoline from about $1.50 to $2.00 per gallon, or by about 33%, and reduce the quantity demanded of gasoline by 6.6% $[(\eta)(\%\Delta P) = (-0.2)(0.33) = -6.6\% = \%\Delta Q]$ in the short run. With the price elasticity equal to 0.6 in the long run, the reduction in the quantity demanded of gasoline in the long run would be three times larger than in the short run, or about 20%.

▲

5.3 INCOME ELASTICITY OF DEMAND

In section 4.1 we defined the **Engel curve** as showing the amount of a commodity that a consumer would purchase per unit of time at various income levels, while holding prices and tastes constant. We can measure the responsiveness or sensitivity in the quantity demanded of a commodity at any point on the Engel curve by the **income elasticity of demand.** This is defined as

$$\eta_I = \frac{\Delta Q/Q}{\Delta I/I} = \frac{\Delta Q}{\Delta I} \cdot \frac{I}{Q} \qquad\qquad [5\text{--}3]$$

where ΔQ is the change in the quantity purchased, ΔI is the change in income, Q is the original quantity, and I is the original money income of the consumer.[5]

A commodity is normal if η_I is positive and inferior if η_I is negative. A normal good can be further classified as a **necessity** is η_I is less than 1 and as a **luxury** is η_I is greater than 1. In the real world, most broadly defined commodities such as food, clothing, housing, health care, education, and recreation are normal goods. Inferior goods are usually narrowly defined inexpensive goods, such as bologna, for which good substitutes are available.

---

[5]For a discussion of the income elasticity of demand using calculus, see section A.5 of the Mathematical Appendix at the end of the book.

TABLE 5–3   **Income Elasticity and Classification of Hamburgers (X) at Various Daily Income Allowances**

I	Q_X	$\% \Delta Q_X$	$\% \Delta I$	η_I	Classification
10	2	. . .	. . .	. . .	. . .
15	4	100	50	2.00	Luxury
20	5	25	33	0.76	Necessity
30	6	20	50	0.40	Necessity
40	4	−33	33	−1.00	Inferior

Among normal goods, food and clothing are necessities while education and recreation are luxuries.

This classification of goods into inferior and normal and necessity and luxury cannot be taken too seriously, however, because the same commodity can be regarded as a luxury by some individuals or at some income levels, and as a necessity or even as an inferior good by other individuals or at other income levels.[6] A simple geometric method can determine if a commodity is a luxury, a necessity, or an inferior good at each income level. If the tangent to the Engel curve is positively sloped and crosses the income axis, η_I exceeds 1 and the good is a luxury at that income level. If the tangent crosses the origin, $\eta_I = 1$. If the tangent crosses the horizontal axis, η_I is less than 1 and the commodity is a necessity at that income level. Finally, if the tangent to the Engel curve is negatively sloped, the commodity is an inferior good.

For example, Table 5–3 and Figure 5–4 show that the student in Chapters 3 and 4 would regard hamburgers as a luxury at income levels (allowances) of up to $15 per day. Hamburgers would become a necessity for daily allowances of between $15 and $30 and would be regarded as an inferior good at higher incomes (where the student can afford steaks and lobsters).

The concept and measurement of the income elasticity of demand and Engel curve can refer to a single customer or to the entire market. When referring to the entire market, Q and ΔQ are the total or the market quantity purchased and its change, while I and ΔI are the total or aggregate money income of all consumers in the market and its change.[7]

As pointed out in section 4.1, the proportion of total expenditures on food declines as family incomes rise. This is referred to as **Engel's law.** Indeed, the higher the proportion of income spent on food, the poorer a family or nation is taken to be. For example, in the United States less than 20% of total family incomes is spent on food as compared with over 50% for India (a much

---

[6]Indeed, some economists feel that the necessity-luxury classification of goods is entirely spurious and meaningless.

[7]Remember, however, that the income elasticity of market demand is not well defined unless it is also specified on which commodities income increments are spent.

FIGURE 5–4   Engel Curve and Income Elasticity

Because the tangent to the Engel curve is positively sloped and crosses the income axis up to the daily income allowance of $15, hamburgers are a luxury for this individual (student). The tangent goes through the origin at $I = \$15$ and $\eta_I = 1$ at that income level. Since the tangent is positively sloped and crosses the quantity axis from $I = \$15$ to $30, hamburgers are a necessity between these income levels. For I higher than $30, the Engel curve is negatively sloped and hamburgers become an inferior good for this individual.

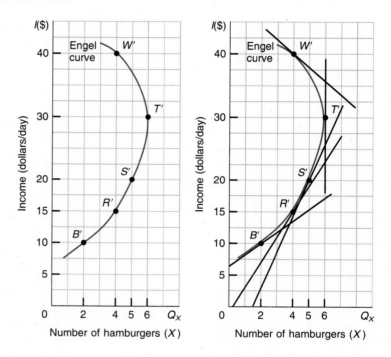

poorer nation). As Example 3 shows, the income elasticity of demand can be very different for different products.

Example 3

Foreign Travel Is a Luxury, Flour an Inferior Good

The third and last rows of Table 5–4 show, respectively, that the income elasticity of demand is 3.09 for foreign travel and -0.36 for flour. This means that a 1% increase in consumers' income leads to a 3.09% increase in expenditures on foreign travel but to a 0.36% *reduction* in expenditures on flour. Thus, foreign travel is a (strong) luxury, while flour is a (weak) inferior good. Indeed, all of the other commodities shown in the table are luxuries, except tobacco products, china and glassware, beef, and pork (which are necessities).

TABLE 5–4   **Selected Income Elasticities of Demand**

Commodity	Income Elasticity	Commodity	Income Elasticity
Radio and TV repairs	5.20	Gasoline	1.36
Motion pictures	3.41	Chicken*	1.06
Foreign travel	3.09	Tobacco products	0.86
Medical insurance	2.02	China and glassware	0.77
Electricity (household)	1.94	Beef*	0.45
Bus transportation (local)	1.89	Pork*	0.18
Stationery	1.83	Flour	−0.36
Jewelry and watches	1.64		

Source: H. S. Houthakker and L. S. Taylor, *op. cit.*
*M. K. Wohlgenant and W. F. Hahn, "Dynamic Adjustment in Monthly Consumer Demand for Meats," *American Journal of Agricultural Economics,* August 1982.

Note that the income elasticities given in Table 5–4 are measured as the percentage change in expenditures on the various commodities (rather than the percentage change in the *quantity* purchased of the various commodities). To the extent that prices are held constant, however, we get the same results as if the percentage change in quantities were used. As pointed out, the interpretation of these income elasticity values is not as clear-cut and precise as for the price elasticity of demand discussed earlier.

▲

5.4 CROSS ELASTICITY OF DEMAND

We have seen in section 2.2 that one of the things held constant in drawing the market demand curve for a commodity is the price of substitute and complementary commodities. Commodities X and Y are **substitutes** if more of X is purchased when the price of Y goes up. For example, consumers usually purchase more coffee when the price of tea rises. Thus, coffee and tea are substitutes. Other examples of substitutes are butter and margarine, hamburgers and hot dogs, Coca-Cola and Pepsi, electricity and gas, and so on.

On the other hand, commodities X and Y are **complements** if less of X is purchased when the price of Y goes up. For example, consumers usually purchase fewer lemons when the price of tea goes up. Thus, lemons and tea are complements. Other examples of commodities that are complements are coffee and cream, hamburgers and buns, hot dogs and mustard, cars and gasoline, and so on.

An increase in the price of a commodity leads to a reduction in the quantity demanded of the commodity (a movement along the demand curve for the commodity) but causes the demand curve for a substitute to shift to the right and the demand curve for a complement to shift to the left. For example, an increase in the price of tea will cause the demand for coffee (a substitute of tea) to shift to the right (so that more coffee is demanded at each coffee price) and the demand for lemons (a complement of tea) to shift to the left (so that fewer lemons are demanded at each lemon price).

We can measure the responsiveness or sensitivity in the quantity purchased of commodity X as a result of a change in the price of commodity Y by the **cross elasticity of demand** (η_{XY}). This is given by:

$$\eta_{XY} = \frac{\Delta Q_X / Q_X}{\Delta P_Y / P_Y} = \frac{\Delta Q_X}{\Delta P_Y} \cdot \frac{P_Y}{Q_X} \qquad\qquad [5\text{--}4]$$

where ΔQ_X is the change in the quantity purchased of X, ΔP_Y is the change in the price of Y, P_Y is the original price of Y, and Q_X is the original quantity of X. Note that in measuring η_{XY}, we hold constant P_X, consumers' incomes, their tastes, and the number of consumers in the market.[8]

If η_{XY} is greater than zero, X and Y are substitutes because an increase in P_Y leads to an increase in Q_X as X is substituted for Y in consumption. On the other hand, η_{XY} is less than zero, X and Y are complements because an increase in P_Y leads to a reduction in (Q_Y and) Q_X. The absolute value (i.e., the value without the sign) of the cross elasticity of demand measures the degree of substitution or complementarity. For example, if η_{XY} between coffee and tea is found to be larger than that between coffee and hot chocolate, this means that coffee and tea are better substitutes than coffee and hot chocolate. If η_{XY} is close to zero, X and Y are independent commodities. This may be the case with cars and pencils, telephones and chewing gum, pocket calculators and beer, and so on.

Several additional things must be kept in mind with respect to the cross elasticity of demand. First, the value of η_{XY} need not equal the value of η_{YX} because the responsiveness of Q_X to a change in P_Y need not equal the responsiveness of Q_Y to a change in P_X. For example, a change in the price of coffee is likely to have a greater effect on the quantity of sugar (a complement of coffee) demanded than the other way around, since coffee is the more important of the two in terms of total expenditures.

Second, a high positive cross elasticity of demand is often used to define an industry since it indicates that the various commodities are very similar. For example, the cross elasticity of demand between Chevrolets and Oldsmobiles is very high, and so they belong to the same (auto) industry. This can lead to some difficulty, however. For example, how high must the positive cross elasticity between two commodities be for them to be in the same industry? Also, if the cross elasticity between cars and station wagons and between station wagons and trucks is "high," but the cross elasticity of de-

---

[8]For a discussion of the cross elasticity of demand using calculus, see section A.5 of the Mathematical Appendix at the end of the book.

mand between cars and trucks is "low," are cars and trucks in the same industry? In these cases the definition of the industry usually depends on the problem to be studied.

Third, the above definition of substitutes and complements is sometimes referred to as a "gross" definition; as such, it refers to the entire market response and reflects both the income and the substitution effects. For an individual consumer, there is a more rigorous definition (in terms of the substitution effect only) discussed in more advanced treaties.[9] Example 4 gives the estimated gross elasticity of demand between a number of products and shows its usefulness in the analysis of important economic issues.

Example 4

Margarine and Butter Are Substitutes, Cereals and Fresh Fish Complements

The first row of Table 5–5 shows that the cross elasticity of demand of margarine with respect to the price of butter is 1.53%. This means that a 1% increase in the price of butter leads to a 1.53% increase in the demand for margarine. Thus, margarine and butter are substitutes in the United States. On the other hand, the last row of Table 5–5 shows that the cross elasticity of demand of cereals with respect to fresh fish is −0.87. This means that a 1% increase in the price of cereals leads to a reduction in the demand for fresh fish by 0.87%. Thus, cereals (for example, bread) and fresh fish are

TABLE 5–5   Selected Cross Elasticities of Demand

Commodity	Estimate
Margarine with respect to the price of butter	1.53*
Natural gas with respect to the price of electricity	0.80†
Pork with respect to the price of beef	0.40*
Chicken with respect to the price of pork	0.29*
Entertainment with respect to price of food	−0.72‡
Cereals with respect to price of fresh fish	−0.87§

*D. M. Heien, "The Structure of Food Demand: Interrelatedness and Duality," *American Journal of Agricultural Economics*, May 1982.
†G. R. Lakshmanan and W. Anderson, *op. cit.*
‡E. T. Fujii et al., "An Almost Ideal Demand System for Visitor Expenditures," *Journal of Transport Economics and Policy*, May 1985.
§A. Deaton, "Estimation of Own- and Cross-Price Elasticities from Household Survey Data," *Journal of Econometrics*, September-October 1987.

[9]See, J. R. Hicks, *Value and Capital* (New York: Oxford University Press, 1946), p. 44.

complements. The table also shows the cross elasticity of demand of other selected commodities in the United States.

Cross price elasticities of demand have important economic applications—even in the courtroom, as the celebrated Cellophane Case shows.[10] In that case, the court decided that DuPont had not monopolized the market for cellophane even though it had 75% of the market. The reason? The cross price elasticity of demand between cellophane and other flexible packaging materials (waxed paper, aluminum foil, and others) was sufficiently high to indicate that the relevant market was not cellophane as such, but flexible packaging materials, and DuPont, with only a 20% market share, had not monopolized that market.

▲

5.5 PRICE AND INCOME ELASTICITIES OF U.S. IMPORTS AND EXPORTS

We have seen that when the price of a commodity falls, consumers purchase more of the commodity. The increase in the quantity purchased of the commodity resulting from a decline in its price (while holding everything else constant) is measured by the price elasticity of demand. The same is true for U.S. imports and exports. When import prices fall, domestic consumers import more from abroad. When the price of U.S. exports fall, foreigners purchase more American goods and U.S. exports rise. The increase in the quantity of U.S. imports and exports resulting from a price decline is measured, respectively, by the **price elasticity of demand for imports** and the **price elasticity of demand for exports.**

One slight complication arises, however, when we deal with imports and exports. The price of imports to U.S. consumers depends not only on prices in exporting nations (expressed in foreign currencies) but also on the rate of exchange between the dollar and foreign currencies. The rate of exchange between the dollar and a foreign currency is called the **exchange rate.** For example, the exchange rate between the U.S. dollar and the British pound sterling (£) is about 2. This means that U.S. consumers must pay $2 to get £1. Thus, the price of a music record that costs £1 in the United Kingdom is $2 to U.S. consumers. If the price of the record falls to £0.50 in the United Kingdom, U.S. consumers will have to pay only $1 for the record. The price of the British record to U.S. consumers can also fall to $1, even if the price remains at £1 in the United Kingdom, if the exchange rate between the dollar and the pound falls from $2 to £1 to $1 to £1.[11]

---

[10]See, *U.S. Reports,* Vol. 351 (Washington, D.C.: U.S. Government Printing Office, 1956), p. 400.

[11]This is only the immediate outcome. Over time, the dollar price of U.S. imports is likely to fall by less than that indicated above because of other forces at work (that need not be examined here).

Exchange rates change very frequently in the real world. How exchange rates are determined and the reasons that they change are not important at this point (they will be explained in the appendix to Chapter 8). What is important is that the *dollar* price of U.S. imports can change because of a change in foreign-currency prices abroad or because of a change in exchange rates. Regardless of the reason for the change in the price of U.S. imports, we can measure the increase in quantity of U.S. imports resulting from a change in their *dollar* price by the price elasticity of demand for imports. This has been estimated to be about 1.06 for U.S. imports of manufactured goods, both in the short run and in the long run. That is, a 1% decline in the dollar price of U.S. imports of manufactured goods can be expected to lead to a 1.06% increase in the quantity demanded and thus leave their dollar value practically unchanged.

On the other hand, the price elasticity of demand for U.S. manufactured goods exports was estimated to be 0.48 in the short run and 1.67 in the long run. This means that a 1% decline in the price of U.S. exports can be expected to lead to an increase in the quantity of U.S. manufactured goods exports of 0.48% within a year or two of the price change and 1.67% in the long run (i.e., in a period of five years or so). Thus, a decline in U.S. export prices leads to U.S. earnings from manufactured exports to fall in the short run and to rise in the long run. Finally, the **income elasticity of demand for imports** was estimated to be 1.68 in the United States. This means that for each 1% increase in U.S. income or GNP, U.S. imports can be expected to increase by about 1.68%. Thus, U.S. imports are normal goods and can be regarded as luxuries. The income elasticity of imports for the six largest industrial countries range from 1.23 for Japan to 2.19 for Italy.[12]

At this point you might ask, "Why deal with these international elasticities in a course on microeconomic theory?" As pointed out in previous chapters, the reasons are that U.S. consumers spend an increasing proportion of their income on foreign products and U.S. firms purchase more and more imported inputs, export an increasing share of their output, and face increasing competition from foreign firms. Furthermore, most (otherwise purely) domestic policies affect and are affected by the international trade and financial position of the country. In short, we can no longer ignore these crucial and pervasive international forces in the study of modern microeconomics.

5.6 MARGINAL REVENUE AND ELASTICITY

Up to this point, we have examined demand from the consumers' side only. However, consumers' expenditures on a commodity are the receipts or the total revenues of the sellers of the commodity. In this section, we look at the

---

[12]See, D. Salvatore, *International Economics*, 4th ed. (New York: Macmillan, 1993), Chapters 15 and 16.

TABLE 5-6   Demand, Total Revenue, and Marginal Revenue

P (1)	Q (2)	TR (3)	MR (4)	Sum of MR's (5)
$11	0	$ 0	. . .	. . .
10	1	10	$10	$10
9	2	18	8	18
8	3	24	6	24
7	4	28	4	28
6	5	30	2	30
5	6	30	0	30
4	7	28	-2	28
3	8	24	-4	24

sellers' side of the market. We begin by defining marginal revenue and showing how the marginal revenue curve can be derived geometrically from the demand curve. Then we examine the relationship between marginal revenue, price, and the price elasticity of demand. Thus, the material of this section represents the link or bridge between the theory of demand (Part Two of the text) and the theory of the firm (Chapters 8–12).

Demand, Total Revenue, and Marginal Revenue

The total amount earned by sellers of a commodity is called **total revenue (TR)**; it is equal to the price per unit of the commodity times the quantity of the commodity sold. **Marginal revenue (MR)** is then the change in total revenue per unit change in the quantity sold; MR is calculated by dividing the change in total revenue (ΔTR) by the change in the quantity sold (ΔQ):[13]

$$MR = \frac{\Delta TR}{\Delta Q} \qquad [5\text{--}5]$$

We can also show that the sum of the marginal revenues on all units of the commodity sold equals total revenue.

In Table 5–6, price (column 1) and quantity (column 2) give the demand schedule of the commodity. Price times quantity gives total revenue (column 3). The change in total revenue resulting from each additional unit of the commodity sold gives the marginal revenue (column 4). As a check on the calculations, we see that the sum of the marginal revenues equals total revenues (column 5). Note that TR/Q equals **average revenue (AR)**, and AR = P (the height of the demand curve).

The information given in Table 5–6 is plotted in Figure 5–5. The top panel

---

[13]For the definition of marginal revenue in terms of calculus, see section A.7 of the Mathematical Appendix at the end of the book.

FIGURE 5–5 Total Revenue, Demand, and Marginal Revenue

Total revenue rises up to 5 units of the commodity sold, remains constant between 5 and 6 units, and declines thereafter. When D is elastic, MR is positive because TR increases. When D is unitary elastic, $MR = 0$ because TR is constant (at its maximum), and when D is inelastic, MR is negative because TR declines (as Q increases).

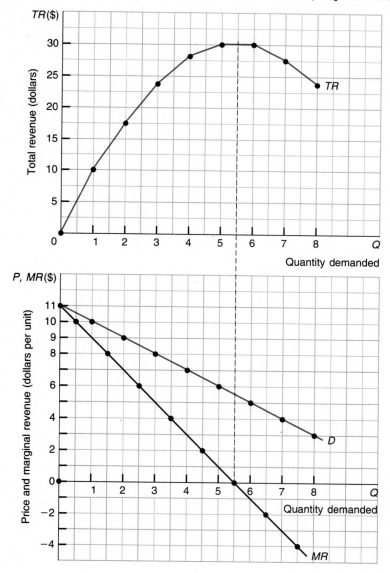

gives the total revenue curve. The bottom panel gives the corresponding demand (D) and marginal revenue curves. Since MR is defined as the change in TR per unit change in Q, the MR values are plotted at the midpoint of each quantity interval in the bottom panel of Figure 5–5. On the other hand, points on the TR and D curves are plotted *at* each level of output. For example, at $P = \$11$, $Q = 0$, and so TR (which equals P times Q) is zero and is plotted at the origin in the top panel of Figure 5–5. At $P = \$10$, $Q = 1$, and so $TR = \$10$ and MR ($\Delta TR/\Delta Q$) is also $\$10$. This TR value is plotted at $Q = 1$ in the top panel, while the corresponding MR is plotted between $Q = 0$ and $Q = 1$ (i.e., at $Q = 0.5$) in the bottom panel.

The MR curve starts at the same point on the vertical axis as the D curve and is everywhere else below the D curve. The reason is that to sell one more unit of the commodity, price must be lowered not only for the additional unit sold but also on all previous units. For example, we see in Table 5–6 that to sell the second unit of the commodity, price must be lowered from $\$10$ to $\$9$ on both units. Therefore, the MR on the second unit is given by $P = \$9$ (a point on D) minus the $\$1$ reduction on the price of the first unit. That is, $MR = \$8$, which is lower than P, so the MR curve is below the D curve (see the bottom panel of Figure 5–5). When D is elastic, MR is positive because an increase in Q increases TR. When D is unitary elastic, $MR = 0$ because an increase in Q leaves TR unchanged (at its maximum level). When D is inelastic, MR is negative because an increase in Q reduces TR (see the bottom panel of Figure 5–5). We will make a great deal of use of the relationship between the demand curve and the marginal revenue curve in Chapters 8–12, where we deal with the theory of the firm and market structure.

Geometry of Marginal Revenue Determination

The marginal revenue curve for a straight-line and for a nonlinear demand curve can easily be found geometrically. This is shown in Figure 5–6. In the left panel, we can find the marginal revenue corresponding to point C on D'_X by dropping perpendicular CJ to the vertical axis and CW to the horizontal axis, and then subtracting distance AJ from CW. This identifies point C'. Thus, at $Q = 3$, $P = WC = \$1.50$, and $MR = WC' = \$1.00$. Similarly, by dropping perpendiculars EK and EE' from point E on D'_X and subtracting distance AK from EE', we get point E'. Thus, at $Q = 6$, $P = E'E = \$1$, and $MR = 0$. By joining points C' and E' we derive the MR'_X curve shown in the left panel of Figure 5–6. Note that the MR'_X curve starts at point A (as the D'_X curve) and every point on it bisects (i.e., cuts in half) the distance from the D'_X curve to the vertical or price axis. (Indeed, this provides an alternative but equivalent method of deriving the MR curve geometrically for a straight-line demand curve.) Thus, $JV = \frac{1}{2}JC$, $KC' = \frac{1}{2}KE$, and $OE' = \frac{1}{2}OH$ (see the figure).

To find the marginal revenue curve corresponding to any point on a nonlinear demand curve, we draw a tangent to the demand curve at that point and then proceed as described. Thus, to find the marginal revenue corresponding to point B on D_X in the right panel of Figure 5–6, we draw the tangent to demand curve D_X at point B and move distance NR downward from point B. This identifies point B' on the MR_X curve. Another point on the MR_X curve is obtained by moving distance RT down from point E. This identifies point E'. Other points on the MR_X curve can similarly be obtained. By joining these points we get the MR_X curve for the D_X curve (see the right panel of Figure

FIGURE 5–6 Marginal Revenue Determination

In the left panel, for point C on the D'_x curve, $MR = C'W$ and is obtained by subtracting distance AJ from price CW. For point E, $MR = 0$ and was obtained by subtracting distance $AK = EE'$ from P_x. In the right panel, to find the MR at point B we draw a tangent to the D_x curve at point B, and then we move down distance NR from point B. This identifies point B' on the MR_x curve. By moving down distance RT from point E on the D_x curve, we define point E' ($MR = 0$) on the MR_x curve.

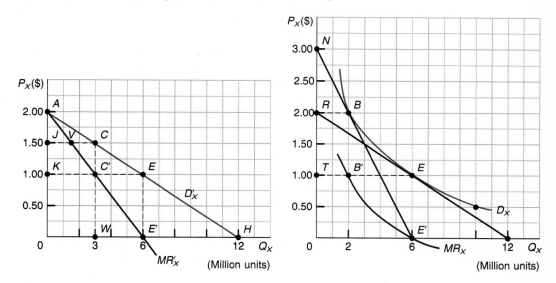

5–6). Note that when the demand curve is nonlinear, the marginal revenue curve is also nonlinear.

Marginal Revenue, Price, and Elasticity

There is an important and often-used relationship among marginal revenue, price, and the price elasticity of demand given by

$$MR = P(1 - 1/\eta) \qquad \text{[5–6]}$$

For example, at point C on D'_x in the left panel of Figure 5–6, $\eta = WH/OW = 9/3 = 3$, and

$$MR = \$1.50(1 - 1/3) = \$1.00$$

(the same as WC' found earlier geometrically). At point E, $\eta = E'H/OE' = 6/6 = 1$, and $MR = \$1.00(1 - 1/1) = \$1.00(0) = 0$. At point A, $\eta = OH/O = 12/0 = \infty$ (infinity), and $MR = \$2.00 (1 - 1/\infty) = \$2.00(1 - 0) = \$2.00$.

Formula [5–6] also applies to nonlinear demand curves. For example, at point B on D_x in the right panel of Figure 5–6, $\eta = 4/2 = 2$ and

$$MR = \$2.00(1 - 1/2) = \$1.00$$

FIGURE 5–7   Demand Curve for the Output of a Perfectly Competitive Firm

The demand curve for the output of a perfectly competitive firm is horizontal or infinitely elastic. Thus, $MR = P$ and the demand curve and the marginal revenue curve coincide

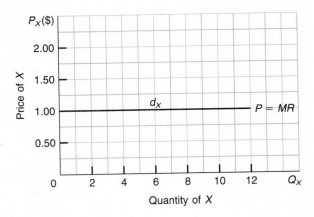

(the same as found earlier geometrically). Similarly, at point E, $\eta = 6/6 = 1$ and $MR = \$1.00(1 - 1/1) = 0$.

Formula [5–6] can be derived with reference to the straight-line demand curve in the left panel of Figure 5–6. Take, for example, point C on D'_x. At point C,

$$\eta = WH/OW = CH/AC = JO/AJ$$

But $JO = CW$ and, by congruent triangles, $AJ = CC'$. Hence,

$$\eta = JO/AJ = CW/CC' = CW/(CW - C'W) = P/(P - C'W) = P/(P - MR).$$

With this result, we manipulate the equation algebraically, to isolate MR on the left-hand side:

$$\eta(P - MR) = P$$
$$P - MR = P/\eta$$
$$-MR = P/\eta - P$$
$$MR = P - P/\eta$$
$$MR = P(1 - 1/\eta) \text{ [expression (5–6)]}[14]$$

So far, we have discussed the market demand curve for a commodity (D'_x or D_x in Figure 5–6). If there is only one producer or seller in the market (a monopolist), the firm faces the market demand curve for the commodity. When there is more than one producer or seller of the commodity, each firm

---

[14]For a more straightforward derivation of expression [5–6] using simple calculus, see section A.7 of the Mathematical Appendix at the end of the book.

will face a demand curve that is more elastic than the market demand curve because of the possible substitution among the products of the different firms. With a very large number of sellers of a homogeneous or identical product, the demand curve for the output of each firm might be horizontal or infinitely elastic (perfect competition). Then the change in total revenue in selling one additional unit of the commodity (i.e., the marginal revenue) equals price. This is confirmed by using formula [5–6]; that is,

$$MR = P(1 - 1/\infty) = P$$

For example, in Figure 5–7, if the firm sells 5X, its TR = \$5. If it sells 6X, TR = \$6. Thus, $MR = P$ = \$1, and the demand curve and the marginal revenue curves coincide. (The perfectly competitive model will be examined in Chapter 8.)

SUMMARY

1. The market demand curve for a commodity is obtained from the horizontal summation of the demand curves of all the individual consumers in the market and shows the total quantity demanded at various prices. It is negatively sloped; and, in drawing it, we must hold constant the consumers' incomes, the price of substitutes and complementary commodities, tastes, and the number of consumers in the market. The market demand curve is flatter or more elastic than otherwise with a bandwagon effect, and steeper and less elastic when a snob effect is present, or with conspicuous expenditures or Veblen effect.

2. By drawing a tangent to a point on a nonlinear demand curve and dropping a perpendicular to either axis, we can measure price elasticity at that point by the ratio of two distances. A straight-line demand curve is unitary elastic at its midpoint, elastic above the midpoint, and inelastic below the midpoint. Total expenditures and price move in opposite directions if demand is elastic and in the same direction if demand is inelastic. A rectangular hyperbola demand curve has unitary elasticity and constant total expenditures throughout. A demand curve is more elastic (a) the closer

and the better are the available substitutes and (b) the longer the adjustment period to the price change.

3. The income elasticity of demand (η_I) measures the percentage change in the quantity purchased of a commodity divided by the percentage change in consumers' incomes. A commodity is usually taken to be a necessity if η_I is between 0 and 1 and a luxury if η_I exceeds 1. η_I exceeds 1 if the tangent to the Engel curve is positively sloped and crosses the income axis. η_I is between 0 and 1 if the tangent to the Engel curve is positively sloped and crosses the quantity axis. If η_I is negative, the commodity is an inferior good and the Engel curve is negatively sloped. According to Engel's law, the proportion of total expenditures on food declines as family incomes rise.

4. Commodities X and Y are substitutes if more of X is purchased when the price of Y goes up, and complements if less of X is purchased when the price of Y goes up. The cross elasticity of demand between commodities X and Y (η_{XY}) measures the percentage change in the quantity purchased of X divided by the percentage change in the price of Y. If η_{XY} is positive,

X and Y are substitutes. If η_{XY} is negative, X and Y are complements, and if $\eta_{XY} = 0$, X and Y are independent commodities.

5. We can measure the increase in U.S. imports and exports as a result of a decline in their prices by their respective price elasticities of demand. The only complication is that the price of U.S. imports and exports is also affected by changes in the exchange rate. This gives the number of units of the domestic currency required to purchase one unit of the foreign currency. We can also measure the income elasticity of demand for U.S. imports and for the imports of other nations.

6. The total revenue (TR) of sellers equals price times quantity. Marginal revenue (MR) is the change in TR per unit change in the quantity of the commodity sold. MR is positive when demand (D) is elastic because a reduction in price increases TR. When D is unitary elastic, $MR = 0$ because TR is constant (at its maximum). When D is inelastic, MR is negative because a reduction in price reduces TR. The MR curve for a straight-line D curve bisects the quantity axis. The MR at a point on a nonlinear D curve is found geometrically by drawing a tangent to the demand curve at that point. Marginal revenue, price, and price elasticity of demand are related by $MR = P(1 - 1/\eta)$. The demand curve facing a perfectly competitive firm is horizontal and $P = MR$ because η is infinite.

KEY TERMS

Market Demand Curve	Engel's Law	Exchange Rate
Bandwagon Effect	Substitutes	Income Elasticity of Demand
Snob Effect	Complements	for Imports
Veblen Effect	Cross Elasticity of Demand	Total Revenue (TR)
Engel Curve	(η_{XY})	Marginal Revenue (MR)
Income Elasticity of Demand	Price Elasticity of Demand for	Average Revenue (AR)
(η_I)	Imports	Identification Problem
Necessity	Price Elasticity of Demand for	Multiple Regression
Luxury	Exports	

REVIEW QUESTIONS

1. Is an individual's or the market demand curve for a commodity more elastic? Why? Is this always true? Explain.

2. Will a fall in a commodity price increase expenditures on it? Why?

3. If the price of china and glassware increases by 10%, by how much can we expect the quantity demanded of and total expenditures on china and glassware to change in the short run and in the long run according to the elasticity values in Table 5–2?

4. Is the price elasticity of demand for Marlboro cigarettes more or less elastic than the demand for all tobacco products? Why? By how much would the quantity demanded of Marlboro cig-

arettes change in the long run if its price rose by 5% and the long-run price elasticity of demand is 3.56? If the price of all tobacco products also increased by 5%, would the quantity demanded of Marlboro cigarettes change by more or less as compared to the case when only the price of Marlboro cigarettes changed?

5. Suppose that a study has found that the price elasticity of demand for subway rides is 0.7 in Washington, D.C., and the mayor wants to cut the operating deficit of the subway system. Should the mayor contemplate increasing or decreasing the price of a subway ride? Why?

6. Can you say with reference to Table 5–2 whether producers and sellers of stationery or

tobacco products would be affected more adversely from a recession?

7. Which of the following are more likely to have a positive cross elasticity of demand: pencils and paper, an IBM PC and a Zenith PC, and automobiles and gasoline?

8. What other demand elasticities, besides those examined in the chapter, are likely to be important for beachwear? How would you measure such elasticities?

9. If the price of books in England falls by 10%, but at the same time the dollar appreciates (i.e., increases in value with respect to the British pound) by 10%, how is the U.S. demand for imported books from the United Kingdom likely to be affected?

10. If prices and exchange rates remain un-

changed, but income rises by 4% in the United States and 3% in the rest of the world during a given year, by how much would U.S. imports from and exports to the rest of the world change if the income elasticity of demand for U.S. imports is 1.68 while the income elasticity of demand for U.S. exports is 1.92? How would the U.S. trade balance (exports minus imports) change over the year if it was in balance at the beginning of the year?

11. If the price of a product is $10 and the marginal revenue is $5, what is the price elasticity of demand for the product at that point?

12. If the demand curve faced by a firm is $d_x = P_x = \$10$, what is the price elasticity of demand at $Q_x = 10$? Between $Q_x = 10$ and $Q_x = 12$?

PROBLEMS

1. Measure graphically the price elasticity of demand curve D_x in the left panel of Figure 5–2.
   a. at point B.
   b. at point G.

2. Using the general formula for the price elasticity of demand (i.e., equation [2–1]), prove that
   a. $\eta = \infty$ at point A on D_x' in the right panel of Figure 5–2.
   b. $\eta = 0$ at point H in the same diagram.

*3. Explain the following.
   a. Of two parallel demand curves, the one further to the right has a smaller price elasticity at each price.
   b. When two demand curves intersect, the flatter of the two is more elastic at the point of intersection.

4. Using only the total expenditures criterion, determine if the demand schedules given in the following table are elastic, inelastic, or unitary elastic.

P($)	5	4	3	2	1
Q_X	100	130	180	275	560
Q_Y	100	120	150	220	430
Q_Z	100	125	167	250	500

5. If the price elasticity of demand for Marlboro cigarettes is 6 and its price rose by 10%
   a. by how much would the quantity demanded decrease?
   b. would the consumers' total expenditures on Marlboro cigarettes increase, decrease or remain unchanged?
   c. If the price of all other brands of cigarettes also increased by 10%, what would happen to the quantity demanded of Marlboro? To consumers' expenditures on Marlboro?

6. From the following table

Q_X	100	250	350	400	300
I	$10,000	15,000	20,000	25,000	30,000

   a. calculate the income elasticity of demand for commodity X between various income levels and determine what type of good is commodity X;
   b. plot the Engel curve; how can you tell from the shape of the Engel curve what type of good is commodity X?

_____

* = Answer found at end of book.

*7. a. Explain why in a two-commodity world both commodities cannot be luxuries.
    b. What would be the effect on the quantity of cars purchased if consumers' incomes rose by 10% and the income elasticity of demand is 2.5?

8. Which of the following sets of commodities are likely to have positive cross elasticity of demand?
    a. aluminum and plastics
    b. wheat and corn
    c. pencils and paper
    d. private and public education
    e. gin and tonic
    f. ham and cheese
    g. men's and women's shoes

*9. Using the values for the price and income elasticity of demand for electricity and for the cross elasticity of demand between electricity and natural gas given in Tables 5–2, 5–4, and 5–5, answer the following questions:
    a. Is the demand for electricity elastic or inelastic in the short run? In the long run? How much would the quantity demanded of electricity change as a result of a 10% increase in its price in the short run? In the long run?
    b. Is electricity a necessity or a luxury? How much would electricity consumption change with a 10% increase in consumers' incomes?
    c. Is natural gas a substitute or complement of electricity? By how much would electricity consumption change with a 10% increase in the price of natural gas?

10. Given the following demand schedule

P	$8	7	6	5	4	3	2	1	0
Q	0	1	2	3	4	5	6	7	8

    a. find the total revenue and the marginal revenue.
    b. plot the total revenue curve, the demand curve, and the marginal revenue curve.
    c. Using the formula relating marginal revenue, price and elasticity, confirm the values of the marginal revenue found geometrically for $P = \$8$, for $P = \$4$, and for $P = \$2$.

11. Explain why a firm should never operate in the inelastic range of its demand curve.

*12. The following proposition (proved in section A.6 of the Mathematical Appendix at the end of the text) is given:

$$K_X\eta_{IX} + K_Y\eta_{IY} = 1$$

where K_X is the proportion of the consumer's income I spent on commodity X (i.e., $K_X = P_X Q_X / I$), $\eta_I X$ is the income elasticity of demand for commodity X, K_Y is the proportion of income spent on Y (i.e., $K_Y = P_Y Q_Y / I$), and η_{IY} is the income elasticity of demand for Y. Also, suppose that a consumer spends 75% of his or her income on commodity X and the income elasticity of demand for commodity X is 0.9. Assume that the individual consumes only commodities X and Y.
    a. Find the income elasticity of demand for commodity Y.
    b. What kind of commodity is Y? X? How high would the income elasticity of demand for X have to be before commodity Y becomes inferior?

APPENDIX   EMPIRICAL ESTIMATION OF DEMAND

So far, we have discussed the theory of demand and theoretical demand curves. To analyze a real-world situation, however, we need the actual or empirical market demand curve. There are several different approaches to estimate market demand curves. One involves *interviews or questionnaires*. These ask consumers how much of a commodity they would purchase at various prices. It is generally agreed today that this procedure yields very biased results, because consumers either cannot or will not give trustworthy answers.

Another approach is *consumer clinics*, in which consumers are given a sum of money and asked to spend it in a simulated store to see how they react to price changes.

FIGURE 5–8   Empirical Estimation of Demand Curves

When the scatter of quantity-price observations (points) falls as in the left panel, we can estimate by regression analysis an average demand curve from the data, such as dashed line D. However, when the points fall as in the right panel, we may be unable to estimate or identify either a reliable demand or supply curve.

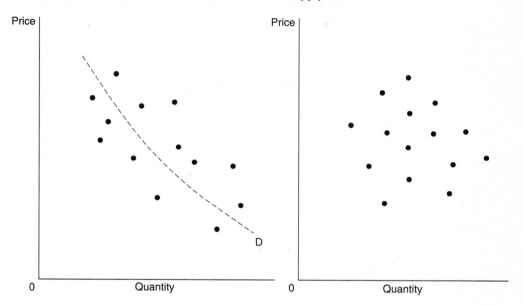

However, the sample of consumers must necessarily be small because this procedure is expensive. Also, the results are questionable because consumers are aware that they are in an artificial situation. Still another approach is a *market experiment*, whereby the seller increases the price of the commodity in one market or store and lowers it in another and then records the different quantities purchased in the two markets or stores. This procedure is questionable because (1) a small sample is involved, (2) the seller can permanently lose customers in the high-priced market or store, and (3) only the immediate or short-run response to the price change is obtained.

Today, market demand curves are generally estimated from actual market data of the quantities purchased of the commodity at various prices over time (i.e., using time series data) or for various consuming units or areas at one point in time (i.e., using cross-section data). However, only when the scatter of quantity-price observations (points) fall as in the left panel of Figure 5–8 can we estimate a demand curve from the data. When the points fall as in the right panel, we face an **identification problem** and may be able to estimate neither a reliable demand curve nor a supply curve for the commodity from the data.[15]

_____

[15]Each quantity-price observation (point) is usually given by the intersection of a different (and unknown) demand and supply curve for the commodity. The reason for this is that demand and supply curves usually shift over time and are usually different for different consumers and in different places. When the points fall as in the left panel, we can correct for the forces that cause the demand curve to shift and derive an average demand curve from the data. When the points fall as in the right panel and the shifts in demand and supply are not independent, we are unable to do so.

When quantity-price observations (points) fall as in the left panel of Figure 5–8, we can estimate the average demand curve for the good by correcting for the forces that cause the demand curve to shift (i.e., by correcting for the changes or differences in incomes and in the prices of related commodities). This is accomplished by the **multiple regression** statistical technique.[16] Regression analysis allows the economist to disentangle the independent effect of the various determinants of demand, so as to identify from the data the average market demand curve for the commodity (such as dashed line D in the left panel).

To conduct the regression analysis, the researcher collects data on the quantity purchased of the good in question, its price, the income of consumers, and the price of one or more related commodities (substitutes and complements). Regression analysis allows the researcher to correct for the effect of changes or differences in consumers' incomes and in the prices of related commodities and permits the estimation of the average demand function that best fits the data (as, for example, D in the left panel of Figure 5–8). The values of all the collected variables are usually first transformed into logarithms because by doing so the estimated coefficients of the demand function are the various elasticities of demand.[17]

By regression analysis we estimate a demand function of the following form:

$$Q_X = a + bP_X + cI + eP_Y \qquad \text{[5–7]}$$

where Q_X, P_X, I, and P_Y usually refer to the logarithm of the quantity purchased of commodity X per unit of time, its price, the consumers' income, and the price of related commodity Y, respectively. $Q_X = a$ (the constant) when P_X, I, and P_Y are all zero. The estimated coefficient of P_X, b, is the price elasticity of demand (when the regression is performed on the data transformed into logarithms). On the other hand, c is the estimated income elasticity of demand, while e is the estimated cross elasticity of demand of good X for good Y.

For the demand curve of good X to obey the law of demand, the estimated b coefficient (η_X) must be negative (so that quantity demanded and price are inversely related). Good X is a necessity if the estimated c coefficient (η_I) is positive but smaller than 1. On the other hand, good X is a luxury if $c > 1$ and an inferior good if $c < 0$. If the estimated e coefficient (η_{XY}) is positive, good Y is a substitute for good X. If $e < 0$, good Y is a complement of good X.

Even though regression analysis is not devoid of problems, it is the most extensively used technique today for the estimation of market demand curves and the one utilized in measuring all elasticities in this chapter. Regression analysis is also used to forecast future demand, as Example 5 illustrates.

---

[16]Regression analysis is explained in a course in statistics. For an introduction to regression analysis, see D. Salvatore, *Statistics and Econometrics* (New York: McGraw-Hill, 1982), Chapters 6 and 7.

[17]In order for the estimated coefficients to be elasticities, the value of each variable collected must first be transformed into the natural logarithm. Natural logs are those to the base 2.718 (as opposed to common logs, which are to the base 10). For example, the natural log of 100, written ln100, is 4.61 (i.e., ln100 = 4.61). This is obtained by looking up the number 100 in a table of natural logs or more simply using a pocket calculator. The time series or the cross-section data of each variable transformed into natural logs are then used to run the regression and obtain the various coefficients of the demand function. These estimated coefficients are themselves the elasticities. Why this is so is explained in a course of mathematics for economists.

Example 5

 Estimating and Forecasting the U.S. Demand for Electricity

Estimating and forecasting the demand for electricity is very important because it takes many years to build new capacity to meet future needs.[18] Many such studies have been conducted during the past 30 years. One of these is by Halvorsen, who used multiple regression analysis to estimate the market demand equation for electricity with cross-sectional data transformed into natural logarithms for the 48 contiguous states in the United States for the year 1969.

Table 5–7 reports the estimated elasticity of demand for electricity for residential use in the United States with respect to the price of electricity, per capita income, the price of gas, and the number of customers in the market. Although the results of various studies differ somewhat, the results reported below indicate that the amount of electricity for residential use consumed in the United States would fall by 9.74% as a result of a 10% increase in the price of electricity, would increase by 7.14% with a 10% increase in per capita income, would increase by 1.59% with a 10% increase in the price of gas, and is proportional to the number of customers in the market. Thus, the market demand curve for electricity is negatively sloped, electricity is a normal good and a necessity, and gas is a substitute for electricity.

Using the above estimated demand elasticities and projecting the growth in per capita income, in the price of gas, in the number of customers in the market, and in the price of electricity, public utilities could forecast the growth in the demand for electricity in the United States so as to adequately plan new capacity to meet future needs. For example, if we assume that per capita income grows at 3% per year, the price of gas at 20% per year, the number of customers at 1% per year, and the price of electricity at 4% per year, we can forecast that the demand for electricity for residential use in the United States will expand at a rate of 2.43% per year. This is obtained by adding the products of the value of each elasticity by the projected growth of the corresponding variable, as indicated in the following equation:

$$Q = (0.714)(3\%) + (0.159)(20\%) + (1.000)(1\%) - (0.974)(4\%)$$

$$= 2.142 + 3.180 + 1.000 - 3.896$$

$$= 6.322 - 3.896 = 2.426$$

With different projections of the yearly growth in per capital income, the price of gas, the number of customers in the market, and the price of electricity, we will get correspondingly different results.

The above results are shown in Figure 5–9, where P_0 and Q_0 are the original

---

[18]"Warding Off an Electricity Shortage," *New York Times*, July 7, 1985, p. F3.

**TABLE 5–7   Elasticities of Demand for Electricity
for Residential Use in the United States**

Variable	Value
Price	$(-)0.974$
Per capita income	0.714
Price of gas	0.159
Number of customers	1.000

Source: R. Halvorsen, "Demand for Electric Energy in the United States," *Southern Economic Journal*, April 1976.

price and quantity of electricity demanded in the United States on hypothetical demand curve D_0 in the base period (say, the current year). Demand curve D' results from the projected increase in per capital income, D'' from the increase in the price of gas also, and D_1 from the increase in the number of

FIGURE 5–9   Forecast of Electricity in the United States

P_0 and Q_0 are the original price and quantity of electricity demanded in the United States on hypothetical demand curve D_0. Demand curve D' results from projecting a 3% increase in per capita incomes, D'' by also projecting a 20% increase in the price of gas, and D_1 from a 1% increase in the number of customers in the market as well. If the price of electricity is also assumed to increase by 4% (from P_0 to P_1), the demand for electricity increases by 2.426% per year (the movement from point A on D_0 to point F on D_1).

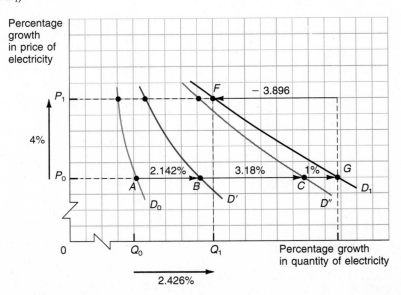

customers in the market as well. Thus, D_1 takes into account or reflects the cumulative effect of all the growth factors considered.

Were the price of electricity to remain constant, the demand for electricity would rise by 6.322% per year (given by the movement from point A on D_0 to point G on D_1 in the figure). The projected increase in the price of electricity by 4% per year (from P_0 to P_1), by itself, will result in a decline in the quantity demanded of electricity by 3.896% (the movement from point G to point F on D_1). The net result of all forces at work gives rise to a net increase in Q of 2.426% per year (the movement from point A on D_0 to point F on D_1).

Data Resources, Wharton Econometrics, and the U.S. Department of Energy have forecast growth in annual electricity demand of 2% to 3% to the turn of the century. To satisfy this increase in demand, from 100 to 200 new large electrical generating power stations are required at the cost of hundreds of billions of dollars by the turn of the century. Since it takes from 6 to 12 years to build a new plant, electrical power companies have little time to waste. In the face of low electricity rates set by many of the nation's state regulatory commissions, however, electrical power companies prefer instead to charge higher electricity rates at times of peak demand to avoid building the new plants. Demand studies have been conducted for practically every major commodity in the United States and are widely used by businesspeople and managers to forecast future demand. This, in turn, greatly affects investments in new plants and equipment and the general level of economic activity.

▲

PART THREE

PRODUCTION, COSTS, AND COMPETITIVE MARKETS

P art Three (Chapters 6–8) presents the theory of production, cost, and pricing in competitive markets. Chapter 6 examines production theory, or how firms combine resources or inputs to produce final commodities. These concepts are then utilized and extended in Chapter 7 to examine costs of production and to derive the short-run and the long-run cost curves of the firm. Finally, Chapter 8 brings together the theory of consumer behavior and demand (from Part Two) with the theory of production and costs (from Chapters 6 and 7) to analyze how price and output are determined under perfect competition. The chapter appendices present more advanced topics in the theory of production, cost, and pricing. The presentation of the theory is reinforced throughout with many real-world examples.

6

PRODUCTION THEORY

In Part Two, we examined the theory of consumer behavior and demand. Our focus of attention was the consumer. In Part Three, we examine the theory of production, cost, and pricing in competitive markets. Here the focus of attention is the firm. This chapter examines the theory of production or how firms organize production; that is, we examine how firms combine resources or inputs to produce final commodities. Chapter 7 builds on the discussion and analyzes the costs of production of the firm. Then Chapter 8 brings together the theory of consumer behavior and demand with the theory of production and costs to analyze how price and output are determined under perfect competition.

This chapter begins with a discussion of the organization of production. We define the meaning of production, examine the reason for the existence of firms and their aim, classify resources or inputs into various categories, and define the meaning of the short run and the long run production. From this, we go on to the theory of production when only one input is variable. This is accomplished by defining the total, the average, and the marginal product curve of the variable input. Production theory is subsequently extended to deal with two variable inputs by the introduction of isoquants.

From the theory of production where only one or two inputs are variable, we proceed to examine cases in which all inputs are variable. Here, we define the meaning of constant, increasing, and decreasing returns to scale, the conditions under which they arise, and their importance. Finally, we examine technological progress and international competitiveness.

The real-world examples included in this chapter highlight the importance and relevance of the theory of production. The optional appendix examines the most used production function (the Cobb-Douglas) and its empirical estimation.

6.1 RELATING OUTPUTS TO INPUTS

In this section, we examine the organization of production and classify inputs into various categories. We begin by focusing on the meaning and organization of production and the reason for the existence of firms and their aim. Then we classify inputs into various broad categories. This section serves as a general background for the theory of production presented in subsequent sections.

Organization of Production

Production refers to the transformation of resources into outputs of goods and services. For example, General Motors hires workers who use machinery in factories to transform steel, plastic, glass, rubber, and so on into automobiles. The output of a firm can either be a final commodity such as automobiles or an intermediate product such as steel (which is used in the production of automobiles and other goods). The output can also be a service rather than a good. Examples of services are education, medicine, banking, legal counsel, accounting work, communications, transportation, storage, wholesaling, and retailing. Production is a flow concept or has a time dimension. In other words, production refers to the rate of output over a given period of time. This is to be distinguished from the stock of a commodity or input, which refers to the quantity of the commodity (such as the number of automobiles) or input (such as the tons of steel) at hand or available at a particular point in time.

More than 80% of all goods and services consumed in the United States are produced by firms. The remainder is produced by the government and such nonprofit organizations as the Red Cross, private colleges, foundations, and so on. A **firm** is an organization that combines and organizes resources for the purpose of producing goods and services for sale at a profit. There are millions of firms in the United States. These include proprietorships (firms owned by one individual), partnerships (owned by two or more individuals), and corporations (owned by stockholders). The way the firm is organized is not of primary concern in the study of microeconomic theory; only what the firm does is. Firms arise because it would be inefficient and costly for workers and for the owners of capital and land to enter into and enforce contracts with one another to pool their resources for the purpose of producing goods and services.

Just as consumers seek to maximize utility or satisfaction, firms generally seek to maximize profits. Both consumers and firms can be regarded as maximizing entities. Profits refer to the revenue of the firm from the sale of the output after all costs have been deducted. Included in costs are not only the actual wages paid to hired workers and payments for purchasing other inputs but also the income that the owner of the firm would earn by working for someone else and the return that he or she would receive from investing his or her capital in the best *alternative* use. For example, the owner of a delicatessen must include in his or her costs not only payments for the rental of the store, hired help, and for the purchase of the hams, cheeses, beers, milk, crackers, and so on in the store. He or she must also include as part of costs the foregone earnings of the money invested in the store as well as the earnings that he or she would receive by working for someone else in a similar capacity (e.g., as the manager of another delicatessen). The owner earns (economic) profits only if total revenue exceeds total costs (which include actual expenses and the alternatives foregone).

The profit-maximizing assumption provides the framework for analyzing the behavior of the firm in microeconomic theory. It is from this assumption that the behavior of the firm can be studied most fruitfully. This assumption has recently been challenged by the so-called "managerial theories of the firm" (discussed in greater detail in Chapter 10), which postulate multiple goals for the firm. That is, after attaining "satisfactory" rather than maximum profits, the large modern corporation is said to seek to maintain or increase its market share, maximize sales or growth, maintain a large staff of executives and lavish offices, minimize uncertainty, create and maintain a good public image as a desirable member of the community and good employer, and so on. However, because many of these goals can be regarded as indirect ways to earn and increase profits in the long run, we will retain the profit-maximizing assumption.

Classification of Inputs

Firms transform inputs into outputs. **Inputs,** resources, or factors of production are the means of producing the goods and services demanded by society. Inputs can be classified broadly into labor or human resources (including entrepreneurial talent), capital, and land or natural resources. This threefold classification of inputs is, however, only a convenient way to organize the discussion, and it does not convey the enormous variety of specific resources in each category. For example, labor includes simple clerks and assembly-line workers as well as accountants, teachers, engineers, doctors, and scientists. And we must consider the specific types of labor and other inputs required for the analysis of production of a particular firm or industry.[1]

Particularly important among inputs is **entrepreneurship,** which refers to the ability on the part of some individuals to see opportunities to combine resources in new and more efficient ways to produce a particular commodity or to produce entirely new commodities. The motivation is the great profit possibilities that an entrepreneur may believe to exist. The entrepreneur either uses his or her resources to exploit these profit opportunities or, more likely, attempts to convince other people with large sums of money to put some of that money at his or her disposal to introduce new production techniques or new products and share in the potential profits. We have many examples of this during the late 1970s and early 1980s in the field of microcomputers. This

---

[1]The reason is that different skills require varying training costs and wages to be supplied. Thus, to analyze the production process of a particular firm or industry, we must consider the *specific* types of labor and other inputs that are required. Yet, for general theoretical work, it is often convenient to deal with the broad input categories of labor, capital, and land.

was a time when some young engineers and computer experts sought to combine new and more powerful chips (the basic memory component of computers) to produce cheaper or better microcomputers. Some of these entrepreneurs were successful and became rich overnight (e.g., the developers of the Apple Computers). Most had to abandon their dreams after huge losses. In any event, entrepreneurs play a crucial role in modern economies. They are responsible for the introduction of new technology and new products and for most of the growth of the economy as a whole.

Inputs can be further classified into fixed and variable. **Fixed inputs** are those that cannot be varied or can be varied only with excessive cost during the time period under consideration. Examples of fixed inputs are the firm's plant and specialized equipment. For example, it takes many years for General Motors to build a new automobile plant and introduce robots to perform many repetitive assembly-line tasks. **Variable inputs,** on the other hand, are those that can be varied easily and on a short notice during the time period under consideration. Examples of these are raw materials and many types of workers, particularly those with low levels of skills. Thus, whether an input is fixed or variable depends on the time horizon being considered. The time period during which at least one input is fixed is called the **short run,** and the time period during which all inputs are variable is called the **long run.** Obviously, the length of time it takes to vary all inputs (i.e., to be in the long run), varies for firms in different industries. For a street vendor of apples, the long run may be a day. For an apple farmer, it is at least five years (this is how long it takes for newly planted trees to begin bearing fruit).

6.2 PRODUCTION WITH ONE VARIABLE INPUT

In this section, we present the theory of production when only one input is variable. Thus, we are dealing with the short run. We begin by defining the total, the average, and the marginal product of the variable input and examining their relationship graphically. We then discuss the important law of diminishing returns and the meaning and importance of the stages of production. Production theory with more than one variable input is taken up in subsequent sections.

Total, Average, and Marginal Product

A **production function** is a unique relationship between inputs and outputs. It can be represented by a table, a graph, or an equation showing the maximum output of a commodity that can be produced per period of time with each set of inputs. Both output and inputs are measured in physical rather than monetary units. Technology is assumed to remain constant. A simple short-run production function is obtained by applying various amounts of labor to farm one acre of land and recording the resulting output or **total product (TP)** per period of time. This is illustrated by the first two columns of Table 6–1.

TABLE 6–1   **Total, Average, and Marginal Product of Labor in the Cultivation of Wheat on One Acre of Land (bushels per year)**

Labor (Workers per Year) (1)	Output or Total Product (2)	Average Product of Labor (3)	Marginal Product of Labor (4)
0	0	. . .	. . .
1	3	3	3
2	8	4	5
3	12	4	4
4	14	3.5	2
5	14	2.8	0
6	12	2	−2

The first two columns of Table 6–1 provide a hypothetical production function for a farm using various quantities of labor (i.e., number of workers per year) to cultivate wheat on one acre of land (and using no other input). When no labor is used, total output or product is zero. With one unit of labor ($1L$), total product (TP) is 3 bushels of wheat per year. With $2L$, $TP = 8$ bushels. With $3L$, $TP = 12$ bushels, and so on.[2]

From the output or total product schedule we can derive the (per-unit) average and marginal product schedules for the input. Specifically, the total (physical) output or total product (TP) divided by the quantity of labor employed (L) equals the **average product** of labor (AP_L). On the other hand, the change in output or total product per-unit change in the quantity of labor employed is equal to the **marginal product** of labor (MP_L).[3] That is,

$$AP_L = \frac{TP}{L} \qquad\qquad \textbf{[6–1]}$$

and

$$MP_L = \frac{\Delta TP}{\Delta L} \qquad\qquad \textbf{[6–2]}$$

Column 3 in Table 6–1 gives the average product of labor (AP_L). This equals TP (column 2) divided by the quantity of labor used (column 1). Thus, with one unit of labor ($1L$), the AP_L equals $\frac{3}{1}$ or 3 bushels. With $2L$, AP_L is $\frac{8}{2}$ or 4 bushels, and so on. Finally, column 4 reports the marginal product of labor (MP_L). This measures the change in total product per-unit change in labor. Since labor increases by one unit at a time in column 1, the MP_L in column 4 is obtained by subtracting successive quantities of the TP in column 2. For

---

[2]The reason for the decline in TP when six units of labor are used will be discussed shortly.

[3]In subsequent chapters, when the possibility arises of confusing the AP and the MP with their monetary values, they will be referred to as the average *physical* product and the marginal *physical* product.

example, *TP* increases from 0 to 3 bushels when we add the first unit of labor. Thus, the MP_L is 3 bushels. For an increase in labor from 1*L* to 2*L*, *TP* increases from 3 to 8 bushels. Thus, the MP_L is 5 bushels. For an increase in labor from 2*L* to 3*L*, the MP_L is 4 bushels (12 − 8), and so on.

Plotting the total, average, and marginal product quantities of Table 6–1 gives the corresponding product curves shown in Figure 6–1. Note that *TP*

FIGURE 6–1   Total, Average, and Marginal Product Curves

The top panel shows the total output or total product (*TP*) curve. The AP_L at point *A* on the *TP* curve is 3 bushels (the slope of *OA*) and is plotted as *A'* in the bottom panel. The AP_L curve is the highest between 2*L* and 3*L*. The MP_L between *A* and *B* on the *TP* curve is 5 bushels (the slope of *AB*) and is plotted between *A* and *B* in the bottom panel. The MP_L is highest at 1.5*L*, $MP_L = AP_L$ at 2.5*L*, $MP_L = 0$ at 4.5*L*, and it is negative thereafter.

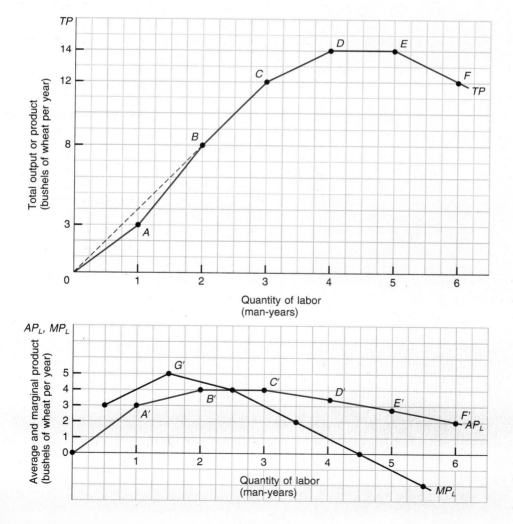

grows to 14 bushels with $4L$. It stays at 14 bushels with $5L$ and then declines to 12 bushels with $6L$ (see the top panel of Figure 6–1). The reason for this is that laborers get into each other's way and actually trample the wheat when the sixth worker is employed. In the bottom panel, we see that the AP_L curve rises to 4 bushels and then declines. Since the marginal product of labor refers to the change in total product per-unit change in labor used, each value of the MP_L is plotted halfway between the quantities of labor used. Thus, the MP_L of 3 bushels, which results from increasing labor from $0L$ to $1L$, is plotted at $0.5L$; the MP_L of 5 bushels, which results from increasing labor from $1L$ to $2L$, is plotted at $1.5L$, and so on. The MP_L curve rises to 5 bushels at $1.5L$ and then declines. Past $4.5L$, the MP_L becomes negative.

The Geometry of Average and Marginal Product Curves

The shape of the average and marginal product of labor curves is determined by the shape of the corresponding total product curve. The AP_L at any point on the TP curve is equal to the slope of the straight line drawn from the origin to that point on the TP curve. Thus, the AP_L at point A on the TP curve in the top panel of Figure 6–1 is equal to the slope of OA. This equals ¾ or 3 bushels and is plotted directly below A, as point A', in the bottom panel of Figure 6–1. Similarly, the AP_L at point B on the TP curve is equal to the slope of dashed line OB. This equals % or 4 bushels and is plotted as point B' in the bottom panel. At point C, the AP_L is again equal to 4. This is the highest AP_L. Past point C, the AP_L declines but remains positive as long as the TP is positive.

The MP_L between any two points on the TP curve is equal to the slope of the TP between the two points. Thus, the MP_L between the origin and point A on the TP curve in the top panel of Figure 6–1 is equal to the slope of OA. This is equal to 3 bushels and is plotted halfway between $0L$ and $1L$ (i.e., at $0.5L$) in the bottom panel of Figure 6–1. Similarly, the MP_L between points A and B on the TP curve is equal to the slope of AB. This is equal to 5 (the highest MP_L) and is plotted as point G' at $1.5L$ in the bottom panel. The MP_L between B and C on the TP curve is equal to the slope of BC. This equals 4 and is the same as the highest AP_L (the slope of OB and OC). Between points D and E, TP remains unchanged and the $MP_L = 0$. Past point E, TP falls and MP_L becomes negative.

We have drawn the curves in Figure 6–1 under the assumption that labor is used in whole units. If this were not the case and labor time were infinitesimally divisible, we would have the smooth TP, AP_L, and MP_L curves shown in Figure 6–2. In this figure, the AP_L (given, as before, by the slope of a ray from the origin to the TP curve) rises up to point H on the TP curve in the top panel and then declines. Thus, the AP_L curve in the bottom panel rises up to point H' and declines thereafter (but remains positive as long as TP is positive). On the other hand, the MP_L at any point on the TP curve is equal to the slope of the tangent to the TP curve at that point. The slope of the TP curve rises up to point G (the point of inflection) and then declines. Thus,

FIGURE 6–2   Geometry of Total, Average, and Marginal Product Curves

With labor time infinitesimally divisible, we have smooth TP, AP_L, and MP_L curves. The AP_L (given by the slope of the line from the origin to a point on the TP curve) rises up to point H' and declines thereafter (but remains positive as long as TP is positive). The MP_L (given by the slope of the tangent to the TP curve) rises up to point G', becomes zero at I', and is negative thereafter. When the AP_L curve rises, the MP_L is above it; when the AP_L falls, the MP_L is below it; and when AP_L is highest, $MP_L = AP_L$.

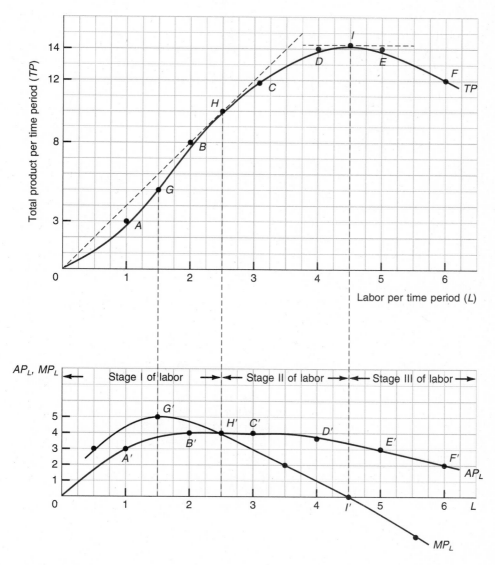

the MP_L curve in the bottom panel rises up to point G' and declines thereafter. The MP_L is zero at point I' directly below point I, where the TP is highest or has zero slope, and it becomes negative when TP begins to decline.[4]

Note that the MP_L curve reaches its maximum point before the AP_L curve. Furthermore, as long as the AP_L curve is rising, the MP_L curve is above it. When the AP_L curve is falling, the MP_L curve is below it, and when the AP_L curve is highest, the MP_L intersects the AP_L curve. The reason for this is that for the AP_L to rise, the MP_L must be greater than the average to pull the average up. For the AP_L to fall, the MP_L must be lower than the average to pull the average down. For the average to be at a maximum (i.e., neither rising nor falling), the marginal must be equal to the average (the slope of line OH). For example, for a student to increase his or her cumulative average test score, he or she must receive a grade on the next (marginal) test that exceeds his or her average. With a lower grade on the next test, the student's cumulative average will fall. If the grade on the next test equals the previous average, the cumulative average will remain unchanged.

The Law of Diminishing Returns and Stages of Production

The decline in the MP_L curve in Figures 6–1 and 6–2 is a reflection of the **law of diminishing returns.** This is an empirical generalization or a physical law, not a proposition of economics. It postulates that as more units of a variable input are used with a fixed amount of other inputs, after a point, a smaller and smaller return will accrue to each additional unit of the variable input. In other words, the marginal (physical) product of the variable input eventually declines. This occurs because each additional unit of the variable input has less and less of the fixed inputs with which to work. Eventually, too much of the variable input is used with the fixed inputs, and so the marginal product of the variable input declines.

In Figure 6–2, the law of diminishing returns for labor begins to operate past point G' (i.e. when more than $1.5L$ is applied to one acre of land). Further additions of labor will eventually lead to zero and then to negative MP_L. Note that to observe the law of diminishing returns, at least one input (here, land) must be held constant. Technology is also assumed to remain unchanged. It should also be noted that when less than $1.5L$ is employed, labor is used too sparsely in the cultivation of one acre of land and the MP_L rises. Had land been kept constant at two acres instead of one, the TP, AP_L, and MP_L curves would retain their general shape but would all be higher, since each unit of labor would have more land to work with (see section 6.3).

---

[4]Note that the TP curve in Figure 6–2 has an initial portion over which it faces up (so that the MP_L increases). That is, up to point G, labor is used so sparsely on one acre of land that the MP_L increases as more labor is employed. This is usual but not always true. That is, in some cases, the TP curve faces down from the origin (so that MP_L falls from the very start). An example of this is discussed in the appendix to this chapter.

The relationship between the AP and the MP curves can be used to define the three stages of production as follows. The range from the origin to the point where the AP is maximum is **stage I of production** for the variable input. **Stage II of production** proceeds from the point where the AP of the variable input is maximum to the point where the MP of that input is zero. The range over which the MP is negative is **stage III of production** for the variable input. In Figure 6–2, stage I for labor extends up to 2.5L (i.e., up to point H'); stage II extends from 2.5L to 4.5L (i.e., from point H' to point I'); stage III extends beyond 4.5L (i.e., beyond point I', in the range where MP_L is negative).

The rational producer would not operate in stage III of labor, even if labor time were free, because the MP_L is negative. That is, adding one additional unit of labor in stage III of labor actually causes output to decline. This means that a greater output or TP could be produced by using *less* labor! Thus, the rational producer will not produce in stage III of labor. Similarly, he or she will not produce in stage I of labor because (as shown in more advanced texts) this corresponds to stage III of land (where the MP of land is negative).[5] Thus, the rational producer will operate in stage II where the MP of both factors is positive but declining. The precise point within stage II at which the rational producer operates will depend on the prices of inputs and output. This is examined in Chapter 8, where we discuss profit maximization by the firm. Sometimes a production function exhibits diminishing returns from the very start and reflects only stage II of production (see the appendix to this chapter).

Example 1

 Economics—The Dismal Science Because of Diminishing Returns

In the early 19th century, Thomas Malthus (in his *Essay on the Principles of Population,* 1798) and other classical economists predicted that population growth in the face of fixed stocks of land and other nonhuman resources could doom humanity to a subsistence standard of living. That is, rapid population growth could reduce the average and the marginal product of labor sufficiently to keep people always near starvation. This gloomy prediction earned for economics the label of the "dismal science."

These predictions have not proved correct, especially for the United States and other industrial nations of the world where standards of living are much higher than a century or two ago. The reasons for the sharply increased standard of living are (1) the quantities of capital, land, and minerals used in

---

[5]Stage I of labor corresponds to stage III of land only under constant returns to scale. This is the case where output changes in the same proportion as the change in all inputs (see section 6.5). As we will see in Chapter 7, average costs of production decrease over stage I of labor, and so it pays for the producer to use more labor until he or she is in stage II of labor.

production have vastly increased since the beginning of the 19th century; (2) population growth has slowed down considerably in the industrial nations; and (3) most importantly, very significant improvements in technology have greatly increased productivity.

Contrary to Malthus's dismal predictions, standards of living have in fact increased over the past century throughout most of the world. Malthus inappropriately applied a short-run law (the law of diminishing returns) to the long run (when technology can improve dramatically) and came up with the wrong prediction! As Table 6-2 shows, food production per capita has increased over the past decade in all major developing-country groups (with the exception of Sub-Saharan Africa) as a result of new high-yielding and disease-resistant grains, better fertilizer, more irrigation, and so on.

TABLE 6–2   **Index of Food Production per Capita in Major Developing-Country Groups in 1990 (1978–1981 = 100)**

Developing-Country Groups	Index
East Asia and Pacific (of which China)	127 (133)
South Asia (of which India)	116 (119)
Latin America (of which Brazil)	106 (115)
Europe (of which Greece)	102 (103)
Middle East and North Africa (of which Egypt)	101 (118)
Sub-Saharan Africa (of which Ethiopia)	94 (84)

Source: World Bank, 1992.

▲

6.3 PRODUCTION WITH TWO VARIABLE INPUTS

In this section, we examine production theory with two variable inputs by introducing isoquants. We also show how to derive total product curves from an isoquant map, thereby highlighting the relationship between production with one and two variable inputs. We then examine the shape of isoquants in section 6.4.

What Do Isoquants Show?

An **isoquant** shows the various combinations of two inputs (say, labor and capital) that can be used to produce a specific level of output. A higher isoquant refers to a larger output, whereas a lower isoquant refers to a smaller output. If the two variable inputs (labor and capital) are the only inputs used in production, we are in the long run. If the two variable inputs are used with other fixed inputs (say, land), we would still be in the short run.

FIGURE 6–3   Production Function with Two Variable Inputs

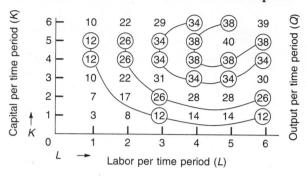

Figure 6–3 gives a hypothetical production function, which shows the outputs (the Q's) that can be produced with various combinations of labor (L) and capital (K) per time period. For example, the table shows that 12 units of output (i.e., 12Q) can be produced with 1 unit of labor (i.e., 1L) and 5 units of capital (i.e., 5K) or with 1L and 4K.[6] Table 6–2 also shows that 12Q can also be produced with 3L and 1K or with 6L and 1K per time period. On the other hand, the table indicates that 26 units of output (26Q) could be produced with 2L and 5K, 2L and 4K, 3L and 2K, and 6L and 2K. From the table, we can also determine the various combinations of L and K to produce 34Q and 38Q. Note that to produce a greater output per time period, more labor, more capital, or both more labor and more capital are required. For visual aid, equal levels of output are joined together by a curve in the body of Figure 6–3.

Plotting the various combinations of labor and capital that can be used to produce 12, 26, 34, and 38 units of output per time period gives the isoquant for each of these levels of output shown in Figure 6–4. The figure shows that 12 units of output (the lowest isoquant shown) can be produced with 1 unit of labor (1L) and 5 units of capital (5K). This defines point J. Twelve units of output can also be produced with 1L and 4K (point M), 3L and 1K (point C), and 6L and 1K (point F). Joining these points with a smooth curve, we obtain the isoquant for 12 units of output. Similarly, by plotting the various combinations of labor and capital that can be used to produce 26 units of output (2L and 5K, 2L and 4K, 3L and 2K, and 6L and 2K) and joining the resulting points by a smooth curve we get the isoquant for 26Q in Figure 6–4. The isoquants for 34Q and 38Q in the figure can be similarly derived from the data in Figure 6–3.

---

[6]Of course, since inputs are not free, a firm would prefer to produce 12Q with 1L and 4K rather than with 1L and 5K.

FIGURE 6–4   Isoquants

The isoquants in the figure are obtained from the data in Figure 6–3. The lowest isoquant shows that 12 units of output can be produced with 1L and 5K (point J), 1L and 4K (point M), 2L and 1.5K (point N), 3L and 1K (point C), or 6L and 1K (point F). Higher isoquants refer to higher levels of output.

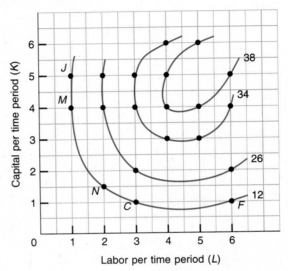

Derivation of Total Product Curves from the Isoquant Map

By drawing a horizontal line across an isoquant map at the level at which the input measured along the vertical axis is fixed, we can generate the total product curve for the variable input measured along the horizontal axis. For example, by starting with the isoquant map of Figure 6–4 and keeping capital constant at $K = 4$, we can derive the total product curve of labor for $K = 4$. This corresponds to the higher of the two TP curves in the bottom panel of Figure 6–5. Thus, from point M (1L and 4K) on the isoquant for 12Q in the top panel, we obtain point M' on the TP curve for $K = 4$ in the bottom panel. From point V (2L and 4K) on the isoquant for 26Q in the top panel, we derive point V' on the TP curve for $K = 4$ in the bottom panel, and so on. This is equivalent to reading across the row for $K = 4$ in Figure 6–3.

With capital held constant at the lower level of $K = 1$, we generate the lower total product curve in the bottom panel of Figure 6–5. This is equivalent to reading across the row for $K = 1$ in Figure 6–3. Note that when capital is held constant at a smaller level, the TP curve for labor is lower because each unit of labor has less capital with which to work.

If, instead, we held the quantity of labor constant and changed the quantity of capital used, we would derive the TP curve for capital. This can be obtained by drawing a vertical line on the isoquant map at the level at which labor is held constant. This is equivalent to reading up to the appropriate column of

FIGURE 6–5 Derivation of Total Product Curves from the Isoquant Map

By keeping capital constant at $K = 4$ in the top panel, we can derive the higher of the two total product curves in the bottom panel. Thus, from point M ($1L$ and $4K$) on the isoquant for $12Q$ in the top panel, we obtain point M' on the TP curve for $K = 4$ in the bottom panel. From point V ($2L$ and $4K$) in the top panel we derive point V' in the bottom panel, and so on. With capital constant at $K = 1$ (i.e., reading across the row for $K = 1$ in Figure 6–3), we get the lower total product curve in the bottom panel.

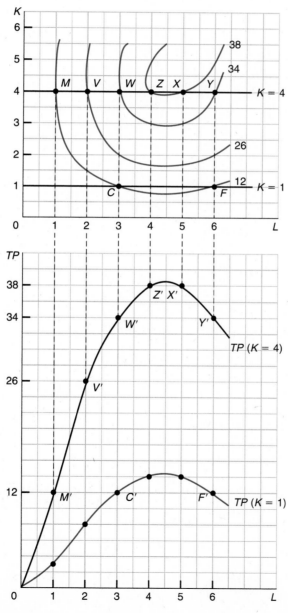

Figure 6–3. The higher the level at which labor is held constant, the higher is the total product curve of capital. From a given total product curve, we could then derive the corresponding average and marginal product curves, as shown in the bottom panel of Figure 6–2. Thus, Figure 6–3 and Figure 6–4 could provide information about the long run as well as the short run, depending on whether labor and capital are the only two inputs and both are variable (the long run), or whether labor and capital are used with other fixed inputs (such as land), or either labor or capital is fixed (the short run).

6.4 THE SHAPE OF ISOQUANTS

In this section, we examine the characteristics of isoquants, define the economic region of production, and consider the special cases where commodities can only be produced with fixed input combinations. We will see that the shape of isoquants plays as important a role in production theory as the shape of indifference curves plays in consumption theory.

Characteristics of Isoquants

The characteristics of isoquants are crucial for understanding production theory with two variable inputs. Isoquants are similar to indifference curves. However, whereas an indifference curve shows the various combinations of two commodities that provide the consumer equal satisfaction (measured ordinally), an isoquant shows the various combinations of two inputs that give the same level of output (measured cardinally, or in actual units of the commodity).[7]

Isoquants have the same general characteristics of indifference curves. That is, they are negatively sloped in the economically relevant range, convex to the origin, and do not intersect. These properties are shown in Figure 6–6.[8] The nonintersecting property of isoquants can easily be explained. Intersecting isoquants would mean that two different levels of output of the same commodity could be produced with the identical input combination (i.e., at the point where the isoquants intersect). This is impossible under our assumption that the most efficient production techniques are always used.

Isoquants are negatively sloped in the economically relevant range. This means that if the firm wants to reduce the quantity of capital used in production, it must increase the quantity of labor in order to continue to produce the same level of output (i.e., remain on the same isoquant). For example, starting at point M (1L and 4K) on the isoquant for 12 units of output (12Q),

---

[7]Compare Figure 6–6 with Figure 3–2.

[8]The positively sloped portions of the isoquants have been omitted in Figure 6–6 because they are irrelevant. The reason for this is discussed in the next subsection.

the firm could reduce the quantity of capital by 2.5K by adding 1L in production and reach point N on the same isoquant (see Figure 6–6). Thus, the slope of the isoquant between points M and N is $-2.5K/1L$. The slope between N and C is $-\frac{1}{2}$.

The absolute value of the slope of the isoquant is called the **marginal rate of technical substitution (MRTS)**. This is analogous to the marginal rate of substitution of one good for another in consumption, which is given by the absolute value of the slope of an indifference curve. For a movement down along an isoquant, the marginal rate of technical substitution of labor for capital ($MRTS_{LK}$) is given by $-\Delta K/\Delta L$. It measures the amount of capital that the firm can give up by using one additional unit of labor and still remain on the same isoquant. Because of the reduction in K, $MRTS_{LK}$ is negative. However, we multiply by -1 and express $MRTS_{LK}$ as a positive value. Thus, the $MRTS_{LK}$ between points M and N on the isoquant for 12Q is 2.5. Similarly, the $MRTS_{LK}$ between points N and C is $\frac{1}{2}$. The $MRTS_{LK}$ at any point on an isoquant is given by the absolute value of the slope of the isoquant at that point. Thus, the $MRTS_{LK}$ at point N is 1 (the absolute value of the slope of the tangent to the isoquant at point N; see Figure 6–6).

The $MRTS_{LK}$ is also equal to MP_L/MP_K. To prove this, we begin by remembering that all points on an isoquant refer to the same level of output. Thus, for a movement down a given isoquant, the gain in output from using more labor must be equal to the loss in output from using less capital. Specifically, the increase in the quantity of labor used (ΔL) times the marginal product of labor (MP_L) must equal the reduction in the amount of capital used ($-\Delta K$) times the marginal product of capital (MP_K). That is,

$$(\Delta L)(MP_L) = -(\Delta K)(MP_K) \qquad [6\text{--}3]$$

FIGURE 6–6   Marginal Rate of Technical Substitution (MRTS)

Between point M and point N on the isoquant for 12 units of output (12Q), the marginal rate of technical substitution of labor for capital ($MRTS_{LK}$) equals 2.5. Between point N and point C, $MRTS_{LK} = \frac{1}{2}$. At point N, $MRTS_{LK} = 1$ (the absolute slope of the tangent to the isoquant at point N).

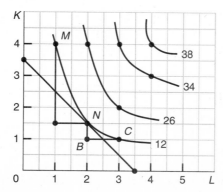

so that

$$MP_L/MP_K = - \Delta K/\Delta L = MRTS_{LK} \qquad \text{[6–4]}$$

Thus $MRTS_{LK}$ is equal to the absolute value of the slope of the isoquant and to the ratio of the marginal productivities.

Although we know that the absolute value of the slope of the isoquant or $MRTS_{LK}$ equals the ratio of MP_L to MP_K, we cannot infer from that the actual value of MP_L and MP_K. For example, at point N on the isoquant for 12Q in Figure 6–6, we know that $MRTS_{LK} = - \Delta K/\Delta L = MP_L/MP_K = 1$ (so that $MP_L = MP_K$), but we do not know what the actual (common) value of MP_L and MP_K is. Similarly, we know that between points N and C on the isoquant for 12Q, $MRTS_{LK} = - \Delta K/\Delta L = MP_L/MP_K = \frac{1}{2}$ (so that $MP_L = \frac{1}{2}MP_K$), but we do not know what the actual value of either marginal product is. They can, however, be calculated from Figure 6–6.

For example, we can find the value of MP_L and MP_K between points N and C on the isoquant for 12Q in Figure 6–6 by comparing point N (2L, 1.5K) and point C (3L, 1K) referring to 12Q to point B (2L, 1K) referring to 8Q (see Table 6–3). The rightward movement from point B to point C keeps capital constant at 1K and increases labor by 1L, and it results in an increase in output of 4Q (from 8Q to 12Q). Thus, $MP_L = 4$. On the other hand, the upward movement from point B to point N keeps labor constant at 2L and increases capital by $\frac{1}{2}K$, and it also results in an increase in output of 4Q. Thus, the $MP_K = 8$. With $MP_L = 4$ and $MP_K = 8$, $MP_L/MP_K = \frac{4}{8} = \frac{1}{2} = MRTS_{LK}$, as found earlier.

Within the economically relevant range, isoquants are not only negatively sloped but also convex to the origin. That is, as we move down along an isoquant, the absolute value of its slope or $MRTS_{LK}$ declines and the isoquant is convex (see Figure 6–6). The reason for this can best be explained by separating the movement down along an isoquant (say, from point N to point C along the isoquant for 12Q in Figure 6–6) into its two components: the movement to the right (from point B to point C) and the movement downward (from point N to point B). The increase in L with constant K (the movement from point B to point C) will lead to a decline in the MP_L since we are in stage II of production. In addition, the reduction in K (the movement from point N to point B), by itself, will cause the entire MP_L curve to shift down. Thus, MP_L declines for both reasons. On the other hand, by using less K and more L, the MP_K rises.[9] With the MP_L declining and the MP_K rising as we move down along an isoquant, the $MRTS_{LK} = MP_L/MP_K$ will fall and the isoquant is convex to the origin.[10]

---

[9]The reasoning is exactly the opposite as for the decline in MP_L.

[10]For a mathematical presentation of isoquants and their characteristics, see section A.8 of the Mathematical Appendix at the end of the book.

Economic Region of Production

The firm would not operate on the positively sloped portion of an isoquant because it could produce the same level of output with less capital and less labor. For example, the firm would not produce 34Q at point P in Figure 6–7 because it could produce 34Q by using the smaller quantity of labor and capital indicated by point R. Similarly, the firm would not produce 34Q at point S because it could produce 34Q at point T with less L and K. Since inputs are not free, the firm would not want to produce in the positively sloped range of isoquants.

Ridge lines separate the relevant (i.e., the negatively sloped) from the irrelevant (or the positively sloped) portions of the isoquants. In Figure 6–7, ridge line ORU joins points on the various isoquants where the isoquants have zero slope (and thus zero $MRTS_{LK}$). The isoquants are negatively sloped to the left of this ridge line and positively sloped to the right. This means that starting, for example, at point R on the isoquant for 34Q, if the firm used more labor it would also have to use more capital to remain on the same isoquant (compare point P to point R on the isoquant for 34Q). Starting from point R, if the firm used more labor with the same amount of capital, the level of output would fall (i.e., the firm would fall back to a lower isoquant; see the dashed horizontal line at K = 2.8 in Figure 6–7). The same is true at all other points on ridge line ORU. Therefore, the MP_L must be negative to the right of this ridge line. This corresponds to stage III of production for

FIGURE 6–7 **Economic Region of Production**

Isoquants are positively sloped to the right of ridge line ORU and to the left of or above ridge line OTU. The firm would never produce at a point such as P or S in the positively sloped portion of the isoquant because it could produce the same output with less of both inputs.

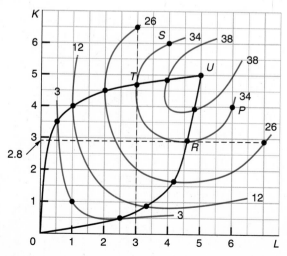

labor. Note that points on ridge line ORU specify the minimum quantity of capital required to produce the levels of output indicated by the various isoquants. Note also that at all points on this ridge line, $MRTS_{LK} = MP_L/MP_K = 0/MP_K = 0$.

On the other hand, ridge line OTU joins points where the isoquants have infinite slope (and thus infinite $MRTS_{LK}$). The isoquants are negatively sloped to the right of this ridge line and positively sloped to the left. This means that starting, for example, at point T on the isoquant for $34Q$, if the firm used more capital it would also have to use more labor to remain on the same isoquant (compare point S to point T on the isoquant for $34Q$). Starting at point T, if the firm used more capital with the same quantity of labor, the level of output would fall (i.e., the firm would fall back to a lower isoquant; see the dashed vertical line at $L = 3$ in Figure 6–7). The same is true at all other points on ridge line OTU. Therefore, the MP_K must be negative to the left of or above this ridge line. This corresponds to stage III of production for capital. Note that points on ridge line OTU indicate the minimum quantity of labor required to produce the levels of output indicated by the various isoquants. Note also that at all points on this ridge line, $MRTS_{LK} = MP_L/MP_K = MP_L/0 = $ infinity.

Thus, we conclude that the negatively sloped portion of the isoquants within the ridge lines represents the economic region of production. This refers to stage II of production for labor and capital, where the MP_L and the MP_K are both positive but declining. Producers will never want to operate outside this region. As a result, from this point on, whenever we will draw isoquants, we will usually show only their negatively sloped portion. Indeed, some special types of production functions have isoquants without positively sloped portions.

Fixed-Proportions Production Functions

So far, we have drawn isoquants as smooth curves, and this indicates that there are many different (really, an infinite number of) input combinations that can be used to produce any output level. There are cases, however, where inputs can only be combined in fixed proportions in production. In such a case, there would be no possibility of input substitution in production and the isoquants would be at a right angle, or L-shaped.

For example, Figure 6–8 shows that 10 units of output ($10Q$) can only be produced at point A with $2L$ and $1K$. Employing more labor will not change output since $MP_L = 0$ (the horizontal portion of the isoquant). Similarly, using more capital will not change output since $MP_K = 0$ (the vertical portion of the isoquant). Here, there is no possibility of substituting L for K in production and the $MRTS_{LK} = 0$. Production would only take place at the constant capital-labor ratio of $K/L = \frac{1}{2}$. A larger output can only be produced by increasing both labor and capital in the same proportion. For example, $20Q$ can be produced at point B by using $4L$ and $2K$ at the constant K/L ratio of $\frac{1}{2}$. Similarly, $30Q$ can only be produced at point C with $6L$ and $3K$ and $K/L = \frac{1}{2}$.

In the real world, some substitution of inputs in production is usually

FIGURE 6–8   **Fixed–Proportions Production Function**

When isoquants are at right angles, or L-shaped, inputs must be used in fixed proportions in production. Thus, 10 units of output (10Q) can only be produced at point A with 2L and 1K. Using more labor or capital would not change output. 20Q can only be produced with 4L and 2K (point B), and 30Q only with 6L and 3K (point C). Thus, output can only be produced at the constant or fixed capital-labor ratio or proportion of $K/L = \frac{1}{2}$.

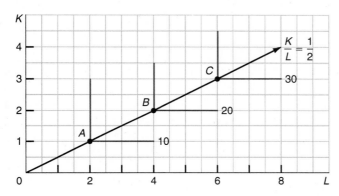

possible. The degree to which this is possible can be gathered from the curvature of the isoquants. In general, the smaller is the curvature of the isoquants, the more easily inputs can be substituted for each other in production. On the other hand, the greater the curvature (i.e., the closer are isoquants to right angles, or L-shape), the more difficult is substitution. To be able to easily substitute inputs in production is extremely important in the real world. For example, if petroleum had good substitutes, users could easily have switched to alternative energy sources when petroleum prices rose sharply in the fall of 1973. Their energy bill would then not have risen very much. As it was, good substitutes were not readily available (certainly not in the short run), and so most energy users faced sharply higher energy costs. As Example 2 shows, gasoline and driving time can also be substituted for each other, and this can be shown by isoquants.

Example 2

Trading Traveling Time for Gasoline Consumption on the Nation's Highways

Higher automobile speed reduces the driving time needed to cover a given distance but reduces gas mileage and thus increases gasoline consumption.[11]

---

[11]It has been estimated that reducing the speed limit on the nation's highways from 65 to 55 MPH reduced gasoline consumption by about 3%. See, "U.S. Progress in Energy Efficiency Is Halting," *New York Times*, February 27, 1989, p. 1.

The trade-off between traveling time and gasoline consumption can be represented by an isoquant such as the one in Figure 6–9. In the figure, the vertical axis measures hours of traveling time, while the horizontal axis measures gallons of gasoline consumed. Gasoline and travel time are thus the inputs into the production of automobile transportation. The isoquant in the figure refers to 600 miles of automobile transportation.

At 50 MPH, the 600 miles can be covered in 12 hours and with 16 gallons of gasoline, at 37.5 miles per gallon (point *A*). At 60 MPH, the 600 miles can be covered in 10 hours and with 20 gallons of gasoline, at 30 miles per gallon (point *B*). Driving at 60 MPH saves 2 hours of travel time (one scarce resource) but increases gasoline consumption by 4 gallons (another scarce resource). Thus, the trade-off or marginal rate of technical substitution (*MRTS*) of gasoline for travel time between point *A* and point *B* on the isoquant in Figure 6–9 is ½. At 66.7 MPH (assuming that the speed limit is above it), the 600 miles can be covered in 9 hours with 30 gallons of gasoline, at 20 miles per gallon (point *C*). Thus, the *MRTS* of gasoline for travel time between points *B* and *C* is ⅒.

In order to determine the most economical (i.e., the least cost) combination of gasoline and travel time to cover the 600 miles, we need to know the price of gasoline and the value of labor to the individual. This is addressed in the next chapter, where we take up costs of production. If the price of gasoline were to increase, the individual would want to substitute traveling time for gasoline (i.e., drive at a lower speed so as to increase gas mileage and save gasoline) to minimize the cost of traveling the 600 miles. This, too, will be

FIGURE 6–9   Speed Limit and Gasoline Consumption

Isoquant *ABC* shows the trade-off between traveling time and gasoline consumption. At 50 MPH, 600 miles can be covered in 12 hours and with 16 gallons of gasoline (point *A*). At 60 MPH, the 600 miles can be covered in 10 hours and with 20 gallons of gasoline (point *B*). At 66.7 MPH, it can be covered in 9 hours with 30 gallons (point *C*).

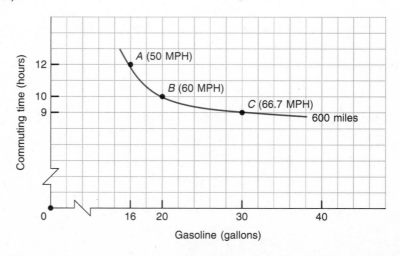

examined in greater detail in the next chapter. Note that there is also a trade-off between travel speed and safety (i.e., lower speeds increase travel time but save lives).

▲

6.5 CONSTANT, INCREASING, AND DECREASING RETURNS TO SCALE

The word "scale" refers to the long-run situation where all inputs are changed in the same proportion. The result might be constant, increasing, or decreasing returns. **Constant returns to scale** refers to the situation where output changes by the *same* proportion as inputs. For example, if all inputs are increased by 10%, output also rises by 10%. If all inputs are doubled, output also doubles. **Increasing returns to scale** refers to the case where output changes by a *larger* proportion than inputs. For example, if all inputs are increased by 10%, output increases by more than 10%. If all inputs are doubled, output more than doubles. Another name for increasing returns to scale is economies of scale. Finally, with **decreasing returns to scale,** output changes by a *smaller* proportion than inputs. Thus, increasing all inputs by 10% increases output by less than 10%, and doubling all inputs, less than doubles output.

Constant, increasing, and decreasing returns to scale can be shown by the spacing of the isoquants in Figure 6–10. The left panel shows constant returns

FIGURE 6–10   Constant, Increasing, and Decreasing Returns to Scale
The left panel shows constant returns to scale. Here, doubling inputs from 3L and 3K to 6L and 6K doubles output from 100 (point A along ray OD) to 200 (point B). Tripling inputs to 9L and 9K triples output to 300 (point C). Thus, OA = AB = BC along ray OD. The middle panel shows increasing returns to scale. Here, output can be doubled or tripled by less than doubling or tripling the quantity of inputs. Thus, OA > AB > BC and the isoquants become closer together. The right panel shows decreasing returns to scale. Here, output changes proportionately less than labor and capital and OA < AB < BC.

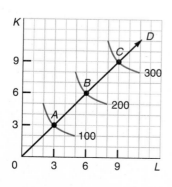
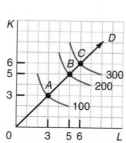
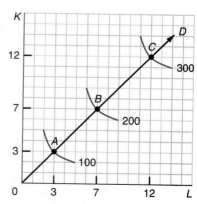

to scale. Here, doubling inputs from $3L$ and $3K$ to $6L$ and $6K$ doubles output from 100 (point A along ray OD) to 200 (point B). Tripling inputs from $3L$ and $3K$ to $9L$ and $9K$ triples output from 100 (point A) to 300 (point C). Thus, $OA = AB = BC$ along ray OD and we have constant returns to scale. The middle panel shows increasing returns to scale. Here, output can be doubled or tripled by less than doubling or tripling the quantity of inputs. Thus, $OA > AB > BC$ along ray OD and the isoquants are compressed closer together. Finally, the right panel shows decreasing returns to scale. In this case, in order to double and triple output we must more than double and triple the quantity of inputs. Thus, $OA < AB < BC$ and the isoquants move farther and farther apart. Note that in all three panels, the capital-labor ratio remains constant at $K/L = 1$ along ray OD.

Constant returns to scale make sense. We would expect two similar workers using identical machines to produce twice as much output as one worker using one machine. Similarly, we would expect the output of two identical plants employing an equal number of workers of equal skill to produce double the output of a single plant. Nevertheless, increasing and decreasing returns to scale are also possible.

Increasing returns to scale arise because, as the scale of operation increases, a greater division of labor and specialization can take place and more specialized and productive machinery can be used. With a large scale of operation, each worker can be assigned to perform only one repetitive task rather than numerous ones. Workers become more proficient in the performance of the single task and avoid the time lost in moving from one machine to another. The result is higher productivity and increasing returns to scale. At higher scales of operation, more specialized and productive machinery can also be used. For example, using a conveyor belt to unload a small truck may not be justified, but it greatly increases efficiency in unloading a whole train or ship. In addition, some physical properties of equipment and machinery also lead to increasing returns to scale. Thus, doubling the diameter of a pipeline more than doubles the flow, doubling the weight of a ship more than doubles its capacity to transport cargo, and so on. Firms also need fewer supervisors, fewer spare parts, and smaller inventories per unit of output as the scale of operation increases.

Decreasing returns to scale arise primarily because, as the scale of operation increases, it becomes ever more difficult to manage the firm effectively and coordinate the various operations and divisions of the firm. The channels of communications become more complex, and the number of meetings, the paper work, and telephone bills increase more than proportionately to the increase in the scale of operation. All of this makes it increasingly difficult to ensure that the managers' directives and guidelines are properly carried out. Thus, efficiency decreases. Decreasing returns to scale must be clearly distinguished from diminishing returns. *Decreasing returns to scale* refers to the long-run situation when all inputs are variable. On the other hand, *diminishing returns* refers to the short-run situation where at least one input is fixed. Diminishing returns in the short run is consistent with constant, increasing, or decreasing returns to scale in the long run.

In the real world, the forces for increasing and decreasing returns to scale often operate side by side. The forces for increasing returns to scale usually prevail at small scales of operation. The tendency for increasing returns to scale may be balanced by the tendency for decreasing returns to scale at intermediate scales of operation. Eventually, the forces for increasing returns to scale may be overcome by the forces for decreasing returns to scale at very large scales of operation. Whether this is true for a particular firm can only be determined empirically. In the real world, most firms seem to exhibit near constant returns to scale (see Table 6–7 in the appendix to this chapter). As Example 3 shows, however, General Motors faces strong decreasing returns to scale and wants to shrink.

Example 3
General Motors Decides Small Is Better

General Motors (GM), the largest corporation and automaker in the world, incurred losses of $2 billion in 1990 and an incredible $4.5 billion in 1991. These losses were the result of a bloated work force and management, low-capacity utilization, too many divisions and models, and high-cost suppliers. For a corporation that had been extolled as the epitome of a successful corporation in 1946, this was a dramatic decline indeed! During the postwar period, however, GM became the victim of managerial methods that had become outmoded and was unable to change. As the data on sales per employee in Table 6–3 seem to indicate, GM is too large and is facing strong decreasing returns to scale. Chrysler, on the other hand, can still expand to take advantage of increasing returns to scale. Ford, with the largest sales per employee, seems to be just about the right size.

As part of its reorganization plan to shrink in size in order to avoid decreasing returns to scale, GM announced in December 1991 that it was closing 21 plants and shedding 74,000 (50,000 blue-collar and 24,000 white-collar) workers from 1992 to 1995. The plants to be closed will eliminate GM's excess capacity of 2 million cars and trucks per year and leave GM with a 5 to 5.5 million capacity in its North American operation. It will also leave GM with about 30% to 32% of the U.S. car market—down from 46% in 1978 and 35% in 1991. The GM market share lost during the past decade, which is larger than the entire Chrysler operation today, was captured by Japanese automobile imports and production in the United States.

In 1992, GM brought the vice president and top purchasing officer from its highly successful and profitable European operation to its headquarters in Detroit. They were put in charge of the reorganization of the North American operation in the hope that they could duplicate their European success. The new team aims at streamlining management, eliminating redundant or irrelevant activities, developing models more quickly and manufacturing them more efficiently, increasing capacity utilization, and forging new and better

TABLE 6–3   Total World Sales, Employees, and Sales per Employee at General Motors, Ford, and Chrysler in 1991

	Sales (in billion dollars)	Employees (in thousands)	Sales per Employee (in thousand dollars)
General Motors	123.1	756	162.7
Ford	88.3	333	265.4
Chrysler	29.4	123	238.8

Source: The Economist, May 2, 1992, p. 78.

relationships with suppliers, dealers, and employees. The job of restructuring GM will not be easy; among the formidable roadblocks are institutional resistance to change, enormous size, and outdated management style. Just closing plants and reducing GM's size will not be sufficient. Nothing short of a complete change in corporate mentality is needed.

Sources: "Automobiles: GM Decides Smaller Is Better," *The Margin,* November/December 1988, p. 29, and "GM Posts Record '91 Loss of $4.45 Billion, Sends Tough Message to UAW on Closings," *New York Times,* February 25, 1992, p. 3.

6.6 TECHNOLOGICAL PROGRESS AND INTERNATIONAL COMPETITIVENESS

In this section, we examine the meaning and importance of technological progress and innovations in general and the crucial role they play in the international competitiveness of firms.

Meaning and Importance of Innovations

In our analyses so far, we have assumed a given technology. Over time, however, technological progress takes place. **Technological progress** refers to the development of new and better production techniques to make a given, improved, or an entirely new product. The introduction of innovations is the single most important determinant of a firm's long-term competitiveness at home and abroad. Innovations are basically of two types: **product innovation,** which refers to the introduction of new or improved products, and **process innovation,** the introduction of new or improved production processes. Contrary to popular belief, most innovations are incremental; that is, they involve more or less continuous small improvements in products or processes rather than a single, major technological breakthrough. Furthermore, most innovations involve the commercial utilization of ideas that may have been around for years. For example, it took a quarter of a century before firms (primarily

Japanese ones) were able to perfect the flat video screen (invented in the mid-1960s by George Heilmeier of RCA) and introduce the screens commercially in portable personal computers (PCs).

Innovations can be examined with isoquants. A new or improved product requires an entirely new isoquant map showing the various combinations of inputs to produce each level of output of the new or improved product. On the other hand, a process innovation can be shown by a shift toward the origin of the firm's given product isoquants, showing that each level of output can be produced with fewer inputs after the innovation than before. Unless a firm aggressively and continuously improves its product or production process, it will inevitably be overtaken by other more innovative firms. To be successful in today's world, firms must adopt a global competitive strategy, which means that they must continuously scout the world for new product ideas and processes. It is also crucial for firms to have a presence, first through exports and then by local production, in the world's major markets. Larger sales mean economies of scale in production and distribution, and they allow the firm to spend more on research and development and thus stay ahead of the competition.

The introduction of innovations is stimulated by strong domestic rivalry and geographic concentration—the former because it forces firms to constantly innovate or lose market share (and even risk being driven entirely out of the market), the latter because it leads to the rapid spread of new ideas and the development of specialized machinery and other inputs for the industry. Sharp domestic rivalry and great geographic concentration make Japanese firms in many high-tech industries fierce competitors in the world economy today.[12]

The risk of failure in introducing innovations is usually high. For example, eight of ten new products fail within a short time of their introduction. Even the most carefully introduced innovations can fail, as evidenced by the failure of RJR Nabisco's "smokeless cigarette" and Coca-Cola's change in 1985 of its 99-year-old recipe. In general, the introduction of a *new* product or concept (such as McDonald's hamburgers and Sony's Walkmans) is more likely to succeed than changing an existing product. Product innovations can also die because of poor planning and unexpected production problems. This happened, for example, to Weyerhauser. Encouraged by market testing that showed its diaper product was better than competitors' products and could be produced more cheaply, Weyerhauser introduced its UltraSoft diapers in 1990, but the product failed within a year because of unexpected production problems.[13]

---

[12]See, M. Porter, *The Competitive Advantage of Nations* (New York: The Free Press, 1990), and "How American Industry Stacks Up," *Fortune*, March 9, 1992, pp. 30–46.

[13]See, "Diaper's Failure Shows How Poor Plans, Unexpected Woes Can Kill New Products," *The Wall Street Journal*, October 9, 1990, p. B1.

Innovations and the International Competitiveness of U.S. Firms

Hardly a technological breakthrough during the past four decades, from TVs to robots, from copiers to fax machines, from semiconductors to flat video screens was not made by an American firm or laboratory. According to the **product cycle model,** however, firms that first introduce an innovation eventually lose their export market and even their domestic market to foreign imitators who pay lower wages and generally face lower costs. In the meantime, however, technologically leading firms introduce even more advanced products and technologies.

The problem is that the period during which firms can exploit the benefits of successful innovations is becoming shorter and shorter before foreign imitators take the market away. In fact, in many cases American discoveries such as the fax machine and the flat video screen were first introduced and exploited commercially by foreign (Japanese) firms. Although many American firms remain world leaders in their industries (e.g., Boeing in commercial aircraft, IBM in mainframe computers, Hewlett-Packard in laser printers, Gillette in razors, Coca-Cola in soft drinks, and McDonald's in fast food—to mention only a few), firms in many other industries such as steel, automobiles, consumer electronics, semiconductors, and portable PCs have lost or are losing to foreign competitors, especially the Japanese. One important reason for this is that American firms generally stress product innovation, whereas Japanese firms stress process innovations. Thus, even when American firms are the first to introduce a new product, Japanese firms are soon able to produce it better and more cheaply and in a few years outsell American competitors at home and abroad. This has happened in industry after industry from steel to textiles, consumer electronics, automobiles, and more recently, portable PCs. A great deal of international trade among industrial nations is now based on **intraindustry trade** in such differentiated products.

Often Japanese firms are prepared to sustain millions of dollars of losses over many years while striving to succeed. American managers and investors, on the other hand, generally have a much shorter time horizon and are excessively concerned with quarterly statements and profits. Japanese firms also face far greater domestic rivalries and geographic concentration than their American counterparts, and thus a greater stimulus to innovate. Furthermore, as Japanese firms gain global market share in many industries, their advantages become cumulative. Nevertheless, many American high-tech firms retain world leadership and others have shown that they are fully capable of regaining lost competitiveness, as Example 4 shows.[14]

---

[14]"In the Realm of Technology, Japan Seizes a Greater Role," *New York Times*, May 28, 1991, p. C1.

Example 4

How Xerox Lost and Regained International Competitiveness

The Xerox Corporation was the first to introduce the copying machine in 1959, based on its patented xerographic technology. Until 1970, Xerox had no competition and thus had little incentive to reduce manufacturing costs, improve quality, and increase customers' satisfaction. Even when Japanese firms entered the low end of the market with better and cheaper copiers in 1970 and began to take over this segment of the market, Xerox did not respond; instead, it concentrated on the mid and high ends of the market where profit margins were much higher. Xerox also used the profits from its copier business to expand into computers and office systems during the 1970s. It was not until 1979 that Xerox finally awakened to the seriousness of the Japanese threat. From so-called *competitive benchmarking* missions to Japan to compare relative production efficiency and product quality, Xerox was startled to find that Japanese competitors were producing copiers of higher quality at far lower costs and were positioning themselves to move up into the more profitable mid- and high-end segments of the market.

Faced with this life-threatening situation, Xerox, with the help of its Japanese subsidiary (Fuji Xerox), mounted a strong response that involved reorganization and integration of development and production and an ambitious companywide quality-control effort. Employee involvement was greatly increased, suppliers were brought into the early stages of product design, and inventories and the number of suppliers were greatly reduced. Constant benchmarking was then used to test progress in the companywide quality-control program and customer satisfaction. By taking these drastic actions, Xerox was able to reverse the trend toward loss of market share to Japanese competitors, even at the low segment of the market. Indeed, in 1991, Xerox had the biggest-selling high-speed paper copier not only in the United States but in Japan! The same turnaround was achieved by American textile firms during the second half of the 1980s by investing heavily in plant modernization.

Sources: The MIT Commission on Industrial Productivity, *Made in America* (Cambridge, Mass.: The MIT Press, 1989), pp. 270–277; "Xerox on the Move," *Forbes*, June 10, 1991, pp. 70–71; and "Japan Is Tough, But Xerox Prevails," *New York Times*, September 3, 1992, p. D1.

SUMMARY

1. *Production* refers to the transformation of resources or inputs into outputs of goods and services. A firm is an organization that combines and organizes resources for the purpose of producing goods and services for sale at a profit. In general, the aim of

firms is to maximize profits. Profits refer to the revenue of the firm from the sale of the output after all costs have been deducted. Inputs can be broadly classified into labor, capital, and land, and into fixed and variable. *Entrepreneurship* refers to the introduction of new technologies and products to exploit perceived profit opportunities. The time period during which at least one input is fixed is called the short run. In the long run, all inputs are variable.

2. The production function is a unique relationship between inputs and output. It can be represented by a table, graph, or equation showing the maximum output or total product (*TP*) of a commodity that can be produced per time period with each set of inputs. Average product (*AP*) is total product divided by the quantity of the variable input used. Marginal product (*MP*) is the change in total output per-unit change in the variable input. The *MP* is above the *AP* when *AP* is rising, *MP* is below *AP* when *AP* is falling, and *MP* = *AP* when *AP* is at a maximum. The declining portion of the *MP* curve reflects the law of diminishing returns. The range over which *AP* rises is stage I of production for the variable input. Stage II covers the range from maximum *AP* to where the *MP* of the input is zero. Stage III covers the range over which the *MP* of the variable input is negative.

3. An isoquant shows the various combinations of two inputs that can be used to produce a specific level of output. From the isoquant map, we can generate the total product curve of each input by holding the quantity of the other input constant.

4. Isoquants are negatively sloped in the economically relevant range, convex to the origin, and do not intersect. The absolute value of the slope of the isoquant is called the marginal rate of technical substitution (*MRTS*). This equals the ratio of the marginal product of the two inputs. As we move down along an isoquant the absolute value of its slope, or *MRTS*, declines and the isoquant is convex. Ridge lines separate the relevant (i.e., the negatively sloped) from the irrelevant (or positively sloped) portions of the isoquants. With right-angled, or L-shaped, isoquants, inputs can only be combined in fixed proportions in production.

5. Constant, increasing, and decreasing returns to scale refer to the situation where output changes, respectively, by the same, by a larger, and by a smaller proportion than do inputs. These can be shown by the spacing of isoquants. Increasing returns to scale arise because of specialization and division of labor and from using specialized machinery. Decreasing returns to scale arise primarily because as the scale of operation increases, it becomes more and more difficult to manage the firm and coordinate its operations and divisions effectively. In the real world, most industries seem to exhibit near-constant returns to scale.

6. The introduction of innovations is the single most important determinant of a firm's long-term competitiveness. Product innovations refer to the introduction of new or improved products, and process innovations refer to the introduction of new or improved production processes. The introduction of innovations is stimulated by taking a strong global view of competition as well as by the existence of strong domestic rivalry and geographic concentration. Many innovations die because of poor planning and unexpected production problems.

KEY TERMS

Production	Inputs	Fixed Inputs
Firm	Entrepreneurship	Variable Inputs

Short Run
Long Run
Production Function
Total Product (*TP*)
Average Product (*AP*)
Marginal Product (*MP*)
Law of Diminishing Returns
Stage I of Production
Stage II of Production

Stage III of Production
Isoquant
Marginal Rate of Technical
   Substitution (*MRTS*)
Ridge Lines
Constant Returns to Scale
Increasing Returns to Scale
Decreasing Returns to Scale
Technological Progress

Product Innovation
Process Innovation
Product Cycle Model
Intraindustry Trade
Cobb-Douglas Production
   Function
Output Elasticity of Labor
Output Elasticity of Capital
Homogeneous of Degree 1

REVIEW QUESTIONS

1. What does the total product curve look like if diminishing returns set in after the first unit of labor is employed?
2. Will all three stages of production exist if the total product curve is concave throughout? If not, which stages would be missing?
3. Do the production principles and theory presented in this chapter need to be changed if a production function exhibits only stage II of production (i.e., if stages I and III are missing)?
4. Would a rational producer be concerned with the average or the marginal product of an input in deciding whether or not to hire the input?
5. Which of the following points (5*L* and 7*K*, 3*L* and 9*K*, 4*L* and 5*K*, and 6*L* and 6*K*) cannot be on the same isoquant? Why?
6. If the marginal product of labor is 6 and the marginal rate of technical substitution between labor and capital is 1.5, what is the marginal product of capital?

7. Is the firm facing increasing, constant, or decreasing returns to scale if it expands the quantity of labor and capital used in production from 10*L* and 10*K* to 13*L* and 13*K*, and output increases from 256 units to 300 units? Why?
8. Can a firm have a production function that exhibits increasing, constant, and decreasing returns to scale at different levels of output? Explain.
9. Is technical efficiency sufficient to determine at what point on an isoquant a firm operates? Why?
10. Is diminishing returns to a single factor of production consistent with constant or nonconstant returns to scale?
11. What is meant by an innovation? What are the different types of innovations? What are some of the factors that determine the rate at which a firm introduces innovations?
12. What is the difference between technological progress and economies of scale?

PROBLEMS

1. From the following production function, showing the bushels of corn raised on one acre of land by varying the amount of labor employed (in man-years),

Labor	1	2	3	4	5	6
Output	8	20	30	34	34	30

   a. derive the average and the marginal product of labor.
   b. plot the total, the average, and the marginal product curves.
2. Plot again the total product curve of problem

1 on the assumption that labor time is infinitesimally divisible, and derive graphically the corresponding average and marginal product curves.

*3. a. On the *same set of axes* redraw the total, the average, and the marginal product curves of problem 2 and indicate the three stages of production for labor.
   b. Where on the total product and on the marginal product of labor curves does the law

---

* = Answer provided at end of book.

of diminishing returns begin to operate? What gives rise to the law of diminishing returns?

4. From the following production function,
   a. derive the isoquants for 8 units of output, $8Q$, $20Q$, $25Q$, $30Q$, and $34Q$.
   b. what is the relationship between Table 6–4 and the table in problem 1?

5. From the isoquant map of problem 4a, derive
   a. the total product curve for labor when the quantity of capital is held fixed at $K = 4$.
   b. the average and the marginal product curves for labor from the total product curve of 5a above.

6. a. From problem 4, redraw the isoquant for 20 units of output ($20Q$) and show how to measure the marginal rate of technical substitution of labor for capital (i.e., $MRTS_{LK}$) between the point where two units of labor and four units of capital (i.e., $2L$ and $4K$) are used (call this point M) and the point where ($3L$, $2K$) are used (call this point N). What is the $MRTS_{LK}$ at point N? At point C ($4L$, $1.5K$)?
   b. Find the value of the MP_L and MP_K for a movement from point N on the isoquant for $20Q$ and point N' ($4L$, $2K$) and N'' ($3L$, $3K$) on the isoquant for $25Q$, and show that $MRTS_{LK} = MP_L/MP_K$.
   c. Explain why the $MRTS_{LK}$ falls as we move down along the isoquant.

7. a. On the isoquant map of problem 4, draw the ridge lines.
   b. Explain why a firm would never produce below the lower ridge line or above the top ridge line.

*8. On the same set of axes draw two isoquants, one indicating that the two inputs must be combined in fixed proportions in production, and the other showing that inputs are perfect substitutes for each other.

9. If the price of gasoline is $1.50 per gallon and travel time is worth $6.00 per hour to the individual, determine at which speed the cost of traveling the 600 miles is minimum in Figure 6–9.

10. Does the production function of problem 4 exhibit constant, increasing, or decreasing returns to scale? Explain.

*11. Suppose that the production function for a commodity is given by

$$Q = 10\sqrt{LK}$$

where Q is the quantity of output, L is the quantity of labor, and K is the quantity of capital:
   a. Indicate whether this production function exhibits constant, increasing, or decreasing returns to scale.
   b. Does the production function exhibit diminishing returns? If so, when does the law of diminishing returns begin to operate? Could we ever get negative returns?

*12. Indicate whether each of the following statements is true or false and give the reason.
   a. A student preparing for an examination should not study after reaching diminishing returns.
   b. If large and small firms operate in the same industry, we must have constant returns to scale.

TABLE 6–4 Production Function with Two Variable Inputs

Capital	(K)	6	6	18	25	30	30	25	
		5	8	20	30	34	34	30	
		4	8	20	30	34	34	30	Q
		3	6	18	25	30	30	25	
		2	4	13	20	25	25	20	
↑		1	1	5	7	8	8	7	
K		0	1	2	3	4	5	6	
			L →			Labor		(L)	

APPENDIX   THE COBB-DOUGLAS PRODUCTION FUNCTION

In this appendix, we present the Cobb-Douglas production function. This is the simplest and most widely used production function in empirical work today. We begin with the formula, which is followed by a simple illustration. Next we consider the methods available to empirically estimate the Cobb-Douglas production function and some of the difficulties involved. We conclude with some empirical results.

The Formula

The formula for the **Cobb-Douglas production function** is

$$Q = AL^{\alpha}K^{\beta} \qquad\qquad [6\text{--}5]$$

where Q = output in physical units, L = quantity of labor, and K = quantity of capital A, α (alpha), and β (beta) are positive parameters estimated in each case from the data. The parameter A refers to technology. The more advanced the technology, the greater is the value of A. The parameter α refers to the percentage increase in Q for a 1% increase in L, while holding K constant. Thus, α is the **output elasticity of labor.** For example, if $\alpha = 0.7$, this means that a 1% increase in the quantity of labor used (while holding the quantity of capital constant) leads to a 0.7% increase in output. Thus, the output elasticity of labor (α) is 0.7. Similarly, the parameter β refers to the percentage increase in Q for a 1% increase in K, while holding L constant. Thus, β is the **output elasticity of capital.** For example, if $\beta = 0.3$, this means that a 1% increase in K, while holding L constant, leads to a 0.3% increase in Q. Thus, the output elasticity of K (β) is 0.3.

In the above example, $\alpha + \beta = 0.7 + 0.3 = 1$. Thus, we have constant returns to scale. That is, a 1% increase in both L and K leads to a 1% increase in Q. Specifically, a 1% increase in L, by itself, leads to a 0.7% increase in Q, and a 1% increase in K, by itself, leads to a 0.3% increase in Q. Thus, with an increase of both L and K by 1%, Q increases by a total of 1% also and we have constant returns to scale. Another name for constant returns to scale is **homogeneous of degree 1.**

On the other hand, if $\alpha + \beta > 1$, we have increasing returns to scale. That is, a 1% increase in L and K leads to a greater than 1% increase in Q. For example, if $\alpha = 0.8$ and $\beta = 0.3$, a 1% increase in L and K leads to a $0.8 + 0.3 = 1.1\%$ increase in Q. Finally, if $\alpha + \beta < 1$, we have decreasing returns to scale (i.e., an increase in L and K by 1% leads to an increase in Q of less than 1%).

Illustration

Suppose $A = 10$, $\alpha = \beta = \frac{1}{2}$, and $\overline{K} = 4$ and is held constant (so that we are dealing with the short run). By substituting these values into equation [6–5], we get

$$Q = 10L^{1/2}4^{1/2} = 10\sqrt{4}\sqrt{L} = 20\sqrt{L} \qquad\qquad [6\text{--}5A]$$

By then substituting alternative quantities of L used in production into equation [6–5A], we derive the total product (TP) schedule, and from it, the average product of labor (AP_L) and the marginal product of labor (MP_L) schedules. The results are given in Table 6–5.

Plotting the TP, the AP_L, and the MP_L schedules of Table 6–5 as Figure 6–11, we see that the Cobb-Douglas production function exhibits only stage II of production. That is, the AP_L and the MP_L decline from the very start (i.e., the law of diminishing

TABLE 6–5   Total, Average, and Marginal Product of Labor

L	TP	AP_L	MP_L
0	0	. . .	. . .
1	20.00	20.00	20.00
2	28.28	14.14	8.28
3	34.64	11.55	6.36
4	40.00	10.00	5.36
5	44.72	8.94	4.72

FIGURE 6–11   Total, Average, and Marginal Product of Labor for the Cobb-Douglas Production Function

The figure shows the TP, the AP_L, and the MP_L schedules given in Table 6–5. From the figure, we see that the Cobb-Douglas production function exhibits only stage II of production. That is, the AP_L and the MP_L decline from the very start and the MP_L never becomes negative. Note that the MP_L is plotted between the various quantities of labor used and capital is held constant at $\overline{K} = 4$.

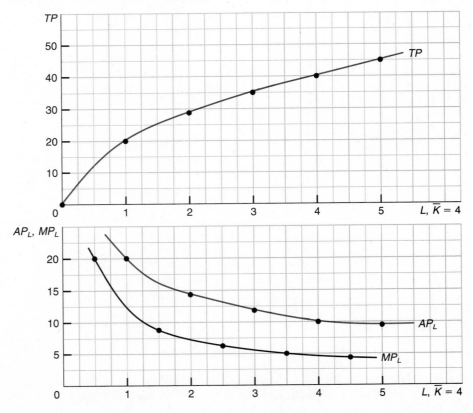

TABLE 6–6   Production in the Long Run

L	K	$10\sqrt{(L)(K)}$	Q
0	0	$10\sqrt{(0)(0)}$	0
1	1	$10\sqrt{(1)(1)}$	10
2	2	$10\sqrt{(2)(2)}$	20
3	3	$10\sqrt{(3)(3)}$	30
4	4	$10\sqrt{(4)(4)}$	40
5	5	$10\sqrt{(5)(5)}$	50

returns begins to operate with the first unit of L used) and the MP_L never becomes negative. Note that the MP_L is plotted between the various quantities of labor used. The AP_L and the MP_L are functions of or depend only on the K/L ratio. That is, they remain the same regardless of how much L and K are used in production as long as the K/L ratio remains the same (as along any given ray from the origin).[15]

In the long run, both L and K are variable. Thus,

$$Q = 10L^{1/2}K^{1/2} = 10\sqrt{L}\,\sqrt{K} = 10\sqrt{LK} \qquad \text{[6–5B]}$$

Since $\alpha + \beta = 0.5 + 0.5 = 1$ in this case, we have constant returns to scale. This is shown in Table 6–6. Here, output grows at the same rate as the rate of increase in both inputs. For example, doubling the quantity of labor and capital used, from 1 to 2 units, doubles output from 10 to 20 units. Increasing L and K by 50%, from 2 to 3 units, increases Q by 50% from 20 to 30 units, and so on.

We can also define the isoquants for this Cobb-Douglas production function. For example, the isoquant for $50Q$ can be defined by substituting 50 for Q in equation [6–5B]. By then substituting various quantities of labor into the resulting equation, we get the corresponding quantities of capital required to produce the $50Q$:

$$\begin{aligned} 50 &= 10\sqrt{LK} \\ 5 &= \sqrt{LK} \\ 25 &= LK \\ 25/L &= K \end{aligned} \qquad \text{[6–5C]}$$

Thus, if $L = 10$, $K = 2.5$; if $L = 5$, $K = 5$; if $L = 2.5$, $K = 10$, and so on. Other isoquants can be similarly derived. Isoquants are parallel along any ray from the origin and are equally spaced to reflect constant returns to scale. If, in addition, the wage rate (w) equals the rental price of capital (r), the slope of the isocost lines is $w/r = -1$, and the expansion path is a straight line through the origin with $K/L = 1$. This is shown in Figure 6–12.

Empirical Estimation

One method of estimating the parameters of the Cobb-Douglas production function (i.e., A, α, and β) applies statistical (i.e., regression) analysis to *time series data* on the

---

[15]This is proved in more advanced texts.

FIGURE 6–12   Expansion Path for the Cobb-Douglas Production Function

If $\alpha = \beta = \frac{1}{2}$ so that $\alpha + \beta = 1$, the Cobb-Douglas production function exhibits constant returns to scale. Isoquants are parallel along any ray from the origin and are equally spaced to reflect constant returns to scale. If $w = r$, the slope of the isocost lines is $w/r = -1$, and the expansion path is a straight line through the origin with $K/L = 1$.

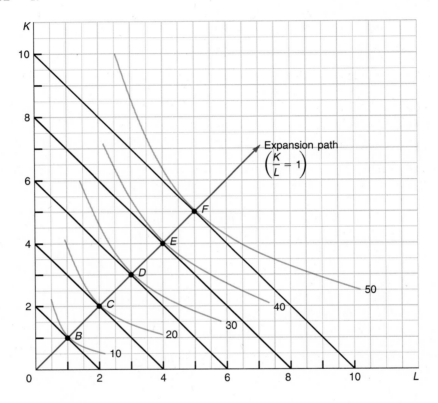

inputs used and the output produced.[16] For example, the researcher may collect data on the number of automobiles produced by an automaker in each year from 1950 to 1993 and on the quantity of labor and capital used in each year to produce the automobiles. The data are usually transformed into natural logarithms (indicated by the symbol ln) and the regression analysis is conducted on the transformed data. The form of the estimated Cobb-Douglas production function is then

$$\ln Q = \ln A + \alpha \ln L + \beta \ln K \qquad \text{[6–5D]}$$

The researcher thus obtains an estimate of the value of $\ln A$, α, and β.[17] Of primary interest to the researcher is the value of α and β.[18]

---

[16]For a general discussion of regression analysis, see the appendix to Chapter 5.

[17]The value of parameter A can then be obtained by finding the antilog of $\ln A$.

[18]In Cobb-Douglas time series estimates, technological progress must also be accounted for. This is usually accomplished by including time (t) as an additional explanatory variable in equation [6–5D].

Another method of estimating the value of A, α, and β is by regression analysis using *cross-section data*. In this case, the researcher collects data for a given year (or other time unit) for each of many producers or firms in a particular industry on the quantity of labor and capital used and the output produced. That is, instead of collecting data for one firm over many years (time series), the researcher now collects data for a given year for many firms in the same industry (cross section). As in the previous case, the researcher usually first transforms the data into natural logarithms and then estimates equation [6–5D] by regression analysis to obtain the values of parameters A, α, and β. Once again the researcher is primarily interested in the value of α and β. Table 6–7 in the section that follows presents the values of α and β estimated for various U.S. manufacturing industries for the year 1957.[19]

Input-output relationships can also be obtained from engineering studies. All of these methods (i.e., regression analysis using time series or cross-section data and engineering studies) face difficulties. One of these is that we must assume that the best production techniques are used by all firms at all times. Due to a lack of information or erroneous decisions, this may not be the case. Another difficulty arises in the measurement of the capital input, since machinery and equipment are of different types, ages (vintage), and productivities. A further shortcoming characteristic of engineering studies is that they typically cover only some production activities of the firm. Despite these and other problems, numerous studies have been conducted over the years using these different approaches. They have provided very useful information on production for the entire economy and for various industries.

Example 5

▽ **Output Elasticity of Labor and Capital in U.S. Manufacturing**

Table 6–7 reports the estimated output elasticities of labor (α) and capital (β) for various U.S. manufacturing industries in 1957. A value of $\alpha = 0.90$ for furniture means that a 1% increase in the quantity of labor used (holding K constant) results in a 0.90% increase in the quantity produced of furniture. A value of $\beta = 0.21$ means that a 1% increase in K (holding L constant) increases Q by 0.21%. Increasing both L and K by 1% increases Q by $0.90 + 0.21 = 1.11\%$. This means that the production of furniture is subject to increasing returns to scale.

The values of α and β reported in Table 6–7 were estimated by regression analysis using cross-section data for many firms in each industry for the year 1957. The value of α ranges from 0.51 for food and beverages to 0.96 for leather. This is the output elasticity of production and nonproduction workers combined. The value of β ranges from 0.08 for leather to 0.56 for food and beverages. Note that most industries exhibit close-to-constant returns to scale (i.e., the value of $\alpha + \beta$ is close to 1).

---

[19]Data for many firms in each of the various U.S. manufacturing industries for the year 1957 were used to estimate the value of α and β for each industry. Thus, these are cross-section estimates.

TABLE 6–7   Estimated Output Elasticity of Labor (α) and Capital (β) in U.S. Manufacturing

Industry	α	β	$\alpha + \beta$
Furniture	0.90	0.21	1.11
Chemicals	0.89	0.20	1.09
Printing	0.62	0.46	1.08
Food, beverages	0.51	0.56	1.07
Rubber, plastics	0.58	0.48	1.06
Instruments	0.84	0.20	1.04
Lumber	0.65	0.39	1.04
Apparel	0.91	0.13	1.04
Leather	0.96	0.08	1.04
Electrical machinery	0.66	0.37	1.03
Nonelectrical machinery	0.62	0.40	1.02
Transport equipment	0.79	0.23	1.02
Textiles	0.88	0.12	1.00
Paper pulp	0.56	0.42	0.98
Primary metals	0.59	0.37	0.96
Petroleum	0.64	0.31	0.95

Source: J. Moroney, "Cobb-Douglas Production Functions and Returns to Scale in U.S. Manufacturing Industry," *Western Economic Journal*, December 1967.

COSTS OF PRODUCTION

In this chapter, we consider the costs of production of the firm and their relationship to production theory (which was discussed in Chapter 6). After examining the nature of costs and how firms should combine inputs to mini-mize costs, we derive short-run and long-run cost curves for the firm. These will be utilized to determine the profit-maximizing level of output for a per-fectly competitive firm in Chapter 8 and for imperfectly competitive firms in Chapters 9–12. This chapter also introduces dynamic changes in costs with learning curves and the international "sourcing" of inputs by firms aimed at keeping costs down. The several real-world examples highlight the importance and relevance of the analysis. In the optional appendix, we examine in a more technical way the relationship between production and costs and the effect of input-price changes on production and costs.

7.1 THE NATURE OF PRODUCTION COSTS

From the firm's production function (showing the input combinations that the firm can use to produce various levels of output) and the price of inputs, we can derive the firm's cost functions. These show the minimum costs that the firm would incur in producing various levels of output. For simplicity, we assume that the firm is too small to affect the prices of the inputs it uses. Thus, the prices of inputs remain constant regardless of the quantity demanded by the firm. (The determination of input prices when the firm does and does not affect input prices is discussed in Part Five, Chapters 13–15.)

In economics, costs include explicit and implicit costs. **Explicit costs** are the actual out-of-pocket expenditures of the firm to purchase or hire the inputs it requires in production. These expenditures include the wages to hire labor, interest on borrowed capital, rent on land and buildings, and the expenditures on raw and semifinished materials. **Implicit costs,** on the other hand, refer to the value of the inputs owned and used by the firm in its own production processes. The value of these owned inputs must be imputed or estimated from what these inputs could earn in their best alternative use.

Implicit costs include the maximum wages that the entrepreneur could earn in working for someone else in a similar capacity (say, as the manager of another firm), and the highest return that the firm could obtain from investing its capital elsewhere and renting out its land and other inputs to others. The inputs owned and used by the firm in its own production processes are not free to the firm, even though the firm can use them without any actual or explicit expenditures. Accountants traditionally include only actual expenditures in costs, whereas economists always include both explicit and implicit costs.[1]

The cost to a firm in using any input is what the input could earn in its best alternative use (outside the firm). This is true for inputs purchased or hired by the firm as well as for inputs owned and used by the firm in its own production. For example, a firm must pay wages of $20,000 per year to one of its employees if that is the amount the worker would earn in his or her best alternative occupation in another firm. If this firm attempted to pay less, the worker would simply seek employment in the other firm. Similarly, if the entrepreneur could earn more in managing another firm than in directing his or her own firm, it would not make much economic sense to continue to be self-employed.[2] Thus, for a firm to retain any input for its own use, it must include as a cost what the input could earn in its best alternative use or employment. This is the **alternative** or **opportunity cost doctrine.** Similarly, the cost of attending college includes not only the explicit cost of tuition, books, and so on, but also the foregone earnings of not working (see Example 1).

Costs are also classified into private and social. **Private costs** are the explicit and the implicit opportunity costs incurred by *individuals and firms* in the process of producing goods and services. **Social costs** are the costs incurred by *society* as a whole. Social costs are higher than private costs when firms are able to escape some of the economic costs of production. For example, a firm dumping untreated waste into the air imposes a cost on society (in the form of higher cleaning bills, more breathing ailments, and so on) that is not reflected in the costs of the firm. Private costs can be made equal to social costs by public regulation that requires the firm to install antipollution equipment. In this and subsequent chapters, we will be primarily concerned with private costs. Social costs will be examined in detail in Chapter 17.

 ### Example 1
The Cost of Attending College

Table 7–1 reports the annual explicit and implicit costs of attending a private college during the 1992–1993 academic year. Explicit costs include tuition,

TABLE 7–1 Annual Cost of Attending a Private College

Explicit costs		
Tuition	$12,000	
Room	3,300	
Meal plan	2,200	
Books and supplies	500	
Subtotal		$18,000
Implicit costs		
Foregone earnings	$12,000	
Foregone interest		
($9,000 at 5%)	450	
Subtotal		$12,450
Total costs		$30,450

Source: Admission Office, Fordham University.

room, meals, and books and supplies. Implicit costs include the student's foregone earnings by attending college rather than entering the labor force. It also includes the foregone interest on half of the explicit costs, if they have to be paid at the beginning of each semester (since these funds could have been lent at the going interest rate).

The annual implicit costs of attending college are nearly as high as the explicit costs. Note that the implicit cost of $450 is 5% of $9,000 which is half of the total explicit costs of $18,000 for the entire year (if we assume that they have to be paid at the beginning of each semester). Attending a public college is cheaper only to the extent that tuition for state residents in many states is about $3,500 (so that the total costs of attending a public college are about $22,000). For out-of-state residents, the annual cost of attending a public college may be close to $25,000 or $26,000. Of course, these costs would be lower if the student continued to live at home while attending college. Most independent colleges and universities also provide financial aid to a large minority of students from low-income families, but this usually amounts to less than half of tuition. The annual total cost of attending an Ivy League College is more than $35,000, since tuition alone exceeds $15,000 per year.

Sources: "Colleges Caught in Tuition Student-Aid Squeeze," *The New York Times,* April 5, 1989, p. B12, and "State College Tuition Soars While Private School Costs Top $23,000 a Year," *Wall Street Journal,* March 26, 1992, p. A1.

▲

7.2 OPTIMAL COMBINATION OF INPUTS

Since cost functions and cost curves provide the minimum cost of producing various levels of output, we must examine the process of cost minimization by the firm. This involves defining isocost lines and the optimal combination of inputs in production. We will then examine how the firm minimizes costs of production in the short run and in the long run.

Isocost Lines

Suppose that a firm uses only labor and capital in production. Then the total cost (TC) of the firm for the use of a specific quantity of labor and capital is equal to the price of labor (w or the wage rate) times the quantity of labor hired (L), plus the price of capital (r or the rental price of capital) times the quantity of capital rented (K). If the firm owns the capital, r is the rent foregone from not renting out the capital (such as machinery) to others. The total cost of the firm can thus be expressed as

$$TC = wL + rK \qquad\qquad [7\text{--}1]$$

That is, the total cost (TC) is equal to the amount that the firm spends on labor (wL) plus the amount that the firm spends on capital (rK).

Given the wage rate of labor (w), the rental price of capital (r), and a particular total cost (TC), we can define an **isocost line** or equal-cost line. This shows the various combinations of labor and capital that the firm can hire or rent for the given total cost. For example, for $TC_1 = \$80$, $w = \$10$, and $r = \$10$, the firm could either hire 8L or rent 8K, or any combination of L and K shown on isocost line RS in the left panel of Figure 7–1. For each unit of capital the firm gives up, it can hire one more unit of labor. Thus, the slope of isocost line RS is -1.

By subtracting wL from both sides of equation [7–1] and then dividing by r, we get the general equation of an isocost line in the following more useful form:

$$K = TC/r - (w/r)L \qquad\qquad [7\text{--}2]$$

The first term on the right-hand side of equation [7–2] is the vertical or Y-intercept of the isocost line, and $-w/r$ is the slope. Thus, for $TC_1 = \$80$ and $w = r = \$10$, the vertical or Y-intercept is $TC_1/r = \$80/\$10 = 8K$, and the slope is $-w/r = -\$10/\$10 = -1$ (see isocost line RS in the left panel of Figure 7–1).

A different total cost will define a different but parallel isocost line, while a different relative price of an input will define an isocost line with a different slope. For example, an increase in total expenditures to $TC_2 = \$100$ with unchanged $w = r = \$10$ will generate isocost line $R'S'$ in the right panel of Figure 7–1. The vertical or Y-intercept of isocost line $R'S'$ is equal to $TC_2/r = \$100/\$10 = 10K$ and its slope is $-w/r = -\$10/\$10 = -1$. With $TC_1 = \$80$ and $r = \$10$ but $w = \$5$, we have isocost line RT with slope of $-\frac{1}{2}$.

Note the symmetry between the isocost line and the budget line. In section 3.4 we defined the *budget line* as showing the various combinations of two commodities that a consumer could purchase with his or her given money income. The *isocost line* shows the various combinations of two inputs that a

FIGURE 7–1   Isocost Lines

With capital measured along the vertical axis, for $TC_1 = \$80$ and $w = r = \$10$, the Y-intercept of the isocost line is $TC_1/r = \$80/\$10 = 8K$ and the slope is $-w/r = -\$10/\$10 = -1$. This gives budget line RS in the left and right panels. With $TC_2 = \$100$ and unchanged $w = r = \$10$, we have isocost line $R'S'$, with Y-intercept of $TC_2/r = \$100/\$10 = 10K$ and slope of $-w/r = -\$10/\$10 = -1$ in the right panel. With $TC_1 = \$80$ and $r = \$10$ but $w = \$5$, we have isocost line RT with slope of $-\frac{1}{2}$.

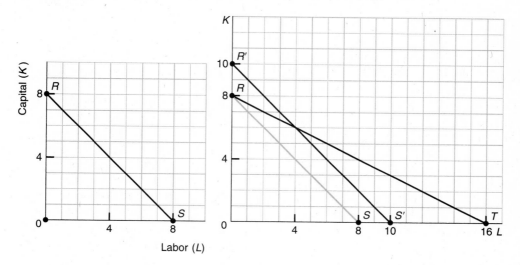

firm can hire at a given total cost. However, whereas an individual's income is usually given and fixed over a specific period of time (so that we usually deal with only one budget line), a firm's total costs of production vary with output (so that we have a whole family of isocost lines).[3]

Least-Cost Input Combination

To minimize the cost of producing a given level of output, the firm must produce at the point where an isocost line is tangent to the isoquant. For example, the left panel of Figure 7–2 shows that the minimum cost of producing four units of output ($4Q$) is \$80 (isocost line RS). This is the lowest isocost line that will allow the firm to reach the isoquant for $4Q$. The firm must produce at point D and use $4L$ (at the cost of $wL = \$40$) and $4K$ (at the cost of $rK = \$40$). This is the least-cost input combination. Any other input combination results in higher total costs for the firm to produce four units of output (i.e., to reach isoquant $4Q$).

---

[3]A consumer's budget line can also change over a given period of time because consumers can save or borrow as well as vary the hours worked and type of job. However, these possibilities are usually not considered in order to keep the analysis simple.

FIGURE 7–2   Optimal Input Combination

The left panel shows that RS is the lowest isocost with which the firm can reach isoquant $4Q$. The firm minimizes the cost of producing four units of output at point D by using $4L$ and $4K$ at a total cost of $80. The right panel shows that isoquant $4Q$ is the highest one that the firm can reach with isocost line RS. Thus, the firm maximizes output with a total cost of $80 by producing at point D and using $4L$ and $4K$.

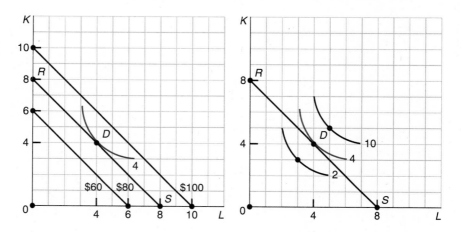

Minimizing the cost of producing a given level of output is equivalent to maximizing the output for a given cost outlay. The right panel of Figure 7–2 shows that the maximum output or highest isoquant that the firm could reach at the total cost of $80 (i.e., with isocost line RS) is the isoquant for $4Q$. Thus, the condition for cost minimization is equivalent to the condition for output maximization. For both, the firm must produce where an isoquant and an isocost are tangent (point D in both panels of Figure 7–2). The concept of output maximization for a given cost outlay for a producer is completely analogous to the concept of consumer utility maximization for a given budget constraint, which was discussed in section 3.5.

At the point of tangency, the (absolute) slope of the isoquant or marginal rate of technical substitution of labor for capital is equal to the (absolute) slope of the isocost line. That is,

$$MRTS_{LK} = w/r \qquad\qquad [7\text{–}3]$$

Since the $MRTS_{LK} = MP_L/MP_K$, we can rewrite the **least-cost input combination** as

$$MP_L/MP_K = w/r \qquad\qquad [7\text{–}3A]$$

Cross multiplying, we get

$$MP_L/w = MP_K/r \qquad\qquad [7\text{–}3B]$$

Equation [7–3B] indicates that to minimize production costs (or maximize output for a given total cost), the extra output or marginal product per dollar spent on labor must be equal to the marginal product per dollar spent on capital. If $MP_L = 5$, $MP_K = 4$, and $w = r$, the firm would not be maximizing output or minimizing costs since it is getting more extra output for a dollar spent on labor than on capital. To maximize output or minimize costs, the firm would have to hire more labor and rent less capital. As the firm does this, the MP_L declines and the MP_K increases (since the firm is in stage II of production for L and K). The process would have to continue until condition [7–3B] held. If w were higher than r, the MP_L would have to be proportionately higher than the MP_K for condition [7–3B] to hold.

The same general condition would have to hold to minimize production costs, no matter how many inputs the firm uses. That is, the MP per dollar spent on each input would have to be the same for all inputs. Another way of stating this is that, for costs to be minimized, an additional or marginal unit of output should cost the same whether it is produced with more labor or more capital.[4]

Cost Minimization in the Long Run and in the Short Run

We have seen in the left panel of Figure 7–2 that the minimum cost of producing four units of output ($4Q$) is $80 when the firm uses four units of labor ($4L$) at $10 per unit and four units of capital ($4K$) at $10 per unit (point D, where the isoquant for $4Q$ is tangent to the isocost for $80). This is repeated in Figure 7–3. Figure 7–3 also shows that in the long run (when both L and K can be varied), the firm can produce $10Q$ with $5L$ and $5K$ at the *minimum* total cost of $100 (point H, where the isoquant for $10Q$ is tangent to the isocost for $100). Points D and H can also be interpreted as the points of maximum output for cost outlays of $80 and $100, respectively. Note that this production function exhibits strong economies of scale (i.e., $4L$ and $4K$ produce $4Q$, while $5L$ and $5K$ produce $10Q$!).

If capital were fixed at $4K$ (in the short run), the *minimum cost* of producing $10Q$ would be higher, or $110, because the firm would have to use $7L$ and $4K$ (point V, where the isoquant for $10Q$ *crosses* the isocost for $110). Thus, the minimum cost of producing a given level of output is lower in the long run when both L and K are variable than in the short run when only L is variable. Note that at point V, the $MRTS_{LK} < w/r$. This means that the rate at which L can be substituted for K *in production* is smaller than the rate at which L can be substituted for K *in the market*. Thus, total costs can be reduced in the long run by using less labor and more capital in production. But this is impossible in the short run. As Example 2 shows, total costs would also be higher if government regulation prevented the attainment of the long-run cost minimization point.

In the next section, we derive short-run cost curves. These show the mini-

---

[4]For a mathematical presentation of cost minimization using rudimentary calculus, see section A.9 of the Mathematical Appendix at the end of the book.

FIGURE 7–3   Long-Run and Short-Run Cost Minimization

Starting from point D, the firm minimizes the long-run cost of producing 10Q at point H, where isoquant 10Q is tangent to the isocost line for $100 and the firm uses 5L and 5K. If capital is fixed at 4K, the firm minimizes the short-run cost of producing 10Q by using 7L and 4K (point V, where the isoquant for 10Q crosses the isocost line for $110).

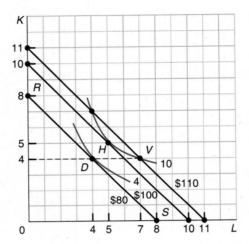

mum cost of producing the various levels of output when at least one input (here, capital) is fixed. Costs are minimized in the sense just discussed. In the section following the next, we derive long-run cost curves. These show the minimum cost (in the sense discussed) of producing various levels of output when all inputs are variable.

Example 2

 The Least-Cost Combination of Gasoline and Driving Time

Figure 7–4 repeats the isoquant of Figure 6–9, showing the various combinations of gasoline consumption and driving time required to cover 600 miles. If the price of gasoline is $1.50 per gallon and the opportunity cost of driving time is $6.00 per hour, the minimum total cost for the trip is $90. This is given by point B, where the isocost line (with absolute slope of $1.50/$6.00 = ¼) is tangent to the isoquant. Thus, to minimize traveling cost, the individual would have to drive 10 hours at 60 MPH and use 20 gallons of gasoline. The individual would spend $30 on gasoline (20 gallons at $1.50 per gallon) and incur an opportunity cost of $60 for travel time (10 hours of driving at $6.00 per hour), for a total cost of $90 for the trip.

If the government set the speed limit at 50 MPH, the trip would require

FIGURE 7–4 The Minimum Cost of a Trip

The minimum cost for the trip is $90 and is given at point *B*, where the isoquant is tangent to the isocost. The individual spends $30 on gasoline (20 gallons at $1.50 per gallon) and $60 in driving time (10 hours at $6.00 per hour).

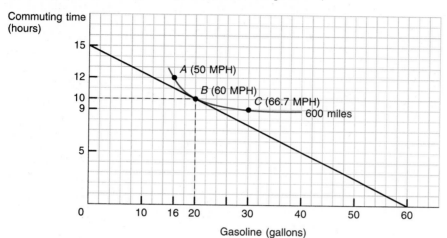

16 gallons of gasoline and 12 hours of driving time (point *A*). The total cost of the trip would then be $24 for gasoline (16 gallons at $1.50 per gallon) plus $72 for the driving time (12 hours at $6.00 per hour), or $96. Thus, enforcing the 50 MPH speed limit saves gasoline but increases driving time and the total cost of the trip.

7.3 THEORY OF COST IN THE SHORT RUN

In this section, we examine the theory of cost in the short run. We first define fixed, variable, and total costs and draw these total cost curves. We then define average fixed cost, average variable cost, average total cost, and marginal cost and draw these per-unit cost curves. Finally, we show how per-unit cost curves can be derived graphically from the corresponding total cost curves.

Total Costs

In the short run, some inputs are fixed and some are variable, and this leads to fixed and variable costs. **Total fixed costs (*TFC*)** are the total obligations of the firm per time period for all fixed inputs. These include payments for renting the plant and equipment (or the depreciation on plant and equipment if the firm owns them), most kinds of insurance, property taxes, and some salaries (such as those of top management, which are fixed by contract and must be paid over the life of the contract whether the firm produces or not). Fixed costs are sometimes referred to as *sunk costs*. **Total variable costs (TVC)** are the total obligations of the firm per time period for all the variable inputs of the firm. These include payments for raw materials, fuels, most types of labor, excise taxes, and so on. **Total costs (TC)** equal TFC plus TVC.

Within the limits imposed by the given plant, the firm can vary its output in the short run by varying the quantity of the variable inputs used per period of time. This gives rise to TFC, TVC, and TC schedules and curves. These show, respectively, the *minimum* fixed, variable, and total costs of producing the various levels of output in the short run. In defining these cost schedules and curves, all inputs are valued at their opportunity cost, which includes both explicit and implicit costs.

Table 7–2 presents hypothetical TFC, TVC, and TC schedules. These schedules are then plotted in Figure 7–5. From Table 7–2, we see that TFC are $30 regardless of the level of output. This is reflected in Figure 7–5 in the horizontal TFC curve at the level of $30. TVC are zero when output is zero and rise as output rises. The shape of the TVC curve follows directly from the law of diminishing returns. Up to point W' (the point of inflection), the firm uses

FIGURE 7–5   Total Cost Curves

The TFC curve is horizontal at the level of $30, regardless of the level of output. The TVC are zero when output is zero and rise as output rises. Past point W', the law of diminishing returns operates and the TVC curve faces upward or rises at an increasing rate. Total costs (TC) equal TFC plus TVC. Thus, the TC curve has the same shape as the TVC curve but is $30 above it at each output level.

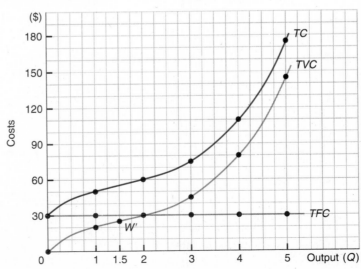

TABLE 7–2   **Fixed, Variable, and Total Costs**

Quantity of Output	Total Fixed Costs	Total Variable Costs	Total Costs
0	$30	$ 0	$ 30
1	30	20	50
2	30	30	60
3	30	45	75
4	30	80	110
5	30	145	175

so little of the variable inputs with the fixed inputs that the law of diminishing returns is not yet operating. As a result, the *TVC* curve faces downward or rises at a decreasing rate. Past point *W'* (i.e, for output levels greater than 1.5), the law of diminishing returns operates and the *TVC* curve faces upward or rises at an increasing rate. Since *TC* = *TFC* + *TVC*, the *TC* curve has the same shape as the *TVC* curve but is $30 (the *TFC*) above it at each output level.

Per-Unit Costs

From total costs we can derive per-unit costs. These are even more important in the short-run analysis of the firm. **Average fixed cost (*AFC*)** equals total fixed costs divided by output. **Average variable cost (*AVC*)** equals total variable costs divided by output. **Average total cost (*ATC*)** equals total costs divided by output. *ATC* also equals *AFC* plus *AVC*. **Marginal cost (*MC*)** equals the change in *TC* or in *TVC* per unit change in output.

Table 7–3 presents the per-unit cost schedules derived from the correspond-

TABLE 7–3   **Total and Per-Unit Costs**

Quantity of Output (1)	Total Fixed Costs (2)	Total Variable Costs (3)	Total Costs (4)	Average Fixed Cost (5)	Average Variable Cost (6)	Average Total Cost (7)	Marginal Cost (8)
1	$30	$ 20	$ 50	$30	$20	$50	$20
2	30	30	60	15	15	30	10
3	30	45	75	10	15	25	15
4	30	80	110	7.50	20	27.50	35
5	30	145	175	6	29	35	65

ing total cost schedules of Table 7–2. The *AFC* values given in column 5 are obtained by dividing the *TFC* values in column 2 by the quantity of output in column 1. *AVC* (column 6) equals *TVC* (column 3) divided by output (column 1). *ATC* (column 7) equals *TC* (column 4) divided by output (column 1). *ATC* also equals *AFC* plus *AVC*. *MC* (column 8) is given by the change in *TVC* (column 3) or in *TC* (column 4) per unit change in output (column 1). Thus, *MC* does not depend on *TFC*.

The per-unit cost schedules given in Table 7–3 are plotted in Figure 7–6. Note that *MC* is plotted *between* the various levels of output. From Table 7–3 and Figure 7–6, we see that the *AFC* curve falls continuously, while the *AVC*, *ATC*, and *MC* curves first fall and then rise (i.e., they are U-shaped). Since the vertical distance between the *ATC* and the *AVC* curve equals *AFC*, a separate *AFC* curve is superfluous and can be omitted from the figure.

The reason the *AVC* curve is U-shaped can be explained as follows. With labor as the only variable input in the short run, *TVC* for any output level (Q) equals the given wage rate ($\overline{w}$) times the quantity of labor (L) used. Then,

$$AVC = \frac{TVC}{Q} = \frac{\overline{w}L}{Q} = \frac{\overline{w}}{Q/L} = \frac{\overline{w}}{AP_L} = \overline{w}\left(\frac{1}{AP_L}\right) \qquad [7\text{–}4]$$

With $\overline{w}$ constant and from our knowledge (from section 6.2) that the average physical product of labor (AP_L or Q/L) usually rises first, reaches a maximum, and then falls, it follows that the *AVC* curve first falls, reaches a minimum, and then rises. Thus, the *AVC* curve is the monetized mirror image, reciprocal, or "dual" of the AP_L curve. Since the *AVC* curve is U-shaped, the *ATC* curve is also U-shaped. The *ATC* curve continues to fall after the *AVC* curve begins to rise because, for a while, the decline in *AFC* exceeds the rise in *AVC* (see Figure 7–6).

The U-shape of the *MC* curve can similarly be explained as follows:

$$MC = \frac{\Delta TVC}{\Delta Q} = \frac{\Delta(\overline{w}L)}{\Delta Q} = \frac{\overline{w}(\Delta L)}{\Delta Q} = \frac{\overline{w}}{\Delta Q/\Delta L} = \frac{\overline{w}}{MP_L} = \overline{w}\left(\frac{1}{MP_L}\right) \qquad [7\text{–}5]$$

Since the marginal product of labor (MP_L or $\Delta Q/\Delta L$) first rises, reaches a maximum, and then falls, it follows that the *MC* curve first falls, reaches a minimum, and then rises. Thus, the rising portion of the *MC* curve reflects the operation of the law of diminishing returns.

The *MC* curve reaches its minimum point at a smaller level of output than the *AVC* and the *ATC* curves, and it intersects from below the *AVC* and the *ATC* curves at their lowest points (see Figure 7–6). The reason is that for average costs to fall, the marginal cost must be lower. For average costs to rise, the marginal cost must be higher. Also, for average costs neither to fall nor rise (i.e., to be at their lowest point), the marginal cost must be equal to them. Although the *AVC*, *ATC*, and *MC* curves are U-shaped, they sometimes have a fairly flat bottom (see Example 3).

FIGURE 7-6 Per-Unit Cost Curves

The average fixed cost (*AFC*) curve falls continuously, while the average variable cost (*AVC*), average total cost (*ATC*), and marginal cost (*MC*) curves are U-shaped. The *MC* is plotted between the various output levels. The *ATC* curve falls as long as the decline in *AFC* exceeds the rise in *AVC*. The rising portion of the *MC* curve intersects from below the *AVC* and the *ATC* curves at their lowest point.

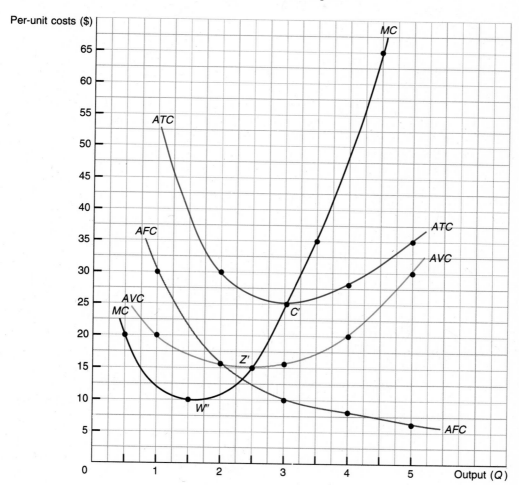

Geometry of Per-Unit Cost Curves

The shapes of the per-unit cost curves are determined by the shapes of the corresponding total cost curves. The *AVC* and *ATC* are given, respectively, by the slope of a line (ray) from the origin to the *TVC* and *TC* curves, while the *MC* is given by the slope of the *TC* and the *TVC* curves. This is similar

FIGURE 7–7 Graphic Derivation of Per-Unit Cost Curves

The *AVC* and *ATC* are given, respectively, by the slope of a line from the origin to the *TVC* and *TC* curves, while the *MC* curve is given by the slope of the *TC* or *TVC* curves. The slope of a ray from the origin to the *TVC* curve (the *AVC*) falls up to point *Z* and rises thereafter. The slope of a ray from the origin to the *TC* curve (the *ATC*) falls up to point *C* and rises thereafter. The slope of the *TC* and *TVC* curves (the *MC*) falls up to point *W* and *W'*, respectively, and then rises and intersects from below the *AVC* and the *ATC* curves at their lowest points.

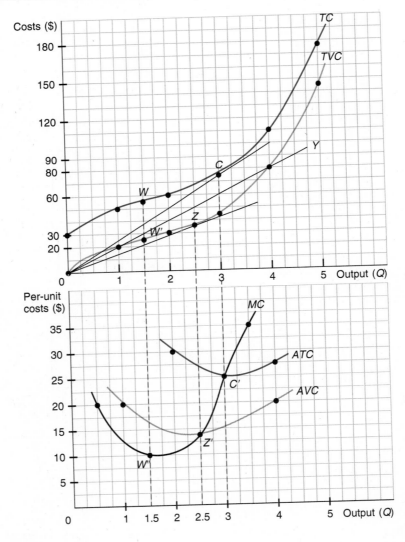

to the derivation of the average and marginal product curves from the total product curve in section 6.2.

Figure 7–7 shows that the AVC at 1 and 4 units of output (Q) is given by the slope of ray OY, which is $20. Note that the slope of a ray from the origin to the TVC curve in the top panel falls up to point Z (where the ray from the origin is tangent to the TVC curve) and then rises. Thus, the AVC curve in the bottom panel falls up to point Z' (i.e., up to Q = 2.5) and rises thereafter. The bottom panel of Figure 7–7 also shows that the ATC at Q = 3 is $25 (the slope of ray OC in the top panel). Note that the slope of a ray from the origin to the TC curve falls up to point C (where the ray from the origin is tangent to the TC curve) and then rises. Thus, the ATC curve falls up to point C' (i.e., up to Q = 3) and rises thereafter.

The top panel of Figure 7–7 also shows that the slope of the TC and TVC curves falls up to point W and W' (the points of inflection) on the TC and TVC curves, respectively, and then rises. Thus, the MC curve in the bottom panel falls up to W" and rises thereafter. At point Z, the MC and AVC are both equal to the slope of ray OZ. This is $35/2.5, or $14, and equals the lowest AVC. At point C, the MC and ATC are both equal to the slope of ray OC. This is $75/3, or $25, and equals the lowest ATC. Note that the AVC, ATC, and MC curves derived geometrically in Figure 7–7 are identical to those in Figure 7–6 and correspond to the values in Table 7–3.

Not shown in Figure 7–7 (in order not to complicate the figure unnecessarily) is the geometrical derivation of the AFC curve. This, however, is very simple. For example, turning back for a moment to Figure 7–5, we can see that the AFC for one unit of output is equal to the slope of the ray from the origin to Q = 1 on the TFC = $30 curve. This is $30/1, or $30. At Q = 2, AFC = $30/2 = $15. At Q = 3, AFC = $30/3 = $10, and so on. Note that because TFC are constant, AFC falls continuously as output rises. Thus, the AFC curve is a rectangular hyperbola (see Figure 7–6). As pointed out earlier, AFC is equal to the vertical distance between the ATC curve and the AVC curve, and so a separate AFC curve is not really necessary.

Example 3
Average and Marginal Cost of Corn

Figure 7–8 shows the actual estimated AVC, ATC, and MC per bushel of corn raised on central Iowa farms in 1971. The per-unit cost curves in the figure have the same general shape as the typical curves examined earlier, but with flatter bottoms. Once MC starts rising, it does so very rapidly. This is true not only in raising corn but also in many other cases. For example, traveling costs (in terms of travel time) rise very steeply during peak hours on highways.

FIGURE 7–8   Estimated Average and Marginal Costs of Corn

The figure shows actual *AVC*, *ATC*, and *MC* curves per bushel of corn raised on Iowa farms. The curves have flat bottoms and the *MC* curve rises steeply.

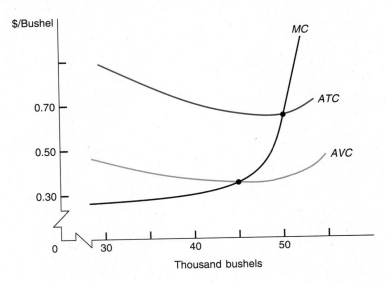

Similarly, landing costs (in terms of landing time) at airports also rise rapidly during peak hours (3–5 P.M.).

Sources: D. Suits, "Agriculture," in W. Adams, *The Structure of the American Economy*, 5th ed. (New York: Macmillan, 1977), p. 17, and A. Carlin and R. Park, "Marginal Cost Pricing of Airport Runway Capacity," *American Economic Review*, June 1970.

7.4 THEORY OF COST IN THE LONG RUN

Now we examine the theory of costs in the long run. We first define the firm's expansion path and, from it, derive the firm's long-run total cost curve. Then we derive the firm's long-run average cost curve. Finally, we show the relationship between the firm's short-run and long-run cost curves.

Expansion Path and the Long-Run Total Cost Curve

With constant input prices and higher total cost outlays by the firm, isocost lines will be higher and parallel. By joining the origin with the points of tangency of isoquants and the isocost lines, we derive the firm's **expansion path**. For example, in the top panel of Figure 7–9, the expansion path of the firm is line *OBDFHJN*. In this case, the expansion path is a straight line, and

FIGURE 7–9   Derivation of the Expansion Path and the Long-Run Total Cost Curve

The expansion path of the firm is line *OBDFHJN* in the top panel. It is obtained by joining the origin with the points of tangency of isoquants with the isocost lines holding input prices constant. Points along the expansion path show the least-cost input combinations to produce various output levels in the long run. The long-run total cost curve in the bottom panel is derived from the expansion path. For example, point *B'* on the *LTC* curve is derived from point *B* on the expansion path. The *LTC* curve shows the minimum long-run total costs of producing various levels of output when the firm can build any desired scale of plant.

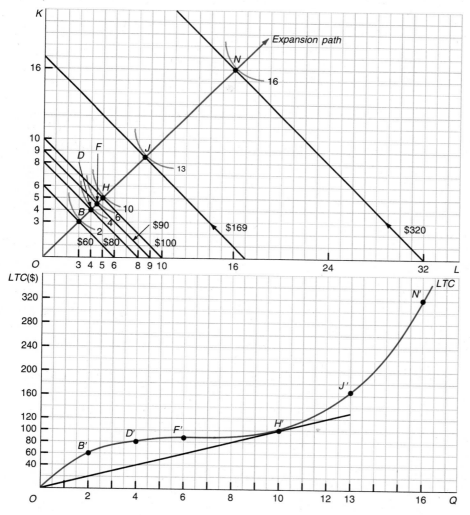

this indicates a constant capital-labor ratio (K/L) for all output levels. At the tangency points, the slope of the isoquants is equal to the slope of the isocost lines. That is, $MRTS_{LK} = MP_L/MP_K = w/r$, and $MP_L/w = MP_K/r$. Thus, points along the expansion path show the least-cost input combinations to produce various levels of output in the long run.

From the expansion path, we can derive the **long-run total cost (LTC)** curve of the firm. This shows the minimum long-run total costs of producing various levels of output. For example, point B in the top panel of Figure 7–9 indicates that the minimum total cost of producing two units of output ($2Q$) is $60 ($30 to purchase $3L$ and $30 to purchase $3K$). This gives point B' in the bottom panel of Figure 7–9, where the vertical axis measures total costs and the horizontal axis measures output. From point D in the top panel, we get point D' in the bottom panel. Other points on the LTC curve are similarly obtained. Note that the LTC curve starts at the origin because in the long run there are no fixed costs.

Derivation of the Long-Run Average Cost Curve

The **long-run average cost (LAC)** curve is derived from the LTC curve in the same way as the short-run average total cost ($SATC$) curve is derived from the short-run total cost (STC) curve. For example, in Figure 7–10, the $LAC =$ $30 for two units of output ($2Q$) is obtained by dividing the LTC of $60 (point B' on the LTC curve in the bottom panel of Figure 7–9) by 2. This is the slope of the ray from the origin to point B' on the LTC curve and is plotted as point B in Figure 7–10. Other points on the LAC curve are similarly obtained. Note that the slope of a line from the origin to the LTC curve falls up to point H' (in the bottom panel of Figure 7–9) and then rises. Thus, the LAC curve in Figure 7–10 falls up to point H ($10Q$) and rises thereafter. However, whereas the U-shape of the $SATC$ curve is explained by the law of diminishing returns, the U-shape of the LAC curve depends on the operation of increasing, constant, and decreasing returns to scale, respectively, as explained in section 6.5.

Figure 7–10 also shows that the LAC curve is tangent to various $SATC$ curves. Each $SATC$ curve represents the plant to be used to produce a particular level of output at minimum cost. The LAC curve is then the tangent to these $SATC$ curves and shows the minimum cost of producing each level of output. For example, the lowest LAC (of $30) to produce two units of output results when the firm operates plant 1 at point B on its $SATC_1$ curve. The lowest LAC (of $20) to produce four units of output results when the firm operates plant 2 at point D on its $SATC_2$ curve. Four units of output could also be produced by the firm operating plant 1 at point D^* on its $SATC_1$ curve (see the figure). However, this would not represent the lowest cost of producing $4Q$ in the long run. Other points on the LAC curve are similarly obtained. Thus, the LAC curve shows the minimum per-unit cost of producing any level of output *when the firm can build any desired scale of plant.* Note that the LAC to produce $3Q$ is the same for plant 1 and plant 2 (point C).

FIGURE 7–10 **Derivation of the Long-Run Average Cost Curve**

The *LAC* of $30 for two units of output (point *B*) is given by the slope of the line from the origin to point *B'* on the *LTC* curve (in the bottom panel of Figure 7–9). Other points on the *LAC* curve are similarly obtained. The slope of a ray from the origin to the *LTC* curve falls up to point *H'* (in the bottom panel of Figure 7–9) and then rises. Thus, the *LAC* curve falls up to point *H* and rises thereafter. The *LAC* curve is tangent to the *SATC* curves, each representing the plant size to produce a particular level of output at minimum cost.

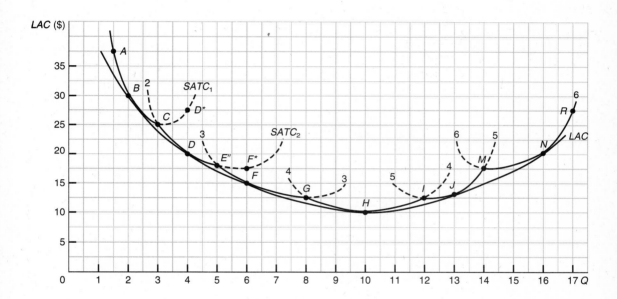

With only six plant sizes, the *LAC* curve would be *ABCDE"FGHIJMNR* (the solid portion of the *SATC* curves). With the infinite or very large number of plant sizes that the firm could build in the long run, the *LAC* curve would be the smooth curve passing through points *BDFHJN* (that is, the "kink" at points *C, E", G, I,* and *M* would be eliminated by having many plant sizes). Mathematically, the *LAC* curve is the "envelope" to the *SATC* curves.

The long run is often referred to as the **planning horizon**. In the long run, the firm has the time to build the plant that minimizes the cost of producing any anticipated level of output. Once the plant has been built, the firm operates in the short run. Thus, the firm plans in the long run and operates in the short run.

Relationship Between Short- and Long-Run Cost Curves

The relationship between the *long-run* total and per-unit cost curves is generally the same as between the *short-run* total and per-unit cost curves. There is also a unique relationship between the *LTC* and *STC* curves and between the long-run and the short-run per-unit cost curves. These are shown in Figure 7–11.

FIGURE 7–11 Relationship Between Short- and Long-Run Cost Curves

The top panel shows the *LTC* curve of Figure 7–9 and the *STC* curve of Figure 7–5. The bottom panel shows the *LAC* curve of Figure 7–10 and the *SATC* and the *SMC* curves of Figure 7–6. The long-run marginal cost (*LMC*) is given by the slope of the *LTC* curve. This falls up to $Q = 7$ (the point of inflection) and rises thereafter. *SATC* = *LAC* at point *B* because *STC* = *LTC* at point *B'*. Also, *SMC* = *LMC* at point *B** because the slope of the *LTC* and *STC* curves are equal at point *B'*. At the lowest point on the *LAC* curve (i.e., at point *H*), *LAC* = *LMC* = *SATC* = *SMC*.

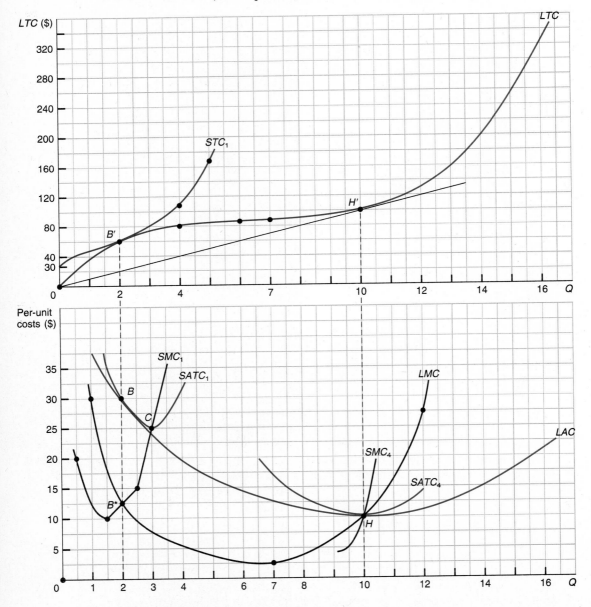

The top panel of Figure 7–11 shows the *LTC* curve of the bottom panel of Figure 7–9 and the *STC* curve of Figure 7–5.[5] The bottom panel of Figure 7–11 shows the *LAC* curve of Figure 7–10 and the *SATC* and the *SMC* curves of Figure 7–6. As previously pointed out, the *LAC* is given by the slope of a ray from the origin to the *LTC* curve. Thus, the *LAC* curve falls up to point *H* and rises thereafter.

The **long-run marginal cost (*LMC*)** curve is given by the slope of the *LTC* curve. From the top panel of Figure 7–11, we see that the slope of the *LTC* curve (the *LMC*) falls up to $Q = 7$ (the point of inflection) and rises thereafter. Also, the slope of the *LTC* curve (the *LMC*) is smaller than the slope of a ray from the origin to the *LTC* curve (the *LAC*) up to point *H'* and larger thereafter. At point *H*, *LMC* = *LAC*. Note that the *LMC* curve intersects from below the *LAC* curve at the lowest point of the latter. The *LMC* is $30 at $Q = 1$ because *LTC* increases from 0 to $60 when output rises from zero (the origin) to two units. Thus, the change in *LTC* per unit change in output (the *LMC*) is $60/2 = $30. The *LMC* is $10 at $Q = 3$ because *LTC* increases from $60 to $80 for a two-unit increase in output (from $Q = 2$ to $Q = 4$). The other *LMC* values shown in Figure 7–11 are obtained in the same way.

The *SATC* = *LAC* at point *B* (in the bottom panel of Figure 7–11) because *STC* = *LTC* at point *B'* in the top panel. Also, *SMC* = *LMC* at point *B** in the bottom panel because the slope of the *LTC* and *STC* curves are equal at point *B'* in the top panel. Also note that at the lowest point on the *LAC* curve (i.e., at point *H*), *LAC* = *LMC* = *SATC* = *SMC*. The reason for this is that the *STC₄* curve (not shown in the top panel) is tangent to the *LTC* curve at the point *H'*.

Example 4
Long-Run Average Cost Curve in Electricity Generation

Figure 7–12 shows the actual estimated *LAC* curve for a sample of 114 firms generating electricity in the United States in 1970. The figure shows that the *LAC* is lowest at the output level of about 32 billion kilowatt-hours. The *LAC*, however, is nearly L-shaped (the reason for and significance of this are explained in section 7.5).

In the future, solar energy may become competitive with coal and oil in the generation of electricity. The attraction of solar energy is that it has no turbines or other moving parts, so maintenance is minimal. Furthermore, solar energy is nonpolluting, silent, and can operate unattended. Even though solar energy has become much more efficient during the past decade (it was 16 times more expensive than coal-powered electricity a decade ago but is

---

[5]It should be noted that an infinite number of *STC* curves could be drawn in the top panel of Figure 7–11—one for each quantity of the fixed input or *TFC*.

FIGURE 7–12   Long-Run Average Cost Curve in Electricity Generation

The figure shows the actual estimated *LAC* curve for a sample of 114 firms generating electricity in the United States in 1970. The lowest point on the *LAC* curve is at the output level of about 32 billion kilowatt-hours. However, the *LAC* curve is nearly L-shaped.

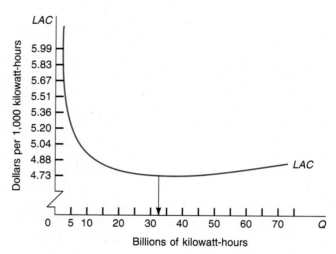

only two to four times as expensive now), American energy corporations, tied as they are to short-term profits, are becoming impatient and unwilling to wait another decade before solar energy might become competitive. And public opposition to nuclear power in the United States means that we cannot rely on this source of energy until safety and waste-disposal problems have been resolved in a more satisfactory way. More promising (don't laugh) is windmill power. After some striking recent technological breakthroughs, windmill power is now fully competitive with traditional sources of energy, is not polluting, and is expected to supply as much as 10% of the nation's energy requirements in 30 years—the same as hydroelectric power today.

Sources: L. Christensen and W. Green, "Economies of Scale in U.S. Electric Power Generation," *Journal of Political Economy*, August 1976; "U.S. Companies Losing Interest in Solar Energy," *New York Times*, March 7, 1989, p. 1; "Disposal of High-Level Nuclear Waste: Is It Possible?" *Science*, September 14, 1990, pp. 1231–1232; and "A New Era for Windmill Power," *New York Times*, September 8, 1992, p. D1.

7.5 SHAPE OF THE LONG-RUN AVERAGE COST CURVE

In Figures 7–10 and 7–11, the *LAC* curve has been drawn as U-shaped, just like the *SATC* curve. The reason for this similarity, however, is entirely different. The *SATC* curve turns upward when the rise in *AVC* (resulting from the operation of the law of diminishing returns) exceeds the decline in *AFC* (see Figure 7–6 and the discussion relating to it). However, in the long run, all inputs are variable (i.e., there are no fixed inputs) and so the law of diminishing returns is not applicable. The U-shape of the *LAC* curve depends instead on increasing and decreasing returns to scale. That is, as output expands from very low levels, increasing returns to scale prevail and cause the *LAC* curve to fall. As output continues to expand, the forces for decreasing returns to scale eventually begin to overtake the forces for increasing returns to scale and the *LAC* curve begins to rise.

As seen in section 6.5, increasing returns to scale means that output rises proportionately more than inputs, and so the cost per unit of output falls if input prices remain constant. On the other hand, decreasing returns to scale means that output rises proportionately less than inputs, and so the cost per unit of output rises if input prices remain constant. Therefore, decreasing *LAC* and increasing returns to scale are two sides of the same coin. Similarly, increasing *LAC* and decreasing returns to scale are equivalent. When the forces for increasing returns to scale are just balanced by the forces for decreasing returns to scale, we have constant returns to scale and the *LAC* curve is horizontal.

Empirical studies seem to indicate that in many industries the *LAC* curve has a very shallow bottom or is nearly L-shaped, as in Figure 7–12. This means that economies of scale are rather quickly exhausted, and constant or near-constant returns to scale prevail over a considerable range of output. This permits relatively small and large firms to coexist in the same industry (see Example 5).

Were increasing returns to scale to prevail over a very large range of output, large (and more efficient) firms would drive smaller firms out of business. In an extreme case, only one firm could most efficiently satisfy the entire market demand for the commodity. This is usually referred to as a "natural monopoly." In such cases, the government allows only one firm to operate in the market, but the firm is subject to regulation. Examples are provided by public utilities (such as electricity, telephone, and so on). This topic is discussed in detail in Chapter 9. On the other hand, the reason we do not often observe steeply rising *LAC* in the real world is that firms may generally know when their *LAC* would begin to rise rapidly and avoid expanding output in that range.

Economies of scale must be distinguished from **economies of scope**. The latter refers to the lowering of costs that a firm often experiences when it produces two or more products together rather than each alone. A small commuter airline, for example, can profitably expand into providing cargo services, thereby lowering the cost of each operation alone. Another example is a firm that produces a second product in order to utilize the by-products (which before, the firm had to dispose at a cost) arising from the production of the first product. A firm must constantly be alert to the possibility of profitably extending its product line to exploit such economies of scope.

Example 5

L-Shaped Long-Run Average Cost Curves from Hospitals to Railroads

Table 7–4 gives the long-run average cost for small firms as a percentage of the long-run average cost of large firms in six U.S. industries. The table shows that the *LAC* of small hospitals is 29% higher than for large hospitals. This implies that small hospitals operate in the declining portion of the *LAC* curve. For most other industries, the *LAC* of small firms is not much different from the *LAC* of large firms in the same industry. These results are consistent with the widespread near-constant returns to scale reported in Table 6–3 and, thus, with L-shaped or at least flat-bottomed *LAC* curves. These results are also consistent with a much more extensive study conducted in India. Of the 29 industries examined, 18 were found to have L- or nearly L-shaped *LAC* curves, 6 were found to have horizontal *LAC* curves or nearly so, and only 5 were found to be U-shaped.

The large number of industries with an L- or nearly L-shaped *LAC* curve does not, however, necessarily contradict the hypothesis of U-shaped *LAC* curves. It may simply reflect the fact that firms normally fail to expand output past the point where they begin to incur rapidly rising long-run average costs. Note that Table 7–4 shows that only in trucking does the *LAC* curve seem mildly U-shaped (since small firms have lower *LAC* costs than large ones). Example 3 in Chapter 6 also implies a U-shaped *LAC* curve in manufacturing automobiles, with Ford near the bottom of the *LAC* curve, General Motors on the rising arm of the *LAC* curve (i.e., because of its large size GM is incurring diseconomies of scale), while Chrysler, being much smaller than both GM and Ford, operates on the falling arm of the *LAC* curve (i.e., is too small to fully take advantage of all economies of scale).

TABLE 7–4   Long-Run Average Cost (*LAC*) of Small Firms as a Percentage of *LAC* of Large Firms

Industry	Percentage
Hospitals	129
Commercial banking	
Demand deposits	116
Installment loans	102
Electric power	112
Airline (local service)	100
Railroads	100
Trucking	95

Sources: H. Cohen, "Hospital Cost Curves with Emphasis on Measuring Patient Care Output," in H. Klarman (ed.), *Empirical Studies in Health Economics* (Baltimore: Johns Hopkins Press, 1979), pp. 279–93; F. Bell and N. Murphy, *Costs in Commercial Banking* (Boston: Federal Reserve Bank of Boston, Research Report No. 41, 1968); L. Christensen and W. Greene, "Economies of Scale in U.S. Electric Power Generation," *Journal of Political Economy*, August 1976; G. Eads, M. Nerlove, and W. Raduchel, "A Long-Run Cost Function for the Local Service Airline Industry," *The Review of Economics and Statistics*, August 1969; Z. Griliches, "Cost Allocation in Railroad Regulation," *The Bell Journal of Economics and Management Science*, Spring 1972; R. Koenker, "Optimal Scale and the Size Distribution of American Trucking Firms," *Journal of Transport Economics and Policy*, January 1977; V. K. Gupta, "Cost Functions, Concentration, and Barriers to Entry in Twenty-Nine Manufacturing Industries in India," *Journal of Industrial Economics*, November 1968; and "Automobiles: GM Decides Smaller Is Better," *The Margin*, November/December 1988, p. 28.

▲

7.6 DYNAMIC CHANGES IN COSTS—THE LEARNING CURVE

As firms gain experience in the production of a commodity or service, their average cost of production declines. In other words, *for a given level of output per time period*, the increasing *cumulative total output* over many time periods often provides the manufacturing experience that enables firms to lower their average cost of production. The **learning curve** shows the decline in the average input cost of production with rising cumulative total outputs over time. For example, it might take 1,000 hours to assemble the 100th aircraft, but only 700 hours to assemble the 200th aircraft because as managers and workers gain production experience they usually become more efficient, especially when the production process is relatively new. Contrast this with economies of scale, which refers to declining average cost as the firm's output *per time period* increases.

The left panel of Figure 7–13 shows a learning curve that indicates the average cost declines from $10 for producing the 10th unit of the product (point *H*), to $7 for producing the 20th unit (point *T*), and to $5 for producing the 40th unit of the product (point *W*). Average cost declines at a decreasing rate so that the learning curve is convex to the origin. This is the usual shape of learning curves; that is, firms usually achieve the largest decline in average input costs when the production process is relatively new and less as the firm matures.

The difference between the reduction in average costs due to learning and to increasing returns to scale is clarified by examining the right panel of Figure 7–13. There, the reduction in long-run average cost (*LAC*) due to increasing returns to scale is shown by a movement, say from point *D* to point *F*, along the *LAC* curve (the same as in Figure 7–10) as output *per time period* increases. The reduction in *LAC* due to learning is instead shown by the downward shift in the *LAC* curve, say from point *D* to point *D**, for a given level of

FIGURE 7–13   Learning and Increasing Returns Compared

The left panel shows that as the total cumulative output of the firm doubles from 10 to 20 units over time, the average cost declines from \$10 to \$7 (the movement from point *H* to point *T* on the learning curve). The right panel shows that *LAC* declines from \$20 to \$15 as output increases from 4 to 6 units per time period (the movement from point *D* to point *F* along the *LAC* curve) due to increasing returns to scale. But *LAC* falls from \$20 to \$12.50 to produce 4 units of output per time period as the firm learns from larger cumulative total outputs (the downward shift of the *LAC* curve from point *D* to point *D**).

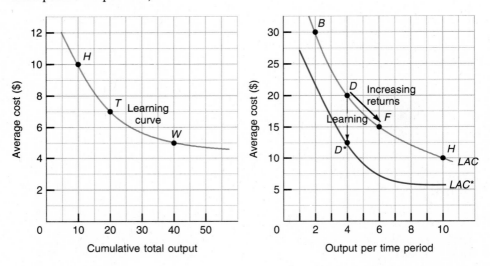

output per time period, but as the firm learns from a larger total cumulative output over many periods.

Learning curves have been documented in many manufacturing and service sectors: manufacturing of airplanes, appliances, ships, and refined petroleum products and the operation of power plants. They have also been used to forecast the need for personnel, machinery, and raw materials and for scheduling production, determining the price at which to sell output, and even to evaluate suppliers' price quotations. For example, in its early days as a producer of computer chips, Texas Instruments adopted an aggressive price strategy based on the learning curve. Believing that the learning curve in chip production was steep, the firm kept unit prices very low to increase its total cumulative output rapidly, thereby learning by doing. The strategy was successful and the rest is history (Texas Instruments became one of the world's major players in this market). How rapidly the learning curve (i.e., average input cost) declines can differ widely among firms and is greater the smaller the rate of employee turnover, the fewer production interruptions (which would lead to "forgetting"), and the greater the ability of the firm to transfer knowledge from the production of other similar products. The average cost typically declines by 20% to 30% for each doubling of cumulative output for many firms.[6]

7.7 MINIMIZING COSTS INTERNATIONALLY—THE NEW ECONOMIES OF SCALE

During the past decade, there has been a sharp increase in international trade in parts and components. More and more firms have opened production facilities abroad to keep production costs as low as possible and be able to meet growing international competition. Today, most products manufactured by international corporations have parts and components made in many different nations. The reason is to minimize production costs. For example, the motors of some Ford Fiestas are produced in the United Kingdom, the transmissions in France, the clutches in Spain, and the parts are assembled in Germany for sales throughout Europe. Similarly, Japanese and German cameras are often assembled in Singapore to take advantage of the much cheaper labor there.

Foreign "sourcing" of inputs is often not a matter of choice to earn higher profits, but simply a requirement to remain competitive. Firms that do not look abroad for cheaper inputs face loss of competitiveness in world markets and even in the domestic market. This is certainly the reason that $625 of the $860 total cost of producing an IBM PC was incurred for parts and components manufactured by IBM outside the United States or purchased from foreign producers during the mid-1980s (see Example 3 in Chapter 1). Such low-cost offshore purchase of inputs is likely to continue to expand rapidly in the future and is being fostered by joint ventures, licensing arrangements, and other nonequity collaborative arrangements. Indeed, this represents one of the most dynamic aspects of the global business environment of today.

Not only are more and more inputs imported, but more and more firms are opening production facilities in more and more nations. For example, Nestlé, the largest Swiss company and the world's second largest food company, has production facilities in 59 countries and America's Gillette has facilities in 22. In 1987, Ford had component factories and assembly plants in 26 different industrial sites in the United Kingdom, Germany, Belgium, France, Spain, and Portugal and employed more people abroad than in the United States (201,000 people abroad as compared with 181,000 in the United States). Bertelsman AG, the $7 billion German media empire, owns printing plants around the world and the Literary Guild Book Club, and it also prints books

---

[6]The classic paper on learning curves is K. Arrow, "The Economic Implication of Learning by Doing," *Review of Economic Studies*, June 1962. A more recent reference is L. Argote and D. Epple, "Learning Curves in Manufacturing," *Science*, February 23, 1990.

at competitors' plants and sells them through Time-owned Book-of-the-Month Club.[7]

So widespread and growing is international trade in inputs and the opening of production facilities abroad that we are rapidly moving toward truly multinational firms with roots in many nations rather than in only one country. This change affects not only the multinational companies. Indeed, more and more firms that until a few years ago operated exclusively in the domestic market are now purchasing increasing quantities of inputs and components and shifting some of their production to foreign nations. For example, Malachi Mixon, the American medical equipment company, now buys parts and components in half a dozen countries, from China to Colombia, when ten years ago it did all of its shopping at home. The popular Mazda Miata automobile, which is manufactured in Japan, was conceived in Mazda's California design lab by an American engineer at the same time that Mazda opened production facilities for other models in the United States.

Firms must constantly explore sources of cheaper inputs and overseas production to remain competitive in our rapidly shrinking world. Indeed, this process can be regarded as manufacturing's new (international) economies of scale in today's global economy. Just as companies were forced to rationalize operations within each country in the 1980s, they now face the challenge of integrating their operations for their entire system of manufacturing around the world to take advantage of the new international economies of scale.[8] What is important is for the firm to focus on those components that are indispensable to the company's competitive position over subsequent product generations and "outsource" other components for which outside suppliers have a distinctive production advantage.[9]

The new international economies of scale can be achieved in five basic areas: product development, purchasing, production, demand management, and order fulfillment. In product development, the firm can design a core product for the entire world economy by building into the product the possibility of variations and derivatives to meet the needs of local markets. Firms can achieve new economies of scale by purchasing raw materials, parts, and components on a global rather than on a local basis—no matter where their operations are located. Firms can also coordinate production in low-cost manufacturing centers with final assembly in high-cost locations near markets. They can forecast the demand for their products and undertake demand management on a world rather than on a national basis. Firms can achieve important economies of scale by shipping products from the plants closest

[7]See, W. H. Davison and J. de la Torre, *Managing the Global Corporation* (New York: McGraw-Hill, 1989).

[8]See, "Manufacturing's New Economies of Scale," *Harvard Business Review*, May-June 1992, pp. 94–102.

[9]See, "Strategic Outsourcing," *Harvard Business Review*, November-December 1992, pp. 98–107.

to customers more quickly and with smaller inventory on a global basis. International economies of scale are likely to become even more important in the future as we move closer and closer to a truly global economy.

SUMMARY

1. In economics, costs include explicit and implicit costs. Explicit costs are the actual expenditures of the firm to purchase or hire inputs. Implicit costs refer to the value (imputed from their best alternative use) of the inputs owned and used by the firm. The cost to a firm in using any input (whether owned or hired) is what the input could earn in its best alternative use. This is the alternative or opportunity cost doctrine. Costs are also classified into private and social. Private costs are those incurred by individuals and firms, while social costs are those incurred by society as a whole.

2. Given the wage rate of labor (w), the rental price of capital (r), and a particular total cost (TC), we can define the isocost line. This shows the various combinations of L and K that the firm can hire. With K plotted along the vertical axis, the Y-intercept of the isocost line is TC/r and its slope is $-w/r$. To minimize production costs or maximize output, the firm must produce where an isoquant is tangent to an isocost line. There, $MRTS_{LK} = w/r$, and $MP_L/w = MP_K/r$. This means the MP per dollar spent on L must be equal to the MP per dollar spent on K. The minimum cost of producing a given level of output is usually lower in the long run than in the short run.

3. In the short run we have fixed, variable, and total costs. Total fixed costs (TFC) plus total variable costs (TVC) equal total costs (TC). The shape of the TVC curve follows directly from the law of diminishing returns. Average fixed cost (AFC) equals TFC/Q, where Q is output. Average variable cost (AVC) equals TVC/Q. Average total cost (ATC) equals TC/Q. $ATC = AFC$ $+ AVC$ also. Marginal cost (MC) equals the change in TC or in TVC per-unit change in output. The AVC, ATC, and MC curves first fall and then rise (i.e., they are U-shaped). AVC and MC move inversely to the AP_L and the MP_L, respectively. The AVC and the ATC are given, respectively, by the slope of a line from the origin to the TVC and to the TC curves, while the MC is given by the slope of the TC and the TVC curves.

4. The expansion path joins the origin with the points of tangency of isoquants and isocost lines with input prices held constant. It shows the least-cost input combination to produce various output levels. From the expansion path, we can derive the long-run total cost (LTC) curve. This shows the minimum long-run total costs of producing various levels of output when the firm can build any desired plant. The long-run average cost (LAC) equals LTC/Q. The LAC curve is tangent to the short-run average cost curves. The long-run marginal cost (LMC) equals $\Delta LTC/\Delta Q$. The relationship between the LAC and LMC curves and their derivation from the LTC curve is similar to that of the short run. When $LTC = STC$, $LAC = SATC$ and $LMC = SMC$. The firm plans in the long run and operates in the short run.

5. The U-shape of the long-run average cost curve of the firm results from the operation of increasing, constant, and decreasing returns to scale, respectively. Empirical studies seem to indicate that in many industries the LAC curve has a very shallow bottom or is nearly L-shaped. This means that economies of scale are quickly exhausted,

and constant or near-constant returns to scale prevail over a considerable range of output. This permits relatively small and large firms to coexist in the same industry. Economies of scope are also possible in production. These refer to the lowering of costs that a firm often experiences when it produces two or more products together rather than producing each product separately.

6. The learning curve shows the decline in the average cost of production with rising cumulative total outputs over time. The learning curve is negatively sloped and convex to the origin, indicating that aver-age input costs decline at a decreasing rate as cumulative total output rises.

7. During the past decade, there has been a sharp increase in international trade in parts and components, and more and more firms have opened production facilities abroad to keep production costs as low as possible and be able to meet growing international competition. This process can be regarded as manufacturing's new (international) economies of scale in today's global economy. These new international economies of scale can be achieved in product development, purchasing, production, demand management, and order fulfillment.

KEY TERMS

Explicit Costs
Implicit Costs
Alternative or Opportunity
  Cost Doctrine
Private Costs
Social Costs
Isocost Line
Least-Cost Input Combination

Total Fixed Costs (TFC)
Total Variable Costs (TVC)
Total Costs (TC)
Averaged Fixed Cost (AFC)
Average Variable Cost (AVC)
Average Total Cost (ATC)
Marginal Cost (MC)
Expansion Path

Long-Run Total Cost (LTC)
Long-Run Average Cost
  (LAC)
Planning Horizon
Long-Run Marginal Cost
  (LMC)
Economies of Scope
Learning Curve

REVIEW QUESTIONS

1. An individual quits his job as a manager of a small photocopying business in which he was earning $30,000 per year and opens his own shop by renting a store for $5,000 per year, using $10,000 of his own to rent the photocopying machines, and hiring a helper for $10,000 per year. How much are the individual's accounting costs? How much are his economic costs?

2. State colleges are more efficient than independent colleges in providing college education because they charge lower tuition. True or false? Explain.

3. Is the annual retainer paid by a firm to a lawyer a fixed or a variable cost?

4. Is it always better to hire a more qualified and productive worker than a less qualified and productive worker? Explain.

5. Is a firm minimizing costs if the marginal product of labor is six, the marginal product of capital is five, the wage rate is $2, and the interest on capital is $1? If not, what must the firm do to minimize costs?

6. How should a firm utilize each of two plants to minimize production costs for the firm as a whole?

7. If the marginal cost of a firm is rising, does this mean that its average cost is also rising?

8. A rational producer never operates in the negatively sloped range of its short-run marginal cost curve. True or false? Explain.

9. Must a firm's long-run average cost curve be

U-shaped if its long-run marginal cost curve is U-shaped?

10. What does the long-run marginal cost curve of a firm look like if its long-run average cost curve is L-shaped?

11. What is the difference between economies of scale, economies of scope, and the reduction in average costs as a result of learning?

12. Should a firm purchase some parts and components abroad even if it creates employment opportunities abroad?

PROBLEMS

*1. A woman working in a large duplicating (photocopying) establishment for $15,000 per year decides to open a small duplicating place of her own. She runs the operation by herself without hired help and invests no money of her own. She rents the premises for $10,000 per year and the machines for $30,000 per year. She spends $15,000 per year on supplies (paper, ink, envelopes), electricity, telephone, and so on. During the year her gross earnings are $65,000.

 a. How much are the explicit costs of this business?

 b. How much are the implicit costs?

 c. Should this woman remain in business after the year, if she is indifferent between working for herself or for others in a similar capacity?

2. Suppose that the marginal product of the last worker employed by a firm is 30 units of output per day and the daily wage that the firm must pay is $20, while the marginal product of the last machine rented by the firm is 80 units of output per day and the daily rental price of the machine is $40.

 a. Why is this firm not maximizing output or minimizing costs in the long run?

 b. How can the firm maximize output or minimize costs?

3. With reference to Figure 7–3, answer the following questions.

 a. If capital were fixed at 5 units, what would be the minimum cost of producing 10 units of output in the short run?

 b. If capital were variable but labor fixed at 4 units, what would be the minimum cost of producing 10 units of output?

4. a. Plot the total fixed cost (TFC) curve, the total variable costs (TVC) curve, and the total costs (TC) curve given in the following table.

Quantity of Output	Total Variable Costs	Total Costs
0	$ 0	$ 30
1	20	50
2	30	60
3	48	78
4	90	120
5	170	200

 b. Explain the reason for the shape of the cost curves in 4a above.

5. a. Derive the average fixed costs (AFC), the average variable costs (AVC), the average total costs (ATC), and the marginal costs (MC) from the total cost schedules given in the table of problem 4.

 b. Plot the AVC, ATC, and MC curves of 5a on a graph and explain the reason for their shape. How are AFC reflected in the figure?

 c. How can the AFC, AVC, ATC, and MC curves be derived geometrically?

*6. Electrical utility companies usually operate their most modern and efficient equipment around the clock and use their older and less efficient equipment only to meet periods of peak electricity demand.

 a. What does this imply for the short-run marginal cost of these firms?

 b. Why do these firms not replace all of their older equipment with newer equipment in the long run?

_____

* = Answer provided at end of book.

7. a. Suppose that $w = \$10$ and $r = \$10$ and the least-cost input combination is $3L$ and $3K$ to produce 2 units of output ($2Q$), $4L$ and $4K$ to produce $4Q$, $4.5L$ and $4.5K$ to produce $6Q$, $5L$ and $5K$ to produce $8Q$, $7.5L$ and $7.5K$ for $10Q$, and $12L$ and $12K$ for $12Q$. Draw the isocost lines, the isoquants, and the expansion path of the firm.

   b. From the expansion path of 7a, derive the long-run total cost curve of the firm.

   c. Redraw your figure of 7b and on it draw the STC curve of problem 4a, the STC curve tangent to the LTC curve at $Q = 8$, and the STC curve tangent to the LTC curve at $Q = 12$.

8. a. From the LTC curve of the firm of problem 7b, derive the LAC and the LMC curves of the firm.

   b. Redraw the figure of 8a, and on the same figure draw the ATC and the MC curves of problem 5b. Also draw the ATC curve that forms the lowest point of the LAC curve at $Q = 8$ and the corresponding SMC curve. On the same figure, draw the ATC curve that is tangent to the LAC curve at $Q = 12$ and the corresponding SMC curve.

*9. a. Under what condition would the LTC curve be a positively sloped straight line through the origin?

   b. What would then be the shape of the LAC and the LMC curves?

c. Would this be consistent with U-shaped STC curves?

   d. Draw a figure showing your answer to 9a, 9b, and 9c.

10. Suppose that in Figure 7–4 the opportunity cost of driving time remained at $6.00 per hour but the price of gasoline increased to $4.50 per gallon.

   a. Approximately how much gasoline and driving time would the individual use for the trip of 600 miles?

   b. What would be the minimum total cost of the trip?

11. a. Draw a figure showing that the best plant for a range of outputs may not be the best plant to produce a given level of output.

   b. Why might the firm build the first rather than the second type of plant?

*12. Given the following learning curve equation,

$$AC = 1,000 \, Q^{-0.3}$$

where AC refers to the average cost of production and Q to the total cumulative output of the firm over time, find the AC of the firm for producing the

   a. 100th unit of the product.

   b. 200th unit of the product.

   c. 400th unit of the product.

   d. Draw the learning curve from the results obtained from parts (a) to (c).

APPENDIX   EXTENSIONS AND USES OF PRODUCTION AND COST ANALYSIS

This appendix shows how the total variable cost curve can be derived from the total product curve, examines input substitution in production to minimize costs, and shows the effect of an increase in input prices on the firm's cost curves.

Derivation of the Total Variable Cost Curve from the Total Product Curve

The top panel of Figure 7–14 reproduces the total product (TP) curve of Figure 6–2. With labor (L) as the only variable input and with the constant wage rate of $10, the total variable cost (TVC) of producing various quantities of output is given by $TVC =$

FIGURE 7–14   **Derivation of the *TVC* Curve from the *TP* Curve**

The top panel reproduces the *TP* curve of Figure 6–2. With labor (*L*) as the only variable input, and with the constant wage rate of $10, *TVC* = $10*L* (the lower horizontal scale in the top panel). If we now transpose the axes and plot *TVC* on the vertical axis and output on the horizontal axis, we obtain the *TVC* curve shown in the bottom panel. At points *G* and *G'*, the law of diminishing returns begins to operate.

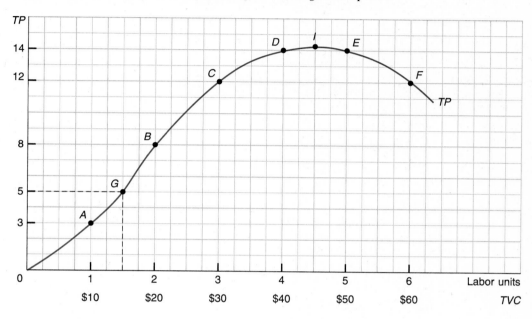

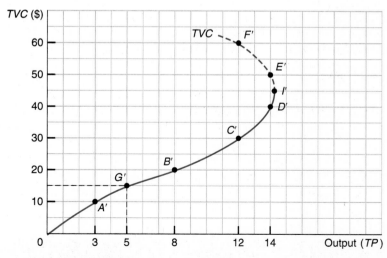

$10L (the lower horizontal scale in the top panel). If we now transpose the axes and plot TVC on the vertical axis and output on the horizontal axis, we obtain the TVC curve shown in the bottom panel of Figure 7–14. Thus, the shape of the TVC curve is determined by the shape of the TP curve.

Note that the slope of the TP curve (or MP_L) rises up to point G (the point of inflection) in the top panel and then declines. On the other hand, the slope of the TVC curve (the MC) falls up to point G' (the point of inflection) in the bottom panel and then rises. At points G and G', the law of diminishing returns begins to operate. The MC is the monetized mirror image or dual of the MP_L. That is, MC falls when MP_L rises, MC is minimum when MP_L is highest, and MC rises when MP_L falls. The same inverse relationship exists between the AVC and the AP_L. Note also that the TVC curve is dashed above point I' in the bottom panel because no firm would want to incur higher TVC to produce smaller outputs.

Input Substitution in Production to Minimize Costs

Figure 7–15 shows that with TC = $140 and w = r = $10, the firm minimizes the cost of producing 10Q by using 7K and 7L (point A, where isocost line FG is tangent to isoquant 10Q). At point A, K/L = 1.

If r remains at $10 but w falls to $5, the isocost line becomes FH and the firm can reach an isoquant higher than 10Q with TC = $140. The firm can now reach isoquant 10Q with TC = $100. This is given by isocost F'H', which is parallel to FH (i.e., w/r = ½ for both) and is tangent to isoquant 10Q at point B. At point B, K/L = ½. Thus, with a reduction in w (and constant r), a lower TC is required to produce a given level

FIGURE 7–15   Input Substitution in Production

With TC = $140 and w = r = $10, the firm minimizes the cost of producing 10Q by using 7K and 7L (point A, where isocost FG is tangent to isoquant 10Q). At point A, K/L = 1. If r remains at $10 but w falls to $5, the firm can reach isoquant 10Q with TC = $100. The least-cost combination of L and K is then given by point B, where isocost F'H' is tangent to isoquant 10Q. At point B, K/L = ½.

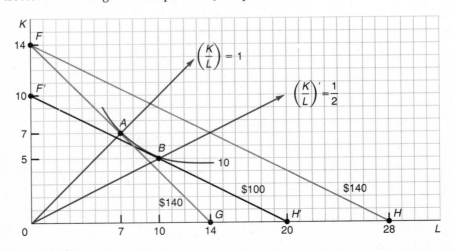

of output. To minimize production costs, the firm will have to substitute L for K in production, so that K/L declines.

The ease with which the firm can substitute L for K in production depends on the shape of the isoquant. The flatter is the isoquant, the easier it is to substitute L for K in production. On the other hand, if the isoquant is at a right angle, or L-shaped (as in Figure 6–8), no input substitution is possible (i.e., $MRTS_{LK} = 0$). In such a case, K/L will then always be constant regardless of input prices.

Input Prices and the Firm's Cost Curves

In deriving the firm's cost curves, input prices are kept constant. Per-unit costs differ at different levels of output because the physical productivity of inputs varies as output varies. If input prices do change, the AC and the MC curves of the firm will shift—up if input prices rise and down if input prices fall.

For example, point B in Figure 7–15 shows that $10Q$ is produced at $TC = \$100$ when $w = \$5$, so that $AC = \$10$. With $w = \$10$, the production of $10Q$ requires $TC = \$140$ (point A in Figure 7–15), so that $AC' = \$14$. This is shown in Figure 7–16 by point B' and A' on average cost curves AC and AC', respectively. Note that the marginal cost curve will also shift up from MC to MC' when w rises.

For simplicity, we assumed in Figure 7–16 that the firm produces at the lowest point on its average cost curve before and after the increase in w. Be that as it may, the minimum cost of producing a given level of output is always achieved by substituting the cheaper input (here, capital) for the input that has become more expensive (labor) until the tangency of the given isoquant with the new (steeper) isocost is reached (point A in Figure 7–15, at which, once again, $MRTS_{LK} = w/r$).

FIGURE 7–16   Input Prices and the AC and MC Curves

Point B' on curve AC shows that with $w = \$5$, $AC = \$10$ for $Q = 10$ (from point B in Figure 7–15). Point A' on curve AC' shows that with $w = \$10$, $AC = \$14$ for $Q = 10$ (from point A in Figure 7–15). Thus, an increase in w from $\$5$ to $\$10$ shifts AC and MC up to AC' and MC'.

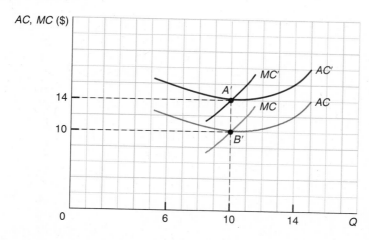

PRICE AND OUTPUT UNDER PERFECT COMPETITION

In this chapter, we bring together the theory of consumer behavior and demand (from Part Two) and the theory of production and costs (from Chapters 6 and 7) to analyze how price and output are determined under perfect competition. As explained in Chapter 1, the analysis of how price and output are determined in the market is a primary aim of microeconomic theory.

The chapter begins by identifying the various types of market structure and defining perfect competition. It then examines price determination in the market period, or the very short run, when the supply of the commodity is fixed. Subsequently, we discuss how the firm determines its best level of output in the short run at various commodity prices. In the process, we derive the short-run supply curve of the firm and industry and show how the interaction of industry demand and supply curves determines the equilibrium price of the commodity. This was already demonstrated in Chapter 2, but now we know what lies behind the market demand and supply curves and how they are derived.

From the analysis of the market period and the short run, we go on to examine the long-run equilibrium of the firm and define constant, increasing, and decreasing cost industries. Subsequently, we consider the very significant effect of international competition on the domestic economy. The chapter concludes with an analysis of perfectly competitive markets. This analysis, together with the real-world examples presented in the theory sections, highlight the great importance and relevance of the analytical tools developed in the chapter. In the optional appendix, the foreign exchange market and the dollar exchange rate are examined.

8.1 MARKET STRUCTURE: PERFECT COMPETITION

In economics, we usually identify four different types of market structure: perfect competition, monopoly, monopolistic competition, and oligopoly. This chapter examines perfect competition. The other three types of market organization are considered in the next three chapters (monopoly in Chapter 9 and monopolistic competition and oligopoly in Chapters 10 and 11). Chapter 12 then analyzes the efficiency implications of market imperfections and regulation.

Perfect competition refers to the type of market organization in which (1) there are many buyers and sellers of a commodity, each too small to affect the price of the commodity; (2) the commodity is homogeneous; (3) there is perfect mobility of resources; and (4) economic agents have perfect knowledge of market conditions (i.e., prices and costs). Let us now examine in detail the meaning of each of the four aspects of the definition.

First, in perfect competition, there are many buyers and sellers of the commodity, each of which is too small (or behaves as if he or she is too small) in relation to the market to have a perceptible effect on the price of the commodity. Under perfect competition, the equilibrium price and quantity of the commodity are determined at the intersection of the market demand and supply curves of the commodity. The equilibrium price will not be affected perceptibly if only one or a few consumers or producers change the quantity demanded or supplied of the commodity.

Second, the commodity is *homogeneous,* identical, or perfectly standardized, so that the output of each producer is indistinguishable from the output of others. An example of this might be grade A winter wheat. Thus, buyers are indifferent as to the output of which producer they purchase.

Third, resources are perfectly mobile. This means that resources or inputs are free to move (i.e., they can move at zero cost) among the various industries and locations within the market in response to monetary incentives. Firms can enter or leave the industry in the long run without much difficulty. That is, there are no artificial barriers (such as patents) or natural barriers (such as huge capital requirements) to entry into and exit from the industry.

Fourth, consumers, firms, and resource owners have perfect knowledge of all relevant prices and costs in the market. This ensures that the same price prevails in each part of the market for the commodity and for the inputs required in the production of the commodity.

Needless to say, these conditions have seldom if ever existed in any market. The closest we might come today to a perfectly competitive market is the stock market (see Example 1) and the foreign exchange market (in the absence of intervention by national monetary authorities) examined in the appendix. Another example might be U.S. agriculture at the turn of the century, when millions of small farmers raised wheat. Despite its rarity, the perfectly competitive model is extremely useful to analyze market situations that approximate perfect competition. More importantly, the perfectly competitive model provides the point of reference or standard against which to measure the economic cost or *inefficiency* of departures from perfect competition. These departures can take the form of monopoly, monopolistic competition, or oligopoly. In the case of monopoly, there is a *single* seller of a commodity for which there are no good substitutes. Under monopolistic competition, there are many sellers of a *differentiated* commodity.[1] In oligopoly, there are *few* sellers of either a homogeneous or a differentiated commodity. Imperfectly competitive markets are examined in Part Four (Chapters 9–12).

The economist's definition of perfect competition is diametrically opposite to the everyday usage of the term. In economics, the term "perfect competition" stresses the *impersonality* of the market. One producer does not care and is not affected by what other producers are doing. The output of all producers is identical, and an individual producer can sell any quantity of the commodity at the given price without any need to advertise. On the other hand, in everyday usage, the term "competition" stresses the notion of *rivalry* among producers or sellers of the commodity. For example, GM managers speak of the fierce competition that their firm faces from other domestic and foreign auto producers with regard to style, mileage per gallon, price, and so on. Because of this, GM mounts elaborate and costly advertising campaigns to convince consumers of the superiority of its vehicles. This is not, however, what the economist means by competition.

Under perfect competition, the firm is a *price taker* and can sell any quantity of the commodity at the given market price. If the firm raised its price by the slightest amount, it would lose all of its consumers. On the other hand, there is no reason for the firm to reduce the commodity price since the firm can sell any quantity of the commodity at the given market price. Thus, the perfectly competitive firm faces a horizontal or infinitely elastic demand curve (as in Figure 5–7) at the price determined at the intersection of the market demand and supply curves for the commodity (as in Figure 2–5).

Example 1

Competition in the New York Stock Market

The market for stocks traded on the New York and other major stock exchanges is as close as we come today to a perfectly competitive market of buyers and sellers. In most cases, the price of the stock is determined by the demand and supply of the stock; and the individual buyer and seller of the stock has no perceptible effect on price (i.e., he or she is a price taker). All stocks within each company category are more or less homogeneous. The frequency with which a particular type of stock is bought and sold is evidence that resources are mobile. Finally, information on prices and quantities traded is readily available. In general, the price of a stock reflects knowledge of the present and expected future net income stream from the stock.

The price of a stock at any point in time usually reflects (though seldom, if ever, perfectly) all the publicly known information about the stock. This is known as the *efficient-market hypothesis*. Information about greater profitability

---

[1]An example of a differentiated commodity is the different brand names of the same commodity.

of a company will be reflected, rather quickly, by a higher price of its stock (as those who first learn of the increased current or expected profitability purchase the stock). On the other hand, expectations of lower profitability will result in a decline in the price of the stock (as those who first learn of the reduced profitability sell the stock). Funds flow into stocks, and resources into uses where the rate of return, corrected for risk, is highest. Thus, stock prices provide the signals for the efficient allocation of investments in the economy.

Today, more and more Americans trade foreign stocks, and more and more foreigners trade American stocks. This has been the result of a communications revolution that linked stock markets around the world into a huge global capital market and around-the-clock trading. Although this provides immense new earning possibilities and sharply increased opportunities for portfolio diversification, it also creates the danger that a crisis in one market will quickly spread to other markets around the world. This actually happened when the New York Stock Exchange collapsed in October 1987. The linking of international stock markets around the world and globalization of capital markets provide further justification for introducing an international dimension in the study of microeconomic theory (see Chapter 15). In recent years, the New York Stock Exchange seems to have lost some of its former ability to anticipate changing economic conditions and its importance as the central source of capital for corporate America, as the latter borrows increasing amounts from banks for takeovers and mergers. Indeed, global markets for securities, featuring automated, round-the-world, round-the-clock trading could eventually eclipse Wall Street's capital-raising dominance.

Sources: The New York Stock Exchange (New York: the New York Stock Exchange, 1987), and ''The Future of Wall Street,'' *Business Week,* November 5, 1990, pp. 119–124.

8.2 PRICE DETERMINATION IN THE MARKET PERIOD

The **market period,** or the very short run, refers to the period of time during which the market supply of a commodity is fixed. This may be a day, a week, a month, or longer, depending on the industry. For example, if milk is delivered every morning to New York City, and no other deliveries can be arranged for the rest of the day, the market period is one day. For wheat, the market period extends from one harvest to the next. For Michelangelo's paintings, the length of the market period is infinite because the supply is fixed forever.

During the market period, costs of production are irrelevant in the determination of price, and the entire stock of a perishable commodity is put up for sale at whatever price it can fetch. Thus, with perfect competition among buyers and sellers, demand alone determines price, while supply alone determines quantity. This is shown in Figure 8–1.

FIGURE 8–1   Price Determination in the Market Period

With the quantity supplied fixed at 350, the market supply curve of the commodity
is S. With D as the market demand curve, the equilibrium price is $35. At prices higher
than $35, there will be unsold quantities, and this will cause the price to fall to the
equilibrium level. At prices below $35, the quantity demanded exceeds the quantity
supplied, and the price will be bid up to $35. With D' as the demand curve, $P = \$50$.
With D'', $P = \$20$.

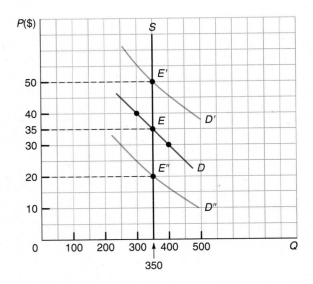

In the figure, S is the fixed or zero-elastic market supply curve for 350 units
of the commodity. With D as the market demand curve, the equilibrium price
is $35. Only at this price does the quantity demanded equal the quantity
supplied, and the market clears. At higher prices, there will be unsold quantities, and this will cause the price to fall to the equilibrium level. For example,
at the price of $40, only 300 units would be demanded (see the figure); hence,
the quantity supplied would exceed the quantity demanded and the commodity price would fall. On the other hand, at lower than the equilibrium price,
the quantity demanded exceeds the quantity supplied, and the price will be
bid up to $35. For example, at the price of $30, 400 units of the commodity
would be demanded; hence, the quantity demanded would exceed the quantity supplied and the price would be bid up to $35 (the equilibrium price at
which the quantity demanded equals the quantity supplied). With D' as the
demand curve, $P = \$50$. With D'', $P = \$20$.

8.3 SHORT-RUN EQUILIBRIUM OF THE FIRM

Even though analysis of the market period is interesting, we are primarily
interested in the short run and in the long run, when the quantity produced

and sold of the commodity can be varied. In this section, we examine the determination of output by the firm in the short run. We first do so with the total approach and then with the marginal approach. Finally, we focus on the process of profit maximization or loss minimization by the firm.

Total Approach: Maximizing the Positive Difference Between Total Revenue and Total Costs

We have seen in section 6.1 that profit maximization provides the framework for the analysis of the firm. The equilibrium output of the firm is the one that maximizes the total profits of the firm. Total profits equal total revenue minus total costs. Thus, total profits are maximized when the positive difference between total revenue and total costs is largest. This is shown in Figure 8–2.

The short-run total cost (STC) curve in the top panel of Figure 8–2 is the one of Figure 7–5. The vertical intercept ($30) gives the fixed costs of the firm. Within the limits imposed by the given plant, the firm can vary its output by varying the quantity of the variable inputs it uses. This generates the STC curve of the firm. The STC curve shows the minimum total costs of producing the various levels of output in the short run. Past point W, the law of diminishing returns begins to operate and the STC curve faces upward or rises at an increasing rate (see section 7.3).

The total revenue curve is a straight line through the origin because the firm can sell any quantity of the commodity at the given price (determined at the intersection of the market demand and supply curves of the commodity). With $P = \$35$, the total revenue ($TR$) of the firm is $35 if the firm sells one unit of output. The $TR = \$70$ if the firm sells two units of output, $TR = \$105$ with $Q = 3$, $TR = \$140$ with $Q = 4$, and so on. Put more succinctly, $TR = (\$35)(Q)$. Thus, the TR of the firm is a straight line through the origin with slope equal to the commodity price of $35 (see the top panel of Figure 8–2).

At zero output, $TR = 0$ while $STC = \$30$. Thus, the firm incurs a total loss of $30 equal to its fixed costs. This gives the negative intercept of $(-)\$30$ of the total profit curve in the bottom panel. At $Q = 1$, $TR = \$35$ and $STC = \$50$, so that total profits are $-\$15$. At $Q = 1.5$, $TR = STC = \$52.50$ (point W in the top panel), and total profits are zero (point W' in the bottom panel). This is called the **break-even point.** Between $Q = 1.5$ and $Q = 5$, TR exceeds STC and the firm earns a profit. Total profits equal the positive difference between TR and STC. Total profits are largest at $31.50 when $Q = 3.5$ (i.e., where the TR and the STC curves are parallel and the total profit curve has zero slope). At Q smaller than 3.5, say, $Q = 3$, $TR = \$105$ and $STC = \$75$, so that total profits are $30. At $Q = 4$, $TR = \$140$, $STC = \$110$, and total profits are again $30. At $Q = 5$, $TR = STC = \$175$, so that total profits are zero (points T and T', respectively). At Q greater than 5, TR is smaller than STC and the firm incurs a loss. Thus, the level of output at which the firm

FIGURE 8–2   Short-Run Equilibrium of the Firm: Total Approach

The STC curve in the top panel is that of Figure 7–5. The TR curve is a straight line through the origin with slope of $P = \$35$. At $Q = 0$, $TR = 0$ and $STC = \$30$, so that total profits are $-\$30$ and equal the firm's TFC (see the bottom panel). At $Q = 1$, $TR = \$35$ and $STC = \$50$, so that total profits are $-\$15$. At $Q = 1.5$, $TR = STC = \$52.50$, and total profits are zero. This is the break-even point. Between $Q = 1.5$ and $Q = 5$, TR exceeds STC and the firm earns (positive) economic profits. Total profits are greatest at $\$31.50$ when $Q = 3.5$ (and the TR and the STC curves are parallel). At $Q = 5$, $TR = STC = \$175$ so that total profits are zero (points T and T'). At Q greater than 5, TR is smaller than STC and the firm incurs a loss.

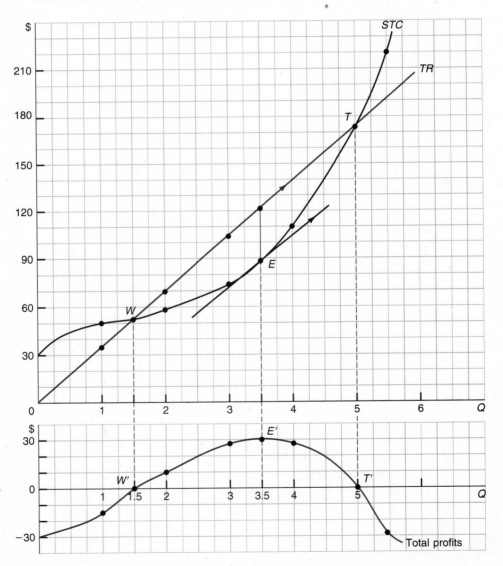

TABLE 8–1   Total Revenue, Total Costs, and Total Profits

Quantity of Output	Price	Total Revenue	Total Costs	Total Profits
0	$35	$ 0	$ 30	$−30
1	35	35	50	−15
1.5	35	52.50	52.50	0
2	35	70	60	+10
3	35	105	75	+30
*3.5	35	122.50	91	+31.50
4	35	140	110	+30
5	35	175	175	0
5.5	35	192.50	220	−27.50

*Output at which firm maximizes total profits.

maximizes total profits is $Q = 3.5$ (point E and E' in the top and bottom panels, respectively). Figure 8–2 is summarized in Table 8–1.[2]

Marginal Approach: Equating Marginal Revenue and Marginal Cost

Although the total approach to determine the equilibrium output of the firm is useful, the marginal approach is even more valuable and more widely used. This approach is shown in Figure 8–3. In the figure, the demand curve facing the firm (d) is horizontal or infinitely elastic at the given price of $P = \$35$. That is, the perfectly competitive firm is a price taker and can sell any quantity of the commodity at $P = \$35$. Since marginal revenue (MR) is the change in total revenue per-unit change in output, and price (P) is constant, then $P = MR$ (see section 5.6). For example, with $P = \$35$ and $Q = 1$, $TR = \$35$. With $P = \$35$ and $Q = 2$, $TR = \$70$. Thus, the change in TR per-unit change in output (the slope of the TR curve or marginal revenue) is $MR = P = \$35$ (see Figure 8–3).

The short-run marginal cost (MC) and the average total cost (ATC) curves of the firm in Figure 8–3 are those of Figure 7–6 (and derived from the STC curve of Figures 7–5 and 8–2). The $MC = \Delta STC/\Delta Q$, while $ATC = STC/Q$. As explained earlier, total profits are maximized where the TR and the STC curves are parallel and their slopes are equal. Since the slope of the TR curve is $MR = P$ and the slope of the STC curve is MC, this implies that when total profits are at a maximum, $P = MR = MC$. Furthermore, since the STC curve

[2]When the firm has no knowledge of the exact shape of its STC curve, it uses a break-even chart to determine the minimum sales volume to avoid losses (see problem 4, with answer at end of book).

FIGURE 8–3   Short-Run Equilibrium of the Firm: Marginal Approach

The demand curve facing the firm (d) is horizontal or infinitely elastic at the given price of $P = \$35$. Since P is constant, marginal revenue (MR) equals P. The firm maximizes total profits where $P = MR = MC$, and MC is rising. This occurs at $Q = 3.5$ (point E). At $Q = 3.5$, $P = \$35$ and $ATC = \$26$. Therefore, profit per unit is $9 (EE'), and total profits are $31.50 (shaded rectangle EE'AB).

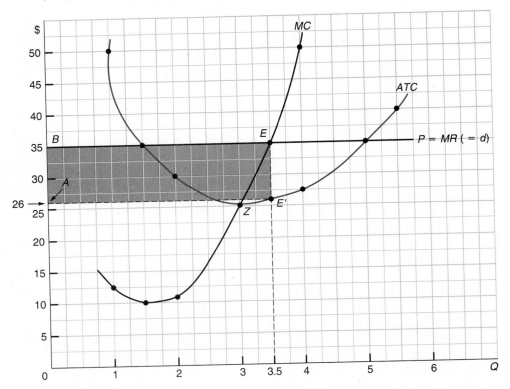

faces upward where profits are maximum, the MC curve must be rising. Thus, the firm is in short-run equilibrium or maximizes total profits by producing the output where $P = MR = MC$, and MC is rising.[3]

For example, the best level of output for the firm in Figure 8–3 is $Q = 3.5$ (point E), and this is the same result as with the total approach. At $Q = 3.5$, $P = \$35$ and $ATC = \$26$. Therefore, profit per unit is $9 (EE' in the figure), and total profits are ($9)(3.5) = $31.50 (shaded rectangle EE'AB). Until point E, MR exceeds MC and so the firm earns higher profits by expanding output. On the other hand, past point E, MC exceeds MR and the firm earns higher profits by *reducing* output. This leaves point E as the profit-maximizing level of output. Note that at point E, P or $MR = MC$ and MC is rising so that the conditions for profit maximization are fulfilled.

[3]For a mathematical presentation of profit maximization using rudimentary calculus, see section A.10 of the Mathematical Appendix at the end of the book.

TABLE 8–2   **Profit Maximization for the Perfectly Competitive Firm: Per-Unit Approach**

Q	P = MR	MC	ATC	Profit per Unit	Total Profits	Relationship Between MR and MC
1	$35	$12.50	$50	$−15	$−15	
1.50	35	10	35	0	0	
2	35	11	30	+5	+10	MR > MC
3	35	25	25	+10	+30	
*3.50	35	35	26	+9	+31.50	MR = MC
4	35	50	27.50	+7.50	+30	
5	35		35	0	0	MR < MC
5.5	35		40	−5	−27.50	

*Output at which firm maximizes total profits.

Also note that at $Q = 3$, $P = \$35$, and $ATC = \$25$, and profit per unit is largest at that point ($10). The firm, however, seeks to maximize total profits, not profit per unit, and this occurs at $Q = 3.5$, where total profits are $31.50, as opposed to $30 at $Q = 3$. The total profits of the firm at various levels of output with $P = \$35$ are summarized in Table 8–2. The MR, MC, and ATC values given in the table are read off Figure 8–3 at various output levels. For example, at $Q = 1$, $MR = \$35$, $MC = \$12.50$, and $ATC = \$50$. At $Q = 2$, $MR = \$35$, $MC = \$11$, and $ATC = \$30$, and so on.

The rule that a firm maximizes profits at the output level at which the marginal revenue to the firm equals its marginal cost is a specific application of the general *marginal* concept that any activity should be pursued until the marginal benefit from the activity equals the marginal cost.

Profit Maximization or Loss Minimization?

We have seen that the best or optimum level of output of the firm is given at the point where P (or MR) equals MC, and MC is rising. At this level of output, however, the firm can either make a profit (as in Figure 8–3), break even, or incur a loss. In Figure 8–3, P was higher than the ATC at the best level of output, and the firm made a profit. If P were smaller than the ATC at the best level of output, the firm would incur a loss. However, as long as P exceeds the average *variable* cost (AVC), it pays for the firm to continue to produce, because by doing so it would *minimize its losses*. That is, the excess of P over the AVC can be used to partially cover the fixed costs of the firm. Were the firm to shut down, it would incur a greater loss equal to its total fixed costs. This is shown in Figure 8–4.

In the figure, the MC and the ATC curves are the same as in Figure 8–3. Figure 8–4 also includes the AVC curve of the firm (from Figure 7–6). In Figure 8–4, we assume that $P = MR = \$20$. The best level of output of the firm is then 2.75 units, given at point F, where $P = MR = MC = \$20$, and MC is

FIGURE 8–4   Profit Maximization or Loss Minimization

At P = \$20, the best level of output of the firm is 2.75 units (point F, where $P = MR$ = MC, and MC is rising). At Q = 2.75, average total cost (ATC) exceeds P and the firm will incur a loss of $F'F$ (about \$5.50) per unit, and a total loss equal to rectangle $F'FNR$ (about \$15). If, however, the firm were to shut down, it would incur the greater loss of \$30 equal to its total fixed costs (the area of the larger rectangle $F'F''GR$). The shutdown point (Z) is at $P = AVC$.

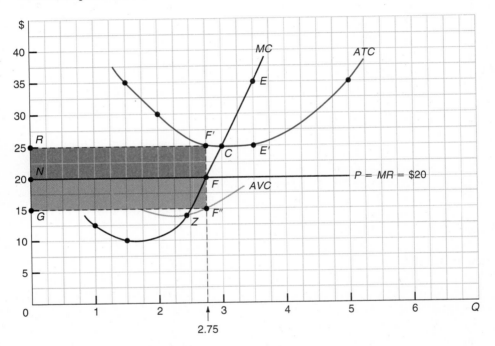

rising. At Q = 2.75, ATC exceeds P and the firm incurs a loss equal to $F'F$ (about \$5.50) per unit, and a total loss equal to the area of rectangle $F'FNR$ (about \$15). Were the firm to shut down, it would incur the greater loss of \$30 (its total fixed costs, given by the area of the larger rectangle $F'F''GR$).

Put another way, by continuing to produce Q = 2.75 at P = \$20, the firm will cover FF'' (about \$5.50) of its fixed costs per unit and $FF''GN$ (about \$15) of its total fixed costs. Thus, it pays for the firm to stay in business even though it incurs a loss. That is, by remaining in business, the firm will incur losses that are smaller than its total fixed costs (which would be the firm's losses by shutting down). Only if P were smaller than the AVC at the best level of output would the firm minimize losses by going out of business. By doing so, the firm would limit its losses to an amount no larger than its total fixed costs. Finally, if $P = AVC$, the firm would be indifferent between producing or going out of business, because in either case it would incur a loss equal to its total fixed costs. The point where $P = AVC$ (point Z in the figure) is called the **shutdown point**.[4]

8.4 SHORT-RUN SUPPLY CURVE AND EQUILIBRIUM

In this section, we derive the short-run supply curve of a perfectly competitive firm and industry. We also examine how the equilibrium price of the commodity is determined at the intersection of the market demand and supply curves for the commodity. This is the price at which the perfectly competitive firm can sell any quantity of the commodity.

Short-Run Supply Curve of the Firm and Industry

We have seen so far that a perfectly competitive firm always produces at the point where $P = MC$ and MC is rising, and this is so as long as $P > AVC$. As a result, the rising portion of the firm's MC curve above the AVC curve is the firm's short-run supply curve of the commodity. This is shown in the left panel of Figure 8–5.

The left panel of Figure 8–5 reproduces the firm's MC curve above point Z (the shutdown point) from Figure 8–4. This is the perfectly competitive firm's short-run supply curve (s) because it shows the quantity of the commodity that the firm would supply in the short run at various prices. For example, the firm supplies 3 units of the commodity at the price of $25 (point C in the left panel). The reason is that at $P = \$25$, $P = MR = MC = \$25$, and MC is rising. At $P = \$35$, the firm supplies 3.5 units of the commodity (point E), while at $P = \$50$, it supplies 4 units (point T). The firm will supply no output at prices below the shutdown point (point Z in the figure). Thus, the rising portion of the firm's MC curve above the shutdown point is the firm's short-run supply curve of the commodity (s in the left panel of Figure 8–5). It shows the quantity of the commodity that the firm would supply in the short run at various prices.

The horizontal summation of the supply curves of all firms in the industry then gives the industry short-run supply curve for the commodity. This is given by the $\Sigma MC = S$ curve in the right panel of Figure 8–5, where the symbol Σ refers to the "summation of." The perfectly competitive industry's short-run supply curve in the right panel is based on the assumption that there are 100 identical firms in the industry (and input prices do not vary with industry output). For example, at $P = \$25$, each firm supplies 3 units of the commodity (point C in the left panel) and the entire industry supplies 300 units (point C^* in the right panel). At $P = \$35$, each firm supplies 3.5 units (point E) and the industry supplies 350 units (point E^*). At $P = \$50$,

---

[4]Recall that $STC = TVC + TFC$ and total profits equal $TR - STC$. When $P = AVC$, $TR = TVC$, so that the firm's total losses would equal its TFC, whether it produces or shuts down. Thus, point Z, at which $P = AVC$ (and $TR = TVC$), is the firm's shutdown point.

FIGURE 8–5   Short-Run Supply Curve of the Firm and Industry

The left panel reproduces the firm's *MC* curve above point Z (the shutdown point) from Figure 8–4. This is the perfectly competitive firm's short-run supply curve *s*. For example, at $P = \$25$, $Q = 3$ (point C); at $P = \$35$, $Q = 3.5$ (point E); at $P = \$50$, $Q = 4$ (point T). The right panel shows the industry's short-run supply curve on the assumption that there are 100 identical firms in the industry and input prices are constant. This is given by the $\Sigma MC = S$ curve. Thus, at $P = \$25$, $Q = 300$ (point C*); at $P = \$35$, $Q = 350$ (point E*); at $P = \$50$, $Q = 400$ (point T*).

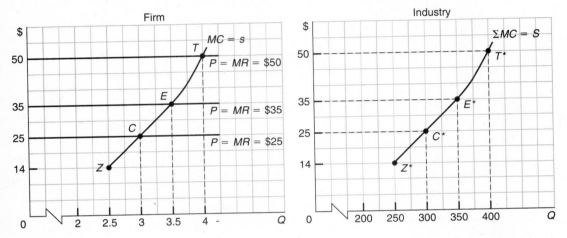

$Q = 4$ for the firm (point T) and $Q = 400$ for the industry (point T*). Note that no output of the commodity is produced at prices below $P = \$14$ (points Z and Z* in the figure).[5]

The derivation of the perfectly competitive industry short-run supply curve of the commodity as the horizontal summation of each firm's short-run supply curve is based on the assumption that input prices are constant regardless of the quantity of inputs that each firm and the industry demand. That is, it is based on the assumption that the firm is able to hire a greater quantity of the inputs (to produce the larger output) at constant input prices. If input prices were to rise as firms demanded more of the inputs, the industry supply curve would be steeper or less elastic than indicated in the right panel of Figure 8–5. An increase in the commodity price will then result in a smaller increase in the quantity supplied of the commodity (see problem 8, with answer at end of book).

Example 2
The Supply of Alaskan Shale Oil

In a 1978 study, Ericsson and Morgan estimated (from engineering studies) that the industry supply curve of shale oil (often called "synthetic fuel") was

---

[5]Point Z in the left panel of Figure 8–5 corresponds to point Z' in Figure 7–6.

as shown in Figure 8–6. This indicates that it would not be economical to produce oil from shale at prices below $10 per barrel. The quantity of oil supplied, in millions of barrels per day, would be 2 at the price of $10 per barrel, 6 at the price of $16 per barrel, and 16 at $18 per barrel. The maximum that would be supplied at any price would be about 16 million barrels per day. Compare this with a consumption of about 18 million barrels per day in the U.S. in 1978 (of which over 3 million were imported at the price of about $13 per barrel).

In 1980, Congress created the Synthetic Fuel Corporation to stimulate the production of oil from shale and reduce American dependence on imported petroleum. The original plan called for the production of one-half million barrels of oil from shale per day by 1987. By the end of 1984, $3 billion of federal subsidies had been spent on four projects. Because of large cost overruns, however, the cost of producing synthetic oil was sharply revised upward in 1984 to be double the price of $28 per barrel for imported oil. This led Exxon, one of the co-sponsors of the project, to withdraw from the project. The entire shale oil project was abandoned at the end of 1985 when the U.S. government refused to provide further subsidies.

FIGURE 8–6   The Supply Curve of Shale Oil

The supply curve of shale oil rises gently up to 16 million barrels per day, where it becomes vertical.

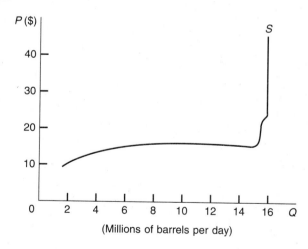

(Millions of barrels per day)

Sources: N. Ericsson and P. Morgan, "The Economic Feasibility of Shale Oil: An Activity Analysis," *Bell Journal of Economics*, August 1978; "Exxon Abandons Shale Oil Project," *New York Times*, May 3, 1982, p. 1, and "Congressional Conferees End Financing of Synthetic Fuels Program," *New York Times*, December 17, 1985, p. B11.

Short-Run Equilibrium of the Industry and Firm

In section 5.1, we showed how the market demand curve for a commodity was derived from the horizontal summation of the demand curves of all the individual consumers of the commodity in the market. We have now shown how to derive the industry or market supply curve of the commodity. In a perfectly competitive market, the equilibrium price of the commodity is determined at the intersection of the market demand curve and the market supply curve of the commodity. This was already explained in section 2.4. Thus, we have traveled a complete circle and returned to the point of departure. We now know, however, what lies behind the market demand curve and the market supply curve of the commodity and how they are derived (i.e., we no longer simply assume that these curves are given, as in Chapter 2).

Given the price of the commodity, the perfectly competitive firm can sell any quantity of the commodity at that price. As noted earlier, the firm will produce at the point where P or $MR = MC$, provided that MC is rising and $P \geq AVC$. This is shown in Figure 8–7.

The right panel of Figure 8–7 shows the short-run market supply curve S (from Figure 8–5) and hypothetical market demand curve D for the commodity. These curves intersect at point E^*, and result in the equilibrium price of $35 and the equilibrium quantity of 350 units. At $P = \$25$, the quantity demanded (400 units) exceeds the quantity supplied (300 units), and the resulting shortage will drive the commodity price up to $P = \$35$. On the other hand, at $P = \$50$, the quantity supplied (400 units) exceeds the quantity

FIGURE 8–7   Short-Run Equilibrium of the Firm and Industry

With S (from Figure 8–5) and D in the right panel, $P = \$35$ and $Q = 350$ (point E^*), and the perfectly competitive firm would produce 3.5 units (point E in the left panel, as in Figure 8–3). If D shifted up to D', $P = \$50$ and $Q = 400$ (point T^*) and the firm would produce 4 units of output (point T in the left panel).

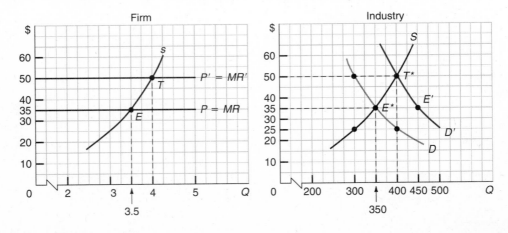

demanded (300 units), and the resulting surplus will drive the price down to
$P = \$35$. The left panel shows that at $P = \$35$, the perfectly competitive firm
will produce 3.5 units (point E, as in Figure 8–3). Note that each firm produces
$\frac{1}{100}$ of the total industry or market output.[6]

If the market demand curve then shifted up to D' (for example, as a result
of an increase in consumers' incomes), there would be a shortage of 100 units
of the commodity at $P = \$35$ (E^*E' in the right panel of Figure 8–7). This
would cause the equilibrium price to rise to $50 and the equilibrium quantity
to 400 units (point T^*). Then, at $P = \$50$, the perfectly competitive firm
maximizes profits at point T by producing 4 units of output (see the left panel).
This is based on the assumption that there are 100 identical firms in the
perfectly competitive industry and that input prices remain constant.

Example 3
The Russian Wheat Deal

In July 1982, the then Soviet Union announced that it would purchase
400 million bushels of winter wheat from the United States. This was
approximately one-quarter of the total U.S. annual production. With the short-
run supply curve for winter wheat fairly price inelastic, the increased demand
for American wheat led to a sharp rise in the price of wheat in the United
States—from about $1.60 per bushel at the end of June 1982 to about $2.25
by the end of September.

The size of the Russian wheat deal caught many farmers by surprise and
angered those who had sold their wheat just before the wheat deal was
announced. The increase in demand for American wheat led to an increase
in the price of wheat, exactly as predicted by our model (see the right panel
of Figure 8–7). Furthermore, since the supply curve for American (winter)
wheat was fairly price inelastic, the price increase was sharp. In the face of
continued difficulties in Russian agriculture and in the expectation of
continued purchases of American wheat by the Soviet Union and high wheat
prices in the United States, American farmers increased their wheat output
in 1983 and 1989 (also as predicted by our model). The same occurred with
corn in 1989.

More recently, the demand for U.S. wheat increased as a result of U.S. aid
to Russia to purchase American food after the fall of communism and as a
result of the subsidies that the U.S. government gave for exporting American
wheat to counter European subsidies. By increasing the demand for American

---

[6]For a mathematical presentation of how equilibrium is determined in a perfectly competitive
industry using rudimentary calculus, see section A.11 of the Mathematical Appendix at the end
of the book.

wheat, these measures also tended to keep wheat prices and production in the United States above what they would have been.

Sources: B. Luttrell, "Grain Export Agreements," *Federal Reserve Bank of St. Louis Review*, August/September 1981; "Signs of Big Soviet Purchase Push Corn Prices Higher," *New York Times*, October 20, 1989, p. D3; "U.S. Offers Russia Aid in Buying Food," *New York Times*, September 15, 1992, p. 6; and "U.S. Wheat Subsidies Are Message to Europe," *New York Times*, September 3, 1992, p. D2.

▲

8.5 LONG-RUN EQUILIBRIUM OF THE FIRM AND INDUSTRY

Having analyzed how equilibrium is reached in the market period and in the short run, we can now go on to examine how the perfectly competitive firm and industry reach equilibrium in the long run. This will set the stage for the analysis of constant, increasing, and decreasing cost industries in section 8.6.

Long-Run Equilibrium of the Firm

In the long run, all inputs are variable and the firm can build the most efficient plant to produce the best or most profitable level of output. The *best (i.e., the profit-maximizing) level of output* of the firm in the long run is the one at which price or marginal revenue equals long-run marginal cost. The *most efficient plant* is the one that allows the firm to produce the best level of output at the lowest possible cost. This is the plant represented by the *SATC* curve tangent to the *LAC* curve of the firm at the best level of output, as shown in Figure 8–8.[7]

The *LAC* curve in Figure 8–8 is the one of Figure 7–10, and the $SATC_1$ curve is that of Figures 7–6, 7–10, and 8–3. At $P = MR = \$35$ in Figure 8–8, the firm is in *short-run* equilibrium at point *E* by producing 3.5 units of output. The firm makes a profit of \$9 per unit (vertical distance *EE'*) and \$31.50 in total (as in Figure 8–3).

In the long run, the firm can increase its profits significantly by producing at point *J'*, where *P* or *MR* = *LMC* (and *LMC* is rising). The firm should build plant $SATC_5$ and operate it at point *J* (at *SATC* = \$13). Plant $SATC_5$ is the best plant (i.e, the one that allows the firm to produce the best level of output at the lowest *SATC*). In the long run, the firm will make profits of \$22 (*J'J*) per unit and \$286 in total (\$22 times 13 units of output). This compares with total profits of \$31.50 in the short run. Note that when the firm is in long-run equilibrium, it will also be in short-run equilibrium since *P* or *MR* = *SMC* =

---

[7]Since in the long run all costs are variable, the firm must at least cover all of its costs to remain in business.

FIGURE 8–8 Long-Run Equilibrium of the Firm

At $P = MR = \$35$, the firm is in short-run equilibrium at point E (as in Figure 8–3). In the long run, the firm can increase its profits by producing at point J', where P or $MR = LMC$ (and LMC is rising) and operating plant $SATC_5$ at point J. In the long run, the firm will make profits of $\$22$ ($J'J$) per unit and $\$286$ in total ($\$22$ times 13 units of output). Since at point J', $P = MR = SMC = LMC$, the firm is also in short-run equilibrium.

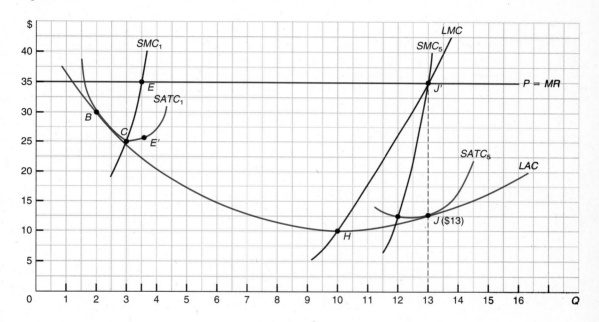

LMC (see point J' in the figure). This analysis assumes that input prices are constant.

Long-Run Equilibrium of the Industry and Firm

Even though the firm would be in long-run equilibrium at point J' in Figure 8–8, the industry would not. This is because the large profits that this and other firms earn at point J' will attract more firms to the industry. As new firms enter the industry (entry is free and resources are mobile), aggregate output expands. This will shift the short-run industry supply curve to the right until it intersects the market demand curve at the commodity price at which all firms make zero economic profits (i.e., they earn only a normal return) in the long run. Then, and only then, will the industry (and the firm) be in equilibrium. In fact, the building of the best plant by the firm and the entrance of new firms into the industry will take place simultaneously in the long run. The final result (equilibrium) is shown in Figure 8–9.

In the figure, the industry (in the right panel) and the firm (in the left panel) are in long-run equilibrium at point H, where $P = MR = LMC = SMC$

FIGURE 8–9   **Long-Run Equilibrium of the Industry and Firm**

The industry (in the right panel) and the firm (in the left panel) are in long-run equilibrium at point H, where $P = MR = SMC = LMC = SATC = LAC = \$10$. The firm produces at the lowest point on its LAC curve (operating optimal plant $SATC_4$ at point H) and earns zero profits.

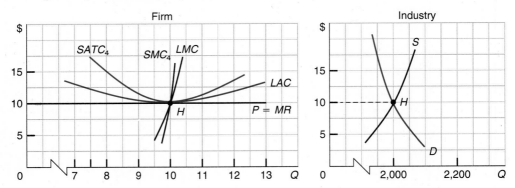

$= LAC = SATC = \$10$.[8] The firm produces at the lowest point on its LAC curve (operating optimal plant $SATC_4$ at point H) and earns zero economic profits. Zero economic profit means that the owner of the firm receives only a normal return on his or her investment when the industry and firm are in long-run equilibrium. That is, the owner receives a return on the capital invested in the firm equal only to the amount that he or she would earn by investing the capital in a similarly risky venture. If the owner manages the firm, zero economic profits also includes what he or she would earn in the best *alternative* occupation (i.e., managing a similar firm for someone else). Thus, zero profits in economics means that the total revenues of the firm just cover all costs (explicit and implicit).[9]

When the perfectly competitive industry is in long-run equilibrium, the firm not only earns zero profits but produces at the lowest point on its LAC curve (point H in the left panel of Figure 8–9). Thus, resources are used most efficiently to produce the goods and services most desired by society at the minimum cost. Since firms also earn zero profits, consumers purchase the commodity at the lowest possible price (\$10 at point H in the figure). In this sense, perfect competition is the most efficient form of market organization.

---

[8]Note that the supply curve labeled S in the right panel of Figure 8–9 is much larger than the supply curve S in the right panel of Figure 8–7 because more firms have entered the industry in the long run and industry output is larger.

[9]As pointed out in section 6.1, the meaning of *profit* in economics is to be distinguished clearly from the everyday use of the term (which considers implicit costs as part of profits). In economics, profits always refer only to the excess of total revenue over total costs, and total costs include both explicit and implicit costs (see section 7.1). In short, in economics, profits mean above-normal returns.

This is to be contrasted to the situation under imperfect competition (discussed in the next four chapters), where we will see that producers seldom, if ever, produce at the lowest point on their *LAC* curve, and they charge a price that also usually includes a profit margin.

We have seen so far that when a perfectly competitive firm earns (economic) profits, more firms will enter the industry in the long run and this will lower the commodity price until all firms just break even (i.e., earn zero profits). On the other hand, if the perfectly competitive firm incurs a loss in the short run and would continue to incur a loss in the long run even by constructing the best plant, some firms would leave the industry. This would shift the industry supply curve to the left until it intersected the industry demand curve at the (higher) commodity price at which the remaining firms made zero economic profits but incurred no losses. The final result would be as shown in Figure 8–9, except that there would now be fewer firms in the industry and the industry output would be smaller. As it is, Figure 8–9 indicates that if all firms had identical cost curves, there would be 200 identical firms in the industry when in long-run equilibrium. Each firm would produce 10 units of output and break even.

Perfectly competitive firms need not have identical cost curves (although we assume so for simplicity), but the *minimum point* on their *LAC* curves must occur at the same cost per unit. If some firms had more productive inputs and, thus, lower average costs than other firms in the industry, the more productive inputs would be able to extract from their employer higher rewards (payments) commensurate to their higher productivity, under the threat of leaving to work for others. As a result, their *LAC* curves would shift upward until the lowest point on the *LAC* curve of all firms is the same. Thus, competition in the input markets as well as in the commodity market will result in all firms having identical (minimum) average costs and zero economic profits when the industry is in the long-run equilibrium.

Example 4

 Long-Run Adjustment in the U.S. Cotton Textile Industry

In studying the U.S. cotton textile industry, Lloyd Reynolds found that this industry was closer to perfect competition than any other U.S. manufacturing industry during the period between World Wars I and II. The product was nearly homogeneous, there were many buyers and sellers of cotton cloth (each too small to affect its price), and entry into and exit from the industry was relatively easy. Reynolds found that the rate of return on investments in the textile industry was about 6% in the South and 1% in the North (due to higher costs for labor and raw cotton in the North). These returns compared to an average rate of return of about 8% for all manufacturing industries in the United States. As a result, many textile firms went out of business in the long run, and capacity declined by more than 33% from 1925 to 1938. The decline was more rapid in the North than in the South.

The decline in capacity in the U.S. cotton textile industry was as predicted by the perfectly competitive model. According to the model, firms would leave an industry in the long run until remaining firms break even (or returns on investment in the industry rise to the average for other industries). Also as predicted by the model, most textile firms going out of business were in the North, where returns were much lower than in the South. Indeed, most U.S. textile firms were able to remain in business during the period after World War II only as a result of U.S. restrictions on cheaper textile imports.

Sources: L. Reynolds, "Competition in the Textile Industry," in W. Adams and T. Traywick, Eds., *Readings in Economics* (New York: Macmillan, 1948), and "Apparel Makes Last Stand," *New York Times*, September 26, 1990, p. D2.

▲

8.6 CONSTANT, INCREASING, AND DECREASING COST INDUSTRIES

In the previous section, we examined how a perfectly competitive industry and firm reach equilibrium in the long run. Starting from a position of long-run equilibrium, we now examine how the perfectly competitive industry and firm adjust in the long run to an increase in the market demand for the commodity. This allows us to define constant, increasing, and decreasing cost industries and analyze their operation graphically.

Constant Cost Industries

Starting from the long-run equilibrium condition of the industry and the firm (point H) in Figure 8–9, if the market demand curve for the commodity increases, the equilibrium price will rise in the short run and firms earn economic profits (i.e., they receive above-normal returns). This will attract more firms into the industry, and the short-run industry or market supply curve of the commodity increases (shifts to the right). If input prices remain constant (as more inputs are demanded by the expanding industry), the new long-run equilibrium price for the commodity will be the same as before the increase in demand and supply. Then, the long-run industry supply curve (*LS*) for the commodity is horizontal at the minimum *LAC*. This is a **constant cost industry** and is shown in Figure 8–10.

In Figure 8–10, point H in the right and left panels show the long-run equilibrium position of the perfectly competitive industry and firm, respectively (as in Figure 8–9), before the increase in demand (*D*) and supply (*S*). The increase in D to D' results in the short-run equilibrium price of $20 (point H' in the right panel). At $P = \$20$, each of the 200 identical firms in the industry will produce $Q = 10.5$ (given by point H' in the left panel at which $P = SMC_4 = \$20$) for a total industry output of 2,100 units.

FIGURE 8–10 Constant Cost Industry

Point H is the original long-run equilibrium point of the industry and firm. An increase in D to D' results in P = $20, and all firms earn economic profits. As more firms enter the industry, S shifts to S' and P = $10 if input prices remain constant. By joining points H and H" in the right panel, we derive horizontal long-run supply curve LS for the (constant cost) industry.

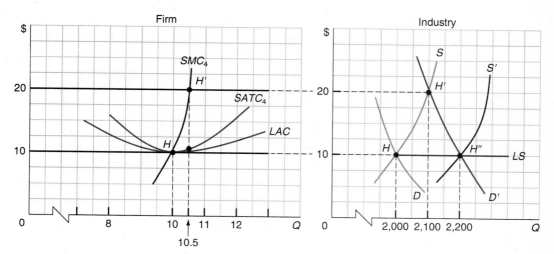

Because each firm earns profits at P = $20 (see the left panel), more firms enter the industry in the long run, shifting S to the right. If input prices remain constant, S shifts to S', reestablishing the original equilibrium price of $10 (point H" in the right panel). At P = $10, each firm produces at the lowest point on its LAC and earns zero economic profit (point H in the left panel). By joining points H and H" in the right panel, we derive the long-run supply curve of the industry (LS). Since LS is horizontal, this is a constant cost industry (with 220 identical firms producing a total output of 2,200 units).

Constant costs are more likely to result in industries that utilize general rather than specialized inputs and that account for only a small fraction of the total quantity demanded of the inputs in the economy. Then, the industry may be able to hire a greater quantity of the general inputs it uses without driving input prices upward.

Increasing Cost Industries

If input prices *rise* as more inputs are demanded by an expanding industry, the long-run industry supply curve for the commodity will be positively sloped and we have an **increasing cost industry**. This means that greater outputs of the commodity per time period will be supplied in the long run only at higher commodity prices (see Figure 8–11).

Starting from point H in the right and left panels of Figure 8–11, the increase

FIGURE 8–11   Increasing Cost Industry

Point *H* is the original long-run equilibrium point of the industry and firm. An increase in *D* to *D'* results in *P* = $20 and all firms earn economic profits. As more firms enter the industry, *S* shifts to *S'* and *P* = $15 if input prices rise. By joining points *H* and *H"* in the right panel, we derive positively sloped long-run supply curve *LS* for the (increasing cost) industry.

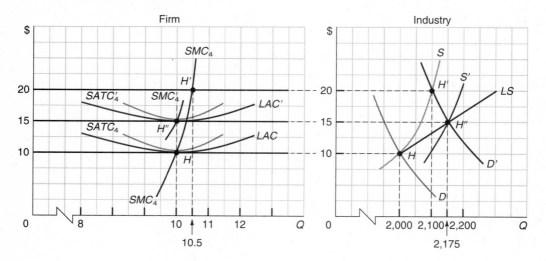

in *D* to *D'* results in *P* = $20 (point *H'* in the right panel), at which all firms earn economic profits (point *H'* in the left panel). More firms enter the industry in the long run, and more inputs are demanded as industry output expands. *So far, this is identical to Figure 8–10.* If input prices now rise, each firm's per-unit cost curves shift up (as explained in the appendix to Chapter 7), and *S* shifts to the right to *S'* so as to establish equilibrium *P* = minimum *LAC'* = $15 (see point *H"* in both panels of Figure 8–11). All profits are squeezed out as costs rise and price falls. By joining points *H* and *H"* in the right panel, we get the long-run industry supply curve (*LS*). Since *LS* is positively sloped, the industry is an increasing cost industry (with 217.5 or 218 identical firms).

Increasing costs are more likely to result in industries that utilize some specialized input such as labor with unique skills (e.g., highly trained lab technicians to conduct experiments in genetics) or custom-made machinery to perform very special tasks (e.g., oil drilling platforms). Then, the industry may have to pay higher prices to bring forth a greater supply of the specialized inputs it requires and we have an increasing cost industry.

Decreasing Cost Industries

If input prices *fall* as more inputs are demanded by an expanding industry, the long-run industry supply curve for the commodity will be negatively sloped and we have a **decreasing cost industry.** This means that greater outputs of the commodity per time period will be supplied in the long run at lower commodity prices (see Figure 8–12).

The movement from point H to point H' in both panels of Figure 8–12 is the same as in Figures 8–10 and 8–11. Since at point H' firms earn profits, more firms enter the industry in the long run. Industry output expands, and more inputs are demanded. If input prices fall, each firm's per-unit cost curves shift down, and S shifts to the right to S' so as to establish equilibrium $P =$ minimum $LAC' = \$5$ (point H'' in both panels). By joining points H and H'' in the right panel, we derive LS, the industry long-run supply curve. Since LS is negatively sloped, we have a decreasing cost industry (with 230 identical firms).

Decreasing costs may result when the expansion of an industry leads to (1) the establishment of technical institutes to train labor for skills required by the industry at a lower cost than firms in the industry do; (2) the setting up of enterprises to supply some equipment used by the industry that was previously constructed by the firms in the industry for themselves at higher cost; (3) the exploitation of some cheaper natural resource that the industry can substitute for more expensive resources but which was not feasible to exploit when the demand for the natural resource was smaller.

In the real world, we have examples of constant, increasing, and decreasing cost industries. In fact, a particular industry could exhibit constant, increasing, or decreasing costs over different time periods and at various levels of de-

FIGURE 8–12   Decreasing Cost Industry

Points H and H' are the same as in the preceding two figures. Starting from point H', as more firms enter the industry, S shifts to S' and $P = \$5$ if input prices fall. By joining points H and H'' in the right panel, we derive the negatively sloped long-run supply curve LS for the (decreasing cost) industry.

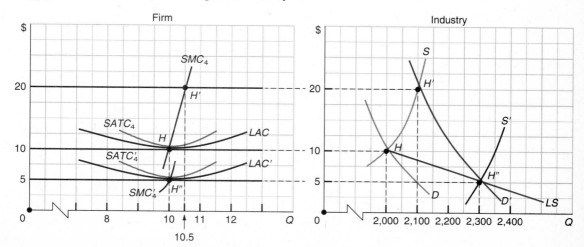

mand.[10] It should also be noted that the shifts in firms' per-unit cost curves in the left panel of Figures 8–11 and 8–12 were vertical (so that the lowest point on both the *LAC* and *LAC'* curves occurred at $Q = 10$). This is the case if the prices of all inputs change in the same proportion. Otherwise, per-unit cost curves would also shift to the right or to the left.

The *downward shift* in the firm's per-unit cost curves (due to a fall in input prices) as the *industry expands* is called an **external economy,** while the *upward shift* in the firm's per-unit cost curves (due to an increase in input prices) as the *industry expands* is called an **external diseconomy.** These are to be clearly distinguished from economies or diseconomies of scale, which are *internal* to the firm and refer instead to a downward or an upward *movement along* a given *LAC* curve (as the firm expands output and builds larger scales of plants). The assumption here is that as only a single firm expands output, input prices remain constant. External economies and diseconomies will be examined in detail in Chapter 17.

8.7 INTERNATIONAL COMPETITION IN THE DOMESTIC ECONOMY

Domestic firms in most industries face a great deal of competition from abroad. Most U.S.-made goods today compete with similar goods from abroad and in turn compete with foreign-made goods in foreign markets. Steel, textiles, cameras, wines, automobiles, television sets, computers, and aircraft are but a few of the domestic products that compete with foreign products for consumers' dollars in the U.S. economy today. As international tastes converge (see section 3.3), multinational corporations grow in size and number, and communications and transportation continue to improve, international competition—already sizable in most domestic markets—is bound to sharply increase. Competition from imports allows domestic consumers to purchase more of a commodity at a lower price than in the absence of imports. This is shown by Figure 8–13.

In the figure, D_X and S_X refer to the domestic market demand and supply curves of commodity X. In the absence of trade, the equilibrium price is given by the intersection of the D_X and S_X at point E, so that domestic consumers purchase $400X$ (all of which is produced domestically) at $P_X = \$5$. With free trade at the world price of $P_X = \$3$, the price of commodity X to domestic consumers will fall to the world price. The foreign supply curve of this nation's imports of commodity X, S_F, is horizontal at $P_X = \$3$ on the assumption that this nation's demand for imports of commodity X is small in relation to the total world supply of exports of commodity X to the nation. From the figure,

---

[10]Of the three cases, increasing cost industries may be, perhaps, somewhat more common than the other two cases.

FIGURE 8–13   Consumption, Production, and Imports Under Free Trade

In the absence of trade, equilibrium is at point E, where D_X and S_X intersect, so that $P_X = \$5$ and $Q_X = 400$. With free trade at the world price of $P_X = \$3$, domestic consumers purchase $IR = 600X$, of which $IK = 200X$ are produced domestically and $KR = 400X$ are imported.

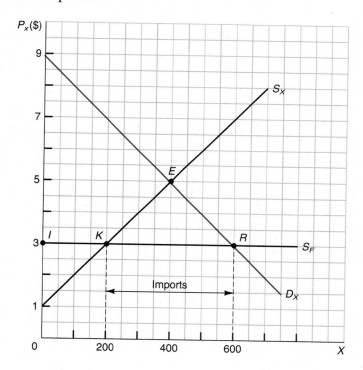

we can then see that domestic consumers will purchase IR or $600X$ at $P_X = \$3$ with free trade (and no transportation costs), as compared with $400X$ at $P_X = \$5$ in the absence of trade (given by point E).

Figure 8–13 also shows that with free trade, domestic firms produce only IK or $200X$, so that KR or $400X$ are imported at $P_X = \$3$. Resources in the nation will then shift from the production of commodity X to the production of other commodities that the nation can produce relatively more efficiently (i.e., in which the nation has a comparative advantage). By doing this, the nation will be able to obtain more of commodity X through exchange than if it had used the same amount of domestic resources to produce commodity X domestically.[11]

---

[11]If the nation's demand for the imports of commodity X is large in relation to the total world supply of the exports of commodity X to the nation, then S_F would be positively sloped and intersect D_X at a higher price, so that the domestic production of commodity X would be higher while domestic consumption and imports would be smaller than indicated in Figure 8–13. Try to pencil in this in Figure 8–13.

8.8 ANALYSIS OF COMPETITIVE MARKETS

In this section, we examine a number of important applications of the tools of analysis developed in this chapter. These include the definition and measurement of producer surplus, examination of the efficiency of perfect competition, and the effects of a per-unit tax and an import tariff. These applications, together with those in Chapter 2 (which presented an introductory overview of the perfectly competitive model) on rent control, U.S. farm-support programs, and the incidence of (i.e., who pays for) an excise tax clearly demonstrate the great usefulness of the perfectly competitive model.

Producer Surplus

Producer surplus is a concept analogous to that of the consumer surplus examined in section 4.5. Consumer surplus is the difference between what consumers are willing to pay for a commodity and what they actually pay and is measured by the area under the demand curve and above the commodity price. **Producer surplus** is defined as the excess of the commodity price over the marginal cost of production and is measured by the area between the commodity price and the producer's marginal cost curve. This is shown in Figure 8–14.

Figure 8–14 shows that a perfectly competitive firm facing a price of $5 produces $4X$ (given by point E at which $d_X = MR_X = P_X = \$5 = MC_X$). This is derived from the optimization rule that a firm should expand production as long as price or marginal revenue exceeds marginal cost and until they are equal. Since the firm sells all four units of commodity X at the market price of $5, but faces a marginal cost (or minimum price at which it will supply the first unit of the commodity) of only $2 on the first unit produced, the firm receives a surplus of $3 (given by the area of the first shaded rectangle in the figure) on the first unit sold. With $P_X = \$5$ but a marginal cost of $3 to produce the second unit of commodity X, the firm receives a surplus of $2 (the area of the second shaded rectangle) on the second unit sold. With $P_X = \$5$ and $MC = \$4$ on the third unit of commodity X produced, the firm receives a surplus of $1 (the area of the third shaded rectangle) on the third unit of X sold. Finally, since $P_X = MC_X = \$5$ on the fourth unit, producer surplus is zero on the fourth unit of X. The firm will not produce the fifth unit of commodity X because the marginal cost of producing the fifth unit ($6) exceeds the commodity price of $5 (see the figure).

By adding the producer surplus of $3 on the first unit of commodity X, $2 on the second unit, $1 on the third unit, and $0 on the fourth unit, we get the total producer surplus of $6 that the firm receives from the sale of $4X$. If commodity X could be produced and sold in infinitesimally small units, the total producer surplus would be given by the total area between the price of the commodity and the firm's marginal cost curve. This is the area of triangle BEC, which is equal to $8 (as compared with $6 found above). At the market price of $P_X = \$5$ and with output of $4X$, the total revenue of the firm is $20

FIGURE 8–14   Producer Surplus

At $P_X = \$5$, the firm produces $4X$ (point E). Since the marginal cost is \$2 on the first unit of X produced, the firm receives a surplus of \$3 (given by the area of the first shaded rectangle). With $MC = \$3$ on the second unit of X, producer surplus is \$2 (the area of the second shaded rectangle). With $MC_X = \$4$ on the third unit, producer surplus is \$1 (the area of the third shaded rectangle). With $MC_X = \$5$ on the fourth unit, producer surplus is zero. Total producer surplus on $4X$ is \$6. If commodity X were infinitesimally divisible, total producer surplus would be \$8 (the area of triangle BEC).

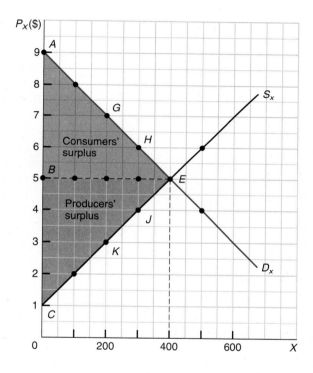

(given by the area of rectangle $BEFO$ in the figure). Of this, $CEFO$ or \$12 represents the opportunity cost of the variable inputs used or the minimum amount that the producer requires to produce $4X$. The difference of \$8 (the area of triangle BEC) thus represents the producer surplus or the amount that is not necessary for the producer to receive in order to induce him or her to supply $4X$.

If the market price of commodity X fell to \$4, we can see from the figure that the best level of output of the firm would be $3X$ and total producer surplus would be \$4.50 (given by the area of the triangle formed by $P_X = \$4$ and the MC_X curve). On the other hand, if the price of commodity X rose to \$6, the best level of output of the firm would be $5X$ and the total producer surplus would be \$12.50 (given by the area of the triangle formed by $P_X = 6$ and the MC_X curve in Figure 8–14). Another producer with lower marginal costs would produce more of the commodity and receive a larger producer surplus at each market price of the commodity. Although this analysis referred to an individual producer, a similar analysis would also apply to a perfectly competitive market. Indeed, the concepts of consumer and producer surplus are used in the next section to demonstrate the efficiency of a perfectly competitive market and in the last two sections of this chapter to show the welfare effects of an excise tax and an import tariff.

Efficiency of Perfect Competition—Consumers' and Producers' Surplus

We have seen in section 8.4 that in a perfectly competitive market, equilibrium occurs at the intersection of the industry or market demand and supply curves for the commodity. Here, the marginal benefit to consumers from the last unit of the commodity purchased just matches the marginal cost to producers, and the combined consumers' and producers' surplus is at a maximum. Thus, perfect competition is the most efficient type of market structure. This is shown in Figure 8–15.

In Figure 8–15, D_X and S_X refer, respectively, to the industry or market demand and supply curves for commodity X. The intersection of D_X and S_X defines equilibrium point E at which $P_X = \$5$ and $Q_X = 400$. The total consumers' surplus (the sum of the surpluses of all the consumers of commodity X

FIGURE 8–15   The Efficiency of Perfect Competition

Expanding output from 300X to 400X increases consumers' plus producers' surplus by $HEJ = \$100$. Expanding output past the competitive equilibrium output of 400X reduces the total surplus, because the marginal benefit to consumers is less than the marginal cost of producers. Thus, consumers' plus producers' surplus is maximized when a perfectly competitive market is in equilibrium.

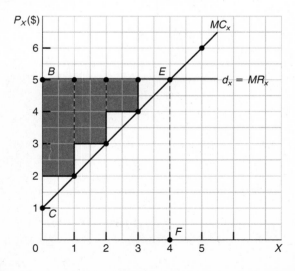

in the market) is given by triangle AEB (the area under D_X and above P_X), which is equal to $800. On the other hand, the total producers' surplus (the sum of the surpluses of all the producers of commodity X in the market) is given by triangle BEC (the area below P_X and above S_X), which is also $800. Thus, the total combined consumers' and producers' surplus is given by area $AEC = \$1,600$.

We can use Figure 8–15 to show that when a perfectly competitive market is in equilibrium, consumers' plus producers' surplus is maximized. For example, expanding output from $200X$ to $300X$ leads to a combined increase of consumers' and producers' surplus equal to $GHJK = \$300$. The increase in consumers' and producers' surplus arises because the marginal benefit to consumers exceeds the marginal cost of producers for each additional unit produced and consumed. Expanding output from $300X$ to $400X$ leads to a further increase in consumers' plus producers' surplus of $HEJ = \$100$. If output expands past the equilibrium output of $400X$, the total surplus declines because consumers value the extra output at less than the marginal cost of producing it. Only at the competitive equilibrium output of $400X$ does the marginal benefit to consumers equal the marginal cost of producers and is the total combined consumers' and producers' surplus maximized. This can also be regarded as the benefit from exchange or trading (i.e., from buying and selling commodity X).

We will see in Part Four (Chapters 9–12) that imperfect competitors restrict output and charge a higher price so that the total combined consumers' and producers' surplus is smaller than under perfect competition. So important are the benefits of competition that market economies have been reducing the number and size of government regulations during the past decade. Even China is increasingly relying on markets and less on planning.[12]

Welfare Effects of an Excise Tax

We will now use changes in consumers' and producers' surplus to measure the net loss in welfare resulting from an excise tax. The production and consumption effects of an excise tax as well as its incidence (i.e., who pays for the tax) were discussed in section 2.7. Here, we expand that discussion to include a measurement of the loss in consumers' and producers' surplus resulting from the imposition of the tax. This is shown in Figure 8–16.

In Figure 8–16, D_X and S_X are, respectively, the market demand and supply curves for commodity X. The intersection of D_X and S_X defines the equilibrium price of $5 and the equilibrium quantity of $400X$ (just as in Figure 8–15). A tax of $2 per unit causes the S_X curve to shift up by $2 to S_X' because producers must now pay the $2 tax in addition to the previous marginal cost of producing

---

[12]See, "The Global March of Free Markets," *New York Times,* July 19, 1987, Section 3, p. 1, and "Support Is Growing in China for Shift to Free Markets," *New York Times,* June 28, 1992, p. 1.

FIGURE 8–16   Welfare Effects of an Excise Tax

With D_X and S_X, equilibrium is at point E at which P_X = $5 and Q_X = 400. A tax of
$2 per unit on commodity X shifts S_X up to S'_X and defines new equilibrium point H
at which P_X = $6 to consumers, Q_X = 300, and producers receive a net price of $4
per unit. The loss of consumers' surplus is $LHEB$ = $350, the loss of producers' surplus
is $BEJN$ = $350, for a combined loss of $LHEJN$ = $700. Since tax revenues are $LHJN$
= $600 ($2 per unit on 300 units), there is a deadweight loss of HEJ = $100.

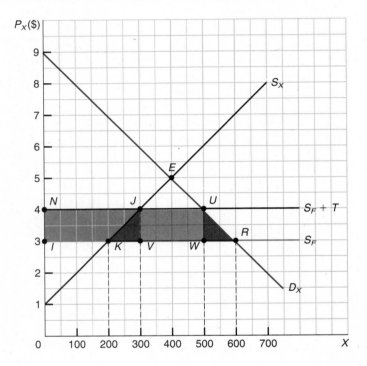

each unit of commodity X shown by the S_X curve. This defines the new
equilibrium point H at which P_X = $6 to consumers and Q_X = 300. Producers,
however, receive a net price of only $4 after paying the tax of $2 per unit.
Thus, the tax raises the price to consumers from $5 to $6 and lowers the net
price received by producers from $5 to $4, so consumers and producers share
equally the burden of the tax. So far, this is the same as in section 2.7.

We can now go further, however, and measure the welfare effect of the
tax by the change in consumers' and producers' surplus resulting from the
tax. From Figure 8–16 we can see that the imposition of the tax leads to a
reduction in consumers' surplus equal to $LHEB$ = $350 and a reduction in
producers' surplus equal to $BEJN$ = $350, for an overall combined loss of
consumers' and producers' surplus of $700. Since the government collects $2
per unit on 300 units of the commodity, or a total of $600 (the area of rectangle
$LHJN$), the tax results in a *net* loss of $100 (the area of triangle HEJ) in consum-
ers' and producers' surplus. This **deadweight loss** remains even if the govern-

ment were to return the entire amount of tax collected in the form of a general income subsidy to consumers. It results because of the distortions resulting from the tax. Specifically, some of society's resources shift from the production of commodity X to the production of other commodities that consumers value less. The provision of a per-unit production *subsidy* to producers has the opposite effect as the excise tax (see problem 11 at the end of this chapter).

Effects of an Import Tariff

We can show the effects of an import tariff with Figure 8–17. In Figure 8–17, D_X and S_X refer, respectively, to the domestic market demand and supply

FIGURE 8–17   Effects of an Import Tariff

D_X and S_X represent the domestic market demand and supply curves of commodity X. At the free trade price $P_X = \$3$, domestic consumers purchase $IR = 600X$, of which $IK = 200X$ are produced domestically and $KR = 400X$ are imported. With a $1 import tariff, P_X to domestic consumers rises to $4. At $P_X = \$4$, domestic consumers purchase $NU = 500X$, of which $NJ = 300X$ are produced domestically and $JU = 200X$ are imported. Thus, the consumption effect of the tariff is $RW = -100X$, the production effect is $KV = 100X$, the trade effect is $RW + KV = -200X$, and the revenue effect is $JUWV = \$200$. Consumers' surplus declines by $NURI = \$550$, of which $NJKI = \$250$ represents an increase in producers' surplus, $JUWV = \$200$ is the tariff revenue, and $URW = \$50$ plus $JKV = \$50$ represents the deadweight loss of the tariff.

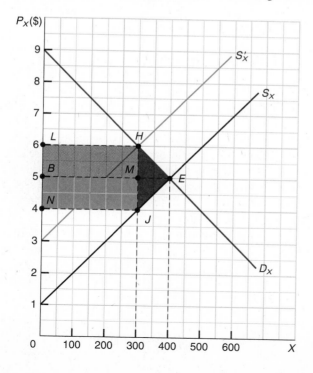

curves of commodity X. S_F is the foreign supply curve of exports of commodity X to the nation at the world price of $3 (on the assumption that the quantity demanded of imports of commodity X by the nation is very small in relation to the total foreign supply of exports of the commodity). With free trade at the world price of P_X = $3, domestic consumers purchase IR = $600X$, of which IK = $200X$ are produced domestically and KR = $400X$ are imported (so far this is the same as in Figure 8–13 in section 8.7).

Suppose that from the free trade position, the nation imposes a 33% import tariff, or a tariff of $1 on each unit of commodity X imported. The new foreign supply curve for the nations' imports now becomes $S_F + T$, where T refers to the tariff. The price of commodity X to domestic consumers now becomes $4 (see Figure 8–17). At P_X = $4, domestic consumers purchase NU = $500X$, of which NJ = $300X$ are produced domestically and JU = $200X$ are imported. Thus, the consumption effect of the tariff (i.e., the reduction in domestic consumption resulting from the tariff) is $RW = -100X$, the production effect (i.e., the expansion of domestic production resulting from the tariff) is $KV = 100X$, the trade effect (i.e., the decline in imports) is $RW + KV = -200X$, and the revenue effect (i.e., the revenue collected by the government) is $JUWV$ = $200 ($JV$ = $1 on each of the $200X$ imported).

We can also measure the welfare effects of the tariff. From Figure 8–17, we see that the tariff leads to a reduction in consumers' surplus equal to $NURI$ = $550. Of this, $NJKI$ = $250 represents a transfer to producers in the form of an increase in producers' surplus, $JUWV$ = $200 is the tariff revenue collected by the nation's government, and the sum of triangles URW = $50 and JKV = $50 represents the protection cost or deadweight loss of the tariff. This results from the production and consumption distortions arising from the tariff.

Results would be similar if, starting from the free trade position in Figure 8–17, the nation imposed an import quota that directly restricted the *quantity* of imports of commodity X into the nation to JU = $200X$. If the nation auctioned off import licenses to the highest bidder, it would collect the same revenue ($JUWV$ = $200) as with the 33% or $1 tariff on each unit of imports. If the nation does not auction off import licenses (as it is often the case), the nation's importers or the foreign exporters would earn that much greater profits. This is exactly what happened when the United States negotiated an agreement with Japan during the 1980s under which Japan "voluntarily" reduced its automobile exports to the United States. Japanese automakers were, therefore, able to sell automobiles in the United States at the world price plus the equivalent tariff (i.e., the tariff that would have reduced imports by the same amount as the quota) and earn huge profits. If trade restrictions were necessary to allow domestic automakers to improve quality and meet Japanese competition, then it would have been better for the United States to impose an equivalent import tariff and collect the tariff revenue.[13]

---

[13]See, D. Salvatore, *International Economics*, 4th ed. (New York: Macmillan, 1993), Section 9.3a.

SUMMARY

1. Economists identify four different types of market organization: perfect competition, monopoly, monopolistic competition, and oligopoly. In a perfectly competitive market, no buyer or seller affects (or behaves as if he or she affects) the price of a commodity, all units of the commodity are homogeneous or identical, resources are mobile, and knowledge of the market is perfect.

2. The market period, or the very short run, refers to the period of time during which the market supply of a commodity is fixed. During the market period, costs of production are irrelevant in the determination of the price of a perishable commodity and the entire supply of the commodity is put up for sale at whatever price it can fetch. Thus, demand alone determines price (while supply alone determines quantity).

3. The TR of a perfectly competitive firm is a straight line through the origin with slope of $MR = P$. The best or profit-maximizing level of output occurs where the positive difference between TR and STC is greatest. The same result is obtained where P or $MR = MC$ and MC is rising, provided that $P \geq AVC$. If P is smaller than ATC at the best level of output, the firm will incur a loss. As long as P exceeds AVC, it pays for the firm to continue to produce because it covers all variable costs and part of its fixed costs. If the firm were to shut down, it would incur a loss equal to its total fixed costs. The shutdown point is where $P = AVC$.

4. The rising portion of the firm's MC curve above the AVC curve (the shutdown point) is the firm's short-run supply curve of the commodity. The industry short-run supply curve is the horizontal summation of the firms' short-run supply curves. The equilibrium price is at the intersection of the market demand and supply curves of the commodity. The firm will then produce the output at which P or $MR = MC$, and MC is rising (as long as P exceeds AVC). With an increase in demand, the equilibrium price will rise and firms will expand their output. If input prices rise, the MC curve of each firm shifts up, and so the short-run supply curve of each firm and of the industry are less elastic.

5. In the long run, the industry and the firm are in long-run equilibrium where $P = MR = SMC = LMC = SATC = LAC$. Each firm operates at the lowest point on its LAC curve and earns zero profits. Competition in the input markets as well as in the commodity market will result in all firms having identical average costs and zero profits when the industry is in long-run equilibrium.

6. One of three possible cases can result as industry output expands and more inputs are demanded. If input prices remain constant, the industry long-run supply curve is horizontal and we have a constant cost industry. If input prices rise (external diseconomy), the industry long-run supply curve is positively sloped and we have an increasing cost industry. This may be more common than the other two cases. If input prices fall (external economy), the industry long-run supply curve is negatively sloped and we have a decreasing cost industry.

7. Domestic firms in most industries face a great deal of competition from imports. International trade leads to a decline in the domestic price of the commodity, and larger domestic consumption and lower domestic production of the commodity than in the absence of trade.

8. Producer surplus equals the excess of the commodity price over the producer's marginal cost of production. The combined consumers' and producers' surplus is maximized when a perfectly competitive mar-

ket is in equilibrium. A tax leads to a deadweight loss. An import tariff increases the domestic price of the importable commodity, reduces domestic consumption and imports, increases domestic production, generates tax revenues, and leads to a deadweight loss.

KEY TERMS

Perfect Competition
Market Period
Break-Even Point
Shutdown Point
Constant Cost Industry

Increasing Cost Industry
Decreasing Cost Industry
External Economy
External Diseconomy
Producer Surplus

Deadweight Loss
Foreign Exchange Market
Exchange Rate
Depreciation
Appreciation

REVIEW QUESTIONS

1. If perfect competition is rare in the real world, why do we study it?
2. A firm's total revenue is $100, its total cost is $120, and its total fixed cost is $40. Should the firm stay in business? Why?
3. Why might a firm remain in business in the short run even if incurring a loss, but will always leave the industry if incurring a loss in the long run?
4. At what level of output is profit per unit maximized for a perfectly competitive firm? Why will the firm not produce this level of output?
5. Why would a firm enter a perfectly competitive industry if it knows that its profits will be zero in the long run?
6. Must a perfectly competitive industry be in long-run equilibrium if a perfectly competitive firm is in long-run equilibrium? Must each perfectly competitive firm be in equilibrium if the industry is in long-run equilibrium? Why?

7. Why should a nation trade if such trade benefits domestic consumers but harms domestic producers?
8. What is the difference between economic profit and producer surplus?
9. What is the combined consumers' and producers' surplus at the output level of 500X in Figure 8–15? Why is this not the best level of output?
10. Is the deadweight loss from an excise tax greater when the market demand and supply curves of the commodity are elastic or inelastic? Why?
11. What is the size of a prohibitive tariff in Figure 8–17? What would be the effects of such a prohibitive tariff?
12. Assuming a two-currency world—the U.S. dollar and the British pound sterling—what does a depreciation of the dollar mean for the pound? Explain.

PROBLEMS

*1. Suppose that the market demand function of a perfectly competitive industry is given by $QD = 4,750 - 50P$ and the market supply function is given by $QS = 1,750 + 50P$, and P is expressed in dollars.
   a. Find the market equilibrium price.
   b. Find the quantity demanded and supplied in the market at $P = $50, $40, $30, 20, and $10.

   c. Draw the market demand curve, the market supply curve, and the demand curve for one of 100 identical perfectly competitive firms in this industry.
   d. Write the equation of the demand curve of the firm.
2. a. If the market supply function of a commodity is $QS = 3,250$, are we in the market period, the short run, or the long run?

b. If the market demand function is $QD = 4{,}750 - 50P$ and P is expressed in dollars, what is the market equilibrium price (P)?

c. If the market demand increases to $QD' = 5{,}350 - 50P$, what is the equilibrium price?

d. If the market demand decreases to $QD' = 4{,}150 - 50P$, what is the equilibrium price?

e. Draw a figure showing parts (b), (c), and (d) of this problem.

3. Using the STC schedule provided in the table for problem 4a in Chapter 7 and $P = \$26$ for a perfectly competitive firm,

a. draw a figure similar to Figure 8–2 and determine the best level of output for the firm.

b. construct a table similar to Table 8–1 showing TR, STC, and total profits at each level of output.

*4. Suppose that a perfectly competitive firm has no knowledge of the exact shape of its STC curve. It knows that its total fixed costs are $\$200$, and it assumes that its average variable costs are constant at $\$5$.

a. If the firm can sell any amount of the commodity at the price of $\$10$ per unit, draw a figure and determine the sales volume at which the firm breaks even.

b. How can an increase in the price of the commodity, in the total fixed costs of the firm, and in average variable costs, be shown in the figure of part a of this problem?

c. What is an important shortcoming of this analysis?

5. Using the per-unit cost schedules derived from the table for problem 4a in Chapter 7 and $P = \$26$,

a. draw a figure similar to Figure 8–3 and show the best level of output of the firm.

b. construct a table similar to Table 8–2 showing P, MR, ATC, and MC at each level of output.

6. For your figure in problem 5a, determine the best level of output, the profit or loss per unit, total profit or losses, and whether the firm should continue to produce or not at

a. $P = \$42$.

b. $P = \$18$.

c. $P = \$12.50$.

7. Graph the quantity supplied (Q) at various

prices (P) by firms 1, 2, and 3 given below, and derive the industry supply curve on the assumptions that the industry is composed only of these three firms and input prices are constant.

Price and Quantity Supplied by Firms 1, 2, and 3

P	Q1	Q2	Q3
$1	0	0	0
2	20	0	0
3	40	10	10
4	60	20	20

*8. Starting from Figure 8–5, suppose that as each of the 100 identical firms in the perfectly competitive industry increases output (as a result of an increase in the market price of the commodity), input prices rise, causing the SMC curve of each firm to shift upward by $\$15$. Draw a figure showing the original and the new MC curve and the quantity supplied by each firm and by the industry as a whole at the original price of $P = \$35$ and at $P = \$50$. On the same figure, show the supply curve of each firm and of the industry.

9. a. For the perfectly competitive firm of problem 5, draw a figure similar to Figure 8–8 showing short-run and long-run equilibrium on the assumption that the firm, but not the industry, is in long-run equilibrium. Assume $P = \$30$, the lowest $LAC = \$12.50$ at $Q = 8$, the best level of output is $Q = 10$, and $LAC = \$15$ with $SATC_5$ and $SMC_5 = LMC = \$30$ when the firm, but not the industry, is in long-run equilibrium.

b. Draw a figure similar to Figure 8–9 for the firm of part (a) showing the long-run equilibrium point for the firm and the industry.

*10. Starting from long-run equilibrium in a perfectly competitive increasing cost industry, show on one diagram the effect on price and quantity of an increase in demand in the market period in the short run and in the long run.

———

* = Answer provided at end of book.

11. Starting with D_X and S_X in Figure 8–16, show all the effects of a production subsidy of $2 per unit given by the government to all producers of commodity X.

12. Starting with D_X and S_X of Figure 8–17, draw a figure similar to Figure 8–17 showing all the effects of a 100% import tariff on commodity X if the free trade price of commodity X is $2.

APPENDIX   THE FOREIGN EXCHANGE MARKET AND THE DOLLAR EXCHANGE RATE

A firm will import a commodity as long as the domestic currency price of the imported commodity is smaller than the price of the identical domestically produced commodity and until they are equal (in the absence of transportation costs, tariffs, or other obstructions to the flow of trade). In order to make the payment, the domestic importer will have to exchange the domestic currency for the foreign currency. Since the dollar is also used as an international currency, however, a U.S. importer could also pay in dollars. In that case, it is the foreign exporter that will have to exchange dollars into the local currency.

The market where one currency is exchanged for another is called the foreign exchange market. The **foreign exchange market** for any currency, say the U.S. dollar, is formed by all the locations (such as London, Tokyo, Frankfurt, as well as New York) where dollars are bought and sold for other currencies. These international monetary centers are connected by a telephone and telex network and are in constant contact with one another. The rate at which one currency is exchanged for another is called the **exchange rate.** This is the price of a unit of the foreign currency in terms of the domestic currency. For example, the exchange rate (R) between the U.S. dollar and the British pound sterling (£) is the number of dollars required to purchase one pound. That is, $R = \$/£$. Thus, if $R = \$/£ = 2$, this means that two dollars are required to purchase one pound.

Under a flexible exchange rate system of the type we have today, the dollar price of the pound (R) is determined (just like the price of any other commodity in a competitive market) by the intersection of the market demand and supply curves of pounds. This is shown in Figure 8–18, where the vertical axis measures the dollar price of pounds, or the exchange rate ($R = \$/£$), and the horizontal axis measures the quantity of pounds. The market demand and supply curves for pounds intersect at point E, defining the equilibrium exchange rate of $R = 2$, at which the quantity of pounds demanded and the quantity supplied of pounds are equal at £300 million per day. At a higher exchange rate, the quantity of pounds supplied exceeds the quantity demanded, and the exchange rate will fall toward the equilibrium rate of $R = 2$. At an exchange rate lower than $R = 2$, the quantity of pounds demanded exceeds the quantity supplied, and the exchange rate will be bid up toward the equilibrium rate of $R = 2$.

The U.S. demand for pounds is negatively inclined, indicating that the lower is the exchange rate (R), the greater is the quantity of pounds demanded by the United States. The reason is that the lower is the exchange rate (i.e., the fewer the number of dollars required to purchase one pound), the cheaper it is for the United States to import from and invest in the United Kingdom, and thus the greater is the quantity of pounds demanded by U.S. residents. On the other hand, the U.S. supply of pounds

FIGURE 8–18   The Foreign Exchange Market and the Dollar Exchange Rate

The vertical axis measures the dollar price of pounds ($R = \$/£$) and the horizontal axis measures the quantity of pounds. Under a flexible exchange rate system, the equilibrium exchange rate is $R = 2$ and the equilibrium quantity of pounds bought and sold is £300 million per day. This is given by point E, at which the U.S. demand and supply curves for pounds intersect.

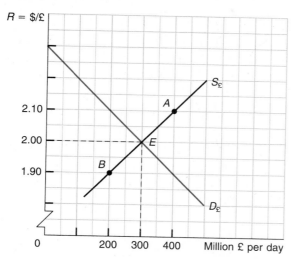

is usually positively inclined, indicating that the higher is the exchange rate (R), the greater is the quantity of pounds earned by or supplied to the United States. The reason is that at higher exchange rates, U.K. residents receive more dollars for each of their pounds. As a result, they find U.S. goods and investments cheaper and more attractive and spend more in the United States, thus supplying more pounds to the United States.

If the U.S. demand curve for pounds shifted up (for example as a result of increased U.S. tastes for English goods) and intersected the U.S. supply curve for pounds at point A (see Figure 8–18), the equilibrium exchange rate would be $R = 2.10$, and the equilibrium quantity would be £400 million per day. The dollar is then said to have depreciated since it now requires $2.10 (instead of the previous $2) to purchase one pound. **Depreciation** thus refers to an increase in the domestic price of the foreign currency. On the other hand, if through time the U.S. demand for pounds shifted down so as to intersect the U.S. supply curve of pounds at point B (see Figure 8–18), the equilibrium exchange rate would fall to $R = 1.90$ and the dollar is said to have appreciated (because fewer dollars are now required to purchase one pound). An **appreciation** thus refers to a decline in the domestic price of the foreign currency. Shifts in the U.S. supply curve of pounds through time would similarly affect the equilibrium exchange rate and equilibrium quantity of pounds.

In the absence of interferences by national monetary authorities, the foreign exchange market operates just like any other competitive market, with the equilibrium price and quantity of the foreign currency determined at the intersection of the market demand and supply curves for the foreign currency. Sometimes, monetary authorities attempt to affect exchange rates by a coordinated purchase or sale of a currency on the foreign exchange market. For example, U.S. and foreign monetary authorities may sell dollars for foreign currencies to induce a dollar depreciation (which makes U.S. goods cheaper to foreigners) in order to reduce the U.S. trade deficit. These official foreign exchange market interventions are only of limited effectiveness, however, because the foreign exchange resources at the disposal of national monetary authorities are very small in relation to the size of daily transactions on the foreign exchange market (now estimated to be over $900 billion per day!).[14]

---

[14]See, "The Last of the Good Times," *The Economist*, August 15, 1992, pp. 61–62.

PART FOUR

IMPERFECTLY COMPETITIVE MARKETS

P art Four (Chapters 9–11) presents the theory of the firm in imperfectly competitive markets. It brings together the theory of consumer behavior and demand (from Part Two) and the theory of production and costs (from Chapters 6 and 7) to analyze how price and output are determined under various types of imperfectly competitive markets. Chapter 9 shows price and output determination under pure monopoly. Chapter 10 does the same for monopolistic competition and oligopoly. Chapter 11 describes how game theory is useful in analyzing oligopolistic behavior. Finally, Chapter 12 examines the efficiency implications of various market structures and regulation. As in previous parts of the text, the presentation of the theory is reinforced with many real-world examples and important applications.

PRICE AND OUTPUT UNDER PURE MONOPOLY

In this chapter, we bring together the theory of consumer behavior and demand (from Part Two) and the theory of production and costs (from Chapters 6 and 7) to analyze how price and output are determined under pure monopoly. Monopoly is the opposite extreme from perfect competition in the spectrum or range of market structure or organization. The monopoly model is useful for analyzing cases that approximate monopoly, and it provides insights into the operation of other imperfectly competitive markets (i.e., monopolistic competition and oligopoly).

The chapter begins by defining pure monopoly, describing the sources of monopoly, and explaining why the monopolist faces the market demand curve for the commodity. It then examines the determination of price and output in the short run and in the long run and compares the long-run equilibrium of the monopolist with that of a perfectly competitive firm and industry. Subsequently, we extend the monopoly model to examine how a monopolist (1) should allocate production among its various plants to minimize production costs and (2) can increase total profits by charging different prices for different quantities and in different markets—at home and abroad. Finally, we discuss some other pricing practices that monopolists often use to increase their profits and present several important applications of the pure monopoly model. As in previous chapters, these applications, together with the real-world examples presented in the chapter, highlight the importance and relevance of the analytical tools developed in the chapter.

9.1 PURE MONOPOLY—THE OPPOSITE EXTREME FROM PERFECT COMPETITION

In this section, we first define the meaning of pure monopoly and discuss the sources of monopoly power. We then examine the shape of the demand and marginal revenue curves facing the monopolist and compare them with those of a perfectly competitive firm.

Definition and Sources of Monopoly

Pure monopoly is the form of market organization in which a *single firm* sells a commodity for which there are *no close substitutes*. Thus, the monopolist represents the industry and faces the industry's negatively sloped demand curve for the commodity. As opposed to a perfectly competitive firm, a monopolist can earn profits in the long run because *entry into the industry is blocked or very difficult*. Monopoly is at the opposite extreme from perfect competition in the spectrum or range of market organizations. Whereas the perfect competitor is a price taker and has no control over the price of the commodity it sells, the monopolist has complete control over price.

Monopoly can arise from several causes. First, a firm may own or control the entire supply of a raw material required in the production of a commodity, or the firm may possess some unique managerial talent. For example, until World War II, the Aluminum Company of America (Alcoa) controlled practically the entire supply of bauxite (the basic raw material necessary for the production of aluminum) and had almost a complete monopoly in the production of aluminum in the United States (see Example 1).

Second, a firm may own a patent for the exclusive right to produce a commodity or to use a particular production process. Patents are granted by the government for 17 years as an incentive to inventors.[1] Some argue that if an invention could be copied freely (thus leaving little, if any, reward for the inventor), the flow of inventions and technical progress would be greatly reduced. Examples of monopolies that were originally based on patents are the Xerox Corporation for copying machines and Polaroid for instant cameras. An alternative to patents might be for the government to financially reward the inventor directly and allow inventions to be freely used. However, it is often difficult to determine the value of an invention: government archives are full of patents that found no commercial use.

Third, economies of scale may operate (i.e., the long-run average cost curve may fall) over a sufficiently large range of outputs as to leave a single firm supplying the entire market. Such a firm is called a **natural monopoly.** Examples of natural monopolies are public utilities (electrical, water, gas, telephone, and transportation companies).[2] To have more than one firm supplying electricity, water, gas, telephone, cable TV, and transportation services in a given market would lead to overlapping distribution systems and much higher per-unit costs. In cases such as these, the government usually allows a single firm to operate in the market subject to some form of government regulation. For example, electricity rates are set so as to leave the local electrical company only a "normal rate of return" (say, 8% to 10%) on its investment. We will examine the regulation of public utilities in section 12.5.

---

[1]As opposed to copyrights, patents are not renewable. Improvement patents are available, however.

[2]In view of the divestiture and restructuring of AT&T, only local telephone companies are natural monopolies. Electrical, water, gas, local telephone, and companies providing transportation services are organized as public utilities because they are natural monopolies.

Fourth, some monopolies are created by government franchise itself. An example of this is the post office (which many believe is *not* a natural monopoly). In addition, licenses are often required by local governments to start a radio or television station, to open a liquor store, to operate a taxi, to be a plumber, a barber, a funeral director, and so on. The purpose of these licenses is to ensure minimum standards of competency. Nevertheless, because the number of licenses issued (e.g., the number of taxi medallions issued in most metropolitan areas) is often restricted by the regulatory agency, licenses also protect present license holders from *new* competition (i.e., confer monopoly power to them as a group). In most cases, local governments turn the regulatory function (such as the issuance of licenses) over to the professional association involved. Examples are the medical and bar associations.

Aside from the few cases just mentioned and for public utilities, pure monopoly is rare in the United States today, and attempts to monopolize the market are forbidden by antitrust laws.[3] Nevertheless, the pure monopoly model is useful for analyzing situations that approach pure monopoly and for other types of imperfectly competitive markets (i.e., monopolistic competition and oligopoly).

A monopolist does not have unlimited market power but faces many forms of direct and indirect competition. On a general level, a monopolist competes for the consumers' dollars with the sellers of all other commodities in the market. Furthermore, while *close* substitutes do not exist for the particular commodity supplied by the monopolist, imperfect substitutes are likely to exist. For example, although Du Pont was the only producer of cellophane in the late 1940s, the company faced a great deal of competition from the producers of all other flexible packaging materials (waxed paper, aluminum foil, and so on). In addition, the market power of the monopolist (or the would-be monopolist) is sharply curtailed by fear of government antitrust prosecution, by the threat of potential competitors, and by international competition.

Example 1
Barriers to Entry and Monopoly by Alcoa

The Aluminum Company of America (Alcoa) is a classic example of how a monopoly was created and maintained for almost 50 years. The monopoly was created in the late 19th century when Alcoa acquired a patent on the method to remove oxygen from bauxite to obtain aluminum. This patent expired in 1906, but in 1903, Alcoa had patented another more efficient method to produce aluminum. This patent expired in 1909. By that time, Alcoa had

---

[3]It should be noted that "monopoly" per se is not illegal; only "monopolizing" or "attempting to monopolize the market" are illegal under U.S. antitrust laws (Section 2, Sherman Antitrust Act, 1890).

signed long-term contracts with producers of bauxite prohibiting them from selling bauxite to any other American firm. At the same time, Alcoa entered into agreements with foreign producers of aluminum not to export aluminum into each other's market. Alcoa even went as far as purchasing electricity only from those power companies that agreed not to sell energy for the production of aluminum to any other firm. In 1912, the courts invalidated all of these contracts and agreements. Nevertheless, Alcoa retained monopoly power by always expanding productive capacity in anticipation of any increase in demand and by pricing aluminum in such a way as to discourage new entrants. The monopoly was finally broken after World War II, when Alcoa was not allowed to purchase government-financed aluminum plants built during the war. This is how Reynolds and Kaiser aluminum came into existence. During the 1960s, Reynolds diversified into plastics, gold, and consumer products, while Alcoa stuck to pure aluminum.

An association of all the producers of a commodity can also operate as a monopoly. This is known as a cartel (discussed in Chapter 10). For example, South Africa's De Beers Consolidated Mines dominates global diamond trading by leading a diamond-trading cartel that controls 80% of world sales (about $4 billion per year). De Beers restricts the quantity of diamonds it puts on the world market, thus keeping diamond prices high. Another cartel, which was highly successful from the fall of 1973 to the early 1980s, is OPEC (the Organization of Petroleum Exporting Countries). Even though monopolistic behavior (such as price fixing) is illegal under U.S. antitrust laws, "tacit collusion" or implicit cooperation among the producers of a commodity is difficult to eradicate (see Chapter 10).

Sources: R. Lanzilotti, "The Aluminum Industry," in W. Adams, ed., *The Structure of American Industry* (New York: Macmillan, 1961); "Reynolds Metals, Alcoa Split on Strategy," *Wall Street Journal*, November 7, 1990, p. A4; "How De Beers Dominates the Diamonds," *The Economist*, February 23, 1980, pp. 101–102; and "Can De Beers Hold to Its Own Hammerlock?" *Business Week*, September 21, 1992, pp. 45–46.

▲

The Monopolist Faces the Market Demand Curve for the Commodity

Because a monopolist is the sole seller of a commodity for which there are no close substitutes, the monopolist faces the negatively sloped industry demand curve for the commodity. In other words, while the perfectly competitive firm is a price taker and faces a demand curve that is horizontal or infinitely elastic at the price determined by the intersection of the industry or market demand and supply curves for the commodity, the monopolist *is* the industry and, thus, it faces the negatively sloped industry demand curve for the commodity. This means that to sell more units of the commodity, the monopolist must lower the commodity price. As a result, marginal revenue (defined as the change in total revenue per-unit change in the quantity sold) is smaller

TABLE 9–1   **Hypothetical Demand, Total Revenue, and Marginal Revenue Faced by a Monopolist**

P	Q	TR	MR
$9	0	$ 0	. . .
8	1	8	$ 8
7	2	14	6
6	3	18	4
5	4	20	2
4	5	20	0
3	6	18	−2
2	7	14	−4
1	8	8	−6
0	9	0	−8

than price, and the monopolist's marginal revenue curve lies below its demand curve (see section 5.6).[4] This is shown in Table 9–1 and Figure 9–1.

The first two columns of Table 9–1 give a hypothetical market demand schedule for the commodity faced by a monopolist. In order to sell more of the commodity, the monopolist must lower the commodity price. Price times quantity gives total revenue (the third column of the table). The change in total revenue per-unit change in the quantity of the commodity sold gives the marginal revenue (the fourth column). For example, at $P = \$8$, the monopolist sells one unit of the commodity, so $TR = \$8$. To sell two units of the commodity, the monopolist must lower the price to $7 on both units of the commodity. TR is then $14. The change in TR resulting from selling the additional unit of the commodity is then $MR = \$14 - \$8 = \$6$. This equals the price of $7 for the second unit of the commodity sold minus the $1 reduction in price (from $8 to $7) on the first unit (since to sell two units of the commodity, the monopolist must lower the price of the commodity to $7 for both units).

The information contained in Table 9–1 is plotted in Figure 9–1. Since MR is defined as the change in TR per-unit change in Q, the MR revenue values are plotted at the midpoint of each quantity interval. Note that the MR curve starts at the same point on the vertical axis as the demand curve and at every point bisects (i.e., cuts in half) the distance between D and the vertical or price axis.[5] The MR is positive when D is elastic (i.e., in the top segment of the demand curve) because an increase in Q increases TR. $MR = 0$ when D

---

[4]At this point, a review of the material in section 5.6 may be helpful.

[5]This is true only when, as in this case, the demand curve that the monopolist faces is a negatively sloped straight line.

FIGURE 9–1   Hypothetical Demand and Marginal Revenue Curves of a Monopolist

Since D is negatively sloped, MR is lower than P. The MR values are plotted at the midpoint of each quantity interval. The MR curve starts at the same point as the D curve and at every point bisects the distance between D and the vertical axis. MR is positive when D is elastic. $MR = 0$ when D is unitary elastic and TR is at a maximum. MR is negative when D is inelastic.

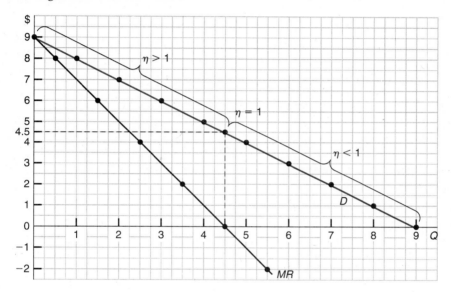

is unitary elastic (i.e., at the geometric midpoint of D) because an increase in Q leaves TR unchanged (at its maximum level). MR is negative when D is inelastic (i.e., the bottom segment of D) because an increase in Q reduces TR (see Figure 9–1 and section 5.6).

Contrast this situation with the case of a perfectly competitive firm (examined in Chapter 8), which faced a horizontal or infinitely elastic demand curve for the commodity at the price determined at the intersection of the market demand and supply curves for the commodity. Since the perfect competitor is a price taker and can sell any quantity of the commodity at the given price, price equals marginal revenue, and the demand and marginal revenue curves are horizontal and coincide.

The relationship between price, marginal revenue, and elasticity (η) can be examined with formula [5–6] introduced in section 5.6:

$$MR = P(1 - 1/\eta) \qquad \text{[5–6]}$$

Using the formula, we see that since $\eta = \infty$ for the perfect competitor, $MR = P$ always. That is, $MR = P(1 - 1/\infty) = P(1 - 0) = P$. Since $\eta < \infty$ (i.e., since the demand curve is not infinitely elastic) for the monopolist, $MR < P$. That is, for any value of η smaller than infinity, MR will be smaller than P, and the MR curve will be below the market demand curve. Furthermore, we can see from the formula that when $\eta = 1$, $MR = 0$; when $\eta > 1$, $MR > 0$; and when $\eta < 1$, $MR < 0$. Since $MR < 0$ when $\eta < 1$, the monopolist can increase its TR by selling a *smaller* quantity of the commodity. Thus, the monopolist would never operate over the inelastic portion of the demand curve. By reducing output, the monopolist would increase total revenue, reduce total costs, and thus increase total profits.

9.2 SHORT-RUN EQUILIBRIUM PRICE AND OUTPUT

In this section, we examine the determination of price and output by a monopolist in the short run. We first do so with the total approach and then with the marginal approach. We also show that a monopolist, like a perfect competitor, can incur losses in the short run. Finally, we demonstrate that, unlike the case of the perfectly competitive firm, the monopolist's short-run supply curve cannot be derived from its short-run marginal cost curve.

Total Approach: Maximizing the Positive Difference Between Total Revenue and Total Costs

As with the perfectly competitive firm, profit maximization provides the framework for the analysis of monopoly. The equilibrium price and output of a monopolist are the ones that maximize its total profits. Total profits equal total revenue minus total costs. Total revenue is given by price times quantity. The total costs of the monopolist are similar to those discussed in Chapter 7 and need not differ from those of the perfectly competitive firm (if the monopolist does not affect input prices). Thus, except for the case of natural monopoly, the basic difference between monopoly and perfect competition lies on the demand side rather than on the production or cost side.

Table 9–2 gives the total revenue (TR), the short-run total costs (STC), and the total profits of a monopolist in the short run at various levels of output.

The total revenue schedule is that of Table 9–1. As usual, short-run total costs rise slowly at first and then more rapidly (when the law of diminishing returns begins to operate). The best or optimum level of output for the monopolist in the short run is where total profits are maximized. For the monopolist of Table 9–2, this is at three units of output per time period. At this level of output, the monopolist charges the price of $6 and earns the maximum total profit of $4.50 per time period.

The data of Table 9–2 are plotted in Figure 9–2. The top panel shows that, unlike the case of a perfectly competitive firm, the monopolist's TR curve is not a straight line, but has the shape of an inverted U. The reason is that the monopolist must lower the price to sell additional units of the commodity. The monopolist's STC faces upward or increases at an increasing rate past $Q = 2$ because of diminishing returns.

TABLE 9–2   **Total Revenue, Short-Run Total
Costs, and Total Profits**

Q	P	TR	STC	Total Profits
0	$9	$ 0	$ 6	$−6
1	8	8	10	−2
2	7	14	12	2
*3	6	18	13.50	4.50
4	5	20	19	1
5	4	20	30	−10
6	3	18	48	−30

*Output at which firm maximizes total profits.

   Total profits are maximized at $Q = 3$, where the positive difference between the *TR* and the *STC* curves is greatest ($4.50). This is the point where the *TR* and the *STC* curves are parallel (see the top panel) and the total profits curve reaches its highest point (see the bottom panel). Total profits are positive between $Q = 1.5$ and $Q = 4.1$ and negative at other output levels. At $Q = 0$, $TR = 0$, while $STC = \$6$. Thus, by going out of business, the monopolist would incur the total loss of $6, which equals its total fixed costs. Note that the monopolist maximizes total profits at an output level smaller than the one at which *TR* is maximum (i.e., at $Q = 3$ rather than at $Q = 4.1$–see Figure 9–2).

Marginal Approach: Equating Marginal Revenue and Marginal Cost

Although the total approach to determine the equilibrium price and output of the monopolist is useful, the marginal approach is even more valuable and widely used. According to the marginal approach, a monopolist maximizes total profits by producing the level of output at which *marginal revenue equals marginal cost*. The difference between the commodity price and the monopolist's average total cost at the best or optimum level of output then gives the profit per unit. Profit per unit times output gives total profits. Thus, to be able to use the marginal approach and to determine the level of total profits, we must calculate the marginal cost and the average total cost of the monopolist.[6]

   From the monopolist's short-run total cost schedule given in Table 9–2, we can derive the marginal cost and the average total cost schedules given

---

[6]Since we already know the monopolist's *MR* (see Figure 9–1), all we need to calculate now is the monopolist's marginal cost to determine the best or profit-maximizing level of output. This is given at the point where $MR = MC$. The average total cost is only required to measure the monopolist's profit at the best level of output.

FIGURE 9–2 Short-Run Equilibrium of the Monopolist: Total Approach

The monopolist's *TR* curve has the shape of an inverted U because the monopolist must lower the commodity price to sell additional units. The *STC* has the usual shape. Total profits are maximized at $Q = 3$, where the positive difference between *TR* and *STC* is greatest ($4.50). This is the point where the *TR* and the *STC* curves are parallel (see the top panel) and the total profit curve is highest (see the bottom panel). Total profits are positive between $Q = 1.5$ and $Q = 4.1$ and negative at other output levels. At $Q = 0$, total loss is $6 and equals total fixed costs.

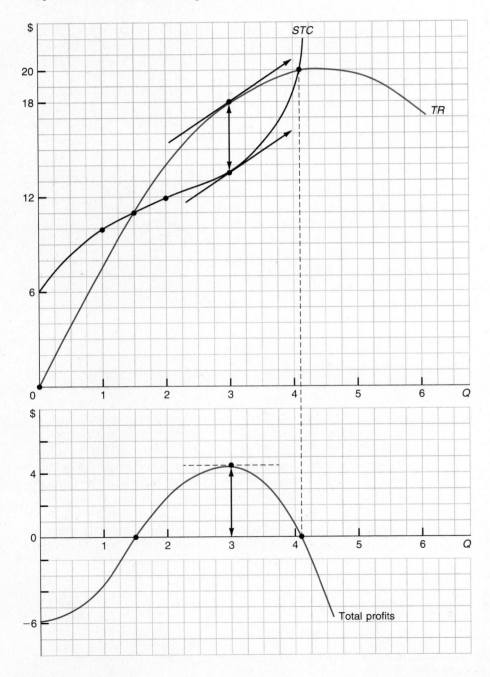

in Table 9–3. Marginal cost equals the change in short-run total costs per-unit change in output. That is, $MC = \Delta STC/\Delta Q$. For example, at $Q = 1$, $STC = \$10$, while at $Q = 2$, $STC = \$12$. Therefore, $SMC = (\$12 - \$10)/1 = \$2$. The other SMC values in Table 9–3 are similarly obtained. On the other hand, average total costs equal short-run total costs divided by the level of output. That is, $ATC = STC/Q$. For example, at $Q = 1$, $STC = \$10$, and so $ATC = \$10/1 = \$10$. At $Q = 2$, $STC = \$12$, and so $ATC = \$12/2 = \$6$.

By plotting the monopolist's D and MR schedules of Table 9–1 and the MC and ATC schedules of Table 9–3 on the same set of axes, we get Figure 9–3. Note that MR and MC are plotted *between* the various levels of output, while D and ATC are plotted *at* the various output levels. In Figure 9–3, the best or optimum level of output of the monopolist is three units. This is given by point G, where $MR = MC$. At $Q = 3$, $P = \$6$ (point A on the demand curve), while $ATC = \$4.50$ (point B on the ATC curve). Thus, the monopolist earns $\$1.50$ (AB) per unit of output sold and $\$4.50$ in total (shaded area $ABCF$ in the figure). Note that at point G, the MC curve cuts the MR curve from below. This is always true for profit maximization, whether the MC curve is rising or falling at the point of intersection (see section 9.8).

At outputs smaller than three units, MR exceeds MC (see the figure). Therefore, by expanding output, the monopolist would be adding more to TR than to STC, and total profits would rise. On the other hand, at outputs larger than three units, MC exceeds MR. A *reduction* in output would reduce STC more than TR and total profits would also rise. Thus, the monopolist must produce where $MR = MC$ (in this case three units of output) to maximize total profits. This is the same result as obtained earlier by the total approach.

Table 9–4 summarizes the marginal approach numerically. Note that the MR and the MC values given in the table are read off Figure 9–3 at various output levels, just as P and ATC. For example, at $Q = 3$, $P = \$6$, $ATC = \$4.50$, and $MR = MC = \$3$. Table 9–4 shows that the monopolist maximizes total profits (equal to $\$4.50$) at $Q = 3$, where $MR = MC = \$3$ (as shown in Figure 9–3).

TABLE 9–3 **Short-Run Total Cost, Marginal Cost, and Average Total Cost**

Q	STC	MC	ATC
0	$ 6	. . .	. . .
1	10	$ 4	$10
2	12	2	6
3	13.50	1.50	4.50
4	19	5.50	4.75
5	30	11	6
6	48	18	8

FIGURE 9–3   Short-Run Equilibrium of the Monopolist: Marginal Approach

The best or optimum level of output of the monopolist is three units. This is given by point G, where MR = MC (and the MC curve intersects the MR curve from below). At Q = 3, P = $6 (point A on the demand curve), ATC = $4.50 (point B on the ATC curve), and the monopolist earns $1.50 (AB) per unit of output sold and $4.50 in total (shaded area ABCF). At Q < 3, MR > MC and total profits rise by increasing Q. At Q > 3, MC > MR and total profits rise by reducing Q.

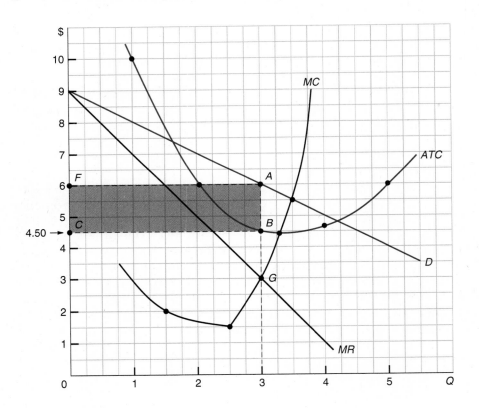

TABLE 9–4   Profit Maximization for the Monopolist: Marginal Approach

Q	P	ATC	Profit per Unit	Total Profits	MR	MC	Relationship of MR to MC
1	$8	$10	$−2	$ −2	$ 7	$ 3	MR > MC
2	7	6	1	2	5	1.50	MR > MC
*3	6	4.50	1.50	4.50	3	3	MR = MC
4	5	4.75	0.25	1	1	8	MR < MC
5	4	6	−2	− 10	−1	15	MR < MC

*Output at which firm maximizes total profits.

Profit Maximization or Loss Minimization?

As for the perfect competitor, the monopolist can earn a profit, break even, or incur a loss in the short run. The monopolist will remain in business in the short run (minimizing losses) as long as price exceeds the average variable cost at the best or optimum level of output. Were the monopolist to shut down, it would incur the higher loss equal to its total fixed costs (TFC).

To show this, assume that, for whatever reason, the monopolist's demand curve shifts down from its level in Figure 9–3 while its cost curves remain unchanged, so that $ATC > P$ at the best level of output. The monopolist will now incur losses at the best level of output. To determine whether the monopolist will minimize losses by remaining in business, we now need to calculate the monopolist's average variable costs. Average variable costs (AVC) equal total variable costs (TVC) divided by output (Q). We can obtain the monopolist's total variable costs by subtracting its total *fixed* costs from its short-run *total* costs. That is, $TVC = STC - TFC$.

The monopolist's TVC and AVC are calculated in Table 9–5 from the STC of Tables 9–2 and 9–3. Specifically, since $STC = \$6$ at $Q = 0$ in Table 9–5, $TFC = \$6$. The TVC schedule is then obtained by subtracting TFC from STC at various output levels, and AVC is calculated by TVC/Q. For example, at $Q = 1$, $TVC = STC - TFC = \$10 - \$6 = \$4$ and $AVC = TVC/Q = \$4/1 = \$4$. At $Q = 2$, $TVC = \$12 - \$6 = \$6$ and $AVC = \$6/2 = \$3$. The other TVC and AVC values in Table 9–5 are calculated in a similar way.

In Figure 9–4, the MC and the ATC curves are those of Figure 9–3, and the AVC curve is obtained by plotting the AVC schedule given in Table 9–5. These per-unit *cost* curves are unchanged from Figure 9–3. The monopolist, however, now faces lower demand curve D' with marginal revenue curve MR'. The best or optimum level of output of the monopolist is now 2.5 units. This is given by point G', where $MR' = MC$ (and the MC curve intersects the MR' curve from below in Figure 9–4). At $Q = 2.5$, $P = \$4$ (point A' on demand curve D') and $ATC = \$5$ (point B' on the ATC curve). Thus, the monopolist incurs a loss of \$1 ($B'A'$) per unit of output sold and \$2.50 in total (the area of rectangle $B'A'F'C'$).

At $Q = 2.5$, $AVC = \$2.60$ (point H' on the AVC curve). Since price (\$4)

TABLE 9–5   **Short-Run Total Cost, Total Variable Costs, and Average Variable Costs**

Q	STC	TFC	TVC	AVC
0	$ 6	$6	$ 0	. . .
1	10	6	4	$4
2	12	6	6	3
3	13.50	6	7.50	2.50
4	19	6	13	3.25

FIGURE 9–4   **Profit Maximization or Loss Minimization**

With D', the best or optimum level of output of the monopolist is $Q = 2.5$ (given by point G', where $MR' = MC$ and the MC curve intersects the MR' curve from below). At $Q = 2.5$, $ATC > P$, and the firm incurs a loss of \$1 ($B'A'$) per unit and \$2.50 in total (the area of rectangle $B'A'F'C'$). If, however, the firm were to shut down, it would incur the greater loss of \$6 equal to its total fixed costs (the area of rectangle $B'H'J'C'$). The shutdown point (Z') is at $P = AVC$.

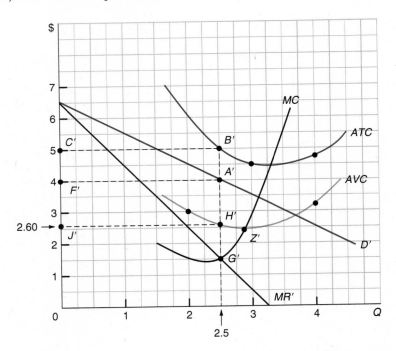

exceeds average variable costs (\$2.60) at the best level of output (2.5 units), the monopolist covers \$1.40 ($A'H'$) of its fixed costs per unit and \$3.50 (the area of rectangle $A'H'J'F'$) of its total fixed costs. If the monopolist were to shut down, it would incur the greater loss of \$6 (its total fixed costs, given by the area of rectangle $B'H'J'C'$). Only if P were smaller than AVC at the best level of output would the monopolist minimize total losses by going out of business (and incurring a loss equal only to its total fixed costs). At $P = AVC$, the monopolist would be indifferent between producing or going out of business because in either case it would incur a loss equal to its total fixed costs. Thus, the point where $P = AVC$ (point Z' in the figure) is the monopolist's shutdown point.

Short-Run Marginal Cost and Supply

While the rising portion of the marginal cost curve over the average variable cost curve (the shutdown point) is a perfect competitor's short-run supply curve (when input prices are constant), this is not the case for the monopolist. The reason is that the monopolist could supply the same quantity of a commodity at different prices depending on the price elasticity of demand. Thus, for the monopolist there is no unique relationship between price and quantity supplied, or no supply curve.

This is shown in Figure 9–5, where D is the original demand curve and D'' is an *alternative* and less elastic demand curve facing the monopolist. In the figure, MR is the marginal revenue curve for demand curve D, while MR'' is the marginal revenue curve for demand curve D''. Since the MC curve

FIGURE 9–5   Short-Run Marginal Cost and Supply

D is the original demand curve, and D'' is an alternative and less elastic demand curve facing the monopolist. Since the MC curve intersects the MR and MR'' curves from below at point G'', the best level of output is three units, whether the monopolist faces D or D''. However, with D, the monopolist charges $P = \$6$, whereas with D'', it would charge $P = \$7.50$. Thus, under monopoly, there is no unique relationship between price and output (i.e., the supply curve is undefined).

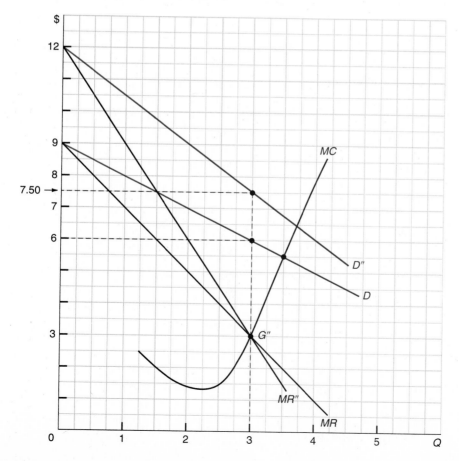

intersects the MR and MR'' curves from below at the same point (point G''), the best level of output is three units whether the monopolist faces D or D''. However, with D, the monopolist would sell the three units of output at $P = \$6$ (as in Figure 9–3), whereas with D'', the monopolist would sell the three units of output at $P = \$7.50$ (see Figure 9–5). Thus, the same quantity (i.e., $Q = 3$) can be supplied at two different prices (i.e., at $P = \$6$ or $P = \$7.50$) depending on the price elasticity of demand (i.e., depending on whether the monopolist faced demand curve D or D''). Therefore, under monopoly, costs are related to the quantity supplied of the commodity, but there is no unique relationship between price and output (i.e., we cannot derive the monopolist's supply curve from its MC curve). Note that the monopolist would charge a higher price if it faces the less elastic demand curve (i.e., D'').

9.3 LONG-RUN EQUILIBRIUM PRICE AND OUTPUT

In this section, we analyze the behavior of the monopolist in the long run and compare it with the behavior of a perfectly competitive firm and industry. We also measure the welfare costs of monopoly.

Profit Maximization in the Long Run

In the long run, all inputs are variable and the monopolist can build the most efficient plant to produce the best level of output. The best or profit-maximizing level of output is given by the point where the monopolist's *long-run* marginal cost curve intersects the marginal revenue curve from below. Thus, the marginal concept is again at work. The most efficient plant is the one that allows the monopolist to produce the best level of output at the lowest possible cost. This is the plant represented by the $SATC$ curve tangent to the LAC curve at the best level of output. As before, we assume that the monopolist does not affect input prices.

Figure 9–6 shows that the monopolist maximizes profits in the long run by producing $Q = 4$; this is given by point M, where the LMC curve intersects the MR curve from below. The monopolist should build plant $SATC_2$ and operate it at point N with $SATC = \$3.50$. Plant $SATC_2$ is the most efficient plant (i.e., the one that allows the monopolist to produce $Q = 4$ at the lowest $SATC$). In the long run, the monopolist will charge $P = \$5$ (point R), and earn a profit of $\$1.50$ (RN) per unit and $\$6$ in total (as opposed to $\$4.50$ in the short run with $SATC_1$–the same as in Figure 9–3).

Even though profits will attract additional firms into the perfectly competitive industry until all firms just break even in the long run, the monopolist can continue to earn profits in the long run because of blocked entry. However, the value of these long-run profits will be capitalized into the market value of the firm. Thus, it is the original owner of the monopoly that directly benefits from the monopoly power. A purchaser of the firm would have to pay a price that reflected the present (discounted) value of the monopoly profits, and so

FIGURE 9–6 Long-Run Equilibrium of the Monopolist

In the long run, the monopolist maximizes profits by producing at point M ($Q = 4$), where the LMC curve intersects the MR curve from below. The monopolist should build plant $SATC_2$, and operate it at point N at $SATC = \$3.50$. The monopolist will earn a profit of \$1.50 (RN) per unit and \$6 in total (as opposed to \$4.50 in the short run).

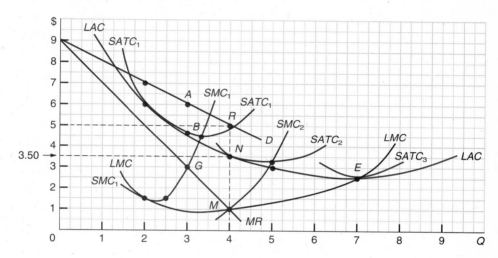

would only break even in the long run. That is, monopoly profits become part of the opportunity costs of the original monopolist (see Example 2).

Note also that the monopolist, as opposed to a perfectly competitive firm, does not produce at the lowest point on its LAC curve (see Figure 9–6). Only if the monopolist's MR curve happened to go through the lowest point on its LAC would this be the case (see problem 7). Furthermore, a monopolist may earn long-run profits. Thus, as compared with a perfectly competitive firm when the industry is in long-run equilibrium (see section 8.5), monopoly is inefficient because the monopolist is not likely to produce at the lowest point on its LAC curve and consumers are likely to pay a price that also usually includes a profit margin. These social costs of monopoly are measured in the next subsection for a perfectly competitive industry that faces constant returns to scale and is subsequently monopolized.

Example 2

Monopoly Profits in the New York Taxi Industry

In order to operate a taxicab in most municipalities (cities) in the United States, a "medallion" or license is needed. Most municipalities are not issuing any more medallions, thereby conferring monopoly power (the ability to earn economic profits) on the original medallion owners. The value of owning a medallion is given by the present (discounted) value of the future stream of earnings resulting from the ownership rights to the monopoly. This process is called *capitalization*. For example, the purchase price of a medallion in New York City was about $134,000 in 1989 (when there were 11,787 medallions). The original owners purchased the medallion by paying only a $10 fee to the city government in 1937! The price of a medallion is lower in other American cities to reflect the lower earning power of the medallion in other cities. For example, the price of a medallion is about $25,000 in Chicago (the next most expensive) where there are 4,600 medallions.

The monopoly power of taxicab license owners arose because of government restrictions on the number of licenses issued. Were municipalities to freely grant a license (medallion) for the asking, the price of the license would drop to zero. Note that only the original owner benefits from the monopoly rights. A buyer of the rights would now have to pay a price that would fully reflect the future stream of earnings from the monopoly power, and so the buyer would only break even in the long run. The only way to prevent further windfall gains to present owners of the monopoly rights (medallions) is for the government to issue additional medallions. While not doing that, New York City has allowed a sharp growth during the 1980s in the number of radio cabs, which can only respond to radio calls and cannot cruise the streets for passengers. This has, nevertheless, sharply increased competition in the New York City taxi industry and curtailed the rise in the price of medallions.

Source: "Owners Bewail Flood of Cabs in New York," *New York Times*, April 10, 1989, p. B1.

Comparison with Perfect Competition: The Social Cost of Monopoly

To measure the long-run social cost of monopoly, we assume that a perfectly competitive industry operating under constant returns to scale is suddenly monopolized and the market demand and cost curves remain unchanged. We will see that in that case output will be smaller and prices will be higher than under perfect competition. In addition, there will be a redistribution of income from consumers to the monopolist and a welfare loss due to less efficient resource use. These are shown in Figure 9–7.

In Figure 9–7, D is the perfectly competitive industry market demand curve, and LS is the perfectly competitive industry long-run supply curve under constant costs. The long-run perfectly competitive equilibrium is at point E, where D intersects LS. At point E, $Q = 6$ and $P = \$3$. Consumers collectively would be willing to pay $LEIO$ ($36) for six units of the commodity, but need only pay $EIOC$ ($18). Thus, the consumers' surplus is LEC or $18 (see section 8.8).

When the perfectly competitive industry is monopolized, the LS curve

FIGURE 9–7   The Social Cost of Monopoly

With perfect competition, D is the market demand curve, and LS is the supply curve under constant costs. Equilibrium is at point E, where D intersects LS, and $Q = 6$ and $P = \$3$. When the perfectly competitive industry is monopolized, the LS curve becomes the monopolist's LAC and LMC curve. Equilibrium is at point M, where $MR = LMC$. At point M, $Q = 3$, $P = \$6$, total profits are $RMCF$, and REM is the social cost to society due to the less efficient resource use under monopoly.

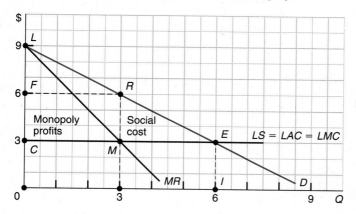

becomes the monopolist's LAC and LMC curves (the monopolist would simply operate the plants of the previously perfectly competitive firms).[7] The best level of output for the monopolist in the long run is then given by point M, where $MR = LMC$. Thus, with monopoly, $Q = 3$, $P = \$6$ (which exceeds $LMC = \$3$), and the monopolist will earn total profits equal to $RMCF$ ($\$9$). The consumers' surplus is now only LRF ($\$4.50$), down from LEC ($\$18$) under perfect competition. Of the $RECF$ ($\$13.50$) reduction in the consumers' surplus, $RMCF$ ($\$9$) represents a redistribution of income from consumers to the monopolist in the form of profits, and REM ($\$4.50$) is the social cost to society due to the less efficient resource use under monopoly.

Specifically, monopoly profits are not a net loss to society as a whole, because they represent simply a redistribution of income from consumers of the commodity to the monopolist producer. This redistribution is "bad" only to the extent that society "values" the welfare of consumers more than that of the monopolist. As we will see later, all of the monopolist's profits could be taxed away and redistributed to consumers of the commodity. On the other hand, the area of welfare triangle REM represents a true welfare or

---

[7]Specifically, a perfectly-competitive, constant cost industry in long-run equilibrium has a horizontal LS curve at the minimum LAC of the individual firms (see Figure 8–10). A monopolist taking over the industry could change output by changing the number of plants previously operated by the independent firms at minimum LAC (where $LAC = LMC$). Thus, the horizontal LS supply curve of the competitive industry is the LAC and LMC curves of the monopolized industry. They show the constant LAC and LMC at which the monopolist can change output.

deadweight loss to society as a whole, which is inherent to monopoly and which society cannot avoid under monopoly.

Welfare triangle *REM* arises because the monopolist artificially restricts the output of the commodity so that some resources flow into the production of other commodities that society values less. Specifically, consumers pay $P =$ \$6 for the third unit of the commodity produced by the monopolist. This is a measure of the social value or marginal benefit of this unit of the commodity to consumers. The marginal cost (*MC*) to produce this unit of the commodity, however, is only \$3. This means that society forgoes one unit of the monopolized commodity valued at \$6 for a unit of another commodity valued at \$3. Thus, some of society's resources are used to produce less valuable commodities under monopoly. Since under perfect competition, production takes place at point *E*, where $P = LMC$ (see Figure 9–7), welfare triangle *REM* represents the social cost or welfare loss from the less efficient use of society's resources under monopoly.

Example 3

Estimates of the Social Cost of Monopoly in the United States

In 1954, Harberger measured the area of the welfare triangle (*REM* in Figure 9–7) in each manufacturing industry in the United States on the assumption that the marginal cost was constant and that the price elasticity of the demand curve was 1. He found that the total social cost of monopoly was only about one-tenth of 1% of GNP. With some refinements of the estimating method, Scherer found that the social welfare loss from monopoly was between 0.5% and 2% of GNP, and most likely about 1%. The reason for these relatively low estimates is that there are few firms in the American economy with a great deal of monopoly power. In fact, Siegfried and Tiemann found that 44% of the total welfare loss due to monopoly power in the United States in 1963 came from the auto industry; the remainder of the loss was mostly due to a few other industries such as petroleum refining, plastics, and drugs.

There are, however, other losses resulting from monopoly power that are not included in the aforementioned measure. One is that, in the absence of competition, monopolists do not keep their costs as low as possible, and they prefer the "quiet life" (*X*-inefficiency). Evidence of this is that when U.S. steel firms started to face increased foreign competition during the 1970s and 1980s, they were able to sharply reduce costs. Another is that monopolists waste a lot of resources (from society's point of view) lobbying, engaging in legal battles, and advertising in the attempt to create and retain monopoly power and to avoid regulation and prosecution under antitrust laws. These are sometimes referred to as the social costs of "rent seeking." In fact, some economists believe that these other social costs of monopoly are larger than those measured by the welfare triangle. But the method of measurement and actual estimates of the size of these social costs are subject to a great deal of disagreement and controversy.

Sources: A. Harberger, "Monopoly and Resource Allocation," *American Economic Review*, May 1954; F. Scherer, *Industrial Market Structure and Economic Performance* (Chicago: Rand McNally, 1980), pp. 459–464; and J. Siegfried and T. Tiemann, "The Welfare Cost of Monopoly: An Interindustry Analysis," *Economic Inquiry*, June 1974. For the social costs of rent seeking, see W. Rogerson, "The Social Costs of Monopoly and Regulation: A Game-Theoretic Analysis," *Bell Journal of Economics* (now *The Rand Journal of Economics*), Autumn 1982, and F. Fisher, "The Social Costs of Monopoly and Regulation: Posner Reconsidered," *Journal of Political Economy*, April 1985.

9.4 PROFIT MAXIMIZATION BY THE MULTIPLANT MONOPOLIST

So far, the discussion has been based on the implicit assumption that the monopolist operated a single plant. This is not always or even usually the case. In this section, we examine how a multiplant monopolist should distribute its best level of output among its various plants, both in the short run and in the long run, to minimize its costs of production and maximize profits.

Short-Run Equilibrium

A multiplant monopolist will minimize the total cost of producing the best level of output in the short run when the marginal cost of the last unit of the commodity produced in each plant is equal to the marginal revenue from selling the combined output. This is shown in Figure 9–8, which refers to a two-plant monopolist.

The left and center panels of Figure 9–8 show the SMC curve of each of the two plants operated by the monopolist. The *horizontal* summation of SMC_1 and SMC_2 yields SMC in the right panel. The SMC curve shows the monopolist's minimum SMC of producing each additional unit of the commodity. Thus, the monopolist should produce the first and second unit of the commodity in plant 1 (at a SMC of \$2 and \$2.50, respectively), the third and fourth unit in plant 1 and plant 2 (one unit in each plant, at $SMC = \$3$), and so on.

If the monopolist were to produce all four units of the commodity in plant 1, it would incur a $SMC = \$4$ for the fourth unit (instead of a $SMC = \$3$ with plant 2). Thus, the monopolist should produce three units of the commodity in plant 1 and one unit in plant 2. By adding the three units of the commodity produced in plant 1 and the one unit produced in plant 2, we get point G on the SMC curve in the right panel of Figure 9–8. Thus, the SMC curve in the right panel is obtained from the horizontal summation of the SMC_1 and SMC_2 curves in the left and center panels, respectively. The SMC shows the monopolist's minimum SMC of producing each additional unit of the commodity.

The best level of output of this monopolist is four units of the commodity and is given by point G, where the SMC curve intersects the MR curve from

FIGURE 9–8 Short-Run Equilibrium of the Multiplant Monopolist

The *SMC* curves of each of two plants of a monopolist are SMC_1 and SMC_2 in the left and center panels, respectively. The horizontal summation of SMC_1 and SMC_2 yields *SMC* in the right panel. *SMC* shows the monopolist's minimum *SMC* of producing each additional unit of the commodity. The best level of output is $Q = 4$, given by point G, where the *SMC* curve intersects the *MR* curve from below. To minimize *STC*, the monopolist should produce three units of the commodity in plant 1 and one unit in plant 2 so that $SMC_1 = SMC_2 = SMC = MR = \$3$.

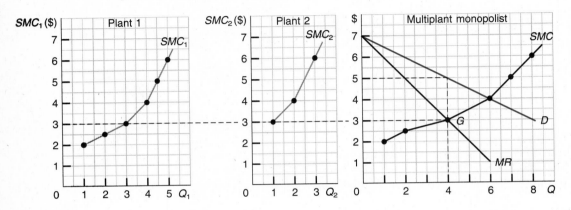

below. The monopolist should produce three units of the commodity in plant 1 and one unit of the commodity in plant 2 so that $SMC_1 = SMC_2 = SMC = MR = \$3$ (see the figure). This minimizes the total cost of producing the best level of output of four units at \$10.50 (\$2 + \$2.50 + \$3 + \$3) in the short run. If the monopolist were to produce all four units in plant 1, it would incur a $STC = \$11.50$ (\$2 + \$2.50 + \$3 + \$4). The *STC* would be even higher if the monopolist produced all four units in plant 2 (see the center panel of the figure).

Whether the monopolist earns a profit, breaks even, or incurs a loss by producing three units of the commodity in plant 1 and one unit in the commodity in plant 2 depends on the value of the *SATC* at $Q = 4$. Even if the monopolist were to incur a loss at its best level of output, it would stay in business in the short run as long as $P > AVC$ (see section 9.2).

Long-Run Equilibrium

In the long run, a monopolist can build as many identical plants of optimal size (i.e., plants whose *SATC* curves form the lowest point of the *LAC* curve) as required to produce the best level of output. This is shown in Figure 9–9. The left panel shows one of the plants of the monopolist. The monopolist will operate this plant at point E', where $SATC_1 = SMC_1 = LAC_1 = LMC_1 = \$1$ and $Q = 3$. To produce larger outputs, the monopolist will build additional identical plants and run them at the optimal rate of output of $Q = 3$. If input prices remain constant, the *LMC* curve of the monopolist is horizontal at $LAC = LMC = \$1$ (see the right panel).

FIGURE 9–9   Long-Run Equilibrium of the Multiplant Monopolist

The left panel shows one of the plants of the monopolist. The monopolist will operate this plant at point E', where $LAC_1 = LMC_1 = \$1$ and $Q_1 = 3$. To produce larger outputs, the monopolist will build additional identical plants and run them at $Q = 3$. If input prices remain constant, the LMC curve of the monopolist is horizontal at $LMC = \$1$ (see the right panel). The best level of output is at point E, where $LMC = MR = \$1$. At point E, $Q = 6$, $P = \$4$, $LAC = \$1$, the monopolist earns a total profit of $18 and operates two plants.

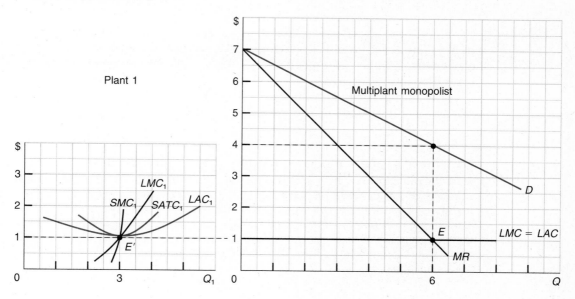

The best level of output of the monopolist in the long run is then given by point E, where $LMC = MR = \$1$ in the right panel. At point E, $Q = 6$, $P = \$4$, $LAC = \$1$, and the monopolist earns a profit of $3 per unit and $18 in total. The monopolist will produce three units of output in each of two identical plants (point E' in the left panel). If the best level of output is not a multiple of three, the monopolist will either have to run some plants at outputs greater than three units or build and run an extra plant at less than three units of output.

If input prices rise when the multiplant monopolist builds additional plants to increase output, then the LAC curve of each plant shifts up (as in Figure 8–11) and the LMC curve of the monopolist will be upward sloping.

9.5   PRICE DISCRIMINATION—A MONOPOLIST'S GIMMICK TO INCREASE PROFITS

In this section, we examine various types of price discrimination. **Price discrimination** refers to the charging of different prices for different quantities of a commodity or in different markets, which are not justified by cost differ-ences. By practicing price discrimination, the monopolist can increase its total revenue and profits. We first examine the charging of different prices by the monopolist for different quantities sold and then the charging of different prices in different markets.

Charging Different Prices for Different Quantities

If a monopolist could sell each unit of the commodity separately and charge the highest price each consumer would be willing to pay for the commodity rather than go without it, the monopolist would be able to extract the entire consumers' surplus from consumers. This is called **first degree** or **perfect price discrimination.**

For example, in Figure 9–10, the consumer would be willing to pay *LRZO* ($22.50) for three units of the commodity. Since he or she only pays *RZOF*

FIGURE 9–10   First and Second Degree Price Discrimination

Since the consumer is willing to pay $22.50 for three units of the commodity, but only pays $18, this consumer's surplus is $4.50. If the monopolist charged $8.50 for the first unit, $7.50 for the second, and $6.50 for the third, it would receive $22.50, thus extracting the entire consumer's surplus. This is first degree price discrimination. If the monopolist set $P = \$7$ for the first two units and $P = \$6$ for additional units, it would sell three units and extract $2 of the consumer's surplus. This is second degree price discrimination.

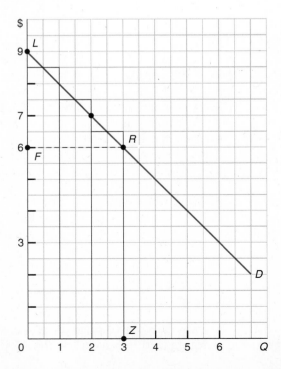

($18), this consumer's surplus is *LRF* ($4.50). If the monopolist, however, charged $8.50 for the first unit (the highest price that this consumer would pay rather than forego entirely the consumption of the commodity), $7.50 for the second unit of the commodity, and $6.50 for the third unit, then the monopolist would receive $22.50 (the sum of the areas of the rectangles above the first three units of the commodity), thereby extracting the entire consumer's surplus from this consumer.[8] The result would be the same if the monopolist made an all-or-nothing offer to the consumer either to purchase all three units of the commodity for $22.50 or none at all.

To be able to practice first degree price discrimination, the monopolist must know the exact shape of each consumer's demand curve and be able to charge the highest price that each and every consumer would pay for each unit of the commodity. Even if this were possible, it would probably be prohibitively expensive to carry out. Thus, first degree price discrimination is not very common in the real world.

More practical and common is **second degree** or **multipart price discrimination.** This refers to the charging of a uniform price per unit for a specific quantity of the commodity, a lower price per unit for an additional batch of block of the commodity, and so on. By doing so, the monopolist will be able to extract part, but not all, of the consumer's surplus. For example, in Figure 9–10, the monopolist could set the price of $7 per unit on the first two units of the commodity and a price of $6 on additional units of the commodity. The monopolist would then sell three units of the commodity to this individual for $20 and extract $2 from the total consumer's surplus of $4.50. Second degree price discrimination is often practiced by public utilities such as electrical power companies (see Example 4).

Charging Different Prices in Different Markets

The charging of a different price in different markets is called **third degree price discrimination.** For simplicity, we will assume that there are only two markets. To maximize profits, the monopolist must produce the best level of output and sell that output in the two markets in such a way that the marginal revenue of the last unit sold in each market is the same. This will require the monopolist to sell the commodity at a higher price in the market with the less elastic demand. This is shown in Figure 9–11.

The left panel of Figure 9–11 shows D_1 and MR_1, which are, respectively, the market demand and the corresponding marginal revenue curves faced by the monopolist in the first market. The middle panel shows the D_2 and MR_2 for the second market. From the horizontal summation of D_1 and D_2, and from MR_1 and MR_2, we get D and MR for the firm as a whole (monopolist) in the right panel. We sum horizontally D_1 and D_2, and MR_1 and MR_2, because

---

[8]Note that the consumer is willing to pay an amount equal to the area under the demand curve between zero and one on the horizontal axis for the first unit of the commodity. This is equal to the area of the rectangle above the first unit of the commodity in Figure 9–10.

FIGURE 9–11   Third Degree Price Discrimination

D_1 in the left panel is the demand curve faced by the monopolist in market 1 (with MR_1 as the corresponding marginal revenue curve). D_2 and MR_2 in the middle panel refer to market 2. By summing horizontally D_1 and D_2, and MR_1 and MR_2, we get the D and MR curves for the monopolist in the right panel. The best level of output is seven units, given where the MC curve intersects the MR curve from below. To maximize total profits the monopolist should sell $Q = 4$ at $P = \$7$ in market 1 and $Q = 3$ at $P = \$4.50$ in market 2, so that $MR_1 = MR_2 = MR = MC = \$3$. With $AC = \$4$ (point Z in the right panel), the monopolist's total profits are \$13.50.

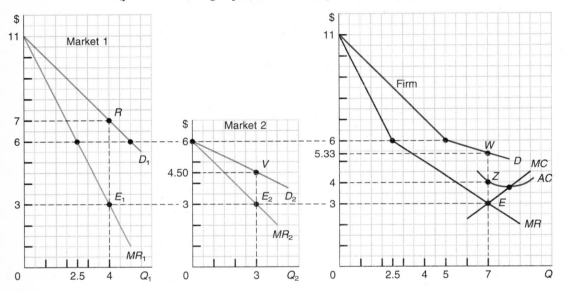

the firm can sell the commodity in and obtain extra revenues from both markets. Note that until $Q = 2.5$, $MR_1 = MR$, and until $Q = 5$, $D_1 = D$.

The best level of output of the monopolist is seven units and is given by the point where the firm's marginal cost curve (MC) intersects the firm's total marginal revenue curve (MR) from below (point E in the right panel). To maximize total profits, the monopolist should then sell four units of the commodity in market 1 (given by point E_1 in the left panel) and the remaining three units in market 2 (given by point E_2 in the middle panel) so that $MR_1 = MR_2 = MR = MC = \$3$ (see the figure). If the MR for the last unit of the commodity sold in one market were different from the MR of the last unit sold in the other market, the monopolist could increase its total revenue and profits by redistributing sales from the market with the lower MR to the market with the higher MR until $MR_1 = MR_2$.

The monopolist should charge $P = \$7$ for each of the four units of the commodity sold in market 1 (point R on D_1) and $P = \$4.50$ for each of the three units of the commodity in market 2 (point V on D_2). Note that the price is higher in market 1, where demand is less elastic. The total revenue of the monopolist would be $41.50 ($28 from selling four units of the commodity at $P = \$7$ in market 1 plus $13.50 from selling three units of the commodity at $P = \$4.50$ in market 2). With total costs of $28 (seven units at $AC = \$4$, given by point Z in the right panel), the monopolist earns a profit of $13.50 (the total revenue of $41.50 minus the total costs of $28). If the monopolist sold the best level of output of seven units at the price of $5.33 (point W on D in the right panel) in both markets (i.e., if it did not practice third degree price discrimination), the monopolist would earn a profit of $WZ = \$1.33$ per unit (the price of $5.33 minus the average cost of $4) and $9.31 in total (the $1.33 profit per unit times the seven units sold) as compared with $13.50 with third degree price discrimination. Any other output or distribution of sales between the two markets would similarly lead to lower total profits for the monopolist. This type of analysis is valid for the long run as well as for the short run.[9]

For a firm to be able to practice third degree price discrimination, three conditions must be met. First, the firm must have some monopoly power (i.e., the firm must not be a price taker). Second, the firm must be able to keep the two markets separate. Third, the price elasticity of demand for the commodity or service must be different in the two markets. All three conditions are met in the sale of electricity. For example, electrical power companies can set prices (subject to government regulation). The market for the industrial use of electricity is kept separate from that of household use by meters installed in each production plant and home. The price elasticity of demand for electricity for industrial use is higher than for household use because industrial users have better substitutes and more choices available (such as generating their own electricity) than households. Thus, electrical power companies usually charge lower prices to industrial users than to households.

Note that without market power the firm would be a price taker and could not practice any form of price discrimination. If the firm were unable to keep the markets separate, users in the lower-priced market could purchase more of the service than they needed and resell some of it in the higher-priced market (thus underselling the original supplier of the service). Finally, if the price elasticity of demand were the same in both markets, the best that the firm could do would be to charge the same price in both markets.

There are many other examples of third degree price discrimination: (1) the lower fees that doctors usually charge low-income people than high-income people for basically identical services; (2) the lower prices that airlines, trains, and cinemas usually charge children and the elderly than other adults; (3) the lower postal rates for third-class mail than for equally heavy first-class

---

[9]If the monopolist knows the price elasticity of demand for the commodity in the two markets, it can determine the price to charge in each market to maximize total profits by utilizing formula [5–6]. See problem 10, with answer at end of book. For a mathematical presentation of price discrimination using rudimentary calculus, see section A.12 of the Mathematical Appendix at the end of the book.

mail; (4) the lower prices that producers usually charge abroad than at home for the same commodity, and so on.

Third degree price discrimination is more likely to occur in service industries than in manufacturing industries because it is more difficult (often impossible) for a consumer to purchase a service in the low-price market and resell it at a higher price in the other market (thus undermining the monopolist's differential pricing in the two markets). For example, a low-income person could not possibly resell a doctor's visit at a higher fee to a high-income person. On the other hand, if an elderly person were charged a lower price for an automobile, he or she could certainly resell it at a higher price to other people. It is not clear that a supermarket's charging of $0.95 for two bars of soap and $0.50 for one bar is price discrimination, because the supermarket saves on clerks' time in marking the merchandise and on cashiers' time in ringing up customers' bills. That is, the charging of different prices to different consumers in different markets is not price discrimination if the different prices are based on different costs.

Example 4
Price Discrimination by Con Edison

Table 9–6 gives the price per kilowatt-hour that Con Edison charged residential and commercial users for various quantities of electricity consumed in New York City in 1993 during winter and summer months. Since Con Edison charged different rates for different quantities of electricity purchased by residential and commercial customers, it practiced both second and third degree price discrimination.

Another way for a seller to practice third degree price discrimination is by offering coupons to consumers for the purchase of some products (such as a box of breakfast cereal) at a discount. This allows a firm to sell the product at a lower price to only the 20% to 30% of consumers who bother to clip, save, and use coupons (these are the consumers who have a higher price elasticity of demand). Offering coupons, then, is a form of third degree price discrimination that the firm can use to increase profits. Firms often offer rebates and airlines charge many different fares for a given trip for the same reason.

One type of price difference that is not price discrimination is *peak-load pricing*. This refers to the charging of higher prices during peak times (such as during summer months) to reflect the higher costs of generating electricity at peak times, when older and less efficient equipment has to be brought into operation to meet peak demand. These price differences do not represent third degree price discrimination because they are in fact based on or reflect cost differences.

TABLE 9–6   Electricity Rates Charged by Con Edison in 1993 (cents per killowatt-hour [kWh])

	kWh	Cents/kWh	kWh	Cents/kWh
Residential rates (single residence)				
Winter	0–250	12.20	Above 250	11.66
Summer	0–250	12.20	Above 250	13.16
Commercial rates (small business)				
Winter	0–900	14.39	Above 900	13.25
Summer	0–900	15.89	Above 900	14.75
Commercial rates (large business)				
Winter	0–15,000	5.60	Above 15,000	5.21
Summer	0–15,000	5.60	Above 15,000	5.21

Sources: Con Edison, *Electric Rates,* New York 1993; C. Narasimhan, "A Price Discriminatory Theory of Coupons," *Marketing Science,* Spring 1984; and "The Art of Devising Air Fares," *New York Times,* March 8, 1987, p. D1.

9.6 INTERNATIONAL PRICE DISCRIMINATION AND DUMPING

Price discrimination can also be practiced between the domestic and the foreign market. International price discrimination is called **dumping.** Dumping refers to the charging of a lower price abroad than at home for the same commodity because of the greater price elasticity of demand in the foreign market. By so doing, the monopolist earns higher profits than by selling the best level of output at the same price in both markets. The price elasticity of demand for the monopolist's product abroad is higher than at home because of the competition from producers from other nations in the foreign market. Foreign competition is usually restricted at home by import tariffs or other trade barriers. These import restrictions serve to segment the market (i.e., keep the domestic market separate from the foreign market) and prevent the reexport of the commodity back to the monopolist's home country (which would under-mine the monopolist's ability to sell the commodity at a higher price at home than abroad). International price discrimination can be viewed in Figure 9–11 if D_1 referred to the demand curve faced by the monopolist in the domestic market and D_2 referred to the demand curve that the monopolist faces in the foreign market.

Besides dumping resulting from international price discrimination (often referred to as *persistent dumping* to distinguish it from other types of dumping), there are two other forms of dumping. These are predatory dumping and sporadic dumping. *Predatory dumping* is the *temporary* sale of a commodity at below cost or at a lower price abroad in order to drive foreign producers out of business, after which prices are raised abroad to take advantage of the newly acquired monopoly power. *Sporadic dumping* is the *occasional* sale of the commodity at below cost or at a lower price abroad than domestically in order to unload an unforeseen and temporary surplus of a commodity without having to reduce domestic prices.

Trade restrictions to counteract *predatory* dumping are justified and allowed to protect domestic industries from unfair competition from abroad. These restrictions usually take the form of antidumping duties to offset price differentials. However, it is often difficult to determine the type of dumping, and domestic producers invariably demand protection against any form of dumping. In fact, the very threat of filing a dumping complaint discourages imports and leads to higher domestic production and profits. This is referred to as the "harassment thesis." Persistent and sporadic dumping benefit domestic consumers (by allowing them to purchase the commodity at a lower price), and these benefits may exceed the possible losses of domestic producers.

Over the past decade, Japan was accused of dumping steel, televisions, and computer chips in the United States, and Europeans of dumping cars, steel, and other products. Most industrial nations (especially those of the European Economic Community) have a tendency of persistently dumping surplus agricultural commodities arising from their farm-support programs. Export subsidies are also a form of dumping which, though illegal by international agreement, often occur in disguised forms. When dumping is proved, the violating firm usually chooses to raise its prices (as Volkswagen did in 1976 and Japanese TV exporters did in 1977) rather than face antidumping duties.

9.7 TWO-PART TARIFF, TYING, AND BUNDLING

In this section, we examine some other pricing practices by monopolists: two-part tariff, tying, and bundling.

Two-Part Tariff

Two-part tariff is another pricing practice that monopolists sometimes use to extract consumer surplus. It requires consumers to pay an initial fee for the right to purchase a product as well as a usage fee or price for each unit of the product they purchase. Consider amusement parks where visitors are charged an admission fee as well as a fee or price for each ride they take. Other examples are telephone companies that charge a monthly fee plus a message-unit fee; computer companies that charge monthly rentals plus a usage fee for renting their mainframe computers; and golf and tennis clubs that charge an annual membership fee plus a fee for each round or game played. In each case, the monopolist wants to charge the initial fee and the usage fee that extracts as much of consumers' surplus as possible and thus maximizes its total profits.

The monopolist maximizes its total profits by charging a usage fee or per-unit price equal to its marginal cost and an initial or membership fee equal to the entire consumer surplus. To see this, assume that initially there is a single consumer in the market with demand curve D in the left panel of Figure 9–12. The monopolist should then charge the usage fee or price (P) equal to the marginal cost (MC) of $2 and an initial or membership fee of $8 (area AEB), which equals the entire consumer surplus at $P = $2. The monopolist would earn lower profits at any other price. For example, charging $P = $3 would provide the monopolist with a profit of $1 for each of the three units of the product or service that the monopolist would sell at $P = $3, but it would allow the monopolist to charge an initial or membership fee of only $4.50 (equal to the consumer surplus of $AE'B'$ for $P = $3). Thus, with $P = $3, the monopolist's total profit would be $7.50 ($3 from the sale of the three units of the product or service and $4.50 from the initial or membership fee) as compared with a profit of $8 (from the initial or membership fee for $P = MC = $2). On the other hand, with a usage fee or price of only $1, the monopolist would incur a loss of $1 on each of the five units of the product or service that it would sell at $P = $1, but it could charge an initial or membership charge of $12.50 (equal to the consumer surplus of $AE''B''$). This

FIGURE 9–12 Two-Part Pricing by a Monopolist

With only one consumer in the market (left panel), the monopolist maximizes its total profits by charging $P = MC = $2 and the initial or membership fee of $AEB = $8. The monopolist can bring the consumer in the right panel into the market by lowering the initial or membership fee to $6 (equal to the surplus of $A^*E^*B^*$ of the second consumer at $P = MC = $2) for each consumer and earn a total profit of $12.

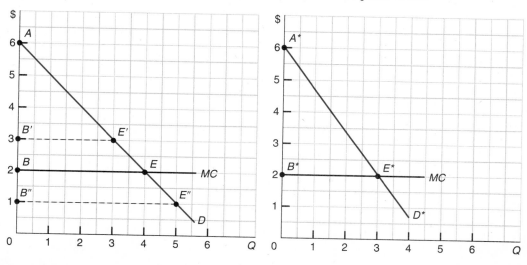

would leave the monopolist with a net profit of $7.50, which is also less than the total profit of $8 with $P = \$2$.

Suppose now that there was a second customer with demand curve D^* in the right panel of Figure 9–12 who could be brought into the market. At $P = MC = \$2$, the consumer surplus for this second customer would be $6 ($A^*E^*B^*$ in the right panel of Figure 9–12), and this is as high an initial fee that the second consumer would be willing to pay. The monopolist would then have to lower the initial fee to $6 for both consumers to bring this second consumer into the market and thus earn the higher total profits of $12 (from the $6 initial fee from each consumer). This leaves $2 of consumer surplus to the first consumer. The monopolist could extract this remaining $2 surplus from the first consumer if it could somehow charge the first consumer a price higher than marginal cost. Another way would be to charge the first consumer an initial fee of $8 and provide a special discount membership of $6 for the second consumer. If both consumers were identical and faced the same demand curve, no such difficulty would arise and the monopolist would set $P = MC$ and charge each consumer an initial fee equal to their (identical) consumer surplus.[10]

Tying and Bundling

Tying refers to the requirement that a consumer who buys or leases a monopolist's product also purchase another product needed in the use of the first. For example, when the Xerox Corporation was the only producer of photocopiers in the 1950s, it required those leasing its machines to also purchase paper from Xerox. Similarly, until it was ordered by the court to discontinue the practice, IBM required by contract that the users of its computers purchase IBM punch cards. Sometimes tying of purchases is done to ensure that the correct supplies are used for the equipment to function properly or to ensure quality. More often, it is used as a form of two-part tariff, whereby the monopolist can charge a price higher than marginal cost for supplies and thus extract more of the consumer surplus from the heavier users of the equipment (those who use more supplies). Often, the courts intervene to forbid these restrictions on competition. For example, MacDonald's was forced to allow its franchises to purchase their materials and supplies from any MacDonald's-approved supplier rather than only from MacDonald's. This increased competition while still ensuring quality and protection of the brand name.[11]

Bundling is a common form of tying in which the monopolist requires customers buying or leasing one of its products or services to also buy or lease another product or service *when customers have different tastes* but the monopolist cannot price discriminate (as in tying). By selling or leasing the

---

[10]For a more in-depth discussion of a two-part tariff, see W. Oi, "A Disneyland Dilemma: Two-Part Tariff for a Mickey Mouse Monopoly," *Quarterly Journal of Economics*, February 1971, pp. 77–96.

[11]See B. Klein and L. F. Saft, "The Law and Economics of Franchise Tying Contracts," *Journal of Law and Economics*, May 1985, pp. 345–361.

TABLE 9–7   Maximum Price Each Theater Would Be Willing to Pay to Lease Each Film Separately or as Bundle

	Theater 1	Theater 2
Movie A	$12,000	$10,000
Movie B	3,000	4,000

products or services as a package—a bundle—rather than separately, the monopolist can increase its total profits. This is shown in Table 9–7.

Table 9–7 shows the prices that theater 1 and theater 2 would be willing to pay to lease movie A and movie B. If the film company cannot price discriminate and leases each movie separately to the two theaters, it will have to lease each movie at the lower of the two prices at which each theater is willing to lease each film. Specifically, the film company would have to charge $10,000 for movie A and $3,000 for movie B for a total of $13,000 to lease both movies to each theater (if the film company charged more for either movie, one of the theaters would not lease the movie). But theater 1 would have been willing to pay $15,000 to lease both movies and theater 2 would have been willing to pay $14,000 for both movies. The film company can thus lease both movies to both theaters as package or a bundle for $14,000 (the lowest of the total amounts at which the two theaters are willing to lease the two movies) rather than individually for $13,000. Thus, by leasing the two movies together as a bundle rather than individually, the film company can extract some of the surplus from theater 1 without price discriminating between the two theaters.

Such profitable bundling is possible only when one theater is willing to pay more for leasing one movie but less for leasing the other movie with respect to the other theater (i.e, when the *relative* valuation for the two movies differs between the two theaters or the demand for the two movies by each theater is negatively correlated). If, in our example, theater 1 had been willing to pay only $9,000 or theater 2 only $8,000 to lease movie A, then the maximum price that the film company could charge either theater without price discrimination would be $12,000, whether it leased the movies as a bundle or separately. In that case, the relative valuation for the two movies would be the same for both theaters and bundling would not be profitable. For bundling to be profitable, one theater must be willing to pay more for one movie and less for another movie with respect to the other theater. This occurs only if the two theaters serve different audiences with different tastes and have different relative valuations for the two movies.[12]

---

[12]For a more detailed discussion of bundling, see, W. J. Adams and J. L. Yellin, "Commodity Bundling and the Burden of Monopoly," *Quarterly Journal of Economics*, August 1976, pp. 475–498; R. L. Schmalensee, "Commodity Bundling by Single-Product Monopolies," *Journal of Law and Economics*, April 1982, pp. 67–71; and A. Lewbel, "Bundling of Substitutes or Complements," *International Journal of Industrial Organization*, No. 3, 1985, pp. 101–107.

9.8 ANALYSIS OF MONOPOLY MARKETS

Now we consider some analyses of monopoly markets. First, we examine a comparison of the effect of a per-unit tax on a monopolist and on a perfect competitor, which shows that some commodities could only be supplied with price discrimination. Then, we answer the question of whether monopolists suppress inventions.

Per-Unit Tax: Perfect Competition and Monopoly Compared

One additional way to compare monopoly with perfect competition is with respect to the incidence of a per-unit tax. A per-unit excise tax (such as on cigarettes, gasoline, and liquor) will fall entirely on consumers if the industry is perfectly competitive and will fall only partly on consumers under monopoly, if both the monopolist and the perfectly competitive industry operate under constant costs.[13] For simplicity, we assume that the perfectly competitive industry and the monopolist face the same demand and cost conditions. Thus, S in Figure 9–13 refers to the long-run supply curve of the perfectly competitive industry and to the $LAC = LMC$ curve of the monopolist under constant costs.

Before the imposition of the per-unit tax, the perfectly competitive industry operates at point E, where D and S intersect, so that $Q = 6$ and $P = \$3$. If a tax of $2 per unit is imposed, S shifts up by \$2 to S'. The perfectly competitive industry would then operate at point E', where D and S' intersect, so that $Q = 4$ and $P = \$5$. Thus, when the industry is perfectly competitive and operates under constant costs, the entire amount of the per-unit tax (\$2 in this case) falls on consumers in the form of higher prices (so that $P = \$5$ instead of \$3).

The case is different under monopoly. Before the imposition of the tax, the monopolist operates at point M, where MR and S (the $LMC = LAC$ of the monopolist) intersect. $Q = 3$, $P = \$6$ (point R), $LAC = \$3$, and the monopolist earns a profit of \$3 (RM) per unit and \$9 in total. If the same tax of \$2 per unit is imposed on the monopolist, S shifts up to S' ($= LMC' = LMC + 2 = LAC' = LAC + 2$). The monopolist would then operate at point M', where MR and S' intersect. At point M', $Q = 2$, $P = \$7$ (point R'), $LAC' = \$5$, and the monopolist earns \$2 per unit ($R'M'$) and \$4 in total. Thus, with monopoly, the price to consumers rises by only \$1 (one-half of the per-unit tax). The remaining half of the tax falls on the monopolist, so that it now only earns a profit of \$2, rather than \$3, per unit. Note also that with the tax, the decline in output under monopoly is half that with perfect competition (i.e., output

---

[13]The fact that a per-unit excise tax falls entirely on consumers under perfect competition but falls only partly on consumers with monopoly does not mean, however, that monopoly is "better" than perfect competition. When all inefficiencies associated with monopoly are considered, perfect competition leads to a higher level of social welfare than monopoly. Furthermore, the incidence of a per-unit tax is entirely on consumers only if the perfectly competitive industry operates under constant costs.

FIGURE 9–13   Per-Unit Tax: Perfect Competition and Monopoly Compared

Before the per-unit tax, the perfectly competitive industry operates at point E, where D and S intersect, so that $Q = 6$ and $P = \$3$. With a \$2 per-unit tax, S shifts up to S', and $Q = 4$ and $P = \$5$, so the tax falls entirely on consumers. Before the tax, the monopolist is in equilibrium at point M. $Q = 3$, $P = \$6$, and the monopolist earns a profit of \$3 (RM) per unit and \$9 in total. With a tax of \$2 per unit, $Q = 2$, $P = \$7$, and half of the per-unit tax falls on the monopolist.

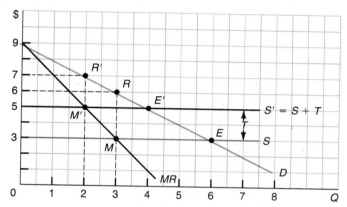

falls from six to four units with perfect competition, but only from three to two units under monopoly).

Price Discrimination and the Existence of the Industry

Sometimes price discrimination is necessary for an industry to exist. For example, in Figure 9–14, D_1 is the demand curve for the commodity for one group of consumers (i.e., in market 1), while D_2 is the demand curve for another group (market 2). The horizontal summation of D_1 and D_2 yields D (ABC). Since the LAC curve is above D at every level of output, the commodity or service would not be supplied in the long run in the absence of price discrimination or a subsidy.

With third degree price discrimination (to the extent that the two markets can be kept separate), the firm could sell one unit of the commodity at $P = \$4$ in market 1 and sell three units of the commodity at $P = \$1.50$ in market 2. The total output would then be four units sold at the (weighted) average price of \$2.13, which equals the LAC of producing four units in the long run (point F in the figure).[14]

---

[14]The weighted average price of \$2.13 is obtained by $[(1)(\$4) + (3)(\$1.50)]/4 = \$8.50/4$. The sale of $Q = 1$ in market 1 and $Q = 3$ in market 2 was obtained from inspection of the figure. This is the only output and distribution of sales (in whole units of the commodity) between the two markets by which this firm covers all costs.

FIGURE 9–14   **Price Discrimination and the Existence of an Industry**

The demand curve is D_1 in market 1 and D_2 in market 2. The horizontal summation of D_1 and D_2 gives D (ABC). Since the LAC curve is above D at every output level, the commodity or service would not be supplied in the long run without price discrimination or a subsidy. With third degree price discrimination, the firm could sell $Q = 1$ at $P = \$4$ in market 1 and sell $Q = 3$ at $P = \$1.50$ in market 2 and break even (since at point F, the weighted average $P = \$2.13$ equals LAC).

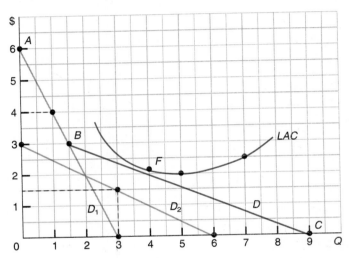

Do Monopolists Suppress Inventions?

A useful invention is one that allows the production of a given-quality product at lower cost or a higher-quality product at the same cost. Many people believe that a monopolist would suppress such inventions. Why, they argue, would a monopolist want to introduce a longer-lasting light bulb that costs the same to produce when that would reduce the number of light bulbs sold, and the total revenue and profits of the monopolist? Such reasoning is wrong. We will see that the introduction of an invention usually increases rather than reduces profits, and so the monopolist has an economic incentive to introduce it rather than to suppress it. This is shown in Figure 9–15.

The vertical axis of the figure measures the price of a kilowatt-hour (kWh) of electric light, and the horizontal axis measures the quantity (in thousands of hours) of kWhs provided either with original light bulbs or with new and longer-lasting light bulbs.[15] Thus, the axes do not refer to the price and quantity of light bulbs; instead they refer to the main attribute or characteristic of light bulbs, which is to provide light. D is the market demand curve for kWhs of

---

[15]See, "Bulb Lighted by Radio Waves May Last for up to 14 Years," *New York Times*, June 1, 1992, p. 1.

FIGURE 9-15   Monopoly and Inventions

The price per kilowatt-hour (kWh) of light is measured vertically and the quantity of kWhs horizontally. D is the market demand curve for kWhs of light. MC is the marginal cost of providing kWhs with the original bulbs and MC' with new bulbs (which last twice as long but cost the same to produce). With the original bulbs, $Q = 4$ kWhs, $P = \$0.80$ per kWh, $AC = \$0.40$, and profit is $\$0.40$ per kWh and $\$1.60$ in total. If original bulbs last ½ kWh, the monopolist sells eight of them at $P = \$0.40$. With new bulbs, $Q = 5$ kWhs, $P = \$0.70$, $AC' = \$0.20$, and profit is $\$0.50$ per kWh and $\$2.50$ in total. The monopolist sells five new bulbs at $\$0.70$ each.

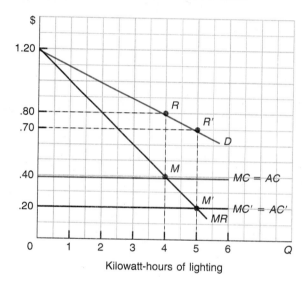

Kilowatt-hours of lighting

light with either the original or new light bulbs, and MR is the corresponding marginal revenue curve. The $MC = AC$ curve shows the marginal and average cost of producing kWhs of light with the original light bulbs (produced under conditions of constant cost). The best level of output of the monopolist is 4 kWhs and is given by point M where $MC = MR$. At $Q = 4$ kWhs, $P = \$0.80$ per kWh, $AC = \$0.40$ per kWh, and the monopolist earns a profit of $\$0.40$ per kWh and $\$1.60$ in total. If each original light bulb provides or lasts ½ kWh, the monopolist sells eight of the original light bulbs at $P = \$0.40$ each.

Suppose that the monopolist considers introducing a new light bulb that costs the same to produce but provides twice as many kWhs (i.e., lasts twice as long) as the original light bulbs. This is shown by the $MC' = AC'$ curve. This is half as high as the $MC = AC$ curve, indicating that each kWh of light could now be provided at half the cost. The best level of output of the monopolist is 5 kWhs and is given by point M' where $MC' = MR$. At $Q = 5$ kWhs, $P = \$0.70$ per kWh, $AC' = \$0.20$ per kWh, and the monopolist earns a profit of $\$0.50$ per kWh and $\$2.50$ in total (as compared with $\$1.60$ previously). Since each of the new light bulbs provides or lasts for 1 kWh (twice as much as the original light bulbs), the monopolist sells five light bulbs at $P = \$0.70$

each. Even though the monopolist sells fewer of the new light bulbs, it earns larger total profits, and so it has an economic incentive to introduce the invention. Consumers are also better off because after the invention they pay $0.70 instead of $0.80 per kWh of light and consume 5 kWh instead of 4 kWh.

Thus, the widespread belief that monopolists suppress inventions does not seem to be true. This is a good example of how dispassionate economic analysis based on the marginal principle can dispel some commonly held, yet incorrect, beliefs. Only when the monopolist is not successful in patenting an invention and the introduction of the invention would lead to loss of monopoly power would the monopolist seek to suppress the invention.

SUMMARY

1. A monopolist is a firm selling a commodity for which there are no close substitutes. Thus, the monopolist faces the industry's negatively sloped demand curve for the commodity, and marginal revenue is smaller than price. Monopoly can be based on control of the entire supply of a required raw material, a patent or government franchise, or declining long-run average costs over a sufficiently large range of outputs so as to leave a single firm supplying the entire market. In the real world, there are usually many forces that limit the monopolist's market power.

2. The best level of output of the monopolist in the short run is the one that maximizes total profits. This occurs where the positive difference between TR and STC is greatest. The same result is obtained where the MC curve intersects the MR curve from below. If P is smaller than ATC, the monopolist will incur a loss in the short run. However, if P exceeds AVC, it pays for the monopolist to continue to produce because it covers part of its fixed costs. There is no unique relationship between price and output or supply curve for the monopolist.

3. The best or profit-maximizing level of output of the monopolist in the long run is given by the point where the LMC curve intersects the MR curve from below. The best plant is the one whose $SATC$ curve is

tangent to the LAC at the best level of output. The monopolist can make long-run profits because of restricted entry and does not usually produce at the lowest point on the LAC curve. The long-run profits of the monopolist will be capitalized into the market value of the firm and benefit only the original owner of the monopoly. As compared with perfect competition, monopoly restricts output, results in a higher price, redistributes income from consumers to the monopolist, and leads to less efficient use of society's resources.

4. A multiplant monopolist minimizes the total cost of producing the best level of output in the short run when the marginal cost of the last unit of the commodity produced in each plant is equal to the marginal revenue from selling the combined output. In the long run, a monopolist can build as many identical plants of optimal size (i.e., plants whose $SATC$ curves form the lowest point of the LAC curve) as required to produce the best level of output.

5. Under first degree price discrimination, the monopolist sells each unit of the commodity separately and charges the highest price that each consumer is willing to pay rather than go without it. By doing so, the monopolist extracts the consumers' entire surplus. More practical and common is second degree price discrimination. This refers to

the charging of a lower price per unit of output for each additional batch or block of the commodity. By doing so, the monopolist will be able to extract part of the consumers' surplus. Third degree price discrimination refers to the charging of a higher price for a commodity in the market with the less elastic demand in such a way as to equalize the *MR* of the last unit of the commodity sold in the two markets. To be able to do this, the firm must have some control over prices, it must be able to keep the two markets separate, and the price elasticity of demand must be different in the two markets.

6. International price discrimination is called (persistent) dumping. Under this type of dumping, the monopolist sells the commodity at a higher price at home (where the market demand curve is less elastic) than abroad where the monopolist faces competition from other nations and the market demand curve for the monopolist's product is more elastic.

7. Two-part tariff is the pricing practice whereby a monopolist maximizes its total profits by charging a usage fee or price equal to its marginal cost and an initial or membership fee equal to the entire consumer surplus. Tying refers to the requirement that a consumer who buys or leases a monopolist's product also purchase another product needed in the use of the first. Bundling is a common form of tying in which the monopolist requires customers buying or leasing one of its products or services to also buy or lease another product or service when customers have different tastes but the monopolist cannot price discriminate (as in tying).

8. A per-unit excise tax will fall on consumers in its entirety under perfect competition, but only in part under monopoly with constant costs. The commonly held view that monopolists suppress inventions is not generally true. Price discrimination may be necessary to permit the existence of an industry.

KEY TERMS

Pure Monopoly
Natural Monopoly
Price Discrimination
First Degree or Perfect Price
    Discrimination

Second Degree or Multipart
    Price Discrimination
Third Degree Price
    Discrimination

Dumping
Two-Part Tariff
Tying
Bundling

REVIEW QUESTIONS

1. a. What forces limit the monopolist's market power in the real world?
   b. Why would a monopolist advertise its product if it has a monopoly power over the product?

2. a. Why would a monopolist never operate in the inelastic range of its demand curve?
   b. What would be the best level of output for a monopolist that faced zero average and marginal costs?

3. a. How does the shape of the monopolist's total revenue curve differ from that of a perfectly competitive firm?
   b. Why doesn't the monopolist produce where total revenue is maximum?

4. Suppose that a monopolist sells a commodity at the price of $10 per unit and that its marginal cost is also $10. Is the monopolist maximizing total profits? Why?

5. If the monopolist's total profits were entirely

taxed away and redistributed to consumers, would any social cost of monopoly remain? Why?

6. If $LS = LAC = LMC = \$3$ in Figure 9–7 shifted up to $5, what would be
   a. the consumers' surplus?
   b. the monopolist's total profits?
   c. the social cost of monopoly?

7. How could the government entirely eliminate the social cost of monopoly in Figure 9–7?

8. Under what condition would a multiplant monopolist keep some of its plants idle?

9. a. Will a monopolist's total revenue be larger with second degree price discrimination when the batches on which it charges a uniform price are larger or smaller? Why?

   b. How does a two-part tariff differ from bundling?

10. If the monopolist of Figure 9–11 sold the best level of output at the same price in market 1 and market 2 (i.e., if the monopolist did not practice third degree price discrimination), how much would it sell in each market?

11. Is persistent dumping good or bad for the receiving country? Against what type of dumping would the nation want to protect itself? Why?

12. Assuming that everything is the same, will a per-unit tax reduce output more under perfect competition or under monopoly? Why?

PROBLEMS

1. Given that the demand function of a monopolist is $Q = \frac{1}{5}(55 - P)$
   a. derive the monopolist's demand and marginal revenue schedules from $P = \$55$ to $P = \$20$, at $5 intervals.
   b. On the same set of axes, plot the monopolist's demand and marginal revenue curves, and show the range over which D is elastic and inelastic and the point where D is unitary elastic.
   c. Using the formula relating marginal revenue, price, and elasticity, find the price elasticity of demand at $P = \$40$.

2. Using the TC schedule of Table 7–2 and the demand schedule of problem 1
   a. construct a table similar to Table 9–2 showing TR, STC, and total profits at each level of output, and indicate by an asterisk the best level of output of the monopolist.
   b. draw a figure similar to Figure 9–2, and determine the best level of output of the monopolist.

3. Using the per-unit cost curves of Figure 7–5 and the demand and marginal revenue curves from problem 1b
   a. draw a figure similar to Figure 9–3, and show the best level of output of the firm.
   b. From your figure in part (a), construct a table similar to Table 9–4 showing P, ATC,

profit per unit, total profits, MR, and MC at each level of output.

*4. Suppose the demand curve facing the monopolist changes to $Q' = \frac{1}{5}(30 - P)$, while cost curves remain unchanged.
   a. Draw a figure similar to Figure 9–4, showing the best level of output.
   b. Does the monopolist make a profit, break even, or incur a loss at the best level of output? Should the monopolist go out of business? Why? Where is the monopolist's shutdown point?

5. Suppose that the monopolist has unchanged cost curves but faces two alternative demand functions:

   $$Q = \frac{1}{5}(55 - P) \text{ and } Q'' = \frac{1}{5}(45 - P)$$

   a. Draw a figure similar to Figure 9–5, showing the best level of output with each demand function.
   b. Which of the two demand functions is more elastic? Where is the monopolist's supply curve?

6. Starting with the cost curves of Figure 7–10 and the demand and marginal revenue curves of problem 1, draw a $SATC$ curve (label it

---

* = Answer provided at end of book.

$SATC_2'$) and its associated SMC curve (label it SMC_2') showing that the monopolist is in long-run equilibrium at $Q = 5$.

*7. Draw two figures and label the best level of output as Q^* and label per-unit profit as AB for a monopolist that

   a. produces at the lowest point on its LAC curve.

   b. overutilizes a plant larger than the one that forms the lowest point on its LAC curve.

8. Given that the market demand function facing a two-plant monopolist is $Q = 20 - 2P$ and the short-run marginal cost for plant 1 and plant 2 *at* various levels of output are

Q	0	1	2	3	4
SMC_1 (\$) . . .	2	4	6	8	
SMC_2 (\$) . . .	2.50	3.50	4.50	5.50	

draw a figure showing D, MR, SMC_1, SMC_2 and MC schedules of this monopolist. What is the best level of output of the monopolist? How much should the monopolist produce in plant 1 and how much in plant 2?

9. Given the following demand curve of a consumer for a monopolist's product

$$Q = 14 - 2P$$

   a. find the total revenue of the monopolist when it sells six units of the commodity without practicing any form of price discrimination. What is the value of the consumers' surplus?

   b. What would be the total revenue of the monopolist if it practiced first degree price discrimination? How much would be the consumers' surplus in this case?

   c. Answer part (a) if the monopolist charged $P = \$5.50$ for the first three units of the commodity and $P = \$4$ for the next three units. What type of price discrimination is this?

   d. With $MC = \$4$, what two-part tariff should the monopolist use to maximize its total profits? What if $MC = 0$?

*10. With reference to Figure 9–11, prove using formula [5–6] that if the monopolist charges $P = \$4.50$ in market 2, it must charge $P = \$7$ in market 1 to maximize total profits with third degree price discrimination.

11. With reference to Figure 9–13, compare the effect of a \$4 per-unit tax if the industry is perfectly competitive or a monopoly.

*12. Starting from Table 9–3 and Figure 9–3, construct a table and draw a figure showing

   a. how a lump-sum tax can be used to eliminate all of the monopolist's profits.

   b. what would happen if the government imposed a per-unit tax of \$2.50.

PRICE AND OUTPUT UNDER MONOPOLISTIC COMPETITION AND OLIGOPOLY

In this chapter, we bring together the theory of consumer behavior and demand (from Part Two) and the theory of production and costs (from Chapters 6 and 7) to analyze how price and output are determined under monopolistic competition and oligopoly. These fall between the two extremes of perfect competition and pure monopoly in the spectrum or range of market organizations, and, as such, they contain elements of both.

As in the case of perfect competition and monopoly, the best level of output for a monopolistic competitor and oligopolist is where marginal revenue equals marginal cost. But, as in the case of monopoly, price exceeds marginal revenue and marginal cost. This means that monopolistically competitive and oligopolistic firms are able to somewhat restrict output and charge consumers a higher price than perfect competitors would, but their market power is not as great as that of the monopolist.

The chapter begins by examining the meaning and importance of monopolistic competition; it shows how the equilibrium price and quantity are determined in the short run and in the long run and analyzes product variation and selling expenses. Then, after discussing the meaning and sources of oligopoly, we examine various models of oligopoly pricing and output. We will see that there is no general theory of oligopoly but a number of models of various degrees of realism. Subsequently, we discuss the long-run efficiency implications of oligopoly, review some other oligopolistic pricing practices, and examine the growth in the number and size of international oligopolists. In the next chapter, we will consider oligopolistic behavior with a novel approach called game theory. Chapter 12 deals with market structure, efficiency, and regulation.

10.1 MONOPOLISTIC COMPETITION: MANY SELLERS OF A DIFFERENTIATED PRODUCT

In Chapter 8 we defined perfect competition as the form of market organization in which there are many sellers of a homogeneous product. In Chapter 9 we defined pure monopoly as the single seller of a commodity for which there are no close substitutes. Between these two extreme forms of market organization lies **monopolistic competition.** This refers to the case in which there are many sellers of a heterogeneous or differentiated product, and entry into or exit from the industry is rather easy in the long run.

Differentiated products are products that are similar but not identical. The similarity of differentiated products arises from the fact that they satisfy the same basic consumption needs. Examples are the numerous brands of breakfast cereals, toothpaste, cigarettes, detergents, cold medicines, and so on, on the market today. The differentiation may be real (as in the case of the various breakfast cereals with greatly different nutritional and sugar contents) or imaginary (as in the case of the different brands of aspirin, all of which contain the same ingredients). Product differentiation may also be based entirely on some sellers being more or less conveniently located or on the kind of service they provide (i.e., more or less friendly).

As the name implies, monopolistic competition is a blend of competition and monopoly. The competitive element arises from the fact that there are many sellers of the differentiated product, each of which is too small to affect the other sellers. Firms can also enter and leave a monopolistically competitive industry rather easily in the long run. The monopolistic element arises from product differentiation. That is, since the product of each seller is similar but not identical, each seller has a monopoly power over the *specific* product it sells. This monopoly power, however, is severely limited by the existence of close substitutes. Thus, if a seller of a particular brand of aspirin charged a price more than a few pennies higher than competitive brands, it would lose a great deal of its sales.

Monopolistic competition is most common in the retail and service sectors of the economy. On the national level, clothing, cotton textiles, and food processing are industries that come closest to monopolistic competition. On the local level, the best examples of monopolistic competition are the many gasoline stations, barber shops, grocery stores, drug stores, newspaper stands, restaurants, pizzerias, liquor stores, and so on, all located near one another. Each of these businesses has some monopoly power over its competitors due to the uniqueness of its product, better location, slightly lower prices, better service, greater range of products, and so on. Yet, this market power is very limited due to the availability of close substitutes.

Because each firm produces a somewhat different product under monopolistic competition, we cannot define the industry (which refers to the producers of an *identical* product). Chamberlin, who introduced the theory of monopolistic competition in the early 1930s, sought to overcome this difficulty by lumping all the sellers of *similar* products into a **product group.** For simplicity, we will continue to use the term "industry" here, but in this broader sense (i.e., to refer to all the sellers of the differentiated products in a product group). However, because of product differentiation, we cannot derive the industry demand and supply curves as we did under perfect competition, and we do not have a single equilibrium price for the differentiated product, but a cluster of prices. Thus, our graphic analysis will have to be confined to the "typical" or "representative" firm rather than to the industry. Under monopolistic competition, firms can affect the volume of their sales by changing the product price, by changing the characteristics of the product, or by varying their selling expenses (such as advertising). We will deal with each of these choice-related variables next.

10.2 MONOPOLISTIC COMPETITION: SHORT-RUN AND LONG-RUN ANALYSIS

In this section, we examine how a monopolistically competitive firm determines its best level of output and price in the short run and in the long run on the assumption that the firm has already decided on the characteristics of the product to produce and on the selling expenses to incur. Later, we examine product variation and selling expenses and evaluate the theory of monopolistic competition.

Price and Output Decisions Under Monopolistic Competition

Because a monopolistically competitive firm produces a differentiated product, the demand curve it faces is negatively sloped; but since there are many close substitutes for the product, the demand curve is highly price elastic. The price elasticity of demand is higher the smaller is the degree of product differentiation. As in the case of monopoly, since the demand curve facing a monopolistic competitor is negatively sloped, the corresponding marginal revenue curve is below it, with the same price intercept and twice the absolute slope. As for firms under any type of market structure, the best level of output of the monopolistically competitive firm in the short run is where marginal revenue equals marginal cost, provided that price exceeds the average variable cost. This is shown in the left panel of Figure 10–1.

The left panel of Figure 10–1 shows that the best level of output of the typical or representative monopolistically competitive firm in the short run is six units and is given by point E, at which $MR = SMC$. At $Q < 6$, $MR > SMC$ and the total profits of the firm increase by expanding output. At $Q > 6$, $SMC > MR$ and the total profits of the firm increase by *reducing* output. To sell the best level of output (i.e., six units) the firm charges a price of $9 per unit (point A on the D curve). Since at $Q = 6$, $SATC = $7 (point B in the figure), the monopolistic competitor earns a profit of $AB = $2 per unit and $ABCF = $12 in total (the shaded area in the figure). As in the case of a

**FIGURE 10–1   Short-Run and Long-Run Price and Output Determination
Under Monopolistic Competition**

The left panel shows that in the short run the firm produces six units, given by point
E, where $MR = SMC$. At $Q = 6$, $P = \$9$ (point A on the D curve) and $SATC = \$7$
(point B), so that the firm maximizes profits of $AB = \$2$ per unit and $ABCF = \$12$ in
total (the shaded area). The right panel shows that in the long run the firm produces
four units, given by point E', where $MR' = LMC = SMC'$. At $Q = 4$, $P = LAC =
SATC' = \$6$ (point A'), so that the firm breaks even. This compares to $Q = 7$, where
$P = $ lowest $LAC = \$5$ (point E'') under long-run perfectly competitive equilibrium.

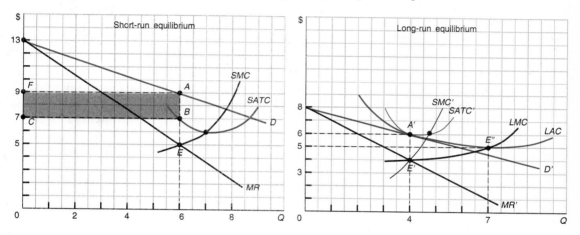

perfectly competitive firm and monopolist, the monopolistic competitor can
earn profits, break even, or incur losses in the short run. If at the best level
of output, $P > SATC$, the firm earns a profit; if $P = SATC$, the firm breaks
even; and if $P < SATC$, the firm incurs losses, but it minimizes losses by
continuing to produce as long as $P > AVC$. Finally, since the demand curve
facing a monopolistic competitor is negatively sloped, $MR = SMC < P$ at the
best level of output, so that (as in the case of monopoly) the rising portion
of the MC curve above the AVC curve does not represent the short-run supply
curve of the monopolistic competitor.

Since the firm in the left panel of Figure 10–1 earns profits in the short
run, more firms will enter the market in the long run. This shifts the demand
curve facing the monopolistic competitor to the left (as its market share decreases) until it becomes tangent to the firm's LAC curve. Thus, in the long
run, all monopolistically competitive firms break even and produce on the
negatively sloped portion of their LAC curve (rather than at the lowest point,
as in the case of perfect competition). This is shown in the right panel of
Figure 10–1.

In the right panel of Figure 10–1, D' is the new demand curve facing the
monopolistically competitive firm in the long run. Demand curve D' is lower
and more price elastic than demand curve D that the firm faced in the short
run. This is because, as more firms enter the monopolistically competitive

market in the long run (attracted by the profits that can be earned), the monopolistic competitor is left with a smaller share of the market and faces greater competition from the greater range of (differentiated) products that becomes available in the long run. Demand curve D' is tangent to the LAC and $SATC'$ curves at point A'—the output at which $MR = LMC = SMC'$ (point E' in the figure). Thus, the monopolistic competitor sells four units of the product at the price of $6 per unit and breaks even in the long run (as compared to $Q = 6$ and $P = \$9$ and profits of $2 per unit and $12 in total in the short run). At any other price, the monopolistically competitive firm would incur losses in the long run, and with a different number of firms it would not break even.

The fact that the monopolistically competitive firm produces to the left of the lowest point on its LAC curve when in long-run equilibrium means that the average cost of production and price of the product under monopolistic competition are higher than under perfect competition ($6 at point A' as compared with $5 at point E'', respectively, in the right panel of Figure 10–1). This difference, however, is not large, because the demand curve faced by the monopolistic competitor is very elastic. In any event, the slightly higher LAC and P under monopolistic competition than under perfect competition can be regarded as the cost that consumers willingly pay for having a variety of differentiated products appealing to different consumer tastes, rather than a single undifferentiated product.

The difference between the level of output indicated by the lowest point on the LAC curve and the monopolistic competitor's output when in long-run equilibrium measures **excess capacity**. In the right panel of Figure 10–1, excess capacity is three units, given by $Q = 7$ at the lowest point on the LAC curve minus $Q = 4$ indicated by point A' on the LAC curve at which the firm produces in the long run. Excess capacity permits more firms to exist (i.e., it leads to some overcrowding) in monopolistically competitive markets as compared with perfect competition. Consumers, however, seem to prefer that firms selling some services operate with some unused capacity (i.e., they are willing to pay a slightly higher price for getting a haircut, filling up on gasoline, checking out at a grocery store, eating at a restaurant, and so on) to avoid waiting in long lines.

Product Variation and Selling Expenses

Under monopolistic competition, a firm can increase its expenditures on product variation and selling effort to increase the demand for its product and make it more price inelastic. **Product variation** refers to changes in some of the characteristics of the product that a monopolistic competitor undertakes in order to make its product more appealing to consumers. For example, producers may reduce the sugar and increase the fiber content of breakfast cereals. **Selling expenses** are all those expenses that the firm incurs to advertise the product, increase its sales force, provide better service for its product, and so on. Product variation and selling expenses can increase the firm's sales and profits, but they also lead to additional costs. A firm should spend more on product variation and selling effort as long as the *MR* from these efforts exceeds the *MC* and until *MR* = *MC*. While spending more on product variation and selling effort (nonprice competition) can increase profits in the short run, monopolistically competitive firms will break even in the long run because of imitation and the entrance of new firms. This is shown in Figure 10–2.

In Figure 10–2, *D″* and *MR″* are demand and marginal revenue curves that are higher than *D′* and *MR′* in the right panel of Figure 10–1 as a result of greater product variation and selling expenses. The *LAC* curve is that of Figure 10–1, while *LAC** and *LMC** are the long-run average and marginal cost curves resulting from greater product variation and selling expenses. Note that the vertical distance between *LAC** and *LAC* increases on the (realistic) assumption that to sell greater quantities of the product requires larger expenses per unit on product variation and selling effort. While these efforts can lead to larger short-run profits, however, our typical or representative firm will break even in the long run. This is shown by point *A** in Figure 10–2, at which Q = 5

FIGURE 10–2   Long-Run Equilibrium with Product Variation and Selling Expenses

Curves *D″* and *MR″*, as well as *LAC** and *LMC**, are higher than in the right panel of Figure 10–1 because of the firm's greater expenses on product variation and selling effort. While these efforts can increase the firm's profits in the short run, in the long run the firm breaks even. This is shown by point *A**, at which Q = 5 units and P = *LAC** = $8, and *MR″* = *LMC** (point *E**). At point *A** the firm charges a higher price and sells a greater quantity than at point *A′* in the right panel of Figure 10–1, but the firm will nevertheless only break even in the long run.

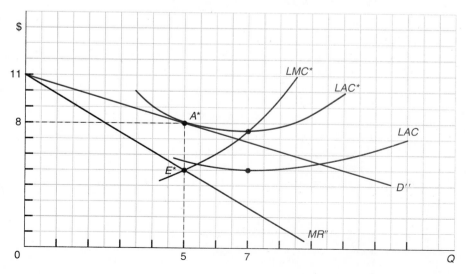

and $P = LAC^\star = \$8$ and $MR'' = LMC^\star$ (point $E^\star$). At point $A^\star$ the firm charges a higher price and sells a greater quantity than at point A' in the right panel of Figure 10–1, but the firm will nevertheless break even in the long run. If all firms selling similar products increase their expenses on product variation and selling effort, each firm may retain only its share of an expanding market in the long run.

Two important questions arise with respect to selling expenses in general and advertising in particular. First, is advertising manipulative, and does it create false needs? Second, does advertising increase or reduce the degree of competition in a market? The manipulative view that advertising creates false needs has been forcefully advanced by Galbraith.[1] Why, Galbraith asks, would firms keep spending millions on advertising if it didn't work? Recent studies on cigarette and beer consumption in the United States and Canada, however, have shown that although advertising does affect brand choices, it does not seem to be very effective in increasing the overall consumption of a product. With regard to the second question, a recent study has found that industries with higher-than-average advertising expenditures relative to sales had lower rates of price increases and higher rates of output increases than the average for 150 major U.S. industries studied during the period from 1963 to 1977.[2] Thus, on balance (and as Example 1 clearly indicates), advertising seems to enhance, rather than restrict, competition. Even though some advertising is manipulative and can act as a barrier to entry, a great deal of it is informative and increases market competition. More will be said about this in Chapter 18, which deals with the economics of information.

Example 1

 ### Advertisers Are Taking on Competitors by Name . . . and Being Sued

Since 1981 when the National Association of Broadcasters abolished its guidelines against making disparaging remarks against competitors' products, advertisers have taken their gloves off and begun to praise the superior qualities of their products—not compared to "Brand X" as before 1981, but by identifying competitors' products by name. The Federal Trade Commission welcomed the change because it anticipated that this would increase competition and lead to better quality products at lower prices. Some of these hopes have in fact been realized. For example, the price of eyeglasses was found to be much higher in New York and Rhode Island, the only two states prohibiting advertising by optometrists and opticians, than in states that

---

[1]J. K. Galbraith, *The Affluent Society* (Boston: Houghton Mifflin, 1958).

[2]E. W. Eckard, "Advertising, Concentration Changes, and Consumer Welfare," *Review of Economics and Statistics*, May 1988, pp. 340–343, and "Cigarette Advertising and Competition," *The Margin*, March/April 1990, p. 22.

allowed such advertising (without any increase in the probability of having the wrong eyeglass prescription). Similarly, the price of an uncontested divorce dropped from $350 to $150 in Phoenix after the Supreme Court allowed advertising for legal services.

Though less sportsmanlike and possibly resulting in legal suits, advertisers have been willing to take on competitors by name because the technique seems effective. Burger King sales soared when it began to attack McDonald's by name. Changes in the federal law in 1988, however, made it easier for firms to win suits against competitors for making misleading statements about their products. As a result, more and more firms are suing rivals who mention their product by name. For example, Gillette sued Wilkinson Sword, MCI sued AT&T, and Alpo Petfoods sued Ralston Purina over allegedly misleading ad claims. The stakes can be very high—legal fees alone in battles between large companies can run as high as $200,000 per month! In the future, we are thus likely to see a return of comparison to "Brand X" in many promotion campaigns.

Sources: "Advertisers Remove the Cover from Brand X," *U.S. News and World Report*, December 19, 1983, pp. 75–76; L. Benham, "The Effect of Advertising on the Price of Eyeglasses," *Journal of Law and Economics*, October 1973, pp. 337–352; "Clearly Wrong on Eye Glasses," *New York Times*, May 16, 1989, p. 16; "Lawyers Are Facing Surge in Competition as Courts Drop Curbs," *Wall Street Journal*, October 18, 1978, p. 1; "A Come Back May Be Ahead for Brand X," *Business Week*, December 4, 1989, p. 35; and "Debate Intensifies Over State Regulations that Restrict TV Advertising by Lawyers," *Wall Street Journal*, August 31, 1992, p. B1.

▲

How Useful Is the Theory of Monopolistic Competition?

When the theory of monopolistic competition was introduced more than 60 years ago, it was hailed as a significant theoretical breakthrough. Today, economists have grown somewhat disenchanted with it. There are several reasons for this.

First, it may be difficult to define the market and determine the firms and products to include in it. For example, should moist paper tissues be included with other paper tissues or with soaps? Are toothpaste, dental floss, toothpicks, and water picks part of the same market or product group?

Second, and more important, in markets where there are many small sellers, product differentiation has been found to be slight. As a result, the demand curve facing the monopolistic competitor is close to being horizontal. Under these circumstances, the perfectly competitive model provides a good approximation to the monopolistically competitive solution, and it is also much easier to use for analysis.[3]

---

[3]The short-run and long-run analysis of monopolistic competition presented here is a simplification of the full-fledged monopolistically competitive model introduced by Chamberlin in 1933 (see E. Chamberlin, *The Theory of Monopolistic Competition* (Cambridge, Mass.: Harvard University Press, 1933).

Third, in many markets where there are strong brand preferences, it usually turns out that there are only a few producers, so that the market is oligopolistic rather than monopolistically competitive. For example, while there are numerous brands of breakfast cereals, cigarettes, toothpaste, detergents, soaps, and many other consumer products on the market today (so that the markets may seem to be monopolistically competitive), on closer examination we find that these products are produced by only four or five very large firms (so that the market is in fact oligopolistic). Millions of dollars are likely to be needed to develop and promote a new product in these markets, and this represents a significant barrier to entry into the market. In fact, only a handful of firms have been able to enter these markets during the past two decades.

Fourth (and related to the third point), even in a market where there are many small sellers of a product or service (say, gasoline stations), a change in price by one of them may have little or no effect on most other gasoline stations that are located far away from it, but it will have a significant impact on those in the immediate vicinity. These nearby stations are, therefore, likely to react to a reduction in price or to an increased promotional effort on the part of the nearby station. The nearby station, for its part, is also likely to be aware of this fact and to take it into consideration in deciding to change its price or in undertaking a new promotional effort. But then the oligopoly model is more appropriate than the model of monopolistic competition to analyze cases such as these.

Despite these serious criticisms, the monopolistically competitive model does provide some important insights, such as the emphasis on product differentiation and selling expenses, which are also applicable to oligopolistic markets, to which we turn next.

10.3 OLIGOPOLY: INTERDEPENDENCE AMONG THE FEW PRODUCERS IN THE INDUSTRY

Oligopoly is the form of market organization in which there are few sellers of a homogeneous or differentiated product. If there are only two sellers, we have a **duopoly.** If the product is homogeneous, we have a **pure oligopoly.** If the product is differentiated, we have a **differentiated oligopoly.** Although entry into an oligopolistic industry is possible, it is not easy (as evidenced by the fact that there are only a few firms in the industry).

Oligopoly is the most prevalent form of market organization in the manufacturing sector of the United States and other industrial countries. Some oligopolistic industries in the United States are automobiles, primary aluminum, steel, electrical equipment, glass, breakfast cereals, cigarettes, soaps and detergents, beer brewing, and many others. Some of the products (such as steel and aluminum) are homogeneous, whereas others (such as automobiles, cigarettes, breakfast cereals, beer, and soaps and detergents) are differentiated. For simplicity, we will deal mostly with pure oligopolies (where products are homogeneous) in this chapter.

Because there are only a few firms selling a homogeneous or differentiated product in oligopolistic markets, the action of each firm affects the other firms in the industry, and vice versa. For example, when GM introduced price rebates in the sale of its automobiles, Ford and Chrysler immediately followed with price rebates of their own. Furthermore, since price competition can lead to ruinous price wars, oligopolists usually prefer to compete on the basis of product differentiation, advertising, and service. Yet, even here, if GM mounts a major advertising campaign, Ford and Chrysler are likely to soon respond in kind. Every time that Coca-Cola or Pepsi mounts a major advertising campaign, the other usually responds with a large advertising campaign of its own.

From what has been said, it is clear that the distinguishing characteristic of oligopoly is the interdependence or rivalry among firms in the industry. This is the natural result of fewness. Since an oligopolist knows that its own actions will have a significant impact on the other oligopolists in the industry, each oligopolist must consider the possible reaction of competitors in deciding its pricing policies, the degree of product differentiation to introduce, the level of advertising to undertake, the amount of service to provide, and so on. Because competitors can react in many different ways (depending on the nature of the industry, the type of product, etc.), we do not have a single oligopoly model but many—each based on the particular behavioral response of competitors to the actions of the first. Because of interdependence, policy decisions on the part of the firm are also much more complex under oligopoly than under other forms of market organization. In this chapter, we present some of the most important oligopoly models. We must keep in mind, however, that each model is usually applicable only to some specific situations, rather than generally, and that most models are more or less unrealistic.

The sources of oligopoly are generally the same as for monopoly: (1) economies of scale may operate over a sufficiently large range of outputs so as to leave only a few firms supplying the entire market; (2) huge capital investments and specialized inputs are usually required to enter an oligopolistic industry (say, automobiles, aluminum, steel, and similar industries), and this acts as an important natural barrier to entry; (3) a few firms may own a patent for the exclusive right to produce a commodity or to use a particular production process; (4) established firms might have a loyal following of customers based on product quality and service that new firms may find very difficult to match; (5) a few firms may own or control the entire supply of a raw material required in the production of the product; and (6) the government may give a franchise to only a few firms to operate in the market. These are not only the sources of oligopoly but also represent the barriers to other firms entering the market in the long run. If entry were not so restricted, the industry would not remain oligopolistic in the long run.

The degree by which an industry is dominated by a few large firms is measured by **concentration ratios,** which give the percentage of total industry sales of the 4, 8, or 12 largest firms in the industry (see Example 2). An industry in which the 4-firm concentration ratio is close to 100 is clearly oligopolistic, and industries where this ratio is higher than 50% or 60% are also likely to be oligopolistic. The 4-firm concentration ratio for most manufacturing industries in the United States is between 20% and 80%. As we will see, however, concentration ratios must be used and interpreted with great caution since they may greatly overestimate the market power of the largest firms in an industry.

Example 2
Industrial Concentration in the United States

Table 10–1 gives the 4-firm and the 8-firm concentration ratios for various industries in the United States from the 1987 Census of Manufacturers (the latest available).

There are several reasons, however, for using these concentration ratios cautiously. First, in industries where imports are significant, concentration ratios may greatly overestimate the relative importance of the largest firms in the industry. For example, since automobile imports are about 35% of the domestic market in the United States, the real 4-firm concentration ratio in

TABLE 10–1   Concentration Ratios in the United States, 1987

Industry	4-Firm Ratio	8-Firm Ratio
Cigarettes	92	D*
Electric lamps	91	94
Motor vehicles	90	95
Breakfast cereals	87	99
Household refrigerators	85	98
Primary aluminum	74	95
Aircraft	72	92
Tires	69	87
Soaps and detergents	65	76
Office machines	47	62
Steel mills	44	63
Household furniture	43	59
Cheese	43	55
Book publishing	38	62
Petroleum refining	32	52
Soft drinks	30	40
Cement	28	47
Newspapers	25	39
Men's clothing	19	29
Women's clothing	6	10

Source: U.S. Bureau of the Census, 1987 Census of Manufacturers, *Concentration Ratios in Manufacturing* (Washington, D.C.: U.S. Government Printing Office, 1992).
*D = Data withheld to avoid disclosing company data.

the automobile industry is not 90% (as indicated in the table) but 59% (i.e., 90% times 0.65). Second, concentration ratios refer to the nation as a whole, even though the relevant market may be local. For example, the 4-firm concentration ratio for the cement industry is 28%, but because of very high transportation costs, only two or three firms may actually compete in many local markets. Third, how broadly or narrowly a product is defined is also very important. For example, concentration ratios in the office machines industry as a whole are higher than in the personal computer segment of the market. Fourth, concentration ratios do not give any indication of potential entrants into the market and of the degree of actual and potential competition in the industry. Indeed, as the *theory of contestable markets* discussed in Chapter 12 shows, vigorous competition can take place even among few sellers. In short, concentration ratios provide only one dimension of the degree of competition in the market, and although useful, they must be used with great caution.

▲

10.4 THE COURNOT AND THE KINKED-DEMAND CURVE MODELS

Now we examine two of the earliest and best known oligopoly models: the Cournot model and the kinked-demand curve model. In the Cournot model, oligopolists never recognize their interdependence or rivalry. As such, the Cournot model is quite unrealistic. The model is, nevertheless, useful in highlighting the interdependence that exists among oligopolistic firms (even though they do not actually recognize it). The Cournot model is also the forerunner of more realistic models. In the kinked-demand curve model, oligopolists do recognize their interdependence or rivalry. This model also faces many shortcomings, but it does represent a step forward in the direction of greater realism in the analysis of oligopolistic behavior.

The Cournot Model: Interdependence Not Recognized

The first formal oligopoly model was introduced by the French economist Augustin Cournot more than 150 years ago.[4] For simplicity, Cournot assumed that there were only two firms (duopoly) selling identical spring water. Consumers came to the springs with their own containers, so that the marginal cost of production was zero for the two firms. With these assumptions, the analysis is greatly simplified without losing the essence of the model.[5]

---

[4]A. Cournot, *Recherches sur les principes mathematiques de la theorie des richess* (Paris: 1838). English translation by N. Bacon, *Researches into the Mathematical Principles of the Theory of Wealth* (New York: MacMillan, 1897).

[5]The model, however, can be extended to deal with more than two firms and nonzero marginal costs.

The basic behavioral assumption made in the **Cournot model** is that each firm, while trying to maximize profits, assumes that the other duopolist holds its *output* constant at the existing level. The result is a cycle of moves and countermoves by the duopolists until each sells one-third of the total industry output (if the industry were organized along perfectly competitive lines). This is shown in Figure 10–3.

In the left panel of Figure 10–3, D is the market demand curve for spring water. Initially, firm A is the only firm in the market, and thus, it faces the total market demand curve. That is, $D = d_A$. The marginal revenue curve of firm A is then mr_A (see the figure). Since the marginal cost is zero, the MC curve coincides with the horizontal axis. Under these circumstances, firm A maximizes total profits where $mr_A = MC = 0$. Firm A sells six units of spring water at $P = \$6$ so that its total revenue (TR) is $\$36$ (point A in the left panel). This is the monopoly solution. Note that point A is the midpoint of demand curve $D = d_A$, at which price elasticity is 1 and TR is maximum (see section 5.6). With total costs equal to zero, total profits equal $TR = \$36$.

FIGURE 10–3   The Cournot Model

In the left panel, D is the market demand curve for spring water. The marginal cost of production is assumed to be zero. When only firm A is in the market, $D = d_A$ and the firm maximizes profits by selling $Q = 6$ at $P = \$6$ (point A, given by $mr_A = MC = 0$). When firm B enters the market, it will face d_B (given by shifting market demand curve D to the left by six units). Firm B maximizes profits by selling $Q = 3$ at $P = \$3$ (point B, the midpoint of d_B at which $mr_B = MC = 0$). Duopolist A now faces $d_{A'}$ (given by D minus 3 in the right panel) and maximizes profits by selling $Q = 4.5$ at $P = \$4.50$ (point A'). The process continues until each duopolist is at point E on d_E and sells $Q = 4$ at $P = \$4$.

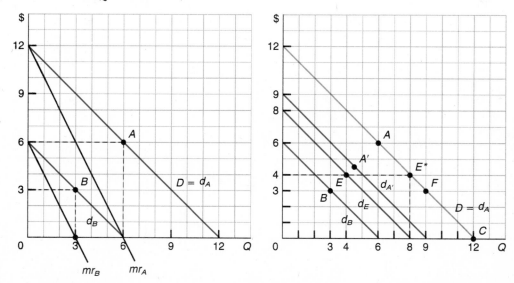

Next, assume that firm B enters the market and believes that firm A will continue to sell six units. Then the demand curve that firm B faces is market demand curve D shifted to the left by the six units sold by firm A, or d_B in the left panel. The marginal revenue curve of firm B is then mr_B. Firm B maximizes total profits where $mr_B = MC = 0$. Therefore, firm B sells three units at $P = \$3$ (point B, the midpoint of d_B). This is also shown in the right panel of Figure 10–3. Assuming that firm B continues to sell three units, firm A reacts and faces $d_{A'}$ (obtained by shifting market demand curve D to the left by three units in the right panel of Figure 10–3). Firm A will then maximize profits by selling 4.5 units (point A', at the midpoint of $d_{A'}$, at which $mr_{A'} = MC = 0$). Firm B now reacts once again and maximizes profits on its new demand curve, which is obtained by shifting market demand curve D to the left by the 4.5 units supplied by firm A (not shown in the figure).

The process continues until each duopolist faces demand curve d_E and maximizes profits by selling four units at $P = \$4$ (point E). This is equilibrium because whichever firm faces demand curve d_E and reaches point E first, the other will also face demand curve d_E (given by $D - 4$) and will also maximize profits at point E. With each duopolist selling four units, a combined total of eight units will be sold in the market at $P = \$4$ (point E* on D). If the market had been organized along perfectly competitive lines, sales would have been twelve units given by point C, where market demand curve D intercepts the horizontal axis. At point C, $P = MR = LMC = LAC = 0$ and all the perfectly competitive firms would break even when in long-run equilibrium.

Thus, the duopolists supply one-third or four units each (and two-thirds or eight units together) of the total perfectly competitive market quantity of twelve units. Note that the Cournot duopoly outcome of $P = \$4$ and $Q = 8$ lies between the monopoly equilibrium of $P = \$6$ and $Q = 6$ and the competitive equilibrium of $P = \$0$ and $Q = 12$. The final Cournot equilibrium reflects the interdependence between the duopolists, even though they (rather naively) do not recognize it.

With three oligopolists, each would supply one-fourth (i.e., three units) of the perfectly competitive market of twelve units and three-fourths (i.e., nine units) in total. Note that when $Q = 9$, $P = \$3$ on market demand curve D (point F). Thus, as the number of firms increases, the total combined output of all the firms together increases and price falls (compare equilibrium point A with only firm A in the market, with equilibrium point E* with firms A and B, and equilibrium point F with three firms). Eventually, as more firms enter, the market will no longer be oligopolistic. In the limit, with many firms, total output will approach twelve units and price will approach zero (the perfectly competitive solution—point C in the right panel of Figure 10–3).[6]

---

[6]The appendix to this chapter presents a more advanced and complete treatment of the Cournot model, as well as an important extension of it (the Stackelberg model).

The Kinked-Demand Curve Model: Interdependence Recognized

The **kinked-demand curve model**, introduced by Paul Sweezy in 1939,[7] attempts to explain the price rigidity that is often observed in some oligopolistic markets.

Sweezy postulated that if an oligopolist raised its price, it would lose most of its customers because the other firms in the industry would not match the price increase. On the other hand, an oligopolist could not increase its share of the market by lowering its price, since its competitors would immediately match the price reduction. As a result, according to Sweezy, oligopolists face a demand curve that is highly elastic for price increases and less elastic for price reductions. That is, the demand curve faced by oligopolists has a kink at the established price; and, because of this, oligopolists tend to keep prices constant even in the face of changed costs and demand conditions. This is shown in Figure 10–4.

In Figure 10–4, the demand curve facing the oligopolist is d or HBC and has a "kink" at the prevailing price of $8 and $Q = 4$ (point B). The demand curve is much more elastic above than below the kink on the assumption that competitors will not match price increases but quickly match price cuts.[8] Thus, the oligopolist's marginal revenue curve is mr or $HJKFG$. Segment HJ of the mr curve corresponds to segment HB of the demand curve, and segment FG of the mr curve corresponds to segment BC of the demand curve (see the figure). The kink at point B on the demand curve results in discontinuity JF in the mr curve.

With SMC as the short-run marginal cost curve, the oligopolist will maximize profits by selling four units of output at $P = \$8$ (given by point K, where the SMC curve intersects the discontinuous segment of the mr curve). Any shift in the oligopolist's SMC curve that falls within the discontinuous segment of the mr curve will leave the oligopolist's price and output unchanged. That is, the oligopolist's best level of output will continue to be four units and price $8 for any shift in the SMC curve up to SMC' or down to SMC'' (see the figure). Only if the SMC curve shifts above the SMC' curve will the oligopolist raise its price, and only if the SMC curve shifts below the SMC'' curve will the oligopolist lower its price (see problem 3). Similarly, a rightward or leftward shift in the demand curve will induce the oligopolist to increase or decrease output, respectively, but to keep its price unchanged

---

[7]P. Sweezy, "Demand under Conditions of Oligopoly," *Journal of Political Economy*, August 1939, pp. 568–573.

[8]That is, since competitors do not match price increases, the quantity demanded from the oligopolist that increases price *falls a great deal*. On the other hand, since competitors quickly match price reductions, the quantity demanded from the oligopolist that cuts price *does not increase very much*. This makes the demand curve faced by an oligopolist more elastic for price increases than for price reductions.

FIGURE 10–4   The Kinked-Demand Curve Model

The demand curve facing the oligopolist is *d* or *HBC* and has a "kink" at the prevailing price of $8 and Q = 4 (point *B*), on the assumption that competitors match price cuts but not price increases. The marginal revenue curve is *mr* or *HJKFG*. The oligopolist maximizes profits by selling Q = 4 at P = $8 (given by point *K*, where the *SMC* curve intersects the discontinuous segment of the *mr* curve). Any shift between *SMC'* and *SMC"* will leave price and output unchanged.

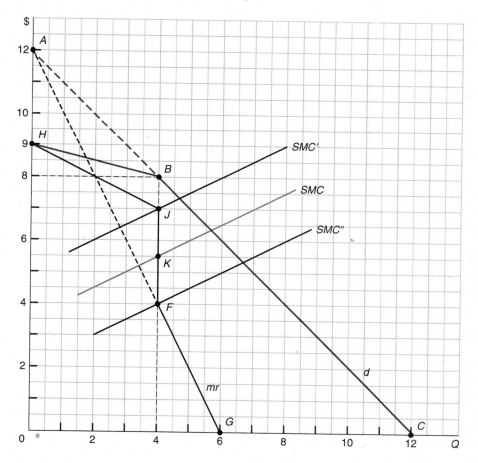

if the kink remains at the same level (see problem 4, with answer at end of book). Note that the marginal principle postulating that the best level of output of the firm occurs where *MR* = *MC* is still valid, even though the *MR* curve is discontinuous in this case.

When the kinked-demand curve model was first introduced, it was hailed by some economists as a general theory of oligopoly. Yet, the model failed to live up to its expectations. For example, Stigler found no evidence that oligopolists were reluctant to match price increases as readily as price reductions, and thus he seriously questioned the existence of the kink.[9] The same was found by other researchers in other oligopolistic industries. Even more serious is the criticism that although the kinked-demand curve model can *rationalize* the existence of rigid prices where they occur, it cannot *explain* at what price the kink occurs in the first place. Since one of the major aims of microeconomic theory is to explain how prices are determined, this theory is, at best, incomplete.

10.5 COLLUSION: CARTELS AND PRICE LEADERSHIP MODELS

In the oligopoly models we examined so far, oligopolists did not collude. In view of the interdependence in oligopolistic markets, however, there is a natural tendency to collude. With **collusion,** oligopolistic firms can avoid behavior that is detrimental to their general interest (for example, price wars) and adopt policies that increase their profits. Collusion can be overt (i.e., explicit), as in a centralized cartel, or tacit (i.e., implicit), as in price leadership models. In this section, we examine oligopolistic models with collusion and provide several real-world examples. (Antitrust laws forbidding collusion in the United States are examined in Chapter 12.)

A Centralized Cartel Operates as a Monopolist

A **cartel** is a formal organization of producers of a commodity. Its purpose is to coordinate the policies of the member firms so as to increase profits. Cartels are illegal in the United States under the provision of the Sherman Antitrust Act passed in 1890 (see section 12.4) but not in some other nations. Of the many types of cartels, the **centralized cartel** is at one extreme. The centralized cartel sets the monopoly price for the commodity, allocates the monopoly output among the member firms, and determines how the monopoly profits are to be shared. The centralized cartel is shown in Figure 10–5.

In Figure 10–5, D is the total market demand curve and MR is the corresponding marginal revenue curve for a homogeneous commodity produced by, say, four firms that have formed a centralized cartel. The ΣSMC curve for the cartel is obtained by summing horizontally the SMC curve of the four firms on the assumption that input prices remain constant. The centralized authority will set $P = \$8$ and sell $Q = 4$ (given by point E, where the ΣSMC curve intersects the MR curve from below). This is the monopoly solution. To minimize production costs, the centralized authority will have to allocate output among the four firms in such a way that the SMC of the last unit

[9]G. Stigler, "The Kinky Oligopoly Demand Curve and Rigid Prices," *Journal of Political Economy,* October 1947, pp. 432–449.

FIGURE 10–5   Centralized Cartel

D is the market demand curve and MR is the corresponding marginal revenue curve for a homogeneous commodity produced by the four firms in a centralized cartel. The ΣSMC curve for the cartel is obtained by summing horizontally the four firms' SMC curves on the assumption that input prices are constant. The centralized authority will set $P = \$8$ and $Q = 4$ (given by point E, where the ΣSMC curve intersects the MR curve from below). This is the monopoly solution.

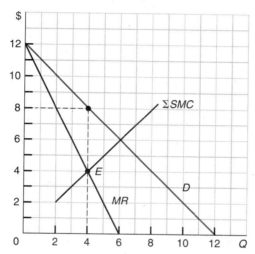

produced by each firm are equal. If the SMC of one firm are higher than for the other firms, the total costs of the cartel as a whole can be reduced by shifting some production from the firm with higher SMC to the other firms until the SMC of the last unit produced by all firms are equal. The cartel will also have to decide on the distribution of profits.

If all firms are of the same size and have identical cost curves, then it is very likely that each firm will be allocated the same output and will share equally in the profits generated by the cartel. In Figure 10–5, each firm would be allocated one unit of output. The result would be the same if a monopolist acquired the four firms and operated them as a multiplant monopolist. If the firms in the cartel are of different sizes and have different costs, it will be more difficult to agree on the share of output and profits. Then the allocation of output is likely to be based on past output, present capacity, and bargaining ability of each firm, rather than on the equalization of the SMC of the last unit of output produced by all member firms. Sometimes the market is divided among the firms in the industry as indicated in the next subsection.

Cartels often fail; there are several reasons for this. First, it is very difficult to organize all the producers of a commodity if there are more than a few of them. Second, as pointed out, it is difficult to reach agreement among the member firms on how to allocate output and profits when firms face different cost curves. Third, there is a strong incentive for each firm to remain outside the cartel or cheat on the cartel by selling more than its quota. Fourth, monopoly profits are likely to attract other firms into the industry and undermine the cartel agreement.

Even though cartels are illegal in the United States, many trade associations and professional associations perform many of the functions usually associated with cartels. Some cartellike associations are in fact sanctioned by the government. An example of this is the American Medical Association, which, by rigidly restricting the number of students admitted to medical schools and forbidding advertising by physicians (until recently), has been able to ensure very high doctors' fees and incomes. Another example is the New York Taxi and Limousine Commission, which restricts the number of taxis licensed, thus conferring monopoly profits to the original owners of the "medallions" (see Example 2 in Chapter 9). The best example of a successful international cartel is OPEC (the Organization of Petroleum Exporting Countries) during the 1970s and early 1980s (see Example 3 in this chapter).

Example 3
 The Organization of Petroleum Exporting Countries (OPEC) Cartel

It is often asserted that OPEC was able to sharply increase petroleum prices and profits for its members by restricting supply and behaving as a cartel. Twelve nations are presently members of OPEC: Algeria, Gabon, Indonesia, Iran, Iraq, Kuwait, Libya, Nigeria, Qatar, Saudi Arabia, the United Arab Emirates, and Venezuela (Ecuador, the thirteenth member, withdrew in November 1992). As a result of supply shocks during the Arab-Israeli war in the fall of 1973 and the Iranian revolution during 1979–1980, OPEC was able to increase the price of petroleum from $2.50 per barrel in 1973 to more than $40 per barrel in 1980. This, however, stimulated conservation in developed nations (by lowering thermostats, switching to small, fuel-efficient automobiles, etc.), expanded exploration and production (by the United Kingdom and Norway in the North Sea, by the United States in Alaska, and by Mexico in newly discovered fields), and switching to other energy sources (such as coal). As a result, OPEC's share of world oil production fell from 55% in 1974 to less than 30% in 1993. Although OPEC meets regularly for the purpose of setting petroleum prices and production quotas, it has seldom succeeded in its effort under the conditions of excess supplies that have prevailed since 1980.

In general, the densely populated and low-petroleum reserve countries such as Indonesia, Nigeria, and Iran want to charge high prices to maximize short-run profits; in contrast, the sparsely populated and large-reserve countries such as Saudi Arabia and Kuwait prefer lower prices to discourage conservation and non-OPEC production to maximize long-run profits. Be that as it may, OPEC was unable to prevent a decline in petroleum prices to the $15 to $20 range and widespread cheating by its members during the

1980s. Thus, while OPEC is often given as the best example of a sometimes successful cartel, many economists are now convinced that OPEC never really controlled the world crude oil market. Under the conditions of tight supply that prevailed during the 1970s, OPEC was given credit for the sharp increase in petroleum prices; but when excess supplies arose, OPEC was unable to prevent almost equally sharp price declines. Even the mini oil shock resulting from Saddam Hussein's invasion of Kuwait in August 1990 was reversed with the quick end to the Persian Gulf War, so that by the middle of 1991 oil prices were as low as before the invasion of Kuwait, and at the end of 1992 the price of oil was $22 a barrel.

Sources: "OPEC's Painful Lessons," *New York Times*, December 29, 1985, p. F3; "OPEC Sets New Policy on Quota," *New York Times*, November 29, 1989, p. D1; "Gulf War: An Energy Defeat?" *New York Times*, June 18, 1991, p. D1; "Crude Oil Prices Fall Slightly on Traders' Belief that OPEC Again Failed to Set Output Strategy," *Wall Street Journal*, September 22, 1992, p. C14; and "Domestic Oil Demand Up in 1992 and Import Rise Filled the Gap," *New York Times*, January 14, 1993, p. D2.

Market-Sharing Cartel

The difficulties encountered by the members of a centralized cartel (such as agreeing on the price to charge, allocating output and profits among members, and avoiding cheating) make a market-sharing cartel more likely to occur. In a **market-sharing cartel** the member firms agree only on how to share the market. Each firm then agrees to operate only in one area or region and not to encroach on the others' territories. An example is the agreement in the early part of this century between Du Pont (American) and Imperial Chemical (English) for the former to have exclusive selling rights for their products in North America (except for British colonies) and the latter in the British Empire. Under certain simplifying assumptions, a market-sharing cartel can also result in the monopoly solution. This is shown in Figure 10–6.

In Figure 10–6, we assume that there are two identical firms selling a homogeneous product and deciding to share the market equally. D is the total market demand for the commodity. Then, d is the half-share demand curve of each firm and *mr* is the corresponding marginal revenue curve. If each firm has the same *SMC* curve as shown in the figure, according to the marginal principle, each will sell two units of output at P = $8 (given by point E', at which *mr* = *SMC*). Thus, the duopolists together will sell the monopolist output of four units at P = $8 (see the figure). In the real world there may be more than two firms, each may have different cost curves, and the market may not be shared equally. Then, we are not likely to have the neat monopoly solution shown above. The firm with greater capacity or operating in an inferior territory may demand a greater share of the market. The result will then depend on bargaining, and the possibility of incursions into each other's territory cannot be excluded.

FIGURE 10–6 Market-Sharing Cartel

D is the total market demand for a homogeneous commodity, d is the half-share demand curve of each firm, and mr is the corresponding marginal revenue curve. If each duopolist also has the same SMC curve shown in the figure, each will sell two units of output at $P = \$8$ (given by point E', at which $mr = SMC$). Thus, the duopolists together will sell the monopolist output of four units at $P = \$8$.

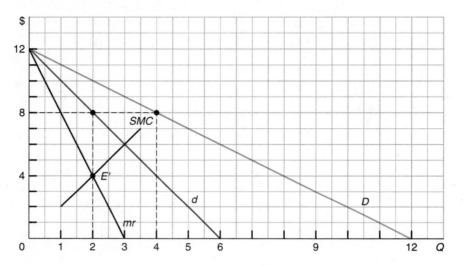

The firms in a market-sharing cartel can also operate in the same geographic area by deciding which is to fill each particular contract. These market-sharing cartels are likely to be unstable due to cheating. Some loose market-sharing cartels are sanctioned by law. For example, local medical and bar associations essentially set the fees that doctors and lawyers are to charge. Similarly, many states had *fair trade laws* (until they became illegal in the mid-1970s), which allowed manufacturers to set the price that each retailer was to charge for the product. The market was then shared by means other than price.

Example 4

The Market-Sharing Ivy Cartel

For more than three decades prior to 1991, the presidents and top financial officers of the eight Ivy League colleges (Brown, Columbia, Cornell, Dartmouth, Harvard, Princeton, Yale, and the University of Pennsylvania), as well as the Massachusetts Institute of Technology (MIT), held yearly meetings at which they exchanged sensitive information about intended tuition increases, the amount of student financial aid packages, and increases in faculty salaries. The result was tuition increases, student financial aid packages, and faculty salary increases that were closely bunched together. For example, the charge for tuition, room, board and fees at the eight Ivy

League colleges and MIT ranged only from $16,841 to $17,100 for the 1988–1989 academic year. The same was true for increases in faculty salaries and for the amount of student aid packages. Specifically, the colleges agreed not to outbid each other in granting aid to top students who had been accepted to more than one school, thus leaving students and their families no reason to shop around for better financial aid packages. In 1986, this "Ivy League cartel" tried to bring Stanford University into the fold—an attempt that failed because (as court documents later showed) Stanford was worried that the Ivies were colluding illegally. Indeed, this is what the U.S. Justice Department subsequently charged.

In May 1991, the Ivy League colleges (while admitting no wrongdoing) signed a consent decree with the Justice Department to stop colluding on tuition, financial aid, and faculty salaries in order to avoid a costly trial, thereby putting an end to their cartel arrangement. The result was clear and immediate: average increases in private-college tuition, which had soared fivefold between 1971–1972 and 1989–1990 in the face of only a tripling of consumer prices, subsided and were much smaller after 1990.

MIT, however, refused to sign the consent decree and chose instead to fight the case in court; it argued that antitrust laws did not apply to the noncommercial and charitable activities of universities. But in a ten-day trial in August 1992 that cost MIT $1 million, the court found MIT guilty of price fixing and restricting competition by reducing students' ability to get the best financial aid possible. Strangely, the Justice Department only pursued the price-fixing arrangement of the financial-aid package and not of the tuition and faculty salary, which should have been much more of a cause for government intervention and for which the government had a much stronger case.

Sources: "Ivy League Discussions on Finances Extended to Tuition and Salaries," *Wall Street Journal*, May 8, 1992, p. A1, and "M.I.T. Ruled Guilty in Antitrust Case," *New York Times*, September 3, 1992, p. 1.

▲

Price Leadership

One way by which firms in an oligopolistic market can make necessary price adjustments without fear of starting a price war and without overt collusion is by **price leadership.** The firm generally recognized as the price leader starts the price change and the other firms in the industry quickly follow. The price leader is usually the dominant or largest firm in the industry. Sometimes, it is the low-cost firm (see problem 9, with answer at end of book) or any other firm (called the **barometric firm**) recognized as the true interpreter or barometer of changes in demand and cost conditions in the industry warranting a price change. Then, an orderly price change is accomplished by other firms following the leader.

In the price leadership model by the dominant firm, the dominant firm sets the price for the commodity that maximizes its profits, allows all the other (small) firms in the industry to sell all they want at that price, and then comes in to fill the market. Thus, the small firms in the industry behave as perfect competitors or price takers, and the dominant firm acts as the residual supplier of the commodity. This is shown in Figure 10–7.

FIGURE 10–7   Price Leadership by the Dominant Firm

D (*ABCFG*) is the market demand curve and ΣSMC_s is the marginal cost curve of all the small firms in the industry. Since the small firms can sell all they want at the price set by the dominant firm, they behave as perfect competitors and produce where $P = \Sigma SMC_s$. The horizontal distance between the D and ΣSMC_s curves then gives the (residual) quantity supplied by the dominant firm at each price. Thus, the demand curve of the dominant firm (*d*) is *HKFG*, and the corresponding marginal revenue curve is mr_d. With SMC_d, the dominant firm will set $P = \$6$ (given by point E, where $mr_d = SMC_d$) to maximize its profits. At $P = \$6$, the small firms will supply four units of the commodity and the dominant firm $JK = LC$ or two units.

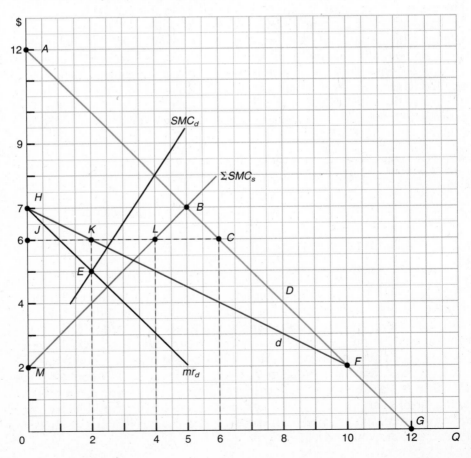

In the figure, D $(ABCFG)$ is the market demand curve for the homogeneous commodity sold in the oligopolist market. Curve ΣSMC_s is the (horizontal) summation of the marginal cost curves of all the small firms in the industry. Since the small firms in the industry can sell all they want at the industry price set by the dominant firm (i.e., they are price takers), they behave as perfect competitors and always produce at the point where $P = \Sigma SMC_s$. Thus, the ΣSMC_s curve (above the average variable cost of the small firms) represents the short-run supply curve of the commodity for all the small firms in the industry as a group (on the assumption that input prices remain constant).

The horizontal distance between D and ΣSMC_s at each price then gives the (residual) quantity of the commodity demanded from and supplied by the dominant firm at each price. For example, if the dominant firm set $P = \$7$, the small firms in the industry together supply HB or five units of the commodity, leaving nothing to be supplied by the dominant firm. This gives the vertical intercept (point H) on the demand curve of the dominant firm (d). If the dominant firm set $P = \$6$, the small firms in the industry supply JL or four units of the commodity, leaving two units ($LC = JK$) to be supplied by the dominant firm (point K on the d curve). Finally, if the dominant firm set $P = \$2$, the small firms together supply zero units of the commodity (point M), leaving the entire market quantity demanded of MF or ten units to be supplied by the dominant firm. Thus, the demand curve of the dominant firm is d or $HKFG$.

With demand curve d, the marginal revenue curve of the dominant firm is mr_d (which bisects the distance from the vertical axis to the d curve). If the short-run marginal cost curve of the dominant firm is SMC_d, the dominant firm will set $P = \$6$ (given by point E, where $mr_d = SMC_d$) to maximize its profits. Note that the industry price set by the dominant firm is determined on the demand curve of the dominant firm (d), not on the market demand curve (D). At $P = \$6$, the small firms together will supply JL or four units of the commodity (see the figure). The dominant firm will then come in to fill the market by selling $JK = LC$ or two units of the commodity at $P = \$6$ which it set.

Among the firms that operated as price leaders are Alcoa (in aluminum), American Tobacco, American Can, Chase Manhattan Bank (in setting the prime rate), GM, Goodyear Tire and Rubber, Gulf Oil, Kellogg (in breakfast cereals), U.S. Steel (now USX), and so on. Many of these industries are characterized by more than one large firm, and the role of the price leader has sometimes changed from one large firm to another. For example, Reynolds has also behaved at times as the price leader in tobacco products. Continental Can, Bethlehem and National Steel, and General Mills (in the breakfast cereals market) also behaved as the price leaders in their respective markets during some periods of time. Finally, note that one important advantage of price leadership is that it can be accomplished informally by tacit collusion, which is much more difficult to prove than overt or explicit collusion.

On the international level, Saudi Arabia was the dominant price leader for petroleum during the 1970s. Saudi Arabia set petroleum prices and satisfied only that portion of the world demand that was left unfilled by others. But with other petroleum exporting countries greatly exceeding their export quotas and cheating by selling oil at discount prices, Saudi Arabia's share of the world's export market shrunk considerably. As the holder of the world's largest proven petroleum reserves and largest exporter, Saudi Arabia threatened to flood the market if other petroleum exporting countries continued to exceed their export quotas and sell at a discount. In 1986, Saudi Arabia made good on its threat and sharply increased petroleum production and exports, which caused a collapse in world oil prices to below $10 a barrel. Some degree of price and production discipline was subsequently reestablished, so that the price of petroleum more than doubled (to $22 a barrel) in 1992.[10]

10.6 LONG-RUN ADJUSTMENTS AND EFFICIENCY IMPLICATIONS OF OLIGOPOLY

Most of the analysis of oligopoly until this point has referred to the short run. In this section, we analyze the long-run adjustments and efficiency implications of oligopoly. We examine the long-run plant adjustments of existing firms and the entry prospects of other firms into the industry, we discuss nonprice competition, and we examine the long-run welfare effects of oligopoly.

Long-Run Adjustments in Oligopoly

As in other forms of market organization, oligopolistic firms can build the best plant to produce their anticipated best level of output in the long run. However, in view of the uncertainty generally surrounding oligopolistic industries, it is even more difficult than under other forms of market organization for firms to determine their best level of output and plant in the long run. An oligopolist would leave the industry in the long run if it would incur a loss even after building the best scale of plant. On the other hand, if existing firms earn profits, more firms will seek to enter the industry in the long run, and, unless entry is blocked or somehow restricted, industry output will expand until industry profits fall to zero. There may then be so many firms in the industry that the actions of each no longer affect the others. In that case, the industry would no longer be oligopolistic.[11]

For an industry to remain oligopolistic in the long run, entry must be somewhat restricted. This may result from many reasons, some natural and some artificial. These are generally the same barriers that led to the existence

---

[10]"Crude Oil Prices Fall Slightly on Traders' Belief that OPEC Again Failed to Set Output Strategy," *Wall Street Journal*, September 22, 1992, p. C14.

[11]As we will see in the theory of contestable markets discussed in section 12.2, vigorous competition can take place even among few sellers.

of the oligopoly in the first place. One of the most important natural barriers to entry is the smallness of the market in relation to the optimum size of the firm. For example, only three or four firms can most efficiently supply the entire national market for automobiles. Potential entrants know that by entering this market they would probably face huge losses and possibly also impose losses on the other established auto makers (see problem 11).

Another important natural barrier to entry in oligopolistic markets is the usually huge investment and specialized inputs required (as, for example, to enter automobile, steel, aluminum, and similar industries). Many artificial barriers to entry may also exist. These include control over the source of an essential raw material (such as bauxite to produce aluminum) by the few firms already in the industry, unwillingness of existing firms to license potential competitors to use an essential industrial process on which they hold a patent, and the inability to obtain a government franchise (for example, to run a bus line or a taxi fleet). Still another artificial barrier to entry is **limit pricing,** whereby existing firms charge a price low enough to discourage entry into the industry.[12] By doing so, they voluntarily sacrifice some short-run profits to maximize their profits in the long run (see section 10.7).

Nonprice Competition Among Oligopolists

Most oligopoly models presented in this chapter predict sticky or infrequent price changes in oligopolistic markets. This conforms to what is often observed in the real world. To be sure, costly price wars do sometimes erupt as a result of miscalculations on the part of one of the oligopolists, but they usually last only short periods. To avoid the possibility of starting a price war, oligopolists prefer to leave price unchanged and compete instead on the basis of **nonprice competition** (advertising, product differentiation, and service). Only when demand and cost conditions make a price change absolutely essential will oligopolists change prices. An orderly price change is then usually accomplished by price leadership.

As pointed out in section 10.2, a firm may use advertising to try to increase (i.e., to shift to the right) the demand curve for its product. If successful, the firm will then be able to sell a greater quantity of the product at an unchanged price. The problem is that other firms, upon losing sales, are likely to retaliate and also increase their advertising expenditures. The result may be simply to increase all firms' costs, with each firm retaining more or less its share of the market and earning less profits. For example, when the government banned cigarette advertising on television, all tobacco companies benefited by spending less on advertising—a step that each firm alone was not willing to take before the ban. Although some advertising provides useful information to

---

[12]See, J. Bain, *Industrial Organization*, rev. ed. (New York: John Wiley, 1967). Perhaps, more than an artificial barrier to entry, limit pricing is a practice that is designed to exploit barriers that do exist (e.g., economies of scale).

consumers on new or improved products and uses, a great deal does not. Examples might be the huge advertising expenditures (running in the hundreds of millions of dollars per year) of beer producers, automakers, and others.

The same is generally true for product differentiation. That is, producers often differentiate their product in order to increase sales, but this usually leads to retaliation and higher costs and prices. Sometimes product changes are simply cosmetic (e.g., the yearly automobile model changes). Other changes may truly improve the product, for example, when a new and longer-lasting razor blade is introduced at the same price. Some product differentiation is introduced to better serve particular segments of the market. For example, the GM Cutlass Supreme is a somewhat cheaper version of the GM Cutlass Sierra. Advertising, product differentiation, and market segmentation can be combined in many different ways and used with still other forms of nonprice competition in oligopolistic markets.

Welfare Effects of Oligopoly

We now turn to some of the long-run welfare effects of oligopoly. First, as in the case of monopoly and monopolistic competition, oligopolists usually do not produce at the lowest point on their LAC curve. This would only occur by sheer coincidence if the oligopolist's MR curve intersected the LAC curve at the lowest point of the latter. Only under perfect competition will firms *always* produce at the lowest point on the LAC curve. Oligopoly, however, often results because of the smallness of the market in relation to the optimum size of the firm, and so it does not make much sense to compare oligopoly to perfect competition. Automobiles, steel, aluminum, and many other products could only be produced at prohibitive costs under perfectly competitive conditions.

Second, as in the case of monopoly, oligopolists can earn long-run profits, and so price can exceed LAC. This is to be contrasted to the case of perfect competition and monopolistic competition where $P = LAC$ in the long run. However, some economists believe that oligopolists utilize a great deal of their profits for research and development (R&D) to produce new and better products and to find cheaper production methods. These are the primary sources of growth in modern economies. These same economists point out that monopolists do not have as much incentive to engage in R&D, and perfect competitors and monopolistic competitors are too small and do not have the resources to do so on a large scale (more will be said on this in section 12.3).

Third, as in imperfect competition in general, $P > LMC$ under oligopoly, and so there is underallocation of resources to the industry. Specifically, since the demand curve facing oligopolists is negatively sloped, $P > MR$. Thus, at the best level of output (give by the point where the LMC intersects the firm's MR curve from below), $P > LMC$. This means that society values an additional unit of the commodity more than the marginal cost of producing it. But again, $P = LMC$ only under perfect competition, and economies of scale may make perfect competition infeasible.

Fourth, while some advertising and product differentiation are useful because they provide information and satisfy the consumers' tastes for diversity, they are likely to be pushed beyond what is socially desirable in oligopolistic markets. It is difficult, however, to determine exactly how much advertising and product differentiation is socially desirable in the real world. For example, the cost of model changes equals about one-fourth of the price of a new automobile during many years.[13] To the extent that consumers purchase new automobiles and choose to have the options introduced into the new models, we can infer that most of the costs of model changes are wanted by consumers and do not represent a waste of resources. Nevertheless, the demand for some model changes and for some new options is surely created by advertising and may not represent true needs. An example of clear manipulative advertising is the attempt by Coca-Cola and Pepsi to persuade young adults to switch from coffee to Coke or Pepsi for breakfast.[14]

Turning to oligopoly theory itself, we can now see why we said earlier that there is no general theory of oligopoly. All the oligopoly models that we have examined are somewhat incomplete and unsatisfactory. This is unfortunate because oligopoly is the most prevalent form of market organization in production in all modern economies. Some hope of further progress in oligopoly theory is now provided by game theory (examined in the next chapter).

10.7 OTHER OLIGOPOLISTIC PRICING PRACTICES

In this section, we examine two other pricing practices often used by oligopolists: limit pricing and cost-plus pricing.

Limit Pricing as a Barrier to Entry

Limit pricing was defined earlier as the charging of a price low enough to discourage entry into the industry. By doing so, existing firms voluntarily sacrifice some short-run profits to maximize their profits in the long run. We can show this with Figure 10–8.

In the left panel of Figure 10–8, D is the total market demand curve for the commodity. Suppose that existing firms are already selling four units of the commodity at $P = \$8$ (point A). The entrance of a new firm would increase industry output and cause the price to fall. That is, a potential entrant assumes that it faces the segment of demand curve D to the right of point A. Subtracting the four units of the commodity supplied by existing firms from the market demand curve (D) gives the potential entrant's demand curve (d_2). If existing

---

[13]See, F. Fisher, Z. Griliches, and C. Kaysen, "The Cost of Automobile Model Changes Since 1949," *The Journal of Political Economy*, October 1962, pp. 433–451.

[14]"A Morning Cola Instead of Coffee?" *New York Times*, January 20, 1988, p. D1, and "Test Shows that Pepsi's Rival to Coffee So Far Isn't Most People's Cup of Tea," *Wall Street Journal*, March 30, 1990, p. B1.

FIGURE 10–8   Limit Pricing

In the left panel, D is the total market demand curve for the commodity. The demand curve of a potential entrant is d_2 if existing firms sell $Q = 4$, and d_1 if they sell $Q = 6$. In the right panel, the $LAC = LMC$ curve refers to the constant costs of the established firms, while $LAC^* = LMC^*$ refers to the constant and higher costs of the potential entrant. Existing firms maximize profits by selling $Q = 4$ at $P = \$8$ (given by point E, at which $MR = LMC$). The demand curve facing the potential entrant is then d_2 and it could earn profits. To discourage entrance, existing firms can set the price at $\$6$ so that d_1 lies everywhere below LAC^*.

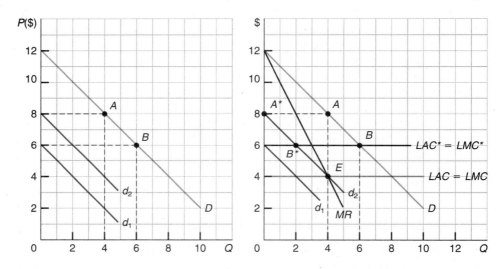

firms were selling instead six units of the commodity at $P = \$6$ (point B), the potential entrant's demand curve would be d_1.

For simplicity, we assume that per-unit costs of existing firms and for the potential entrant are constant. We also assume (quite realistically) that the per-unit costs of the potential entrant are somewhat higher than for the established firms. These are shown in the right panel of Figure 10–8, where the horizontal $LAC = LMC$ curve refers to the constant costs of the established firms and the horizontal $LAC^* = LMC^*$ curve refers to the constant and higher costs of the potential entrant.

Existing firms maximize profits by selling $Q = 4$ at $P = \$8$ (given by point E, at which $LMC = MR$) and earn profits of AE or $\$4$ per unit and $\$16$ in total. The demand curve facing the potential entrant is then d_2. Since over the range A^*B^* of d_2, $P > LAC^*$, the potential entrant would find it profitable to enter the industry. However, this would increase industry output and lower price so that the profits of existing firms would fall. To avoid this, existing firms may choose to sell $Q = 6$ at $P = \$6$ so that the demand curve facing the potential entrant is d_1. Since d_1 lies everywhere below the LAC^* curve, the potential entrant would incur losses at all output levels and would not enter the industry. Therefore, $P = \$6$ is the entry-limit price. This is the highest price that existing firms can charge without inducing entry. By setting the limit price, existing firms sacrifice some profits in the short run (they now make a profit of \$12 rather than \$16) to maximize their profits in the long run.

Note that existing firms may only charge the limit price when they believe entry is imminent and set their profit-maximizing price of $P = \$8$ at other times. Sometimes existing firms, faced with the entry of another firm, may voluntarily reduce their output to accommodate the new entrant and avoid a price reduction. Finally, note that limit pricing assumes some form of collusion (such as price leadership) on the part of existing firms.[15]

Cost-Plus Pricing: A Common Short-Cut Pricing Practice

In the real world, firms often lack exact information to set the price that maximizes their profits (given by the point where the firm's MC curve intersects its MR curve from below). In those cases, firms usually adopt **cost-plus pricing.** Here, the firm estimates the average variable cost for a "normal" output level (usually between 70% and 80% of capacity output) and then adds a certain percentage or **markup** over average variable cost to determine the price of the commodity. The markup is set sufficiently high to cover average variable and fixed costs and also provide a profit margin for the firm. The markup varies depending on the industry and demand conditions. For example, the markup is about 20% in the steel industry in general, but it is higher for products facing less elastic demand or in periods of high demand.

Cost-plus pricing is fairly common in oligopolistic industries, and, under certain conditions, it is not inconsistent with profit maximization. That is, because of the lack of adequate data, firms often cannot generally follow the $MR = MC$ rule to maximize profits. To the extent that the markup is varied inversely with the elasticity of demand of the product, however, it leads to a price which is approximately the profit-maximizing price. This can be shown as follows:

$$m = \frac{P - AVC}{AVC} \qquad [10\text{--}1]$$

where, P is price, AVC is average variable cost, and m is the markup over AVC, expressed as a percentage of AVC.

Solving for P, we get

$$m(AVC) = P - AVC$$
$$P = AVC + m(AVC) \qquad [10\text{--}2]$$
$$P = AVC(1 + m)$$

---

[15]For more dynamic theories of limit pricing that predict that the limit price will be above the existing firms' *LAC*, see R. T. Masson and J. Shaanan, "Stochastic-Dynamic Limiting Pricing: An Empirical Test," *The Review of Economics and Statistics*, August 1982, pp. 413–422.

But from section 5.6 we know that:

$$MR = P(1 - 1/\eta) \qquad \text{[10–3]}$$

where, MR is marginal revenue, P is price, and η is the price elasticity of demand.

Solving for P we get

$$P = \frac{MR}{1 - 1/\eta}$$

Since profits are maximized where $MR = MC$, we can substitute MC for MR in the above formula and get

$$P = \frac{MC}{1 - 1/\eta}$$

To the extent that the firm's MC is constant over a wide range of outputs, $MC = AVC$. Substituting AVC for MC in the above formula, we get

$$P = \frac{AVC}{1 - 1/\eta} \qquad \text{[10–4]}$$

Formula [10–4] for profit maximization equals formula [10–2] for the markup, if $1 + m = \dfrac{1}{1 - 1/\eta}$ or if $m = 1/(\eta - 1)$. Thus, the firm will maximize profits if its markup is inversely related to the price elasticity of demand for the commodity. For example, when $\eta = 3$, m should be ½, or 50%. For $\eta = 5$, $m = $ ¼, or 25%. This means that if $AVC = \$100$, P should equal $\$125$ (so that the markup is 25% of AVC) for the firm to cover all costs and maximize profits.

Cyert and March found that firms in the retailing sector adjusted prices on the basis of feedback from the market and did reduce the markup and price when the demand for a product declined and became more elastic.[16] Thus, using cost-plus pricing with a markup that varies inversely with the price elasticity of demand is consistent with profit maximization. In any event, those firms that choose a markup and price that is not near the profit-maximizing price are less likely to grow and may go out of business in the long run, as compared to firms that choose the appropriate markup. Cost-plus pricing is one of many *rules of thumb* that firms are forced to use in the real world because of the frequent lack of adequate data.

10.8 THE MARCH OF GLOBAL OLIGOPOLISTS

During the past decade, the trend toward the formation of global oligopolies has accelerated as the world's largest corporations have been getting even

---

[16]R. M. Cyert and J. G. March, *A Behavioral Theory of the Firm* (Englewood Cliffs, N.J.: Prentice-Hall, 1963).

bigger through internal growth and mergers. Indeed, in more and more industries and sectors the pressure to become one of the largest global players seems irresistible. No longer are corporations satisfied to be the largest or the next-to-the-largest national company in their industry or sector. Now many corporations operate on the belief that their survival requires that they become one of a handful of world corporations or global oligopolists in their sector. Smaller corporations are merging with larger ones in the belief that either they grow or become a casualty of sharply increased global competition. A strong impetus toward globalization has been provided by the sharp and rapid improvements in communications and transportation, the movement toward globalization of tastes, and the reduction of barriers to international trade and investments.

The sector in which the size of the largest firms has grown the most during the past decades is banking. From 1966 to 1992, the total deposits of the world's ten largest banks grew from $87 billion to nearly $4,000 billion. Even after accounting for the quintupling of prices and exchange rate changes (to convert local currency values into dollar values), this means that the size of the ten largest banks increased by more than 9 times during the past 25 years. In 1969, six of the world's largest banks (including the first four) were American. By 1992, the largest seven banks were Japanese, the eighth and the ninth were French, and the tenth was German. The largest American bank (Citicorp) was 26th! There is a great deal of disagreement, however, about whether American banks are too small to compete in the global market. It is often pointed out that after a certain size (already achieved by the largest four or five U.S. banks), stability and profitability are more important than size per se. Nevertheless, the growth in the size of the world's largest banks has been nothing but spectacular.[17]

Another sector where corporations have grown sharply in size and have become global is communications. The merger of Time, Inc. and Warner Communications, Inc. to form the world's largest communications company (American) and Japan's Sony Corporation's purchase of American Paramount Pictures for $3.4 billion in 1989 are only two examples of the growth and globalization that swept the communications industry worldwide during the 1980s. Most of the recent mergers involved the purchase of American companies by foreigners: Sony bought CBS Records, West Germany's Bertelsmann acquired RCA Records as well as Doubleday and Bantam Books, Britain's Robert Maxwell (now deceased) purchased Macmillan Publishing Company, and Ruppert Murdoch (from Australia but now residing in the United States) bought Harper & Row Publishers, Triangle Publications, and Twentieth Century Fox. The reason given for most mergers in the communications industry is to become more competitive globally. "Competitive, according to the current conventional wisdom, means being equipped to become one of the five to eight

---

[17]"The World's Biggest Commercial Banks," *Fortune*, July 31, 1989, p. 286, and "The World's 100 Largest Banks," *Wall Street Journal*, September 24, 1992, p. R27.

giant corporations expected to dominate the world communication industry by the year 2000 or so. . . . These enterprises, the reasoning goes, will be able to produce and distribute information and entertainment in virtually any medium: books, magazines, news, television, movies, videos, cinemas, electronic data networks and so on."[18] Important synergies or cross benefits are expected from joint operation.

The same growth toward globalization has occurred in the industrial arena. The total sales in real terms (i.e., after taking inflation into account) of the world's 25 largest *industrial* corporations increased 70% faster than the combined index of real total industrial production in all industrial countries from 1969 to 1979 and 50% faster from 1979 to 1990.[19] Thus, the tendency for the largest industrial corporations to become relatively larger during the past two decades is clear. In automobiles, for example, only a handful of global players survive. General Motors with 1991 sales of $105 billion and Ford with sales of $88 billion are the world's number one and number two largest industrial corporations. They are followed (with 1991 sales in billions of dollars) by Toyota (71), Daimler-Benz (62), Volkswagen (50), Fiat (50), Nissan (42), Renault (32), Honda (31), Peugeot (31), Chrysler (29), and Volvo (14)—all in the world's largest top fifty corporations (except for Volvo, which was 70th).[20] Even some of these are likely to merge. Globalization has proceeded even more rapidly in tires, where Goodyear (American), Bridgestone (Japanese), and Michelin (French) command more than half of the world's total sales, and further consolidation is expected.

The same type of globalization has been taking place in consumer products, food, drugs (see Example 5 in this chapter), electronics, and commercial aircraft. In 1989, Gillette introduced its Sensor razor, which took 20 years and $300 million to develop, and is now marketing it in 19 countries around the world (see Example 2 in Chapter 3). Nestlé has production plants in 37 countries and sells its food products in more than 40 countries. America's Phillip Morris, the world's largest tobacco and food company, Britain's Unilever, and Switzerland's Nestlé are among the world's 30 largest corporations, and America's RJR Nabisco, Sara Lee, and Pepsico are among the top 100. Coca-Cola has 40% of the U.S. market and an incredible 33% of the world's soft drink market. Despite the need to cater to local food tastes (Nestlé has more than 200 blends of Nescafé to cater to different local tastes), there is a clear trend toward global supermarkets. This has been the result of the cross-fertilization of cultures and convergence of tastes made possible by the tremendous improvements in communications and transportation. The same is true in drugs, chemicals, electronics, commercial aircraft, and other products, where a

---

[18]"Media Mergers: An Urge to Get Bigger and More Global," *The New York Times*, March 19, 1989, Section 4, p. 7; "American Banking Dinosaurs," *Wall Street Journal*, March 18, 1992, p. A14.

[19]See, *Fortune*, August 1970, May 1980, and July 1990.

[20]See, "The Global 1000," *Business Week*, July 13, 1992, pp. 57–108.

handful of huge corporations literally control the world market. It no longer makes sense to talk about or be concerned only with national rather than global competition in these sectors. Bluntly, a large corporation can even be a monopolist in the national market and face deadly competition from larger and more efficient global oligopolists. The ideal global corporation is strongly decentralized, to allow local units to develop products that fit into local cultures, and yet at its core is centralized, to coordinate activities around the globe.[21]

Example 5
Globalization of the Pharmaceutical Industry

The past few years have witnessed more than 15 mergers of large pharmaceutical companies. The largest of these were the merger of Bristol-Myers with Squib, Marion with Merrel, Dow SmithKline with Beecham, and Rhone-Poulec with Rorer. As a result, the industry today is dominated by global firms, the largest of which is U.S. Johnson & Johnson with 1991 sales of more than $12 billion. Competition is likely to lead to further consolidation and globalization of the industry. Some industry analysts are predicting that one-third of today's 20 largest U.S. drug companies will have merged, been bought, or disappeared by the end of the 1990s. The same is likely to take place in Europe and Japan.

The urge to merge, even by today's largest industry players, arises from the incredibly high cost of developing new drugs. It has been estimated that it now costs about $230 million (including failures and lost opportunity costs) to bring a new commercial drug to market. This is expected to rise to over $400 million by the end of the decade. Despite average return on sales of 20%, these huge development costs are becoming out of reach for even the largest drug companies. Hence, further consolidation and globalization in the industry are becoming a necessity.

Faced with growing competition at home and abroad, U.S. pharmaceutical companies are looking to increase sales abroad as never before. Nowhere is this more apparent than at Johnson & Johnson, which already has 175 operating units in 55 countries. Indeed, the company's fastest-growing drug in the United States (Hismanal, a nonsedating antihistamine) was discovered and developed by the company's Belgian unit and is now sold in 116 countries. While in the past it licensed drugs to companies abroad in exchange for royalties (which are usually small), Johnson & Johnson now sells new drugs directly through its growing international sales force. Indeed, half of the company's sales and 60% of profits were generated outside the United States

[21]See, "A View from the Top: Survival Tactics for the Global Business Arena," *Management Review*, October 1992, pp. 49–53.

in 1989. Expansion abroad allows the firm to spread research costs over larger sales and reach a break-even point on new drugs sooner.

Sources: "Johnson and Johnson Looks Abroad," *The New York Times*, September 3, 1990, p. 27; "Drug Industry Still Has Room to Merge," *The Wall Street Journal*, June 25, 1991, p. A2; "An Industry Top?" *Forbes*, April 15, 1991, pp. 48–52; and "The 500 Ranked by Performance," *Fortune*, April 20, 1992, p. 280.

▲

SUMMARY

1. Monopolistic competition is the form of market organization in which there are many sellers of a differentiated product, and entry into and exit from the industry are rather easy in the long run. Differentiated products are those that are similar but not identical and satisfy the same basic need. The competitive element arises from the many firms in the market. The monopoly element results from product differentiation. The monopoly power, however, is severely limited by the availability of many close substitutes. Monopolistic competition is most common in the retail sector of the economy. Because of product differentiation, we cannot derive the market demand curve and we have a cluster of prices. The choice-related variables for a monopolistically competitive firm are product variation, selling expenses, and price.

2. Since a monopolistically competitive firm produces a differentiated product for which there are many close substitutes, the demand curve that the firm faces is negatively sloped but highly price elastic. The best level of output in the short run is given by the point at which $MR = SMC$, provided that $P > AVC$. If firms earn profits in the short run, more firms enter the market in the long run. This shifts the demand curve facing each firm to the left until all firms break even. Because of product differentiation, P and LAC are somewhat higher than if the market had been orga-

nized along perfectly competitive lines, there is excess capacity, and this allows more firms to exist in the market. A monopolistically competitive firm can increase the degree of product variation and selling expenses in an effort to increase the demand for its product and make it less elastic. The optimal level of these efforts is given by the point at which $MR = MC$. In the long run, however, the monopolistically competitive firm breaks even. In recent years, economists have preferred to use the perfectly competitive and oligopoly models.

3. Oligopoly is the form of market organization in which there are few sellers of either a homogeneous or a differentiated product, and entry into or exit from the industry is possible but difficult. Oligopoly is the most prevalent form of market organization in the manufacturing sector of industrial countries, including the United States. The distinguishing characteristic of oligopoly is the interdependence or rivalry among the firms in the industry. The sources of oligopoly as well as the barriers to entry are economies of scale, the huge investments and specialized inputs required to enter the industry, patents and copyrights, the loyalty of customers of existing firms, control over the supply of a required raw material, and government franchise. The degree by which an industry is dominated by a few large firms is mea-

sured by concentration ratios. These, however, can be very misleading as a measure of the degree of competition in the industry and must be used with great caution.

4. Cournot assumed that two firms sold identical spring water produced at zero marginal cost. Each duopolist, in its attempt to maximize profits, assumes the other will keep output constant at the existing level. The result is a sequence of moves and countermoves until each duopolist sells one-third of the total output that would be sold if the market were perfectly competitive. In the kinked-demand or Sweezy model, it is assumed that oligopolists match the price reductions but not the price increases of competitors. Thus, the demand curve has a kink at the prevailing price. Oligopolists maintain the price as long as the SMC curve intersects the discontinuous segment of the MR curve. Some empirical studies do not support the existence of the kink, and the model does not explain how the price is set in the first place.

5. A centralized cartel is a formal organization of suppliers of a commodity that sets the price and allocates output and profits among its members so as to increase their joint profits. A market-sharing cartel is an organization of suppliers of a commodity that overtly or tacitly divides the market among its members. Cartels can result in the monopoly solution but are unstable and often fail. A looser form of collusion is price leadership by the dominant, the low-cost, or the barometric firm. Under price leadership by the dominant firm, the small firms are allowed to sell all they want at the price set by the dominant firm, and

then the dominant firm comes in to fill the market.

6. In the long-run, oligopolistic firms can build their best scale of plant and firms can leave the industry. Entry, however, has to be blocked or restricted if the industry is to remain oligopolistic. There can be several natural and artificial barriers to entry. Oligopolists seldom change prices for fear of starting a price war and prefer instead to compete on the basis of advertising, product differentiation, and service. In oligopolistic markets, production does not usually take place at the lowest point on the LAC curve, $P > LAC$, $P > LMC$, and too much may be spent on advertising, product differentiation, and service. Oligopoly, however, may result from the limitation of the market, and it may lead to more research and development.

7. Limit pricing refers to the charging by existing firms of a sufficiently low price to discourage entry into the industry. Cost-plus pricing refers to the setting of a price equal to average variable cost plus a markup.

8. During the past decade, the trend toward the formation of global oligopolies has accelerated as the world's largest corporations have been getting even bigger through internal growth and mergers. More and more, corporations operate on the belief that their survival requires that they become one of a handful of world corporations, or global oligopolists, in their sector. This globalization of production and distribution has important implications for the concept of efficiency (to be explored in section 12.3).

KEY TERMS

Monopolistic Competition
Differentiated Products

Product Group
Excess Capacity

Product Variation
Selling Expenses

Oligopoly
Duopoly
Pure Oligopoly
Differentiated Oligopoly
Concentration Ratios
Cournot Model
Kinked-Demand Curve Model

Collusion
Cartel
Centralized Cartel
Market-Sharing Cartel
Price Leadership
Barometric Firm
Limit Pricing

Nonprice Competition
Cost-Plus Pricing
Markup
Reaction Function
Cournot Equilibrium
Nash Equilibrium
Stackelberg Model

REVIEW QUESTIONS

1. a. Why is it that we cannot define the industry in monopolistic competition?
   b. How can cross elasticities of demand help define a product group under monopolistic competition?
2. Can the short-run supply curve of a monopolistically competitive firm be derived? Why?
3. What effect will product variation and selling expenses have on
   a. the firm's demand and cost curves?
   b. short-run and long-run equilibrium?
4. a. What is the usefulness and cost of product variation?
   b. Is advertising good or bad for consumers? Why?
5. Why does excess capacity arise in monopolistic competition? What is its economic significance?
6. What is the distinction between interdependence and rivalry in oligopoly?

7. How much would be produced by each oligopolist and in total in Figure 10–3 if there were
   a. four firms in the market?
   b. five firms in the market?
8. What general conclusion can you draw from the results in the text and from your answer to question 7 with regard to the proportion of the perfectly competitive total quantity sold by
   a. each oligopolist?
   b. all oligopolists together?
9. a. What is the usefulness of the kinked-demand curve model?
   b. What are its disadvantages?
10. Why do we study cartels and price leadership if they are illegal?
11. Why is there no general theory of oligopoly?
12. What are the advantages and disadvantages of oligopoly?

PROBLEMS

1. Suppose that SATC were $10 and AVC were $8 at the best level of output for the firm in the left panel of Figure 10–1.
   a. How much profit or loss per unit and in total would the firm have if it chose to remain in business?
   b. Should the firm remain in business in the short run? Why?
   c. What would be the total loss of the firm if it went out of business in the short run and if it didn't?
*2. Excess capacity is inversely related to the price elasticity of demand faced by a monopolistically competitive firm. True or false? Explain.
3. Starting with the assumptions of the Cournot model, explain what would happen if each

duopolist assumed that the other kept its price rather than its output constant (as in the Cournot model).
4. Draw a figure showing the best level of output and price for the oligopolist of Figure 10–4 if its SMC curve shifts
   a. up by $3.50;
   b. down by $4.
5. Draw a figure showing the best level of output and price for the oligopolist of Figure 10–4 if the government sets a price ceiling of
   a. $8;
   b. $7.

———

* = Answer provided at end of book.

*6. Draw a figure showing the best level of output and price for the oligopolist of Figure 10–4 if the demand curve it faces shifts
   a. up by $0.50 but the kink remains at $P = \$8$.
   b. down by $0.50 but the kink remains at $P = \$8$ and the SMC curve shifts up to SMC'.

7. Assume that (1) the four identical firms in a purely oligopolistic industry form a centralized cartel; (2) the total market demand function facing the cartel is $QD = 20 - 2P$, and P is given in dollars; and (3) each firm's SMC function is given by $\$\frac{1}{4}Q$, and input prices are constant.
   a. Find the best level of output and price for this centralized cartel.
   b. How much should each firm produce if the cartel wants to minimize production costs?
   c. How much profit will the cartel make if the average total cost of each firm at the best level of output is $4?

8. Redraw Figure 10–6, and show on it the MR and the ΣSMC curves for the cartel as a whole. How are the best levels of output and price for the cartel as a whole determined? On the same figure, draw the $SATC$ curve of one of the duopolists if $SATC = \$6$ at $Q = 2$ and $Q = 4$. How much profit does each duopolist earn?

*9. Start with Figure 10–6 where the duopolists share equally the market for a homogeneous product.
   a. Draw a figure such that duopolist 1's short-run marginal cost (SMC_1) is as shown in Figure 10–6 and duopolist 2's short-run marginal cost is given by $SMC_2 = 6 + 2Q$.

What quantity of the commodity will each duopolist produce? What price would each like to charge? What is the actual result likely to be?
   b. If $SATC_1 = \$5$ at $Q = 2$ and $SATC_2 = \$8$ at $Q = 1$, how much profit will each duopolist earn?

10. Assume that (1) in a purely oligopolistic industry, there is one dominant firm and ten small identical firms; (2) the market demand curve for the commodity is $Q = 20 - 2P$, where P is given in dollars; (3) $SMC_d = 1.5 + Q/2$, while $SMC_s = 1 + Q/4$; and (4) input prices remain constant. Based on the above assumptions
   a. draw a figure similar to Figure 10–7 showing the market demand curve, SMC_d, SMC_s, and the demand curve that the dominant firm faces.
   b. What price will the dominant firm set? How much will the small firms supply together? How much will the dominant firm supply?

11. Draw a figure showing that when two identical firms share the market equally for a homogeneous product they both earn profits, but if a third identical firm entered the industry, they would all face losses. How is this related to the existence of oligopoly?

*12. If an oligopolist knows that the price elasticity of demand of the product it sells (η) is 4 and its $AVC = \$10$, determine
   a. the markup that the oligopolist should use in pricing its product;
   b. the price the oligopolist should charge.

APPENDIX   THE COURNOT AND STACKELBERG MODELS

This appendix is a more advanced and complete treatment of the Cournot model presented in section 10.4, as well as an important extension of it known as the Stackelberg model.

The Cournot Model—An Extended Treatment

We begin by writing the equation for market demand curve D shown in both panels of Figure 10–3 as

$$Q = 12 - P \qquad \text{[10–5]}$$

where Q is the total quantity of spring water sold in the market per unit of time (say per week) and P is the market price. For example, applying formula [10–5], $Q = 0$ when $P = \$12$ (the vertical intercept of market demand curve D in the right panel of Figure 10–3, repeated below for ease of reference as the left panel of Figure 10–9). On the other hand, when $P = \$0$, $Q = 12$ (point C on market demand curve D in the left panel of Figure 10–9).

Given the quantity of spring water supplied by duopolist B (Q_B), duopolist A will supply one-half of the difference between 12 (the total that would be supplied to the market at $P = \$0$) and Q_B in order to maximize total profits. That is,

$$Q_A = \frac{12 - Q_B}{2} \qquad [10–6]$$

For example, when $Q_B = 0$, $Q_A = 12/2 = 6$ (point A on d_A in the left panel of Figure 10–9). On the other hand, when $Q_B = 3$, $Q_A = (12 - 3)/2 = 4.5$ (point A' on d_A in the left panel of Figure 10–9). With total costs equal to zero, duopolist A always maximizes total revenue and total profits by producing one-half of 12 minus the amount supplied by duopolist B (formula [10–6]). The reason is that (as shown in the left panel of Figure 10–3) this is the quantity at which $mr = MC = 0$.

Similarly, duopolist B maximizes total revenue and total profits by selling

$$Q_B = \frac{12 - Q_A}{2} \qquad [10–7]$$

FIGURE 10–9   Duopolists' Demand Curves and Reaction Functions in the Cournot Model

The left panel shows the demand curves faced by duopolists A and B and the quantity sold by each, given the quantity sold by the other (exactly as in the right panel of Figure 10–3). The right panel shows duopolist A's and B's reaction functions. The intersection of the two reaction functions at point E gives the Cournot equilibrium of $Q_A = Q_B = 4$ (in the right panel), so that $Q_A + Q_B = 8$ and $P = \$4$ (point F in the left panel).

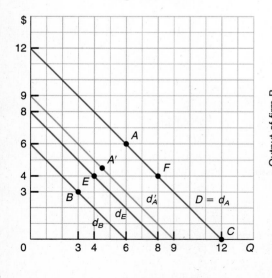
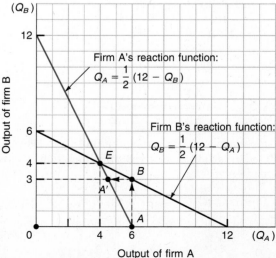

For example, when $Q_A = 6$, $Q_B = (12 - 6)/2 = 3$ (point B on d_B in the left panel of Figure 10–9) because (as shown in the left panel of Figure 10–3) that is the quantity at which $mr = MC = 0$.

Equation [10–6] is duopolist A's **reaction function.** It shows how duopolist A reacts to duopolist B's action and is plotted in the right panel of Figure 10–9. It shows that if $Q_B = 0$, $Q_A = 6$ (given by point A at which duopolist A's reaction function crosses the horizontal or Q_A axis in the right panel of Figure 10–9) in order for duopolist A to maximize total revenue and total profits. If $Q_B = 3$, $Q_A = 4.5$ (point A' on duopolist A's reaction function).

Similarly, equation [10–7] is duopolist B's reaction function and is also plotted in the right panel of Figure 10–9. It shows that if $Q_A = 6$, $Q_B = 3$ (given by point B on duopolist B's reaction function in the right panel of Figure 10–9) in order for duopolist B to maximize total revenue and total profits. Thus, a duopolist's reaction function shows the quantity that the duopolist should sell to maximize its total profits, given the amount sold by the other duopolist.

The two reaction functions intersect at point E, giving the **Cournot equilibrium** of $Q_A = Q_B = 4$. That is, if $Q_B = 4$, then $Q_A = 4$ (point E on duopolist A's reaction function) for duopolist A to maximize total profits. Similarly, if $Q_A = 4$, then $Q_B = 4$ (point E on duopolist B's reaction function) for duopolist B to maximize total profits. Thus, point E (where the two reaction functions intersect) is the Cournot equilibrium point because there is no tendency for either duopolist to change the quantity it sells. A situation such as the Cournot equilibrium where each player's strategy is optimal, given the strategy chosen by the other player, is called a **Nash equilibrium.**

The right panel of Figure 10–9 can also be used to show the time path or movement toward equilibrium. With $Q_B = 0$, $Q_A = 6$ (point A on duopolist A's reaction function). With $Q_A = 6$, $Q_B = 3$ (point B on duopolist B's reaction function). With $Q_B = 3$, $Q_A = 4.5$ (point A' on duopolist A's reaction function). Note how the direction of the arrows from point A to point B and from point B to point A' moves the duopolists toward the final Cournot equilibrium point E at the intersection of the two reaction functions.

The Cournot equilibrium point E can be obtained algebraically by substituting duopolist B's reaction function (i.e., equation [10–7]) into duopolist A's reaction function (equation [10–6]). Doing this, we get

$$Q_A = \frac{12 - (12 - Q_A)/2}{2} \qquad \qquad \textbf{[10–8]}$$

$$= \frac{12 - 6 + Q_A/2}{2}$$

$$= 3 + Q_A/4$$

Multiplying both sides by 4, we get

$$4Q_A = 12 + Q_A$$

so that

$$3Q_A = 12$$

and

$$Q_A = 4 \qquad \qquad \textbf{[10–9]}$$

With $Q_A = 4$

$$Q_B = \frac{12 - 4}{2} = 4 \qquad \qquad \textbf{[10–10]}$$

so that

$$Q_A = 4 = Q_B \text{ (Cournot equilibrium)} \qquad \textbf{[10-11]}$$

and

$$Q = Q_A + Q_B = 4 + 4 = 8 \qquad \textbf{[10-12]}$$

Solving equation [10-5] for P, we get

$$P = 12 - Q \qquad \textbf{[10-13]}$$

With $Q = 8$ at Cournot equilibrium, the price at which each duopolist will sell spring water is

$$P = 12 - 8 = \$4 \qquad \textbf{[10-14]}$$

which is shown by point F in the left panel of Figure 10-9.

The Stackelberg Model

In 1934, the German economist Heinrich von Stackelberg made an important extension to the Cournot model. This became known as the **Stackelberg model.** Stackelberg assumed that one of the duopolists, say duopolist A, knows that duopolist B behaves in the naive Cournot fashion (i.e., A knows B's reaction function) and uses that knowledge in choosing its own output. Duopolist A is then called the *Stackelberg leader*, and duopolist B is referred to as the *Stackelberg follower*. All the other assumptions of the Cournot model hold. The Stackelberg model shows that duopolist A (the Stackelberg leader) will have higher profits than under the Cournot solution at the expense of duopolist B (the Stackelberg follower).

To examine the Stackelberg model, we begin by rewriting equation [10-5] for market demand function D:

$$Q = 12 - P \qquad \textbf{[10-5]}$$

Since Q refers to the total output of duopolists A and B, we can rewrite equation [10-5] as

$$Q_A + Q_B = 12 - P \qquad \textbf{[10-15]}$$

Because duopolist A knows duopolist B's reaction function, we can substitute equation [10-7] for Q_B into equation [10-15]. When we do this, we get

$$Q_A + (12 - Q_A)/2 = 12 - P \qquad \textbf{[10-16]}$$

$$Q_A + 6 - Q_A/2 = 12 - P$$

$$Q_A/2 = 6 - P$$

$$Q_A = 12 - 2P \qquad \textbf{[10-17]}$$

Equation [10-17] is now the demand function facing duopolist A when duopolist A knows duopolist B's reaction function and behavior. Plotting equation [10-17], we get the (residual) demand curve facing duopolist A, d_A^*, and its corresponding marginal revenue curve, mr_A^* (which, as usual, is twice as steep as the corresponding demand curve) as shown in Figure 10-10. Since marginal cost equals zero, duopolist A maximizes its total revenue and profits by selling six units of output (given by point E^* where $mr_A^* = MC = 0$).

FIGURE 10–10   Demand and Marginal Revenue Curves of Stackelberg Duopolist A

d_A^* and mr_A^* are, respectively, the demand curve and the marginal revenue curve facing Stackelberg duopolist A. Since $MC = 0$, duopolist A maximizes its total revenue and total profits by selling six units. This is given by point E^* where $m_A^* = MC = 0$. Duopolist B would then sell three units. With $Q = 9$, $P = \$3$, duopolist A earns $18 and duopolist B earns $9.

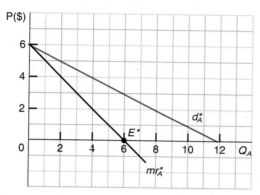

With $Q_A = 6$, $Q_B = 3$ (according to B's reaction function given by equation [10–7]). With $Q = Q_A + Q_B = 6 + 3 = 9$, $P = 12 - Q = 12 - 9 = 3$. Thus, duopolist A earns a total revenue and total profit of $18 (six units at $P = \$3$), while duopolist B earns a total revenue and profit of $9 (three units times $P = \$3$). This compares with the four units of output sold by each duopolist at $P = \$4$ (with each earning a total revenue and profit of $16) under the Cournot model. Thus, duopolist A (the Stackelberg leader) gains at the expense of duopolist B (the Stackelberg follower) with respect to the Cournot solution. Note, however, that what duopolist A gains is less than what duopolist B loses. Of course, if duopolist B were the Stackelberg leader and duopolist A were the Stackelberg follower, duopolist B would earn $18 and duopolist A would earn $9. By allowing one of the firms to behave strategically, the Stackelberg is thus superior to the Cournot model.

When duopolist A is the Stackelberg leader, the solution is the same as point B on duopolist B's reaction function in Figure 10–9. However, while point B is not the Cournot equilibrium, it does represent the Stackelberg solution. Note that under the Stackelberg solution (whether duopolist A or B is the Stackelberg leader), the combined total revenue and profits of both firms would be $27 ($18 + $9). By colluding and operating as a centralized cartel or monopoly (see section 10.5), the combined output of both firms could be cut from nine units in the Stackelberg solution to six units, which could be sold at $P = \$6$, so that the total combined revenue and profits that both firms could share would be $36 (rather than $27). This is sometimes referred to as the *Chamberlin model*.[22]

[22]See, D. Salvatore, Schaum's Outline, in *Microeconomic Theory*, 3rd ed. (New York: McGraw-Hill, 1992), pp. 262–263.

GAME THEORY AND OLIGOPOLISTIC BEHAVIOR

In this chapter, we extend our analysis of firm behavior in oligopolistic markets using game theory. As we will see, game theory offers many insights into oligopolistic interdependence and strategic behavior that could not be examined with the traditional tools of analysis presented in the previous chapter.

The chapter begins with an explanation of the basic concepts, objectives, and usefulness of game theory. It then defines a dominant strategy and a Nash equilibrium and examines their usefulness in the analysis of oligopolistic behavior. Next, the chapter describes the prisoners' dilemma and its applicability to the analysis of price and nonprice competition and cartel cheating. We conclude our discussion of game theory by analyzing multiple and strategic moves. The examples and applications presented in the chapter clearly highlight the importance of game theory to the understanding of many aspects of oligopolistic behavior that could not otherwise be explained.

11.1 GAME THEORY: DEFINITION, OBJECTIVES, AND USEFULNESS

We have seen that oligopolists must consider the reactions of the other firms in the industry to their own actions. Some have likened the behavior of oligopolists to that of players in a game and to the strategic actions of warring factions. It is this crucial aspect of oligopolistic interdependence that game theory seeks to capture and explain (see Example 1).

Game theory was introduced by John von Neumann and Oskar Morgenstern in 1944, and it was soon hailed as a breakthrough in the study of oligopoly.[1] In general, **game theory** is concerned with the choice of an optimal

---

[1]J. von Neumann and O. Morgenstern, *Theory of Games and Economic Behavior* (Princeton, N.J.: Princeton University Press, 1944). More recent and in-depth presentations of game theory and with applications to economics are found in J. W. Friedman, *Game Theory with Applications to Economics* (New York: Oxford University Press, 1990), and D. Fudenberg and J. Tirole, *Game Theory* (Cambridge, Mass.: MIT Press, 1991).

strategy in conflict situations. Specifically, game theory can help an oligopolist choose the course of action (e.g., the best price to charge) that maximizes its benefits or profits after considering all possible reactions of its competitors. For example, game theory can help a firm determine (1) the conditions under which lowering its price would not trigger a ruinous price war; (2) whether the firm should build excess capacity to discourage entry into the industry, even though this lowers the firm's short-run profits; and (3) why cheating in a cartel usually leads to its collapse. Game theory can be of great use in the analysis of such conflict situations. In short, game theory shows how an oligopolistic firm can make strategic decisions to gain a competitive advantage over its rivals or how it can minimize the potential harm from a strategic move by a rival. Before we examine concrete examples, however, let us consider some of the common elements in all game theory.

Every game theory model includes players, strategies, and payoffs. The **players** are the decision-makers (here, the managers of oligopolist firms) whose behavior we are trying to explain and predict. **Strategies** are the potential choices to change price, to develop new or differentiated products, to introduce a new or a different advertising campaign, to build excess capacity, and all other such actions that affect the sales and profitability of the firm and its rivals. The **payoff** is the outcome or consequence of each strategy. For each strategy adopted by a firm, there is usually a number of strategies (reactions) available to a rival firm. The payoff is the outcome or consequence of each *combination* of strategies by the two firms. The payoff is usually expressed in terms of the profits or losses of the firm that we are examining as a result of the firm's strategies and the rivals' responses. A table that gives the payoffs from all the strategies open to the firm and the rivals' responses is called the **payoff matrix**.

Example 1
Military Strategy and Strategic Business Decisions

According to William E. Peackock, the president of two St. Louis companies and former assistant secretary of the army under Jimmy Carter, decision-making in business has much in common with military strategy and can thus be profitably analyzed using game theory. Of course, business managers' actions are restricted by laws and regulations to prevent unfair practices, and the objective of managers is not to literally destroy the competition. Nevertheless, they can learn from military strategists. Peackock points out that throughout history, military conflicts have produced a set of Darwinian basic principles that can serve as an excellent guideline to business managers about how to compete in the marketplace. Neglect of these principles can mean business failure instead of success.

In business as in war, it is crucial for the organization to have a clear objective and to explain this objective to all of its employees. The benefits of a simple marketing strategy that all employees can understand are clearly evidenced by the success of McDonald's. Both business and war also require the development of a strategy for attacking. Aggressiveness is important, because few competitions are won by being passive. Both business and warfare require unity of command to pinpoint responsibility. Even in decentralized companies with informal lines of command, there are always key individuals who must make important decisions. Furthermore, in business as in war, the element of surprise and security (keeping your strategy secret) is crucial. For example, Lee Iacocca stunned the competition in 1964 by introducing the immensely successful (high payoff) Mustang. Finally, in business as in war, spying to discover a rival's plans or steal a rival's new technological breakthrough is becoming more common.

Today's business leaders must learn how to tap employees' ideas and energy, manage large-scale rapid change, anticipate business conditions five or ten years down the road, and muster the courage to steer the firm in radical new directions when necessary. Above all, firms must think and act strategically in a world of increasing global competition. Game theory can be particularly useful and can offer important insights in the analysis of oligopolistic interdependence.

Sources: W. E. Peackock, *Corporate Combat* (New York: Facts on File Publication, 1984); W. B. Wriston, "The State of American Management," *Harvard Business Review*, Vol. 68, January–February 1990; and "The Valley of Spies," *Forbes*, October 26, 1992, pp. 200–204.

11.2 DOMINANT STRATEGY AND NASH EQUILIBRIUM

In this section, we discuss the meaning of a dominant strategy and Nash equilibrium and examine their usefulness in the analysis of oligopolistic interdependence.

Dominant Strategy

Let us begin with the simplest type of game with an industry (duopoly) composed of two firms, firm A and firm B, and a choice of two strategies for each—advertise or don't advertise. Firm A, of course, expects to earn higher profits if it advertises than if it doesn't. But the actual level of profits of firm A depends also on whether firm B advertises or not. Thus, each strategy by firm A (i.e., advertise or don't advertise) can be associated with each of firm B's strategies (also to advertise or not to advertise). The four possible outcomes from this simple game are illustrated by the payoff matrix in Table 11–1.

In the payoff matrix in Table 11–1, the first number in each of the four cells refers to the payoff (profit) for firm A, while the second is the payoff (profit) for firm B. From Table 11–1, we see that if both firms advertise, firm A will earn a profit of 4, and firm B will earn a profit of 3 (the top left cell of

TABLE 11–1   Payoff Matrix for the Advertising Game

		Firm B	
		Advertise	**Don't Advertise**
Firm A	**Advertise**	4,3	5,1
	Don't Advertise	2,5	3,2

the payoff matrix).[2] The bottom left cell of the payoff matrix, on the other hand, shows that if firm A doesn't advertise and firm B does, firm A will have a profit of 2, and firm B will have a profit of 5. The other payoffs in the second column of the table can be interpreted similarly.

What strategy should each firm choose? Let us consider firm A first. If firm B does advertise (i.e., moving down the left column of Table 11–1), we see that firm A will earn a profit of 4 if it also advertises and 2 if it doesn't. Thus, firm A should advertise if firm B advertises. If firm B doesn't advertise, (i.e., moving down the right column in Table 11–1), firm A would earn a profit of 5 if it advertises and 3 if it doesn't. Thus, firm A should advertise whether firm B advertises or not. Firm A's profits would always be greater if it advertises than if it doesn't, regardless of what firm B does. We can then say that advertising is the dominant strategy for firm A. The **dominant strategy** is the optimal choice for a player no matter what the opponent does.

The same is true for firm B. Whatever firm A does (i.e., whether firm A advertises or not), it would always pay for firm B to advertise. We can see this by moving across each row of Table 11–1. Specifically, if firm A advertises, firm B's profit would be 3 if it advertises and 1 if it does not. Similarly, if firm A does not advertise, firm B's profit would be 5 if it advertises and 2 if it doesn't. Thus, the dominant strategy for firm B is also to advertise.

In this case, both firm A and firm B have the dominant strategy of advertising and this will, therefore, be the final equilibrium. Both firm A and firm B will advertise regardless of what the other firm does and will earn a profit of 4 and 3, respectively (the top left cell in the payoff matrix in Table 11–1). The advertising solution or final equilibrium for both firms holds whether firm A or firm B chooses its strategy first or if both firms decide on their best strategy simultaneously.

Nash Equilibrium

Not all games have a dominant strategy for each player, however. An example of this is shown in the payoff matrix in Table 11–2. This table is same as the

---

[2]The profits of 4 and 3 could refer, for example, to $4 million and $3 million, respectively.

TABLE 11–2   Payoff Matrix for the Advertising Game

		Firm B	
		Advertise	Don't Advertise
Firm A	Advertise	4,3	5,1
	Don't Advertise	2,5	6,2

payoff matrix in Table 11–1, except that the first number in the bottom right cell was changed from 3 to 6. Now firm B has a dominant strategy but firm A does not. The dominant strategy for firm B is to advertise whether firm A advertises or not, because the payoffs for firm B are the same as in Table 11–1. Firm A, however, has no dominant strategy now. If firm B advertises, firm A earns a profit of 4 if it advertises and 2 if it does not. Thus, if firm B advertises, firm A should also advertise. On the other hand, if firm B does not advertise, firm A earns a profit of 5 if it advertises and 6 if it does not.[3] Thus, firm A should advertise if firm B does, and it should not advertise if firm B doesn't. Firm A no longer has a dominant strategy. What firm A should do now depends on what firm B does.

In order to firm A to determine whether to advertise, firm A must first try to determine what firm B will do (and advertise if firm B does and not advertise if firm B does not). If firm A knows the payoff matrix, it can figure out that firm B has the dominant strategy of advertising. Therefore, the optimal strategy for firm A is also to advertise (because firm A will earn a profit of 4 by advertising and 2 by not advertising—see the first column of Table 11–2). This is the Nash equilibrium, named after John Nash, the Princeton University mathematician who first formalized the notion in 1951.

The **Nash equilibrium** is a situation in which each player chooses his or her optimal strategy, *given the strategy chosen by the other player*. In our example, the high advertising strategy for firm A and firm B is the Nash equilibrium, because given that firm B chooses its dominant strategy of advertising, the optimal strategy for firm A is also to advertise. Note that when both firms had a dominant strategy, each firm was able to choose its optimal strategy regardless of the strategy adopted by its rival. Here, only firm B has a dominant strategy; firm A does not. As a result, firm A cannot choose its optimal strategy independently of firm B's strategy. Only when each player has chosen its optimal strategy given the strategy of the other player do we have a Nash equilibrium. The Cournot equilibrium examined in section 10.4 was an example of a Nash equilibrium. Not all games have a Nash equilibrium, and some

---

[3]This might result, for example, if firm A's advertisement is not effective or if advertising adds more to firm A's costs than to its revenues.

games can have more than one Nash equilibrium (see problem 3 with answer at end of book).

Example 2
Dell Computers and Nash Equilibrium

Dell Computers of Austin, Texas, a company created by 27-year old Michael Dell in 1984, ended its latest fiscal year with revenues of more than $2 billion and very healthy profits, at a time when other computer companies (including the giant IBM) are struggling with sluggish sales or heavy losses. By offering a 30-day, money-back guarantee on next-day, free, on-site service through independent contractors for the first year of ownership and unlimited calls to a toll-free technical support line, Dell established a solid reputation for reliability, thus taking the fear and uncertainty out of mail-order computers. Dell will even mail a $25 check to any customer who does not get a Dell technician within five minutes of calling Dell's technical support line! Ordering a computer from Dell by mail is now like ordering a Big Mac at McDonald's: you know exactly what you get. By eliminating intermediaries, Dell was also able to charge lower prices than its larger and more established competitors. For example, Dell's selling and administrative expenses are 14 cents for each dollar of sales, compared with 24 cents for Apple and 30 cents for IBM. Dell ships computers by mail by adding only a 2% shipping charge to the sale price. When receiving a mail order, Dell technicians simply pick up the now-standard components from the shelf to assemble the particular PC ordered. It is simple, quick, and inexpensive. Thus, Dell has developed a dominant strategy—one that is optimal regardless of what competitors do.

Traditional computers firms such as IBM, Apple, Zenith Data Systems, and others always thought that customers were willing to pay a substantial retail markup for the privilege of being able to go to a store and feel and touch the machine before buying it. Some still do. But by reducing fears and uncertainty from ordering computers through the mail, Dell was able to convince a growing number of customers to bypass the middleman and order directly from Dell by mail at lower prices. Given Dell's dominant and profitable strategy, IBM, Apple, and Zenith are now busy setting up their own mail-order departments and 800 phone lines. Their dominant strategy of selling exclusively through retail outlets was knocked out by Dell's market strategy, so we now can say that the computer industry is in a Nash equilibrium. Given Dell's dominant strategy, the other major computer companies have decided to change their strategy and also accept orders by mail.

Sources: "Why Dell Is a Survivor," *Forbes*, October 12, 1992. pp. 82–91, and "Compaq Also to Sell Its PC's Direct," *New York Times*, March 12, 1993, p. D3.

11.3 THE PRISONERS' DILEMMA, PRICE AND NONPRICE COMPETITION, AND CARTEL CHEATING

In this section, we examine the meaning of the prisoners' dilemma and see how it can be applied to explain oligopolistic behavior in the form of price and nonprice competition and cartel cheating.

The Prisoners' Dilemma: Definition and Importance

Oligopolistic firms often face a problem called the **prisoners' dilemma.** This refers to a situation in which each firm adopts its dominant strategy, but each could do better (i.e., earn larger profits) by cooperating. Consider the following situation. Two suspects are arrested for armed robbery; if convicted, each could receive a maximum sentence of 10 years imprisonment. Unless one or both suspects confess, however, the evidence is such that they could only be convicted of possessing stolen goods, which carries a maximum sentence of 1 year in prison. Each suspect is interrogated separately and no communication is allowed between the two suspects. The district attorney promises each suspect that by confessing, he or she will go free while the other suspect (who does not confess) will receive the full 10-year sentence. If both suspects confess, each gets a reduced sentence of 5 years imprisonment. The (negative) payoff matrix in terms of years of detention is given in Table 11–3.

From Table 11–3, we see that confessing is the best or dominant strategy for suspect A no matter what suspect B does. The reason is that if suspect B confesses, suspect A revives a 5-year jail sentence if he also confesses and a 10-year sentence if he does not. Similarly, if suspect B does not confess, suspect A goes free if he confesses and receives a 1-year sentence if he does not. Thus, the dominant strategy for suspect A is to confess. Confessing is also the best or dominant strategy for suspect B. The reason is that if suspect A confesses, suspect B gets a 5-year jail sentence if he also confesses and a 10-year jail sentence if he does not. Similarly, if suspect A does not confess, suspect B goes free if he confesses and gets 1 year if he does not. Thus, the dominant strategy for suspect B is also to confess.

TABLE 11–3   Negative Payoff Matrix for Suspect A and Suspect B (Years of Detention)

		Suspect B	
		Confess	Don't Confess
Suspect A	**Confess**	5,5	0,10
	Don't Confess	10,0	1,1

With each suspect adopting his or her dominant strategy of confessing, each ends up receiving a 5-year jail sentence. But if each suspect did not confess, each would get only a 1-year jail sentence! Each suspect, however, is afraid that if he or she does not confess, the other will confess, and so he or she would end up receiving a 10-year jail sentence. Only if each suspect was sure that the other would not confess, and he or she does not confess, would each get only a 1-year sentence. Because it is not possible to reach an agreement not to confess (remember, the suspects are already in jail and cannot communicate), each suspect adopts his or her dominant strategy to confess and receives a 5-year jail sentence. Even if an agreement not to confess could be reached, the agreement could not be enforced. Therefore, each suspect will end up confessing and receiving a 5-year jail sentence.

Price and Nonprice Competition, Cartel Cheating, and the Prisoners' Dilemma

The concept of the prisoners' dilemma can be used to analyze price and nonprice competition in oligopolistic markets, as well as the incentive to cheat in a cartel (i.e., the tendency to secretly cut prices or to sell more than the allocated quota). Oligopolistic price competition in the presence of the prisoners' dilemma can be examined with the payoff matrix in Table 11–4.

The payoff matrix of Table 11–4 shows that if firm B charged a low price (say, $6), firm A would earn a profit of 2 if it also charged the low price ($6) and 1 if it charged a high price (say, $8). Similarly, if firm B charged a high price ($8), firm A would earn a profit of 5 if it charged the low price and 3 if it charged the high price. Thus, firm A should adopt its dominant strategy of charging the low price. Turning to firm B, we see that if firm A charged the low price, firm B would earn a profit of 2 if it charged the low price and 1 if it charged the high price. Similarly, if firm A charged the high price, firm B would earn a profit of 5 if it charged the low price and 3 if it charged the high price. Thus, firm B should also adopt its dominant strategy of charging the low price. However, both firms could do better (i.e., earn the higher profit

TABLE 11–4   Payoff Matrix for Pricing Game

		Firm B	
		Low Price	High Price
Firm A	Low Price	2,2	5,1
	High Price	1,5	3,3

of 3) if they cooperated and both charged the high price (the bottom right cell).

Thus, the firms are in a prisoners' dilemma: each firm will charge the low price and earn a smaller profit because if it charges the high price, it cannot trust its rival to also charge the high price. Specifically, suppose that firm A charged the high price in the expectation that firm B would also charge the high price (so that each firm would earn a profit of 3). Given that firm A has charged the high price, however, firm B has now an incentive to charge the low price, because by doing so it can increase its profits to 5 (see, the bottom left cell). The same is true if firm B started by charging the high price in the expectation that firm A would also do so. The net result is that each firm charges the low price and earns a profit of only 2. Only if the two firms learned to cooperate and both charged the high price would they earn the higher profit of 3 (and overcome their dilemma).

Although the payoff matrix of Table 11–4 was used to examine oligopolistic price competition in the presence of the prisoners' dilemma, by simply changing the heading of the columns and rows of the payoff matrix, we can use the same payoff matrix to examine nonprice competition and cartel cheating. For example, if we changed (pencil in) the heading of "low price" to "advertise" and the heading of "high price" to "don't advertise" in Table 11–4, we can utilize the same matrix to analyze advertising as a form of nonprice competition in the presence of the prisoners' dilemma. We would then see that each firm would adopt its dominant strategy of advertising and (as in the case of charging a low price) would earn a profit of 2. Both firms, however, would do better by not advertising because they would then earn (as in the case of charging a high price) the higher profit of 3. The firms then face the prisoners' dilemma. Only by cooperating in not advertising would each increase its profits to 3. For example, when cigarette advertising on television was banned in 1971, all tobacco companies benefitted by spending less on advertising and earning higher profits. While the intended effect of the law was to encourage people not to smoke, the law had the unintended effect of solving the prisoners' dilemma for cigarette producers!

Similarly, if we now changed the heading of "low price" or "advertise" to "cheat" and the heading of "high price" or "don't advertise" to "don't cheat" in the columns and rows of the payoff matrix of Table 11–4, we could use the same payoffs in the table to analyze the incentive for cartel members to cheat in the presence of the prisoners' dilemma. In this case, each firm adopts its dominant strategy of cheating and (as in the case of charging the low price or advertising) earns a profit of 2. But by not cheating, however, each member of the cartel would earn the higher profit of 3. The cartel members then face the prisoners' dilemma. Only if cartel members do not cheat will each share the higher cartel profits of 3. A cartel can prevent or reduce the probability of cheating by monitoring the sales of each member and punishing cheaters. However, the greater the number of members in the cartel and the more differentiated is the product, the more difficult it is for the cartel to do this and prevent cheating.

Example 3
The Airlines' Fare War and the Prisoners' Dilemma

In April 1992, American Airlines, the nation's largest carrier with a 20% share of the domestic market, introduced a new simplified fare structure that included only 4 kinds of fares instead of 16, and it lowered prices for most business and leisure travelers. Coach fares were cut by an average of 38% and first-class fares were lowered by 20% to 50%. Other domestic airlines quickly announced similar fare cuts. American and other carriers hoped that the increase in air travel resulting from the fare cuts would more than offset the price reductions and eventually turn losses into badly needed profits. (During 1990 and 1991, domestic airlines lost more than $6 billion, Pan Am and Eastern Airlines went out of business, and Continental, Trans World Airlines [TWA], and America West filed for bankruptcy protection.)

Rather than establishing price discipline, however, American's new fare structure started a process of competitive fare cuts that led to another disastrous price war during the summer of 1992. It started when TWA, operating under protection from creditors and badly needing quick revenues, began to undercut American's fares by 10% to 20%. American and other airlines responded by matching TWA's price cuts. Then, on May 26, 1992, Northwest, in an effort to stimulate summer leisure travel, announced that an adult and child could travel on the same flight within the continental United States for the price of one ticket. The next day, American countered by cutting all fares by 50%. The other big carriers immediately matched American's 50% price cut for all summer travel. Another full-fledged price war had been unleashed.

Even though deep price cuts increased summer travel sharply, all airlines incurred losses. The low fares meant that passengers paid only 10.6 cents per mile, the lowest since 1980 and well below the industry average cost. American was also sued by three of its rivals (Continental, Northwest, and American West) who charged predatory pricing designed to force them out of business (after which, American would increase prices and return to profitability). Furthermore, three attempts to increase fares by 30% above presale levels in fall 1992 failed when one or more of the carriers did not go along. Having become used to deep discounts, passengers were simply unwilling to pay higher fares, especially in a weak economy.

This example illustrates how all domestic airlines could have benefitted in the long run from the new fare structure established by American in April 1992. But some weak airlines, in desperate need for cash, wanted to do better by lowering prices. Other airlines, however, soon matched the price cuts to avoid losing market share, and all airlines ended up facing even larger losses than before. In short, the airlines faced the prisoners' dilemma and, unable to cooperate, ended up with heavy losses.

Sources: "American Air Cuts Most Fares in Simplification of Rate System," *New York Times,* April 10, 1992, p. 1; "The Airlines Are Killing Each Other Again," *Business Week,* June 8, 1992, p. 32;

"Death Struggle in the Sky," *Newsweek*, June 15, 1992, pp. 43–45; "Continental Sues American Over New Strategy on Fares," *New York Times*, June 10, 1992, p. D2; "Airlines Tally the Damage from Summer's Fare War," *New York Times*, September 12, 1992, p. 1; and "AMR's Airline-Industry Fare Structure Heads for that Big Hangar in the Sky," *Wall Street Journal*, October 9, 1992, p. B1.

▲

11.4 REPEATED GAMES AND TIT-FOR-TAT STRATEGY

We have seen how two firms facing the prisoners' dilemma can increase their profits by cooperating. Such cooperation, however, is not likely to occur in the single-move prisoners' dilemma games discussed so far. Cooperation is more likely to occur in repeated or many-move games, which are more realistic in the real world. For example, oligopolists do not decide on their pricing strategy only once but many times over many years. Axelrod found that in such **repeated games** the best strategy is that of tit-for-tat.[4] **Tit-for-tat** behavior can be summarized as follows: do to your opponent what he or she has just done to you. That is, begin by cooperating and continue to cooperate as long as your opponent cooperates. If he betrays you, the next time you betray him back. If he then cooperates, the next time you also cooperate. This strategy is retaliatory enough to discourage noncooperation but forgiving enough to allow a pattern of mutual cooperation to develop. In fact, Axelrod found through computer simulation experiments that tit-for-tat is the best strategy in repeated prisoners' dilemma games.

For a tit-for-tat strategy to be best, however, certain conditions must be met. First, a reasonably stable set of players is required. If the players change frequently, there is little chance for cooperative behavior to develop. Second, there must be a small number of players (otherwise, it becomes difficult to keep track of what each is doing). Third, it is assumed that each firm can quickly detect (and is willing and able to quickly retaliate for) cheating by other firms. Cheating that goes undetected for a long time encourages cheating. Fourth, demand and cost conditions must be relatively stable (for if they change rapidly, it is difficult to define what is cooperative behavior and what is not). Fifth, it must be assumed that the game is repeated indefinitely, or at least a very large and *uncertain* number of times. If the game is played for a finite number of times, each firm has an incentive not to cooperate in the final period because it cannot be harmed by retaliation. Each firm knows this and thus will not cooperate on the next-to-the-last move. Indeed, in an effort to gain a competitive advantage by being the first to start cheating, the entire situation will unravel and cheating begins from the first move.[5]

---

[4]See, R. Axelrod, *The Evolution of Cooperation* (New York: Basic Books, 1984).

[5]See, D. Kreps, P. Milgron, J. Roberts, and R. Wilson, "Rational Cooperation in the Finitely Repeated Prisoners' Dilemma," *Journal of Economic Theory*, Vol. 27, 1982, pp. 245–252.

There are, of course, times when a firm finds that it is to its advantage not to cooperate. For example, if a supplier is near bankruptcy, a firm may find every excuse for not paying its bills to the near-bankrupt firm (claiming, for example, that supplies were defective or did not meet specification) in the hope of avoiding payment altogether if the firm does go out of business. It is the necessity to deal with the same suppliers and customers in the future and their ability to retaliate for noncooperative behavior that often forces a firm to cooperate. With a tit-for-tat strategy, however, it is possible for firms to cooperate without actually resorting to collusion. As we will see in the next chapter, this can be a nightmare for antitrust officials.

11.5 STRATEGIC MOVES

In this section, we examine strategic games involving threats, commitments, credibility, and entry deterrence. In the next section, we discuss strategic games and international competitiveness. These concepts greatly enrich game theory and provide an important element of realism and relevance.

Threats, Commitments, and Credibility

Oligopolistic firms often adopt strategies to gain a competitive advantage over their rivals, even if it means constraining their own behavior or temporarily reducing their own profits. For example, an oligopolist may threaten to lower its prices if its rivals lower theirs, even if this means reducing its own profits. This threat can be made credible, for example, by a written commitment to customers to match any lower price by competitors. Schelling defined such a **strategic move** as one that "influences the other person's choice in a manner favorable to one's self by affecting the other person's expectations of how one's self would behave."[6] There must be a *commitment* that the firm making the *threat* is ready to carry it out for the threat to be *credible*.

For example, suppose that the payoff matrix of firms A and B is given by Table 11–5. This payoff matrix indicates that firm A has the dominant strategy of charging a high price. The reason is that if firm B charged a low price, firm A would earn a profit of 2 if it charged a low price and a profit of 3 if it charged a high price. Similarly, if firm B charged a high price, firm A would earn a profit of 2 if it charged a low price and a profit of 5 if it charged a high price. Therefore, firm A charges a high price regardless of what firm B does. Given that firm A charges a high price, firm B will want to charge a low price because by doing so it will earn a profit of 4 (instead of 2 with a high price).

---

[6]See, T. Schelling, *The Strategy of Conflict* (New York: Oxford University Press, 1960). Another important volume examining strategic moves is M. Porter, *Competitive Strategy* (New York: Free Press, 1980).

TABLE 11–5   Payoff Matrix for Pricing Game with a Threat

		Firm B	
		Low Price	High Price
Firm A	Low Price	2,2	2,1
	High Price	3,4	5,3

This is shown by the bottom left cell of Table 11–5. Now firm A can threaten to lower its price and also charge a low price. However, firm B does not believe this threat (i.e., the threat is not credible) because by lowering its price firm A would lower its profits from 3 (with a high price) to 2 with the low price (the top left cell in the table).

One way to make its threat credible is for firm A to develop a *reputation* for carrying out its threats, even at the expense of its profits. Does this seem irrational? If firm A actually carries out its threat several times, it would earn a reputation for making credible threats. This is likely to induce firm B to also charge a high price, which would possibly lead to higher profits for firm A in the long run. In that case, firm A would earn a profit of 5 and firm B a profit of 3 (the bottom right cell) as opposed to a profit of 3 for firm A and 4 for firm B (the bottom left cell). Even if firm B earns a profit of 3 by charging the high price (as compared with a profit of 4 by charging the low price), the profit is still higher than the profit of 2 that it would earn if firm A carries out the threat of charging the low price if firm B does (see the top left cell of the table). By showing a commitment to carry out its threats, firm A makes its threats credible and increases its profits over time. The same result would follow if firm A develops a reputation for being irrational and charging a low price to deter entry even if this means lower profits in the long run.

Entry Deterrence

One important strategy that an oligopolist can use to deter market entry is to threaten to lower its price and thereby impose a loss on the potential entrant. Such a threat, however, works only if it is credible. *Entry deterrence* can be examined with the payoff matrices of Tables 11–6 and 11–7.

The payoff matrix of Table 11–6 shows that firm A's threat to lower its price is not credible and does not discourage firm B from entering the market. The reason is that firm A earns a profit of 4 if it charges the low price and a profit of 7 if it charges the high price. Unless firm A makes a credible commitment to fight entry even at the expense of profits, it would not deter firm B from entering the market. Firm A could make a credible threat by expanding its capacity before it is needed (i.e., to build excess capacity). The new payoff matrix might then look like the one in Table 11–7.

TABLE 11–6   Payoff Matrix without Credible Entry Deterrence

		Firm B	
		Enter	Don't Enter
Firm A	**Low Price**	4, −2	6,0
	High Price	7, 2	10,0

The payoff matrix of Table 11–7 is the same as in Table 11–6, except that firm A's profits are now lower when it charges a high price because idle or excess capacity increases firm A's costs without increasing its sales. On the other hand, in the payoff matrix of Table 11–7, we assume that charging a low price would allow firm A to increase sales and utilize its newly built capacity, so that costs and revenues *increase* leaving firm A's profits the same as in Table 11–6 (i.e., the same as before firm A expanded capacity).[7] Building excess capacity in anticipation of future need now becomes a credible threat, because with excess capacity firm A will charge a low price and earn a profit of 4 instead of a profit of 3 if it charged the high price. By now charging a low price, however, firm B would incur a loss of 2 if it entered the market, and so firm B would stay out. Entry deterrence is now credible and effective. An alternative to building excess capacity could be for firm A to cultivate a reputation for irrationality in deterring entry by charging a low price even if this means earning lower profits indefinitely.[8]

TABLE 11–7   Payoff Matrix with Credible Entry Deterrence

		Firm B	
		Enter	Don't Enter
Firm A	**Low Price**	4, −2	6,0
	High Price	3, 2	8,0

---

[7]Revenues and profits need not increase exactly by the same amount, so that profits can change even when firm A charges a low price. The conclusion would remain the same, however (i.e., firm B would be deterred from entering the market) as long as firm A earns a higher profit with a low price than with a high price after increasing its capacity.

[8]For a more detailed analysis of the use of excess capacity to deter entry, see J. Tirole, *The Theory of Industrial Organization* (Cambridge, Mass.: MIT Press, 1988).

▽ **Example 4**
Wal-Mart's Preemptive Expansion Marketing Strategy

Rapid expansion during the 1980s (from 153 stores in 1976 to 1,738 at the beginning of 1993) propelled Wal-Mart, the chain of discount retail stores started by Sam Walton in 1969, to become the nation's largest and most profitable retailer at a time when most other retailers were making razor-thin profits or incurring losses as a result of stiff competition. How did Wal-Mart do it? By opening discount retail stores in small towns across America and adopting an every-day low-price strategy.

The conventional wisdom had been that a discount retail outlet required a population base of at least 100,000 people to be profitable. Sam Walton showed otherwise. By relying on size, low costs, and high turnover, Wal-Mart earned high profits even in towns of only a few thousand people. Since a small town could only support one large discount store, Wal-Mart did not have to worry about competition from other national chains (which would drive prices and profit margins down). At the same time, Wal-Mart was able to easily undersell small, local, specialized stores out of existence (Wal-Mart has been labeled the "merchant of death" by local retailers), thereby establishing a virtual local retailing monopoly.

The success of Wal-Mart did not go unnoticed by other national discount retailers such as K-Mart and Target, and so a frantic race to open discount stores in rural America ahead of the competition was started. By adopting such an aggressive expansion or *preemptive investment strategy*, Wal-Mart was able to expand at breathtaking speed and beat the competition. Sales at Wal-Mart reached $26 billion in 1992 and are projected to surpass $100 billion by the turn of the century. As Wal-Mart expands to suburban areas and as a revitalized K-Mart and Target push into rural areas, however, the paths of these mammoth chains are likely to cross more frequently across America in what promises to be some of retailing's fiercest fights.

Sources: "3 Discounters on a Collision Course," *New York Times*, September 23, 1991, p. D1; "Can Wal-Mart Keep Growing at Breakneck Speed?" *New York Times*, August 9, 1992, p. F5; and "Wal-Mart," *New York Times*, November 17, 1992, p. D4.

▲

11.6 STRATEGIC MOVES AND INTERNATIONAL COMPETITIVENESS

Game theory is also applicable to strategic trade and industrial policies that a nation could use to gain a competitive advantage over other nations, particularly in the field of high technology. This is best shown through an example.

Suppose that Boeing (the American commercial aircraft company) and Airbus Industrie (a consortium of German, French, English, and Spanish compa-

TABLE 11–8   Two-Firm Competition and Strategic Trade Policy

		Airbus	
		Produce	Don't Produce
Boeing	**Produce**	−10, −10	100, 0
	Don't Produce	0, 100	0, 0

nies) are both deciding whether to produce a new aircraft. Suppose also that because of the huge cost of developing the new aircraft, a single producer would have to have the entire world market for itself to earn a profit, say of $100 million. If both firms produce the aircraft, each loses $10 million. This information is shown in Table 11–8. The case in which both firms produce the aircraft and each incurs a loss of $10 million is shown in the top left cell of the table. If only Boeing produces the aircraft, Boeing makes a profit of $100 million while Airbus makes a zero profit (the top right cell of the table). On the other hand, if Boeing does not produce the aircraft while Airbus does, Boeing makes zero profit while Airbus makes a profit of $100 million (the bottom left cell). Finally, if neither firm produces the aircraft, each makes a zero profit (the bottom right cell).

Suppose that for whatever reason, Boeing enters the market first and earns a profit of $100 million (we might call this the first-mover advantage). Airbus is now locked out of the market because it could not earn a profit. This is the case shown in the top right cell of the table. If Airbus entered the market, both firms would incur a loss (and we would have the case shown in the top left column of the table). Suppose now that European governments give a subsidy of $15 million per year to Airbus. Airbus would then produce the aircraft even though Boeing is already producing the aircraft, because with the $15 million subsidy, Airbus would turn a loss of $10 million into a profit of $5 million. Without a subsidy, however, Boeing will go from making a profit of $100 million (without Airbus in the market) to incurring a loss of $10 million afterwards (we are still in the top left corner of the table, but with the Airbus entry changed from −10 without the subsidy to +5 with the subsidy). Because of its unsubsidized loss, Boeing will stop producing the aircraft, thereby leaving the entire market to Airbus, which will make a profit of $100 million without any further subsidy (the bottom left cell of the table).[9]

The U.S. government could, of course, retaliate with a subsidy of its own to keep Boeing producing the aircraft. Except in cases of national defense,

---

[9]This type of analysis was first introduced into international trade by J. Brander and B. Spencer. See their "International R & D Rivalry and Industrial Strategy," *Review of Economic Studies*, October 1983, pp. 707–722. See also, M. Porter, *The Competitive Advantage of Nations* (New York: The Free Press, 1990).

however, the U.S. government is much less disposed to grant subsidies to firms than European governments. Although the real world is certainly much more complex than this example, we can see how a nation could overcome a market disadvantage and acquire a strategic comparative advantage in a high-tech field by means of an industrial and strategic trade policy. In fact, Airbus is now exploring the possibility of developing an aircraft capable of carrying 500 to 600 passengers, which would compete head on with the Boeing 747 (which can carry up to 475 passengers). For its part, the United States is lobbying the governments of France, Germany, England, and Spain to sharply reduce development subsidies to Airbus (which, over the past decade amounted to more than $26 billion dollars). Boeing, however, continued to earn high profits even as it lost market share to Airbus.[10]

One serious shortcoming of our analysis is that it is usually very difficult to accurately forecast the outcome of government industrial and trade policies (i.e., get the data to fill a table such as Table 11–8). Even a small change in the table could completely change the results. For example, suppose that if both Airbus and Boeing produce the aircraft, Airbus incurs a loss of $10 million (as before) but Boeing makes a profit of $10 million (without any subsidy), say because of superior technology. Then, even if Airbus produces the aircraft with the subsidy, Boeing will remain in the market because it is able to earn a profit without any subsidy. Since Airbus would require a subsidy indefinitely year after year to continue to produce the aircraft, giving it a subsidy does not seem to be such a good idea. The difficulties in correctly carrying out this type of analysis are apparent. We would have to be able to forecast the precise outcome of different strategies, and that is extremely difficult to do. This is why most U.S. economists are wary of supporting the adoption of a full-fledged industrial policy and still regard free trade as the best policy for the United States.[11]

SUMMARY

1. Game theory is concerned with the choice of an optimal strategy in conflict situations. Every game theory model includes players, strategies, and payoffs. The players are the decision-makers (here, the managers of oligopolist firms) whose behavior we are trying to explain and predict. The strategies are the potential choices that can be made by the players (firms). The payoff is the outcome or consequence of each combination of strategies by the two players. The payoff matrix refers to all the outcomes of the players' strategies.

2. The dominant strategy is the optimal

---

[10]See, "Will Boeing Build a Behemoth to Defend Its Turf?" *Business Week*, August 19, 1991, pp. 28–30; "Airbus Takes Off," *Fortune*, June 1, 1992, pp. 102–108; and "Now Airbus Is Cruising Comfortably," *Business Week*, July 27, 1992, p. 33.

[11]See, "Industrial Policy," *Business Week*, April 6, 1992, pp. 70–78; "U.S. Industrial Policy: Inevitable and Ineffective," *Harvard Business Review*, July-August 1992, pp. 104–112; and P. Krugman, "Is Free Trade Passe?" *The Journal of Economic Perspectives*, Fall 1987, pp. 131–144.

choice for a player, no matter what the opponent does. The Nash equilibrium occurs when each player has chosen his or her optimal strategy, *given the strategy chosen by the other player*. The Cournot solution is an example of a Nash equilibrium. Not all games have a Nash equilibrium and some games have more than one.

3. Oligopolistic firms often face a problem called the prisoners' dilemma. This refers to a situation in which each firm adopts its dominant strategy but could do better (i.e., earn larger profit) by cooperating. Oligopolistic firms deciding on their pricing or advertising strategy, or on whether to cheat on a cartel face the prisoners' dilemma.

4. The best strategy for repeated or multiple-move prisoners' dilemma games is tit-for-tat. This strategy postulates that each firm should start by cooperating and continue to do so as long as the rival cooperates; the firm should stop cooperating once the rival stops cooperating.

5. Oligopolists often make strategic moves. A strategic move is one in which a player constrains its own behavior in order to make a threat credible so as to gain a competitive advantage over a rival. The firm making the threat must be committed to carrying it out for the threat to be credible. This may involve accepting lower profits or building excess capacity.

6. Just like firms, nations can make strategic moves, such as subsidizing and providing export subsidies to a high-tech industry or adopting an industrial policy for the entire nation, to gain a competitive advantage over other nations. Industrial policies can also lead to waste, however, if industries that are subsidized or otherwise supported do not become internationally competitive.

KEY TERMS

Game Theory

Players

Strategies

Payoff

Payoff Matrix

Dominant Strategy

Nash Equilibrium

Prisoners' Dilemma

Repeated Games

Tit-for-Tat

Strategic Move

REVIEW QUESTIONS

1. In what way does game theory extend the analysis of oligopolistic behavior presented in Chapter 10?

2. a. Can game theory be used only for oligopolistic interdependence?
   b. In what way is game theory similar to playing chess?

3. Do we have a Nash equilibrium when each firm chooses its dominant strategy?

4. a. Why is the Cournot equilibrium a Nash equilibrium?
   b. In what way does the Cournot equilibrium differ from the Nash equilibrium given in Table 11–2?

5. In what way is the prisoners' dilemma related to the choice of dominant strategies by the players in a game and to the concept of Nash equilibrium?

6. How can the concept of the prisoners' dilemma be used to analyze price competition?

7. How can introducing yearly style changes lead to a prisoners' dilemma for automakers?

8. a. What is the incentive for the members of a cartel to cheat on the cartel?
   b. What can the cartel do to prevent cheating?
   c. Under what conditions is a cartel more likely to collapse?

9. Do the duopolists in a Cournot equilibrium face a prisoners' dilemma? Explain.

10. How did the 1971 law that banned cigarette

advertising on television solve the prisoners' dilemma for cigarette producers?

11. a. What is the meaning of "tit-for-tat" in game theory?
    b. What conditions are usually required for tit-for-tat strategy to be the best strategy?

12. a. How is a strategic move differentiated from a Nash equilibrium?
    b. What is a credible threat? When is a threat not credible?

PROBLEMS

1. From the following payoff matrix, where the payoffs are the profits or losses of the two firms, determine
   a. whether firm A has a dominant strategy.
   b. whether firm B has a dominant strategy.
   c. the optimal strategy for each firm.

		Firm B	
		Low Price	High Price
Firm A	Low Price	1,1	3, −1
	High Price	−1,3	2, 2

2. From the following payoff matrix, where the payoffs are the profits or losses of the two firms, determine
   a. whether firm A has a dominant strategy.
   b. whether firm B has a dominant strategy.
   c. the optimal strategy for each firm.
   d. the Nash equilibrium, if there is one.

		Firm B	
		Low Price	High Price
Firm A	Low Price	1,1	3, −1
	High Price	−1,3	4, 2

*3. From the following payoff matrix, where the payoffs are the profits or losses of the two firms, determine
   a. whether firm A has a dominant strategy.
   b. whether firm B has a dominant strategy.
   c. the optimal strategy for each firm.
   d. the Nash equilibrium.
   e. under what conditions is the situation indicated in the payoff matrix likely to occur?

		Firm B	
		Small Cars	Large Cars
Firm A	Large Cars	4, 4	−2, −2
	Small Cars	−2, −2	4, 4

*4. Provide a hypothetical payoff matrix for example 2 in this chapter.

5. From the following payoff matrix, where the payoffs (the negative values) are the years of possible imprisonment for individuals A and B, determine
   a. whether individual A has a dominant strategy.
   b. whether individual B has a dominant strategy.
   c. the optimal strategy for each individual.
   d. Do individuals A and B face a prisoners' dilemma?

		Individual B	
		Confess	Don't Confess
Individual A	Confess	−5, −5	−1, −10
	Don't Confess	−10, −1	−2, −2

6. Explain why the payoff matrix in problem 1 indicates that firms A and B face the prisoners' dilemma.

7. Do firms A and B in problem 2 face the prisoners' dilemma? Why?

*8. From the following payoff matrix, where the

---

* = Answer provided at end of book.

payoffs refer to the profits that firms A and B earn by cheating and not cheating in a cartel,
a. determine whether firms A and B face the prisoners' dilemma.
b. What would happen if we changed the payoff in bottom left cell to (5,5)?

		Firm B	
		Cheat	Don't Cheat
Firm A	Cheat	4,3	8,1
	Don't Cheat	2,6	6,5

*9. Starting with the payoff matrix of problem 1, show what the tit-for-tat strategy would be for the first five of an infinite number of games if firm A starts by cooperating but firm B does not cooperate in the next period.

10. Given the following payoff matrix
a. indicate the best strategy for each firm.
b. Why is the entry-deterrent threat by firm A to lower price not credible to firm B?

c. What could firm A do to make its threat credible without building excess capacity?

		Firm B	
		Enter	Don't Enter
Firm A	Low Price	3, −1	3,1
	High Price	4, 5	6,3

11. Show how the payoff matrix in the table of problem 10 might change for firm A to make a credible threat to lower price by building excess capacity to deter firm B from entering the market.

12. What strategic industrial or trade policy would be required (if any) in the United States and in Europe if the entries in the top left cell of the payoff matrix in Table 11–8 were changed to
a. 10,10?
b. 5,0?
c. 5, −10?

MARKET STRUCTURE, EFFICIENCY, AND REGULATION

"People of the same trade seldom meet together, even for merriment and diversion, but the conversation ends in a conspiracy against the public, or in some contrivance to raise prices."[1] This is one of the most famous quotations in economics, and it is as relevant today as two centuries ago when it was written. It explains in a nutshell why we are so interested in market structure, efficiency, antitrust, and regulation. In this chapter, we examine the relationship between market structure and efficiency, antitrust, and regulation. We begin by reviewing the reason that inefficiency and social costs arise in imperfect markets. We then consider how to measure market imperfections and ways to minimize, prevent, or overcome (through antitrust and regulation) the most serious social costs that arise from those market imperfections. The examples and applications in the chapter show the importance of the theory and its uses.

12.1 MARKET STRUCTURE AND EFFICIENCY

The concept and measure of **efficiency** as well as the need for antitrust and regulation are based on marginal analysis. Specifically, we have seen in previous chapters that the best level of output for a firm under any form of market organization (be it perfect competition, monopoly, monopolistic competition, or oligopoly) is where marginal revenue equals marginal cost. If marginal revenue exceeds marginal cost, it pays for the firm to expand output because by doing so the firm will add more to its total revenue than to its total costs. On the other hand, if marginal cost exceeds marginal revenue, it pays for the firm to reduce output because by doing so its total costs will decline more than its total revenue. Thus, the best level of output is where marginal revenue equals marginal cost.

---

[1]A. Smith, *The Wealth of Nations* (Toronto: Random House Edition, 1937), p. 128.

Chapter 8 showed that a perfectly competitive firm faces an infinitely elastic demand curve and so price equals marginal revenue. Thus, at the best level of output, $P = MR = MC$. Since price measures the marginal benefit that consumers receive for the last unit of the commodity consumed, at the output where $MR = MC$, the marginal benefit to consumers equals the marginal cost to producers under perfect competition. If less of the commodity is produced, $P = MR > MC$, so that consumers' satisfaction would increase if firms produced more of the commodity. On the other hand, if more of the commodity is produced, $P = MR < MC$. This means that consumers would benefit if some inputs were shifted to the production of some other commodity. Thus, application of the $P = MR = MC$ rule by the firm leads to the highest consumer satisfaction when all markets are perfectly competitive. As pointed out in Figure 8–9, in long-run perfectly competitive equilibrium, consumers can purchase the commodity at the lowest possible price (i.e., at $P =$ lowest LAC).

In imperfectly competitive markets (monopoly, monopolistic competition, and oligopoly), however, the firm faces a negatively sloped demand curve, and so price exceeds marginal revenue. Thus, at the best level of output $P > MR = MC$. This means that the marginal benefit to consumers from the last unit of the commodity consumed exceeds the marginal cost that the firm incurs in producing it. Consumers want more of the commodity than is available, but producers have no incentive to produce more. As a result, consumers' satisfaction is not maximized. Furthermore, imperfect competitors do not usually produce at the lowest point on their LAC curve when in long-run equilibrium, and (except for monopolistic competitors) the price that they charge for the commodity may also include a profit margin. The social cost resulting when a constant-cost perfectly competitive industry is suddenly monopolized was shown in Figure 9–7. In the real world, we seldom if ever have (unregulated) monopoly, but firms in various industries have various degrees of monopoly power. Thus, it becomes important to examine ways to measure the degree of monopoly power in order to assess the social costs resulting from it. This topic is explored in section 12.2. Section 12.3 then compares the social costs with the alleged dynamic benefits of monopoly power.

In many industries, however, technological conditions require such a large scale of production (to take advantage of economies of scale) that only one firm (natural monopoly) or a handful of firms (oligopoly) arise. For example, it would be wasteful to have more than one local telephone or electrical company (duplicating transmission lines would be very costly indeed), and it would be inconceivable and highly inefficient to have numerous small producers of automobiles, steel, aircraft, and many other products. In the case of oligopolies, the government usually relies on the enforcement of anti-trust laws aimed at attaining some degree of workable competition. This is examined in section 12.4. In the case of natural monopoly, on the other hand, the single firm is usually allowed to operate, but with the government regulating the price and the quality of service. This is examined in section 12.5. The rest of the chapter deals with the deregulation movement, the

TABLE 12–1 Comparison of Market Structures

Type of Market	Number of Firms	Type of Product	Conditions of Entry	Firm's Influence over Price	Interdependence Among Firms	Examples
Perfect competition	Many	Homogeneous	Easy	None	None	Some agricultural products and stock market
Monopolistic competition	Many	Differentiated	Easy	Little	None	Some retail trade and services
Oligopoly	Few	Homogeneous or differentiated	Difficult	Considerable	A great deal	Steel, automobiles
Monopoly	One	No good substitutes	Difficult or impossible	Substantial	No direct competitor	Local telephone service

regulation of international competition, and price regulation. Table 12–1 summarizes and compares the various types of market structure that we have examined in previous chapters, from perfect competition to monopoly.

12.2 MEASURING MONOPOLY POWER

In this section, we first define the Lerner index as a measure of the degree of a *firm's* monopoly power and the Herfindahl index as a measure of the degree of monopoly power in an *industry*. We then discuss how effective competition can occur even when there are only a few firms, according to the contestable market theory.

The Lerner Index as a Measure of Monopoly Power

We have seen in Chapter 8 that $P = MR = MC$ for a perfectly competitive firm but $P > MR = MC$ for an imperfectly competitive firm (i.e., for a monopolistic competitor, oligopolist, or monopolist). The greater is the degree of monopoly power that a firm has, the more inelastic is the demand curve for the product that it faces, and so the larger is the degree by which the commodity price exceeds the firm's marginal revenue and marginal cost. Thus, one way of measuring monopoly power is by the **Lerner index.** This is given by the ratio of the difference between price and marginal cost to price, as shown by formula [12–1].[2]

$$L = \frac{P - MC}{P} \qquad \text{[12–1]}$$

The Lerner index can have a value between zero and one. For a perfectly

[2]A. P. Lerner, "The Concept of Monopoly and the Measurement of Monopoly Power," *Review of Economic Studies*, June 1934, pp. 157–175.

competitive firm, $P = MC$ and $L = 0$. On the other hand, the more price exceeds marginal cost (i.e., the greater is the degree of monopoly power), the more the value of L approaches the value of one.

The Lerner index can also be expressed in terms of the price elasticity of the demand curve facing the firm. We can see this as follows. Since at the best level of output $MR = MC$, we can substitute MR for MC in [12–1]. But from [5–6], we know that $MR = P(1 - 1/\eta)$, where η is the absolute value of the price elasticity of demand. Substituting this value of MR for MC in [12–1], we get

$$L = \frac{P - P(1 - 1/\eta)}{P}$$

Simplifying, we get

$$L = 1/\eta \qquad \qquad [12\text{–}2]$$

For a perfectly competitive firm, $\eta = \infty$ and $L = 0$. The fewer and the more imperfect are the substitutes available for the firm's product (i.e., the smaller is the value of η), the larger is the value of L. For example, if $\eta = 4$, $L = 0.25$, but if $\eta = 2$, $L = 0.5$. Note that a high value for L (implying a great deal of monopoly power) is not necessarily associated with high profits for the firm, because profits refer to the excess of price over *average* cost, and average costs can be high or low in relation to the commodity price at the output level where $MR = MC$ (see problem 2, with answer at end of book).

Some difficulties may arise, however, in using the Lerner index. For example, a firm with a great deal of monopoly power may keep its price low to avoid legal scrutiny or to deter entry into the industry (limit pricing). Furthermore, the Lerner index is applicable in a static context, but it is not very useful in a dynamic context when the firm's demand and cost functions shift over time.

Concentration and Monopoly Power: The Herfindahl Index

One method of estimating the degree of monopoly power *in an industry as a whole* is by the **Herfindahl index** (named after Orris Herfindahl, who introduced it). This is given by the sum of the squared values of the market sales shares of all the firms in the industry, as shown by

$$H = S_1^2 + S_2^2 + \ldots S_N^2 \qquad \qquad [12\text{–}3]$$

where S_1 is the market sales share of the largest firm in the industry, S_2 is the market sales share of the second largest firm in the industry, and so on, in such a way that the sum of the market sales shares of all firms in the industry total 1 or 100%. In general, the greater is the value of the Herfindahl index, the greater is the degree of monopoly power in the industry.

For example, if we have a monopoly or a single firm in the industry, so that its market share is 100%, $H = (100)^2 = 10,000$. On the other hand, if there are 1,000 equal-sized firms in the (competitive) industry, each with 0.1% of the market, $H = 1,000(0.1)^2 = 10$. If there are 100 equal-sized firms in the

TABLE 12–2   Herfindahl Index for Selected U.S. Industries in 1987

Industry	Index*
Food and kindred products	68
Industrial machinery and equipment	70
Leather and leather products	95
Textile mill products	113
Primary metal industries	121
Electronic and other electric equipment	129
Paper and allied products	172
Petroleum and coal products	375
Transport equipment	1,044
Tobacco products	2,345

Source: U.S. Bureau of Census, 1987 Census of Manufacturers, *Concentration Ratios in Manufacturing* (Washington, D.C.: U.S. Government Printing Office, 1992).
*Index refers only to the largest 50 firms in each industry.

(still competitive) industry, each with 1% of the market, $H = 100$. For an industry with 10 equal-sized firms, each with 10% market share, $H = 1,000$. But for an industry with 11 firms, one with 50% market share and the other ten firms with 5% market share each, $H = 2,750$. This points to the advantage of the Herfindahl index over the concentration ratios discussed in section 10.3. The Herfindahl index uses all the information and takes into account the size distribution of firms. Specifically, by squaring the market share of each firm, the Herfindahl index gives a much larger weight to larger than to smaller firms in the industry.

The Herfindahl index has become of great practical importance since 1982 when the Justice Department announced new guidelines (revised in 1984) for evaluating proposed mergers based on this index. According to these guidelines, if the postmerger Herfindahl index is 1,000 or less, the industry is regarded as relatively unconcentrated and a merger is unchallenged. On the other hand, an industry where the postmerger Herfindahl index is greater than 1,800 is regarded as highly concentrated and a merger is likely to be challenged (the full set of guidelines is given in section 12.4). Table 12–2 shows the Herfindahl index (for the 50 largest rather than for all firms) in each of a selected number of industries in the United States in 1987. The table shows that for some industries, such as food and kindred products, the Herfindahl index is very low; but for others, such as tobacco products, the Herfindahl index is very high.

Just as with concentration ratios, however, the Herfindahl index must be used with caution. First, in industries (such as automobiles) where imports are significant, the Herfindahl index greatly overestimates the relative importance of concentration in the domestic industry. Indeed, Raymond Vernon found that the Herfindahl index for the *world* automobiles, petroleum, aluminum-smelting, and pulp-and-paper industries declined sharply from 1950 to 1970, pointing to sharply increased international competition at home.[3] Second, the Herfindahl index for the nation as a whole may not be relevant when the market is local (as in the case of cement where transportation costs are very high). Third, how broadly or narrowly a product is defined is also very important. Fourth, the Herfindahl index does not give any indication of potential entrants into the market and of the degree of actual and potential competition in the industry. Indeed, as the *theory of contestable markets* discussed next shows, vigorous competition can take place even among few sellers.

Contestable Markets: Effective Competition Even with Few Firms

According to the **theory of contestable markets** developed during the 1980s, even if an industry has a single firm (monopoly) or only a few firms (oligopoly), it would still operate as if it were perfectly competitive if entry is "absolutely free" (i.e., if other firms can enter the industry and face exactly the same costs as existing firms) and if exit is "entirely costless" (i.e., if there are no sunk costs so that the firm can exit the industry without facing any loss of capital).[4] An example might be an airline that establishes a service between two cities already served by other airlines, *if* the new entrant faces the same costs as existing airlines and could subsequently leave the market by simply reassigning its planes to other routes without incurring any loss of capital.

When entry is absolutely free and exit is entirely costless, the market is contestable. Firms will then operate as if they were perfectly competitive and sell at a price that only covers their average costs (so that they earn zero economic profit) even if there is only one firm or a few of them in the market. In this view, competition within the market is less important than the potential competition for the market. This can be seen in Figure 12–1.

In Figure 12–1, D is the market demand curve, and AC and MC are the average and marginal cost curves, respectively, of each of two identical firms in the market. If the market is contestable (i.e., if entry is absolutely free and exit is entirely costless), each firm will sell 60 units of output at $P = AC = MC = \$6$ (point E in the figure) and behave as a perfect competitor facing horizontal demand curve AEE' and earn zero economic profits. The duopolists will not collude to charge a higher price and earn profits because they know that other firms would quickly enter the market and sell at a slightly lower price. This would lower price to equal marginal cost at the lowest average cost and quickly eliminate all profits. This is true whether the potential entrants are domestic or foreign.

---

[3]R. Vernon, "Competition Policy Toward Multinational Corporations," *American Economic Review*, May 1974, pp. 276–282.

[4]See, W. J. Baumol, "Contestable Markets: An Uprising in the Theory of Industrial Structure," *American Economic Review*, March 1982, pp. 1–5.

FIGURE 12–1   Two Firms in a Contestable Market

D is the market demand curve, and AC and MC are the average and marginal cost curves, respectively, of each of two identical firms in a contestable market. Each firm will sell 60 units of output at $P = AC = MC = \$6$ (point E in the figure) and behave as a perfect competitor facing horizontal demand curve AEE' and earn zero economic profits. Any higher price invites hit-and-run entrants.

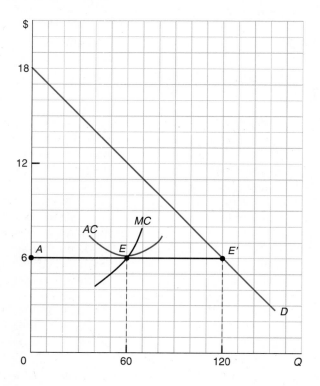

The theory of contestable markets is similar to limit pricing (discussed in section 10.7). With limit pricing, a firm charges a lower-than-the-profit-maximizing price to discourage potential entrants into the market. But whereas profits can still be earned (even though they are not maximized) with limit pricing (because the market is not entirely contestable), economic profits are zero in a contestable market because entry is absolutely free and exit is entirely costless. Even purely transitory profits will not be disregarded but result in entry-exit or hit-and-run behavior on the part of potential entrants into the industry until all profit opportunities are entirely exhausted.

The extreme assumptions on which the theory of contestable markets is based have been sharply criticized as unrealistic. That is, entry is seldom if ever absolutely free and exit is seldom if ever entirely costless in the real world, and so the theory is thought to be of limited applicability and usefulness.[5] Nevertheless, we have seen in section 1.5 that a hypothesis need not be based on entirely realistic assumptions to be acceptable and useful. Thus, the theory of contestable markets can still be acceptable and useful even if entry into and exit from the industry are only reasonably easy rather than absolutely free and costless. Perhaps the importance of the theory lies more in cautioning us against uncritically accepting the view that a market with only one or a few firms must necessarily be noncompetitive and in suggesting that easy entry and exit can severely limit the exercise of monopoly power in contestable markets.

Functioning of Markets and Experimental Economics

During the past two decades, some economists have been conducting experiments to determine how markets actually work in the real world.[6] The experiments are conducted with volunteers, often college students, who are provided money to buy and sell a fictitious commodity within a simple specified institutional framework. The participants are allowed to keep some of the money that they earn by acting in an economically rational way. For example, participants are allowed to retain the profit from buying the commodity at a lower price from the experimenter or from other participants and reselling it at a higher price to others in the simulated market. These experiments are part of the fast-growing field of **experimental economics,** which has already provided very interesting results.

In a simple experiment, it was shown that under certain conditions, the commodity price quickly converges to the equilibrium price even when there are only a few buyers and sellers of the commodity. This would seem to confirm the conclusion of the theory of contestable markets, but from a completely different approach. Whereas the theory of contestable markets reached this conclusion in a purely deductive manner, experimental economics reaches the same conclusion by pure empirical evidence within a simple experimental framework. The results seem to suggest that the perfectly competitive model may have much wider applicability than previously thought. This would go a long way toward overcoming the problems arising from the indeterminacy of oligopoly theory. It is, however, too early to know how widely acceptable and influential both the theory of contestable markets and experimental economics will be in the future.

In one experiment, Vernon Smith handed out several thousand dollars of

---

[5]W. G. Shepherd, "Contestability vs. Competition," *American Economic Review*, September 1984, pp. 572–587.

[6]See, V. L. Smith, "Theory, Experiment and Economics," *The Journal of Economic Perspectives*, Winter 1989, pp. 151–170, and C. R. Plott, "Industrial Organization and Experimental Economics," *Journal of Economic Literature*, December 1982, pp. 1485–1527.

his own money to a group of students participating in a simulated stock market study, which provided some interesting results.[7] One is that stock market or speculative "bubbles" occur regularly within the experimental framework. Traders seem to be carried away in a rising market and continue to bid stock prices up far past the expected dividend and price-earnings ratio of the stock—inevitably leading to an eventual crash. Despite the very simple setting in which these experiments were conducted, their outcome closely mimics the actual stock market crash of 1987. Only after the participants have been through several boom-bust cycles do bubbles seem to disappear. As time passes, however, and the busts fade in investors' memories, great volatility in stock prices reappears.

In an attempt to eliminate the bubbles, Smith modified the experiment by adding futures trading (i.e., agreements to purchase or sell a stock at a specified price for delivery at a specified future time), margin buying (i.e., requiring a down payment when buying a stock on credit), and rules to stop trading when the market falls by a specified percentage. Smith's experiments showed that imposing limits on price declines only postpones the crash and makes it deeper when it comes. Only the availability of futures trading seemed to reduce the size and duration of speculative bubbles. These experimental results could have important practical implications in devising regulations to make the stock market less volatile in the real world. Remember, however, that experimental economics is still in its infancy, and many economists remain skeptical of the real-world usefulness of results obtained in simplistic institutional settings and of their applicability in devising regulatory policies in the real world. The number of converts is growing, however, and the field has boomed in recent years.[8] Most economists seem to be watching hopefully from the sidelines.

12.3 SOCIAL COSTS AND DYNAMIC BENEFITS OF MONOPOLY POWER

We have seen before that in imperfectly competitive markets the best level of output is where $P > MR = MC$. This means that the marginal benefit to consumers (as measured by the commodity price) from the last unit of the commodity consumed exceeds the marginal cost that the firm incurs in producing it. Consumers want more of the commodity than is available, but producers have no incentive to produce more. The social cost resulting when a constant-cost perfectly competitive industry is suddenly monopolized was shown by triangle REM in Figure 9–7. It was also pointed out in section 9.3 that there are other losses or social costs resulting from monopoly power. The first of these is that monopolists do not have much incentive to keep their costs as

---

[7]R. Bailey, "The Economists' New Guinea Pigs," *Forbes*, November 13, 1989, pp. 148, 152.

[8]See, C. R. Plott, "Will Economics Become an Experimental Science?" *Southern Economic Journal*, April 1991, pp. 901–919.

low as possible and prefer instead the quiet life (X-inefficiency).[9] Second, monopolists waste a lot of resources lobbying and engaging in legal battles to avoid or defend themselves against regulation and antitrust prosecution, installing excess capacity to discourage entry, and advertising in the attempt to create and retain the monopoly power (i.e., engaging in rent-seeking activities). Some economists believe that these other social costs of monopoly are larger than those measured by the welfare triangle *REM* in Figure 9–7, but, as pointed out in section 9.3, there is disagreement on the exact size of these social costs.[10]

Measuring the social costs of imperfect competition by comparing it with perfect competition begs the question, however, because the need for large-scale production often precludes the existence of perfect competition. We could not, for example, produce steel, automobiles, aluminum, aircraft, and most industrial products with numerous firms under perfect competition—except at exorbitant costs. The benefits that would result if cost conditions made perfect competition possible are thus irrelevant in these cases. Furthermore, there are many alleged benefits that result from large firm size (i.e., with firms with monopoly power) that just would not be possible under perfect competition. These were emphasized by Schumpeter 50 years ago and remain very controversial today.[11]

According to Schumpeter and others, perfect competition is not the market structure most conducive to long-run growth through technological change and innovations. Since long-run profits tend toward zero in perfectly competitive markets, firms will not have the necessary resources to undertake sufficient R&D to maximize growth. Furthermore, with free entry under perfect competition, a firm introducing a cost-reducing innovation or a new product would quickly lose its source of profits through imitation. Thus, Schumpeter argued that large firms with some degree of monopoly power are essential to provide the financial resources required for R&D and to protect the resulting source of profits. Although monopoly leads to some inefficiency at one point in time (static inefficiency), over time, it is likely to lead to much more technological change and innovation (dynamic efficiency) than perfect competition.[12]

---

[9]See, H. Leibenstein, "Allocative Efficiency vs. X-Inefficiency," *American Economic Review*, June 1966, pp. 392–415.

[10]The charge often heard that monopolists suppress inventions (e.g., that they would avoid introducing a longer-lasting light bulb) is not correct, however, since consumers would be willing to pay a higher price for such light bulbs and this could lead to higher profits for the monopolist. Only if the monopolist believed that the invention could not be patented and that this would result in loss of monopoly power, would the monopolist suppress the invention. See section 9.8.

[11]See, J. Schumpeter, *Capitalism, Socialism, and Democracy* (New York: Harper & Row, 1942), p. 106, and Z. J. Acs and D. B. Audretsch, "Innovation in Large and Small Firms: An Empirical Analysis," *American Economic Review*, September 1988, pp. 678–690.

[12]The question of what is the institutional setting most conducive to technological change and innovations over time is a crucial one, because technological change and innovations are the forces responsible for most of the long-term growth in standards of living in modern societies.

In addition, according to Schumpeter, large firms with some monopoly power are not sheltered from competition. On the contrary, they face powerful competition from new products and new production techniques introduced by other large firms. For example, aluminum is replacing steel in many uses, and plastic is replacing aluminum. Such competition is much more dangerous and affects the very existence of the firm. This is the process of "creative destruction" as new products and technologies constantly lead to new investments and the obsolescence of some existing capital stock. In this process, the role of the entrepreneur is crucial. Indeed, the entrepreneur is the star performer in the dynamic process of creative destruction and growth in the economy.

Other economists disagree. They point out that it is not at all clear that monopoly power leads to more R&D and innovations and faster long-run growth than perfectly competitive markets. They also point out that a more decentralized market economy is more adaptable and flexible to changes and is much more consistent with individual freedom of choice than an economy characterized by great economic concentration. The challenge, according to these economists, is to devise policies that correct the most serious economic distortions in the economy resulting from monopoly power and encourage a high level of R&D, while retaining and encouraging a large degree of decentralization, equity, and individual freedoms.

After a careful review of the empirical evidence, Scherer and Ross conclude that Schumpeter was right in asserting that perfect competition cannot be the model for dynamic efficiency. But neither can powerful monopolies and tightly knit cartels. What is needed for rapid technical progress is a subtle blend of competition and monopoly, with more emphasis on the former than on the latter, especially in those industries in which technical progress is relatively rapid. In other words, although some monopoly power may be more conducive to innovation than perfect competition when technical progress is relatively slow, a great deal of monopoly power is likely to retard innovations and growth, especially when technical progress is rapid.[13]

12.4 CONTROLLING MONOPOLY POWER: ANTITRUST POLICY

Starting in 1890, a number of *antitrust laws* were passed in the United States aimed at preventing monopoly or undue concentration of economic power, protecting the public against the abuses and inefficiencies resulting from monopoly or the concentration of economic power, and maintaining a workable degree of competition in the economy. The two basic antitrust laws were the Sherman Antitrust Act and the Clayton Act.

---

[13]F. M. Scherer and D. Ross, *Industrial Market Structure and Economic Performance* (Boston: Houghton and Mifflin, 1990), pp. 644–660.

According to Section I of the **Sherman Antitrust Act** passed in 1890: "Every contract, combination . . . , or conspiracy in restraint of trade or commerce among the several states, or with foreign nations, is hereby declared to be illegal" in the United States. The Sherman Antitrust Act does not make monopoly, as such, illegal. What is illegal is collusion (i.e., formal or informal agreements or arrangements in restraint of trade). These refer to all types of cartels, but also to informal understandings to share the market, price fixing, and price leadership. An illustration of these is provided by the market-sharing cartel of the Ivy League colleges in Example 4 in Chapter 10. What the courts did *not* rule as illegal is **conscious parallelism,** or the adoption of similar policies by oligopolists in view of their recognized interdependence. Specifically, the courts have ruled that parallel business behavior does not, in and of itself, constitute proof of collusion or an offense under the Sherman Antitrust Act.

The most difficult part of applying Section I of the Sherman Antitrust Act is to prove tacit or informal collusion. Sometimes the case is clear-cut. For example, in 1936, the U.S. Department of the Navy received 31 closed bids to supply a batch of steel and all of which quoted a price of $20,727.26. Also in 1936, the U.S. Engineer's Office received 11 closed bids to supply 6,000 barrels of cement, each quoting a price of $3.286854 per barrel! The probability of identical prices, down to the sixth decimal, occurring without some form of collusion is practically zero. Most antitrust cases are seldom so clear-cut, however.

Section II of the Sherman Antitrust Act, on the other hand, makes attempts to monopolize the market illegal. The most famous of the recent court cases applying Section II of the Sherman Antitrust Act is that against AT&T (discussed in Example 1). But monopolization can also occur through merger. Section 7 of the **Clayton Act** passed in 1914 (and amended by the Celler-Kefauver Act of 1950) prohibits mergers that "substantially lessen competition" or tend to lead to monopoly. According to its 1984 guidelines, the Justice Department will not usually challenge a horizontal merger (i.e., a merger of firms in the same product line) if the postmerger Herfindahl index is less than 1,000. If the postmerger index is between 1,000 and 1,800 and the increase in the index as a result of the merger is less than 100 points, the merger will usually also go unchallenged. But if the postmerger index is between 1,000 and 1,800 and the merger leads to an increase in the index of more than 100 points, or if the postmerger index is more than 1,800 and the merger leads to an increase in the index of more than 50 points, the Justice Department is likely to challenge the merger.

The guidelines based on the Herfindahl index are not the only factors that the Justice Department considers in horizontal mergers. Other factors considered include the financial condition of the firm being acquired, the ease of entry into the industry, the degree of foreign competition, and the expected gains in efficiency that the merger would make possible. The Justice Department is more likely to bend its Herfindahl index guidelines if the merger would prevent the failure of the acquired firm, if entry into the industry is easy, if the degree of foreign competition is strong, and if the acquisition would lead to substantial economies of scale.[14] Less clear-cut are the guidelines on vertical and conglomerate mergers. As a result of the relaxed guidelines and in the face of sharply increased foreign competition, especially from Japan, the number and size of corporate acquisitions in the United States increased sharply during the 1980s.

Since antitrust laws are often broad and general, however, a great deal of judicial interpretation based on economic analysis has often been required in their enforcement. The problems of defining what is meant by "substantially lessening competition," defining the relevant product and geographic markets, and deciding when competition is "unfair" have not been easy to determine and often could not be resolved in a fully satisfactory and uncontroversial way. The fact that many antitrust cases lasted many years, involved thousands of pages of testimony, and cost millions of dollars to prosecute is ample evidence of their great complexity. Perhaps the most significant effect of the antitrust laws is deterring collusion rather than fighting it after it occurs.

Be that as it may, Shepherd found that market concentration seems to have declined from 1958 to 1980.[15] Furthermore, as pointed out in section 12.2, Vernon has found that the Herfindahl index for the *world* automobile, petroleum, aluminum-smelting, and paper-pulp industries has *fallen* sharply from 1950 to 1970. Thus, international competition in these industries has increased sharply during this period. International competition seems to have even intensified since the 1980s in these and most other industries.

Example 1

 Antitrust Policy in Action—The Breakup of AT&T and the Creation of Competition in Long-Distance Telephone Service

In 1974, the Justice Department filed suit (under Section II of the Sherman Antitrust Act) against AT&T for illegal practices aimed at eliminating competitors in the markets for telephone equipment and long-distance telephone service. At the time, AT&T was the largest private firm in the world. After eight years of litigation and a cost of $25 million to the government (and $360 million incurred by AT&T to defend itself), the case was settled on January 8, 1982. By consent decree, AT&T agreed to divest itself of the 22 local telephone companies (which represented two-thirds of its total assets) and lose its monopoly on long-distance telephone service. In return, AT&T was allowed to retain Bell Laboratories and its manufacturing arm, Western

---

[14]See, "Symposium on Mergers and Antitrust," *Economic Perspectives*, Fall 1987, pp. 3–54.

[15]W. G. Shepherd, "Causes of Increased Competition in the U.S. Economy, 1958–1980," *Review of Economics and Statistics*, November 1982, pp. 613–626.

Electric, and was allowed to enter the rapidly growing fields of cable TV, electronic data transmission, video-text communications, and computers. The settlement also led to an increase in local telephone charges (which had been subsidized by long-distance telephone service by AT&T in the past) and a reduction in long-distance telephone charges.

AT&T began to face increasing competition from MCI Communication Corporation and U.S. Sprint Service for long-distance telephone business. By 1993, these two competitors had captured 27% of the long-distance telephone market (17% by MCI and 10% by Sprint) by charging lower rates and mounting aggressive advertising campaigns. AT&T responded with a huge marketing campaign of its own (in 1991 AT&T spent $2.6 billion on revenues of $34 billion compared with MCI's $1.2 billion on revenues of $8.4 billion). This shows how market power that is presumably unassailable can be destroyed by government action and how strong competition can be created where there was none. In a decade, AT&T was forced from a secure monopoly to a very competitive situation. Despite the increase in cost resulting from the huge marketing expenditures, competition has generally been good for consumers. It has lowered rates and helped speed the introduction of advanced services such as customized billing and calling-card plans. Indeed, regulators are now moving to break up *local* telephone monopolies.

Sources: "Ma Bell's Big Breakup," *Newsweek,* January 18, 1982, pp. 58–63; "Regulators Moving to Break Up Local Telephone Monopolies," *New York Times,* December 27, 1991, p. 1; and "AT&T, MCI, Sprint Raise the Intensity of Their Endless War," *Wall Street Journal,* October 20, 1992, p. A1.

▲

12.5 PUBLIC-UTILITY REGULATION

In this section, we consider the need for regulating natural monopolies (such as public utilities) and the dilemma faced by regulatory commissions in determining the appropriate method and degree of regulation.

Public Utilities as Natural Monopolies

As defined in section 9.1, *natural monopoly* refers to the case in which a single firm can supply a service to the entire market more efficiently than a number of firms could. Natural monopoly arises when the firm's long-run average cost curve is still declining at the point where it intersects the market demand curve. Examples of natural monopolies are *public utilities* (local electrical, gas, water, telephone, cable TV, and transportation companies). To have more than one such firm in a given market would lead to duplication of supply lines and to much higher costs per unit. To avoid this, local governments usually allow a single firm to operate in the market but regulate the price and quantity of the services provided so as to allow the firm only a normal rate of return (say, 10% to 12%) on its investment. This is shown in Figure 12–2.

FIGURE 12–2   Natural Monopoly Regulation

A regulatory commission usually sets $P = LAC = \$3$ (point G), at which output is 6 million units per time period and the public utility breaks even in the long run. This, however, would result in a welfare loss to society or social cost equal to about \$1.75 million (the area of shaded triangle GKH), since only at point H is $P = LMC$. This cost could be avoided if the commission set $P = LMC = \$1$. But that would result in a loss of \$1 (JH) per unit and \$8 million in total for the company, and the public utility would not supply the service in the long run without a subsidy of \$1 per unit.

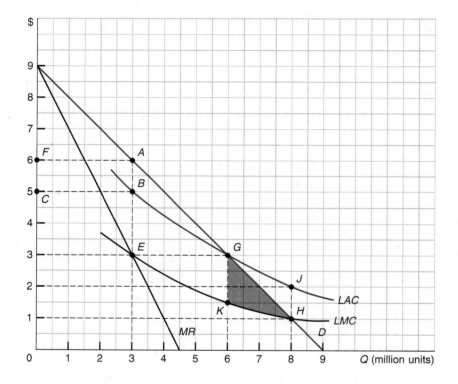

In Figure 12–2, the D and MR curves are, respectively, the market demand and marginal revenue curves for the service faced by the public utility; the LAC and LMC curves are its long-run average and marginal cost curves. The best level of output for the unregulated monopolist in the long run is 3 million units per time period and is given by point E, at which the LMC and MR curves intersect. For $Q = 3$ million units, the monopolist would charge the price of \$6 (point A on the D curve) and incur a $LAC = \$5$ (point B on the LAC curve), thereby earning a profit of \$1 (AB) per unit and \$3 million (the area of rectangle $ABCF$) in total. Note that at $Q = 3$ million units, the LAC curve is still declining. Note also that at the output level of 3 million units, $P > LMC$, so that more of the service is desirable from society's point of view. There is, however, no incentive for the unregulated monopolist to expand output beyond $Q = 3$ million units per time period because its profits are maximized at $Q = 3$ million.

To ensure that the monopolist earns only a normal rate of return on its investment, the regulatory commission usually sets $P = LAC$. In Figure 12–2, this is given by point G, at which $P = LAC = \$3$ and output is 6 million units per time period. While the price is lower and the output is greater than at point A, $P > LMC$ at point G. Thus, consumers pay a price for the last unit of the service purchased which exceeds the LMC of producing it (see the figure). The welfare loss to society or social cost of setting $P = LAC = \$3$ is about $(0.5)(1.75)(2) = \$1.75$ million (the area of shaded triangle GKH). The only way to avoid this social cost is for the regulatory commission to set $P = LMC = \$1$ so that output is 8 million units per time period (point H in the figure). At $Q = 8$ million, however, the $LAC = \$2$ (point J on the LAC curve); and the public utility would incur a loss of $\$1$ (JH) per unit and $\$8$ million in total per time period. As a result, the public utility would not supply the service in the long run without a subsidy of $\$1$ per unit. In general, regulatory commissions set $P = LAC$ (point G in Figure 12–2) so that the public utility breaks even in the long run without a subsidy.

Difficulties in Public-Utility Regulation

Although our discussion of public-utility regulation seems fairly simple and straightforward, the actual determination of prices (rates) for public-utility services by regulatory commissions (often called the *rate case*) is complex. For one thing, it is very difficult to determine the value of the plant or fixed assets on which to allow a normal rate of return. Should it be the original cost of the investment or the replacement cost? More often than not, regulatory commissions decide on the former. Furthermore, since public-utility companies supply the service to different classes of customers, each with different price elasticities of demand, many different rate schedules could be used to allow the public utility to break even. Even more troublesome is the fact that a public utility usually provides many services that are jointly produced, and so it is impossible to allocate costs in any rational way to the various services provided and customers served.

Regulation can also lead to inefficiencies. These result from the fact that, having been guaranteed a normal rate of return on investment, public-utility companies have little incentive to keep costs down. For example, managers may grant salary increases to themselves in excess of what they would get in their best alternative employment, and they may provide luxurious offices and large expense accounts for themselves. Regulatory commissions must, therefore, scrutinize costs to prevent such abuses. Regulated public utilities also have little incentive to introduce cost-saving innovations because they would not be able to keep the increased profits. An example of this is provided by the slowness with which AT&T introduced automatic switching equipment.

Other inefficiencies arise because if rates are set too high, public utilities will overinvest in fixed assets and use excessively capital-intensive production methods to avoid showing above-normal returns (which would lead to rate reductions). On the other hand, if public-utility rates are set too low, public-utility companies will underinvest in fixed assets (i.e., in plant and equipment) and overspend on variable inputs, such as labor and fuel, and tend to reduce the quality of services. Overinvestment or underinvestment in plant and equipment resulting from the wrong public-utility rates being set is known as the **Averch-Johnson (A-J) effect** (from Harvey Averch and Leland Johnson, who first identified this problem) and can lead to large inefficiencies.[16] And yet, it is difficult indeed for regulatory commissions to come up with correct utility rates in view of the difficulty of valuing the fixed assets of public utilities and because of the long planning and gestation period of public-utility investment projects.[17]

Finally, there is usually a lag of 9 to 12 months from the time the need for a rate change is recognized and the time it is granted. This *regulatory lag* results because public hearings must be conducted before a regulatory commission can approve a requested rate change. Since the members of the regulatory commissions are either political appointees or elected officials and are thus subject to political pressures from consumer groups, they usually postpone a rate increase as long as possible and tend to grant rate increases that are smaller than necessary. During inflationary periods, this leads to underinvestment in fixed assets and to the inefficiencies discussed earlier. To avoid these regulatory lags, rates are sometimes tied to fuel costs and are automatically adjusted as variable costs change.

Example 2
Regulated Electricity Rate Increases for Con Edison

On February 23, 1983, after nearly six months of public hearings and deliberations, the New York Public Service Commission approved a 6.5% increase in electricity rates for the 2.7 million customers served by the Consolidated Edison Company. This rate increase, which took effect on March 12, 1983, increased the basic monthly electricity charge by $2.60 in New York City and $3.75 in Westchester County, where the average resident uses more electricity. The increase in the monthly electricity charge was about half of the 12.4% that Con Edison had asked for and far lower than the 15.5% increase that the commission granted Con Edison in 1981. The commission indicated that the decision to grant rate increases that would generate additional revenues of only $240 million per year for Con Edison rather than the requested $491 million was based on the fact that the borrowing and operating costs of the public utility had fallen sharply since it had made the request for a rate increase as the result of the decline in fuel costs, interest rates, and inflation.

Both Con Edison and consumer advocates immediately criticized the rate

---

[16]H. Averch and L. Johnson, "Behavior of the Firm under Regulatory Constraint," *American Economic Review*, December 1962, pp. 1052–1069.

[17]In recent years, regulatory commissions have begun to pay more attention to the structure of rates so as to avoid undue price discrimination against any class of customers.

increase—the former as inadequate and the latter as too high. Because of even lower fuel costs, greater demand for electricity, and higher productivity increases than anticipated, the rate increase actually generated $267 million in additional revenues per year for Con Edison, which represented a 15.2% return on its investment instead of the projected 13.67% return. In 1986, the city administration threatened to sue Con Edison to have the excess profits returned to customers, but it dropped its plan when Con Edison agreed not to seek another rate increase until March 1987. In fact, Con Edison did not ask for a rate increase even after 1987, so that electricity rates in 1993 were the same as a decade earlier.

Sources: "Con Edison Wins 6.5% Rise in Rates, Half of Its Request," *New York Times*, February 24, 1983, p. B4; "Con Edison Puts Freeze on Its Electricity Rates," *New York Times*, January 13, 1986, p. B1; and "Electricity Rates," *Con Edison*, January 1993.

▲

12.6 THE DEREGULATION MOVEMENT

Regulation in the U.S. economy is not confined to cases of natural monopolies, where there is a single seller of a commodity or service, but extends to many other sectors, especially transportation, banking and financial services, where more than one firm operates. For example, airlines needed government approval to enter a market and to change fares, railroads need government approval to abandon a service or a line and change rates, the services that banks can provide and the interest that they can pay on deposits are also regulated, and so are the rates set by insurance companies and other financial institutions. Regulation was justified to ensure that industries operate in a manner consistent with the public interest, ensure a minimum standard of quality of services, and prevent the establishment of monopoly.

Many economists, however, oppose regulation because it restricts competition, contributes to high prices, and reduces economic efficiency. One estimate put the social cost of regulation at more than $100 billion in the year 1979 (of this, about 5% were administrative costs and the rest were the costs of compliance).[18] Even though these estimates have been challenged as grossly exaggerated,[19] compliance costs are surely very high, particularly in the area of social regulation (such as job safety), energy and the environment, and consumer safety and health. Regulation often leads to inefficiencies because regulators do not specify the desired result, but only the method of compliance (such as the type of pollution-abatement equipment to use), in the absence of adequate information and expertise. It is now generally agreed that it would

---

[18]M. Weidenbaum, "The High Cost of Government Regulation," *Challenge*, November–December 1979, pp. 32–39.

[19]See, W. K. Tabb, "Government Regulation: Two Sides of the Story," *Challenge*, November–December 1980, pp. 40–48.

be much better if regulators specified the results wanted and left to industry the task of determining the most efficient way to comply.

From the mid-1970s, a growing **deregulation movement** has sprung up in the United States, which led to deregulation in air travel, trucking, railroads, banking, and telecommunications. The *Airline Deregulation Act of 1978* removed all restrictions on entry, scheduling, and pricing in domestic air travel in the United States, and so did the *Motor Carrier Act of 1980* in the trucking industry. The *Depository Institutions and Monetary Control Act of 1980* allowed banks to pay interest on checking accounts and increased competition for business loans. The *Railroad Revitalization and Regulatory Reform Act of 1976* greatly increased the flexibility of railroads to set prices and determine levels of service and areas of operation. Natural gas pipelines are now deregulated, and there is even talk of deregulating the electric power generation industry. The settlement of the AT&T antitrust case in 1982 (see Example 1) opened competition in long-distance telephone service and in telecommunications. Starting in July 1989, the Federal Communications Commission gave AT&T more freedom in setting long-distance telephone rates in order to provide greater incentives to cut costs. Instead of allowing rates that provided AT&T only a fixed normal return on investment (as in the past), the commission set a floor (to protect competitors) and a ceiling (to protect customers) on the rates that AT&T may charge and allowed AT&T to retain any excess return on investment arising from cost cutting.

The general purpose of deregulation is to increase competition and efficiency in the affected industries and lead to lower prices without sacrificing the quality of service. Although it is too early to assess the full impact of deregulation, most observers would probably conclude that, on balance, the net effect has been positive. Competition has generally increased and prices have fallen in the industries that were deregulated. As expected, however, deregulation has also resulted in some difficulties and strains in the industries affected, to the point where some consumer groups and some firms in recently deregulated industries are asking Congress to reregulate the industries. Nowhere is this more evident than in the airline industry (see Example 3). The rash of failures in the savings and loans associations in the late 1980s and early 1990s has also led to some reregulation.

Example 3
Deregulation of the Airline Industry: An Assessment

By 1993, all but one (America West) of the 15 air carriers that had been established since the 1978 deregulation had gone out of business or had merged with established carriers. Several mergers also took place among large established carriers, and Eastern Airlines and Pan Am went out of business. The result was that by 1993, 7 carriers handled more than 93% of all domestic air travel in the United States (as compared with 11 carriers handling 87% of the traffic in 1978). Since 1985, the market share of the top 5 carriers jumped from 61% to 75%. Instead of a large number of small and highly competitive airlines envisioned by deregulation, the airline industry has become even more concentrated than it was before deregulation. Entry into the industry is increasingly being restricted by established airlines by (1) long-term leasing of the limited number of gates at most airports; (2) frequent-flyer programs, which increase passengers' loyalty to a given airline; (3) computerized reservations systems, which give a competitive advantage in attracting loyal customers to the airlines owning the system; and (4) the emergence of "hub and spoke" operations in which airlines funnel passengers through centrally located airports where one or two companies often dominate service.

It is true that airfares, after adjusting for inflation, have declined an average of 20% since deregulation and that this greatly stimulated domestic air travel (from about 250 million passengers in 1976 to more than 450 million in 1992). It is also true that airlines could not possibly continue to charge fares as low as those charged during the latter part of the 1970s and the early part of the 1980s and continue to incur large losses. Nevertheless, the sharp reduction in the number of airlines is beginning to worry even the stoutest supporters of deregulation. Furthermore, although safety does not seem to have suffered and many small cities have not lost air service (as the opponents of deregulation had warned), delays at airports and passenger complaints about lost luggage, canceled flights, and general declines in the quality of service have increased significantly since deregulation. Bills are now pending in Congress to reimpose some regulation in the industry. The shift of regulatory authority from the Transportation Department to the Justice Department in 1989 also led to a tougher stance on mergers in the industry. But with the list of distressed airlines increasing, we are likely to see further consolidation in the industry.

The Darwinian struggle in the sky may ultimately leave just three giants—American, United, and Delta—to serve the national market. But according to the theory of contestable markets, this may be adequate to keep prices in line with costs.

Sources: "Airline Deregulation," *Federal Reserve Bank of San Francisco Review*, March 9, 1990; "As Airline Competition Drops, Washington Takes Note," *New York Times*, June 11, 1989, p. E4; "Death Struggle in the Sky," *Newsweek*, June 15, 1992, pp. 43–45; and "Waiting Out the Airline Shake Out," *New York Times*, May 22, 1992, p. 2.

▲

12.7 REGULATING INTERNATIONAL COMPETITION: VOLUNTARY EXPORT RESTRAINTS

One of the most important nontariff trade barriers is **voluntary export restraints (VER)**.[20] These refer to the case in which an importing country induces

[20]The effects of an import tariff were examined in section 8.8.

another nation to reduce its exports of a commodity "voluntarily," under the threat of higher all-around trade restrictions, when these exports threaten an entire domestic industry. Voluntary export restraints have been negotiated since the 1950s by the United States and other industrial countries to curtail textile exports from Japan, and more recently also to curb exports of automobiles, steel, shoes, and other commodities from Japan and other nations. These are the mature industries that faced sharp declines in employment in the industrial countries during the 1980s. Sometimes called "orderly marketing arrangements," these voluntary export restraints have allowed the United States and other industrial nations making use of them to save at least the appearance of continued support for the principle of free trade.

When voluntary export restraints are successful, they have all the economic effects of equivalent import tariffs, except that they are administered by the exporting country, and so the revenue effect or monopoly profits are captured by foreign exporters. An example of this is provided by the "voluntary" restraint on Japanese automobile exports to the United States negotiated in 1981 (see Example 4). The United States also negotiated voluntary export restraints with major steel suppliers in 1984 that limit imports to about 20% of the U.S. steel market. It has been estimated that these agreements saved from 35,000 to 40,000 jobs but raised the price of steel in the United States by 20% to 30%.

Voluntary export restraints are likely to be less effective in limiting imports than import quotas, because the exporting nations agree only reluctantly to curb their exports. Foreign exporters are also likely to fill their quotas with higher-quality and higher-priced units of the product over time. This *product upgrading* was clearly evident in the case of the Japanese voluntary restraint on automobile exports to the United States. Furthermore, as a rule, only major supplier countries are involved, which leaves the door open for other nations to replace part of the exports of the major suppliers and also for transshipments through third countries.

Example 4

 ### Voluntary Export Restraints on Japanese Automobiles to the United States

From 1977 to 1981, U.S. automobile production fell by about one-third, the share of imports rose from 18% to 29%, and nearly 300,000 autoworkers in the United States lost their jobs. In 1980 the Big Three U.S. automakers suffered combined losses of $4 billion. As a result, the United States negotiated an agreement with Japan that limited Japanese automobile exports to the United States to 1.68 million units per year from 1981 to 1983 and to 1.85 million units for 1984 and 1985. Japan "agreed" to restrict its automobile exports out of fear of still more stringent import restrictions by the United States.

U.S. automakers generally used the time from 1981 to 1985 wisely to lower break-even points and improve quality, but the cost improvements were not passed on to consumers, and Detroit reaped profits of nearly $6 billion in 1983, $10 billion in 1984, and $8 billion in 1985. Japan gained by exporting higher-priced autos and earning higher profits. The big loser, of course, was the American public, which had to pay substantially higher prices for domestic and foreign automobiles. The U.S. International Trade Commission (USITC) estimated that the agreement resulted in a price $660 higher for U.S.-made automobiles and $1,300 higher for Japanese cars in 1984. The USITC also estimated that the total cost of the agreement to U.S. consumers was $15.7 billion from 1981 through 1984, and that 44,000 U.S. auto jobs were saved at a cost of more than $100,000 each. This is more than two to three times the yearly earnings of a U.S. autoworker.

The United States has not asked for a renewal of the agreement, but Japan unilaterally limited its auto exports (to 2.3 million from 1986 to 1991 and 1.65 million afterwards) to avoid more trade frictions with the United States. Since the late 1980s, however, Japan has been producing an increasing number of automobiles in the United States in so-called transplant factories. By 1993, Japan was producing more than 1 million cars in the United States and had captured 27% of the U.S. market (16% from exports and 11% from production in the United States). The increased efficiency of U.S. automakers (especially Ford and Chrysler), now seems to have arrested and even reversed the growth in the Japanese share of the U.S. market.

Sources: U.S. International Trade Commission, *A Review of Recent Developments in the U.S. Automobile Industry Including an Assessment of the Japanese Voluntary Export Restraint Agreements* (Washington, D.C.: February 1985); J. de Melo and D. Tarr, "Welfare Costs of U.S. Quotas in Textiles, Steel, and Autos," *Review of Economics and Statistics*, March 1990, pp. 489–497; "Detroit Takes the Offensive," *Forbes*, September 28, 1992, pp. 108–112; and "Japan to Continue Restraints on Auto Exports to the United States," *New York Times*, January 8, 1993, p. D10.

▲

12.8 SOME APPLICATIONS OF MARKET STRUCTURE, EFFICIENCY, AND REGULATION

In this section, we discuss some important applications of the theory presented in the chapter: the regulation of monopoly price, peak-load pricing, and transfer pricing. These applications highlight the importance and relevance of the tools introduced in the chapter.

Regulating Monopoly Price

One way for the government to regulate a monopoly is to set a price below the price that the monopolist would charge in the absence of regulation. This leads to a larger output and lower profits for the monopolist, as shown in Figure 12–3.

The figure shows that, in the absence of regulation, the best level of output of the monopolist is given by point M, where the LMC curve intersects the

FIGURE 12–3   Regulating Monopoly Price

In the absence of regulation, $Q = 3$, $P = \$6$, $LAC = \$4$, and profits are \$2 per unit
(*RN*) and \$6 in total. If the government set the maximum price at $P = \$5$, the demand
curve becomes *CID* and the *MR* curve is *CIKW*. Then, $Q = 4$, $P = \$5$, $LAC = \$3.60$,
and profits are \$1.40 per unit (*IJ*) and \$5.60 in total.

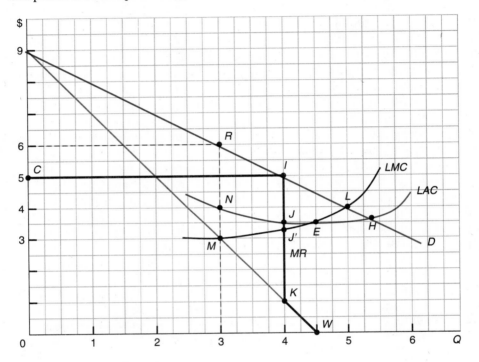

MR curve from below. Thus, $Q = 3$, $P = \$6$ (point R), $LAC = \$4$ (point N),
and profits are \$2 per unit (*RN*) and \$6 in total.

If the government now set the maximum price that the monopolist could
charge at $P = \$5$, the demand curve facing the monopolist would become
CID (see the figure). Thus, the monopolist's demand curve would be horizontal until $Q = 4$ (since the monopolist cannot charge a price higher than
\$5) and would resume its usual downward shape at $Q > 4$ (since the monopo-
list can charge prices lower than \$5). As a result, the monopolist's *MR* curve
is also horizontal and coincides with the demand curve until point I and
resumes its usual downward shape when the demand curve does. That is,
the monopolist's *MR* curve becomes *CIKW*. Note that the *MR* curve has a
discontinuous (vertical) section at point I, where the demand curve has a
kink.

With price set at $P = \$5$, the best level of output of the monopolist is given
by point J', where $LMC = MR$. Thus, $Q = 4$, $P = \$5$ (point I), $LAC = \$3.60$
(point J), and profits are \$1.40 per unit and \$5.60 in total. Price is lower, output
is larger, and the monopolist's profits are lower than without regulation.

If the government set the maximum price at point L, where the LMC curve intersects the D curve (so that $P = LMC = \$4$), the best level of output of the monopolist would be five units (see the figure). The monopolist would then earn a profit of \$0.50 per unit and \$2.50 in total. If the government, in an effort to eliminate all monopoly profits, were to set the lower price (about \$3.50) given by point H, where the monopolist's LAC curve intersects the D curve, a shortage of the commodity (and a black market) would arise. This is because consumers would demand nearly 5.5 units of the commodity while the monopolist would only produce about 4.5 units (given by the point where $P = LMC$ at about \$3.50 in the figure).

Regulation and Peak-Load Pricing

The demand for some services (such as electricity) is higher during some periods (such as in the evening and in the summer) than at other times (such as during the day or in the spring). Electricity is also a nonstorable service (i.e., it must be generated when it is needed). In order to satisfy peak demand (as required by public-utility regulation), electrical power companies must bring into operation older and less efficient equipment and thus incur higher costs during peak periods. Power companies should, therefore, charge a higher price during peak than during off-peak periods to reflect their higher marginal costs in the former than in the latter periods. Since such price differences would be based on cost differences, they are not technically price discrimination (nevertheless, they have sometimes been referred to as *intertemporal* price discrimination).

The problem, however, is that regulatory commissions often do not permit the public utility to charge different prices during peak and off-peak periods, but require it to charge a constant given price that covers the average of the generating costs during both periods together. Such a constant price, in the face of different generating costs, does not represent the best pricing policy. Assuming that the public utility is operating in the short run with a given plant and other equipment, the best pricing policy would be to charge the lower price equal to the lower marginal cost during off-peak periods and the higher price equal to the higher marginal cost in peak periods. By adopting such **peak-load pricing,** consumer welfare will be higher than by the policy of constant pricing during both off-peak and peak periods, and consumers generally will end up spending less on electricity for the peak and off-peak periods combined. This is shown in Figure 12–4.

In the figure, D_1 is the market demand curve for electricity during the off-peak period, and D_2 is the higher market demand curve for electricity during the peak period. The short-run marginal cost of the firm is given by SMC. The regulatory commission sets the price of 4 cents per kWh at all times to cover average total costs in both periods together. At $P = 4$ cents, the firm would sell 4 million kWh during the off-peak period (point A_1 on D_1) and 8 million kWh during the peak period (point A_2 on D_2). At point A_1, however, the marginal benefit to consumers from one additional kWh (given by the

FIGURE 12–4   Peak-Load Pricing

At the constant price of 4 cents per kWh, the public utility sells 4 million kWh of electricity (point A_1) during the off-peak period and 8 million during the peak period (point A_2). But at A_1, $P > SMC$, while at A_2, $P < SMC$. With peak-load pricing, $P = SMC = 3$ cents (point E_1) in the off-peak period and $P = SMC = 5$ cents (point E_2) in the peak period. The gain in consumer welfare with peak-load pricing is thus given by the sum of the two shaded triangles.

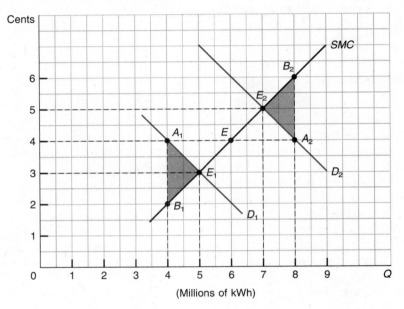

price of 4 cents per kWh) exceeds the marginal cost of generating the last unit of electricity produced (given by point B_1 on the SMC curve). From society's point of view, it would pay if the firm supplied more electricity until $P = SMC = 3$ cents (point E_1 at which D_1 and SMC intersect). The social benefit gained would be equal to the shaded triangle $A_1B_1E_1$.

On the other hand, at point A_2, the marginal benefit to consumers from one additional kWh (given by the price of 4 cents per kWh) is smaller than the marginal cost of generating the last unit of electricity produced (point B_2 on the SMC curve). From society's point of view, it would pay if the firm supplied less electricity until $P = SMC = 5$ cents (point E_2 at which D_2 and SMC intersect). The social benefit gained (by using the same resources to produce some other service that society values more) would be equal to the shaded triangle $B_2A_2E_2$. Charging $P = SMC = 3$ cents in the off-peak period (point E_1 in the figure) and $P = SMC = 5$ cents in the peak period (point E_2) would be the most efficient pricing policy. But, as pointed out earlier, regulatory commissions usually do not allow such peak-load pricing.

There are other effects from peak-load pricing, which are not shown in Figure 12–4. The first results from the substitution of electricity consumption from peak to off-peak periods to take advantage of the lower price during the off-peak period. This tends to reduce the benefit of peak-load pricing (see problem 12, with answer at end of book). Another effect not shown in Figure 12–4 is that with peak-load pricing the scale of plant to meet peak-load demand is smaller (7 million kWh with peak-load pricing as compared with 8 million kWh without peak-load pricing). Thus, in the long run, when the public utility needs to replace the present plant, it can do so with a smaller and more efficient one. One factor that militates against peak-load pricing is that it requires meters to measure consumption at different times of the day, week, or year, and these can be quite expensive to install.

Peak-load pricing is not confined to public utilities. It is equally applicable to such private enterprises as hotels, restaurants, airlines, movie theaters, and so on, which face a demand that fluctuates sharply and in a predictable way during peak and off-peak periods. These enterprises usually charge lower rates during off-season or in periods of naturally low demand (when marginal costs are lower) than during in-season or periods of high demand (when marginal costs are higher).

Some regulatory commissions are now moving toward allowing peak-load or time-of-day pricing for electricity (telephone companies have been practicing second and third degree price discrimination for sometime already). For example, Con Edison charges 13.07 cents per kWh for electricity from 9 A.M. to 9 P.M. and 4.71 cents from 9 P.M. and 9 A.M. and on weekends. Electrical public utilities are also purchasing increasing amounts of electricity from smaller independent companies to meet their peak demand.[21] What is surprising is that it took so long for regulatory commissions to recognize peak-load pricing. The economic analysis of peak-load pricing is an example of the increased efficiency and great benefit that can result from the application of microeconomic analysis. It is microeconomics at its best!

Regulation and Transfer Pricing

The rapid rise of modern large-scale enterprises has been accompanied by decentralization and the establishment of semi-autonomous profit centers. This occurred because of the need to contain the tendency toward increasing costs for communications and coordination among various divisions. Decentralization and the establishment of semi-autonomous profit centers also gave rise to the need for **transfer pricing,** or the need to determine the price of intermediate products sold by one semi-autonomous division of a large-scale enterprise and purchased by another semi-autonomous division of the same enterprise. The appropriate pricing of intermediate products or transfer pricing is of crucial importance to the efficient operation of the individual divisions

---

[21]See, ''Paying for Electric Power by Time of Day,'' *New York Times,* June 9, 1990, p. 48, and ''Unseating the Electrical Utilities Monopoly,'' *New York Times,* March 11, 1990, p. 12.

FIGURE 12–5   Transfer Pricing of the Intermediate Product with No External Market

The marginal cost of the firm, MC, is equal to the vertical summation of MC_p and MC_m, the marginal cost curves of the firm's production and marketing divisions. D_m is the external demand for the final product faced by the firm, and MR_m is the corresponding marginal revenue curve. The firm's best level of output is 40 units and is given by point E_m, at which $MR_m = MC$, so that $P_m = \$14$. Since each unit of the final product requires one unit of the intermediate product, the transfer price for the intermediate product, P_t, is set equal to MC_p at $Q_p = 40$ (point E_p). Thus, $P_t = \$6$.

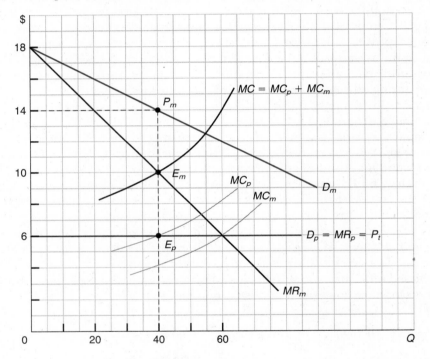

as well as the enterprise as a whole. If the wrong transfer prices are set, the various divisions and the firm as a whole will not produce the optimum or profit-maximizing level of output and will not maximize total profits.

Transfer pricing has also been used by multinational corporations to increase their profits. Specifically, by artificially overpricing components shipped *to* an affiliate in a higher-tax nation and underpricing products shipped *from* the affiliate in the high-tax nation, the multinational corporation can minimize its tax bill and increase its profits. To overcome this problem, government regulators usually apply the "arm's length" test, under which the price of parts shipped from one affiliate of a multinational corporation in one country to another affiliate in another country is priced by regulators for taxing purposes according to the price that the same part would be sold to nonaffiliates.

For simplicity, we assume that the firm has two divisions, a production division (indicated by the subscript p) and a marketing division (indicated by the subscript m). The production division sells the intermediate product only to the marketing division (i.e., there is no external market for the intermediate product). The marketing division purchases the intermediate product from the production division, completes the production process, and markets the final product for the firm. We further assume that one unit of the intermediate product is required to produce each unit of the final product.

In Figure 12–5, MC_p and MC_m are the marginal cost curves of the production and marketing divisions of the firm, respectively, while MC is the vertical summation of MC_p and MC_m and represents the total marginal cost curve for the firm as a whole. The figure also shows the external demand curve for the final product sold by the marketing division, D_m, and its corresponding marginal revenue curve, MR_m. The firm's best or profit-maximizing level of output for the final product is 40 units and is given by point E_m, at which $MR_m = MC$. Therefore, $P_m = \$14$. Since 40 units of the intermediate product are required to produce the 40 units of the final product, the transfer price for the intermediate product, P_t, is set equal to the marginal cost of the intermediate product (MC_p) at $Q_p = 40$. Thus, $P_t = \$6$ and is given by point E_p at which $Q_p = 40$. The demand and marginal revenue curves faced by the production division of the firm are then equal to the transfer price (i.e., $D_p = MR_p = P_t$). Note that $Q_p = 40$ is the best level of output of the intermediate product by the production division of the firm because at $Q_p = 40$, $D_p = MR_p = P_t = MC_p = \$6$. Thus, the correct transfer price for an intermediate product for which there is no external market is the marginal cost of production.[22]

SUMMARY

1. In this chapter we made use of the basic principle that any activity should be carried out until the marginal benefit equals the marginal cost, to examine the relationship between market structure and efficiency, public-utility regulation, and antitrust.

2. The Lerner index measures the degree of a *firm's* monopoly power by the ratio of the difference between price and marginal cost to price. The Herfindahl index estimates the degree of monopoly power in an *industry* as a whole by the sum of the squared values of the market sales shares of all the firms in the industry. According to the theory of contestable markets, even if an industry has only one or a few firms, it would still operate as if it were perfectly competitive if entry is absolutely free and if exit is entirely costless. Experimental economics has been developing during the past two decades. This field seeks to determine how real markets work by using paid volunteers within a simple experimental institutional framework.

---

[22]For a more detailed discussion of transfer pricing, including the case where there is an external market for the intermediate product of the firm, see D. Salvatore, *Managerial Economics in a Global Economy*, 2nd ed. (New York: McGraw-Hill, 1993), Chapter 12.

3. Static social costs of monopoly power arise because imperfect competitors produce where $P > MR = MC$ and from rent-seeking activities. These must be balanced with the benefits of economies of scale resulting from large-scale production and the possibility that firms with monopoly power are more innovative than small firms without market power. A great deal of disagreement exists, however, about the alleged dynamic benefits that larger firms have over smaller ones.

4. Section I of the Sherman Antitrust Act passed in 1890 declared that "Every contract, combination . . . , or conspiracy in restraint of trade or commerce among the several states, or with foreign nations, is hereby declared to be illegal." This does not make monopoly as such, or conscious parallelism, illegal. What is illegal is collusion to restrain trade. Section II of the Sherman Antitrust Act makes attempts to monopolize the market illegal. Section 7 of the Clayton Act passed in 1914 (and amended by the Celler-Kefauver Act of 1950) prohibits mergers that "substantially lessen competition" or tend to lead to monopoly.

5. Natural monopolies such as public utilities arise when the firm's LAC curve is still declining at the point where it intersects the market demand curve. The government then usually allows a single firm to operate but sets $P = LAC$ (so that the firm earns only a normal return on investment). Economic efficiency, however, requires that $P = LMC$, but this would result in a loss and the company would not supply the service in the long run without a subsidy. Therefore, P is usually set equal to LAC. Many difficulties arise in public-utility regulation, especially to ensure that the utilities keep costs as low as possible.

6. Since the mid-1970s, the government has deregulated airlines and trucking and reduced the level of regulation for financial institutions, telecommunications, and railroads in order to increase competition and avoid some of the heavy compliance costs of regulation. Even though the full impact of deregulation has yet to be felt, deregulation seems to have led to increased competition and lower prices, but it has also resulted in some problems such as deterioration in the quality of the services provided.

7. Voluntary export restraints (VER) refer to the case in which an importing country induces another nation to reduce its exports of a commodity "voluntarily," under the threat of higher all-around trade restrictions. When successful, their economic impact is the same as that of an equivalent import tariff, except for the revenue effect, which is now captured by foreign suppliers. Voluntary export restraints have been negotiated to curtail exports of textiles, automobiles, steel, shoes, and other commodities to the United States and other industrial countries.

8. By setting price below the monopoly price, a monopolist can be induced to produce a larger output and have lower profits. Peak-load pricing refers to the charging of a price equal to short-run marginal cost, both in the peak period when demand and marginal cost are higher and in the off-peak period when both are lower. The transfer price for an intermediate product for which there is no external market is the marginal cost of production.

KEY TERMS

Efficiency
Lerner Index

Herfindahl Index
Theory of Contestable Markets

Experimental Economics
Sherman Antitrust Act

Conscious Parallelism
Clayton Act
Averch-Johnson (A-J) Effect

Deregulation Movement
Voluntary Export Restraints
  (VER)

Peak-Load Pricing
Transfer Pricing

REVIEW QUESTIONS

1. Under what conditions will an economy be operating most efficiently? Why?
2. What can be done to increase efficiency if the price of the last unit consumed of a commodity exceeds the marginal cost of producing it?
3. What is the value of the Lerner index if $\eta = 5$? If $\eta = 3$?
4. What is the value of the Lerner index (L) if $P = \$10$ and $MR = \$5$?
5. What is the value of the Herfindahl index
   a. in a duopoly with one firm having 60% of the market?
   b. with 1,000 equal-sized firms?
6. What is the difference between limit pricing and the theory of contestable markets?
7. What are the most important
   a. social costs of monopoly power?
   b. benefits associated with monopoly power?
8. How does the government decide whether to subject a very large firm to antitrust action or regulation?

9. The settlement of the AT&T antitrust case in 1982 involved both good news and bad news for AT&T and its customers. What was
   a. the bad news and good news for AT&T?
   b. the good news and bad news for users of telephone services?
10. a. How could a regulatory commission induce a public-utility company to operate as a perfect competitor in the long run?
   b. To what difficulty would this lead?
   c. What compromise does a regulatory commission usually adopt?
11. Given the difficulties that the regulation of public utilities faces, would it not be better to nationalize public utilities, as some European countries have done? Explain your answer.
12. Peak-load pricing can be regarded as an application of the marginal principle. True or false? Explain.

PROBLEMS

1. Explain why the value of the Lerner index can seldom if ever be equal to one (i.e., the value of L usually ranges from zero to smaller than one).
*2. Show with the use of a diagram that a given value of the Lerner index is consistent with different rates of profits for the firm.
3. In measuring the Herfindahl index, the market share of each firm in the industry is sometimes expressed in ratio form rather than in percentages (as in the text). Find the Herfindahl index if the market share of each firm is expressed as a ratio when
   a. there is a single firm in the industry.
   b. there is duopoly with one firm having 0.6 of the total industry sales.
   c. there is one firm with sales equal to 0.5 of total industry sales and ten other equal-sized firms.

   d. there are ten equal-sized firms.
   e. there are 100 equal-sized firms in the industry.
   f. there are 1,000 equal-sized firms in the industry.
4. Starting with demand curve D in Figure 12–1, draw a figure showing three identical firms in the contestable market.
*5. Draw a figure similar to Figure 9–7 showing the net social losses of monopoly when the firm's marginal cost curve is rising, rather than horizontal as in Figure 9–7.
6. Determine if the Justice Department would challenge a merger between two firms in an industry with ten equal-sized firms, based on its Herfindahl-index guidelines only.

———

* = Answer provided at end of book.

*7. Suppose that the market demand curve for the public-utility service shown in Figure 12–2 shifts to the right by 1 million units at each price level but the *LAC* and *LMC* curves remain unchanged. Draw a figure showing the price of the service that the public-utility commission would set and the quantity of the service that would be supplied to the market at that price.

8. Suppose that the market demand curve for the public-utility service shown in Figure 12–2 shifts to the right by 1 million units at each price level, and, at the same time, the *LAC* curve of the public-utility company shifts up by $1 throughout because of production inefficiencies that escape detection by the public-utility commission. Draw a figure showing the price of the service that the public-utility commission would set and the quantity of the service that would be supplied to the market at that price.

9. Compare the effects of a voluntary export restraint that restricts the export of commodity *X* to the nation to 200 units, with the effects of a $1 import tariff imposed by the nation on commodity *X* shown in Figure 8–17.

10. Draw a figure showing how a regulatory commission could induce the monopolist of Figure 12–3 to behave as a perfect competitor in the short run by setting the appropriate price.

11. Explain why the problems arising in public-utility regulation do not arise in the case of a monopoly that is not a natural monopoly.

*12. a. Starting from Figure 12–4, draw a figure showing peak-load pricing when substitution in consumption is taken into consideration.

b. Is the benefit of peak-load pricing greater or smaller when substitution in consumption is taken into consideration than when it is not? Why is this so?

PRICING AND EMPLOYMENT OF INPUTS

Part Five (Chapters 13–15) presents the theory of input pricing and employment. Until this point, in the text, we assumed input prices to be given. In this part, we examine how input prices and the level of their employment are determined in the market. Chapter 13 deals with input pricing and employment under perfect competition in the output and input markets. Chapter 14 examines input pricing and employment under imperfect competition in the output and/or input markets. Chapter 15 deals with financial microeconomics, that is, the allocation of inputs over time and the cost of capital. As in previous parts of the text, the presentation of theory is reinforced with many real-world examples and important applications.

INPUT PRICE AND EMPLOYMENT UNDER PERFECT COMPETITION

In Chapters 6 and 7 we examined how firms combine inputs to minimize production costs on the assumption of given input prices. In Chapters 8 through 12 we dealt with the product market and examined the pricing and output of consumers' goods, again, on the assumption of given input prices. We now turn our attention to the input market and examine how the price and employment of inputs are actually determined.

In many ways the determination of input prices and employment is similar to the pricing and output of commodities. That is, the price and employment of an input is generally determined by the interaction of the forces of market demand and supply for the input.

There are several important qualifications, however. First, whereas consumers demand commodities because of the utility or satisfaction they receive in consuming the commodities, firms demand inputs in order to produce the goods and services demanded by society. That is, the demand for an input is a derived demand; it is derived from the demand for the final commodity that the input is used in producing. Second, while consumers demand commodities, firms demand the *services* of inputs. That is, firms demand the *flow* of input services (e.g., labor time), not the stock of the inputs themselves. The same is generally true for the other inputs. Third, the analysis in this chapter and the next deals with inputs in general; that is, it refers to all types of labor, capital, raw materials, and land inputs. However, since the various types of labor receive more than three-quarters of the national income, the discussion is couched in terms of labor.

We begin the chapter with a summary discussion of profit maximization and optimal input employment. Then we derive the demand curve for an input by a firm. By adding the demand curves for the input of all firms, we get the market demand curve for the input. Next we discuss an individual's decision between work and leisure and the market supply curve of an input in general. The chapter describes how the interaction of the market demand and supply of an input determines its price and employment under perfect competition (the case of imperfect competition is examined in the next chapter). Subsequently, the chapter shows the process by which input prices are equalized among industries and regions of a country, and internationally among countries. A discussion of rent and quasi-rent follows. This chapter includes several important applications and extensions of the theory.

13.1 PROFIT MAXIMIZATION AND OPTIMAL INPUT EMPLOYMENT

In this section, we bring together and summarize the discussion of Chapters 6, 7, and 8 on the conditions for profit maximization and optimal input employment by firms operating under perfect competition. This is the first step in the derivation of the demand curve for an input by a firm.

In section 7.2, we saw that the least-cost input combination of a firm was given by equation [7–3B], repeated below as [13–1]:

$$MP_L/w = MP_K/r \qquad\qquad \textbf{[13–1]}$$

where MP refers to the marginal (physical) product, L refers to labor, K to capital, w to wages or the price of labor time, and r to the interest rate or the rental price of capital. Equation [13–1] indicates that to minimize production costs, the extra output or marginal product per dollar spent on labor must be equal to the marginal product per dollar spent on capital. If $MP_L = 5$, $MP_K = 4$, and $w = r$, the firm would not be minimizing costs, because it is getting more extra output for a dollar spent on labor than on capital. To minimize costs, the firm would have to hire more labor and rent less capital. As the firm does this, the MP_L declines and the MP_K increases (because the firm operates in stage II of production). The process would have to continue until condition [13–1] held. If w were higher than r, the MP_L would have to be proportionately higher than the MP_K for condition [13–1] to hold. The same general condition would have to hold to minimize production costs, no matter how many inputs the firm uses. That is, the MP per dollar spent on each input would have to be the same for all inputs.

Going one step further, we can show that the reciprocal of each term (ratio) in equation [13–1] equals the marginal cost (MC) of the firm to produce an additional unit of output. That is,

$$w/MP_L = r/MP_K = MC \qquad\qquad \textbf{[13–2]}$$

Consider labor first. The wage rate (w) is the addition to the total costs of the firm from hiring one additional unit of labor, while MP_L is the resulting increase in the total output of the commodity of the firm. Thus, w/MP_L gives the change in total costs (in terms of labor) per unit increase in output. This is the definition of marginal cost. That is, $w/MP_L = MC$.[1] For example, if the

---

[1]Specifically,

$$\frac{w}{MP_L} = \frac{\Delta TC/\Delta L}{\Delta Q/\Delta L} = \frac{\Delta TC}{\Delta L} \cdot \frac{\Delta L}{\Delta Q} = \frac{\Delta TC}{\Delta Q} = MC$$

hourly wage is \$10 and the firm produces five additional units of the commodity with an additional hour of labor time, the marginal cost per unit of output is \$2 ($w/MP_L = \$10/5 = \$2 = MC$). The same is true for capital. That is, $r/MP_K = MC$.[2]

To maximize profits, the firm must use the optimal or least-cost input combination to produce the *best level of output*. We saw in section 8.3 that the best level of output for a perfectly competitive firm is the output at which marginal cost equals marginal revenue (*MR*) or price (*P*).[3] Thus, it follows that to maximize profits

$$w/MP_L = r/MP_K = MC = MR = P \qquad \text{[13–3]}$$

By cross multiplication and rearrangement of the terms, we get equations [13–4] and [13–5]:

$$MP_L \cdot MR = w \text{ or } MP_L \cdot P = w \qquad \text{[13–4]}$$

$$MP_K \cdot MR = r \text{ or } MP_K \cdot P = r \qquad \text{[13–5]}$$

Thus, the profit-maximizing rule is that the firm should hire labor until the marginal product of labor times the firm's marginal revenue or price of the commodity equals the wage rate. Similarly, the firm should rent capital until the marginal product of capital times the firm's marginal revenue or price of the commodity is equal to the interest rate. To maximize profits, the same rule would have to hold for all inputs that the firm uses. In the next section, we will see that this provides the basis for the firm's demand curve for an input.

13.2 THE DEMAND CURVE OF A FIRM FOR AN INPUT

In this section, we build on the discussion of the last section and derive the demand curve of a firm for an input—first, when the input is the only variable input and then, when the input is one of two or more variable inputs.

The Demand Curve of a Firm for One Variable Input

We have stated earlier that a firm demands an input in order to produce a commodity demanded by consumers. Thus, the demand for an input is a **derived demand**—derived, that is, from the demand for the final commodities

---

[2]Specifically,

$$\frac{r}{MP_K} = \frac{\Delta TC/\Delta K}{\Delta Q/\Delta K} = \frac{\Delta TC}{\Delta K} \cdot \frac{\Delta K}{\Delta Q} = \frac{\Delta TC}{\Delta Q} = MC$$

[3]Remember that with perfect competition in the commodity market, $MR = P$.

that the input is used in producing. The demand for an input by a firm shows the quantities of the input that the firm would hire at various alternative input prices. We begin by assuming that only one input is variable (i.e., the amount used of the other inputs is fixed and cannot be changed). This assumption will be relaxed in the next subsection.

According to the marginal concept, a profit-maximizing firm will hire an input as long as the extra income from the sale of the output produced by the input is larger than the extra cost of hiring the input. The extra income is given by the marginal product (MP) of the input times the marginal revenue (MR) of the firm. This is called the **marginal revenue product (MRP)**. That is,

$$MRP = MP \cdot MR \qquad [13-6]$$

When the firm is a perfect competitor in the product market, its marginal revenue is equal to the commodity price (P). In this case, the marginal revenue product is called the **value of the marginal product (VMP)**. That is, when the firm is a perfect competitor in the product market (so that $MR = P$),

$$MRP = MP \cdot MR = MP \cdot P = VMP \qquad [13-6A]$$

If the variable input is labor, we have

$$MRP_L = MP_L \cdot MR = MP_L \cdot P = VMP_L \qquad [13-6B]$$

Thus, the MRP_L or VMP_L is the left-hand side of equation [13-4]. Similarly, the MRP_K or VMP_K is the left-hand side of equation [13-5].

The extra cost of hiring an input or **marginal resource cost (MRC)** is equal to the price of the input if the firm is a perfect competitor in the input market. Perfect competition in the input market means that the firm demanding the input is too small, by itself, to affect the price of the input. In other words, each firm can hire any amount of the input (service) at the given market price for the input. Thus, the firm faces a horizontal or infinitely elastic *supply* curve for the input. For example, if the input is labor, this means that the firm can hire any quantity of labor time at the given wage rate. Thus, a profit-maximizing firm should hire labor as long as the marginal revenue product of labor exceeds the marginal cost of labor or wage rate and until $MRP_L = MRC_L = w$, as indicated by equation [13-4]. Note that the $MRP = MRC$ rule is entirely analogous to the MR-MC profit-maximizing rule employed throughout our discussion of price and output determination in Chapters 8–12.

The actual derivation of a firm's demand schedule for labor, when labor is the only variable input (i.e., when capital and other inputs are fixed), is shown with Table 13–1. In Table 13–1, L refers to the number of workers hired by the firm per day. Q_X is the total output of commodity X produced by the firm by hiring various numbers of workers. The MP_L is the marginal or extra output generated by each additional worker hired. The MP_L is obtained by the change in Q_X per unit change in L. Note that the law of diminishing returns begins to operate with the hiring of the second worker. P_X refers to the price of the final commodity, which is constant (at $10) because the firm is a perfect

TABLE 13–1   Marginal Revenue Product of Labor as the Firm's Demand Schedule for Labor

L	Q_X	MP_L	P_X	$MRP_L = VMP_L$	$MRC_L = w$
0	0	. . .	$10	. . .	$40
1	12	12	10	$120	40
2	22	10	10	100	40
3	30	8	10	80	40
4	36	6	10	60	40
5	40	4	10	40	40
6	42	2	10	20	40

competitor in the product market. The marginal revenue product of labor (MRP_L) is obtained by multiplying the MP_L by MR_X (the marginal revenue from the sale of commodity X) and is equal to the value of the marginal product of labor (VMP_L) because $P_X = MR_X$.[4] The last column gives the marginal resource cost of labor (MRC_L), which is equal to the constant wage rate (w) of $40 per day that the firm must pay to hire each additional worker (since the firm is a perfect competitor in the labor market).

Looking at Table 13–1, we see that the first worker contributes an extra $120 to the firm's revenue (i.e., $MRP_L = \$120$), while the firm incurs an extra cost of only $40 to hire this worker (i.e., $MRC_L = w = \$40$). Thus, it pays for the firm to hire the first worker. The MRP_L of the second worker falls to $100 (because of diminishing returns), but this still greatly exceeds the daily wage of $40 that the firm must pay the second (and all) worker(s) hired. According to equation [13–4], the profit-maximizing firm should hire workers until the $MRP_L = MRC_L = w$. Thus, this firm should hire five workers, at which $VMP_L = w = \$40$. The firm will not hire the sixth worker because he or she will contribute only an extra $20 to the firm's total revenue while adding an extra $40 to its total costs.

Thus, the MRP_L schedule gives the firm's demand schedule for labor. It indicates the number of workers that the firm would hire at various wage rates. For example, if $w = \$120$ per day, the firm would hire only one worker per day. If $w = \$100$, the firm would hire two workers. At $w = \$80$, the firm would hire three workers. At $w = \$40$, $L = 5$, and so on. If we plotted the MRP_L values of Table 13–1 on the vertical axis and L on the horizontal axis, we would get the firm's negatively sloped demand *curve* for labor when labor is the only variable input. This is shown next.

---

[4]Note also that $MRP_L = MP_L \cdot MR = \dfrac{\Delta Q}{\Delta L} \cdot \dfrac{\Delta TR}{\Delta Q} = \dfrac{\Delta TR}{\Delta L}$.

The Demand Curve of a Firm for One of Several Variable Inputs

We have seen that the declining MRP_L schedule given in Table 13–1 gives the firm's demand schedule for labor in the short run when labor is the only variable input. This is shown by the negatively sloped MRP_L curve in Figure 13–1 (on the assumption that labor is infinitesimally divisible or that workers can be hired for any part of a day). The MRP_L or demand for labor curve when labor is the only variable input shows that the firm will hire three workers at $w = \$80$ (point A in Figure 13–1) and five workers at $w = \$40$ (point B).

However, when labor is not the only variable input (i.e., when the firm can also change the quantity of capital and other inputs), the firm's demand curve for labor can be derived from the MRP_L curve, but it is not the MRP_L curve itself. Figure 13–1 shows the derivation of the demand curve for labor by a firm when both labor and capital are variable. As a first step, recall that at $w = \$80$, the profit-maximizing firm would hire three workers (point A on the MRP_L curve in Figure 13–1). This gives the first point on the firm's demand curve for labor when only labor is variable and when both labor and capital are variable. When the daily wage rate falls from $w = \$80$ to $w = \$40$, the firm does not move to point B on the given MRP_L curve and hire five workers (as shown before) if labor is not the only variable input.

FIGURE 13–1   Demand Curve for Labor of a Firm with Labor and Capital Variable

At $w = \$80$, the firm will employ three workers per day (point A on the MRP_L curve). At $w = \$40$, the firm would employ five workers if labor were the only variable input (point B on the MRP_L curve). However, since capital is also variable and complementary to labor, as the firm hires more labor, the MRP_K shifts to the right and the firm also employs more capital (not shown in the figure). But as the firm employs more capital, the MRP_L curve shifts to the right to MRP'_L and the firm employs eight workers per day at $w = \$40$ (point C on MRP'_L). By joining point A and point C, we derive d_L (the firm's demand curve for labor).

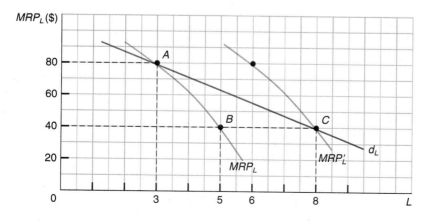

To get another point on the firm's demand curve for labor when both labor and capital are variable, we should realize that labor and capital are usually **complementary inputs** in the sense that when the firm hires more labor, it will also employ more capital (e.g., rent more machinery). For example, when the firm hires more computer programmers, it will usually also pay for the firm to rent more computer terminals, and vice versa. Recall also that the MRP_L curve is drawn on the assumption that the quantity of capital used is fixed at a given level. Similarly, the MRP_K curve is drawn on the assumption of a given amount of labor being used. If the quantity of labor used with various amounts of capital increases (because of a reduction in wages), the entire MRP_K curve will shift outward or to the right. The reason for this is that with a greater amount of labor, each unit of capital will produce more output (see section 6.3). Given the (unchanged) rental price of capital or interest rate, the profit-maximizing firm will then want to expand its use of capital.

But the increase in the quantity of capital used by the firm will, in turn, shift the entire MRP_L curve outward or to the right because each worker will have more capital with which to work (and produce more output). This is shown by the MRP_L' in Figure 13–1. Thus, when the daily wage rate falls to $w = \$40$, the profit-maximizing firm will hire eight workers (point C on the MRP_L' curve) rather than five workers (point B on the MRP_L curve). Thus, point C is another point on the firm's demand curve for labor when labor and capital are both variable. Other points can be similarly obtained. Joining point A and point C gives the firm's demand curve for labor (d_L in Figure 13–1) when labor and capital are both variable and complementary.

To summarize, when $w = \$80$, the firm will hire three workers (point A in Figure 13–1). Point A is a point on the firm's demand curve for labor, whether or not labor is the only variable input. When the wage rate falls to $w = \$40$, the firm will hire five workers (point B on the MRP_L curve) if labor is the only variable input. Thus, the MRP_L curve gives the firm's demand curve for labor when labor is only variable input. If capital is also variable and complementary to labor, as the firm hires more labor because of the reduction in the wage rate, the MRP_K curve (not shown in Figure 13–1) shifts to the right and the firm uses more capital at the unchanged interest rate. However, as the firm uses more capital, its MRP_L curve shifts outward or to the right to MRP_L' and the firm hires not just five workers (point B on the MRP_L curve), but eight workers (point C on the MRP_L' curve). The reason is that only by hiring eight workers will $MRP_L' = w = \$40$. Joining points A and C gives the demand curve for labor of the firm d_L (see the figure) when labor and capital are both variable and complementary.

If capital or other inputs are substitutes for labor, the increase in the quantity of labor used by the firm as a result of a reduction in the wage rate will cause the MRP curves of these other inputs to shift to the *left* (as the utilization of more labor substitutes for, or replaces, some of these other inputs). This, in turn, will cause the MRP_L curve to shift outward and to the right as in Figure 13–1. Thus, whether other inputs are complements or substitutes for labor, the MRP_L shifts outward and to the right when the wage rate falls (and the price of these other inputs remains unchanged). As a result, the firm will hire more labor than indicated on its original MRP_L curve at the lower wage rate (see Figure 13–1).

Thus, the d_L curve is negatively sloped and generally more elastic than the MRP_L curve in the long run when all inputs are variable (whether the other inputs are complements or substitutes of labor, or both). In general, the better the complement and substitute inputs available for labor, the greater the outward shift of the MRP_L curve as a result of a decline in the wage rate, and the more elastic is d_L. The negative slope of the d_L curve means that when the wage rate falls, the profit-maximizing firm will hire more workers. The same is generally true for other inputs. That is, as the price of any input falls, the firm will hire more units of the input (i.e., the demand curve of the input of the firm is negatively sloped). In the process, however, the firm will also make marginal adjustments in the use of all complementary and substitute inputs as well.

13.3 THE MARKET DEMAND CURVE FOR AN INPUT AND ITS ELASTICITY

In this section, we examine how to derive the market demand curve for an input from the individual firms' demand curves for the input. The determination of the market demand curve for an input is important because the equilibrium price of the input is determined at the intersection of the market demand and supply curves of the input under perfect competition. After deriving the market demand curve for an input, we will discuss the determinants of the price elasticity of the demand for the input.

The Market Demand Curve for an Input

The market demand curve for an input is derived from the individual firms' demand curves for the input. Although the process is similar to the derivation of the market demand curve for a commodity, the market demand curve for an input is not simply the horizontal summation of the individual firms' demand curves for the input. The reason is that when the price of an input falls, not only this firm but all other firms will employ more of this and other (complementary) inputs, as explained in section 13.2. Thus, the output of the *commodity* increases and its price falls. Since the MRP of an input is equal to the marginal product of the input times the marginal revenue (which is here equal to the commodity price), the reduction in the commodity price will cause each firm's MRP and demand curves of the input to shift down or to the left. The market demand curve for an input is then derived by the horizontal summation of the individual firm's demand curves for the input *after the effect of the reduction in the commodity price has been considered*. This is shown in Figure 13–2.

FIGURE 13–2   Derivation of the Market Demand Curve for Labor

In the left panel, d_L is the firm's demand curve for labor derived in Figure 13–1. At $w = \$80$ the firm hires three workers (point A on d_L). One hundred identical firms employ 300 workers (point A' in the right panel). Point A' is one point on the market demand curve for labor. When w falls to $w = \$40$, all firms employ more labor, the output of the commodity rises, and its price falls. Then d_L shifts to the left to d'_L, so that at $w = \$40$ the firm hires $6L$ (point E on d'_L), and all firms together will employ $600L$ (point E' in the right panel). By joining points A' and E', we get D_L.

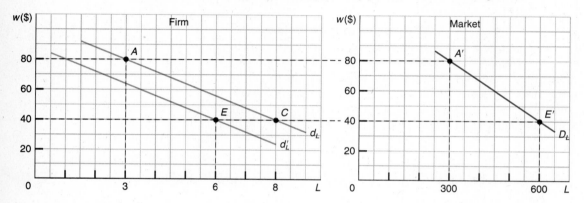

In the left panel of Figure 13–2, d_L is the individual firm's demand curve for labor time derived in Figure 13–1. The d_L curve was derived from the MRP_L of the firm, which itself depended on the marginal product of labor (i.e., MP_L) and the commodity price of $P_x = \$10$. The d_L curve shows that at the wage rate of $w = \$80$ per day the firm would hire three workers per day (point A on d_L). If there were 100 identical firms demanding labor, all firms together would employ 300 workers at $w = \$80$ (point A' in the right panel of Figure 13–2). Point A' is then one point on the market demand curve for labor.

When the wage rate falls to $w = \$40$, the firm would employ eight workers per day (point C on d_L). However, when we consider that all firms will be employing more labor (and capital) when the wage rate falls, they will produce more of the commodity, and the commodity price falls. The reduction in the commodity price will cause a leftward shift in d_L, say to d'_L in the left panel, so that when the wage rate falls to $w = \$40$, the firm will not hire eight workers per day but six workers (point E on d'_L). With 100 identical firms in the market, all firms together will employ 600 workers (point E' in the right panel). By joining points A' and E' in the right panel, we get the market demand curve for labor, D_L. Note that D_L is less elastic than if it were obtained by the straightforward horizontal summation of the d_L curves.

Determinants of the Price Elasticity of Demand for an Input

In section 2.2, we defined the price elasticity of demand for a commodity as the percentage change in the quantity demanded of the commodity resulting from a given percentage change in its price. The price elasticity of demand for an input can similarly be defined as the percentage change in the quantity demanded of the input resulting from a given percentage change in its price. The greater the percentage change in quantity resulting from a given percentage change in price, the greater is the price elasticity of demand. For example, if 2% more workers are employed as a result of a 1% reduction in the wage rate, the price (wage) elasticity of the market demand for labor is 2. If the quantity demanded of labor increased by only ½%, the wage elasticity of labor would be ½.

The determinants of the price elasticity of demand for an input are generally the same as the determinants of the price elasticity of demand for a commodity (discussed in section 5.2). First, the price elasticity of demand for an input is larger the closer and the greater are the number of available substitutes for the input. For example, the price elasticity of demand for copper is greater than the price elasticity of demand for chromium (a metallic element used in alloys and in electroplating) because copper has better and more substitutes (silver, aluminum, fiber glass) than chromium. Thus, the same percentage change in the price of copper and chromium elicits a larger percentage change in the quantity demanded of copper than of chromium.

Second, since the demand for an input is derived from the demand for the final commodity produced with the input, the price elasticity of demand for the input is greater the larger is the price elasticity of demand of the commodity. The reason is that (as we have seen in the previous section) a reduction in the price of an input results in a reduction in the price of the final commodity produced with the input. The more elastic is the demand for the final commodity, the greater is the increase in the quantity demanded of the commodity, and so the greater is the quantity demanded of the input used in the production of the commodity. For example, if the wage rate falls, the price of new homes also declines. If the price elasticity of demand for new homes is very high, then a price reduction for new homes increases very much the quantity demanded of new homes and greatly increases the demand for labor and other inputs going into the production of new homes.

Third, the price elasticity of demand for an input, say aluminum, is greater the larger the price elasticity of *supply* of other inputs for which aluminum is a very good substitute in production. The reason is as follows. A reduction in the price of aluminum will lead producers to substitute aluminum for these other inputs. This is the same as the first reason discussed above, but it is not the end of the story. If the supply curves of these other inputs are very elastic, the reduction (i.e., leftward shift) in their demand curves will not result in a large decline in their prices, and so a great deal of the original increase in the quantity demanded of aluminum as a result of a reduction in its price will persist. This makes the demand curve for aluminum price elastic (if aluminum is a good substitute for these other inputs). Had the supply of these other inputs been inelastic, a reduction in their demand would have reduced their price very much, and checked the increase in the quantity demanded (and the price elasticity of demand) for aluminum.

Fourth, the price elasticity of demand for an input is *lower* the smaller the percentage of the total cost spent on the input. For example, if the percentage of the total cost of the firm spent on an input is only 1%, a doubling of the price of the input will only increase the total costs of the firm by 1%. In that case, a firm is not likely to make great efforts to economize on the use of the input. Therefore, the price elasticity of an input on which the firm spends only a small percentage of its costs is likely to be low. This is usually, but not always, the case, however.

Finally, the price elasticity of an input is greater the longer the period of time allowed for the adjustment to the change in the input price. For example, an increase in the wage of unskilled labor may not reduce their employment very much in the short run because the firm must operate the given plant built to take advantage of the low wage of unskilled labor. In the long run, however, the firm can build a plant using more capital-intensive production techniques to save on the use of the now more expensive unskilled labor. Thus, the reduction in the employment (and the wage elasticity of the demand) of unskilled labor is likely to be greater in the long run than in the short run. In Figure 13–1, the d_L curve (which is the firm's demand curve for labor when labor and other inputs are variable) is more elastic than the MRP_L curve (which is the firm's short-run demand curve for labor when labor is the only variable input).

Example 1

Wage Elasticity of the Demand for Labor in U.S. Manufacturing

Table 13–2 presents the wage elasticity of the demand for labor in some U.S. manufacturing industries. These elasticities are measured by the percentage change in the number of man-hours of labor demanded divided by the

TABLE 13–2   Wage Elasticity of Production Workers in Some U.S. Manufacturing Industries

Industry	Wage Elasticity
Food	−0.51
Chemicals	−0.65
Petroleum	−1.53
Instruments	−1.69
Stone, clay, glass	−1.97
Electrical machinery	−2.14
Fabricated metals	−2.37

Source: R. Waud, "Man-Hour Behavior in U.S. Manufacturing: A Neo-classical Interpretation," *Journal of Political Economy*, May/June 1968.

percentage change in the hourly wages of production workers. The wage elasticities have not been premultiplied by -1 (as in section 2.2) in order to clearly show the inverse relationship between wages and employment. These wage elasticities range from -0.51 in the food industry to -2.37 in the fabricated metals industry.

According to the data in Table 13–2, a 10% increase in the hourly wage of production workers in the U.S. food industry reduces the number of man-hours of production workers demanded by 5.1%. In the fabricated metals industry, a 10% increase in wages reduces the quantity demanded of labor by 23.7%. Thus, the ability to substitute other inputs for labor is much greater in the fabricated metals industry than in the food industry. Explaining the reason for these large differences requires a detailed knowledge of the various industries.

More recent studies have found that the wage elasticity of the demand for labor in U.S. manufacturing as a whole ranges from -0.09 to -0.62.[5] Thus, it seems that the wage elasticity of labor in manufacturing declined during the past two decades. The wage elasticity of demand for labor in retail trade, on the other hand, was found to range between -0.34 and -1.20. The higher wage elasticity in retail trade than in manufacturing is due to the greater substitutability between capital and labor in retail trade than in manufacturing. Finally, the average wage elasticity of demand for labor for the economy as a whole was estimated to be -0.30.

▲

13.4 THE SUPPLY CURVE OF AN INPUT

In this section, we first derive an individual's supply curve of labor. Then, we examine the substitution and the income effects of a wage increase. Finally, we discuss the market supply curve of an input in general, and the market supply of labor in particular. In the next section, we will use the market supply curve examined in this section and the market demand curve derived in section 13.3 to determine the equilibrium price of an input (the wage rate).

The Supply of Labor by an Individual

The short-run supply curve of an input (like the supply curve of a final commodity) is generally positively sloped, indicating that a greater quantity of the input is supplied per unit of time at higher input prices. For example, if the price of iron ore rises, mining firms will supply more iron ore per time period. The same is true for an **intermediate good** such as steel (produced

---

[5]See, R. G. Ehrenberg and R. S. Smith, *Modern Labor Economics: Theory and Public Policy* (New York: HarperCollins, 1991), Chapter 4.

with iron ore), which is itself used as an input in the production of many final commodities such as automobiles. That is, steel producers will supply more steel at higher steel prices. However, while natural resources (such as iron ore) and intermediate goods (such as steel) are supplied by firms, and their supply curves are generally positively sloped, labor is supplied by individuals and their supply curve may be backward-bending. That is, after some wage rate, higher wage rates may result in individuals demanding more leisure time and supplying fewer *hours* of work per day. This is shown in Figure 13–3.

FIGURE 13–3   Derivation of an Individual's Supply Curve of Labor

In the left panel, U_1, U_2, U_3, and U_4 show the trade-off between leisure and income for the individual, while the straight budget lines show the trade-off between leisure and income in the market. The absolute slope of the budget lines gives the wage rates. The individual maximizes satisfaction at point H (with 18 hours of leisure per day and a daily income of $15) on U_1 with $w = \$2.50$, at point E (with 16 hours of leisure and income of $40) on U_2 with $w = \$5$, and so on. By plotting hours of work per day at various wage rates, we get the individual's backward-bending supply curve of labor (s_L) in the right panel.

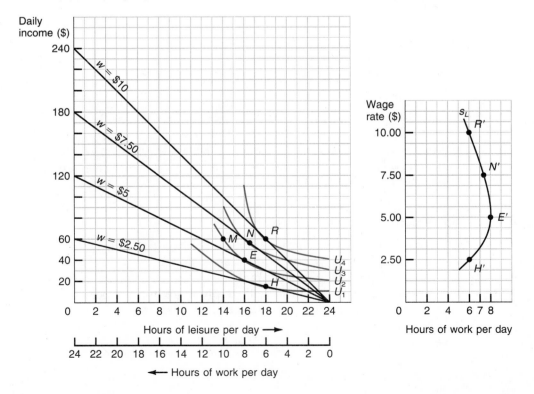

The left panel of Figure 13–3 is used to derive the backward-bending supply curve of labor of an individual shown in the right panel. The movement from left to right on the horizontal axis of the figure in the left panel measures hours of leisure time for the individual (the top scale at the bottom of the figure). Subtracting hours of leisure from the 24 hours of the day, we get the hours worked by the individual per day (the bottom scale in the left panel). Hours of leisure plus hours of work always equal 24. On the other hand, the vertical axis in the left panel measures money income.

Indifference curves U_1, U_2, U_3, and U_4 in the left panel show the trade-off between leisure and income for the individual. They are similar to the individual's indifference curves between two commodities, discussed in section 3.2. For example, the individual is indifferent between 14 hours of leisure (10 hours of work) and a daily income of $60 (point M on U_2) on the one hand, and 16 hours of leisure (8 hours of work) and a daily income of $40 (point E on U_2) on the other. Thus, the individual is willing to give up $20 of income to increase his or her leisure time by 2 hours. Indifference curves U_3 and U_4 provide more utility or satisfaction to the individual than U_2, and U_2 provides more utility or satisfaction than U_1.

Given the wage rate, we can easily define the budget line of the individual. When the individual takes all 24 hours in leisure (i.e., works zero hours), the individual's income is zero regardless of the wage rate. Thus, any budget line of the individual starts at this point on the horizontal axis in the left panel. On the other hand, if the individual worked 24 hours per day, his or her income would be $60 if the wage rate were $2.50 (the lowest budget line), his or her income would be $120 if $w = $5 (the second budget line), $180 if $w = $7.50 (the third budget line), and $240 if $w = $10 (the highest budget line). Note that the wage rate is given by the absolute value of the slope of the budget line. Thus, $w = $60/24 hours = $2.50/hour for the lowest budget line, $w = $120/24 hours = $5 for the second budget line, $w = $180/24 hours = $7.50 for the third budget line, and $w = $240/24 hours = $10 for the highest budget line. These budget lines are similar to the individual's budget lines derived in section 3.3.

As shown in section 3.5, an individual maximizes utility or satisfaction by reaching the highest indifference curve possible with his or her budget line. Thus, if the wage rate is $2.50, the individual will take 18 hours in leisure (i.e., work 6 hours) and earn an income of $15 per day (point H on U_1 in the left panel of Figure 13–3). This gives point H' on the individual's supply curve of labor (s_L) in the right panel. With $w = $5, the individual takes 16 hours of leisure (i.e, works 8 hours) and earns an income of $40 per day (point E on U_2 in the left panel). This gives point E' on s_L in the right panel. At $w = $7.50, the individual chooses 16.5 hours of leisure (works 7.5 hours) and has an income of $56.25 per day (point N on U_3 and N' on s_L). Finally, at $w = $10, the individual chooses 18 hours of leisure (works 6 hours) and has an income of $60 per day (point R on U_4 and R' on s_L).

Note that the individual's supply curve of labor (s_L in the right panel of

Figure 13–3) is positively sloped until the wage rate of $5, and it bends backward at higher wage rates. Thus, the individual works *more* hours (i.e., takes less leisure) until the wage rate of $5 per hour and works *fewer* hours (i.e., takes more leisure) at higher wage rates.

Substitution and Income Effects of a Wage Increase

The reason that an individual's supply curve of labor is backward-bending can be explained by separating the substitution effect from the income effect of the wage increase. That is, an increase in wages (just like an increase in a commodity price) gives rise to a substitution effect and an income effect. In the case of an increase in the price of a normal good, the substitution and the income effects work in the same direction (to reduce the quantity demanded of the commodity). On the other hand, in the case of an increase in the wage rate, the substitution and the income effects operate in opposite directions, and (as explained next) this causes the individual's supply curve of labor to be backward-bending.

According to the substitution effect, an increase in the wage rate leads an individual to work more (i.e., to substitute work for leisure). That is, as the wage rate rises, the price of leisure increases and the individual takes less leisure (i.e., works more). Thus, the substitution effect of the wage increase always operates to make the individual's supply curve of labor *positively* sloped. However, an increase in the wage rate also raises the individual's income, and with a rise in income, the individual demands more of every normal good, including leisure (i.e., supplies fewer hours of work). Thus, the income effect of a wage increase always operates to make the individual's supply curve *negatively* sloped.

The substitution and income effects operate over the entire length of the individual's supply curve of labor. Until the wage rate of $w = \$5$ in Figure 13–3, the substitution effect overwhelms the opposite income effect and the individual works more (i.e., his or her supply curve of labor is positively sloped). At $w = \$5$, the substitution effect is balanced by the income effect and s_L is vertical (point E' in the figure). At wage rates higher than $w = \$5$, the (positive) substitution effect is overwhelmed by the (negative) income effect and s_L bends backward. Note that theory does not tell us at what wage rate the bend occurs. It only says that at some sufficiently high wage rate this is likely to occur. Since individuals' tastes differ, the wage rate at which an individual's supply curve of labor bends backward is likely to differ from individual to individual.

Also note that although the substitution effect is usually greater than the income effect for a *commodity*, this is not the case for labor. The reason is that a consumer spends his or her income on many commodities, so that an increase in the price of any one commodity is not going to greatly reduce his or her real income (i.e., the income effect is small in relation to the substitution effect). On the other hand, since most individuals' incomes come primarily from wages, an increase in wages will greatly affect the individuals' incomes (so that the income effect may overwhelm the opposite substitution effect). At the wage rate at which this occurs, s_L will bend backward. The separation of the substitution and the income effects of a wage increase is shown graphically in section 13.8.

It might be argued that individuals do not have a choice of the number of hours they work per day, and so the above analysis is not relevant. Yet, this is not entirely true. For example, an individual may choose to work any number of hours on a part-time basis, may choose an occupation that requires six or seven hours of work per day instead of eight, may choose an occupation that allows more or less vacation time, and may or may not agree to work overtime (see section 13.8), and so on. All that is required for the analysis to be relevant is for *some* occupations to require different hours of work per day and/or some flexibility in hours of work.

Note that as workers' wages and incomes have risen over time, the average workweek (and the length of the average workday) has declined from ten hours per day for six days per week at the turn of the century to eight hours per day for five days per week, or even slightly less, today. However, the trend toward fewer hours of work per day and per week seems to have come to an end or to have considerably slowed down over the past half a century. Thus, the substitution and income effects of higher wages must have been more or less in balance in recent decades. Over the same period of time, however, the participation rate (i.e., the percentage of the population in the labor force) has increased.

The Market Supply Curve for an Input

The market supply curve for an input is obtained from the straightforward horizontal summation of the supply curve of individual suppliers of the input, just as in the case of the supply curve of a final commodity (see section 8.4). In the case of inputs of natural resources and intermediate goods, which are supplied by firms, the short-run market supply curve of the input is generally positively sloped (as is the firm's supply curve). The market supply curve of labor is usually also positively sloped, but it may bend backward at very high wages (see Example 2).

Figure 13–4 shows a hypothetical market supply curve of labor (S_L) measuring the *number* of workers on the horizontal axis and the *daily* wage rate on the vertical axis. It shows that at the wage of $20 per day, 400 people are willing to work in this market (point H). At $w = $40 per day, 600 people are willing to work (point E'). At $w = $60, 700 are willing to work (point G), and so on. Note that S_L is positively sloped over the range of daily wages shown in the figure but becomes less elastic at high wage rates (and may eventually bend backward at still higher wage rates).

The shape of S_L is also the net result of two opposing forces. Higher daily wages will, on one hand, induce some individuals to enter the labor market (to take advantage of the higher wages), but it will also result in some individuals leaving the job market as their spouse's wages and income rise. Note that

FIGURE 13–4   **Market Supply Curve of Labor**

Market supply curve of labor S_L shows that at the wage of $20 per day, 400 people are willing to work in this market (point H). At $w = $40 per day, 600 people are willing to work (point E'). At $w = $60, 700 are willing to work (point G), and so on. S_L is positively sloped over the range of daily wages shown but becomes less elastic at high wage rates (and may eventually bend backward at still higher wage rates).

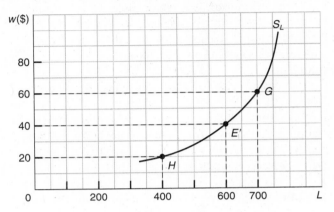

the supply curve of labor is less likely to be backward-bending for a particular industry than for the economy as a whole, because workers can always be attracted to an industry from other industries by raising wages sufficiently.

Example 2

 The Backward-Bending Supply Curve of Physicians' Services

The enactment of Medicare (a subsidy for the medical care of the elderly) and Medicaid (a subsidy for the medical care of the poor) in 1965, as well as the increased insurance coverage for physicians' bills, greatly increased the ability of broad segments of the population to pay for medical services and resulted in a sharp rise in medical fees. The rise in medical fees, however, seems to have led to a reduction, rather than to an increase, in the quantity supplied of physicians' services (i.e., the supply curve for physicians' services seems to be backward-bending).

In fact, Feldstein found that the price elasticity of supply of physicians' services in the United States was between -0.67 and -0.91 over the 1948–1966 period. This means that a 10% increase in the price of physicians' services results in a *reduction* in the quantity supplied of services of between 6.7% and 9.1%. Thus, according to Feldstein's results, the sharp increase in the fees for physicians' services in recent years actually resulted in a reduction in the quantity of services supplied.

More recently, Borjas and Heckman found that the wage elasticity of the labor supply of adult males was between -0.1 and -0.2. Thus, the supply curve of adult males seems to be backward-bending but quite inelastic. On the other hand, most studies found (see Ehrenberg and Smith) that adult females and teenagers work more when the real wage rate rises (i.e., their supply curves are positively sloped) and so does the total population as a whole, but supply elasticities are again quite small (i.e., supply curves are close to being vertical).

Sources: M. Feldstein, "The Rising Price of Physicians' Services," *The Review of Economics and Statistics*, May 1970; G. J. Borjas and J. J. Heckman, "Labor Supply Estimates for Public Policy Evaluation," *Working Paper No. 299*, National Bureau of Economic Research, November 1978; and R. G. Ehrenberg and R. S. Smith, *Modern Labor Economics: Theory and Public Policy* (New York: HarperCollins, 1991), Chapter 6.

13.5 PRICING AND EMPLOYMENT OF AN INPUT

Just as in the case of a final commodity, the equilibrium price and employment of an input is given at the intersection of the market demand and the market supply curve of the input in a perfectly competitive market. This is shown in Figure 13–5 for labor.

In Figure 13–5, D_L is the market demand curve for labor (from the right panel of Figure 13–2), and S_L is the market supply curve of labor (from Figure 13–4). The intersection of D_L and S_L at point E' gives the equilibrium (daily)

FIGURE 13–5 Determination of the Equilibrium Wage Rate and Level of Employment

D_L is the market demand curve for labor (from the right panel of Figure 13–2), and S_L is the market supply curve of labor (from Figure 13–4). The intersection of D_L and S_L at point E' gives the equilibrium (daily) wage rate of \$40 and the equilibrium level of employment of 600 workers per day.

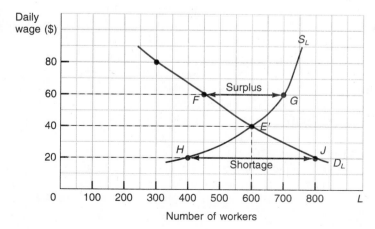

wage of $40 and level of employment of 600 workers per day. At the lower wage rate of $20 per day, firms would like to employ 800 workers per day, but only half that number are willing to work. Thus, there is a shortage of 400 workers per day (*HJ* in the figure), and the wage rate rises. At the high wage of $60 per day, 700 workers are willing to work, but firms would like to employ only 450. There is a surplus of 250 workers (*FG*), and the wage rate falls. Only at $w = $40 is the number of workers who are willing to work equal to the number of workers that firms want to employ (600), and the market is in equilibrium.

Note that at the equilibrium daily wage of $40, each of the 100 identical firms in the market will employ six workers per day (point *E* on d'_L in the left panel of Figure 13–2). In a perfectly competitive input market, each firm is too small to perceptibly affect the wage rate (i.e., the firm can employ any number of workers per day at the equilibrium market wage rate of $40 per day). Another way of saying this is that the firm faces a horizontal or infinitely elastic supply curve of labor at the given wage rate. Since the price of an input equals the marginal revenue product (*MRP*), the theory of input pricing and employment has been called the **marginal productivity theory.**

Finally, note that we have implicitly assumed that all units of the input are identical (have the same productivity) and receive the same price. In the case of labor, the wages of all workers would be the same only if all occupations were equally attractive (or unattractive), if all workers had identical qualifications and productivity, and if there was no interference with the operation of the market. These topics are discussed in section 13.8.

Example 3
The Glut of Lawyers and Doctors in the United States

There were 780,000 lawyers in the United States in 1992—up from 355,000 in 1971—and spending on legal services increased from $10 billion to $100 billion over the same period. Although some increase in the number of lawyers was justified by population growth, the proliferation of laws and regulations, and the greater propensity on the part of citizens to bring legal action, 70% of the members of the American Bar Association believe that the boom has gotten out of hand and that something must be done to limit their number. As predicted by economic theory, the larger increase in the supply, relative to the demand, of law services resulted in a reduction in the price of many law services, such as for uncontested divorces, wills, small personal injury cases, and nonbusiness bankruptcy cases. (It is primarily in large *corporate* disputes that costs are rising sharply and multimillion dollar fees are becoming the rule rather than the exception.) Competition for business has resulted in attorneys setting up legal clinics, often in drugstores and shopping malls, to handle simple cases at cut-rate prices. Lawyers' search for business has also been blamed by some for the rash of lawsuits in recent years. In their search for business, lawyers have also increasingly turned to advertising since 1977, when the U.S. Supreme Court abolished state prohibitions against advertising. Despite the reduction in the price of many legal services and in lawyers' relative incomes, the number of applications to and graduates of law schools kept increasing, and so we can expect a further decline in the price of legal services and in the relative income of lawyers in the coming years.

A similar situation may be developing in the medical profession. A recent American Medical Association (AMA) report indicated that in the 20 years from 1965 to 1985 the number of physicians for each 100,000 people in the United States has grown by 51% and is expected to increase by another 22% by the turn of the century, when there would be 176 doctors per 100,000 residents. This, together with pressure to control the rise in health costs, has led to an "impending surplus" of physicians and a decline in their real incomes (i.e., the earnings adjusted for inflation). The AMA's report called for cutbacks in medical school enrollment and limits on the number of foreign physicians entering the country. The Federal Trade Commission, however, has ruled (and its ruling has been upheld by the Supreme Court) that the AMA, as any other professional group, is subject to the antitrust laws prohibiting restraints of trade. To be sure, not all medical specialties are equally affected. For example, a "shortage" of psychiatrists (especially child psychiatrists) is developing, but a major "surplus" of surgeons, obstetricians, pediatricians, cardiologists, and diagnostic radiologists is expected. While doctors are not unemployed, some are having trouble getting enough patients and are recommending more unnecessary treatment. Economic theory predicts that, under these circumstances, a completely free market would result in lower (or less rapidly rising) prices for medical services and physicians' incomes. This is to be contrasted to the situation in some other fields such as engineering and nursing which face a serious shortage and rising real incomes (see Example 14.1).

Sources: "A Glut of Lawyers—Impact on U.S.," *U.S. News & World Report*, December 19, 1983, pp. 59–61; "The Legal Profession," *The Economist*, July 18, 1992, pp. 3–18; "Jobless New Lawyers Seek Other Venues," *Wall Street Journal*, January 22, 1993, p. B1; "A.M.A. Board Studies Ways to Curb Supply of Physicians," *New York Times*, June 16, 1986, p. 1; "Rising Supply of Doctors May Be Bad for Health Costs," *Wall Street Journal*, May 8, 1991, p. B1; and "Inflation Outpaced Doctors' Incomes in 1991," May 24, 1992, p. 29.

▲

13.6 INPUT PRICE EQUALIZATION AMONG INDUSTRIES, REGIONS, AND COUNTRIES

In this section, we examine the process whereby input prices are equalized through the movement of inputs among industries and regions, rather than through trade among countries. We deal specifically with the equalization of the wage rate across industries, regions, and countries on the assumption that all labor is identical. The same price-equalizing process generally operates for each type of labor and capital.

Input Price Equalization Among Industries and Regions of a Country

If the wage rate differs between two industries or regions of a country, some labor will leave the low-wage industry or region for the high-wage industry or region until the wage difference is eliminated. This is shown in Figure 13–6.

In Figure 13–6, the left panel refers to industry or region A while the right panel refers to industry or region B. The vertical axes measure the daily wage while the horizontal axes measure the number of workers. In the left panel, the intersection of the industry demand curve (D_A) and supply curve (S_A) at point E gives the equilibrium daily wage of $30 in industry or region A. On the other hand, the right panel shows that the equilibrium daily wage (given by point E at the intersection of D_B and S_B) in industry or region B is $50. Some workers will then leave industry or region A to take advantage of the higher wages in industry or region B. As this occurs, the supply of labor declines (i.e., the supply curve shifts to the left) in industry or region A and simultaneously increases (i.e., shifts to the right) in industry or region B. This

FIGURE 13–6   Wage-Equalizing Shifts in Domestic Supply

The left panel shows that D_A and S_A intersect at point E defining the equilibrium daily wage of $30 in industry or region A, while the right panel shows that D_B and S_B intersect at point E defining the equilibrium daily wage of $50 in industry or region B. As labor leaves industry or region A, attracted by the higher wage in B, S_A shifts to the left to S'_A in the left panel while S_B shifts simultaneously to the right to S'_B in the right panel, so that the daily wage in the two industries or regions becomes equal at $40 (point E' in both panels).

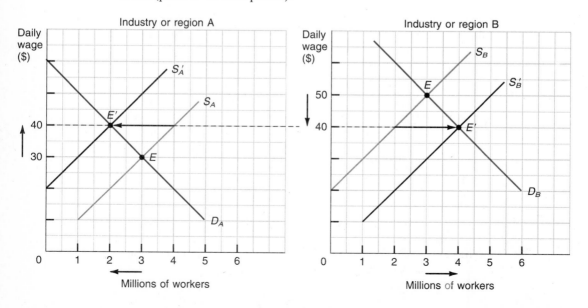

continues until S_A has shifted to S'_A in the left panel and S_B has shifted to S'_B in the right panel, so that the wage rate is equal at $40 per day in both industries (see point E' where D_A and S'_A intersect in the left panel and where D_B and S'_B intersect in the right panel). In total, 1 million workers move from industry or region A to industry or region B (see the direction and the length of the arrows on the quantity axes in both panels).

If there are some obstructions to the movement of labor, or if workers—other things being equal—prefer working in industry or region A rather than in B, then less than 1 million workers will move from industry or region A to industry or region B, and wage differences will only be reduced rather than be entirely eliminated. What is important, however, is the process whereby changes or shifts in input supply in the two industries or regions reduce interindustry or interregional wage differences. The same is true for each particular type of labor and other mobile inputs. They always tend to flow or move to find employment in the industries or regions where returns or earnings are higher. In the process, they reduce interindustry and interregional differences in the returns to homogeneous factors or inputs (i.e., the earnings of inputs of the same quality and productivity). In fact, Bellante has found that when adjustment is made for regional differences in costs of living, North-South real wage differences for the same type of labor have been eliminated for the most part in the United States.[6]

Input Price Equalization Among Countries

The equalization in the returns or earnings of homogeneous inputs also operates internationally, but it occurs mostly through international trade rather than through the flow or migration of inputs from low- to high-return countries. The reason is that most countries impose serious restrictions on the international flow of some inputs, especially the migration of labor. Figure 13–7 shows how wage equalization occurs internationally through trade. For simplicity, we assume that we have only two homogeneous inputs, labor and capital.

The left panel shows that D_1 (the demand curve for labor in country 1) intersects S_1 (the supply curve of labor in country 1) at point E, giving the equilibrium daily wage of $20 in country 1 in the absence of trade. The right panel shows that D_2 and S_2 intersect at point E, giving the equilibrium daily wage of $40 in country 2 in the absence of trade. We assume that labor cannot migrate from country 1 to country 2. Wages can still be equalized between the two countries through trade, however.

Because of lower wages, country 1 has a relative comparative advantage in labor-intensive commodities (i.e., commodities that require a relative abun-

[6]See, D. Bellante, "The North-South Wage Differential and the Migration of Heterogeneous Labor," *American Economic Review*, March 1979.

FIGURE 13-7   International Wage-Equalization Through International
Trade

The left panel shows that in the absence of trade D_1 and S_1 intersect at point E, defining
the equilibrium daily wage of $20 in country 1; while the right panel shows that D_2
and S_2 intersect at point E, defining the equilibrium daily wage of $40 in country 2.
As country 1 specializes in the production of and exports labor-intensive commodities,
D_1 shifts to the right to D_1' and defines the new equilibrium daily wage of $30 at point
E' in the left panel. On the other hand, as country 2 replaces some domestic production
of labor-intensive commodities with imports from country 1, D_2 shifts to the left to
D_2' and defines the new equilibrium daily wage of $30 at point E' in the right panel.

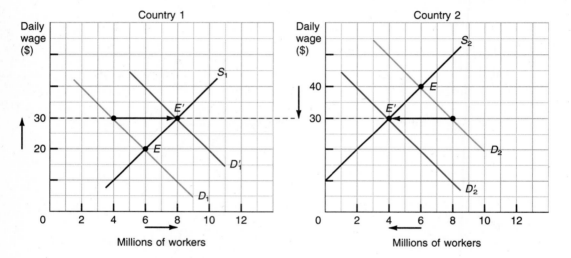

dance of labor in production). Country 2 will then have a comparative advantage in capital-intensive commodities. With trade, country 1 will specialize in
the production of and export labor-intensive commodities in exchange for
capital-intensive commodities from country 2. The left panel shows that the
demand curve for labor will then increase or shift to the right from D_1 to
D_1' in country 1 and defines the new equilibrium daily wage of $30 at point
E' (where D_1' intersects S_1). On the other hand, the right panel shows that
the demand curve for labor will decrease or shift to the left from D_2 to D_2' in
country 2 (as country 2 replaces some domestic production of labor-intensive
commodities with imports from country 1) and defines the new equilibrium
daily wage of $30 at point E' (where D_2' intersects S_2).

Note that now wages have been equalized in the two countries through
international trade and without any migration of labor from country 1 to
country 2. The reason for this is that as long as wages are lower in country
1, labor-intensive commodities will be cheaper in country 1 than in country
2, and country 1 will expand its exports of the labor-intensive commodity.
But as trade expands, country 1 will demand more labor until D_1 has shifted
all the way to the right to D_1' (see the left panel). The demand for labor in
country 2, on the other hand, simultaneously will decline until it reaches

TABLE 13–3   Real Hourly Wages in Manufacturing in Leading Industrial Countries as a Percentage of the U.S. Wage

Country	1959	1970	1983	1990
Japan	11	24	51	108
Italy	23	42	62	100
France	27	41	62	101
United Kingdom	29	35	53	82
Germany	29	56	84	118
Unweighted average	24	40	62	102
United States	100	100	100	100

Sources: Calculated from indices from: IMF, *International Financial Statistics;* OECD, *Economic Outlook;* U.N., *Monthly Bulletin of Statistics;* and U.S. Bureau of Labor Statistics, *Bulletin.*

D_2' (see the right panel), so that wages are equalized at $30 in both countries. Thus, international trade is a substitute for, or has the same effect on, wages as the international migration of labor (which is often seriously restricted). However, while trade operates on the demand for labor (i.e., shifts the demand curves for labor) in the two countries, international migration operates through the supply (i.e., shifts the supply curves) of labor in the two countries. If some labor is allowed to migrate from country 1 to country 2, this will reinforce the tendency of international trade to equalize wages in the two countries. Although we have dealt with labor in general, the same process would operate to equalize the wages of each particular type of labor and the price of each other type of input internationally.

As predicted by theory, Table 13–3 shows that real manufacturing wages have indeed converged among the leading industrial countries during the past three decades.[7] The existence of transportation costs, trade restrictions, and other market imperfections prevented the complete equalization of wages internationally, however. One question remains unanswered. That is, if trade reduces wages in a higher-wage country, why should the higher-wage country trade with a lower-wage country? The reason (not shown in Figure 13–7) is that the higher-wage country will have a comparative advantage in capital-intensive commodities. As it specializes in the production of these commodities for export, the demand and returns on capital increase by more than wages fall, and so this country also benefits from trade.[8]

---

[7]There are many other forces besides international trade that contributed to this convergence, however, including some international labor migration from relatively low- to relatively high-wage industrial countries.

[8]Some of the capital owners' gains from trade can be taxed away and redistributed to labor in such a way that both labor and capital gain from trade in the higher-wage country. This is possible because, as each country specializes in the production of the commodities of its comparative advantage, total world output increases and both countries share in this increase in output.

13.7 ECONOMIC RENT: AN UNNECESSARY PAYMENT TO BRING FORTH THE SUPPLY OF AN INPUT

Economic rent differs from the everyday meaning of the term "rent," which is a payment made to lease an apartment, an automobile, or any other durable asset. Economic rent originally referred only to the payment made to landowners to lease their land (which was assumed to be in fixed supply). Today, **economic rent** is defined as that portion of the payment to the supplier of any input (not just land) that is in excess of the minimum amount necessary to retain the input in its present use. If the market supply of an input is fixed, demand alone determines the input price and all of the payment made to the input is rent. If the market supply of an input is positively sloped, only the area above the supply curve and below the price of the input represents rent. This is shown in Figure 13–8.

In the left panel of Figure 13–8, the market supply of the input, say, land, is fixed at 600 acres (i.e., S is vertical). If the market demand curve is D, the (rental) price is $40 per acre (point E), and the entire payment of $24,000 ($40 times 600) per month made to the owners of land is economic rent. If the market demand were D', the rental price would be $60 (point E'), and rent $36,000 per month. If the market demand for the input were D'', the rental price would be $20 (point E''), and rent $12,000 per month. Note that regardless of the level of demand and price, the same quantity of land is supplied per month, even at an infinitesimally small rental price. Thus, all of the payments

FIGURE 13–8   Measurement of Economic Rent

The left panel shows 600 acres of land supplied per month regardless of the rental price. With D, the price is $40 (point E) and the entire payment of $24,000 ($40 times 600) is rent. With D', $P = $60 (point E') and rent is $36,000. With D'', $P = $20 and rent is $12,000. In the right panel, S_L is positively sloped. With D_L, $w = $40 and 600 workers are employed (point E). Shaded area $ENR = $6,000 represents economic rent or a payment that is not needed to retain the 600 workers in the particular industry.

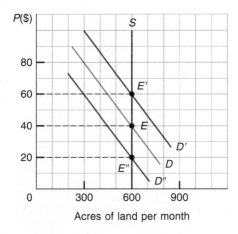
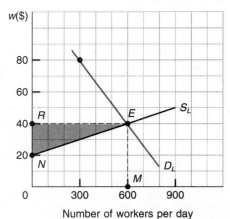

Acres of land per month   Number of workers per day

made to the landowners represent economic rent. This is true not only for land but for any input in fixed supply. For example, since the supply of Picasso paintings is fixed, they will be supplied (sold) at whatever price (including the retention price of present owners) they can fetch. Therefore, all payments made to purchase Picassos represent economic rent.

In the right panel, the supply of the input, say, labor, to an industry is positively sloped. This means that higher daily wages will induce more individuals to work in the industry. The equilibrium wage of $40 is determined at the intersection of D_L and S_L (point E in the figure, at which 600 workers are employed). Each of the 600 (identical) workers receives a wage of $40 per day. Yet, one worker could be found who would work for a wage of only $20, and 300 workers would be willing to work at a daily wage of $30 each (see the S_L curve in the right panel). Thus, the shaded area above the supply curve and below the equilibrium wage of $40 represents economic rent. It is the workers' excess earnings over their next-best employment. That is, the 600 workers receive a total wage of $24,000 (the area of rectangle $EMOR$), but they only need to be paid $EMON$ to be retained in the industry. Therefore, the area of shaded triangle ENR ($6,000) represents economic rent or the payment that need not be made by the particular industry to retain 600 workers in the long run.

Note that even land may not be fixed in supply to any industry, because some land could be bid away from other uses. Land may not even be fixed for the economy as a whole, since over time, land can be augmented through reclamation and drainage and depleted through erosion and loss of fertility. Thus, the payment to lease land, too, may be only partly rent. In general, the more inelastic is the supply curve of an input to the industry, the greater is the proportion of economic rent. In the extreme case, the supply curve is vertical and all the payment to the input is rent. The importance of this is that rent could all be taxed away without reducing the quantity supplied of the input. This is an excellent tax since it does not discourage work or reduce the supply of labor (or other inputs) even in the long run. Note that economic rent is analogous to the concept of *producer surplus* (see section 8.8). Producer surplus was defined as the excess of the commodity price over the *marginal cost of producing a given level of the commodity*. Economic rent is the excess payment that an *input owner* receives and the minimum he or she requires to continue to keep the input in its present use.

While all or some of the payment made by an industry to the suppliers of an input is rent, all payments made by an *individual firm* to employ an input are a *cost* to the firm, which the firm must pay to retain the use of the input. If the firm tried to pay less than the market price for the input, the firm would be unable to retain any unit of the input. For example, if a firm tried to employ workers at less than the $40 daily wage prevailing in the market, the firm would lose all of its workers to other firms. Finally, note that any payment made to *temporarily* fixed inputs is sometimes called **quasi-rent.** Thus, the returns to fixed inputs in the short run are quasi-rents (see problem 8). These payments need not be made in order for these fixed inputs to be supplied in the short run. In the long run, however, all inputs are variable, and unless they receive a price equal to their next-best alternative, they will not be supplied. To the extent that they receive more than this, the inputs receive economic rent. In long-run, perfectly competitive equilibrium, all inputs receive payments equal to their marginal revenue product and the firm breaks even.

13.8 ANALYSIS OF LABOR MARKETS UNDER PERFECT COMPETITION

In this section, we discuss some important applications of the theory presented in the chapter: separation of the substitution from the income effect of a change in wages, the analysis of overtime pay, the cause of wage differentials, and the effect of minimum wages. These applications clearly indicate the usefulness and applicability of the theory.

Substitution and Income Effects of a Wage Rate Change

We have seen in section 13.4 that an increase in wages gives rise to a substitution effect and an income effect. That is, when the wage rate rises, on one hand, the individual tends to substitute work for leisure (since the price of leisure has increased). On the other hand, the increase in income resulting from the wage rise leads the individual to demand more of every normal good, including leisure (i.e., to work fewer hours). We can separate the substitution effect from the income effect as in section 4.3. This is shown in Figure 13–9.

The movement from point E to point R in Figure 13–9 is the combined substitution and income effects of the wage increase from $5 to $10 (as in Figure 13–3). The substitution effect can be isolated by drawing the hypothetical budget line that is tangent to U_2 at point M and with the slope reflecting the higher wage of $10. Since the consumer is on original indifference curve U_2, his or her income is the same as before the wage rise, and the movement along U_2 from point M to point E measures the substitution effect. By itself, it shows that when w rises from $5 to $10, the individual reduces leisure time from 16 to 12 hours (i.e., increases hours of work from 8 to 12 per day). Then, the shift from point M on U_2 to point R on U_4 is the income effect of the wage increase. In this case, the increase in wages raises the individual's income by $50 ($240–$190; see the vertical axis of the figure). By itself, the income effect leads the individual to increase leisure from 12 to 18 hours (i.e., to work 6 hours less). The net result is that the individual increases leisure (works less) by 2 hours per day (ER).

Overtime Pay and the Supply of Labor Services

The hourly wage of many workers increases after a specific number of hours worked per day. This is called **overtime pay.** Figure 13–10 shows the additional

FIGURE 13–9   Separation of the Substitution Effect from the Income Effect of a Wage Increase

The movement from point E to point R is the combined substitution and income effects of the wage increase from \$5 to \$10 (as in Figure 13–3). We can isolate the substitution effect by shifting the highest budget line down parallel to itself until it is tangent to indifference curve U_2 at point M. The movement along U_2 from point M to point E measures the substitution effect of the wage increase. The shift from point M on U_2 to point R on U_4 is the income effect.

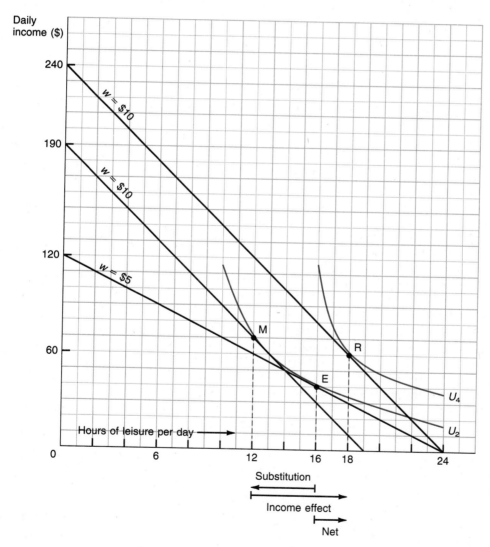

FIGURE 13–10   Overtime Pay and the Supply of Labor Services

Initially, at $w = \$5$, the individual demands 16 hours of leisure (works 8 hours per day) and earns an income of $40 (point E on U_2, as in Figures 13–3 and 13–9). With overtime pay of $w = \$20$ per hour (the slope of ET), the individual will work 2 additional hours per day and have a total income of $80 (point T on U_3).

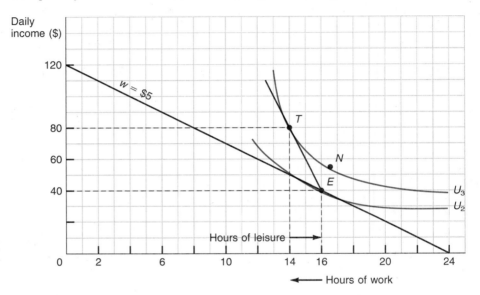

number of hours worked per day by an individual as a result of overtime pay.

Initially, at the wage rate of $5 per hour, the individual demands 16 hours of leisure (works eight hours per day) and earns an income of $40 (point E on U_2, as in Figures 13–3 and 13–9). With an overtime pay of $20 per hour (the slope of ET in Figure 13–10), the individual can be induced to work two additional hours per day and have a total income of $80 per day (point T on higher indifference curve U_3). Thus, the substitution effect (which encourages work) exceeds the income effect (which discourages work), and the individual works more hours with overtime pay.

Wage Differentials

Up to this point we have generally assumed that all occupations are equally attractive and that all units of an input, say, labor, are homogeneous (i.e., have the same training and productivity), so that the wages of all workers are the same. If all jobs and workers were identical, wage differences could not persist among occupations or regions of a country under perfect competition. As pointed out in section 13.6, workers would leave lower-wage occupations and regions for higher-wage occupations and regions until all wage differentials disappeared.

In the real world, jobs differ in attractiveness, workers have different qualifications and training, and markets may not be perfectly competitive. All of these can result in different wages for different occupations and for workers with different training and abilities. More formally, wages differ among different jobs and categories of workers because of (1) equalizing differentials, (2) the existence of noncompeting groups, and (3) imperfect competition. We will now briefly examine each of these.

Equalizing wage differentials are wage differences that compensate workers for the nonmonetary differences among jobs. Even though some jobs (such as garbage collection and being a porter in a hotel) may require equal qualifications, one job (garbage collection) may be more unpleasant than another (being a porter). Hence, the more unpleasant job must pay a higher wage to attract and retain workers. These wage differentials equalize or compensate for the nonmonetary differences among jobs and will persist in time. In the real world, many wage differences are of this type.

For example, police officers' salaries are usually higher than firefighters' salaries because of the alleged greater risk in being a police officer. Similarly, construction work generally pays more than garbage collection because of less job security in the former. Note that a particular individual may prefer being a police officer or a construction worker even if the salary were the same as (or lower than) that of a firefighter or garbage collector, respectively. But it is the intersection of the market demand and supply curves of labor for each occupation that determines the equilibrium wage in the occupation, and the equalizing wage differentials among occupations that require the same general level of qualifications and training.

Noncompeting groups are occupations requiring different capacities, skills, education, and training, and, therefore, receiving different wages. That is, labor in some occupations is not in direct competition with labor in some other occupations. For example, physicians form one noncompeting group not in direct competition with lawyers (which form another noncompeting group). Other noncompeting groups are engineers, accountants, musicians, electricians, and so on. Engineers and electricians belong to different noncompeting groups because, although engineers could probably work easily as electricians, engineers' productivity and wages are so much higher when working as engineers than as electricians that they form a separate noncompeting group. On the other hand, electricians do not have the training and may not have the ability to be engineers.

Each noncompeting group has a particular wage structure as determined by the intersection of its demand and supply curves. Some mobility among noncompeting groups is possible (as, for example, when an electrician becomes an engineer by attending college at night), and this possibility is greater in the long run than in the short run. However, mobility among noncompeting groups is limited, even in the long run, especially if based on innate ability (e.g., not everyone can be a brain surgeon or an accomplished violinist).

An imperfect labor market can also result in wage differences for identical jobs requiring the same ability and level of training. A labor market is imperfect if workers lack information on wages and job opportunities in other occupations, if they are unwilling to move to other jobs and occupations, or if there are labor unions and large employers able to affect wages. These topics will be explored in detail in the next chapter.

Effect of Minimum Wages

In 1938, Congress passed the Fair Labor Standard Act, which established a minimum wage of $0.25 per hour. Since then, the minimum wage has been raised many times. It was $3.35 from January 1981 to March 1989; it was raised to $3.80 in April 1990 and to $4.25 in April 1991. Coverage was also extended over the years, so that today 85% of all workers in the United States are covered. Since skilled workers generally have wages well above the minimum wage, they are not affected by it. Thus, most of the effect of minimum wages is on unskilled workers. We can analyze the effect of the minimum wage on unskilled workers (assuming for the moment that all unskilled workers are identical) with the aid of Figure 13–11.

FIGURE 13–11   Effect of Minimum Wages

D_L is the market demand curve, and S_L is the market supply curve for unskilled workers. The equilibrium wage is $3.00 per hour at which 4 million workers are employed (point E). A minimum wage of $4.25 results in 3.9 million workers being employed as opposed to 4.1 million willing to work, leaving an unemployment gap of 200,000 workers (MN). The disemployment effect is 100,000 workers (the movement from point E to point M on D_L). The increase in the minimum wage from $3.35 in 1989 to $4.25 in 1991 was estimated to increase the unemployment gap by 100,000 (MN minus FG).

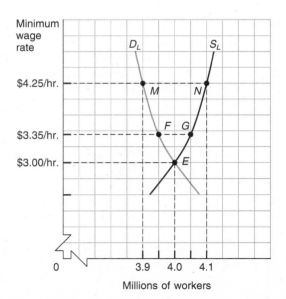

In Figure 13–11, D_L is the market demand curve, and S_L is the market supply curve for unskilled workers. In a perfectly competitive labor market, the equilibrium wage would be $3.00 per hour ($24 per day with an 8-hour workday) and the equilibrium level of employment would be 4 million workers (point E in the figure). The imposition of a federal minimum wage of $4.25 per hour would result in firms hiring only 3.9 million workers (point M on D_L) as opposed to the 4.1 million workers (point N on S_L) willing to work at this minimum wage. Thus, the minimum wage of $4.25 per hour would lead to a total **unemployment gap** of 200,000 workers (MN) from the equilibrium rate of $3.00 per hour. This is composed of the 100,000 additional workers who would like to work at the minimum wage (the movement from point E to point N on the S_L curve) plus the **disemployment effect** of another 100,000 workers as firms employ fewer workers at the above-equilibrium minimum wage (the movement from point E to point M on the D_L curve). On the other hand, the increase in the minimum wage from $3.35 to $4.25 per hour increases the unemployment gap by 100,000 jobs (MN minus FG in Figure 13–11). While the imposition or an increase of a minimum wage benefits those unskilled workers who remain employed, some unskilled workers would lose their jobs, and still more would like to work but could not find employment.

In 1988, 4 million workers of the 60 million Americans paid by the hour worked at the minimum wage. Of these, 30% were teenagers and 70% were women. The U.S. Labor Department estimated that the increase in the minimum wage from $3.35 at the beginning of 1981 to $4.25 in April 1991 would lead to a loss of 100,000 jobs, mostly teenagers and women in two- or three-earner families, rather than breadwinners from poor families. Thus, the increase in the minimum wage was expected to have only a modest and temporary effect on minimum-wage employment and poverty. A growing number of economists are now coming to believe that higher minimum wages would force firms to purchase new equipment, improve productivity, and eventually create more jobs requiring higher skills and providing higher wages over time.[9]

There are other ways by which the imposition or the raising of a minimum wage rate can harm the very people it is supposed to help. An increase in the minimum wage may lead some employers to reduce or cut other fringe benefits (such as some health benefits, free or subsidized meals, free uniforms, and so on). Some employers may suspend apprenticeships and on-the-job training for unskilled workers who they were hiring at a lower minimum wage. The harmful effect of an increase in the minimum wage is even greater in the long run, when employers have a greater opportunity to substitute more capital-intensive production techniques for unskilled labor. The problem

---

[9]See, C. Brown, "Minimum Wage Laws: Are They Overrated?", *Journal of Economic Perspectives*, Summer 1988; "Forging New Insights on Minimum Wages and Jobs," *New York Times*, June 29, 1992, p. D1; and "Higher Minimum Wage: Minimal Damage," *Business Week*, March 22, 1993, p. 92.

can be addressed by training or efforts to improve the skills of minimum-wage workers so that they can qualify for higher-paying jobs.

SUMMARY

1. To maximize profits a firm must produce the best level of output with the least-cost input combination. The optimal or least-cost input combination is the one at which the marginal product per dollar spent on each input is the same. The ratio of the input price to the marginal product of the input gives the marginal cost of the commodity. The best level of output of the commodity for a perfectly competitive firm is the output at which the firm's marginal cost equals its marginal revenue or price.

2. A profit-maximizing firm will employ an input only as long as it adds more to its total revenue than to its total cost. If only one input is variable, the firm's demand curve for the input (d) is given by the marginal revenue product (MRP) curve of the input. The MRP equals the marginal product (MP) of the input times the marginal revenue (MR). If the firm is a perfect competitor in the product market (so that $MR = P$), then $MRP = VMP$ (the value of the marginal product). With more than one variable input, as the input price falls, the demand curve for the input is obtained by points on different MRP curves of the input and will be more elastic than the individual MRP curves.

3. When the price of an input falls, all firms will hire more of the input and produce more of the final commodity. This will reduce the commodity price and shift the individual firm's demand curves for the input to the left. This has to be taken into account in summing the individual firm's demand curves for the input to obtain the market demand curve. The price elasticity of demand for an input is greater (1) the more and better are the available substitutes for the input, (2) the more elastic is the demand for the final commodity made with the input, (3) the more elastic is the supply of other inputs, and (4) the longer is the period of time under consideration.

4. The market supply curve of an input is obtained by the straightforward horizontal summation of the supply curves of the individual suppliers of the input. While natural resources and intermediate goods are supplied by firms and their supply curves are generally positively sloped, labor is supplied by individuals and their supply curves may be backward-bending. That is, as the wage rate rises, eventually the substitution effect (which, by itself, leads individuals to substitute work for leisure) may be overwhelmed by the opposite income effect, so that the individual's supply curve of labor bends backward. The market supply curve of labor is usually positively sloped, but it may bend backward at very high wages.

5. Under perfect competition, the equilibrium price and the level of employment of an input are determined at the intersection of the market demand curve and the market supply curve of the input. Each firm can then employ any quantity of the input at the given market price of the input. Since each firm employs an input until the marginal revenue product equals its price, this theory is usually referred to as the marginal productivity theory. If all inputs were identical (and all occupations equally attractive for labor), all units of the same input would have the same price.

6. With perfect mobility of inputs among industries and regions of a country, input prices will be equalized by input flows

(supply shifts) from the low-return to the high-return industries and regions. On the other hand, free trade in commodities and services among countries under perfect competition, and no transportation costs, would equalize input prices internationally by shifts in input demands resulting from trade.

7. Economic rent is that portion of the payment made to the supplier of an input that is in excess of the minimum amount necessary to retain the input in its present employment. When the supply of an input is fixed, demand alone determines its price and all the payment made to the input is rent. When the market supply curve of an input is positively sloped, the area above the supply curve and below the input price is rent. The return or payment to inputs that are fixed in the short run are sometimes called quasi-rents.

8. By correcting for the income effect of an input-price change, we can graphically isolate the substitution effect as a movement along a consumer leisure-income indifference curve. The same type of analysis can also be used to show the additional number of hours an individual is willing to work per day with overtime pay. Wage differentials can be equalizing, and they can be based on the existence of noncompeting groups and imperfect competition. Minimum wages lead to a disemployment effect and to an even greater unemployment gap.

KEY TERMS

Derived Demand	Complementary Inputs	Equalizing Wage Differentials
Marginal Revenue Product (MRP)	Intermediate Good	Noncompeting Groups
	Marginal Productivity Theory	Unemployment Gap
Value of Marginal Product (VMP)	Economic Rent	Disemployment Effect
	Quasi-Rent	
Marginal Resource Cost (MRC)	Overtime Pay	

REVIEW QUESTIONS

1. What is the function of input prices in the operation of a free-enterprise system?
2. Why is the marginal revenue product of a firm negatively sloped?
3. What happens to a firm's marginal revenue product of labor curve if the rental price of capital falls and capital is complementary to labor? If capital is a substitute for labor?
4. Why does the market price of a commodity fall with a reduction in the price of an input used in the production of the commodity?
5. What effect will a fall in a commodity price have on the firm's demand curve for an input used in the production of the commodity?
6. How can indifference curve analysis be used to explain an individual's supply curve of labor?
7. Under what condition will an individual's labor supply curve be backward-bending?

8. Interregional trade can be a substitute for interregional labor migration in reducing or eliminating interregional wage differences. True or false? Explain.
9. Mexican migrant or seasonal workers to the United States take away jobs from American workers, and so immigration should be stopped. Evaluate.
10. How is a higher interest on capital in industry or region A than in industry or region B eliminated?
11. Can higher wages persist for technicians in nuclear plants as compared with technicians with the same qualifications and training working in aircraft-engine plants? Explain.
12. Why do we have minimum-wage laws if they increase unemployment among unskilled workers?

PROBLEMS

*1. a. Express in terms of equation [13–1] the condition for a firm utilizing too much labor or too little capital to minimize production costs. What is the graphic interpretation of this?

  b. What is the graphic interpretation of a firm utilizing the least-cost input combination but with its marginal cost exceeding its MR?

  c. Express in terms of equation [13–3] the condition for a firm minimizing the cost of producing an output that is too small to maximize profits. What is the graphic interpretation of this?

2. You are given the following production function of a firm, where L is the number of workers hired per day (the only variable input) and Q_X is the quantity of the commodity produced per day, and the constant commodity price of $P_X = \$5$ is assumed:

L	0	1	2	3	4	5
Q_X	0	10	18	24	28	30

  a. Find the marginal revenue product of labor and plot it.

  b. How many workers per day will the firm hire if the wage rate is $50 per day? $40? $30? $20? $10? What is the firm's demand curve for labor?

3. Assume that (1) labor is infinitesimally divisible (i.e., workers can be hired for any part of the day) in the production function of the previous problem; (2) both labor and capital are variable and complementary; and (3) when the wage rate falls from $40 per day to $20 per day, the firm's value of the marginal product curve shifts to the right by two labor units. Derive the demand curve for labor of this firm. How many workers will the firm hire per day at the wage rate of $20 per day?

4. Derive the market demand curve for labor if there are 100 firms identical to the firm of problem 3 demanding labor, and each individual firm's demand curve for labor shifts to the left by one unit when the wage rate falls from $w = \$40$ to $w = \$20$ per day.

*5. Assume that (1) U_1, U_2, U_3, and U_4 given in

the following table are the indifference curves of an individual, where H refers to hours of leisure per day and Y to the daily income and (2) the wage rate rises from $1 per hour of work to $2, $3, and then to $4.

U_1		U_2		U_3		U_4	
H	Y	H	Y	H	Y	H	Y
10	20	10	32	12	40	14	48
16	8	14	20	15	27	17	28
24	4	24	12	24	16	24	20

  a. Derive the individual's supply curve of labor.

  b. Why is the individual's supply curve of labor backward-bending?

6. Given that the market demand curve is the one derived in problem 3 and that 400 individuals will work at $w = \$10$, 500 at $w = \$20$, and 600 at $w = \$30$, determine the equilibrium wage rate and the level of employment. What would happen if $w = \$10$? If $w = \$30$?

7. Given the industry demand function for labor, $D_L = 800 - 15\,w$, where w is given in dollars per day, draw a figure showing the equilibrium wage and find the amount of economic rent if the supply function of labor to the industry is $S_L = 500$, $S_L' = 25w$, or $S_L'' = 50w - 500$.

8. Draw a figure for a perfectly competitive firm in the product and input markets, and label the price at which quasi-rent is (1) negative as P_1; (2) zero as P_2; (3) smaller than total fixed costs as P_3; (4) equal to total fixed costs as P_4; and (5) exceeds total fixed costs as P_5. (Hint: See Figure 13–4.)

*9. Separate the substitution effect from the income effect of an increase in wages from $w = \$2$ to $w = \$4$ in problem 5.

10. Starting with your answer to problem 5 (also provided at the end of the book), draw a figure showing how many additional hours the individual will work and his or her total income (1) starting from $w = \$1$ and overtime $w =$

---

* = Answer provided at end of book.

$4 and (2) starting from $w = \$2$ and overtime $w = \$10$.

*11. Starting from Figure 13–7, draw a figure showing the total demand and supply for labor in both industries or regions, the equilibrium wage rate, and the level of total employment.

12. Starting with Figure 13–7, draw a figure showing that wages will not be equalized when we take transportation costs into consideration.

INPUT PRICE AND EMPLOYMENT UNDER IMPERFECT COMPETITION

In the previous chapter, we analyzed the pricing and employment of inputs when the firm was a perfect competitor in both the product and input markets. In this chapter, we extend the discussion to the pricing and employment of inputs when the firm is (1) an imperfect competitor in the product market but a perfect competitor in the input market and (2) an imperfect competitor in both the product and input markets. As in Chapter 13, the analysis deals with all inputs in general but is geared toward labor because of the greater importance of labor.

The presentation in this chapter proceeds along the same general lines as that of the previous chapter. We begin the chapter with a summary discussion of profit maximization and optimal input employment under imperfect competition in the product market. Then, we derive the demand curve for an input by a firm and by the market as a whole, and we examine how the interaction of the forces of demand and supply determines the price and employment of the input under imperfect competition in the product market but perfect competition in the input market. We next turn to the case of imperfect competition in input markets and examine the pricing and employment of an input when only that input is variable and when all inputs are variable. A discussion of international migration and the "brain drain" follows. Finally, the chapter presents several important applications of the theory.

14.1 PROFIT MAXIMIZATION AND OPTIMAL INPUT EMPLOYMENT

In this section, we extend the discussion of profit maximization and optimal input employment of section 13.1 to the case where the firm is an imperfect competitor in the product market but is still a perfect competitor in the input markets. A firm that is an imperfect competitor in the product market (a monopolist, an oligopolist, or a monopolistic competitor) faces a negatively sloped demand curve for the commodity it sells, and its marginal revenue is smaller than the commodity price. Such a firm, however, can still be one of many firms hiring inputs. That is, the firm can still be a perfect competitor in the input markets, so that it can hire any quantity of an input at the given market price of the input. This is the case we examine in this and in the next two sections of this chapter.

We have seen in section 13.1 that to maximize profits, a firm must use the optimal or least-cost input combination to produce the best level of output. The profit maximizing condition was given by equation [13–3], which is repeated below as [14–1]:

$$w/MP_L = r/MP_K = MC = MR \qquad \text{[14–1]}$$

where w is the wage rate, r is the rental price of capital, MP is the marginal (physical) product, L refers to labor time, K refers to capital, MC is the marginal cost of the firm, and MR is its marginal revenue. The only difference between equations [13–3] and [14–1] is that equation [13–3] and the discussion in section 13.1 referred to the case where the firm was a perfect competitor in both the product and input markets. Thus, the marginal revenue of the firm equaled the product price (P). Since the firm is now an imperfect competitor in the product market, $MR < P$, and equation [14–1] is the relevant condition for profit maximization.

By cross multiplying and rearranging the terms of equation [14–1], we get equations [14–2] and [14–3]:

$$MP_L \cdot MR = w \qquad \text{[14–2]}$$

$$MP_K \cdot MR = r \qquad \text{[14–3]}$$

Thus, the profit maximizing rule is that the firm should hire labor until the marginal product of labor times the firm's marginal revenue from the sale of the commodity equals the wage rate. Similarly, the firm should rent capital until the marginal product of capital times the firm's marginal revenue equals the rental price of capital. To maximize profits, the same rule would have to hold for all inputs that the firm uses. The condition is the same as when the firm is a perfect competitor in the product market, except that in that case, $MR = P$. In the next section, we will see that equation [14–2] provides the basis for the derivation of the firm's demand curve for labor.

14.2 THE DEMAND CURVE OF A FIRM FOR AN INPUT

We now extend the discussion of the last section and derive the demand curve of a firm for an input, first when the input is the only variable input and then when the input is one of two or more variable inputs.

The Demand Curve of a Firm for One Variable Input

We have seen in section 13.2 that a profit-maximizing firm will hire more units of a variable input as long as the income from the sale of the extra output produced by the input is larger than the extra cost of hiring the input. When the firm is an imperfect competitor (say, a monopolist) in the product market, the extra income earned by the firm is called the **marginal revenue product (MRP)** *and is equal to the marginal product of the input times the marginal revenue of the firm.* That is,

$$MRP = MP \cdot MR \qquad\qquad \text{[14–4]}$$

If the variable input is labor, we have

$$MRP_L = MP_L \cdot MR \qquad\qquad \text{[14–4A]}$$

Thus, the MRP_L is the left-hand side of equation [14–2]. Similarly, the MRP_K is the left-hand side of equation [14–3]. Note that when the firm is a perfect competitor in the product market, the firm's marginal revenue equals the product price (i.e., $MR = P$) and the marginal revenue product equals the value of the marginal product (i.e., $MRP = VMP$). Since we are now dealing with a firm that is an imperfect competitor in the product market and $MR < P$, $MRP < VMP$.

Because the firm is a perfect competitor in the input market (i.e., faces a horizontal or infinitely elastic supply curve of the input), the extra cost or marginal resource cost (MRC) of hiring each additional unit of the variable input is equal to the price of the input. If the variable input is labor, a profit-maximizing firm should hire labor as long as the marginal revenue product of labor exceeds the wage rate and until $MRP_L = w$, as indicated by equation [14–2].

The actual derivation of a firm's demand schedule for labor when labor is the only variable input (i.e., when capital and other inputs are fixed), and when the firm is an imperfect competitor (monopolist) in the product market but a perfect competitor in the labor market is shown with Table 14–1. In

TABLE 14–1   The Marginal Revenue Product of Labor and the Firm's Demand Schedule for Labor

L	Q_X	MP_L	P_X	TR_X	MRP_L	$MRC_L = w$
1	12	12	$13	$156	. . .	$40
2	22	10	12	264	$108	40
3	30	8	11	330	66	40
4	37	7	10	370	40	40
5	43	6	9	387	17	40
6	48	5	8	384	−3	40

Table 14–1, L refers to the number of workers hired by the firm per day. Q_X is the total output of commodity X produced by the firm by hiring various numbers of workers. The MP_L is the marginal or extra output generated by each additional worker hired. The MP_L is obtained by the change in Q_X per unit change in L. Note that the law of diminishing returns begins to operate with the hiring of the second worker. P_X refers to the price for the final commodity, and it declines because the firm is an imperfect competitor (monopolist) in the product market. Total revenue (TR_X) is obtained by multiplying P_X by Q_X. The marginal revenue product of labor (MRP_L) is then given by the change in the firm's total revenue by selling the output of commodity X that results from the hiring of an additional worker. More briefly, $MRP_L = \Delta TR_X/\Delta L$. This is the same as MP_L times MR_X (not given in the table; see problem 3, with answer at end of the text). The MRP_L declines because both the MP_L and MR_X decline. That is, as the firm hires more labor and produces more units of the commodity, the MP_L declines (because of diminishing returns) and MR_X also declines (because the firm must lower the commodity price to sell more units of the commodity). The last column of Table 14–1 gives the daily wage rate (w) that the firm must pay to hire each worker. Since the firm is a perfect competitor in the labor market, w is constant (at $40 per day) and is equal to the increase in the firm's total costs (the marginal resource cost) of hiring each additional worker.

Looking at Table 14–1, we see that the second worker contributes $108 extra revenue to the firm (i.e., $MRP_L = \$108$), while the firm incurs a cost of only $40 to hire this worker. Thus, it pays for the firm to hire the second worker. (Since the MRP of the first worker is even greater than the MRP of the second worker, the firm should certainly hire the first worker.) The MRP of the third worker falls to $66, but this still exceeds the daily wage of $40 that the firm must pay each worker. Thus, the firm should also hire the third worker. According to equation [14–2], the profit-maximizing firm should hire workers until the $MRP_L = w$. Thus, this firm should hire four workers, at which $MRP_L = w = \$40$. The firm will not hire the fifth worker because he or she will contribute only $17 to the firm's total revenue while adding $40 to its total costs.

Thus, the MRP_L schedule gives the firm's demand schedule for labor. It indicates the number of workers that the firm would hire at various wage rates. For example, if $w = \$108$ per day, the firm would hire only two workers per day. If $w = \$66$, the firm would hire three workers. At $w = \$40$, $L = 4$, and so on. If we plotted the MRP_L values of Table 14–1 on the vertical axis and L on the horizontal axis, we would get the firm's negatively sloped demand curve for labor when labor is the only variable input. This is shown in the next section.

Note that since the firm is a monopolist in the product market, the MRP_L is smaller than the VMP_L and the MRP_L curve lies below the VMP_L curve. As a result, the firm hires less labor and produces less of the commodity than if the firm were a perfect competitor in the product market. Joan Robinson called

FIGURE 14–1   **Demand Curve for Labor of a Monopolist with All Inputs Variable**

As the wage rate falls and the firm hires more labor (i.e., moves down its MRP_L curve), the MRP curve of inputs that are complements to labor shifts to the right and the MRP curve of inputs that are substitutes for labor shifts to the left. Both of these shifts cause the MRP_L curve to shift to the right to MRP'_L. Thus, when the daily wage falls from $66 to $40, the firm increases the number of workers hired from three (point A on the MRP_L curve) to six (point C on the MRP'_L curve). By joining points A and C, we get the firm's demand curve for labor (d_L).

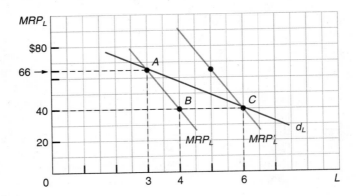

the excess of the VMP_L over the MRP_L at the point where $MRP_L = w$ (the level of employment) **monopolistic exploitation.**[1] Yet, this emotionally laden term is somewhat misleading, because the firm does not pocket the difference between the VMP_L and the MRP_L (see problem 3, with answer at end of the text). That is, the last worker hired receives the entire increase in the total revenue of the firm (the MRP) that he or she contributes.

The Demand Curve of a Firm for One of Several Variable Inputs

We have seen that the declining MRP_L schedule given in Table 14–1 gives the firm's demand schedule for labor in the short run when labor is the only variable input. This is shown by the negatively sloped MRP_L curve in Figure 14–1 (on the assumption that labor is infinitesimally divisible or that workers can be hired for any part of a day). The MRP_L or demand for labor curve when labor is the only variable input shows that the firm will hire three workers at $w = $66 (point A in Figure 14–1) and four workers at $w = $40 (point B).

When labor is not the only variable input (i.e., when the firm can also change the quantity of capital and other inputs), the firm's demand curve for

---

[1]J. Robinson, *The Economics of Imperfect Competition* (London: Macmillan, 1933), Chapter 25.

labor can be derived from the MRP_L curve, but it is not the MRP_L curve itself. The derivation is basically the same as explained in section 13.2 and is shown in Figure 14–1. That is, as the wage rate falls and the firm hires more labor (i.e., moves down its MRP_L curve), the MRP curve of inputs that are complements to labor shifts to the right, and the MRP curve of inputs that are substitutes for labor shifts to the left (exactly as explained in section 13.2). Both of these shifts cause the MRP_L to shift to the right, say, from MRP_L to MRP_L' in Figure 14–1. Thus, when the daily wage falls from \$66 to \$40, the firm will increase the number of workers hired from three (point A on the MRP_L curve) to six (point C on the MRP_L' curve) rather than to four (point B on the original MRP_L curve). By joining points A and C, we get the firm's demand curve for labor (d_L in Figure 14–1) when other inputs besides labor are variable.

Note that the d_L curve is negatively sloped and generally more elastic than the MRP_L curve in the long run, when all inputs are variable. In general, the better the complementary and substitute inputs available for labor are, the greater is the outward shift of the MRP_L curve as a result of a decline in the wage rate, and the more elastic is d_L.

14.3 THE MARKET DEMAND CURVE, AND INPUT PRICE AND EMPLOYMENT

The market demand curve for an input is derived from the individual firms' demand curves for the input. If all the firms using the input are monopolists in their respective product markets, the market demand for the input is derived by the straightforward horizontal summation of the individual firms' demand curves for the input. The reason is that the reduction in the commodity price (as each monopolist produces and sells more of its commodity by hiring more inputs) has already been considered or incorporated in full into the calculation of the MRP of the input.

The case is different when a commodity market is composed of oligopolists and monopolistic competitors. That is, when all the oligopolists or monopolistic competitors in a product market hire more inputs and produce more of the commodity, the commodity price will decline. This decline in the price of the commodity causes a downward shift in each firm's demand curve for labor, exactly the same as when firms are perfect competitors in the product market (see section 13.3). It is by adding the quantity demanded of each input on these downward shifting demand curves of the input of each firm that the market demand curve is obtained. The process is identical to that shown in Figure 13–3 in section 13.3, and so it is not repeated here (see problem 6).

The equilibrium price and employment of an input are then given at the intersection of the market demand and the market supply curves of the input, as described in section 13.5. When all firms are perfect competitors in the input market, each firm can hire any quantity of the input at the given market price of the input. Each firm will then hire the input until the MRP of the input on the firm's demand curve for the input equals the MRC or input price.

If, for whatever reason, the market demand curve for the input rises (i.e., shifts up) from the equilibrium position, the market price and employment of the input will also increase until a new equilibrium price is reached at which the *MRP* of the input equals the *MRC* or input price. This usually does not occur instantaneously. During the adjustment period, there will be a temporary shortage of the input (see Example 1).

Example 1
The Dynamics of the Engineers' Shortage

During the late 1950s and early 1960s a shortage of engineers existed in the United States, which might have endangered winning the "space race" with the former Soviet Union. This can be analyzed with the aid of Figure 14–2. The intersection of the hypothetical market demand curve for engineers D_G and the market supply curve of engineers S_G at point E determines the equilibrium daily wage of $40 for engineers. At $w = \$40$, the 600,000 engineers employed match the number of engineers demanded, and there is no shortage. In the late 1950s and early 1960s, the demand for engineers unexpectedly increased (i.e., shifted up, say, to D'_G) because of the space race. At the original equilibrium wage rate of $w = \$40$, there is a shortage of 500,000 (EF) engineers and engineers' wages rise. As this occurs, employers economize on the use of engineers, and more students enter engineering studies. Thus, the shortage is somewhat alleviated. For example, at $w = \$50$, the shortage declines to

FIGURE 14–2   Dynamics of the Engineer Shortage

The intersection of D_G and S_G at point E determines the equilibrium daily wage of $40 for engineers. There are 600,000 engineers employed, and there is no shortage. If D_G shifts up to D'_G, a temporary shortage of 500,000 (EF) results at $w = \$40$ and wages rise. As this occurs, the shortage is somewhat alleviated. At $w = \$50$, the shortage declines to 250,000 (CM). Only after the wage rises to $66 and enough new engineers are trained, is the temporary shortage eliminated and new equilibrium point E' reached.

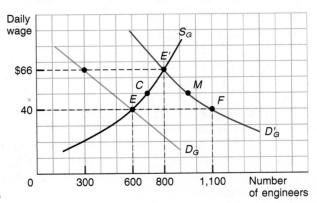

250,000 (*CM*). Only after several years, as wages rise to $66 and enough new engineers are trained, is the shortage eliminated and new equilibrium point *E'* reached with 800,000 engineers employed. If, within this time, the demand for engineers increases again, a new temporary shortage emerges.

On the other hand, if the demand for engineers declines by the time an increasing number of them graduate in response to higher wages, or if the supply repsonse turns out to be excessive, a surplus of engineers develops. This is indeed what occurred during the 1970s and 1980s. Because of the reduced pool of the college-age population and high incomes in other occupations, the National Science Foundation predicts that a shortfall of about half a million engineers and scientists will again develop by the end of the century in the United States. Thus, because of the lag in the supply response to a change in demand and possible subsequent shifts in demand, alternating shortages or surpluses may arise rather than the market moving smoothly toward long-run equilibrium.

The same type of dynamic disequilibrium exists in the market for nurses. That is, because of the sharp increase in the demand for nurses and the reduced supply (as the pool of 18- to 24-year-olds declined, and a smaller percentage of them opted to become nurses because of increased job opportunities elsewhere), the percentage of full-time nursing positions that were vacant increased from 4.5% in 1984 to 14% in 1989, even though average salaries for nurses increased by more than 50% during the period. The higher salaries increased nursing school enrollment, however, so that unfilled vacancies declined to 11% in 1991 and 9% in 1992. As a delayed and continued response to the surplus of Ph.D.s in the humanities (typified by the taxi driver who has a liberal arts Ph.D.) during the 1970s, a shortage of humanities Ph.D.s entering college teaching is also expected to develop during the late 1990s. Such dynamic market disequilibria are common in most occupations requiring long training periods.

Sources: K. Arrow and W. Capron, "Dynamic Shortages and Price Rises: The Engineer-Scientist Case," *Quarterly Journal of Economics*, May 1959; C. Holden, "Wanted: 675,000 Future Scientists and Engineers," *Science*, June 30, 1989; "Nursing Shortage, Tasks and Tasks Grow," *New York Times*, December 4, 1989, p. B1; "Market Struggles to Cure Nursing Shortage," *The Margin*, Fall 1991; "The Nurse Shortage," *Wall Street Journal*, December 15, 1992, p. A1; "Remember the Ph.D. Glut? Colleges Will Go Begging," *U.S. News and World Report*, September 25, 1989, p. 55; and American Association of University Professors (AAUP), *The Ph.D. Shortage: The Federal Role* (Washington, D.C.: AAUP, 1990).

▲

14.4 MONOPSONY: A SINGLE FIRM HIRING AN INPUT

Until this point we have assumed that the firm is a perfect competitor in the input market. This means that the firm faces an infinitely elastic or horizontal supply curve of the input and that the firm can hire any quantity of the input at the given market price of the input. We now examine the case in which the firm is an imperfect competitor in the input market. When there is a single firm hiring an input, we have a **monopsony**. Thus, while *monopoly* refers to the single seller of a commodity, *monopsony* refers to the single buyer of an input. As such, the monopsonist faces the (usually) positively sloped *market* supply curve of the input. This means that to hire more units of the input, the monopsonist must pay a higher price per unit of the input.

An example of monopsony is provided by the "company towns" in 19th century America, where a mining or textile firm was practically the sole employer of labor in many isolated communities. A present-day example of monopsony might be an automaker that is the sole buyer of some specialized automobile component or part, such as radiators, from a number of small local firms set up exclusively to supply these components or parts to the large firm (the automaker).

Monopsony arises when an input is specialized and thus much more productive to a particular firm or use than to any other firm or use. This allows the firm (in which the input is more productive) to pay a much higher price for the input than other firms and so become a monopsonist. Monopsony can also result from lack of geographic and occupational mobility. For example, people often become emotionally attached to a given locality because of family ties, friends, and so on, and are unwilling to move to other areas. Also, people may lack the information, the money, or the qualifications to move to other areas or occupations. In general, monopsony can be overcome by providing information about job opportunities elsewhere, by helping to pay for moving expenses, and by providing training for other occupations.

We have said that the monopsonist faces the usually positively sloped market supply curve of the input, so that it must pay a higher price to hire more units of the input. However, as all units of the input must be paid the same price, the monopsonist will have to pay a higher price, not only for the last unit hired, but for all units of the input it hires. As a result, the **marginal resource cost (MRC)** of the input exceeds the input price. This is shown in Table 14–2 for labor.

In Table 14–2, w is the daily wage rate that a monopsonist must pay to

TABLE 14–2   Marginal Resource Cost of Labor

L	w	TC_L	MRC_L
1	$10	$10	. . .
2	20	40	$30
3	30	90	50
4	40	160	70
5	50	250	90

hire various numbers of workers (L). Thus, the first two columns of the table give the market supply schedule of labor faced by the monopsonist. TC_L is the total cost incurred by the monopsonist to hire various numbers of workers and is obtained by multiplying L by w. MRC_L is the **marginal resource cost of labor** and gives the extra cost that the monopsonist faces to hire each additional worker. That is $MRC_L = \Delta TC_L/\Delta L$.

Note that $MRC_L > w$. For example, the monopsonist can hire one worker at the wage rate of $10 for a total cost of $10. To hire the second worker, the monopsonist must increase the wage rate from $10 to $20 and incur a total cost of $40. Thus, the increase in the total cost (i.e., the marginal cost) of hiring the second worker is $30 and exceeds the wage rate of $20 that the monopsonist must pay for each of the two workers.

Figure 14–3 gives the positively sloped market supply curve of labor (S_L) faced by the monopsonist (from columns 1 and 2 of Table 14–2) and the marginal resource cost of labor curve (MRC_L, from the first and the last columns of Table 14–2). Since the MRC_L measures the changes in TC_L per unit change in L used, the MRC_L values given in Table 14–2 are plotted between the various units of labor hired. Note also that the MRC_L curve is everywhere above the S_L curve. Similarly, a firm that is the single renter of a particular type of specialized capital (i.e., a monopsonist in the capital market) faces the positively sloped market supply curve of capital, so that the firm's **marginal**

FIGURE 14–3   A Monopsonist's Supply and Marginal Resource Cost of Labor Curves

S_L is the positively sloped market supply curve of labor faced by the monopsonist (from columns 1 and 2 of Table 14–2) and MRC_L is the marginal resource cost of labor curve (from the first and the last columns of Table 14–2). The MRC_L values are plotted between the various units of L used, and the MRC_L curve is everywhere above the S_L curve.

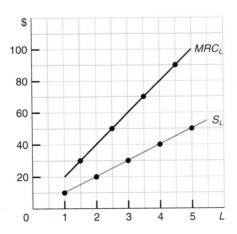

resource cost of capital (MRC_K) curve is above the supply curve of capital (S_K).[2]

Although our discussion has been exclusively in terms of monopsony, there are other forms of imperfect competition in input markets. Just as we have monopoly, oligopoly, and monopolistic competition in product markets, so we can have monopsony, oligopsony, and monopsonistic competition in input markets. **Oligopsony** refers to the case where there are only a few firms hiring a homogeneous or differentiated input. **Monopsonistic competition** refers to the case where there are many firms hiring a differentiated input. As for the monopsonist, oligopsonists and monopsonistic competitors must also pay higher prices to hire more units of an input, and so the marginal resource cost of the input exceeds the input price for them also.

Finally, note that when the firm is a perfect competitor in the input market, the marginal resource cost of the input is equal to the input price, and the marginal resource cost curve of the input is horizontal and coincides with the supply curve of the input that the firm faces. That is, since the firm hires such a small quantity of the input, the supply curve of the input that the firm faces is infinitely elastic, even though the market supply curve of the input is positively sloped. For example, if $w = \$10$ no matter how many workers a firm hires, then $MRC_L = w = \$10$ and the MRC_L curve is horizontal at $w = \$10$ and coincides with the S_L curve (the supply curve of labor faced by the firm).

Example 2

▽ ## Occupational Licensing, Mobility, and Imperfect Labor Markets

Many states do not recognize the occupational license obtained in other states to practice law and dentistry in the state. Invariably, these nonreciprocity regulations are the result of lobbying on the part of the professions involved as a way of restricting the possible competition that would arise from an inflow of professionals from other states. Pashigian estimated that, with reciprocity, interstate migration would increase by 5% for lawyers and from 3% to 4% for dentists, over a five-year period. Reciprocity would thus eliminate one source of imperfection in these labor markets.

On theoretical grounds, we would expect that the income of professionals in states without reciprocity agreements would be higher than in states with reciprocity. In fact, Shepard found that the fees and income of dentists in the

---

[2]In section A.14 of the Mathematical Appendix, we derive an important relationship among input price, marginal resource cost, and the price elasticity of input supply. This is analogous to the relationship among commodity price, marginal revenue, and the price elasticity of commodity demand derived in section 5.5.

35 states that have no reciprocity agreements were 12% to 15% higher than in states with reciprocity. If all states adopted reciprocity agreements, some lawyers and dentists in states with lower fees and incomes would migrate to those states with higher fees and incomes. This would reduce (and in the limit eliminate) all interstate differences in fees and incomes and increase the degree of competition in these labor markets.

Sources: B. Pashigian, "Occupational Licensing and the Interstate Mobility of Professionals," *Journal of Law and Economics,* April 1979, and L. Shepard, "Licensing Restrictions and the Cost of Dental Care," *Journal of Law and Economics,* October 1978.

▲

14.5 MONOPSONY PRICING AND EMPLOYMENT OF ONE VARIABLE INPUT

As pointed out in section 13.2, a firm using only one variable input maximizes profits by hiring more units of the input until the extra revenue from the sale of the commodity equals the extra cost of hiring the input. This is a general marginal condition and applies whether the firm is a perfect or imperfect competitor in the product and/or input market. If the variable input is labor and the firm is a monopsonist in the labor market, the monopsonist maximizes its total profits by hiring labor until the marginal revenue product of labor equals the marginal resource cost of labor. That is, the monopsonist should hire labor until equation [14–5] or, equivalently, equation [14–5A) holds:

$$MRP_L = MRC_L \qquad\qquad \textbf{[14–5]}$$

$$MP_L \cdot MR = MRC_L \qquad\qquad \textbf{[14–5A]}$$

The wage rate paid by the monopsonist is then given by the corresponding point on the market supply curve of labor (S_L). This is shown in Figure 14–4.

In Figure 14–4, the S_L and the MRC_L curves are those of Figure 14–3. With the firm's MRP_L curve shown in Figure 14–4, the monopsonist maximizes profits by hiring three workers (given by point E, at which the MRP_L curve intersects the MRC_L curve and $MRP_L = MRC_L = \$60$). To prove this, consider that the second worker adds \$80 (point A) to the monopsonist's total revenue but only \$40 (point A') to its total costs. Thus, the monopsonist's profits rise (by $AA' = \$40$) by hiring the second worker. On the other hand, the monopsonist would not hire the fourth worker because he or she would add more to toal costs (\$80, given by point B) than to total revenue (\$40, given by point B'), so that the monopsonist's total profits would fall by \$40 (BB' in the figure). Only at $L = 3$, $MRP_L = MRC_L = \$60$ (point E) and the monopsonist maximizes total profits.

Figure 14–4 also shows that to hire three workers, the monopsonist must pay the wage of \$30. This is given by point E' on the S_L curve at $L = 3$. Thus, the intersection of the MRP_L and MRC_L curves gives only the profit-maximizing number of worker that the firm should hire. The wage rate is then given by

FIGURE 14–4   **Optimal Employment of Labor and the Wage Rate Paid by a Monopsonist**

The S_L and the MRC_L curves are those of Figure 14–3. With MRP_L, the monopsonist maximizes profits by hiring three workers (given by point E, at which the MRP_L curve intersects the MRC_L curve and $MRP_L = MRC_L = \$60$). The monopsonist then pays $w = \$30$ to each worker (given by point E' on S_L). The excess of MRP_L over w ($EE' = \$30$) at $L = 3$ is called monopsonistic exploitation.

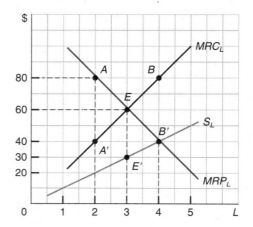

the amount that the firm must pay each worker, and this is given by the point on the market supply curve of labor at the level of employment. Note that $MRP_L = \$60$ (point E) exceeds $w = \$30$ (point E') at $L = 3$.

Joan Robinson called the excess of the marginal revenue product of the variable input over the input price ($EE' = \$30$ at $L = 3$ in Figure 14–4) **monopsonistic exploitation**.[3] It arises because the monopsonist produces where the $MRP_L = MRC_L$ in order to maximize profits. Since the S_L curve is positively sloped, the MRC_L curve is above it, and $MRC_L > w$. The more inelastic is the market supply curve that the monopsonist faces, the greater is the degree of monopsonistic exploitation. If the firm in Figure 14–4 had been a perfect competitor in the labor market, it would have hired four workers (given by point B', at which $MRP_L = MRC_L = w = \$40$). As we have seen, the monopsonist maximizes total profits by restricting output and employment and by hiring only three workers (point E). In section 14.8, we will see how government regulation and/or union power can reduce or eliminate monopsonistic exploitation.

––––––––––
[3]J. Robinson, *The Economics of Imperfect Competition* (London: Macmillan, 1933), Chapter 26.

Example 3
Monopsonistic Exploitation in Major League Baseball

Table 14–3 gives the net marginal revenue product (*MRP*) and the salary of mediocre, average, and star hitters and pitchers in major league baseball calculated by Scully for the year 1969. Scully found that the team's winning record increased attendance and revenues and that a team's performance depended primarily on the "slugging average" for hitters and on the ratio of "strikeouts to walks" for pitchers. Using these data, Scully calculated the net *MRP* or extra gate revenues and broadcast receipts resulting from each type of player's performance after subtracting the player's development cost. In 1969, development costs were as high as $300,000 per player. Table 14–3 shows that for mediocre players, the net *MRP* was negative (−$32,300 for hitters and − $13,400 for pitchers). Of course, the team's scouts and managers could not precisely foresee which players would turn out to be mediocre, average, or stars. The table also shows the average of players' salaries in each category.

Mediocre players reduced the team's profits. Average players received salaries far lower than their net *MRP*. Star players received salaries that were more than six times lower than their net *MRP*. Thus, monopsonistic exploitation was large for average players and very large for star players. On the other hand, mediocre players exploited their team! Note that even though star players received very large salaries (for 1969), they contributed so much more to the team's revenue (after subtracting the cost for their development) that they were greatly "exploited" by their teams. This exploitation was made possible by the "reserve clause," under which the player became the exclusive property of the team that first signed him. Aside from being traded, a player could only play for the team for whatever salary the team offered. Thus, the reserve clause practically eliminated all competition in hiring and

TABLE 14–3   Net Marginal Revenue Product and Salaries in Major League Baseball, 1969 Average

Type of Player	Quality of Player	Net *MRP*	Salary
Hitters	Mediocre	$ − 32,300	$15,200
	Average	129,500	28,000
	Star	313,900	47,700
Pitchers	Mediocre	$ − 13,400	$13,700
	Average	159,900	31,800
	Star	397,000	61,000

Source: G. Scully, "Pay and Performance in Major League Baseball," *American Economic Review*, December 1974, p. 928.

remuneration and essentially established a cartel of employers (teams) for major league baseball players. As such, the cartel behaved much like a monopsonist and exploited players.

In 1975, the reserve clause was substantially weakened. After six years of playing for a team, players could declare themselves "free agents" and negotiate their salaries and the team for which they would play. As anticipated, competition resulted in startling increases in players' salaries and sharply reduced the monopsonistic power of baseball clubs. For example, Summers and Quinton found that free-agent star pitchers had an average marginal revenue product of nearly $300,000 and received salaries of nearly $258,000 in 1980. Even after adjusting for inflation, this represented a doubling of the 1969 salary of star pitchers. In an attempt to reduce these huge salaries and restore some of their previous monopsony power, in 1986 club owners did not sign any player that had become a free agent in 1985. The players' union filed a grievance in 1986, charging that the clubs had acted collusively and thus illegally. In fall 1987, an arbitrator for major league baseball ruled that the clubs had indeed conspired to destroy the free-agent market and that the affected players should be awarded financial damages. By 1991, players' salaries had shot up to more than $500,000 per year and were equal, on the average, to their marginal revenue product (thus essentially putting an end to exploitation in major league baseball). Thirty-five players earned $3 million or more per year, with Boston Red Sox pitcher Roger Clemens and New York Mets pitcher Dwight Gooden topping the list with earnings in excess of $5 million per year.

Sources: G. Scully, "Pay and Performance in Major League Baseball," *American Economic Review,* December 1974; P. M. Summers and N. Quinton, "Pay and Performance in Major League Baseball: The Case of the First Family of Free Agents," *Journal of Human Resources,* Summer 1982; T. Tregarthen, "Players Head for the Courts," *The Margin,* November 1987; and T. Tregarthen, "Baseball's $5 Million Man: Is He Worth It?" *The Margin,* Fall 1991.

▲

14.6 MONOPSONY PRICING AND EMPLOYMENT OF SEVERAL VARIABLE INPUTS

We have seen in section 14.5 that when labor is the only variable input, a monopsonist maximizes profits by hiring labor until the marginal revenue product of labor equals the marginal resource cost of labor. This was given by equations [14–5] and [14–5A]. The same condition holds when there is more than one variable input. That is, the monopsonist maximizes profits by hiring each input until the marginal revenue product of the input equals the marginal resource cost of hiring it. With labor and capital as the variable inputs, the monopsonist should hire labor and capital until equations [14–6A] and [14–6B] hold:

$$MP_L \cdot MR = MRC_L \qquad \text{[14–6A]}$$

$$MP_K \cdot MR = MRC_K \qquad\qquad [14\text{--}6B]$$

Dividing both sides of equations [14–6A] and [14–6B] by MP_L and MP_K, respectively, and combining the results we get [14–7]:

$$MRC_L/MP_L = MRC_K/MP_K = MC = MR \qquad\qquad [14\text{--}7]$$

This is identical to equation (14–1), expect that w has been replaced by the MRC_L and r has been replaced by the MRC_K to reflect the fact that the firm is now a monopsonist in the labor and capital markets, and it must pay a higher wage and rental price to hire more labor and rent more capital, respectively. That is, the optimal input combination is now given by equation [14–7] rather than by equation [13–2], and each ratio in equation [14–7] equals the MC of the firm:

$$MRC_L/MP_L = MRC_K/MP_K = MC \qquad\qquad [14\text{--}8]$$

For example, if MRC_L/MP_L is smaller than MRC_K/MP_K, the monopsonist would not be minimizing production costs. The monopsonist can reduce the cost of producing any level of output by substituting labor for capital in production at the margin. As the monopsonist hires more labor, MRC_L rises and MP_L declines, so that MRC_L/MP_L rises. As the monopsonist rents less capital, MRC_K falls and MP_K rises, so that MRC_K/MP_K falls. To minimize the cost of producing any level of output, the monopsonist should continue to substitute labor for capital in production until equation [14–8] holds.

Note that the MRC_L/MP_L and MRC_K/MP_K measure the extra cost (in terms of labor and capital, respectively) to produce an extra unit of the commodity. This is the marginal cost of the firm. For example, if $MRC_L = \$10$ and $MP_L = 5$, the marginal cost of the firm is $MRC_L/MP_L = \$10/5 = \$2$. This means that it costs the monopsonist \$2 extra to hire the additional labor to produce one extra unit of the commodity. The same is true for capital. That is, $MRC_K/MP_K = MC$ or the marginal cost of the firm (in terms of capital). The best level of output is then given by the point where $MC = MR$ (see equation [14–7]).

Example 4

 ## Imperfect Competition in Labor Markets and the Pay of Top Executives

Table 14–4 gives the earnings of the 12 highest-paid executives in the United States in 1991. The earnings ranged from nearly \$59 million for Roberto Goizueta of Coca-Cola to more than \$10 million for Richard Wood of Eli Lilly. Even though these sums pale in comparison to the \$550 million made in 1987 by junk-bond king Michael R. Milken of Drexel Burnham and Lambert, Inc., they do establish a new standard for chief executive officers' (CEOs') compensation. Most of these incredible incomes resulted from stock option and bonus plans for CEOs (which are less visible to stockholders). While the

TABLE 14-4   Earnings of the 12 Highest-Paid Executives in 1991 (in thousands of dollars)

Executive/Company	Salary and Bonus	Stock Grants	Total Compensation
1. Roberto C. Goizueta Coca-Cola	$2,962	$55,971	$58,933
2. Hamish Maxwell Philip Morris	1,741	28,201	29,942
3. Stanley C. Gault Goodyear Tire & Rubber	735	21,801	22,536
4. Lawrence A. Bossidy Allied-Signal	809	21,393	22,202
5. William A. Schreyer Merrill Lynch	5,850	9,908	15,758
6. Stephen M. Wolf United Airlines	575	13,605	14,180
7. Noland D. Archibald Black & Decker	1,336	12,194	13,529
8. Robert E. Allen American Telephone & Telegraph	2,061	10,716	12,777
9. Richard J. Mahoney Monsanto	1,530	9,078	10,608
10. John F. Welch Jr. General Electric	3,207	7,047	10,254
11. William D. Smithburg Quaker Oats	1,405	8,805	10,210
12. Richard D. Wood Eli Lilly	2,218	7,893	10,111
Average	2,036	17,218	19,254

Source: "What CEOs Really Make," *Fortune*, June 15, 1992, pp. 94–99.

average remuneration of CEOs was equal to 41 times the average pay for the factory worker in 1960, it was nearly 100 times as large in 1991. Union leaders have denounced these multimillion-dollar yearly compensations as the "annual executive pig-out."

The question is, "Are these executives worth to their employer the huge salaries and bonuses that they are paid?" One answer is that since firms voluntarily pay these salaries and bonuses, the marginal revenue product of these top executives must be at least as high. These huge compensations, however, also result because of a conflict of interests (i.e., collusion) between CEOs and compensation committees, and because the latter often have inadequate information or fail to comprehend how rapidly the compensation from a complicated, long-term compensation package can escalate if all goes well.

14.7 INTERNATIONAL MIGRATION AND THE BRAIN DRAIN

International migration affects the supply of labor of the nations of emigration and immigration. Migration can take place for economic as well as for noneconomic reasons. Most of the international labor migration into the United States since the end of World War II has been motivated by the prospects of earning higher real wages and incomes in the United States than in the country of origin. Labor migration to the United States, however, is highly restricted (i.e., international labor markets are not perfectly competitive).

We can examine the effect of labor immigration on a nation with Figure 14–5. The figure is based on the assumption that the nation's output is pro-

FIGURE 14–5   Effects of Immigration on the Earnings of Labor and Capital

Before immigration, the nation employs 3 million workers at the daily wage of $60. Total output is $OFAG$ = $270 million, of which $OHAG$ = $180 million goes to labor and HFA = $90 million goes to the owners of capital. With 1 million immigrants, the wage falls to $40 and the share of total output going to capital increases to JFB = $160 million, or by $HABJ$ = $70 million. Since the original workers' earnings decline by $HACJ$ = $60 million, the nation receives a net gain equal to the area of triangle ABC = $10 million.

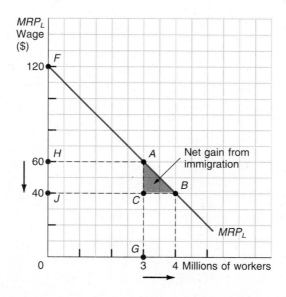

duced under conditions of constant returns to scale with labor and capital inputs only. Before immigration, the nation employs 3 million workers at the daily wage of $60. The total value of output is, therefore, $OFAG$ = $270 million, of which $OHAG$ = $180 million goes to labor and the remainder, or HFA = $90 million, goes to the owners of capital. With 1 million immigrants, the daily wage rate in the nation falls to $40 and the share of total output going to capital owners increases to JFB = $160 million or by $HABJ$ = $70 million. Since the original workers' earnings decline by the area of rectangle $HACJ$ = $60 million, the nation as a whole gains a net amount equal to the area of triangle ABC = $10 million. With income redistribution (i.e., with taxes on earnings of capital and subsidies to labor), both workers and owners of capital can gain from immigration.

The analysis is based on the implicit assumption that all labor is homogeneous and of average productivity. This is not the case in the real world. Some labor is much more productive because of better education and training. The immigration laws of the United States and other industrial countries favor the immigration of skilled labor (such as nurses and technicians) and professional people (doctors, engineers, scientists, etc.) and impose serious obstacles to the immigration of unskilled labor, except temporary migrants. The immigration of skilled workers and professionals is likely to provide even greater benefits to the country of immigration because it saves the nation the costs of education and training.

For example, from 1983 to 1988, more than 200 well-known scholars in the fields of history, philosophy, political science, and physics left British universities to take positions in some of the top universities in the United States. Their departure resulted from a combination of "push" and "pull" forces. Among the push forces in Britain were the budget cuts that froze professors' salaries and left many vacancies unfilled, the abolishment of tenure and the suspension of promotions, and reductions in funds for libraries and assistants. The pull forces were U.S. salaries that often were more than three times higher than those in Britain, as well as the availability of large research funds, assistants, and sophisticated laboratories. This **brain drain** is a serious loss to British universities and an important gain for American universities. The same is true for the more than 300 top Russian mathematicians who emigrated to the United States during 1990 and 1991 after the fall of communism and the collapse of the Soviet Union.[4]

Although these might not be dramatic examples, they are by no means the only forms of the brain drain to the United States. For example, in recent years nearly 37% of the students earning doctorates in the United States have been foreigners. The figures are 51% in computer science, 45% in engineering, 40% in mathematics, and 30% in physical sciences. Since many of these stu-

[4]"British Brain Drain Enriches U.S. Colleges," *New York Times*, November 22, 1988, p. 1, and "The Immigrants," *Business Week*, July 13, 1992, pp. 114–122.

dents remain in the United States after receiving their degrees, this represents a brain drain on their country of origin. Not all migration represents a brain drain on the country of emigration, however; and some (such as illegal migration and the migration of unskilled workers to the United States) may in fact be harmful to the country of immigration.[5]

14.8 ANALYSIS OF IMPERFECT INPUT MARKETS

In this section, we discuss some important applications of the theory presented in the chapter: the regulation of monopsony, bilateral monopoly, the effect of unions on wages, and discrimination in employment. These applications clearly indicate the usefulness and applicability of the theory presented in this chapter.

Regulation of Monopsony

By setting a minimum price for an input at the point where the marginal revenue product curve of the input intersects the market supply curve of the input, the monopsonist can be made to behave as a perfect competitor in the input market, and monopsonistic exploitation is eliminated. If the input is labor, the minimum wage that would eliminate labor exploitation can be set by the government or negotiated by the union. This is shown in Figure 14–6.

In the absence of a minimum wage, the monopsonist of Figure 14–6 hires three workers (given by point E, where the MRP_L curve intersects the MRC_L curve) and the daily wage is \$30 (point E' on S_L) exactly as explained in section 14.5 and Figure 14–4. Monopsonistic exploitation of labor is given by the excess of the MRP_L over w at $L = 3$ and is equal to \$30 per worker (EE' in the figure). If the daily wage is set at \$40 (point B' in the figure, at which the MRP_L curve intersects S_L), $CB'F$ becomes the new supply of labor curve facing the monopsonist. The new MRC_L curve is then $CB'BG$, with the vertical or discontinuous portion directly above and caused by the kink (at point B') on the new S_L curve.

To maximize total profits when the minimum wage of \$40 is imposed, the monopsonist hires four workers (given by point B', at which the MRP_L curve intersects the new MRC_L curve) and $w = MRP_L = \$40$. Thus, the monopsonist behaves as a perfect competitor in the input market (operates at point B', where the MRP_L curve intersects S_L), and the monopsonistic exploitation of labor is entirely eliminated. With a daily wage between \$30 and \$40, the monopsonist will hire three or four workers per day and only part of the labor exploitation will be eliminated. Setting a wage above \$40 will eliminate

[5]For a more detailed analysis of the causes and effects of international migration, see D. Salvatore, *International Economics*, 4th ed. (New York: Macmillan, 1993), Chapter 12.

FIGURE 14-6   Regulation of Monopsony

By setting $w = \$40$, $CB'F$ becomes the new supply of labor curve facing the monopsonist. The new MRC_L curve is then $CB'BG$, with the vertical or discontinuous portion directly above and caused by the kink (at point B') on the new S_L curve. To maximize total profits, the monopsonist now hires four workers (given by point B', at which the MRP_L curve intersects the new MRC_L curve) and $w = MRP_L = \$40$ (so that monopsonistic exploitation is zero).

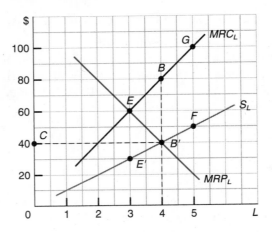

all labor exploitation, but the monopsonist will hire fewer than four workers (see problem 9, with answer at end of the text).

Bilateral Monopoly: A Monopsonistic Buyer Facing a Monopolistic Seller

Bilateral monopoly is said to exist when the single buyer of a product or input (the monopsonist) faces the single seller of the product or input (the monopolist). While this is a rare occurrence in the real world, it is approximated by the "one-mill town" of yesteryears facing the union of all of the town's workers; by some military contractors such as the McDonnell Douglas Corporation, which is the sole seller of the F-18, and the U.S. Navy, the sole purchaser; and (until 1982) by Western Electric, the sole producer of telephone equipment in the United States, and AT&T, the sole buyer of telephone equipment.

In bilateral monopoly, price and output are indeterminate, in the sense that they cannot be established by the profit-maximizing marginal calculations employed by economists. Rather, they are determined by the relative bargaining strength of the monopsonist buyer and the monopolist seller of the product or input. This is shown in Figure 14–7.

In the figure, D is the monopsonist's demand (MRP) curve for the product or input. Curve D is also the market demand curve faced by the monopolist seller of the product or input. Then MR is the corresponding marginal revenue

FIGURE 14–7   **Bilateral Monopoly**

D is the monopsonist's demand (MRP) curve for the product or input that the monopolist seller faces. MR is the monopolist's marginal revenue curve. The monopolist maximizes profits at $Q = 5$ (given by point B', where $MC = MR$) at $P = \$15$ (point B on the D curve). The monopolist's MC curve is the supply curve of the product that the monopsonist faces, and MRC is its marginal resource cost curve. The monopsonist maximizes profits at $Q = 4$ (given by point E, where $MRP = MRC$) and $P = \$8$ (given by point E' on the supply curve that the monopsonist faces). The solution is indeterminate and will be within area $E'B'BE$.

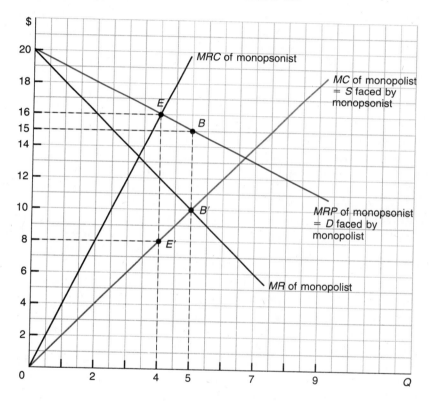

curve of the monopolist. If the monopolist's marginal cost curve is as shown in the figure, the monopolist will maximize profits by selling five units of the product (given by point B', where its MC curve intersects its MR curve from below) at the price of $15 per unit (point B on its D curve).

To determine the monopsonist's profit-maximizing purchase of the product, we must realize that the monopolist's marginal cost curve is the supply curve of the product that the monopsonist faces. It shows the price at which the monopsonist can purchase various quantities of the product. Thus, the monopsonist's marginal resource cost curve for the product is higher, as indicated by the MRC curve in the figure. To maximize profits, the monopsonist must buy four units of the product [given by point E, at which the monopsonist demand (D or MRP) curve intersects its MRC of the product curve] and pay the price of $8 (given by point E' on the supply curve of the product that the monopsonist faces).

Thus, to mazimize profits, the monopolist seller of the product wants to sell $Q = 5$ at $P = \$15$, while the monopsonist buyer of the product wants to purchase $Q = 4$ at $P = \$8$. The solution is indeterminate and depends on the relative bargaining strength of the two firms. All we can say is that the level of output and sales of the product will be between four and five units and the price will be between $8 and $16 (i.e., the solution will be within area $E'B'BE$). The greater the relative bargaining strength of the monopolist seller of the product, the closer output will be to five units and price to $15. The greater the relative bargaining strength of the monopsonist buyer of the product, the closer the purchase of the product will be to four units and the price to $8.

Effect of Labor Unions on Wages

A **labor union** is an organization of workers that seeks to increase the wages and the general welfare of union workers through collective bargaining with employers. The Wagner Act passed in 1935 prohibited firms from interfering with the workers' rights to form unions. Union membership as a percentage of the nonagricultural labor force of the United States peaked at 35.5% in 1947, but it had declined to 16% in 1992 and is expected to decline even further during the rest of the 1990s. Among the reasons for the decline is the increase in the proportion of workers in service industries and women in the labor force, both of whom are less likely to join unions than male production workers. Workers are also less likely to join a union if the union does not have much bargaining clout or if workers lose their jobs when they strike. Furthermore, many workers feel that unions were needed when they started, but with more and more companies setting up work-involvement programs (to avoid unionization), unions are less needed now.

A labor union can try to increase the wages of its members by (1) restricting the supply of union labor that employers must hire, (2) bargaining for an above-equilibrium wage, or (3) increasing the demand for union labor. These are shown in Figure 14–8. In each of the three panels in the figure, the intersection of the market demand curve for labor (D_L) and market supply curve of labor (S_L) at point E determines the equilibrium wage rate of $40 and the equilibrium level of employment of 600 workers in the absence of the union.

The left panel shows that if the union can reduce the supply of union labor that employers must hire from S_L to S_L', the equilibrium daily wage will rise to $66, at which 300 workers are hired (point F, where S_L' intersects D_L). The union can restrict the number of union members by high initiation fees and by long apprenticeship periods. The center panel shows that the union can achieve the wage of $66 through bargaining with employers. The result is the same as if the government set the minimum wage of $66. Note that at $w =$

FIGURE 14–8   **Methods by Which Labor Unions Can Increase Wages**

The union can increase wages from $40 to $66 by reducing the supply of union labor from S_L to S_L' (the left panel), by bargaining with employers for $w = 66 (the center panel), or by increasing the demand for union labor from D_L to D_L' (the right panel). Employment falls from 600 workers to 300 workers with the first two methods (the left and center panels) and increases to 800 workers with the last method (the most difficult to accomplish).

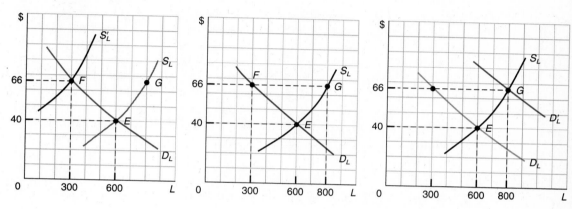

$66, 800 workers would like to work, but only 300 find employment. Thus, there is an unemployment gap of 500 workers (FG in the center panel), 300 of whom represent the disemployment effect (see section 13.8).

Finally, the right panel of Figure 14–8 shows that by shifting D_L up to D_L', the union can increase wages to $66 and employment to 800 workers (given by point G, where D_L' intersects S_L). The union can increase the demand for union labor by advertising to buy "union labels" and by lobbying to restrict imports. Thus, trying to increase union wages by increasing the demand for union labor is the most advantageous method to raise wages, from the point of view of union labor, because it also increases employment. This, however, is also the most difficult for unions to accomplish.

There is a great deal of disagreement regarding the amount by which labor unions have increased the wages of their members. To be sure, unionized workers do receive, on the average, higher wages than nonunionized workers. At least to some extent, however, this is due to the fact that unionized labor is generally more skilled than nonunion labor, is employed in more efficient large-scale industries, and received higher wages even before unionization. On the other hand, wage differences between union and nonunion labor underestimate the effectiveness of labor unions in raising wages because nonunionized firms tend to increase wages when union wages rise in order to retain their workers and avoid unionization. Empirical studies seem to indicate that labor unions, on the average, have been able to increase union wages by 10% to 15% over what they would have been in the absence of unions, but this varies according to occupations, industry, race, and sex. Only during the 1970s and early 1980s were unions able to increase union-nonunion wage differentials to 20% to 30%. By the late 1980s, however, union-nonunion wage differentials returned to the traditional 10% to 15%.

In their actual negotiations with management, labor unions usually "demand" higher wage increases than they really expect to leave room for bargaining. The wage increases in a few major industries, such as the automobile and steel industries, often set the pattern for wage demands in other industries. Union wage demands are also likely to be larger in periods of high profits and employment than in recessionary periods. In the final analysis, the actual wage settlement in a particular industry or firm depends on the relative bargaining strength of the union and the employer, along the lines of the bilateral monopoly model. In making wage demands, unions do take into account the effect of wage increases on employment. Labor unions also seem to have reduced wage differentials among union workers of different skills and among different regions of the country. By bargaining with management for higher wages, unions also tend to reduce monopsonistic exploitation.[6]

Economics of Discrimination in Employment

Discrimination in employment can take many forms, but in this section we will consider only discrimination between male and female workers of equal productivity and its effect on their wages and employment. This is shown in Figure 14–9, where S_F and S_M are the supply curves of female and male labor to a particular industry, respectively; S_L is the total supply of female and male labor; and D_L is the total demand for labor by the industry. The figure shows that in the absence of sex discrimination, the equilibrium wage is $40 for males and females (given by point E, at which S_L intersects D_L), and 200 females (point A) and 400 males (point B) are employed.

However, if employers in the industry refused to hire females, the supply curve of labor to the industry would be only S_M, and 500 male workers would be hired at $w = $50 (point E', where S_M intersects D_L). No females would now be hired by the industry. Females would have to find employment in other industries that do not practice sex discrimination, and this would depress wages for all workers in these other industries. Thus, the gains of male workers from sex discrimination in the industry come at the expense of workers (both males and females) in other industries where there is no sex discrimination.

With a less extreme form of sex discrimination against females, employers

---

[6]For a discussion of labor unions and their effect on wages, see C. J. Parsley, "Labor Unions Effects on Wage Gains: A Survey of Recent Literature," *Journal of Economic Literature*, March 1980; R. B. Freeman and J. L. Medoff, *What Do Unions Do?* (New York: Basic Books, 1984); R. Edwards and P. Swaim, "Union-Nonunion Earnings Differentials and the Decline of Private Sector Unionism," *American Economic Review*, May 1986; M. W. Reder, "The Rise and Fall of Unions: The Public Sector and the Private," *Journal of Economic Perspectives*, Spring 1988; and "Unions' Woes Suggest How the Labor Force in the U.S. Is Shifting," *Wall Street Journal*, May 5, 1992, p. A1.

FIGURE 14–9 Effect of Sex Discrimination in Employment

Without discrimination, $w = \$40$ for males and females (given by point E, at which S_L intersects D_L), and 200 females (point A) and 400 males (point B) are employed. If employers refused to hire females, 500 males would be hired at $w = \$50$ (point E', where S_M intersects D_L). Females would have to find employment in other industries, and this would depress wages for all workers in these other industries. With a less extreme form of discrimination, employers may hire females if their wage is, say, $10 less than for males of the same productivity. Employers would then hire 150 females at $w = \$35$ (point A') and 450 males at $w = \$45$ (point B').

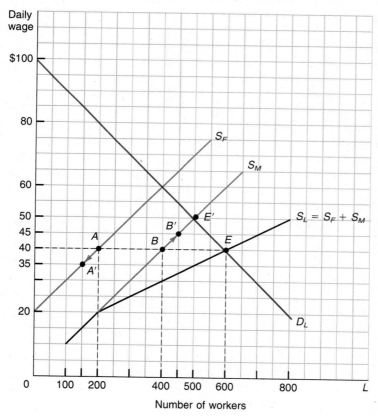

in the industry may prefer to hire males over females at the same wage rate, but the employer's "taste for discrimination" is not absolute and can be overcome by a sufficiently lower wage for female labor than for male labor. For example, employers may also hire females if the wage of female workers is, say, $10 less than for male workers of the same productivity. Compared with the no-discrimination case, employers hire more males (and their wages rise) and fewer females (and their wages fall) until the male-female wage difference is $10. In Figure 14–9, employers hire 150 females at $w = \$35$ (point A') and 450 males at $w = \$45$ (point B'), as compared with 200 females and

400 males at $40 (points *A* and *B*, respectively) without discrimination. Once again, males gain at the expense of females and other employees of this and other industries. The gain is larger the greater is the employers' taste for discrimination in the industry.

If only some employers in the industry discriminated against females, they would employ only male workers while nondiscriminating employers would employ mostly females. If there are enough nondiscriminating employers in the industry to employ all the female workers, no male-female wage differences need arise in the industry. Even if all employers in the industry discriminated against females so that female wages tended to be lower than the wages of male workers, more firms would enter the industry (attracted by the lower female wages), and this, once again, would tend to eliminate sex-based wage differences in the industry. Note that discrimination may also be practiced by employees and by customers.

In 1991, the median weekly earnings of females were 74% of those of males; the earnings of blacks were 78% of those of whites.[7] Empirical studies seem to indicate that from one-half to three-quarters of the male-female and white-black wage differences are due to differences in productivity based on different levels of education, training, age, hours of work, region of employment, and so on. Whether and to what extent the remaining difference is due to discrimination or to other still-unmeasured productivity factors has not yet been settled. The suspicion is that at least part of the unexplained difference is due to discrimination—despite the *Equal Pay Act of 1964*, which prohibits such discrimination.

To overcome possible discrimination, the "comparable-worth doctrine" proposes the evaluation of jobs in terms of the knowledge and skills required, working conditions, accountability, and the enforcement of equal pay for "comparable worth." Many economists, however, consider this too difficult or impossible to do. For example, many of the male-female wage differences are due to fewer work interruptions and longer job tenure for males than for females of equal age and comparable training. Others, however, point out that these work choices themselves are the result of discrimination against females.[8]

SUMMARY

1. A firm that is an imperfect competitor in the product market but a perfect competitor in the input market will maximize profits by hiring any input until the marginal

---

[7]U.S. Department of Commerce, Bureau of the Census, *Statistical Abstract of the United States* (Washington, D.C.: U.S. Government Printing Office, 1992), Table 654, p. 412.

[8]See, G. Becker, *The Economics of Discrimination*, 2nd ed. (Chicago: University of Chicago Press, 1971); "Wage Gap Between Sexes Is Cut in Test, but at a Price," *New York Times*, May 31, 1990, p. 18; and R. Ehrenberg and R. Smith, *Modern Labor Economics* (New York: HarperCollins, 1991), Chapter 14.

product of the input times the firm's marginal revenue from the commodity equals the price of the input.

2. If only one input is variable and the firm is a monopolist in the product market but a perfect competitor in the input market, the firm's demand curve for the input is given by the marginal revenue product (MRP) curve of the input. MRP equals the marginal product (MP) of the input times the marginal revenue (MR) from the commodity. The excess of an input's VMP over MRP at the level of utilization of the input is called monopolistic exploitation. When all inputs are variable, the demand curve of an input is obtained by points on different MRP curves of the input and will be more elastic than the MRP curves. A perfect competitor in an input market will employ the input until the input's MRP on its demand curve equals the input price.

3. When all firms hiring an input are monopolists in their respective product markets, the market demand curve of the input is obtained by the straightforward horizontal summation of all the firms' demand curves for the input. On the other hand, when the firms are oligopolists or monopolistic competitors in the product market, the market demand curve of the input is derived as in section 13.3. The equilibrium price and employment of the input are then determined at the intersection of the market demand and the market supply curve of the input.

4. Monopsony refers to the case where there is a single buyer of an input. The monopsonist faces the positively sloped market supply curve of the input so that its marginal resource cost for the input exceeds the price of the input. Oligopsonists and monopsonistic competitors must also pay higher prices to hire more units of an input. Monopsony arises when an input is much more productive to a particular firm or use than to other firms or uses. It can also result

from lack of geographic or occupational mobility.

5. A monopsonist hiring a single variable input maximizes profits by hiring the input until the marginal revenue product (MRP) of the input equals the marginal resource cost (MRC) of the input. The price of the input is then determined by the corresponding point on the market supply curve of the input. A monopsonist hires less of the variable input and pays the input a lower price than would a perfectly competitive firm in the input market. The excess of the MRP over the price of the input at the point where MRP = MRC is called monopsonistic exploitation.

6. To maximize profits a firm should hire any variable input until the marginal revenue product of the input equals the marginal resouce cost of hiring it. If the firm is a perfect competitor in the product market, the marginal revenue product of the input is identical to the value of the marginal product of the input. If the firm is a perfect competitor in the input market, the marginal resource cost of the input equals the input price.

7. Immigration usually increases the earnings of capital and reduces those of labor. Since the former usually exceeds the latter, however, the nation of immigration as a whole receives a net gain. The emigration of skilled labor and professionals represents a brain drain on the nation of emigration and an even greater gain for the nation of immigration.

8. Monopsonistic exploitation can be eliminated by the government setting the minimum price of an input at the point where the MRP curve intersects the market supply curve of the input. Bilateral monopoly occurs when the monopsonist buyer of a product or input faces the monopolist seller of the product or input. Unions seem to have increased wages only slightly. Among the most important goals of unions

are higher wages and greater employment of union labor. Discrimination in employment reduces the wages and/or the employment of the discriminated category.

The marginal resource cost of an input is related to the price of the input and the price elasticity of the input supply.

KEY TERMS

Marginal Revenue Product
    (MRP)
Monopolistic Exploitation
Monopsony
Marginal Resource Cost (MRC)
Marginal Resource Cost of
    Labor (MRC_L)

Marginal Resource Cost of
    Capital (MRC_K)
Oligopsony
Monopsonistic Competition
Monopsonistic Exploitation
Brain Drain
Bilateral Monopoly

Labor Union
Discrimination in Employment

REVIEW QUESTIONS

1. Why is the demand curve for an input less elastic when the firm is an imperfect rather than a perfect competitor in the product market?

2. Why are real average wages higher in the United States than in most other countries? Why have real wages in West Germany and Japan been catching up with U.S. wages during the period after World War II?

3. Can a demand curve for an input be derived for a monopsonist? Why?

4. Monopsonistic exploitation is true exploitation while monopolistic exploitation is not. True or false? Explain.

5. What is the general rule for a firm to maximize profits in hiring an input? What does the rule become when the firm is a perfect competitor in the product market and/or in the input market?

6. A firm that is a perfect competitor in the product market hires more labor than a firm that is

an imperfect competitor in the product market, everything else being equal. True or false? Explain.

7. How does immigration benefit the United States?

8. What trade alternative can the United States use to slow down the inflow of illegal aliens from Mexico?

9. Why are wages and employment indeterminate when a monopsonistic employer faces a monopolistic union?

10. Why might unionization in some industries lead to lower wages in other industries?

11. What are some of the ways by which labor unions can increase and reduce labor productivity?

12. What are the difficulties in establishing the existence and measuring the extent of discrimination in a labor market?

PROBLEMS

1. For a firm that is a monopolist in the product market but a perfect competitor in the input markets, express the condition prevailing if the firm
    a. utilizes too much labor or too little capital

at the best output level. What is the graphic interpretation of this?
    b. utilizes the least-cost input combination but with its marginal cost exceeding its MR. What is the graphic interpretation of this?

c. minimizes the cost of producing an output that is too small to maximize profits. What is the graphic interpretation of this?

2. You are given the following data where L is the number of workers hired per day by a firm (the only variable input), Q_X is the quantity of the commodity produced per day, and P_X is the commodity price:

L	1	2	3	4	5
Q_X	10	20	28	34	38
P_X	$5.00	4.50	4.00	3.50	3.00

a. Find the marginal revenue product of labor and plot it.
b. How many workers per day will the firm hire if the wage rate is $40 per day? $22? $7? What is the firm's demand curve for labor?

*3. From Table 14–1 in the text
a. find the MR_X, the MRP_L by multiplying MR_X by MP_L, and the VMP_L.
b. On the same graph, plot the VMP_L and the MRP_L on the assumption that labor is infinitesimally divisible. How many workers would the firm employ if it were a perfect competitor in the product market? What is the amount of monopolistic exploitation?

4. Repeat the procedure in problem 3 for the data in problem 2 and on the assumption that the daily wage is $22.

5. Assume that (1) labor is infinitesimally divisible (i.e., workers can be hired for any part of the day) in the production function of problems 2 and 4, (2) all inputs are variable, and (3) when the wage rate falls from $40 to $22 per day, the firm's value of the marginal product curve shifts to the right by two labor units. Derive the demand curve for labor of this firm. How many workers will the firm hire per day at the daily wage rate of $22?

6. a. Derive the market demand curve for labor if there are 100 monopolistically competitive firms identical to the firm of problem 5 in the labor market and each individual firm's demand curve for labor shifts to the left by one unit when the wage rate falls from $w = $40 to $w = $22 per day.
b. If 200 workers are willing to work at the

daily wage of $10, and 600 are willing to work at the daily wage of $40, what is the equilibrium wage and level of employment? How many workers would each firm hire at the equilibrium wage?

7. a. From the following market supply schedule of labor faced by a monopsonist, derive the firm's marginal resource cost of labor schedule.
b. Plot on the same set of axes the firm's supply and marginal resource cost of labor schedules.

L	1	2	3	4	5
w	$10	11	16	40	100

8. On your graph for problem 7b, superimpose the monopsonist's value of marginal product and marginal revenue product of labor curves from problem 14–4. Assuming that labor is the only variable input, determine the number of workers that the firm hires, the wage rate, and the amount of monopolistic and monopsonistic exploitation if the firm is a monopolist in the product market and a monopsonist in the input market.

*9. Starting with Figure 14–4, explain what happens if the government sets the minimum wage at
a. $35.
b. $50.

*10. Assume that all workers in a town belong to the union and there is a single firm hiring labor in the town. Suppose that the supply for labor function of the firm (monopsonist) is $S_L = 2w$ (where w refers to wages, measured in dollars per day) and the demand of labor function by the union (the monopolist seller of labor time) is $D_L = 120 - 2w$. Find the wage rate and number of workers that the firm would like to hire and the wage and level of employment that the union would seek if it behaved as a monopolist. What is the likely result?

*11. Draw a figure showing that an increase in

---

* = Answer provided at end of book.

union wages usually reduces employment in unionized industries and increases employment and lowers wages in nonunionized industries.

12. Given that (1) $MRC_L = w(1 + 1/\epsilon_L)$ where ϵ_L is the price (wage) elasticity of the supply curve of labor (this formula is derived in section A.14 of the Mathematical Appendix), and (2) S_L is a straight line through the origin, find the value of MRC_L if

   a. $w = \$40$.

   b. $w = \$80$.

FINANCIAL MICROECONOMICS: INTEREST, INVESTMENT, AND THE COST OF CAPITAL

In this chapter, we consider intertemporal choices or the optimal allocation of resources *over time*. We examine the choice between consuming now or saving a portion of this year's income in order to consume more in the future. The other side of the coin is borrowing against future income to increase present consumption. The ability of an individual to exchange present for future income or consumption (by lending or borrowing) enables him or her to maximize the total or joint satisfaction of present and future income and consumption. For example, people individually and collectively (through the Social Security system) save during their working lives to provide for retirement, and by doing so, they maximize the lifetime satisfaction from their earnings. On the other hand, students often borrow against their future income (i.e., they dissave).

Another way by which present income can be exchanged for future income is to free some resources from the production of final commodities for present consumption (i.e., save) to produce more capital goods (i.e., invest in machinery, factories, and so on), which will lead to larger output and consumption in the future. The ability of individuals and firms to trade present for future income and output and vice versa (through lending and borrowing, saving and investing) is very crucial in all societies. Indeed, a great deal of the increase in the standards of living in modern societies is the result of investments in physical capital (machinery, factories, etc.) and human capital (education, skills, health, and so on).

An individual usually requires a reward for postponing present consumption (i.e., saving) and lending a portion of this year's income. The reward takes the form of a repayment that exceeds the amount lent. This premium is the interest payment. The other side of the coin is the borrowing of a given sum today and the repaying of a larger sum in the future (the principal plus the interest). Similarly, individuals and firms will only invest in machinery, factories, or in acquiring or providing skills if they can expect a return on their investment in the form of higher future incomes or outputs than the amounts invested.

In this chapter, we examine the determination of the rate of interest that will balance the quantity of resources lent and borrowed and that equilibrates saving and investment. We also analyze the criteria used by individuals, business firms, and government agencies in their investment decisions. Subsequently, we discuss the reasons for differences in interest rates in the same nation, in different nations, and over time. The chapter explains how to measure the cost of capital and describes the effects of foreign investments. Finally, several important applications of the theory introduced in the chapter are presented. These range from investment in human capital to the pricing and management of renewable and nonrenewable resources.

15.1 LENDING-BORROWING EQUILIBRIUM

In this section, we examine how an individual maximizes the total or joint satisfaction from spending his or her present and future income by lending or borrowing. We also show how the equilibrium market rate of interest is determined at the level at which the total quantity demanded of loans (borrowings) equals the total quantity supplied of loans (lendings).

Lending

We begin by considering how a consumer can maximize satisfaction over time by lending. For simplicity, we assume that the consumer's income is measured in terms of the quantity of a commodity (say corn) that he or she has or expects to receive. Also, to simplify matters, we will deal with only two time periods: this year and the next. (This assumption is relaxed in section 15.4.) We also begin by assuming that the consumer has an **endowment position,** or receives $Y_0 = 7.5$ units of corn this year and $Y_1 = 3$ units of corn next year (point A in the left panel of Figure 15–1).[1]

The consumer, however, is not bound to consume the $Y_0 = 7.5$ units of corn this year and the $Y_1 = 3$ units of corn next year, because he or she can lend part of this year's corn or borrow against next year's corn. The question is how should the consumer distribute his or her consumption between this year and next so as to maximize the total or joint satisfaction over the two periods. This is analogous to the consumer's choice between hamburgers (commodity X) and soft drinks (commodity Y) examined in section 3.5 and Figure 3–8. The only difference is that here the choice is between the consumption of corn this year or next.

In the left panel of Figure 15.1, the consumer's tastes between consumption this year and next are given by indifference curves U_1, U_2, and U_3. The consumer also faces budget line FW_0. The latter shows the various combinations

---

[1]Uncertainty is ruled out here so that the consumer knows exactly how much of the commodity he or she gets this year and next year. This assumption is relaxed in section 15.4. In what follows, subscripts 0 and 1 denote, respectively, this year (or the present) and next year (or the future).

FIGURE 15–1 Lending

Starting from endowment A ($Y_0 = 7.5$ and $Y_1 = 3$), the consumer maximizes satisfaction at point E, where budget line FW_0 is tangent to indifference curve U_2 in the left panel. The consumer reaches point E by lending $Y_0 - C_0 = 2.5$ units from this year's endowment and receiving 3 additional units next year. Thus, the slope of the budget line is $3/(-2.5) = -1.2$ or $-1(1 + 0.2)$ and the interest rate $r = 0.2$ or 20%. At $r = 50\%$, the optimal point is E' (in the right panel), where the steeper budget line through point A is tangent to indifference curve U_3. Point E' is reached by lending 3 units (instead of 2.5).

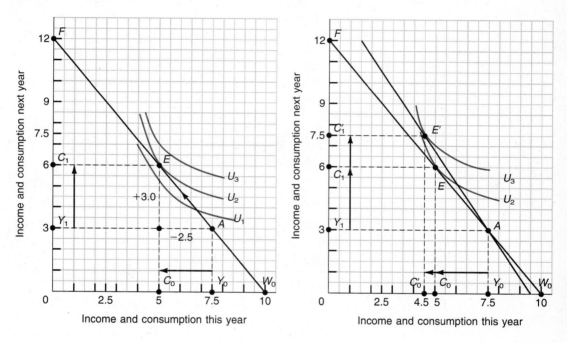

of present and future income and consumption available to the consumer. Starting from endowment position A ($Y_0 = 7.5$ and $Y_1 = 3$), the consumer can lend part of this year's corn endowment so that he or she will consume less this year and more next year. This is represented by an upward movement from point A along budget line FW_0. On the other hand, the consumer could increase consumption this year by borrowing against next year's endowment or income by moving downward from point A along FW_0.

The consumer maximizes satisfaction by reaching the highest indifference curve possible with his or her budget line. The optimal choice is given by point E, where budget line FW_0 is tangent to indifference curve U_2. At point E, the individual consumes $C_0 = 5$ units of corn this year and $C_1 = 6$ units next year (see the left panel of Figure 15–1). The consumer reaches point E by lending $Y_0 - C_0 = 2.5$ units of corn out of this year's endowment or output and receiving 3 additional units next year.

The slope of the budget line gives the premium or the rate of interest that the lender receives. For example, the movement from point A to point E

indicates that the consumer recieves 3 units of the commodity next year by lending 2.5 units this year. Thus, the slope of the budget line is $3/(-2.5) = -1.2$ or $-1(1 + 0.2)$, so that the interest rate $r = 0.2$ or 20%. That is,

$$\frac{C_1 - Y_1}{C_0 - Y_0} = -(1 + r) = -(1 + 0.2) \qquad \text{[15–1]}$$

The negative sign reflects the downward-to-the-right inclination of the budget line. This simply means that for the consumer to be able to consume more next year, he or she will have to consume less this year. In this case, the consumer lends (i.e., reduces consumption by) 2.5 units this year and gets $2.5(1 + 0.2) = 3$ next year. If the consumer lends all of this year's income or endowment of $Y_0 = 7.5$ units at 20% interest, he or she will receive $7.5(1 + 0.2) = 9$ additional units next year (and reaches point F on budget line FW_0). The consumer could do this, but does not, because he or she would not be maximizing satisfaction.

Returning to the slope of the budget line, we can say more generally that the **rate of interest (r)** is the premium received by an individual next year by lending $1.00 today. Another way of stating this is that the rate of interest is the excess in the price next year (P_1) of $1.00 this year ($P_0$). That is,

$$P_1 = P_0 (1 + r) \qquad \text{[15–2]}$$

The individual receives ($1) $(1 + r)$ next year (P_1) by lending $1.00 this year ($P_0$). If the interest rate r is 0.2 or 20%, the individual receives ($1) $(1 + 0.2)$ = $1.20 next year by lending $1.00 this year. Of course, the person who borrows $1.00 today must repay $1.20 next year if the rate of interest is 20%. Thus, the interest rate can be viewed as the excess in the price next year of $1.00 lent or borrowed this year.

If the interest rate rises (i.e., if the budget line becomes steeper), lenders will usually lend more. For example, starting with endowment position A in the *right* panel of Figure 15–1, if the interest rate rises to 50% so that the slope of the budget line becomes $-(1 + 0.5)$, the optimal choice of the consumer is at point E', where the new steeper budget line through point A is tangent to higher indifference curve U_3. The consumer can reach point E' by lending $Y_0 - C_0' = 3$ units (instead of 2.5), for which he or she receives $C_1' - Y_1 = 4.5$ units next year. That is, by lending 3 units at 50% interest, the consumer receives $3(1 + 0.5) = 4.5$ units next year. Thus, the increase in the rate of interest from 20% to 50% leads this individual (the lender) to increase lending from 2.5 to 3 units.[2]

---

[2]The increase in the rate of interest will usually, but not always, increase the amount of lending. The reason is that (as in the case of an increase in the wage rate), an increase in the rate of interest gives rise to a substitution effect and an income effect. According to the substitution effect, the increase in the rate of interest leads the individual to lend more. However, by increasing the future income of the individual, the increase in the rate of interest also gives rise to an income effect, which leads the individual to lend less. At a sufficiently high rate of interest, the negative income effect exceeds the positive substitution effect and the individual's supply curve of loans bends backward. This is examined in problem 5a, with answer at end of the text.

Borrowing

We will now show that if the endowment position of the consumer in the left panel of Figure 15–1 had been to the left of point E on the budget line FW_0 (rather than at point A), the consumer would have been a borrower rather than a lender. This is shown in the left panel of Figure 15–2. Specifically, suppose the endowment position of the consumer had been at point B ($Y_0 = 2.5$ and $Y_1 = 9$) on budget line FW_0. The consumer would maximize satisfaction at point E ($C_0 = 5$ and $C_1 = 6$), where budget line FW_0 is tangent to indifference curve U_2 (the highest the consumer can reach with budget line FW_0). To reach point E, the consumer would have to borrow $C_0 - Y_0 = 2.5$ units of the commodity this year and repay $Y_1 - C_1 = 3$ units next year.

Since $3/2.5 = 1.2$, the rate of interest $r = 0.2$ or 20%, as in the lending example. This means that in order to borrow 2.5 units this year, the individual must repay 3 units next year if the market rate of interest is 20%. That is, $2.5 = 3/(1 + 0.2)$. The reason for this is that 2.5 units this year will grow to 3 units next year at $r = 0.2$ or 20%. More generally, we can say that the price

FIGURE 15–2   Borrowing

Starting from endowment B ($Y_0 = 2.5$ and $Y_1 = 9$), the consumer maximizes satisfaction at point E, where budget line FW_0 is tangent to indifference curve U_2 in the left panel. The consumer reaches point E by borrowing $C_0 - Y_0 = 2.5$ and repaying $Y_1 - C_1 = 3$ next year. Thus, the slope of the budget line is $3/(-2.5) = -1.2$ or $-1(1 + 0.2)$ and the interest rate $r = 0.2$ or 20%. At $r = 50\%$, the optimal point is E^* in the right panel, where the steeper budget line through point B is tangent to indifference curve U_1. Point E^* is reached by borrowing 2 units (instead of 2.5).

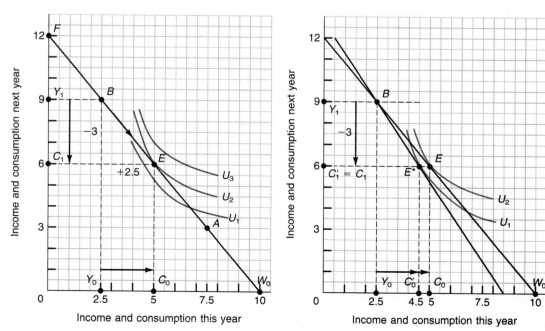

of \$1.00 today (P_0) is equal to \$1.00 next year (P_1) divided by $(1 + r)$. That is,

$$P_0 = P_1/(1 + r) \qquad [15\text{--}3]$$

This is obtained by dividing both sides of equation [15–2] by $(1 + r)$. For example, at $r = 20\%$, \$1.00 next year is equivalent to $\$1/(1 + 0.2) = \$0.83$ this year, because \$0.83 lent this year at 20% will grow to \$1.00 next year.

If the individual borrowed all of next year's income of $Y_1 = 9$, he or she could increase consumption this year by $\$9/(1 + 0.2) = 7.5$ and be at point $W_0 = 10$. Point $W_0 = 10$ gives the **wealth** of the individual. This is equal to the individual's income or endowment this year plus the present value of next year's income or endowment. That is, the consumer's wealth is given by

$$W_0 = Y_0 + [Y_1/(1 + r)] \qquad [15\text{--}4]$$

In our example, the income this year is $Y_0 = 2.5$ and the present value of next year's income is $Y_1/(1 + r) = 9/(1 + 0.2) = 7.5$, resulting in the individual's wealth of 10. Graphically, the wealth of the individual or consumer is given by the intersection of the budget line with the horizontal axis. Thus, wealth plays the same role in intertemporal choice as the consumer's income plays in the consumer's choice between two commodities during the same year. An increase in wealth, like an increase in income, will shift the consumer's budget line outward and allows the consumer to purchase more of every normal good or to consume more, both this year and next.

An increase in the rate of interest leads to a reduction in the amount the individual wants to borrow. Since present consumption becomes more expensive in terms of the future consumption that must be given up, the borrower will borrow less. This is shown in the right panel of Figure 15–2. Starting once again with endowment position B in the right panel of Figure 15–2, an increase in the rate of interest to 50% will result in a new budget line with slope of $-(1 + 0.5)$. The optimal choice of the consumer is then at point E^*, where the steeper budget line through point B is tangent to lower indifference curve U_1. Indifference curve U_1 is the highest that the consumer can reach with his or her initial endowment position B and $r = 50\%$. To reach point E^* ($C_0' = 4.5$ and $C_1' = C_1 = 6$), the consumer will have to borrow C_0' $- Y_0 = 2$ units (instead of 2.5) this year, and will have to repay $C_1' - Y_1 = (-) 3$ units next year. That is, $2 = 3/(1 + 0.5)$. Thus, the increase in the rate of interest from 20% to 50% leads this individual to borrow less.[3]

The Market Rate of Interest with Borrowing and Lending

We now examine how the equilibrium rate of interest is determined in the market for borrowing and lending. For simplicity, we assume that we have

---

[3]As opposed to the supply curve of loans, which could bend backward at a sufficiently high rate of interest, the demand curve for loans is always negatively sloped (see problem 5b, with answer at end of the text).

only two individuals in the market for loans: individual B with endowment position B and individual A with endowment position A on budget line FW_0 (see the left panel of Figure 15–2). That is, instead of assuming as above that an individual has either endowment B (and is a borrower) or endowment A (and is a lender), we now assume that we have two individuals, one with endowment B (the borrower) and the other with endowment A (the lender) on FW_0. We also assume for now that both individuals have the same tastes or time preferences for present (this year) versus future (next year) consumption, as shown by indifference curves U_1, U_2, and U_3 in the left panel of Figure 15–2.

As we can see from the left panel of Figure 15–2, the optimal choice for individual B is to move from point B to point E along budget line FW_0 by borrowing 2.5 units of the commodity this year at the rate of interest of 0.20 or 20% (so that he or she will have to repay 3 units next year). Thus, the quantity demanded of loans (borrowing) by individual B is 2.5 units at $r = 20\%$. On the other hand, the optimal choice of individual A is to move from point A to point E along budget line FW_0 by lending 2.5 units of the commodity this year at the rate of interest of 0.20 or 20% (so that he or she will receive an additional 3 units next year). Thus, the quantity supplied of loans (lending) by individual A is 2.5 units at $r = 20\%$.

Since we have assumed that A and B are the only two individuals in the market, the equilibrium market rate of interest is 0.20 or 20%. This is the only market rate of interest at which the desired quantity demanded of loans (borrowing) of 2.5 units equals the desired quantity supplied of loans (lending) of 2.5 units, and the market for loanable funds is in equilibrium. This is shown by point E in Figure 15–3, where the demand curve for borrowing (D_B) intersects the supply curve for lending (S_L). The figure also shows that at $r = 50\%$, individual B wants to borrow only 2 units (point E^* on D_B, from the right panel of Figure 15–2) and individual A wants to lend 3 units (point E' on D_L, from the right panel of Figure 15–1). The resulting excess in the quantity supplied over the quantity demanded of loans of 1 unit ($E^* E'$) at $r = 50\%$ causes the rate of interest to fall to the equilibrium level of $r = 20\%$ (point E).

In the above analysis, we have assumed for simplicity that there are only two individuals, A and B, in the market and that both have identical tastes or time preference.[4] In the real world, however, there are many individuals with different tastes. Yet, the process by which the equilibrium market rate of interest is determined is basically the same. That is, the equilibrium market rate of interest is the one at which the total or aggregate quantity demanded of borrowing matches the aggregate quantity supplied of lending. At a market rate of interest above the equilibrium rate, the supply of lending exceeds the

---

[4]The determination of the market rate of interest when consumers have different time preferences is examined in problem 4 (with answer at end of the text).

FIGURE 15–3   Borrowing-Lending Equilibrium

Borrowing-lending equilibrium occurs at point E, where the demand curve for borrowing (D_B) intersects the supply curve for lending (S_L). Point E shows that $r = 20\%$ and 2.5 units are borrowed and lent. At $r = 50\%$, the quantity supplied of lending of 3 units (point E') exceeds the quantity demanded of borrowing of 2 units (point E^*) and the rate of interest falls to 20% (point E). The opposite is true at r lower than 20%.

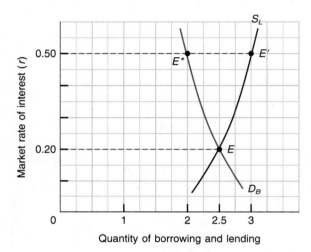

demand for borrowing and the interest rate falls. On the other hand, at a market rate of interest below the equilibrium rate, the demand for borrowing exceeds the supply of lending and the market rate of interest rises toward equilibrium. Only at the equilibrium market rate of interest does the quantity demanded match the quantity supplied and there is no tendency for the interest rate to change.

Example 1

Personal Savings in the United States

Table 15–1 shows the total aggregate amount of personal savings (PS) and the level of disposable (i.e., after tax) personal income (DPI) in 1987 prices, and PS as a percentage of DPI in the United States for 1960, 1970, 1980, and 1985 through 1991. Personal savings ranged from $75 billion in 1960 to $167 billion in 1991, or from 5.7% of disposable personal income in 1960 to 4.7% in 1991.

Prior to the establishment of Social Security in 1935, individuals provided for their retirement by voluntarily saving a portion of their earnings during their working years. Social Security provided retirement income through a forced savings (Social Security tax) program, thus reducing the need for personal savings. If the government had saved the Social Security taxes it

TABLE 15–1   Personal Savings and Disposable Personal Income (in billions of 1987 dollars)

Year	PS	DPI	PS as a % of DPI
1960	$ 75.0	$1,313.0	5.7
1970	161.3	2,025.3	8.0
1980	215.3	2,733.6	7.9
1985	203.3	3,162.1	6.4
1986	195.4	3,261.9	6.0
1987	142.0	3,289.5	4.3
1988	149.3	3,404.3	4.4
1989	139.2	3,464.9	4.0
1990	152.8	3,516.5	4.3
1991	166.5	3,509.0	4.7

Source: Council of Economic Advisors, *Economic Report of the President* (Washington, D.C.: U.S. Government Printing Office, 1993), pp. 377–378.

levied, net savings (personal plus government) would have been more or less unchanged. Because the government chose not to "fund" the system, but to use Social Security taxes for current expenditures and pay future Social Security benefits out of future taxes, the nation's level of aggregate savings declined. Michael Darby estimated that the Social Security program has reduced the nation's savings by 5% to 20%.

Source: Michael R. Darby, *The Effects of Social Security on Income and Capital Stock* (Washington, D.C.: American Enterprise Institute, 1979).

15.2 SAVING-INVESTMENT EQUILIBRIUM

In section 15.1 we analyzed borrowing-lending equilibrium. For simplicity, we assumed that no part of the current endowment or output was invested to increase future productive capacity. In this section, we begin with the opposite situation and examine saving-investment equilibrium without borrowing or lending. That is, we begin by examining the case in which an isolated individual (a Robinson Crusoe) consumes less than he or she produces in this period (saves) in order to have more seeds, or to produce a piece of equipment, to increase production in the next period (invests). Then, we relax the assumption that the individual is isolated and that he or she cannot borrow or lend and examine saving-investment equilibrium with borrowing and lending. Finally, we show how the equilibrium rate of interest is determined with saving and investment and with borrowing and lending.

Saving-Investment Equilibrium Without Borrowing and Lending

Suppose that an individual lives alone on an island and produces and consumes a single commodity. This Robinson Crusoe has no possibility to borrow or lend (or trade) the commodity and can only consume what he produces. Suppose that under present conditions he can count on producing $Y_0 = 7.5$ units of the commodity during this year and $Y_1 = 3$ units next year. This is shown by point A on his production-possibilities curve FQ in Figure 15–4.

Production-possibilities curve FQ shows how much Crusoe can produce and consume next year by saving part of this year's output and investing it to increase next year's output. **Saving** refers to the act of refraining from present consumption. **Investment** refers to the formation of new capital assets. For example, Crusoe may use part of the year to construct a rudimentary net rather than catch fish with a spear. Since he is not catching fish while he is building the net, he is refraining from present consumption (saving). The net is an investment that will allow him to catch more fish in the future. In this case, the saving and the investment are done by the same person, and are one and the same thing.

Disregarding for the moment the indifference curves in Figure 15–4, we see that the FQ curve shows that if the individual consumes $C_0 = 6$ units of the commodity this year, he can produce and consume $C_1 = 6.5$ units of the commodity next year (point G on FQ). Starting from point A, this means that by saving and investing $Y_0 - C_0 = 7.5 - 6 = 1.5$ units of the commodity this year, the individual can increase output by $C_1 - Y_1 = 6.5 - 3 = 3.5$ units next year. Thus, the average yield or return on investment (in terms of next year's output) is $3.5/1.5 = 2.33 = (1 + 1.33)$ or 133%. Should the individual save and invest 3 units of the commodity this year, his output will increase by 6 units next year (the movement from point A to point H on FQ), so that the average yield or rate of return would be $6/3 = 2 = (1 + 1)$ or 100%. Note that the larger is the amount invested, the lower is the rate of return (because of the operation of the law of diminishing returns).

Starting at point A on production-possibilities curve FQ, the question is, "What is the optimal amount of saving and investment for this individual?" The answer is 1.5 units. The reason is that this will permit the individual to reach point G on indifference curve U_4. Indifference curve U_4 is the highest that Crusoe can reach with his production-possibilities curve. Note that indifference curves here show the trade-off or time preference between consumption this year and next. Thus, starting from point A, Crusoe should save and invest 1.5 units of this year's output so as to reach point G next year and maximize his total or joint utility or satisfaction over the two years.

Saving-Investment Equilibrium with Borrowing and Lending

Suppose that more people get stranded on Crusoe's island, and they also start producing and consuming the commodity. Now, borrowing and lending

FIGURE 15–4   Saving-Investment Equilibrium Without Borrowing or Lending

Production-possibilities curve FQ shows how much an isolated individual can produce and consume next year by saving and investing part of this year's output. Starting at point A on FQ, the optimal level of saving and investment is 1.5 units. This allows the individual to reach point G on the highest indifference curve possible (U_4). Saving and investing 1.5 units this year allows the individual to produce and consume 3.5 more units next year. Thus, the average yield on investment is 133%.

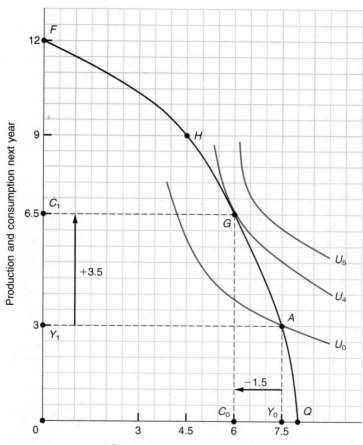

become possible. The optimal choice of Crusoe is now to save and invest, borrow or lend, so as to reach the highest indifference curve possible (higher than U_4).

To show this, we must realize that from every point of the production-possibilities curve there is a **market line,** the slope of which shows the rate at which the individual (Crusoe) can borrow or lend in the market. For example, starting at point A on the FQ curve in Figure 15–5, the individual can borrow or lend along market line FAW_0 at the rate of interest of $r = 20\%$ (as in the left panel of Figures 15–1 and 15–2). If starting from point A the individual only borrows or lends (or does neither), his wealth is $W_0 = 10$ (given by the intersection of market line FAW_0 with the horizontal axis).

However, with the possibility of saving and investment, and borrowing or lending now open, the optimal choice for Crusoe is to invest first (so as to

FIGURE 15–5   Saving-Investment Equilibrium with Borrowing and Lending

Starting from point A, the individual maximizes wealth (at $W_0' = 12$ units) by investing 3 units of the commodity and reaching point H, where market line $HE''W_0'$ (with slope reflecting the market rate of interest) is tangent to production-possibilities curve FQ. The individual then borrows 2.5 units (i.e., moves to the right of point H on market line $HE''W_0'$) and reaches point E'' on U_5 (the highest indifference curve possible). The individual invests 3 units, borrows 2.5, and saves 0.5.

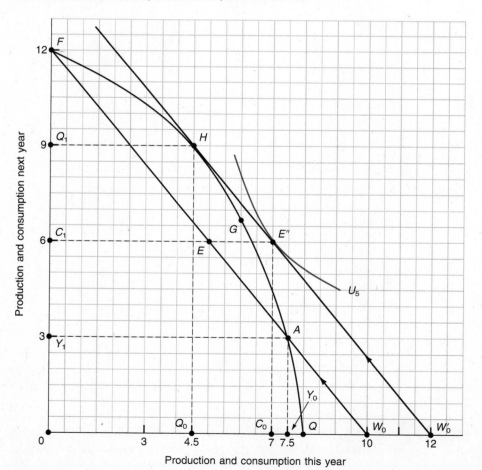

maximize wealth) and then to borrow (so as to reach the highest indifference curve possible). Wealth is maximized by reaching the highest market line (with slope reflecting the market rate of interest) that is possible with the FQ curve. This is given by market line $HE''W_0'$, which is parallel to market line FAW_0 (so that $r = 20\%$) and tangent to production-possibilities curve FQ at point H. Market line $HE''W_0'$ shows that the maximum attainable wealth is $W_0' = 12$. Starting from point A on the FQ curve, the individual can attain market line $HE''W_0'$ and maximize wealth by investing $Y_0 - Q_0 = 3$ units of this year's output. This allows him to reach point H on this production-possibilities curve and produce $Q_1 = 9$ units of the commodity next year.

Having attained the highest wealth possible by investing 3 units of the commodity (point H on market line $HE''W_0'$), the individual can then borrow $C_0 - Q_0 = 2.5$ units (i.e., move to the right of point H on market line $HE''W_0'$) and reach point E'' on U_5. This is the highest indifference curve that the individual can reach with optimal investment and borrowing. Point E'' on indifference curve U_5 is superior to point A on U_0 (see Figure 15–4) without borrowing or investing, it is superior to borrowing alone (to the right of point A along budget line FEW_0), and it is superior to point G on U_4 (see Figure 15–4) with saving equal to investment and no borrowing.

To summarize, the optimal choice of the individual is to invest $Y_0 - Q_0 = 3$ units (i.e., to move from point A to point H on the FQ curve) in order to maximize wealth (at $W_0' = 12$) and to borrow $C_0 - Q_0 = 2.5$ units (the movement from point H to point E'' on indifference curve U_5) to maximize his total or joint satisfaction or utility over both years. Of the total amount of $Y_0 - Q_0 = 3$ invested, the individual borrows $C_0 - Q_0 = 2.5$ and saves $Y_0 - C_0 = 0.5$. That is, the individual is saving a portion of his current output, but not enough to "finance" all of his investment. Therefore, other individuals must be saving 2.5 units of the commodity more than they invest in order to lend this amount to our individual.

If the market rate of interest rises above $r = 20\%$, the market line becomes steeper and tangent to production-possibilities curve FQ to the right of point H, and the individual will invest less (see Figure 15–6 and problem 6). If the individual borrows more than he invests, he will be dissaving (see problem 7). If indifference curve U_5 had been tangent to market line HW_0' to the left of point H in Figure 15–5, the individual would have been investing and lending (rather than investing and borrowing) so that his saving would equal the sum of the two (see problem 8).

The Market Rate of Interest with Saving and Investment, Borrowing and Lending

We now examine how the equilibrium rate of interest is determined in the market with borrowing and lending, and saving and investment. For simplicity, we assume that only our individual borrows and invests while all other individuals collectively only want to lend 2.5 units of the commodity at the rate of interest of $r = 20\%$. The equilibrium rate of interest is then 20% and is shown in Figure 15–6 in two different ways: (1) by point E, where the

FIGURE 15–6   **Rate of Interest with Borrowing and Lending, Saving and Investment**

The equilibrium rate of interest is 20% and is shown (1) by point E, where the demand curve for borrowing (D_B) intersects the supply curve of lending (S_L), and (2) by point E'', where the demand curve for investment (D_I) intersects the total supply curve of savings (S_S). At $r > 20\%$, desired lending exceeds desired borrowing, and desired saving exceeds desired investments, and r falls. The opposite is true at $r < 20\%$.

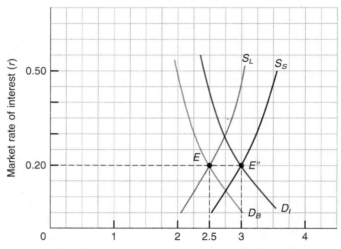

Quantity of borrowing and lending, investment and saving

demand curve of borrowing of our individual (D_B) intersects the supply curve of lending of all other individuals (S_L) as in Figure 15–3, or equivalently, (2) by point E'', where the demand curve for investment of our individual (D_I) intersects the total supply curve of savings of this and other individuals (S_S).

At the equilibrium market rate of interest of $r = 20\%$, the quantity of desired borrowing of 2.5 units (done exclusively by our individual) equals the quantity of desired lending of 2.5 units (supplied by all other individuals). In addition, at $r = 20\%$, the total amount of desired savings of 3 units (2.5 units by other individuals and 0.5 units by our individual) matches the desired level of investment of 3 units (undertaken exclusively by our individual). That is, at equilibrium, desired borrowing equals desired lending (point E) and desired savings equals desired investment (point E''). Note that the excess between the saving-investment equilibrium and the borrowing-lending equilibrium refers to the amount of investment that is self-financed from the investor's own savings rather than from borrowing in the market.[5]

---

[5]Just as some people can borrow more than they invest so that they dissave, so some individuals can consume more than the sum of what they produce, borrow, and invest. Such individuals would be *disinvesting* or failing to maintain (i.e., not replacing depreciated) capital stock. To some extent, these individuals are "living off their capital." This may also be true for society as a whole during periods of war or natural disaster, or when it borrows abroad to increase present consumption.

At a rate of interest above equilibrium, there will be (1) an excess in the quantity supplied of lending over the quantity demanded of borrowing and (2) an excess in the total quantity supplied of savings over the total quantity demanded of investment (see Figure 15–6). As a result, the interest rate will fall to the equilibrium level. The opposite is true at rates of interest below equilibrium. Of course, in the real world, there are many borrowers and many lenders, and many savers and investors, but the principles by which the equilibrium rate of interest is determined are the same (when capital markets are perfectly competitive). That is, at equilibrium, aggregate desired borrowing equals aggregate desired lending, and aggregate desired investment equals aggregate desired saving.

Example 2

▽ **Personal and Business Savings and Gross and Net Private Domestic Investment in the United States**

Table 15–2 presents the total or aggregate amount of personal savings (PS), business savings (BS), gross private domestic investment (GPDI), and net private domestic investment (NPDI) in the United States in terms of 1987 prices for the years 1960, 1970, 1980, and 1985 through 1991. NPDI equals GPDI minus capital consumption allowances or depreciation resulting from the production of the given year's output. Table 15–2 also shows the level of real net national product (NNP) and NPDI as a percentage of NNP during the same years.

Business savings are from two to four times larger than personal savings.

TABLE 15–2   Personal and Business Savings and Gross and Net Private Domestic Investment in the United States (in billions of 1987 dollars)

Year	PS	BS	GPDI	NPDI	NNP	NPDI as a % of NNP
1960	$ 75.0	$221.8	$290.8	$117.1	$1,712.5	6.8
1970	161.3	303.5	429.7	171.7	2,603.9	6.6
1980	215.3	484.0	594.4	193.7	3,402.3	5.7
1985	203.3	586.8	745.9	274.4	3,865.4	7.1
1986	195.4	556.3	735.1	248.4	3,958.8	6.3
1987	142.0	588.7	749.3	247.1	4,042.4	6.1
1988	149.3	620.1	773.4	254.9	4,194.9	6.1
1989	139.2	610.6	784.0	238.5	4,288.1	5.6
1990	152.8	590.3	739.1	184.2	4,297.9	4.3
1991	166.5	585.4	661.1	91.8	4,227.4	2.2

Source: Council of Economic Advisors, *Economic Report of the President* (Washington, D.C.: U.S. Government Printing Office, 1993), pp. 365, 370, 377–378.

Net private domestic investment is the net addition to society's capital stock and an important contributor to the growth of the economy and standards of living. Personal and business savings are required to provide for the replacement of the capital consumed during the course of producing current output and for the net additions to the capital stock of the country. Not included in the table are government savings and investments and foreign investments. As indicated in the previous example, Michael Darby estimated that the establishment of Social Security in 1935 reduced the nation's savings by 5% to 20%. He also estimated that this reduced the level of national income by 2% to 7%.

Source: **Michael R. Darby**, *The Effects of Social Security on Income and Capital Stock* (Washington, D.C.: American Enterprise Institute, 1979).

▲

15.3 INVESTMENT DECISIONS

The previous discussion has important practical applications and is the basis for very valuable decision rules used by firms and government agencies in determining which investment project to undertake. For example, a bank may have to decide whether to purchase or rent a large computer, a government agency whether or not to build a dam, and a manufacturing firm whether it should purchase a more expensive machine that lasts longer or a cheaper one that lasts a shorter period of time. The decision rule to answer these questions and to rank various investment projects is called **capital budgeting.**. Our discussion of capital budgeting begins by considering a two-period time framework. We then extend and generalize the discussion to a multiperiod time horizon.

Net Present Value Rule for Investment Decisions: The Two-Period Case

An investment project involves a cost (to purchase the machinery, build the factory, acquire a skill, and so on) and a return in the form of an increase in output or income in the future. In a two-period framework, the cost is usually incurred in the current year and the return or benefit comes the following year. However, since one unit of a commodity or a dollar next year is worth less than a unit of the commodity or a dollar today, costs and benefits occurring at different times cannot simply be added together to determine whether or not to undertake the project.

For example, for a project that involves the expenditure of $1.00 this year and results in $1.50 return next year, we cannot simply add the $-$1.00 of cost this year to the $1.50 return next year and say that the net value of the project is $0.50. The reason is that $1.50 next year is worth less than $1.50

today.[6] Specifically, if the rate of interest is 20%, $1.50 next year is worth $1.50/(1.2) = $1.25 today. The reason is that $1.25 today will grow to $1.50 next year. That is, $1.25(1 + 0.2) = $1.50. Thus, to determine the net return of an investment we must compare the cost incurred today with the value of the benefits *today*.

The **net present value (*NPV*)** of an investment is the value today of all the *net* cash flows of the investment. Expenditures or outflows are subtracted from revenues or inflows in each year to find the net cash flow. For a two-period time horizon, *NPV* is given by

$$NPV = -C + \frac{R_1}{1 + r}$$ [15–5]

where C is the capital investment cost in the current year when the investment is made, R_1 is the net cash flow next year, and r is the rate of interest. For example, suppose that a firm purchases a machine this year for $100, and this increases the firm's net income by $120 next year. Suppose also that the rate of interest is 10%, and the machine has no salvage or scrap value at the end of the next year. The net present value of the machine (*NPV*) is

$$NPV = -\$100 + \frac{\$120}{(1 + 0.1)} = -\$100 + \$109.09 = \$9.09$$

This means that the purchase of the machine will increase the wealth of the firm by $9.09.

Suppose the firm had to decide between the above project (with net present value of $9.09) and another project that costs $150 and generates a net income of $180 next year. The firm should choose the second project because its net present value of $-\$150 + \$180/(1 + 0.1) = \$13.64$ exceeds the net present value of $9.09 for the previous project. Such a choice arises because firms do not usually have or cannot usually borrow all of the resources required to undertake all of the projects that have a positive net present value.

We will see in the next section that the rule to undertake a project if its net present value is positive or to choose the project with the highest net present value is a general rule and applies to all projects, regardless of the number of periods or years over which the costs and returns of the project are spread. Furthermore, this rule is independent of the tastes or time preference of the investor. That is, regardless of the shape and location of the indifference curves of investors, the general investment or capital budgeting rule is to maximize the wealth of the firm. This is achieved by investing in projects with the highest (positive) net present value. The tastes of investors will then determine whether they will borrow or lend and how they will choose to use their (maximized) wealth. This means that if capital markets

---

[6]We assume throughout this discussion that there is no price inflation. This assumption is relaxed in section 15.4.

are perfect and costless (i.e., if borrowers and lenders are too small individually to affect the rate of interest and can borrow or lend at the same rate), then individuals' production and consumption decisions can be kept completely separate. This is sometimes called the **separation theorem**.

Net Present Value Rule for Investment Decisions: The Multiperiod Case

Most investment projects last longer than (i.e., give rise to net cash flows over more than) two periods. Thus, the investment rule given above must be extended to consider many periods (years). This can easily be done by "stretching" equation [15–5] to deal with many (n) years. This is given by

$$NPV = -C + \frac{R_1}{1 + r} + \frac{R_2}{(1 + r)^2} + \cdots + \frac{R_n}{(1 + r)^n} \qquad [15\text{–}6]$$

where NPV is the net present value of the investment, C is the capital investment cost incurred this year when the investment is made, R_1 is the net cash flow from the investment next year, R_2 is the net cash flow in two years, R_n is the net cash flow in n years, and r is the rate of interest. Net cash flows refer to the revenue of the firm resulting from the investment during any given year minus the expenses or costs of the project during the same year. Thus, formula [15–5] is a special case of formula [15–6] applicable when there is no net cash flow after the first year.[7]

For example, suppose that a firm purchases a machine this year for $150, and this increases the firm's net income by $100 in each of the next two years. If the rate of interest is 10% and the machine has no salvage value after two years, the net present value of the machine (NPV) is

$$NPV = -C + \frac{R_1}{1 + r} + \frac{R_2}{(1 + r)^2} = -\$150 + \frac{\$100}{1 + 0.1} + \frac{\$100}{(1 + 0.1)^2}$$

$$= -\$150 + \$90.91 + \$82.64 = \$23.55$$

This means that the purchase of the machine will increase the wealth of the firm by $23.55. Specifically, $100 received next year is worth $100/(1 + 0.1) = $90.91 this year, because $90.91 this year grows to $100 next year at r = 10%. On the other hand, $100 received two years from now is worth $100/(1 + 0.1)^2 = $82.64 this year because $82.64 this year grows to $90.91 next year

---

[7]If we simply wanted to find the present discounted value (PDV) of a given sum (R) to be received in each of n years, starting with the next year, the formula would simply be

$$PDV = \frac{R}{(1+r)} + \frac{R}{(1+r)^2} + \cdots + \frac{R}{(1+r)^n}$$

If the given sum (R) were to be received in each year indefinitely or in perpetuity (an example of this is the British "consols"), then $PDV = \frac{R}{r}$ (see section A.15 of the Mathematical Appendix).

at $r = 10\%$,[8] and the $90.91 next year grows to $100 the year after (i.e., two years from now) at $r = 10\%$. Another way of saying this is that $82.64 today times $(1 + 0.1)^2$ or 1.21 equals $100 two years from now.

If the project generated a net cash flow of $100 in the third year also, this would be "worth" $100/(1 + 0.1)^3 = \$100/(1.331) = \$75.13$ this year because $75.13 this year will grow to $100 (except for rounding errors) in three years at $r = 10\%$. Similarly, $100 in 10 years is worth $100/(1 + 0.1)^{10} = \$38.55$ this year because $38.55 this year will grow to $100 in 10 years at $r = 10\%$. Finally, $100 in n years (where n is any number of years) is worth $100/(1 + 0.1)^n$ this year because this sum today will grow to $100 in n years at $r = 10\%$.

The *NPV* for any net cash flow is inversely related to r. For example, if r had been 5% in the previous example, the net present value of the investment (*NPV'*) would have been

$$NPV' = -\$150 + \frac{\$100}{(1 + 0.05)^1} + \frac{\$100}{(1 + 0.05)^2}$$

$$= -\$150 + \$95.24 + \$90.70 = \$35.94$$

(as compared with the *NPV* of $23.55 with $r = 10\%$). On the other hand, if r had been 20%,

$$NPV'' = -\$150 + \frac{\$100}{(1 + 0.2)^1} + \frac{\$100}{(1 + 0.2)^2}$$

$$= -\$150 + \$83.33 + \$69.44 = \$2.77$$

The lower *NPV* when r is higher is due to the fact that with a higher r, the net cash flows from the project are "discounted" more heavily than the cost, because the net cash flows arise later in time than cost. Also note that the *net* cash flows should include the extra income generated by the machine minus the extra expense (such as maintenance and the higher cost of hiring more skilled workers) to operate the machine during each year. Similarly, the value today of the salvage value of the machine (if any) must also be included.

For example, suppose that the benefits and costs of an investment project (the purchase of a piece of machinery) are as given in Table 15–3. The table shows that the machine costs $1,000 to purchase this year and also gives rise to $200, $300, $300, and $400 maintenance and other expenses in each of the subsequent four years. The revenues from the investment are $600, $800, $800, and $800, and the salvage value of the machine is $200 at the end of the fourth year. The net revenue is the revenue from the investment minus the expenses in each year. The present value coefficient is $1/(1 + 0.1)^n$. For example, for the first year the present value coefficient is $1/(1 + 0.1)^1 = 0.909$. For the second year, it is $1/(1 + 0.1)^2 = 0.826$, and so on. The present value of the net revenue in each year is obtained by multiplying the net revenue

---

[8]Actually ($82.64) (1.1) equals $90.904 rather than $90.91 (as indicated) because of rounding errors.

TABLE 15-3   Benefit-Cost Analysis of an Investment Project

End of Year	Investment (year 0) and Cost	Revenue	Net Revenue	Present Value Coefficient $1/(1 + 0.1)^n$	Present Value of Net Revenue
0	$1,000	. . .	−$1,000	. . .	−$1,000
1	200	$600	400	0.909	364
2	300	800	500	0.826	413
3	300	800	500	0.751	376
4	400	800	400	0.683	273
4	. . .	200*	200	0.683	137
					$563

*Salvage value.

(R) by the present value coefficient for that year. By adding together all present values of the net revenues, we get the net present value of the project (V_0) of $563. Since *NPV* is positive, the firm should purchase the machine.

Sometimes, complications may arise in applying the net present value rule for investment decisions. First, projects may be interdependent, so that the stream of net cash flows from a project depends on whether or not other projects are undertaken at the same time. In such a case, the net present value of a group of projects may have to be evaluated together and compared with the net present value of other groups of projects. Second, it may sometimes be difficult to accurately forecast the future stream of net cash flows from a project. Third, the firm may not have the resources and may not be willing or able to borrow to undertake all of the projects that have a positive net present value. The firm should then choose those projects with the highest net present value.

Example 3

 Fields of Education and Higher Lifetime Earnings in the United States

Table 15-4 gives the present value of the higher lifetime earnings with a college degree in various fields in the United States in 1992. Present values were calculated by capitalizing (i.e., finding the present discounted value of) the difference between the higher yearly salaries with a bachelor's degree in the various fields over the average salary of workers with only a high school diploma. The interest rate used to find the present values was 5%. Only the benefits of going to college were included; the earnings forgone or opportunity costs and other costs (tuition, books, and so on) of going to college were not

TABLE 15–4   Present Values of Higher Lifetime Earnings with Bachelor's Degree in Various Fields, 1992

Field of Study	Higher Lifetime Earnings
Electrical engineering	$355,080
Nursing	314,460
Computer science	290,460
Mathematics	248,700
Chemistry	231,140
Accounting	223,580
Economics/finance	202,440
Marketing	158,280
Communications	105,240
Education	93,780

Source: Calculated from data reported in *Salary Survey*, Council Placement Council, 1992.

included. To be pointed out is that the higher earnings of the recipients of the bachelor's degree over the earnings of non-college graduates cannot be attributed entirely to college education. At least in part, the higher incomes of college graduates may be due to their higher level of intelligence, longer working hours, and more inherited wealth than for non-college graduates. Earnings differentials with and without a college degree declined during the 1970s and increased during the 1980s.

Source: "Soaring Payoff from Higher Education," *The Margin*, January/February 1990, p. 6, and J. Bound and G. Johnson, "Changes in the Structure of Wages in the 1980s: An Evaluation of Alternative Explanations," *American Economic Review*, June 1992, pp. 371–392.

15.4 DETERMINANTS OF THE MARKET RATES OF INTEREST

Until now we have discussed "the" interest rate; however, the rate of interest varies at different times and in different markets. Even at a given point in time and in a specific capital market, there is not a single rate of interest but many. That is, there is a different interest rate on different loans or investments depending on differences in (1) risk, (2) duration of the loan, (3) cost of administering the loan, and (4) tax treatment. We now briefly examine each of these in turn.

The major reason for differences in rates of interest at a given point in time and place is the risk of the loan. In general, the greater is the risk, the higher is the rate of interest. Two types of risk can be distinguished: default risk and variability risk. **Default risk** refers to the possibility that the loan will not be repaid. If the chance of default is 10%, the lender will usually charge a rate of interest 10% higher than on a loan with no risk of default, such as a government bond. Similarly, loans unsecured by collateral (such as installment credit) usually charge higher rates of interest than loans secured by collateral (such as home mortgages). **Variability risk** refers to the possibility that the yield or return on an investment, such as a stock, may vary considerably above or below the average. Given the usual aversion to risk, investors generally demand a premium or a higher yield for investments whose returns are more uncertain.

The second reason for differences in rates of interest is the duration of the loan. Loans for longer periods of time usually require higher rates of interest than loans for shorter durations. The reason is that the lender has less flexibility or liquidity with loans of longer duration, and so he or she will require a higher rate of interest. It is for this reason that savings deposits offer lower rates of interest than six-month certificates of deposit.[9]

The third reason for differences in rates of interest is the cost of administering the loan. Smaller loans and loans requiring frequent payments (such as installment loans) usually involve greater bookkeeping and service costs per dollar of the loan and, as a result, usually involve a higher interest charge. Finally, the tax treatment of interest and investment income can lead to differences in rates of interest among otherwise comparable loans and investments. For example, state and municipal bonds are exempted from federal income tax, and since investors look at the after-tax return, state and local governments can usually borrow at lower interest rates than corporations.

Thus, at a given point in time and in a given capital market there is a large number of interest rates depending on relative risk, term structure, administration costs, and tax treatment. Yet, all of these rates of interest are related. If individuals and firms collectively decide to save less (a leftward shift in the aggregate supply curve of savings), interest rates will rise. Interest rates will also rise if the time preference of consumers shifts in favor of the present or if the net productivity or yield of capital increases. In addition, a rise in short-term rates will lead to higher long-term rates, and vice versa. Furthermore, higher interest rates for comparable instruments in one market than in another market will lead to an outflow of funds from the latter to the former. These flows of funds will reduce (and may eventually eliminate) interest rate differences between the two markets. Specifically, the supply curve of funds will shift to the left (i.e., the supply of funds decreases) and interest rates will rise in the market with lower rates of interest. The opposite occurs in the market with the higher rates of interest and interest rates will fall there.

Finally, a distinction must be made between real and nominal or money interest rates. Until this point, we have been discussing the **real rate of interest**

---

[9]Regulation may also account for part of the difference.

(*r*). This refers to the premium on a unit of a commodity or real consumption income today compared to a unit of the commodity or real consumption income in the future. However, in the everyday usage of the term, the interest rate refers to the nominal or money rate of interest. The **nominal rate of interest (*r'*)** refers to the premium on a unit of a monetary claim today compared to a unit of monetary claim in the future. The nominal rate of interest (*r'*) is affected by the anticipated rate of price inflation (*i*), while the real rate of interest is not. Thus, the nominal rate of interest equals the real rate of interest plus the anticipated rate of price inflation. That is,

$$r' = r + i \qquad\qquad [15–7]$$

The reason for this is that during the period of the loan, the general price level may rise (i.e., inflation may occur) so that the loan is repaid with dollars of lower purchasing power than the dollars borrowed. Therefore, the nominal rate of interest must be sufficiently high to cover any increase in the price level (or in the price of real claims) during the loan period. It is primarily to avoid this complication (and to deal with the real rate of interest) that we chose to borrow and lend a *commodity* in sections 15.1 and 15.2.

Anyone who borrows money now and repays in money in the future must expect to pay an additional monetary amount to cover any anticipated increase in the monetary price of real claims by the time of repayment. Only if anticipated inflation is zero will $r' = r$. Since some price inflation is always occurring, r' usually exceeds r. For example, if $r' = 11\%$ and $i = 6\%$, then $r = 5\%$. We concentrated on the real rate of interest throughout most of the chapter because it is the real, and not the nominal, rate of interest that primarily affects incentives to borrow and lend and to save and invest.

Example 4

Nominal and Real Interest Rates in the United States: 1974–1992

Table 15–5 shows the nominal annual interest rates on three-month U.S. Treasury bills, the change in the Consumer Price Index, and the real interest rate (the difference between the nominal interest rate and the change in the Consumer Price Index) in the United States from 1974 to 1991. The implicit assumption made here is that the anticipated rate of inflation is equal to the actual rate of inflation. During the highly inflationary period from 1974 to 1982, the nominal interest rate was smaller than the change in the Consumer Price Index, and so the real interest rate was negative, except for 1981 and 1982. On the other hand, during the low-inflation period from 1983 to 1991, the nominal interest rate was greater than the change in the Consumer Price Index, and so the real interest rate was positive. Note that the nominal interest rate moved in the same direction as the change in the Consumer Price Index,

TABLE 15–5   **Nominal and Real Interest Rates on Three-Month U.S.**
Treasury Bills: 1974–1991

Year	Nominal Interest Rate	Change in Consumer Price Index	Real Interest Rate
1974	7.9%	11.0%	−3.1%
1975	5.8	9.1	−3.3
1976	5.0	5.8	−0.8
1977	5.3	6.5	−1.2
1978	7.2	7.6	−0.4
1979	10.0	11.3	−1.3
1980	11.5	13.5	−2.0
1981	14.0	10.3	3.7
1982	10.7	6.2	4.5
1983	8.6	3.2	5.4
1984	9.6	4.3	5.3
1985	7.5	3.6	3.9
1986	6.0	1.9	4.1
1987	5.8	3.6	2.2
1988	6.7	4.1	2.6
1989	8.1	4.8	3.3
1990	7.5	5.4	2.1
1991	5.4	4.2	1.2

Source: Council of Economic Advisers, *Economic Report of the President* (Washington, D.C.: U.S. Government Printing Office, 1993), pp. 416, 428.

except in 1981–1982, 1986–1987, and 1990–1991. As a result, the real interest rate in general reflected changes in the nominal interest rate and in the Consumer Price Index, as expected.

▲

15.5   THE COST OF CAPITAL

We now examine how a firm estimates the cost of raising capital to invest. This is an essential element of the capital budgeting process. The firm can raise investment funds internally (i.e., from undistributed profits) or externally (i.e., by borrowing and/or from selling stocks). The cost of using internal funds is the opportunity cost or foregone return on these funds outside the firm. The cost of external funds is the lowest rate of return that lenders and stockholders require to lend to or invest their funds in the firm. In this section, we examine how the cost of debt (i.e., the cost of raising capital by borrowing) and the cost of equity capital (i.e., the cost of raising capital by selling stocks) are determined. The estimation of the cost of debt is fairly straightforward. On the other hand, there are at least three methods of estimating the cost of equity capital: the risk-free rate plus premium, the dividend valuation model, and the capital asset pricing model (CAPM). These methods will be examined in turn.

Cost of Debt

The **cost of debt** is the return that lenders require to lend their funds to the firm. Since the interest payments made by the firm on borrowed funds are deductible from the firm's taxable income, the *after-tax* cost of borrowed funds to the firm (k_d) is given by the interest paid (r) multiplied by 1 minus the firm's marginal tax rate, t. That is,

$$k_d = r(1 - t) \qquad\qquad \text{[15–8]}$$

For example, if the firm borrows at a 12.5% interest rate and faces a 40% marginal tax rate on its taxable income, the after-tax cost of debt capital to the firm is

$$k_d = 12.5\%(1 - 0.40) = 7.5\%$$

Cost of Equity Capital: The Risk-Free Rate Plus Premium

As pointed out earlier, the cost of equity capital is the rate of return that stockholders require to invest in the firm. The cost of raising equity capital externally usually exceeds the cost of raising equity capital internally by the flotation costs (i.e., the cost of issuing the stock). For simplicity, we disregard these costs in the following analysis and treat both types of equity capital together. Since dividends paid on stocks (as opposed to the interest paid on bonds) are not deductible as a business expense (i.e., dividends are paid out after corporate taxes have been paid), there is no tax adjustment in determining the equity cost of capital.

One method employed to estimate the cost of equity capital (k_e) is to use the risk-free rate (r_f) plus a risk premium (r_p). That is,

$$k_e = r_f + r_p \qquad\qquad \text{[15–9]}$$

The risk-free rate (r_f) is usually taken to be the six-month U.S. Treasury bill rate.[10] The reason for this is that the obligation to make payments of the interest and principal on government securities is assumed to occur with certainty. The risk premium (r_p) that must be paid in raising equity capital has two components. The first component results because of the greater risk that is involved in investing in a firm's securities (such as bonds) as opposed to investing in federal government securities. The second component is the additional risk resulting from purchasing the common stock rather than the bonds of the firm. Stocks involve a greater risk than bonds because dividends

---

[10]Some securities analysts prefer to use instead the long-term government bond rate for r_f.

on stocks are paid only after the firm has met its contractual obligations to make interest and principal payments to bondholders. Because dividends vary with the firm's profits, stocks are more risky than bonds, so that their return must include an additional risk premium. If the premiums associated with these two types of risk are labeled p_1 and p_2, we can restate the formula for the cost of equity capital as

$$k_e = r_f + p_1 + p_2 \qquad \text{[15–10]}$$

The first type of risk (i.e., p_1) is usually measured by the excess of the rate of interest on the firm's bonds (r) over the rate of return on government bonds (r_f). The additional risk involved in purchasing the firm's stocks rather than bonds (i.e., p_2) is usually taken to be about four percentage points. This is the historical difference between the average yield (dividends plus capital gains) on stocks as opposed to the average yield on bonds issued by private companies. For example, if the risk-free rate of return on government securities is 8% and the firm's bonds yield 11%, the total risk premium (r_p) involved in purchasing the firm's stocks rather than government bonds is

$$r_p = p_1 + p_2 = (11\% - 8\%) + 4\% = 3\% + 4\% = 7\%$$

so that the firm's cost of equity capital is

$$k_e = r_f + p_1 + p_2 = 8\% + 3\% + 4\% = 15\%.$$

Cost of Equity Capital: The Dividend Valuation Model

The equity cost of capital to a firm can also be estimated by the **dividend valuation model**. To derive this model, we begin by pointing out that, with perfect information, the value of a share of the common stock of a firm should be equal to the present value of all future dividends expected to be paid on the stock, discounted at the investor's required rate of return (k_e). If the dividend per share (D) paid to stockholders is expected to remain constant over time, the present value of a share of the common stock of the firm (P) is then

$$P = \sum_{t=1}^{\infty} \frac{D}{(1 + k_e)^t} \qquad \text{[15–11]}$$

If dividends are assumed to remain constant over time and to be paid indefinitely, equation 15–11 can be rewritten as

$$P = \frac{D}{k_e} \qquad \text{[15–12]}$$

If dividends are instead expected to increase over time at the annual rate of g, the price of a share of the common stock of the firm will be greater and is given by

$$P = \frac{D}{k_e - g} \qquad \text{[15–13]}$$

Solving equation [15–13] for k_e, we get the following equation to measure the equity cost of capital to the firm:

$$k_e = \frac{D}{P} + g \qquad\qquad [15\text{–}14]$$

That is, the investor's required rate of return on equity is equal to the ratio of the dividend paid on a share of the common stock of the firm to the price of a share of the stock (the so-called dividend yield) plus the expected growth rate of dividend payments by the firm (g). The value of g is the firm's historic growth rate or the earnings growth forecasts of securities analysts (based on the expected sales, profit margins, and competitive position of the firm) published in *Business Week*, *Forbes*, and other business publications.

For example, if the firm pays a dividend of $20 per share on common stock that sells for $200 per share and the growth rate of dividend payments is expected to be 5% per year, the cost of equity capital for this firm is

$$k_e = \frac{\$20}{\$200} + 0.05 = 0.10 + 0.05 = 0.15 \text{ or } 15\%$$

Cost of Equity Capital: The Capital Asset Pricing Model (CAPM)

Another method commonly used to estimate the equity cost of capital is the **capital asset pricing model (CAPM)**. This takes into consideration not only the risk differential between common stocks and government securities but also the risk differential between the common stock of the firm and the average common stock of all firms or broad-based market portfolio. The risk differential between common stocks and government securities is measured by $(k_m - r_f)$, where k_m is the average return on all common stocks and r_f is the return on government securities.

The risk differential between the common stock of a particular firm and the common stock of all firms is called the **beta coefficient, β**. This is the ratio of the variability in the return of the common stock of the firm to the variability in the average return on the common stocks of all firms. Beta coefficients for individual stocks can be obtained from the *Value Line Investment Survey*, Merrill Lynch, or other brokerage firms.

A beta coefficient of 1 means that the variability in the returns on the common stock of the firm is the same as the variability in the returns on all stocks. Thus, investors holding the stock of the firm face the same risk as holding a broad-based market portfolio of all stocks. A beta coefficient of 2 means that the variability in the returns on (i.e., risk of holding) the stock of the firm is twice that of the average stock. On the other hand, holding a stock with a beta coefficient of 0.5 is half as risky as holding the average stock.

The cost of equity capital to the firm estimated by the capital asset pricing model (CAPM) is then measured by

$$k_e = r_f + \beta(k_m - r_f) \qquad\qquad [15\text{–}15]$$

where k_e is the cost of equity capital to the firm, r_f is the risk-free rate, β is the beta coefficient, and k_m is the average return on the stock of all firms. Thus, CAPM postulates that the cost of equity capital to the firm is equal to the sum of the risk-free rate plus the beta coefficient (β) times the risk premium on the average stock ($k_m - r_f$). Note that multiplying β by ($k_m - r_f$) gives the risk premium on holding the common stock of the particular firm.

For example, suppose that the risk-free rate (r_f) is 8%, the average return on common stocks (k_m) is 15%, and the beta coefficient (β) for the firm is 1. The cost of equity capital to the firm (k_e) is then

$$k_e = 8\% + 1(15\% - 8\%) = 15\%$$

That is, since a beta coefficient of 1 indicates that the stock of this firm is as risky as the average stock of all firms, the equity cost of capital to the firm is 15% (the same as the average return on all stocks). If $\beta = 1.5$ for the firm (so that the risk involved in holding the stock of the firm is 1.5 times larger than the risk on the average stock), the equity cost of capital to the firm would be

$$k_e = 8\% + 1.5(15\% - 8\%) = 18.5\%$$

On the other hand, if $\beta = 0.5$

$$k_e = 8\% + 0.5(15\% - 8\%) = 11.5\%$$

In this example, and in the examples using the risk-free rate plus premium and the dividend valuation model, the equity cost of capital was found to be the same (15%). This is seldom the case. That is, the different methods of estimating the equity cost of capital to a firm are likely to give somewhat different results. Firms are thus likely to use all three methods and then attempt to reconcile the differences to arrive at an equity cost of capital for the firm.

Weighted Cost of Capital

In general, a firm is likely to raise capital from undistributed profits, by borrowing, and by the sale of stocks, and so the marginal cost of capital to the firm is a weighted average of the cost of raising the various types of capital. Since the interest paid on borrowed funds is tax deductible while the dividends paid on stocks are not, the cost of debt is generally less than the cost of equity capital. The risk involved in raising funds by borrowing, however, is greater than the risk on equity capital because the firm must regularly make payments of the interest and principal on borrowed funds before paying dividends on stocks. Thus, firms do not generally raise funds only by borrowing but also by selling stock (as well as from undistributed profits).

Firms often try to maintain or achieve a particular long-term capital structure of debt to equity. For example, public utility companies may prefer a capital structure involving 60% debt and 40% equity, whereas auto manufacturers may prefer 30% debt and 70% equity. The particular debt-equity ratio that a firm prefers reflects the risk preference of its managers and stockholders and the nature of the firm's business. Public utilities accept the higher risk involved in a higher debt-to-equity ratio because of their more stable flow of earnings than automobile manufacturers. When a firm needs to raise investment capital, it borrows and sells stocks so as to maintain or achieve a desired debt-to-equity ratio.

The **composite cost of capital** to the firm (k_c) is then a weighted average of the cost of debt capital (k_d) and equity capital (k_e) as given by

$$k_c = w_d k_d + w_e k_e \qquad \text{[15–16]}$$

where w_d and w_e are, respectively, the proportion of debt and equity capital in the firm's capital structure. For example, if the (after-tax) cost of debt is 7.5%, the cost of equity capital is 15%, and the firm wants to have a debt-to-equity ratio of 40:60, the composite or weighted marginal cost of capital to the firm is

$$k_c = (0.40)(7.5\%) + (0.60)(15\%) = 3\% + 9\% = 12\%$$

That is, the proportion of debt to equity that the firm seeks to achieve or maintain in the long run is not usually defined for individual projects but for all the investment projects that the firm is considering. Note that the marginal cost of capital eventually rises as the firm raises additional amounts of capital by borrowing and selling stocks because of the higher risk that lenders and investors face as the firm's debt-to-equity ratio rises.

15.6 EFFECTS OF FOREIGN INVESTMENTS ON THE RECEIVING NATION

Foreign investments reduce the supply of investment funds in the investing nation and increase them in the receiving nation. Foreign investments flow from the nation where the rate of return on investment is lower to the nation where the rate of return is higher. In recent years, the United States has been the recipient of a large net inflow of foreign investments because of the higher rate of return on investments in the United States than abroad. We can examine the effect of foreign investments on the receiving nation with Figure 15–7. For simplicity, we assume that the rate of interest on borrowed capital is the same as the rate of return on both borrowed and equity capital in the nation.

In Figure 15–7, D is the nation's demand curve for, while S is the domestic supply curve of, investment funds. D and S intersect at point E indicating that, in the absence of foreign investments, $300 billion is invested in the nation at the rate of return (r) of 0.15 or 15%. With $150 billion of foreign investment, the nation's supply curve shifts to the right to S'. The intersection of D and S' defines the new equilibrium point of E', which indicates that total investments in the nation are $400 billion and the rate of return on domestic and foreign investments is 0.10 or 10%. Thus, foreign investments reduced the rate of return on domestic investments from 15% to 10% (and this led to a reduction in the quantity supplied of domestic investments to $250 billion).

FIGURE 15–7   Effects of Foreign Investments on the Receiving Nation

D is the demand curve for and S is the supply curve of investment funds in the nation in the absence of foreign investments. D and S intersect at point E, defining the equilibrium rate of return (r) of 0.15 or 15% and level of investments of $300 billion. With $150 billion of foreign investments, S shifts to S', defining the new equilibrium point of E', at which total investments in the nation rise to $400 billion ($250 billion domestic and $150 billion foreign) and r falls to 0.10 or 10%. The $150 billion foreign investment increases the total output of the nation by $GEE'M$ (about $12.5 billion), of which $GCE'M$ = $10 billion is the return on foreign investments and $EE'C$ (about $2.5 billion) is the net gain of the nation.

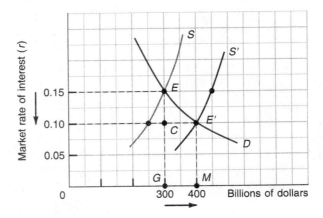

The $150 billion foreign investment increases the total output of the receiving nation by $GEE'M$ (about $12.5 billion), of which $GCE'M$ = $10 billion is paid out to foreign investors as the return on their investment, and $EE'C$ (about $2.5 billion) represents the net benefit or gain to the nation receiving the foreign investments. Some of this net benefit goes to domestic labor because the inflow of foreign investments increases the capital-labor ratio and thus the productivity and wages of domestic labor. Another benefit (not shown in the figure) accruing to the nation receiving the foreign investments is the taxes paid by foreigners on the income (the return on investments) earned in the nation.

In 1985, the United States changed from being a net creditor to being a net debtor nation (i.e, the amount that foreigners lent and invested in the United States began to exceed the amount that the United States lent and invested abroad) for the first time since 1914. Indeed, with a net foreign debt of about $400 billion in 1992, the United States was the most indebted nation in the world. This gave rise to a lively debate among economists, politicians, and government officials in the United States regarding the benefits and risks of this recent development.

On the benefit side, foreign investments allowed the United States to finance about half of its budget deficit without the need for still higher interest rates and more "crowding out" of private investments. To the extent that foreign investments went into directly productive activities and the return on this investment was greater than the interest and dividend payments flowing to foreign investors, this investment was beneficial to the United States.[11] To the extent, however, that foreign investments simply financed larger consumption expenditures in the United States, the interest and dividend payments flowing to foreign investors represent a real burden or drain on future consumption and growth in the United States. Some experts are concerned that a growing share of capital inflows to the United States since 1983 cannot be clearly identified as productive investments, and to that extent they may represent a real burden on the U.S. economy in the future.

There is also the danger that foreigners, for whatever reason, may suddenly withdraw their funds. This would lead to a financial crisis and much higher interest rates in the United States. Some economists and government officials also fear that foreign companies operating in the United States will transfer advanced American technology abroad. They further fear some loss of domestic control over political and economic matters. The irony is that these were precisely the complaints usually heard from Canada, smaller European nations, and developing countries with regard to the large American investments in their countries during the 1950s and 1960s. With the great concern often voiced in the United States today about the danger of foreign investments, the tables seem now to have turned.[12]

15.7 SOME APPLICATIONS OF FINANCIAL MICROECONOMICS

In this section, we discuss some important applications of the theory presented in the chapter. These include investment in human capital, the effect of investment in human capital on hours of work, the pricing of exhaustible resources, and the management of nonexhaustible resources. The applications clearly indicate the usefulness and applicability of the theory.

Investment in Human Capital

Investment in human capital is any activity on the part of a worker or potential worker that increases his or her productivity. It refers to expenditures on education, job training, health, migration to areas of better job opportunities,

---

[11]Of course, the United States would have benefited even more if it had financed its domestic investments entirely through domestic savings. But with inadequate domestic savings, the second best situation was to receive foreign investments and pay the return on investments to foreign investors.

[12]See, "A Note on the United States as a Debtor Nation," *Survey of Current Business* (Washington, D.C.: U.S. Government Printing Office, 1985), p. 28.

and so on. Like any other investment, investments in human capital involve costs and entail returns. For example, going to college involves explicit and implicit, or opportunity, costs. The explicit costs are tuition, books, fees, and all other out-of-pocket expenses of attending college. The implicit costs are the earnings or opportunities foregone while attending college (the individual could have worked or could have worked more by not attending college). As we have seen in the example in section 7.1, the implicit costs of attending college are nearly as high as the explicit costs. The returns of attending college take the form of higher lifetime earnings with a college education than without a college education (see Example 3 in this chapter).

As with any other investment, we can find the present value of the stream of net cash flows from the college degree. Net cash flows are negative during the college years (because of the explicit and implicit or opportunity costs of attending college) and positive during the working life of the college graduate until retirement. The same is generally true for other investments in human capital. That is, they also lead to a stream of net cash flows and should be undertaken only if their net present value is positive or higher than the present value of other investments (such as the purchasing of a stock). Using this method, it was estimated that the return to a college education was about 10% to 15% per year during the 1950s and 1960s. This was substantially higher than the return on similarly risky investments (such as the purchasing of a stock). During the 1970s, and as a result of the sharp increases in tuition and relatively lower starting salaries, the returns to a college education declined to about 7% per year, but they increased during the 1980s.[13]

These studies, however, face a number of statistical problems. For example, not all expenditures for education represent an investment (as, for example, when a physics student takes a course in Shakespeare). In addition, at least part of the higher earnings of college graduates may be due to their being more intelligent or from working harder than non-college graduates (see the next section). On the other side of the coin, there are benefits from a college education that cannot be easily measured. For example, college graduates seem to enjoy their jobs more than non-college graduates, have happier marriages, and generally suffer less mental illness. In spite of these measurement difficulties, however, the concept of investment in human capital is very important and commonly used. Most differences in labor incomes can be explained by differences in human capital. Juries routinely determine the amount of damages to award injury victims (or their survivors, in case of fatal accidents) on the basis of the human capital or income lost by the injured party. Developing countries complain about the brain drain or the emigration to rich nations of their young and skilled people (who embody a great deal of human capital), and so on.

---

[13]R. B. Freeman, "The Decline in the Economic Rewards to College Education," *The Review of Economics and Statistics*, February 1977, pp. 18–29; "The Soaring Payoff from Higher Education," *The Margin*, January/February, 1990, p. 6; and "Managing Your Career," Special Edition of the National Employment Weekly, *The Wall Street Journal*, Fall 1992.

Investment in Human Capital and Hours of Work

People may work more hours as a result of investment in human capital. This can be shown with the aid of Figure 15–8. In Figure 15–8, the movement from left to right on the horizontal axis measures hours of leisure per day. The movement from right to left measures the hours of work. The sum of the hours of leisure and the hours of work always adds up to the 24 hours of the day. The vertical axis measures the daily income of the individual.

We begin by assuming that the individual portrayed in Figure 15–8 has a daily property income of FC ($30). If the hourly wage is $2.50, the individual's budget line is FB (so that the negative of the slope of the budget line gives the wage rate). Before investing in education, the individual maximizes utility or satisfaction at point E, where indifference curve U is tangent to budget line FB. The individual works 8 hours per day and has a daily income of $50 (FC or $30 from property income plus HE or $20 from working 8 hours at the wage rate of $2.50 per hour).

Suppose that now the individual decides to invest all of his or her endowed property income in education (i.e., sacrifice all of his or her nonhuman capital) and that as a result he or she can earn a wage rate of $5 per hour. The budget line of the individual is now CA (see the figure), reflecting zero property income available for consumption and the wage of $5 per hour (the negative of the slope of budget line CA). Assuming that the individual's tastes remain unchanged as a result of the education, the individual will now maximize utility at point G, where indifference curve U is tangent to budget line CA. The individual now works 14 hours per day for a daily income of $70 (all of which is labor income).

Thus, education seems to induce individuals to work more hours (i.e., have fewer leisure hours) and earn higher incomes. Having made the investment in education, the individual will work more hours and earn a higher income to maximize utility. This seems to be confirmed in empirical studies. For example, Lindsay found that physicians work on average 62 hours per week, far more than the average worker.[14] The same seems to be true for other professionals as opposed to nonprofessionals.

Pricing of Exhaustible Resources

One of the great concerns of modern societies is that the world's resources will become depleted. Resources can generally be classified as exhaustible or nonexhaustible. **Exhaustible resources** are those, such as petroleum and other minerals, that are available in fixed quantities and are nonreplenishable. **Nonexhaustible resources** are those such as fertile land, forests, rivers, and fish, which can last forever if they are properly managed. We first examine the

---

[14]C. M. Lindsay, "Real Returns to Medical Education," *Journal of Human Resources*, Summer 1982, p. 338.

FIGURE 15–8   Education and Hours of Work

The individual has a daily property income of $FC = \$30$ and faces budget line FB (with the negative of the slope giving the wage of $2.50 per hour). The individual maximizes utility at point E, where indifference curve U is tangent to FB. He or she works 8 hours and has a daily income of $50 (of which $HE = \$20$ is labor income). Suppose the individual invests all property income in education and as a result earns $5 per hour. The budget line is now CA. The individual maximizes utility at point G, where U is tangent to CA and works 14 hours for a daily income of $70.

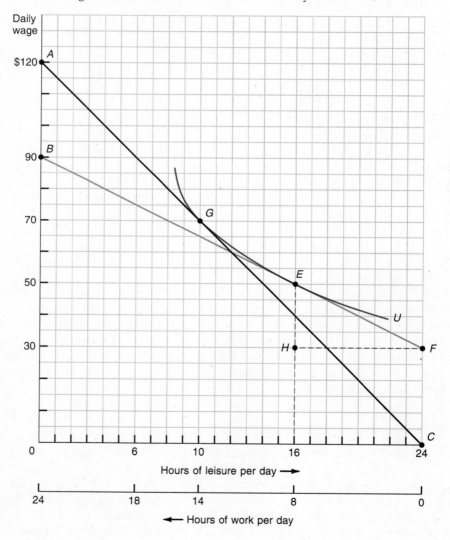

pricing of exhaustible or nonrenewable resources and then look at the pricing of nonexhaustible or renewable resources, under proper management.

During the 1970s (and to large extent as a result of the petroleum crisis), there was great concern that exhaustible resources would soon be depleted. Doomsday models were built that predicted when various exhaustible resources would run out, thereby threatening the living standard and the very future of humanity.[15] Economists, while not entirely shrugging off the danger, were skeptical for the most part. They pointed out that as the prices of exhaustible resources tend to rise over time, this would lead to conservation and to the discovery of substitutes. Thus, doomsday models were not to be taken too seriously. Let us see why economists proved to be generally right.

We begin by pointing out that the owner of an exhaustible resource will keep it in the ground and available for future use if the present value of the resource in future use is greater than its current price. For example, suppose that the price of the resource is $100 per unit today, it is expected to be $120 next year, and the market rate of interest is 10% per year. The owner will sell the resource next year, since the present value of a unit of the resource sold next year is $120/(1 + 0.1) = $109.09 and this exceeds its price of $100 today.

In a perfectly competitive market, the net price of the resource (i.e., the price minus the cost of extraction) will rise at a rate equal to the market rate of interest, and this will spread available supplies over time. If the net price of a resource is expected to rise faster than the market rate of interest, more of the resource will be held off the market for future sale. This increases the current price and reduces the future price until the present value of the future net price is equal to the present net price. On the other hand, if the net price of the resource is expected to rise at a slower rate than the market rate of interest, more of the resource will be sold in the present. This will reduce the present price and increase the future price until the present value of the expected future net price equals the present net price. This is shown in Figure 15–9.

In the left panel of the figure, time is measured along the horizontal axis, and the price of the exhaustible resource and its average total cost (assumed to be constant, and thus equal to marginal cost) are measured along the vertical axis. The right panel shows the market demand curve for the resource (input). The net price or benefit to the owners of the resource is given by the difference (AB at time zero) between the (gross) price of the resource and the assumed constant cost of extracting it. The owner can obtain these net benefits now or in the future (by leaving the resource in the ground). For the owner of the resource to be indifferent between extracting the resource now or in the future,

---

[15]See, J. W. Forrester, *World Dynamics* (Cambridge, Mass.: Wright-Allen Press, 1971); D. H. Meadows et al., *The Limits to Growth: A Report for the Club of Rome's Project on the Predicament of Mankind* (New York: Universe Books, 1972); and M. Mesarovic and E. Pestel, *Mankind at the Turning Point: The Second Report to the Club of Rome* (New York: The American Library, 1974).

FIGURE 15–9   The Price of Exhaustible Resources

In the left panel, time is measured along the horizontal axis, and the price of the exhaustible resource and its average cost (assumed constant and equal to *MC*) is measured along the vertical axis. The right panel shows the demand curve for the resource. At *P* = *OB*, the net benefit is *AB* per unit and the quantity demanded is *OC*. Over time, the net benefit or net price rises at the same rate as the market rate of interest until at *P* = *OF* the supply of the resource is exhausted (point *G* in the left panel) and the quantity demanded is zero (point *F′* in the right panel).

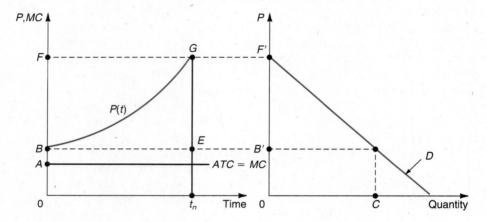

the net benefit or net price of the resource must appreciate over time at a rate equal to the market rate of interest.

The right panel of Figure 15–9 shows that at the resource (gross) price *P* = *OB′*, the quantity demanded of the resource is *OC*. Over time, the net price rises at the same rate as the market rate of interest (from *AB* to *EG* in the left panel) until at *P* = *OF′* the supply of the resource is exhausted (point *G* in the left panel) and the quantity demanded of the resource is zero (point *F′* in the right panel). Thus, in perfectly competitive markets, exhaustion of the resource coincides with zero quantity demanded. If exhaustion occurs before time *t_n* at *P* = *OF*, owners of the resource could have sold the resource at a higher price (and net benefit) over time than indicated by line *BG*. On the other hand, if the resource is not exhausted by *t_n* at *P* = *OF*, owners would have gained by selling the resource at a lower price over time.[16] In the real world, the net price of most resources increased at a smaller rate than the market rate of interest (and the net price of many resources actually fell) over time because of new discoveries, technological improvements in extraction, and conservation.

---

[16]See, H. Hotelling, "The Economics of Exhaustible Resources," *Journal of Political Economy*, April 1931, pp. 137–175.

Management of Nonexhaustible Resources

Nonexhaustible or renewable resources such as forests and fish grow naturally over time. Unless the rate of utilization of the resource exceeds its rate of natural growth, the resource will never be depleted.[17] If the renewable resource is trees, the question is when should the trees be cut? The answer (as you might suspect by now) is that the trees should be allowed to grow as long as the rate of growth in the net value of the trees exceeds the market rate of interest. Cutting the trees when the rate of growth in their net value exceeds the market rate of interest would be equivalent to taking money out of a bank paying a higher rate of interest and depositing the money in another bank that pays a lower rate of interest. We can analyze this with the aid of Figure 15–10.

The top panel of Figure 15–10 shows the net value of the trees if harvested at time t. This is given by the $V(t)$ curve. The net value is the total market value of the trees minus the cost of harvesting them. We assume zero maintenance or management costs. The top panel shows that $V(t)$ grows at an increasing rate at first. At time $t = 3$ (point A), diminishing returns begin. $V(t)$ reaches the maximum value of $14 million at $t = 9$ (point B), after which disease, age, and decay set in.

When should the trees be cut? The answer is not at $t = 9$ when $V(t)$ is maximum. That would be the case only if the market rate of interest were zero. With a positive market rate of interest, the correct answer is to cut the trees when the growth in the net value of the standing trees (ΔV) is equal to the growth of the net receipts from cutting the trees and investing the proceeds at the market rate of interest (rV). That is, the trees should be cut when

$$\Delta V = rV \qquad\qquad \textbf{[15–17]}$$

or

$$\Delta V/V = r \qquad\qquad \textbf{[15–17A]}$$

This says that trees should be cut when the *rate* of growth in the value of the standing trees ($\Delta V/V$) equals the market *rate* of interest (r).

In terms of Figure 15–10, the trees should be cut at $t = 6$ when the ΔV curve crosses the rV curve (point C' in the bottom panel). The ΔV curve (in the bottom panel) is the marginal value curve or slope of the $V(t)$ curve in the top panel (i.e., $\Delta V = MV$). The rV curve in the bottom panel is 0.25 or 25% of the $V(t)$ curve, at $r = 25\%$. To the left of point C', MV exceeds rV (i.e., $\Delta V/V > r$) and it pays for the firm to leave the trees to continue to grow. To the right of point C', MV is smaller than rV (i.e, $\Delta V/V < r$) and it pays

---

[17]The term "renewable" is, perhaps, more appropriate than "nonexhaustible" because if the rate of utilization of the resource exceeds its natural growth rate, the resource can be exhausted. For example, if you cut all trees or catch all the fish now, there will be no trees or fish in the future.

for the firm to cut the trees. The optimal choice is to cut the trees at point t = 6 (point C', where $MV = rV$). This is the usual marginal rule applicable in all optimization decisions.

FIGURE 15–10   Optimal Management of a Standing Forest

The top panel shows the net value of the trees if harvested at time t, $V(t)$. The trees should be cut when the growth in the net value of the standing trees (ΔV) is equal to the growth in the net receipts from cutting the trees and investing the proceeds at the market rate of interest (rV). This occurs at t = 6 when the ΔV or MV curve crosses the rV curve (point C' in the bottom panel) and $\Delta V/V = r$.

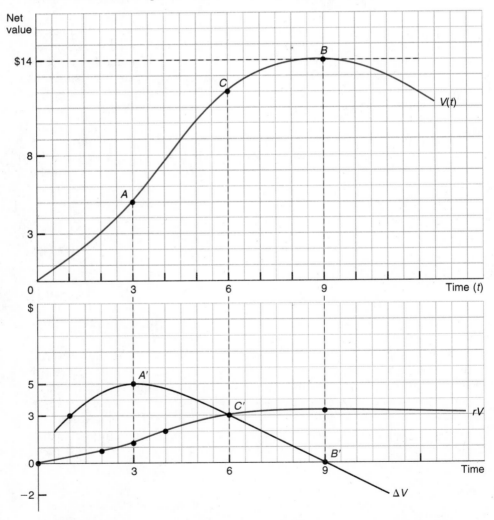

SUMMARY

1. Given the consumer's income or endowment for this year and the next, and the rate of interest, we can define the consumer's budget line. The rate of interest is the premium received next year for lending or borrowing one dollar this year. The optimal consumer's choice involves lending or borrowing so as to reach the highest possible indifference curve showing the consumer's time preference between present and future consumption. The wealth of an individual is given by the sum of the present income and the present value of future income. If the rate of interest rises, the borrower will borrow less and the lender will usually lend more. The equilibrium rate of interest is determined at the intersection of the market demand curve for borrowing and the market supply curve for lending.

2. For an isolated individual, the optimal saving and investment is given by the point where the production-possibilities curve is tangent to an indifference curve. With saving and investment, and borrowing and lending, the optimal choice of the individual is first to maximize wealth (by reaching the market line that is tangent to the production-possibilities curve) and then to borrow or lend along the market line until he or she reaches the highest indifference curve possible. The equilibrium rate of interest is given by the intersection of (1) the aggregate demand curve for borrowing and the aggregate supply curve of lending, or (2) the aggregate demand curve for investment and the aggregate supply curve of savings.

3. A firm should undertake an investment only if the net present value of the investment is positive. The net present value (NPV) of the investment is the value today from the stream of the net cash flows (positive and negative) from the investment. In choosing between any two projects, the firm will maximize attained wealth by undertaking the project with the highest net present value. The separation theorem refers to the independence of the optimum production decision from the individual's preferences in perfect capital markets.

4. The rate of interest usually varies at different times and in different markets. Even at a given point in time and in a specific capital market, there is not a single rate of interest, but many. That is, there is a different interest rate on loans or investments depending on differences in (1) default and variability risks, (2) duration of the loan, (3) cost of administering the loan, and (4) tax treatment. Interest rates rise if society decides to save less or to borrow and invest more. The nominal rate of interest equals the real rate of interest plus the anticipated rate of price inflation.

5. The cost that a firm incurs for using internal funds is the foregone return on these funds invested outside the firm. The cost of external funds is the rate of return that lenders and stockholders require to lend or invest funds in the firm. The after-tax cost of borrowed funds is given by the interest paid times $(1 - t)$, where t is the firm's marginal tax rate. The cost of equity capital can be measured by (1) the risk-free rate plus a risk premium, (2) the dividend valuation model, and (3) the capital asset pricing model (CAPM). The composite cost of capital is the weighted average of the cost of debt and equity capital.

6. Foreign investments result in a reduction in the rate of return on domestic investments but a net gain for the recipient nation. Labor in a nation receiving foreign investments shares in the gains through higher wages from the higher productivity resulting from an increased capital-labor ratio. The nation also collects taxes on foreign earnings. The United States is now the

largest debtor nation in the world. Concern has been voiced on the dangers arising from a sudden withdrawal of foreign investments, technology transfer, and foreign domination. These dangers seem exaggerated.

7. Investment in human capital refers to expenditures on education, job training, health, or migration to areas of better job opportunities that increase the productivity of an individual. Like any other invest-

ment, investments in human capital involve costs and entail returns. Education seems to induce people to work more hours. The net price of exhaustible resources tends to rise at the same rate as the market rate of interest, and this spreads the available supply over time and stimulates the discovery of substitutes. A nonexhaustible resource should be harvested when the growth in its net value equals the market rate of interest.

KEY TERMS

Endowment Position
Rate of Interest (*r*)
Wealth
Production-Possibilities Curve
Saving
Investment
Market Line
Capital Budgeting

Net Present Value (*NPV*)
Separation Theorem
Default Risk
Variability Risk
Real Rate of Interest (*r*)
Nominal Rate of Interest (*r'*)
Cost of Debt
Divident Valuation Model

Capital Asset Pricing Model
 (CAPM)
Beta Coefficient (β)
Composite Cost of Capital
Investment in Human Capital
Exhaustible Resources
Nonexhaustible Resources

REVIEW QUESTIONS

1. How much interest must an individual be paid to save part of his or her income this year if his or her time preference is zero? What happens to the individual's satisfaction this year and next if the individual saves part of this year's income and spends it next year? What happens to the individual's combined satisfaction for this year and next if the individual saves part of this year's income and spends it next year?

2. In what way is intertemporal optimum consumer choice analogous or similar to optimum consumer choice at one point in time?

3. Is microeconomic theory concerned primarily with the real or with the nominal interest rate? Why?

4. What is the present discounted value of an inheritance of $10,000 to be paid in two years, if the market rate of interest is 10%?

5. Should you prefer $100 one year from today

or $110 two years from today if the market rate of interest is 5% per year? Why?

6. What is the rate of interest or discount if an individual is indifferent between receiving $11,111.11 today or $1,000 at the end of each year in perpetuity?

7. Why is the cost of debt capital usually lower than the cost of equity capital for a firm?

8. What additional risks do the stockholders of a firm face in comparison to holders of government securities?

9. A corporation can sell bonds at an interest rate of 9%, and the interest rate on government securities is 7%. What is the cost of equity capital for this firm?

10. If labor and capital are the only inputs, what are the total gains of labor in Figure 15–7 when the nation receives $100 billion of foreign investments?

11. What are some of the benefits and costs of

foreign investments not captured by Figure 15–7? When all benefits and costs are considered, can we still say that foreign investments are beneficial for the receiving nation?

12. Does a nation gain or lose from foreign investments when all benefits and costs from foreign investments are considered?

PROBLEMS

1. Suppose that an individual is endowed with $Y_0 = 7.5$ units of a commodity this year and $Y_1 = 2.75$ units next year. Draw a figure showing that the individual lends 2.5 units of this year's endowment for 2.75 units next year. What is the rate of interest? On the same figure show that the individual lends 3 units for 4.2 units. What would the rate of interest be then?

2. Suppose that an individual is endowed with $Y_0 = 2.5$ units of a commodity this year and $Y_1 = 8.25$ units next year. Draw a figure showing that the individual borrows 2.5 units this year and repays 2.75 units next year. What is the rate of interest? On the same figure, show that the individual borrows 2 units this year and repays 2.80 units next year. What would the rate of interest be then?

3. Assume that (1) the consumer of problem 2 (call him or her individual B or the borrower) is a different individual from the consumer of problem 1 (call him or her individual A or the lender), and (2) both individual A and B have the same tastes or time preference. Draw a figure showing how the equilibrium rate of interest is determined if A and B are the only individuals in the market. What would happen at $r = 40\%$? At $r = 5\%$?

*4. Assume that (1) individuals A and B have identical endowments of a commodity of $Y_0 = 5$ this year and $Y_1 = 6$ next year, and (2) the optimal choice for individual B is to borrow 2.5 units this year and repay 3 units next year, while the optimal choice for individual A is to lend 2.5 units this year and receive 3 units next year. Draw a figure similar to Figures 15–1 and 15–2 for the above. What is the equilibrium rate of interest if A and B are the only individuals in the market? On the same figure show that at $r = 50\%$, individual B wants to borrow 2 units instead of 2.5 this year and

repay 3 units next year, while individual A wants to lend 3 units this year and receive 4.5 units next year. Why is $r = 50\%$ not the equilibrium rate of interest?

*5. a. Why does a lender's supply curve of loans (lending) bend backward at sufficiently high rates of interest?

  b. Why is a borrower's demand curve for loans (borrowing) negatively sloped throughout?

6. Draw a figure similar to Figure 15–5 showing that a rise in the rate of interest will reduce the individual's level of investment and borrowing.

7. Starting from Figure 15–5, draw a figure showing that if indifference curve U_5 had been tangent to market line HW_0' to the right of point A, the individual would have been dissaving.

8. Starting from Figure 15–5, draw a figure showing that if indifference curve U_5 had been tangent to market line HW_0' to the left of point H, the individual would have been saving more than he or she invested.

*9. Reestimate the net present value of the project given in Table 15–3 for $r = 5\%$.

*10. A firm expects to earn $200 million after taxes for the current year. The company has a policy of paying out half of its net after-tax income to the holders of the company's 100 million shares of common stock. A share of the common stock of the company currently sells for eight times current earnings. Management and outside analysts expect the growth rate of earnings and dividends for the company to be 7.5% per year. Calculate the cost of equity capital to this firm.

————————

* = Answer provided at end of book.

11. A company pays the interest rate of 11% on its bonds, the marginal income tax rate that the firm faces is 40%, the rate on government bonds is 7.5%, the return on the average stock of all firms in the market is 11.55%, the estimated beta coefficient for the common stock of the firm is 2, and the firm wishes to raise 40% of its capital by borrowing. Determine:

a. The cost of debt.
b. The cost of equity capital.
c. The composite cost of capital for this firm.

12. Draw a figure showing the effect of the following on the price of an exhaustible resource.
a. A decrease in the market rate of interest.
b. An increase in the demand for the resource.

PART SIX

GENERAL EQUILIBRIUM, EFFICIENCY, AND PUBLIC GOODS

P art Six (Chapters 16–18) presents the theory of general equilibrium and welfare economics, examines the role of government, and deals with the economics of information. Chapter 16 describes general equilibrium theory and welfare economics. It examines the interdependence or relationship among all products and input markets and shows how the various individual markets (studied in Parts Two through Five) fit together to form an integrated economic system. The chapter also considers questions of equity in the distribution of income. Chapter 17 concentrates on externalities, public goods, and the role of government. It studies why externalities (such as pollution) and the existence of public goods (such as national defense) lead to economic inefficiencies and discusses policies that can be used to overcome these inefficiencies. It also presents the theory of public choice. Finally, Chapter 18 deals with the economics of information. It examines the economics of search and the problems arising from asymmetric information (i.e., the situation where one party to a transaction has more information than another) and moral hazard (i.e., the increased probability of a loss when an economic agent can shift some of its costs to others).

GENERAL EQUILIBRIUM AND WELFARE ECONOMICS

Until this point we have examined the behavior of individual decision-making units (individuals as consumers of commodities and suppliers of inputs, and firms as employers of inputs and producers of commodities) and the workings of individual markets for commodities and inputs under various market structures. Generally missing from our presentation was an examination of how the various individual pieces fit together to form an integrated economic system.

In this chapter, we take up the topic of interdependence or relationship among the various decision-making units and markets in the economy. This allows us to trace both the effect of a change in any part of the economic system on every other part of the system, and the repercussions from the latter on the former. We begin the chapter by distinguishing between partial equilibrium analysis and general equilibrium analysis and examining the conditions under which each type of analysis is appropriate. Then, we discuss the conditions required for the economy to be in general equilibrium of exchange, production, and production and exchange simultaneously, and we examine their welfare implications.

16.1 PARTIAL VERSUS GENERAL EQUILIBRIUM ANALYSIS

In Parts Two to Five (Chapters 3–15) we conducted **partial equilibrium analysis**. That is, we studied the behavior of individual decision-making units and individual markets *viewed in isolation*. We examined how an individual maximizes satisfaction subject to his or her income constraint (Part Two: Chapters 3–5), how a firm minimizes its costs of production (Part Three: Chapters 6–8) and maximizes profits under various market structures (Part Four: Chapters 9–12), and how the price and employment of each type of input is determined (Part Five: Chapters 13–15). In doing so, we have abstracted from all the interconnections that exist between the market under study and the rest of the economy (the *ceteris paribus* assumption). In short, we have shown how demand and supply in each market determine the equilibrium price and quantity in that market *independently of other markets*.

However, a change in any market has spillover effects on other markets, and the change in these other markets will, in turn, have repercussions or feedback effects on the original market. These are studied by **general equilibrium analysis**. That is, general equilibrium analysis studies the **interdependence** or interconnections that exist among all markets and prices in the economy and attempts to give a complete, explicit, and simultaneous answer to the questions of what, how, and for whom to produce. In terms of section 1.3 (examining the circular flow of economic activity), general equilibrium analysis examines simultaneously the links among all commodity and input markets, rather than studying each market in isolation.

For example, a change in the demand and price for new, domestically produced automobiles will immediately affect the demand and price of steel, glass, and rubber (the inputs of automobiles), as well as the demand, wages, and income of autoworkers and of the workers in these other industries. The demand and price of gasoline and of public transportation (as well as the wages and income of workers in these industries) are also affected. These affected industries have spillover effects on still other industries, until the entire economic system is more or less involved, and all prices and quantities are affected. This is like throwing a rock in a pond and examining the ripples emanating in every direction until the stability of the entire pond is affected. The size of the ripples declines as they move farther and farther away from the point of impact. Similarly, industries further removed or less related to the automobile industry are less affected than more closely related industries.

What is important is that the effect that a change in the automobile industry has on the rest of the economy will have repercussions (through changes in relative prices and incomes) on the automobile industry itself. This is like the return of feedback effect of the ripples in the pond after reaching the shores. These repercussions or feedback effects are likely to significantly modify the original partial equilibrium conclusions (price and output) reached by analyzing the automobile industry in isolation (see Example 1).

When (as in the automobile example) the repercussions or feedback effects from the other industries are significant, partial equilibrium analysis is inappropriate. By measuring only the *impact* effect on price and output, partial equilibrium analysis provides a misleading measure of the total, final effect after all the repercussions or feedback effects from the original change have occurred. On the other hand, if the industry in which the original change occurs is small and the industry has few direct links with the rest of the economy (for example, the U.S. wristwatch industry), then partial equilibrium analysis provides a good first approximation to the results sought.

The logical question is why not use general equilibrium analysis all the time and immediately obtain the total, direct, and indirect results of a change on the industry (in which the change originated) as well as on all the other industries and markets in the economy. The answer is that general equilibrium analysis, dealing with each and all industries in the economy at the same time, is by its very nature difficult, time consuming, and expensive. Happily for the practical economist, partial equilibrium analysis often suffices. In any event, partial equilibrium analysis represents the appropriate point of departure, both for the relaxation of more and more of the *ceteris paribus* or "other things equal" assumptions, and for the inclusion of more and more industries in the analysis, as required.

The first and simplest general equilibrium model was introduced in 1874 by the great French economist, Léon Walras.[1] This and subsequent general equilibrium models are necessarily mathematical in nature and include one equation for each commodity and input demanded and supplied in the economy, as well as market clearing equations.[2] More recently, economists have extended and refined the general equilibrium model theoretically and proved that under perfect competition, a general equilibrium solution of the model usually exists, under which all markets are *simultaneously* in equilibrium.[3]

Example 1

Effect of a Reduction in Demand for Domestically Produced Automobiles in the United States

With the sharp increase in the price of imported petroleum from 1973 to 1980, the demand for new and large domestically produced automobiles declined, as from D to D' in panel (a) of Figure 16–1, while the demand for small fuel-efficient, foreign-produced automobiles increased. This reduced the real (i.e., the inflation-adjusted) price and quantity of domestically produced automobiles, as from P to P' and from Q to Q', respectively, in panel (a). This impact effect is what partial equilibrium analysis measures. However, the reduction in the demand for the domestically produced automobiles had spillover effects that disturbed the equilibrium in the steel [panel (b)] and other industries that supply inputs to the domestic automobile industry, as well as in the petroleum industry [panel (c)]. The inflation-adjusted price and quantity of steel and other inputs fell, and part of the original increase in the price of gasoline was neutralized. Other industries related to these industries were also affected. But this is not the end of the story. The demand for workers in the automobile industry [panel (d)] and other affected industries fell, and so did real wages, employment, and incomes. The reduction in real incomes

---

[1]L. Walras, *Elements of Pure Economics*, translated by William Jaffé (Homewood, Ill.: Irwin, 1954).

[2]See section A.16 of the Mathetmatical Appendix at the end of the text.

[3]K. J. Arrow and G. Debreu, "Existence of an Equilibrium for a Competitive Economy," *Econometrica*, July 1954, pp. 265–290, and L. W. McKenzie, "On the Existence of General Equilibrium for a Competitive Market," *Econometrica*, January 1959, pp. 54–71.

FIGURE 16-1   General Equilibrium Implications of a Reduction in the Demand for New Domestically Produced Automobiles

The impact or partial equilibrium effect of a reduction in the demand for new domestically produced automobiles is to reduce price from P to P' and quantity from Q to Q' [panel (a)]. This reduces the demand for (and price and quantity of) steel [panel (b)] and gasoline [panel (c)], and the demand for (and wages and employment of) workers in the automobile [panel (d)] and other affected industries. This, in turn, has spillover effects on the market for steaks [panel (e)] and other commodities, and feedback effects on the domestic automobile industry itself [panel (f)].

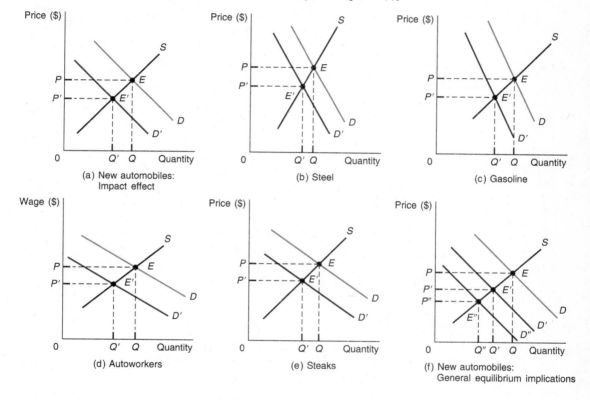

(a) New automobiles: Impact effect

(b) Steel

(c) Gasoline

(d) Autoworkers

(e) Steaks

(f) New automobiles: General equilibrium implications

reduced the demand, price, and quantity of steaks [panel (e)] and other normal goods purchased. To be sure, the demand for public transportation (buses, trains, and drivers and other attendants) and cheaper substitutes for steaks increased, but the net effect of the reduction in the demand for domestically produced cars was to reduce the demand and real income of labor. This, in turn, had feedback effects on the automobile industry, further reducing the demand, the inflation-adjusted price, and the ouput of domestically produced automobiles [panel (f)]. The same process continued throughout the 1980s (long after the petroleum crisis ended), as Japanese automobile exports to and production in the United States displaced more and more domestic production by the big three U.S. automakers. Only since 1992, has the Japanese gain in U.S. market share seemed to have come to a halt as a result of the U.S. automakers' improved efficiency.

Panel (f) of Figure 16–1 shows that the feedback effects on the domestic automobile industry were significant. The inflation-adjusted price fell from P to P'' rather than to P', and quantity fell from Q to Q'' instead of falling only to Q'. Thus, partial equilibrium analysis gives only a rough first approximation to the final solution. Note that a first round of spillover and feedback effects (as shown in the above analysis) can be measured by the cross and income elasticities (see sections 5.3 and 5.4), but these only carry us part of the way. The complete, final effects on the domestic automobile and on all other industries can only be measured through full-fledged general equilibrium analysis. This is necessarily mathematical in nature—words and graphs simply fail us.

Sources: "U.S. Giving Up on Making Small Cars," *U.S. News and World Report*, December 19, 1983, p. 56; "Auto Industry in U.S. Is Sliding Relentlessly into Japanese Hands," *Wall Street Journal*, February 16, 1990, p. 1; and "Detroit Takes the Offensive," *Forbes*, September 28, 1992, pp. 108–112.

▲

16.2 GENERAL EQUILIBRIUM OF EXCHANGE AND PRODUCTION

In this section, we examine separately general equilibrium of exchange and of production, and we derive the production-possibilities frontier. In the next section, we then examine how both equilibria are achieved *simultaneously* and the conditions for maximum economic efficiency.

General Equilibrium of Exchange

Let us begin by examining general equilibrium of exchange for a very simple economy composed of only two individuals (A and B), two commodities (X and Y), and no production. This allows us to present the general equilibrium of exchange graphically.[4] The general equilibrium of exchange for this simple economy of two individuals, two commodities, and no production was presented earlier in section 4.5. That analysis is now summarized and extended, and it will be utilized in the rest of the chapter.

The **Edgeworth box diagram for exchange** of Figure 16–2 is that of Figure 4–9, except that the indifference curves of individual A, convex to origin O_A, are given by A_1, A_2, and A_3 (rather than by U_1, U_2, and U_3 as in Figure 4–9) and the indifference curves of individual B, convex to origin O_B, are given by

---

[4]However, the analysis can be generalized mathematically to more than two individuals and more than two commodities. The graphic presentation in the text follows the well-known article by F. M. Bator, "The Simple Analytics of Welfare Maximization," *American Economic Review*, March 1957, pp. 22–59.

FIGURE 16–2   **Edgeworth Box Diagram for Exchange**

A point such as C indicates that individual A has $3X$ and $6Y$ (viewed from origin O_A), while individual B has $7X$ and $2Y$ (viewed from origin O_B) for a total of $10X$ and $8Y$ (the dimensions of the box). A's indifference curves (A_1, A_2, and A_3) are convex to O_A, while B's indifference curves (B_1, B_2, and B_3) are convex to O_B. Starting from point C where A_1 and B_1 intersect, individuals A and B can reach points on DEF, where one or both individuals gain. Curve $O_A DEFO_B$ is the contract curve for exchange. It is the locus of tangencies of the indifference curves (at which the MRS_{XY} are equal) for the two individuals and the economy is in general equilibrium of exchange.

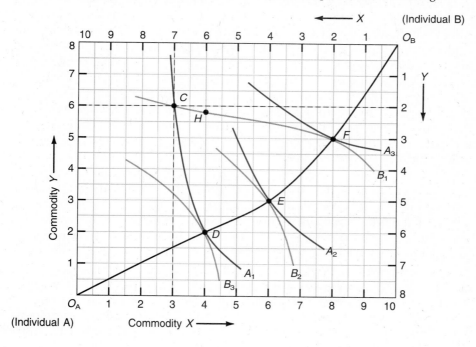

B_1, B_2, and B_3 (rather than by U_1', U_2', and U_3'). The dimensions of the box are given by the total amount of the two commodities ($10X$ and $8Y$) owned by the two individuals together.[5] Any point inside the box indicates how the total amount of the two commodities is distributed between the two individuals. For example, point C indicates that individual A has $3X$ and $6Y$, while individual B has $7X$ and $2Y$, for the combined total of $10X$ and $8Y$ (the dimensions of the box).

Suppose that point C does in fact represent the original distribution of commodities X and Y between individuals A and B. Since at point C, indiffer-

---

[5]As explained in section 4.5, the Edgeworth box was obtained by rotating individual B's indifference curves diagram by 180 degrees (so that origin O_B appears in the top right-hand corner) and superimposing it on individual A's indifference curves diagram (with origin at O_A) in such a way that the size of the box refers to the combined amount of the X and Y owned by the two individuals together.

ence curves A_1 and B_1 intersect, their slope or marginal rate of substitution of commodity X for commodity Y (MRS_{XY}) differs. Starting at point C, individual A is willing to give up 4Y to get one additional unit of X (and move to point D on A_1), while individual B is willing to accept 0.2Y in exchange for one unit of X (and move to point H on B_1).[6] Because A is willing to give up much more Y than necessary to induce B to give up 1X, there is a basis for exchange that will benefit either or both individuals. This is true whenever, as at point C, the MRS_{XY} for the two individuals differs.

For example, starting from point C, if individual A exchanges 4Y for 1X with individual B, A moves from point C to point D along his or her indifference curve A_1, while B moves from point C on B_1 to point D on B_3. Thus, individual B receives all of the gains from exchange while individual A gains or loses nothing (since A remains on A_1). At point D, A_1 and B_3 are tangent, so that their slopes (MRS_{XY}) are equal, and there is no further basis for exchange.[7]

Alternatively, if individual A exchanged 1Y for 5X with individual B, individual A would move from point C on A_1 to point F on A_3, while individual B would move from point C to point F along B_1. Then, A would reap all of the benefits from exchange while B would neither gain nor lose. At point F, MRS_{XY} for A equals MRS_{XY} for B and there is no further basis for exchange. Finally, if A exchanges 3Y for 3X with B and gets to point E, both individuals gain from exchange since point E is on A_2 and B_2. Thus, starting from point C, which is not on line DEF, both individuals can gain through exchange by getting to a point on line DEF between D and F. The greater is A's bargaining strength, the closer the final equilibrium point of exchange will be to point F, and the greater will be the proportion of the total gains from exchange going to individual A (so that less will be left over for individual B).

Curve O_ADEFO_B is the **contract curve for exchange**. It is the locus of tangency points of the indifference curves of the two individuals.[8] That is, along the contract curve for exchange, the marginal rate of substitution of commodity X for commodity Y is the same for individuals A and B, and the economy is in general equilibrium of exchange. Thus, for equilibrium,

$$MRS_{XY}^A = MRS_{XY}^B \qquad\qquad \text{[16–1]}$$

Starting from any point not on the contract curve, both individuals can gain from exchange by getting to a point on the contract curve. *Once on the contract curve, one of the two individuals cannot be made better off without making the other worse off.* For example, a movement from point D (on A_1 and B_3) to point E (on A_2 and B_2) makes individual A better off but individual B worse off. Thus,

---

[6]That is, $MRS_{XY} = 4$ for A, and $MRS_{XY} = 0.2$ for B.

[7]At point D, the amount of Y that A is willing to give up for 1X is exactly equal to what B requires to give up 1X. Any further exchange would make either individual worse off than he or she is at point D.

[8]Such tangency points are assured because indifference curves are convex and the field is dense (i.e., there is an infinite number of indifference curves).

the consumption contract curve is the locus of general equilibrium of exchange. For an economy composed of many consumers and many commodities, the general equilibrium of exchange occurs where the marginal rate of substitution between every pair of commodities is the same for all consumers consuming both commodities.

General Equilibrium of Production

Now that we have examined general equilibrium in a pure exchange economy with no production, we turn to general equilibrium of production in a simple economy in which no exchange takes place.

To examine general equilibrium of production, we deal with a very simple economy that produces only two commodities (X and Y) with only two inputs, labor (L) and capital (K). We construct an Edgeworth box diagram for production from the *isoquants* for commodities X and Y in a manner completely analogous to the Edgeworth box diagram for exchange of Figure 16–2. This is shown in Figure 16–3.

The **Edgeworth box diagram for production** shown in Figure 16–3 was obtained by rotating the isoquant diagram for commodity Y by 180 degrees (so that origin O_Y appears in the top right-hand corner) and superimposing it on the isoquant diagram for commodity X (with origin O_X) in such a way that the size of the box refers to the total amount of L and K available to the economy ($12L$ and $10K$). Any point inside the box indicates how the total amount of the two inputs is utilized in the production of the two commodities. For example, point R indicates that $3L$ and $8K$ are used in the production of X_1 of commodity X, and the remaining $9L$ and $2K$ are used to produce Y_1 of Y. Three of X's isoquants (convex to origin O_X) are X_1, X_2, and X_3. Three of Y's isoquants (convex to origin O_Y) are Y_1, Y_2, and Y_3.

If this economy was initially at point R, it would not be maximizing its output of commodities X and Y because, at point R, the marginal rate of technical substitution of labor for capital ($MRTS_{LK}$) in the production of X (the absolute slope of X_1) exceeds the $MRTS_{LK}$ in the production of Y (the absolute slope of Y_1).[9] By simply transferring $6K$ from the production of X to the production of Y and $1L$ from the production of Y to the production of X, the economy can move from point R (on X_1 and Y_1) to point J (on X_1 and Y_3) and increase its output of Y without reducing its output of X.

Alternatively, this economy can move from point R to point N (and increase its output of X from X_1 to X_3 without reducing its output of Y_1) by transferring $2K$ from the production of X to the production of Y and $6L$ from Y to X. Or, by transferring $4K$ from the production of X to the production of Y and $4L$ from Y to X, this economy can move from point R (on X_1 and Y_1) to point M (on X_2 and Y_2), and increase its output of both X and Y. At points J, M, and

---

[9]Review, if necessary, the definition and measurement of the marginal rate of technical substitution in section 6.4.

FIGURE 16–3   Edgeworth Box Diagram for Production

A point such as R indicates that $3L$ and $8K$ (viewed from origin O_X) are used to produce X_1 of commodity X, and the remaining $9L$ and $2K$ (viewed from origin O_Y) are used to produce Y_1 of Y. The isoquants for X (X_1, X_2, and X_3) are convex to O_X, while the isoquants of Y (Y_1, Y_2, and Y_3) are convex to O_Y. Starting from point R, where X_1 and Y_1 intersect, the economy can produce more of X, more of Y, or more of both by moving to a point on JMN. Curve O_XJMNO_Y is the contract curve for production. It is the locus of tangencies of the isoquants (at which the $MRTS_{LK}$ are equal) for both commodities, and the economy is in general equilibrium of production.

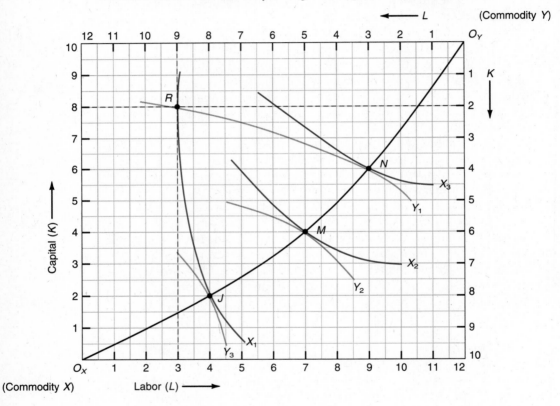

N, an X isoquant is tangent to a Y isoquant so that the $MRTS_{LK}$ in the production of X equals $MRTS_{LK}$ in the production of Y.

Curve O_XJMNO_Y is the **contract curve for production**. It is the locus of tangency points of the isoquants for X and Y at which the marginal rate of technical substitution of labor for capital is the same in the production of X and Y. That is, the economy is in general equilibrium of production when

$$MRTS_{LK}^X = MRTS_{LK}^Y \qquad\qquad \text{[16–2]}$$

Thus, by simply transferring some of the given and fixed amounts of available L and K between the production of X and Y, this economy can move from a point not on the contract curve for production to a point on it and increase its output of either or both commodities. Once on its production contract curve, the economy can only increase the output of either commodity by reducing the output of the other. For example, by moving from point J (on X_1 and Y_3) to point M (on X_2 and Y_2), the economy increases its output of commodity X (by transferring $3L$ and $2K$ from the production of Y to the production of X), but its output of commodity Y falls. For an economy of many commodities and many inputs, the general equilibrium of production occurs where the marginal rate of technical substitution between any pair of inputs is the same for all commodities and producers using both inputs.

Derivation of the Production-Possibilities Frontier

From the production contract curve, we can derive the corresponding production-possibilities frontier or transformation curve by simply plotting the various combinations of outputs directly. For example, if isoquant X_1 in Figure 16–3 referred to an output of 4 units of commodity X and isoquant Y_3 referred to an output of 13 units of commodity Y, we can go from point J (X_1, Y_3) in Figure 16–3 to point J' ($4X$, $13Y$) in Figure 16–4. Similarly, if isoquant X_2

FIGURE 16–4   **Production-Possibilities Frontier**

The production-possibilities frontier or transformation curve TT is derived by mapping the production contract curve of Figure 16–3 from input to output space. Starting from point R', the economy could increase its output of Y (point J'), of X (point N'), or of both X and Y (point M'). The absolute slope or $MRT_{XY} = \frac{1}{2}$ at point M' means that $\frac{1}{2}$ of Y must be given up to produce one additional unit of X. MRT_{XY} increases as we move down the frontier. Thus, at point N', $MRT_{XY} = 3$.

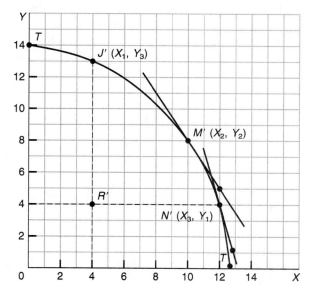

referred to an output of 10X and isoquant Y_2 to an output of 8Y, we can go from point M (X_2, Y_2) in Figure 16–3 to point M' (10X, 8Y) in Figure 16–4. Finally, if $X_3 = 12X$ and $Y_1 = 4Y$, we can plot point N (X_3, Y_1) from Figure 16–3 as point N' (12X, 4Y) in Figure 16–4. By joining points $J'M'N'$ and other points similarly obtained, we derive the production-possibilities frontier or transformation curve of X for Y, TT, shown in Figure 16–4. Thus, the production-possibilities frontier is obtained by simply mapping or transferring the production contract curve from input space to output space.

The **production-possibilities frontier** or transformation curve shows the various combinations of commodities X and Y that the economy can produce by fully utilizing all of the fixed amounts of labor and capital with the best technology available. Since the production contract curve shows all points of general equilibrium of production, so does the production-possibilities frontier. That is, the production-possibilities frontier shows the maximum amount of either commodity that the economy can produce, given the amount of the other commodity that the economy is producing. For example, given that the economy is producing 10X, the maximum amount of commodity Y that the economy can produce is 8Y (point M' in Figure 16–4), and vice versa.

A point inside the production-possibilities frontier corresponds to a point off the production contract curve and indicates that the economy is not in general equilibrium of production, and it is not utilizing its inputs of labor and capital most efficiently. For example, point R', inside production-possibilities frontier TT in Figure 16–4, corresponds to point R in Figure 16–3, at which isoquant X_1 and Y_1 intersect. By simply reallocating some of the fixed labor and capital available between the production of X and Y, this economy can increase its output of Y only (and move from point R' to point J' in Figure 16–4), it can increase the output of X only and move from point R' to point N'), or it can increase its output of both X and Y (the movement from point R' to point M'). On the other hand, a point outside the production-possibilities frontier cannot be achieved with the available inputs and technology.

Once on the production-possibilities frontier, the output of either commodity can be increased only by reducing the output of the other. For example, starting at point J' (4X and 13Y) on the production-possibilities frontier in Figure 16–4, the economy can move to point M' and produce 10X only by reducing the amount produced of Y by 5 units (i.e., to 8Y). The amount of commodity Y that the economy must give up, at a particular point on the production-possibilities frontier, so as to release just enough labor and capital to produce one additional unit of commodity X, is called the **marginal rate of transformation of X for Y (MRT_{XY})**. This is given by the absolute value of the slope of the production-possibilities frontier at that point. For example, at point M' on production-possibilities frontier TT in Figure 16–4, $MRT_{XY} = \frac{3}{2}$ (the absolute value of the slope of the tangent to the production-possibilities frontier at point M').

The marginal rate of transformation of X for Y is also equal to the ratio of the marginal cost of X to the marginal cost of Y. That is, $MRT_{XY} = MC_X/MC_Y$. For example, at point M', $MRT_{XY} = \frac{3}{2}$ This means that $\frac{3}{2}$ of Y must be given up to produce one additional unit of X. Thus, $MC_X = \frac{3}{2} MC_Y$, and $MRT_{XY} = \frac{3}{2}$. Another way of looking at this is that if $MC_Y = \$10$ and $MC_X = \$15$, this means that to produce one additional unit of X requires 1.5 or $\frac{3}{2}$ more units of labor and capital than to produce one additional unit of Y, so that $\frac{3}{2}$ of Y must be given up to produce one additional unit of X. This is exactly what the MRT_{XY} measures. Thus, at point M', $MRT_{XY} = MC_X/MC_Y = \frac{3}{2}$.

As we move down the production-possibilities frontier (and produce more X and less Y), the MRT_{XY} increases, indicating that more and more Y must be given up to produce each additional unit of X. For example, at point N', the MRT_{XY} or absolute value of the slope of the production-possibilities frontier is 3 (up from $\frac{3}{2}$ at point M'). The reason for this is that, as the economy reduces its output of Y (in order to produce more of X), it releases labor and capital in combinations that become less and less suited for the production of more X. Thus, the economy incurs increasing MC_X in terms of Y. It is because of this imperfect input substitutability between the production of X and Y (and rising MC_X in terms of Y) that the production-possibilities frontier is concave to the origin.[10]

16.3 GENERAL EQUILIBRIUM OF PRODUCTION AND EXCHANGE AND PARETO OPTIMALITY

In this section, we examine general equilibrium of production and exchange and define the concept of Pareto optimality, which summarizes the marginal conditions for economic efficiency.

General Equilibrium of Production and Exchange Simultaneously

We now can use the production-possibilities frontier and the contract curve for exchange to examine how our very simple economy composed of two individuals (A and B), two commodities (X and Y), and two inputs (L and K) can reach *simultaneously* general equilibrium of production and exchange. This is shown in Figure 16–5.

The production-possibilities frontier of Figure 16–5 is that of Figure 16–4, which was derived from the production contract curve of Figure 16–3. Thus, every point on production-possibilities frontier TT is a point of general equilibrium of production. Suppose that this economy produces $10X$ and $8Y$, given by point M' on production-possibilities frontier TT in Figure 16–5.[11] By dropping perpendiculars from point M' to both axes, we can construct in Figure 16–5

---

[10]If labor and capital were perfectly substitutable in the production of X and Y, MC_X would be constant in terms of Y, and the production-possibilities frontier would be a negatively sloped straight line.

[11]How this particular output level is determined is examined in section 16.4.

the Edgeworth box diagram for exchange between individuals A and B of Figure 16–2. Note that the top right-hand corner of the Edgeworth box diagram for exchange of Figure 16–2 coincides with point M' on production-possibilities frontier TT in Figure 16–5. Given the indifference curves of individuals A and B and the output of 10X and 8Y, we derived contract cuve $O_A DEFO_B$ for exchange in Figure 16–2. This is reproduced in Figure 16–5. Every point on the contract curve for exchange in Figure 16–5 is a point of general equilibrium of exchange.

Thus, every point on production-possibilities frontier TT in Figure 16–5 is a point of general equilibrium of production, and every point on the contract curve for exchange is a point of general equilibrium of exchange. However, to be *simultaneously* in general equilibrium of production and exchange, the marginal rate of transformation of commodity X for commodity Y in production must be equal to the marginal rate of substitution of commodity X for commodity Y in consumption for individuals A and B. That is,

$$MRT_{XY} = MRS^A_{XY} = MRS^B_{XY} \qquad \text{[16–3]}$$

FIGURE 16–5   **General Equilibrium of Production and Exchange**

Production-possibilities frontier TT is that of Figure 16–4. Every point on TT is a point of general equilibrium of production. Starting from point M' (10X, 8Y) on the production-possibilities frontier, we constructed in the above figure the Edgeworth box diagram for exchange between individuals A and B of Figure 16–2. Every point on contract curve $O_A DEFO_B$ is a point of general equilibrium of exchange. Simultaneous general equilibrium of production and exchange is at point E, at which $MRT_{XY} = MRS^A_{XY} = MRS^B_{XY} = \frac{3}{2}$.

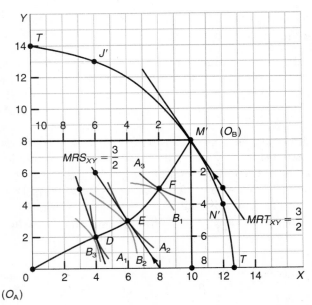

Geometrically, this corresponds to the point on the contract curve for exchange at which the common slope of an indifference curve of individual A and individual B equals the slope of production-possibilities frontier TT at the point of production. In Figure 16–5, this occurs at point E, where

$$MRS^A_{XY} = MRS^B_{XY} = MRT_{XY} = \tfrac{1}{2} \qquad \text{[16–3A]}$$

Thus, when producing $10X$ and $8Y$ (point M' on production-possibilities frontier TT), this economy is simultaneously in general equilibrium of production and exchange when individual A consumes $6X$ and $3Y$ (point E on his or her indifference curve A_2) and individual B consumes the remaining $4X$ and $5Y$ (point E on his or her indifference curve B_2).

If condition [16–3] did not hold, the economy would not be simultaneously in general equilibrium of production and exchange. For example, suppose that individuals A and B consumed at point D on the contract curve for exchange rather than at point E in Figure 16–5. At point D, the MRS_{XY} (the common absolute value of the slope of indifference curves A_1 and B_3) is 3. This means that individuals A and B are willing (indifferent) to give up $3Y$ to obtain one additional unit of X. Since in production, only $\tfrac{1}{2}Y$ needs to be given up to produce an additional 1 unit of X, society would have to produce more of X and less of Y to be simultaneously in general equilibrium of production and exchange. Put in another way, if $MRS_{XY} = 3$, this society would not have chosen to produce at point M', but would have produced at point N' ($12X$ and $4Y$), where $MRS_{XY} = MRT_{XY} = 3$.

The opposite is true at point F. That is, at point F, $MRS_{XY} = \tfrac{1}{2}$. Since $MRT_{XY} = \tfrac{1}{2}$ at point M' (the point of production), more of Y needs to be given up in production to obtain one additional unit of X than individuals A and B are willing to give up in consumption. If this were the case, this society would have chosen to produce at point J' ($4X$ and $13Y$) where $MRS_{XY} = MRT_{XY} = \tfrac{1}{2}$, rather than at point M'. Only by consuming at point E will $MRT_{XY} = MRS_{XY}$ for both individuals, and society will be simultaneously in general equilibrium of production and exchange when it produces at point M'.

We conclude the following about this simple economy when it is in general equilibrium of production and exchange: (1) it produces $10X$ and $8Y$ (point M' in Figure 16–5)[12]; (2) individual A receives $6X$ and $3Y$, and individual B receives the remaining $4X$ and $5Y$ (point E in Figure 16–5); (3) to produce $10X$, $7L$ and $4K$ are used, while to produce $8Y$, the remaining $5L$ and $6K$ are used (see point M in Figure 16–3).[13]

---

[12]As pointed out in footnote 11, we will see how this level of output is determined in section 16.4.

[13]In section 16.4, we will also determine the relative price of commodity X (i.e., P_X/P_Y) and the relative price of labor time (i.e., P_L/P_K or w/r) for this simple economy when it is simultaneously in general equilibrium of production and exchange.

Marginal Conditions for Economic Efficiency and Pareto Optimality

With general equilibrium of production and exchange, **economic efficiency** is maximum and we have **Pareto optimality**.[14] According to this concept, *a distribution of inputs among commodities and of commodities among consumers is Pareto optimal or efficient if no reorganization of production and consumption is possible by which some individuals are made better off (in their own judgment) without making someone else worse off.* Any change that improves the well-being of some individuals without reducing the well-being of others, clearly improves the welfare of society as a whole and should be undertaken. This will move society from a Pareto nonoptimal position to Pareto optimum. Once at Pareto optimum, no reorganization of production and exchange is possible that makes someone better off without, at the same time, making someone else worse off. To evaluate such changes requires interpersonal comparisons of utility, which are subjective and controversial.

In a very simple economy of two individuals, two commodities (X and Y), and no production, the contract curve for exchange (along which the MRS_{XY} is the same for both individuals) is the locus of Pareto optimum in exchange and consumption. As we have seen in section 16.2, a movement from a point off the contract curve to a point on it improves the condition of either or both individuals, with the given quantities of the two commodities. Once on the contract curve, the economy is in general equilibrium or Pareto optimum in exchange, in the sense that either individual can be made better off only by making the other worse off. In an economy of many individuals and many commodities, Pareto optimum in exchange requires that the marginal rate of substitution between any pair of commodities be the same for all individuals consuming both commodities.

In a very simple economy of two commodities, two inputs (L and K), and no exchange, the production contract curve (along which the $MRTS_{LK}$ is the same for both commodities) is the locus of Pareto optimum in production. As we have seen in section 16.2, a movement from a point off the production contract curve to a point on it makes it possible for the economy to produce more of either or both commodities, with the given inputs and technology. Once on the production contract curve, the economy is in general equilibrium or Pareto optimum in production in the sense that the economy can increase the output of either commodity only by reducing the output of the other. In an economy of many commodities and many inputs, Pareto optimum in production requires that the marginal rate of technical substitution between any pair of inputs be the same for all commodities and producers using both inputs.

Finally, Pareto optimum in production and exchange simultaneously in an

---

[14]Vilfredo Pareto was the great Italian economist of the turn of the century who, in 1909, expressed the condition for maximum economic efficiency, which became known as Pareto optimality. See, V. Pareto, *Manual of Political Economy*, translated by William Jaffé (New York: August Kelly, 1971).

FIGURE 16–6   Efficiency in Production and Exchange in a "Robinson Crusoe" Economy

In a single-person economy, economic efficiency in production and exchange (and maximum social welfare) is achieved at point M^*, at which indifference curve A_2 for individual A (the only individual in society) is tangent to his or her production-possibilities frontier, $T'T'$. Output is 6X and 3Y, and $MRT_{XY} = MRS_{XY} = \frac{3}{2}$.

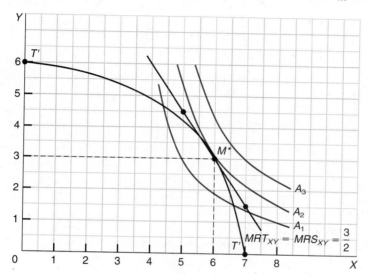

economy of many inputs, many commodities, and many individuals requires that the marginal rate of transformation in production equals the marginal rate of substitution in consumption for every pair of commodities and for every pair of individuals consuming both commodities. In the case of a very simple economy composed of only two commodities and two individuals (A and B), Pareto optimality in production and consumption requires that

$$MRT_{XY} = MRS^A_{XY} = MRS^B_{XY}.$$

This was shown graphically in Figure 16–5 by the point on the contract curve for exchange at which the common slope of an indifference curve of individual A and individual B is equal to the slope of the production frontier at the point of production.

If we assume that there is only one individual (a Robinson Crusoe) in society, we achieve considerable graphic simplification in showing the point of economic efficiency in production and consumption.[15] This is given by point M^* in Figure 16–6, at which indifference curve A_2 for individual A (the only individual in society) is tangent to his or her production-possibilities

---

[15]Since in this very special case, there is no problem of interpersonal comparison of utility; the point of maximum economic efficiency in production and consumption also represents the point of maximum social welfare.

frontier, $T'T'$. Any point on $T'T'$ represents a point of efficient production. Given $T'T'$, A_2 is the highest indifference curve that the individual can reach with his or her production-possibilities frontier. At point M^* (the tangency point of A_2 to $T'T'$), output is $6X$ and $3Y$, and $MRT_{XY} = MRS_{XY} = \frac{1}{2}$. Production and consumption is economically efficient, and society (the individual) maximizes welfare.

16.4 PERFECT COMPETITION, ECONOMIC EFFICIENCY, AND EQUITY

In this section, we show why perfect competition leads to economic efficiency or Pareto optimum, but not necessarily to equity.

Perfect Competition and Economic Efficiency

With perfect competition in all input and commodity markets, the three marginal conditions for economic efficiency or Pareto optimum in production and exchange (section 16.3) are automatically satisfied. This is the basic argument in favor of perfect competition. We can easily prove that perfect competition leads to economic efficiency.

We have seen in section 3.5 that a consumer maximizes utility or satisfaction when he or she reaches the highest indifference curve possible with his or her budget line. This occurs where an indifference curve is tangent to the budget line. At the tangency point, the slope of the indifference curve (the MRS_{XY}) is equal to the slope of the budget line (P_X/P_Y). Since P_X and P_Y, and thus P_X/P_Y, are the same for all consumers under perfect competition, the MRS_{XY} is also the same for all consumers consuming both commodities. This is the first marginal condition for economic efficiency or Pareto optimum in exchange. We can now also establish that for the simple economy examined in section 16.3, $P_X/P_Y = \frac{1}{2}$ (the absolute value of the slope of the common tangent to indifference curves A_2 and B_2 at point E in Figure 16–5).

We have also seen in section 7.2 that efficiency in production requires that the $MRTS_{LK}$ (the absolute value of the slope of an isoquant) be equal to P_L/P_K or w/r (the ratio of the input prices given by the absolute value of the slope of the isocost line). Since P_L or w and P_K or r, and thus P_L/P_K or w/r, are the same for all producers under perfect competition, the $MRTS_{LK}$ is also the same for all producers using both inputs. This is the second marginal condition for economic efficiency or Pareto optimum in production. We can now also establish that for the simple economy examined in section 16.3, P_L/P_K or w/r = $\frac{2}{3}$ (the absolute value of the common tangent to isoquants X_2 and Y_2 at point M in Figure 16–3).[16]

---

[16]Note that in microeconomic theory, we are only concerned with *relative*, not absolute, input and commodity prices. This means that proportionate changes in (e.g., doubling or halving) all input prices and/or all commodity prices do not change the solution to the general equilibrium model. If we want to get unique absolute (dollar) values for P_X, P_Y, P_L, (or w), and P_K (or r), we would have to add a monetary equation, such as Fisher's "equation of exchange" to our model. This is done in a course in macroeconomic theory but is not needed in microeconomics.

Finally, we have seen in section 16.3 that $MRT_{XY} = MC_X/MC_Y$, and in section 8.3 that perfectly competitive firms produce where $MC_X = P_X$ and $MC_Y = P_Y$. Therefore, $MC_X/MC_Y = P_X/P_Y = MRT_{XY}$. Since we have also seen above that under perfect competition $MRT_{XY} = P_X/P_Y$ for all consumers consuming both commodities, we conclude that $MRTS_{XY} = MRS_{XY}$ for all consumers consuming both commodities. This is the third marginal condition for economic efficiency and Pareto optimum in production and exchange. Thus, when the simple economy examined in section 16.3 produces $10X$ and $8Y$ (point M' in Figure 16–5), $MRT_{XY} = MRS_{XY}^A = MRS_{XY}^B = 3/2$. Individual A should then consume $6X$ and $3Y$, and individual B should consume the remaining $4X$ and $5Y$ (point E in Figure 16–5), for the economy to be simultaneously at Pareto optimum in production and exchange.

The output of $10X$ and $8Y$ at point M' in Figure 16–5 is based on a particular distribution of inputs (income) between individuals A and B and on their tastes. A different distribution of income and/or tastes for individuals A and B would lead to a different combination of goods X and Y demanded. This would result in a different P_X/P_Y, different quantities of X and Y produced, and different levels of satisfaction for A and B. For example, suppose that individuals A and B demanded $12X$ and $4Y$ (point N' in Figure 16–5). Then, general equilibrium of production and exchange or Pareto optimality requires that $MRT_{XY} = P_X/P_Y = MRS_{XY}^A = MRS_{XY}^B = 3$ (the absolute slope of TT at point N'). This involves constructing an Edgeworth box diagram from point N' and retracing all the steps of the analysis in section 16.3. In a purely exchange economy (i.e., one in which there is no production), the equilibrium P_X/P_Y is the one that exactly matches the desired quantity of X and Y that each individual wants to exchange. If B wants more of X for a given amount of Y than A is willing to exchange, then P_X/P_Y will rise until the demand for the quantities of X and Y to be exchanged match. Similarly, if B wants less of X for a given amount of Y than A is willing to exchange, P_X/P_Y will fall until equilibrium is reached.

Efficiency and Equity

The fact that perfect competition leads to optimum economic efficiency and Pareto optimum in production and exchange is no small achievement. It proves Adam Smith's famous **law of the invisible hand** stated more than 200 years ago. Smith's law postulates that in a free market economy, each individual by pursuing his or her own selfish interests is led, as if by an *invisible hand*, to promote the well-being of society more so than he or she intends or even understands.[17] This leads to the **first theorem of welfare economics**, which postulates that *an equilibrium produced by competitive markets exhausts all possible gains from exchange,* or that *equilibrium in competitive markets is Pareto*

---

[17]See, A. Smith, *The Wealth of Nations* (Toronto: Random House, 1937), Book IV, Chapter 2, p. 423, and J. Persky, "Adam Smith's Invisible Hand," *Journal of Economic Perspectives*, Fall 1989, pp. 195–201.

optimal. There is also a **second theorem of welfare economics**. This postulates that *when indifference curves are convex to their origin, every efficient allocation (every point on the contract curve for exchange) is a competitive equilibrium for some initial allocation of goods or distribution of inputs (income)*. The significance of the second welfare theorem is that the issue of equity in distribution is logically separable from the issue of efficiency in allocation. This means that whatever the redistribution of income that society wants would lead to the exhaustion of all possible gains from exchange under perfect competition. Pareto optimality does not, therefore, imply equity. Society can use taxes and subsidies to achieve what it considers to be a more equitable distribution of income. These may discourage work, however, and show that there is usually a trade-off between efficiency and equity.[18]

For economic efficiency and Pareto optimum to be reached, there should be no market failure. **Market failures** arise in the presence of imperfect competition, externalities, and public goods. *Externalities* and *public goods* will be examined in the next chapter. Here, we examine why imperfect competition in the product and input markets leads to economic inefficiency and Pareto nonoptimality.

To show that imperfect competition in the product market leads to economic inefficiency and Pareto nonoptimality, remember that in Part Four of the text it was shown that a profit-maximizing firm always produces where marginal revenue (*MR*) equals marginal cost (*MC*). If commodity *Y* is produced in a perfectly competitive market, $P_Y = MR_Y = MC_Y$. On the other hand, if commodity *X* is produced by a monopolist (or other imperfect competitor), $P_X > MR_X = MC_X$. Then,

$$MRT_{XY} = \frac{MC_X}{MC_Y} = \frac{MR_X}{MR_Y} < \frac{P_X}{P_Y} = MRS_{XY}$$

That is, $MRT_{XY} < MRS_{XY}$, so that the third condition for Pareto optimum and economic efficiency (discussed in section 16.3) is violated.

To show that imperfect competition in the input market leads to economic inefficiency and Pareto nonoptimality, remember that in Part Five of the text it was shown that a profit-maximizing firm always produces where the marginal revenue product (*MRP*) of each input equals the marginal resource cost (*MRC*) for the input. If *P* is the price of the input, and the input market is perfectly competitive, $MRP = MRC = P$. Otherwise, $MRP = MRC > P$. Now suppose that all markets in the economy are perfectly competitive, except that the firm producing commodity *X* is a monopsonist in its labor market (i.e, it is the sole employer of labor in its labor market). Therefore, $MRP = MRC > P$ in the production of commodity *X*, while $MRP = MRC = P$ in the production of *Y*. That is, $MRTS^X_{LK} > MRTS^Y_{LK}$, so that the first of the conditions

---

[18]See, A. Okun, *Equality and Efficiency: The Big Tradeoff* (Washington, D.C.: The Brookings Institution, 1975). We will return to questions of equity in sections 16.6 and 16.7.

for Pareto optimum and economic efficiency (discussed in section 16.4) is violated.

Finally, note that perfect competition leads to efficiency and Pareto optimum in production and exchange *at a particular point in time*. Over time, tastes, the supply of inputs, and technology change; and what is most efficient at one point in time may not be most efficient over time. In short, perfect competition leads to *static, but not necessarily to dynamic, efficiency*. (This was discussed in section 12.3.)

Example 2
Watering Down Efficiency in the Pricing of Water

In some cities (Los Angeles, for example), the price of water is lower for irrigation than for most other purposes. This reduces economic efficiency because the marginal rate of technical substitution between water and other inputs differs in irrigation than in other uses. For example, suppose that the price of 1,000 cubic feet of water when used for irrigation is equal to the daily wage of an unskilled worker, but when used to wash cars it is twice the daily wage of the unskilled worker. So, a farmer will use water until the marginal rate of technical substitution between water and labor is equal to 1, but a car-washing firm will do so until *MRTS* = 2. Water and labor inputs are then utilized at a point (such as *R* in Figure 16–3) at which the isoquants intersect off the production contract curve, and production is inefficient. In this case, the farmer will use too much water and too little labor, whereas the car-washing firm will underutilize water and overutilize labor.

If the price of water were the same for both the farmer and the car-washing firm, economic efficiency in production would increase. Each producer would then use water and labor until the *MRTS* between water and labor would be equal to the relative price of these two inputs. The result is that the output of either or both commodities or services would increase, with the given quantity of water and unskilled labor available. This is equivalent to moving from point *R* to a point from *J* to *N* on the production contract curve of Figure 16–3. With the sharp increase in the demand for water in California as a result of rapid population growth and with the reduced supply due to drought, the efficient use of scarce water resources became even more important in California during the 1980s and early 1990s. This has generally meant an increase in the *relative* availability of water for nonirrigation purposes and an increase in the relative price of water in all uses.

Sources: J. Hirschleifer, J. C. DeHaven, and W. J. Milliman, *Water Supply: Economics, Technology, and Policy* (Chicago: University of Chicago Press, 1960), and "California Moves to Revitalize San Francisco Bay," *New York Times*, December 11, 1992, p. 28.

16.5 GENERAL EQUILIBRIUM OF PRODUCTION AND EXCHANGE WITH INTERNATIONAL TRADE

General equilibrium of production and exchange can conveniently be shown for international trade. We will first examine this concept intuitively and then graphically.

General Equilibrium with International Trade

An important example of general equilibrium of production and exchange is provided by international trade, say, between nations A and B. Suppose that nation A is endowed with an abundance of labor (L) relative to capital (K) with respect to nation B, and commodity X is labor intensive (i.e, the L/K ratio in the production of X is greater than in the production of Y). Given the same technology and tastes in the two nations, the cost (in terms of the amount of Y to be given up) of producing an additional unit of X (i.e., $MRT_{XY} = P_X/P_Y$) is lower in nation A than in nation B. We say that nation A has a **comparative advantage** in commodity X and nation B has a comparative advantage in commodity Y.

With trade, nation A specializes in the production of commodity X (i.e., it produces more of X than it demands for internal consumption) in order to exchange it for commodity Y from nation B. On the other hand, nation B specializes in the production of commodity Y (i.e., it produces more of Y than it demands for internal consumption) in order to exchange it for commodity X from nation A. With each nation specializing in the production of the commodity of its comparative advantage (nation A in commodity X and B in Y), the combined output of X and Y by the two nations is larger than without specialization. Both nations then share the increased output of X and Y through voluntary exchange (trade), and both are better off than without trade.

As each nation specializes in the production of the commodity of its comparative advantage, it will incur increasing opportunity costs. Specialization in production reaches the equilibrium level when $MRT_{XY} = P_X/P_Y$ is the same in both nations. The two nations are then simultaneously in general equilibrium of production and exchange (trade) when $MRT_{XY} = P_X/P_Y = MRS_{XY}^A = MRS_{XY}^B$.[19]

General Equilibrium with International Trade—Graphic Analysis

We can show general equilibrium of production and exchange and the gains from specialization in production and trade with the aid of Figure 16–7. The production-possibilities frontier is AA for nation A and BB for nation B. The

---

[19]See, D. Salvatore, *International Economics*, 4th ed. (New York: Macmillan, 1993), Chapter 5.

FIGURE 16–7   Graphic Analysis of General Equilibrium with Trade

The production-possibilities frontier is AA for nation A and BB for nation B. In the absence of trade, A is at point C and B is at point C'. Since $MRT_{XY} = P_X/P_Y$ (the absolute value of the slope of the production-possibilities frontier) is lower at point C than at point C', nation A has a comparative advantage in X while nation B has a comparative advantage in Y. With trade, A produces at point D, exchanges $40X$ for $40Y$ with B, and consumes at $E > C$. B produces at point D', exchanges $40Y$ for $40X$ with A, and consumes at $E' > C'$.

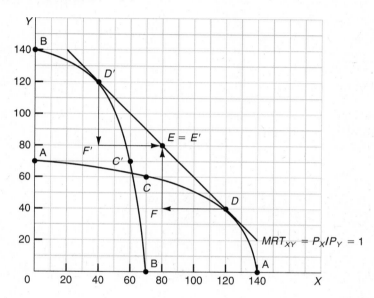

different shapes of the two production-possibilities frontiers result from nation A having a relative abundance of labor and commodity X being the labor-intensive commodity, with nation B having a relative abundance of capital and commodity Y being the capital-intensive commodity. For simplicity, we assume that both technology and tastes are the same in both nations. Suppose that in the absence of trade, nation A is observed to be producing and consuming at point C, while nation B is observed to be at point C'.[20] Since $MRT_{XY} = P_X/P_Y$ (the absolute slope of the production-possibilities frontier) is lower at point C for nation A than at point C' for nation B, nation A has a comparative advantage in commodity X, while nation B has a comparative advantage in commodity Y.

With the opening of trade, nation A specializes in the production of X (moves down its production-possibilities frontier from point C) and incurs increasing opportunity costs in the production of more X (i.e., the $MRT_{XY} =$

---

[20]This means that $MRT_{XY} = MRS_{XY} = P_X/P_Y$ in each country, so that each country is simultaneously in equilibrium of production and exchange in isolation (i.e., in the absence of trade).

P_X/P_Y rises). Nation B specializes in the production of Y (moves up its production-possibilities frontier from point C') and incurs increasing opportunity costs in the production of more Y (i.e., the $MRT_{YX} = P_Y/P_X$ rises, which means that $MRT_{XY} = P_X/P_Y$ falls). Specialization in production proceeds until nation A has reached point D and nation B has reached point D', at which $MRT_{XY} = P_X/P_Y$ is the same in both nations. Nation A might then exchange $40X$ (DF) for $40Y$ (FE) with nation B and reach point E. At point E, nation A consumes $10X$ and $20Y$ more than at point C without trade. With trade, nation B consumes at point E' ($= E$) or $20X$ and $10Y$ more than at point C' without trade. Production and trade is in (general) equilibrium, and both nations gain.

Note that with trade, both nations consume $80X$ and $80Y$ (i.e., point E for nation A coincides with point E' for nation B). This would be true if both nation not only had the same technology and tastes but were also of equal size. These simplifying assumptions were made to simplify the graphic analysis. However, we can show comparative advantage (i.e., the basis for trade) and the gains from trade graphically even if the two nations have different technologies and tastes, and if they are unequal in size.[21]

16.6 WELFARE ECONOMICS AND UTILITY-POSSIBILITIES FRONTIERS

After examining the meaning of welfare economics, we will derive the utility-possibilities frontier and the grand utility-possibilities frontier.

The Meaning of Welfare Economics

Welfare economics studies the conditions under which the solution to the general equilibrium model as presented in this chapter can be said to be optimal. It examines the conditions for economic efficiency in the production of output and in the exchange of commodities, and equity in the distribution of income. This is to be clearly distinguished from the everyday usage of the term "welfare," which refers mostly to government programs to aid low-income families. That topic is only a very small part of what welfare economics covers.

The maximization of society's well-being requires the optimal allocation of inputs among commodities and the optimal allocation of commodities (i.e., distribution of income) among consumers. The conditions for the optimal allocation of inputs among commodities and exchange of commodities among consumers have already been discussed. These are objective criteria devoid of ethical connotations or value judgements. On the other hand, it is impossible to objectively determine the optimal distribution of income. This necessar-

[21]See, D. Salvatore, *International Economics, op. cit.,* Chapter 3.

ily requires interpersonal comparisons of utility and value judgments on the relative "deservingness" or merit of various members of society, and different people will inevitably have different opinions on this. For example, taxing $100 away from individual A and giving it as a subsidy to individual B will certainly make B better off and A worse off. But who is to say that the society composed of both individuals is better or worse off as a whole? This involves comparing the utility lost by individual A to the utility gained by individual B (i.e., making interpersonal comparison of utility). And even if A has a high income and B has a low income to begin with, different people will have different opinions on whether this increases social welfare, reduces it, or leaves it unchanged. Therefore, no entirely objective or scientific rule can be defined. The difficulty in making interpersonal comparisons of utility is clearly demonstrated in rationing hospital care discussed in Example 3.

Example 3

"The Painful Prescription: Rationing Hospital Care"

The great difficulty with interpersonal comparison of utility in making social choices is aptly exemplified by the need to ration hospital care. New therapeutic techniques (such as open-heart surgery) and new diagnostic devices (such as CAT scanners) have improved medical care but have greatly added to costs. For example, open-heart surgery costs tens of thousands of dollars and replaces the much cheaper (but somewhat less effective) use of drugs in treating patients with heart disease. This raises difficult choices for society in general, and for physicians and hospitals in particular, as they try to contain the ever-rising costs of medical care. In England, only a handful of patients over the age of 55 with chronic kidney failure are referred for expensive dialysis; the others are simply allowed to die of chronic renal failure. The idea of rationing medical care is generally alien to Americans, accustomed as they are to expect the best care that can be medically provided. Nevertheless, ever-increasing medical costs are likely to lead to rationing in the use of some new and expensive techniques and diagnostic devices.

   As pointed out by Fuchs, medical care has always been rationed in the United States and elsewhere, because "no nation is wealthy enough to provide all the care that is technically feasible and desirable. . . ." Therefore, the change is not between "no rationing and rationing, but rather in the way rationing takes a place—who does the rationing and who is affected by it." The way hospital care (particularly the use of the more advanced and costly new diagnostic techniques) is to be rationed in the future is likely to give rise to a prolonged national debate and a period of great turmoil. One proposal favored by the Clinton administration is to introduce "managed competition" in health care. This would allow insurance companies to provide consumers with incentives to "price shop" when choosing doctors and hospitals. Such a competition is expected to keep health-care costs down. In addition, unless the courts redefine negligence in view of the need to restrain rising medical costs, physicians are likely to face more and more malpractice suits.

Sources: V. R. Fuchs, "The 'Rationing' of Medical Care," *The New England Journal of Medicine,* December 13, 1984, pp. 1572–1573; H. J. Aaron and W. B. Schwartz, *The Painful Prescription: Rationing Hospital Care* (Washington, D.C.: Brookings Institute, 1984); "Changes in Medicine Bring Pain to Healing Profession," *New York Times,* February 18, 1990, p. 1; "Demands to Fix U.S. Health Care Reaches a Crescendo," *New York Times,* April 19, 1991, Section 4, p. 1; "Yes, the Market Can Curb Health Costs," *Fortune,* December 28, 1992, pp. 84–88; and "Managed Competition—Too Little Competition," *Wall Street Journal,* January 7, 1993, p. A14.

▲

Utility-Possibilities Frontier

By assigning utility rankings to the indifference curves of individual A and individual B in Figure 16–5, we can map or transfer the contract curve for exchange of Figure 16–5 from output or commodity space to utility space, and thus derive utility-possibilities frontier $U_{M'} U_{M'}$ in Figure 16–8. Specifically, if indifference curve A_1 in Figure 16–5 refers to 200 units of utility for individual

FIGURE 16–8   Utility-Possibilities Frontier

Utility-possibilities frontier $U_{M'}U_{M'}$ shows the various combinations of utilities received by individuals A and B (i.e, U_A and U_B) when the economy composed of individuals A and B is in general equilibrium or Pareto optimum in exchange. It is obtained by mapping exchange contract curve $O_A DEFO_B$ in Figure 16–5 from output or commodity space to utility space. Specifically, if A_1 refers to $U_A = 200$ utils and B_3 to $U_B = 600$ utils, point D in Figure 16–5 can be plotted as point D' in the above figure. Point E can be plotted as point E', and point F as F'. By joining points $D'E'F'$, we get utility-possibilities frontier $U_{M'}U_{M'}$.

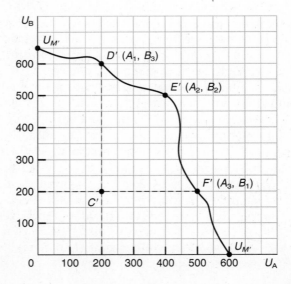

A (i.e., U_A = 200 utils) and B_3 refers to U_B = 600 utils, we can go from point D (on A_1 and B_3) in commodity space in Figure 16–5 to point D' in utility space in Figure 16–8. Similarly, if A_2 refers to U_A = 400 utils and B_2 refers to U_B = 500 utils, we can go from point E (on A_2 and B_2) in Figure 16–5 to point E' in Figure 16–8. Finally, if A_3 refers to U_A = 500 utils and B_1 refers to U_B = 200 utils, we can go from point F (on A_3 and B_1) in Figure 16–5 to point F' in Figure 16–8.[22] By joining points $D'E'F'$ and other points similarly obtained, we derive utility-possibilities frontier $U_M'U_M'$ in Figure 16–8. Thus, the utility-possibilities frontier is obtained by mapping or transferring the contract curve for exchange from output or commodity space into utility space.

The **utility-possibilities frontier** shows the various combinations of utilities received by individuals A and B (i.e., U_A and U_B) when this simple economy is in general equilibrium or Pareto optimum in exchange. It is the locus of maximum utility for one individual for any given level of utility for the other individual. For example, given that U_A = 400 utils, the maximum utility of individual B is U_B = 500 utils (point E'). A point such as C in Figure 16–2 (at which indifference curves A_1 and B_1 intersect off exchange contract curve O_ADEFO_B) corresponds to point C' inside utility-possibilities frontier $U_M'U_M'$ in Figure 16–8. By simply redistributing the 10X and 8Y available to the economy (point M' in Figure 16–5) between individuals A and B, the economy can move from point C' to point D' in Figure 16–8 and increase U_B, to point F' and increase U_A, or to point E' and increase both U_A and U_B. A point outside the utility-possibilities frontier cannot be reached with the available amounts of commodities X and Y. Of all points of Pareto optimality in exchange along utility-possibilities frontier $U_M' U_M'$, in Figure 16–8, only point E' (which corresponds to point E in Figure 16–5) is also a point of Pareto optimality in production. That is, at point E', $MRS_{XY}^A = MRS_{XY}^B = MRT_{XY} = P_X/P_Y = 3/2$.

Grand Utility-Possibilities Frontier

We have seen that utility-possibilities frontier $U_M' U_M'$, in Figure 16–8 (repeated in Figure 16–9) was derived from the contract curve for exchange drawn from point O to point M' on the production-possibilities frontier in Figure 16–5. If we pick another point on the production-possibilities frontier of Figure 16–5, say, point N', we can construct another Edgeworth box diagram and get another contract curve for exchange, this one drawn from point O to point N' in Figure 16–5. From this different contract curve for exchange (not shown in Figure 16–5), we can derive another utility-possibilities frontier ($U_N' U_N'$ in Figure 16–9) and obtain another Pareto optimum point in produc-

---

[22]Note that the scale along the horizontal axis refers only to individual A, while the scale along the vertical axis refers only to B. Thus, U_A = 400 utils is not necessarily smaller than U_B = 500 utils, since no interpersonal comparison of utility is implied. Furthermore, the scale along either axis is ordinal, not cardinal. That is U_A = 300 utils is greater than U_A = 200 utils, but not necessarily 1.5 times larger. Note also that utility-possibilities frontier $U_M U_M'$ is negatively sloped, but irregularly rather than smoothly shaped.

FIGURE 16–9   Grand Utility-Possibilities Frontier

Utility-possibilities frontier $U_M U_{M'}$ is that of Figure 16–8. Utility-possibilities frontier $U_{N'} U_{N'}$ is derived from the contract curve for exchange in the Edgeworth box diagram constructed from point N' on the production-possibilities frontier of Figure 16–5. By joining E', H', and other Pareto optimum points of production and exchange similarly obtained in the above figure, we get grand utility-possibilities frontier $GE'H'G$.

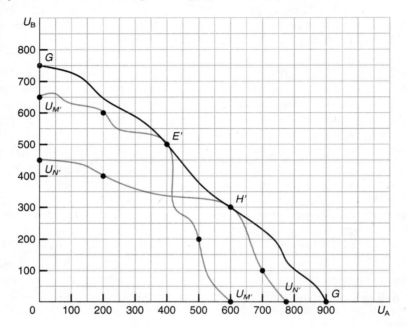

tion and exchange (point H' in Figure 16–9). By then joining points E', H', and other points similarly obtained, we can derive grand utility-possibilities frontier $GE'H'G$ in Figure 16–9.[23]

Thus, the **grand utility-possibilities frontier** is the envelope to the utility-possibilities frontiers at Pareto optimum points of production and exchange. The grand utility-possibilities frontier indicates that no reorganization of the production-exchange process is possible that makes someone better off without, at the same time, making someone else worse off. This is as far as objective analysis goes. To determine the Pareto optimum point in production and exchange at which social welfare is maximum, we need a social welfare function. However, since this is based on interpersonal comparisons of utility (which is not allowed), we cannot determine the point of maximum social welfare.

---

[23]Note that the various utility-possibilities frontiers and the grand utility-possibilities frontier derived from them are negatively sloped but are usually irregularly shaped (as in Figure 16–9).

16.7 SOCIAL POLICY CRITERIA

In this section, we examine some very important criteria for measuring changes in social welfare and Arrow's impossibility theorem.

Measuring Changes in Social Welfare

There are four different criteria to determine whether or not a particular policy raises social welfare. The *first* is the **Pareto criterion**, discussed in section 16.3 and accepted by nearly all economists. According is this criterion, a policy increases social welfare if it benefits some members of society (in their own judgment) without harming anyone. In terms of Figure 16–10, a movement from point C*, inside grand utility-possibilities frontier GG, to points E', H', or any point between E' and H' (such as point V) on GG, benefits one or both individuals and harms none; thus, it passes the Pareto criterion. In contrast, a movement from point C* to point Z on GG makes individual B much better off but individual A a little worse off, and so it does not pass the Pareto criterion. Because most policies will benefit some and harm others,[24] the Pareto criterion does not go very far, and it is biased in favor of the *status quo*.

To overcome this limitation of the Pareto criterion, Kaldor and Hicks introduced the *second* welfare criterion, which is based on the **compensation principle**.[25] According to the **Kaldor-Hicks criterion**, a change is an improvement if those who gain from the change can fully compensate the losers and still retain some gain. In terms of the movement from point C* to point Z in Figure 16–10, individual B (the gainer) could fully compensate individual A for his or her loss, so that society could move from point C* to point E' (instead of from point C* to Z) on GG, and we can determine that social welfare is higher.[26] Yet, this conclusion is not as clear-cut as it may seem.

First of all, it is possible (though unusual) for the Kaldor-Hicks criterion to indicate that a given policy increases social welfare but also to indicate that, after the change, a movement back to the original position also increases social welfare. This limitation can be overcome with the *third* or **Scitovsky criterion**.[27] This is a double Kaldor-Hicks test. That is, according to Scitovsky, a change is an improvement if it satisfies the Kaldor-Hicks criterion, and after the

---

[24]For example, a tax on high-income people to finance aid to low-income families benefits the latter but harms the former. Even the breakup of a monopoly harms someone (the monopolist who loses the source of profits).

[25]N. Kaldor, "Welfare Propositions in Economics and Interpersonal Comparisons of Utility," *Economic Journal*, December 1939, pp. 549–552; and J. R. Hicks, "The Foundations of Welfare Economics," *Economic Journal*, December 1939, pp. 696–712.

[26]One real-world example of actual compensation is given by the trade adjustment assistance provided since 1962 by the Trade Expansion Act for U.S. workers displaced by negotiated tariff reductions. This assistance was justified by the much greater benefits to society as a whole resulting from trade liberalization. See, D. Salvatore, *International Economics, op. cit.*, Chapter 9.

[27]T. Scitovsky, "A Note on Welfare Propositions in Economics," *Review of Economics and Statistics*, November 1941, pp. 77–78.

FIGURE 16–10   Measuring Changes in Social Welfare

A movement from point C^* to a point from E' to H' on grand utility-possibilities frontier GG benefits one or both individuals and harms no one. Thus, it increases social welfare according to the Pareto criterion. A movement from point C^* to point Z increases social welfare according to the Kaldor-Hicks criterion, since individual B could fully compensate individual A for his or her loss and still retain some gain. However, since this type of reasoning is based on interpersonal comparisons of utility, social welfare need not be higher.

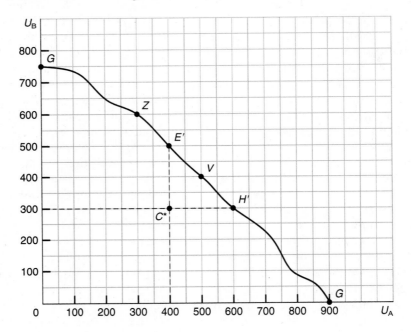

change, a movement back to the original position *does not* satisfy the Kaldor-Hicks criterion.

Another shortcoming of the Kaldor-Hicks criterion is more serious. It arises because the compensation principle measures the welfare changes of the gainers and losers in monetary units. For example, if a policy increases the income of individual B by $100 but lowers the income of individual A by $60, social welfare has increased according to the Kaldor-Hicks criterion (because individual B could transfer $60 of his or her $100 income gain to individual A and retain $40).[28] Since compensation is not actually required, the Kaldor-Hicks criterion is based on the assumption that the gain in utility of individual B (when his or her income rises by $100) is greater than the loss of utility to

---

[28]If compensation actually took place (something that is not required by the Kaldor-Hicks criterion), the Pareto criterion would suffice (since individual B is better off and individual A is not harmed), and the Kaldor-Hicks criterion would be superfluous.

individual A (when his or her income falls by $60). Yet, this line of reasoning is based on interpersonal comparisons of utility, and social welfare need not be higher.

The only way to overcome this limitation of the Kaldor-Hicks criterion is to squarely face the problem of interpersonal comparison of utility. This leads us to the *fourth* welfare criterion, which is based on the construction of a **Bergson social welfare function** from the explicit value judgments of society.[29] A particular policy can then be said to increase social welfare if it puts society on a higher social indifference curve. However, as we will see in the next section, a social welfare function is extremely difficult or impossible to construct by democratic vote.

Arrow's Impossibility Theorem

Nobel laureate Kenneth Arrow proved that a social welfare function cannot be derived by democratic vote (i.e., reflecting the preferences of all the individuals in society). This is known as **Arrow's impossibility theorem**.[30]

Arrow lists the following four conditions that he believes must hold for a social welfare function to reflect individual preferences:

1. Social welfare choices must be transitive. That is, if X is preferred to Y and Y is preferred to Z, then X must be preferred to Z.
2. Social welfare choices must not be responsive in the opposite direction to changes in individual preferences. That is, if choice X moves up in the ranking of one or more individuals and does not move down in the ranking of any other individual, then choice X cannot move down in the social welfare ranking.
3. Social welfare choices cannot be dictated by any one individual inside or outside the society.
4. Social choices must be independent of irrelevant alternatives. For example, if society prefers X to Y and Y to Z, then society must prefer X to Y even in the absence of alternative Z.

Arrow showed that a social welfare function cannot be arrived at by democratic voting without violating at least one of the four conditions. This can easily be proved for the first of the conditions. For example, suppose that Ann, Bob, and Charles (the three individuals in a society) rank alternatives X, Y, and Z as in Table 16–1.

Consider first the choice between alternatives X and Y. The majority (Ann and Charles) prefers X to Y. Now consider the choice between alternatives Y and Z. The majority (Ann and Bob) prefers Y to Z. It might then be concluded

---

[29]A. Bergson, "A Reformulation of Certain Aspects of Welfare Economics," *Quarterly Journal of Economics*, February 1938, pp. 310–334.

[30]K. J. Arrow, *Social Choice and Individual Values* (New York: Wiley, 1951).

TABLE 16–1   **Rankings of Alternatives** X, Y, **and** Z **by Ann, Bob, and Charles**

	Alternative		
Individuals	X	Y	Z
Ann	1st	2nd	3rd
Bob	3rd	1st	2nd
Charles	2nd	3rd	1st

that since the majority prefers X to Y and Y to Z, the society composed of Ann, Bob, and Charles would prefer X to Z. However, from Table 16–1, we see that the majority (Bob and Charles) prefers Z to X. Therefore, the preference of the majority is inconsistent with the preferences of the individuals making up the majority. In short, this society cannot derive a social welfare function by democratic voting even if individual preferences are consistent. This is sometimes referred to as the "voting paradox."

While disturbing, it must be noted that the above conclusion is based on considering only the rank and not the intensity with which various alternatives are preferred. Thus, if half of society *mildly* preferred more space exploration while the other half *strongly* preferred more aid to low-income families instead, the difference in the intensities of these preferences would have to be disregarded in the decision process according to Arrow.

16.8 TRADE PROTECTION AND ECONOMIC WELFARE

By increasing the commodity price, trade protection benefits domestic producers and harms domestic consumers (and usually the nation as a whole). However, since producers are few and stand to gain a great deal from protection, they have a strong incentive to lobby the government to adopt protectionist measures. On the other hand, since the losses are diffused among many consumers, each of whom loses very little from the protection, they are not likely to effectively organize to resist protectionist measures. Thus, there is a bias in favor of protectionism. For example, the sugar quota raises individual expenditures on sugar by only a few dollars per person per year in the United States. But with nearly 270 million people in the United States, the quota generates more than $600 million in rents to the few thousand sugar producers in the United States.

In industrial countries, protection is more likely to be provided to labor-intensive industries employing unskilled, low-wage workers who would have great difficulty in finding alternative employment if they lost their present jobs. Some empirical support has also been found for the *pressure-group* or *interest-group* theory, which postulates that industries that are highly organized (such as the automobile industry) receive more trade protection than less organized industries. An industry is more likely to be organized if it is composed of only a few firms. Also, industries that produce consumer products generally are able to obtain more protection than industries producing intermediate products used as inputs by other industries, because the latter industries can exercise *countervailing power* (i.e., apply opposing pressure) and block protection (since that would increase the price of their inputs).

Furthermore, more protection seems to go to geographically decentralized industries that employ large numbers of workers than to industries that operate in only some regions and employ relatively few workers. The large number of workers have strong voting power to elect government officials who support protection for the industry. Decentralization ensures that elected officials from many regions support the trade protection. Another theory suggests that trade policies are biased in favor of maintaining the status quo. That is, it is more likely for an industry to be protected now if it was protected in the past. Governments also seem reluctant to adopt trade policies that result in large changes in the distribution of income, regardless of who gains and who loses.

Example 4
Welfare Effects of Removing U.S. Trade Restrictions

Table 16–2 shows that removing all quantitative restrictions (QRs) on textile and apparel exports to the United States would result in a gain of $11.92 billion for the United States at 1984 prices. Retaining QRs but capturing the

TABLE 16–2   Welfare Benefits and Employment Effects of Removing Quantitative Restrictions (QRs) on Exports of Textile, Steel, and Automobiles to the United States

	Welfare Gain (billions of dollars)	Employment Change in Industry (1,000 work-years)	Employment Change in Rest of Economy (1,000 work-years)
Textile and apparel			
Remove QRs	11.92	−157.2	157.2
Capturing rents from foreigners	6.05	−3.1	28.4
Automobiles			
Remove QRs	7.50	−1.2	1.3
Capturing rents from foreigners	7.15	+1.3	37.2
Steel			
Remove QRs	0.86	−20.7	22.3
Capturing rents from foreigners	0.74	−0.1	3.5

Source: J. de Melo and D. Tarr. "Welfare Costs of U.S. Quotas on Textile, Steel, and Apparel," *Review of Economics and Statistics*, August 1990.

rents from foreigners (e.g., by auctioning off export quotas to foreign firms) would result instead in a gain of $6.05 billion for the United States. The gains are smaller for automobiles and much smaller for steel. Removing QRs also leads to employment losses in the industry losing the QRs, but these employment losses are matched or more than matched by economywide employment gains. Removing QRs on all three products leads to a total welfare gain of $20.28 ($11.92 + $7.50 + $0.86) billion for the United States. Also, eliminating all tariffs on industrial products after the above QRs have been removed results in a further gain of $0.6 billion for the United States (not shown in the table). The effects of removing agricultural protection, however, are not included.

▲

SUMMARY

1. Partial equilibrium analysis studies the behavior of individual decision-making units and individual markets, viewed in isolation. On the other hand, general equilibrium analysis studies the interdependence that exists among all markets in the economy. Only when an industry is small and has few direct links with the rest of the economy is partial equilibrium analysis appropriate. The first general equilibrium model was introduced by Walras in 1874. Under perfect competition, a solution to the general equilibrium model usually exists.

2. A simple economy of two individuals (A and B), two commodities (X and Y), and two inputs (L and K) is in general equilibrium of exchange when it is on its contract curve for exchange. This is the locus of tangency points of the indifference curves (at which the MRS_{XY} are equal) for the two individuals. The economy is in general equilibrium of production when it is on its production contract curve. This is the locus of the tangency points of the isoquants (at which $MRTS_{LK}$ are equal) for the two commodities. By mapping or transferring the production contract curve from input to output space, we derive the corresponding production-possibilities frontier.

3. For the economy to be simultaneously in general equilibrium of production and exchange, the marginal rate of transformation of X for Y in production must be equal to the marginal rate of substitution of X for Y in consumption for individuals A and B. That is, $MRT_{XY} = MRS^A_{XY} = MRS^B_{XY}$. Geometrically, this corresponds to the point on the contract curve for exchange at which the common slope of the indifference curve of the two individuals equals the slope of the production-possibilities frontier at the point of production. A distribution of inputs among commodities and of commodities among consumers is Pareto optimal or efficient if no reorganization of production and consumption is possible by which some individuals are made better off without making someone else worse off. Thus, the conditions for Pareto optimality are the conditions for general equilibrium of production and exchange.

4. Under perfect competition in all input and output markets, all the conditions for Pareto optimum are automatically satisfied. This is the basic argument in favor of perfect competition and proof of Adam Smith's law of the invisible hand. The first theorem of welfare economics postulates that equilibrium in competitive markets is

Pareto optimal. The second theorem of welfare economics postulates that equity in distribution is logically separable from efficiency in allocation. Perfect competition leads to maximum economic efficiency only in the absence of market failures (which arise from imperfect competition, externalities and public goods). Perfect competition leads to static but not necessarily to dynamic efficiency.

5. Starting from the general equilibrium condition at which $MRT_{XY} = P_X/P_Y = MRS_{XY}$ in each country in the absence of trade, the country with the lower MRT_{XY} or P_X/P_Y will have a comparative advantage in commodity X. With trade, each nation will specialize in the production of the commodity of its comparative advantage until MRT_{XY} or P_X/P_Y becomes equal in both countries. Then each country will trade until $MRT_{XY} = P_X/P_Y = MRS_{XY}$ so as to be in general equilibrium once again. But by specializing in production and trading, each country can consume more of both commodities than it can without trade.

6. Welfare economics studies the conditions under which the solution to the general equilibrium model can be said to the optimal. It examines the conditions for economic efficiency in the production of output and in the exchange of commodities, and for equity in the distribution of income. A utility-possibilities frontier is derived by mapping or transferring a contract curve for exchange from output or commodity space to utility space. It shows the various combinations of utilities received by two individuals at which the economy is in general equilibrium or Pareto optimum in exchange. We can construct an Edgeworth box and contract curve for exchange from each point on the production-possibilties frontier. From each contract curve for exchange, we can then construct the corresponding utility-possibilities frontier and determine on it the point of Pareto optimum in production and exchange. By joining points of Pareto optimality in production and exchange on each utility-possibilities frontier, we can derive the grand utility-possibilities frontier.

7. A change that benefits some but harms others can be evaluated with the Kaldor-Hicks-Scitovsky criterion. However, this is based on the compensation principle, which measures the welfare changes of the gainers and the losers in monetary units. The only way to overcome this shortcoming is with a social welfare function. Arrow proved that a social welfare function cannot be derived by democratic vote. This is known as Arrow's impossibility theorem.

8. By increasing the commodity price, trade protection benefits producers and harms consumers (and usually the nation as a whole). Protection is more likely to be provided to industries that (1) are labor-intensive and employ unskilled, low-wage workers, (2) are highly organized (such as the automobile industry), (3) produce consumer products rather than intermediate products, and (4) are geographically decentralized.

KEY TERMS

Partial Equilibrium Analysis
General Equilibrium Analysis
Interdependence
Edgeworth Box Diagram for
   Exchange
Contract Curve for Exchange
Edgeworth Box Diagram for

Production
Contract Curve for Production
Production-Possibilities
   Frontier
Marginal Rate of
   Transformation of X for Y
   (MRT_{XY})

Economic Efficiency
Pareto Optimality
Law of the Invisible Hand
First Theorem of Welfare
   Economics
Second Theorem of Welfare
   Economics

Market Failures
Comparative Advantage
Welfare Economics
Utility-Possibilities Frontier
Grand Utility-Possibilities
    Frontier

Pareto Criterion
Compensation Principle
Kaldor-Hicks Criterion
Scitovsky Criterion

Bergson Social Welfare
    Function
Arrow's Impossibility
    Theorem

REVIEW QUESTIONS

1. Are all points on the contract curve for exchange equally desirable from society's point of view? Why?
2. How will an increase in the quantity of labor available to society affect its Edgeworth box diagram for production? What effect will that have on the contract curve for production?
3. How can we show a 10% improvement in technology in the production of commodities X and Y in the Edgeworth diagram and production-possibilities frontier?
4. Why would the economy of Figure 16–5 not be at general equilibrium if production took place at point M' and consumption at point D?
5. If $MRT_{XY} = \frac{1}{2}$ while $MRS_{XY} = 2$ for individuals A and B, should the economy produce more of X or more of Y to reach equilibrium of production and exchange simultaneously? Why?
6. What makes general equilibrium analysis ob-

jective while welfare economics is subjective?
7. Would the Robinson Crusoe of Figure 16–6 maximize utility or welfare by producing and consuming $5X$ and $4.5Y$? Why?
8. What is the relationship between Adam Smith's law of the invisible hand and Pareto optimum?
9. Why do market disequilibria lead to inefficiencies and non-Pareto optimum?
10. Perfect competition is the best form of market organization at one point in time but not over time. True or false? Explain.
11. What is meant by the "voting paradox?" How is this related to Arrow's impossibility theorem?
12. Why is international trade often restricted if it benefits few domestic producers but harms many domestic consumers?

PROBLEMS

1. Starting from a position of general equilibrium in the entire economy, if the supply curve of commodity X falls (i.e., S_X shifts up), examine what happens
   a. in the markets for commodity X, its substitutes, and complements.
   b. in the input markets.
   c. to the distribution of income.
*2. Suppose that the indifference curves of individuals A and B are given by A_1, A_2, A_3, and B_1, B_2, B_3, respectively, in the accompanying table. Suppose also that the total amount of commodities X and Y available to the two individuals together are $12X$ and $9Y$. Draw the Edgeworth box diagram for exchange, and show the contract curve for exchange.
3. For the Edgeworth box diagram of problem 2 (shown at the end of the text):

A's Indifference Curves

A_1		A_2		A_3	
X	Y	X	Y	X	Y
3	7	5	6	6	7.5
4	3	6	4	8	6
6	1	8	3	9.5	5.5

B's Indifference Curves

B_1		B_2		B_3	
X	Y	X	Y	X	Y
7	2	6	4	8	4
2	3	4	5	6	6
1	4	3	7	5.5	8

a. Explain how, starting from the point at which A_1 and B_1 intersect, mutually advantageous exchange can take place between individuals A and B.

b. What is the value of the MRS_{XY} at point E, D, and F?

*4. Suppose that the isoquants for commodities X and Y are given by X_1, X_2, X_3, and Y_1, Y_2, Y_3, respectively, in the table below. Suppose also that the total of 14L and 9K are available to produce commodities X and Y. Draw the Edgeworth box diagram for exchange and show the production contract curve.

X's Isoquants					
X_1		X_2		X_3	
L	K	L	K	L	K
5	7	8	5	10	7
6	2	9	3	11	5
7	1	11	2	13	4.5

Y's Isoquants					
Y_1		Y_2		Y_3	
L	K	L	K	L	K
9	2	7	4	10	4
3	4	5	6	8	7
1	6	4	8	7.5	8.5

5. For the Edgeworth box diagram of problem 4 (shown at the end of the text):

a. Explain how, starting from the point at which X_1 and Y_1 intersect, the output of both commodities can be increased by simply reallocating some of the fixed amounts of L and K available between the production of X and Y.

b. What is the value of the $MRTS_{LK}$ at points M, J, and N?

6. Suppose that in the figure in the answer to problem 4, $X_1 = 4X$ and $Y_3 = 13Y$, $X_2 = 10X$ and $Y_2 = 9Y$, and $X_3 = 14X$ and $Y_1 = 4Y$. Derive the production-possibilities frontier corresponding to the production contract curve given in the figure in the answer to

problem 4. What does a point inside the production-possibilities frontier indicate? A point outside?

7. a. Find the MRT_{XY} at points J' M', and N' for the production-possibilities frontier of problem 6.

b. If $MC_Y = \$100$ at point M', what is MC_X?

c. Why is the production-possibilities frontier concave to the origin?

d. When would the production-possibilities frontier be a straight line?

*8. Superimpose the Edgeworth box diagram for exchange of problem 2 on the production-possibilities frontier of problem 4 (both shown at the end of the text), and determine the general equilibrium of production and exchange.

9. Explain why the economy portrayed in the answer to problem 8 would not be simultaneously in general equilibrium of production and exchange at points D and F.

10. Given that the economy of problem 8 produces at point M' on its production-possibilities frontier, determine

a. how much of commodities X and Y it produces.

b. how this output is distributed between individuals A and B.

c. how much labor (L) and capital (K) are used to produce commodities X and Y.

d. What questions have been left unanswered in the model?

11. Suppose that the economy represented by the figure in the answer to problem 8 (shown at the end of the text) grows over time and/or has available a more advanced technology. Explain how this affects the figure and general equilibrium analysis.

12. Suppose that in the figure in the answer to problem 8 (see Figure 16c in Appendix B), A_1 refers to 100 utils, $A_2 = 300$ utils, $A_3 = 450$ utils, and $B_1 = 200$ utils, $B_2 = 400$ utils, and $B_3 = 450$ utils.

a. Derive the utility-possibilities frontier corresponding to contract curve $O_A DEFO_B$ for exchange in Figure 16c in Appendix B.

b. Derive the grand utility-possibilities frontier.

---

* = Answer provided at end of book.

17

EXTERNALITIES, PUBLIC GOODS, AND THE ROLE OF GOVERNMENT

In this chapter, we examine why the existence of externalities and public goods leads to economic inefficiencies and to an allocation of inputs and commodities that is not Pareto optimum. We then consider how the government (through regulation, taxes, and subsidies) could attempt to overcome or at least reduce the negative impact of these distortions on economic efficiency. Because these distortions and government attempts to overcome them are fairly common in most societies, including our own, the importance of the topics presented in this chapter can hardly be overstated. We also discuss in this chapter the theory of public choice (i.e., how government decisions are made and implemented) and strategic trade policy (i.e., how comparative advantage can be created by subsidies, trade protection, and other government policies). We conclude by applying the tools of analysis developed in the chapter to the problem of environmental pollution.

17.1 EXTERNALITIES

In this section, we define externalities and examine why their existence prevents the attainment of maximum economic efficiency or Pareto optimum, even under perfect competition.

Externalities Defined

In the course of producing and consuming some commodities, harmful or beneficial side effects arise that are borne by firms and people not directly involved in the production or consumption of the commodities. These are called **externalities** because they are felt by economic units (firms and individuals) not directly involved with (i.e., that are external to or outside) the economic units that generate these side effects.[1] Externalities are called **external costs**

---

[1]The presentation of this section and of section 17.3 follows F. M. Bator's "The Anatomy of Market Failure," *Quarterly Journal of Economics*, August 1958, pp. 351–379.

when they are harmful and **external benefits** when they are beneficial. An example of an external cost is the air pollution that may accompany the production of a commodity. An example of an external benefit is the reduced chance of the spreading of a communicable disease when an individual is inoculated against it.

Externalities are classified into five different types. These are external diseconomies of production, external diseconomies of consumption, external economies of production, external economies of consumption, and technical externalities. Each of these will be examined in turn. **External diseconomies of production** are uncompensated costs imposed on others by the expansion of output by some firms. For example, the increased discharge of waste materials by some firms along a waterway may result in antipollution legislation that increases the cost of disposing of waste materials for all firms in the area. **External diseconomies of consumption** are uncompensated costs imposed on others by the consumption expenditures of some individuals. For example, the riding of a snowmobile by an individual imposes a cost (in the form of noise and smoke) on other individuals who are skiing, hiking, or ice fishing in the area.

On the other hand, **external economies of production** are uncompensated benefits conferred on others by the expansion of output by some firms. An example of these arises when some firms train more workers to increase output, and some of these workers go to work for other firms (which, therefore, save on training costs). **External economies of consumption** are uncompensated benefits conferred on others by the increased consumption of a commodity by some individual. For example, increased expenditures to maintain his or her lawn by a homeowner increases the value of the neighbor's house. Finally, **technical externalities** arise when declining long-run average costs as output expands lead to monopoly, so that price exceeds marginal cost. Not even regulation to achieve competitive marginal cost pricing is then viable (see section 12.5).

Externalities and Market Failure

We have seen in section 16.4 that perfect competition leads to maximum economic efficiency and Pareto optimum. However, this is true only when private costs equal social costs and when private benefits equal social benefits (i.e., in the absence of externalities). This was implicitly assumed to be the case until now. When externalities are present, the "invisible hand" is led astray and Pareto optimum is not achieved, even under perfect competition. This is shown in Figure 17–1.

We assume that commodity X in Figure 17–1 is produced by a competitive industry. The industry supply curve (S) is the horizontal summation (above minimum average variable costs) of the individual firm's marginal (private) cost curves (i.e., $S = \Sigma MPC$). Given market demand curve D for the commodity, the equilibrium price is $12 and the equilibrium quantity is 6 million units per time period (given by the intersection of D and S at point E in the figure). Suppose that the production of commodity X involves rising external costs

FIGURE 17–1   Competitive Overproduction with External Costs

With perfect competition, $P_X = \$12$ and $Q_X = 6$ million units (given by point E at which D and S intersect). S reflects only marginal private costs, while S' equals marginal private (internal) costs plus marginal external costs. Efficiency and Pareto optimality require that $P_X = \$14$ and $Q_X = 4$ million units (given by point E', at which D and S' intersect). This can be achieved with a \$4 per-unit corrective tax on producers that shifts S to S''.

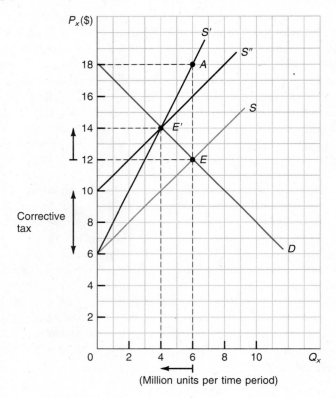

(in the form of air pollution, water pollution, traffic congestion, and so on) that the firms producing commodity X do not take into account. The industry supply curve that includes both the private and external costs might then be given by S' (see the figure). Curve S' shows that the marginal *social* cost (*MSC*) of producing 6 million units of commodity X exceeds the marginal private cost (*MPC*) of \$12 by an amount equal to the marginal external cost (*MEC*) of \$6 (*AE* in the figure).

Thus, efficiency or Pareto optimality requires that $P_X = \$14$ and $Q_X = 4$ million (given by the intersection of D and S' at point E' in the figure). Only then would the commodity price reflect the full social cost of producing it. Starting with S (showing the *MPC*), this could be achieved with a \$4 per-unit corrective tax on producers of commodity X, which shifts S up to S'' and defines equilibrium point E' at the intersection of D and S''.[2] As we will see in the next section, efficiency and Pareto optimality might also be achieved by the proper specification of property rights. Without any such corrective action, the perfectly competitive industry would charge too low a price and produce too much of commodity X (compare point E with E' in the figure).

Efficiency and Pareto optimality are not achieved whenever private and social costs or benefits differ. With external diseconomies of consumption, consumers do not pay the full marginal social cost of the commodity and consume too much of it. Corrective action would then require a tax on consumers rather than on producers. On the other hand, with external economies of production and consumption, the commodity price exceeds the marginal social cost of the commodity so that production and consumption fall short of the optimum level. Efficiency and Pareto optimum in production and in consumption would then require a subsidy (rather than a tax) on producers and on consumers, respectively (see problems 3 and 5, with answers at end of the text). Finally, technical externalities (economies of large-scale production) over a sufficiently large range of outputs lead to the breakdown of competition (natural monopoly). In that case, marginal cost pricing is neither possible nor viable, and Pareto optimum cannot be achieved.

Example 1
The Case for Government Support for Basic Research

Basic research refers to efforts to discover fundamental relationships in nature, such as natural laws. Often, these cannot be patented and do not have immediate commercial applications. It is also practically impossible for the firm that makes a discovery of this nature to take advantage of the full range of commercial applications that might result from its discovery. Thus, the social benefits from basic research greatly exceed private benefits. As a result, there is likely to be underinvestment in basic research by the private sector. Since technological change and innovations are the most important contributors to growth in modern societies, there is a strong case for government support for basic research. Indeed, past government expenditures in basic research, such as for space exploration, laid the foundations of many of today's most productive industries, from aerospace to computers.

The same arguments that apply to firms in a nation apply to nations in the world. That is, the government of a nation may support less than the optimal level of basic research because additions to fundamental knowledge made by

---

[2]However, the marginal external costs created by firms in different areas of the market are likely to be different, so that different corrective per-unit taxes may be required to achieve Pareto optimality. Furthermore, MEC may be constant rather than rising. The corrective tax may also have some unintended side effects that lead to inefficiency (such as the utilization of a less efficient technology).

a nation can easily be utilized by other nations. For example, until recently, Japan stressed the finding of commercial applications for basic discoveries made by other nations, mostly the United States, rather than doing basic research itself. Primarily to overcome this problem, since 1990 the United States has been supporting generic and precompetitive technologies, such as superconductivity, that could have widespread industrial applications but which take many years to develop and commercialize. However, unless American firms improve their ability to bring these new generic technologies to market more rapidly, U.S. international competitiveness will erode no matter how ambitious and far-reaching government technology policy is.

Sources: National Academy of Science, *Basic Research and National Goals* (Washington, D.C.: U.S. Government Printing Office, 1965); The MIT Commission on Industrial Productivity, *Made in America: Regaining the Productive Edge* (Cambridge, Mass.: The MIT Press, 1989), Chapter 5; "Clinton Proposes Changes in Policy to Aid Technology," *New York Times*, February 23, 1993, p. 1; and "When the State Picks Winners," *The Economist*, January 9, 1993, p. 13.

▲

17.2 EXTERNALITIES AND PROPERTY RIGHTS

We have seen in the previous section that externalities, by driving a wedge between private and social costs or benefits, prevent the attainment of economic efficiency and Pareto optimality. But why do externalities arise in some cases and not in others? To see this, suppose that you own a car. You have a clear property right in the car and anyone ruining it is liable for damages. The courts will uphold your right to compensation. In this case there are no externalities. Private and social costs are one and the same thing. Compare this with the case of a firm polluting the air. Neither the firm nor the people living next to the firm own the air. That is, the air is **common property.** Since no resident owns the air, he or she cannot sue the firm for damages resulting from the air pollution generated by the firm. The firm imposes an external (i.e., an uncompensated) cost on the individual. These two simple examples clearly demonstrate that externalities arise when property rights are not adequately specified. In the first case, you have a clear property right to the car and there are no externalities. In the second case, no one owns the air and externalities arise. This leads to the famous Coase theorem.[3]

The **Coase theorem** postulates that when property rights are clearly defined and transaction costs are zero, perfect competition results in the internalization of externalities, regardless of how property rights are assigned among the parties (individuals or firms). For example, suppose that a brewery is located downstream from a paper mill that dumps waste into the stream. Suppose also that in order to filter and purify the water to make beer, the brewery

---

[3]R. R. Coase, "The Problems of Social Cost," *Journal of Law and Economics*, October 1960, pp. 1–44.

incurs a cost of $1,000 per month, while the paper mill would incur a cost of $400 to dispose of its waste products by other means and not pollute the stream. If the brewery has the property right to clean water, the paper mill will incur the added cost of $400 per month to dispose of its waste without polluting the stream (lest the brewery sue it for damages of $1,000 per month). On the other hand, if the paper mill has the property right to the stream and can freely use it to dump its wastes in it, the brewery will pay to the paper mill $400 per month not to pollute the stream (and thus avoid the larger cost of $1,000 to purify the water later).

The cost of avoiding the pollution is *internalized* by the paper mill in the first instance and by the brewery in the second. That is, the $400 cost per month of avoiding the pollution becomes a regular business expense of one party or the other and *no externalities result.* The socially optimal result of **internalizing external costs** and avoiding the pollution at $400 per month, rather than cleaning up afterwards at a cost of $1,000 per month, is achieved regardless of who has the property right to the use of the stream.[4] Thus, externalities are avoided (and economic efficiency and Pareto optimum achieved) under perfect competition, if property rights are clearly defined and transferable, and if transaction costs are zero.[5]

Transaction costs are the legal, administrative, and informational expenses of drawing up, signing, and enforcing contracts. These expenses are small when the contracting parties are few (as in the above example). When the contracting parties are numerous (as in the case of a firm polluting the air for possibly millions of people in the area), it would be practically impossible or very expensive for the firm to sign a separate contract with each individual affected by the pollution it creates. Contracting costs are then very large, and externalities (and inefficiencies) arise. This is especially true in the case of environmental pollution (see section 17.7).[6]

Example 2

Commercial Fishing: Fewer Boats but Exclusive Rights?

As a response to catastrophic overfishing by foreigners during the 1960s, the United States passed the Fisheries Conservation and Management Act of

---

[4]Note that the cost of pollution abatement is minimized rather than entirely eliminated. The only way to completely avoid the cost of pollution is for the paper mill to stop production. But this would result in the greater social cost of the lost production. The above conclusion is also based on the assumption of a zero income effect on the demand curve for the use of the stream regardless of who has the property right of it.

[5]Even if neither the brewery nor the paper mill had a property right to the use of the stream, the conclusion would generally be the same as long as transaction costs are zero. That is, it pays for the brewery to pay the paper mill $400 per month not to pollute. This is equivalent to the paper mill having the right to the use of the stream.

[6]However, the development of class action lawsuits has greatly reduced transaction costs in this area.

1976. The act extended the U.S. exclusive economic (fishing) zone from the traditional 3-mile limit to 200 miles and created eight U.S. regional councils dominated by local fishing interests to distribute exclusive rights to the catch. Economists strongly supported the plan to move from public to private ownership as the best method of preventing overfishing and preserving fisheries for future generations. However, strong disagreement as to who should benefit from the distribution of the rights to the catch (the government, current owners of fishing boats, or fishermen) has so far prevented the privatization plan from being implemented. As a result, the act has only eliminated overfishing by foreigners but not by Americans, so the catches have remained above biologically sustainable limits. Even though a small number of boats could catch the maximum sustainable yield at the lowest possible cost, there remains a strong incentive to overinvest in the industry as long as it is profitable to bring new boats into operation.

At present, the attempt to reduce overfishing takes the form of sharply reducing the length of the fishing seasons. For example, off Alaska, the halibut season consists of only two or three days per year. A far more efficient way to curb overfishing would be to sell private harvesting rights to those who can fish most efficiently or cheaply. Owners of such rights would then have a strong incentive to prevent overfishing or pollution to protect the market value of their rights. Furthermore, if rights to the catch were sold so as to keep individual boats operating at full capacity, three-quarters of the boats could be retired, and this would lead to cost savings exceeding $1 billion per year for the Alaskan fisheries alone. Only part of these cost savings would be sufficient to compensate the owners of the boats to be retired for their loss. Thus, we see how the establishment of property rights would eliminate overfishing, reduce costs, and increase efficiency in U.S. fisheries.

Source: "A Change in Commercial Fishing: Fewer Boats but Exclusive Rights," *New York Times,* April 2, 1991, p. 1.

17.3 PUBLIC GOODS

We have seen in section 16.4 that perfect competition leads to maximum economic efficiency and Pareto optimum in the absence of market failures. One type of market failure results from the existence of public goods. In this section, we examine the nature of public goods and their provision.

Nature of Public Goods

If consumption of a commodity by one individual does not reduce the amount available for others, the commodity is a public good. That is, once the good is provided for someone, others can also consume it at no extra cost. Examples of **public goods** are national defense, law enforcement, fire and police protection, and flood control (provided by the government), but also radio and TV broadcasting (which are provided by the private sector in many nations, including the United States).

The distinguishing characteristic of public goods is **nonrival consumption.** For example, when one individual watches a TV program, he or she does not interfere with the reception of others. This is to be contrasted to private goods, which are rival in consumption, in that if an individual consumes a particular quantity of a good, such as apples, these *same* apples are no longer available for others to consume.

Nonrival consumption must be distinguished for nonexclusion. **Nonexclusion** means that it is impossible or prohibitively expensive to confine the benefits of the consumption of a good (once produced) to selected people (such as only to those paying for it). Whereas nonrival consumption and nonexclusion often go hand in hand, a public good is defined in terms of nonrival consumption only. For example, since national defense and TV broadcasting are nonrival in consumption (i.e., the same amount can be consumed by more than one individual at the same time), they are both public goods. However, national defense also exhibits nonexclusion (i.e., when it is provided for some individuals, others cannot be excluded from also enjoying it free), while TV broadcasting can be exclusive (e.g., only paying customers can view cable TV). We will see in the next section that public goods (i.e., goods that are nonrival in consumption) will not be provided in the optimal amount by the private sector under perfect competition, thus requiring government intervention. First, however, we must determine what is the optimal amount of a public good.

Because a given amount of a public good can be consumed by more than one individual at the same time, the aggregate or total amount of a public good is obtained by the vertical (rather than by the horizontal) summation of the demand curves of the various individuals who consume the public good. This is shown in Figure 17–2. In the figure, D_A is the demand curve of Ann and D_B is the demand curve of Bob for public good X. If Ann and Bob are the only two individuals in the market, the aggregate demand curve for good X, D_T, is obtained by the *vertical* summation of D_A and D_B. The reason for this is that each unit of public good X can be consumed by both individuals at the same time.[7]

Given market supply curve S_X for public good X, the optimal amount of X is eight units per time period (given by the intersection of D_T and S_X at point E in the figure). At point E, the sum of the individuals' marginal benefits or marginal social benefit equals the marginal social cost (i.e., $AB + AC = AE$). Thus, note once again that the marginal principle is at work. The problem is that, in general, less than the optimal amount of public good X will be

---

[7]This is to be contrasted with the *market* demand curve for a private or rival good, which, as we have seen in section 5.1, is obtained from the *horizontal* summation of the individuals' demand curves (see problem 10, with answer at end of the text).

FIGURE 17–2   Optimal Amount of a Public Good

Aggregate demand curve D_T for public good X is obtained by the vertical summation of individual demand curves, D_A and D_B. The reason for this is that each unit of public good X can be consumed by both individuals at the same time. Given market supply curve S_X, the optimal amount of X is eight units per time period (given by the intersection of D_T and S_X at point E). At point E, the sum of the individuals' marginal benefits equals the marginal social costs (i.e., $AB + AC = AE$).

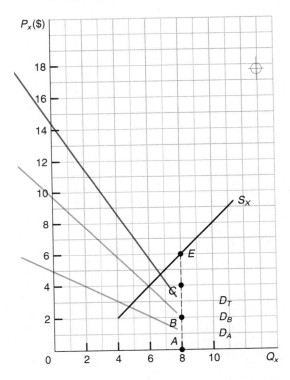

supplied under perfect competition, and this prevents the attainment of maximum efficiency and Pareto optimum.

Example 3
The Economics of a Lighthouse and Other Public Goods

A lighthouse is a good example of a public good. Once a lighthouse is built, it can send signals to ships during storms at practically zero extra cost. That is, lighthouse signals are nonrival in consumption. Lighthouse signals are not exclusive, however, as it was originally believed. That is, each user *can* be charged for the service. Indeed, historical research has shown that lighthouses were privately owned in England from 1700 to 1834, and that they must have been doing a good business because their number increased over the period.

Lighthouse owners charged ships at dock (according to their tonnage) for their land-demarcation light signals during storms. Usually only one ship at a time was in sight of the lighthouse and ships were identified by their flag. If a ship had not paid for the service, the light signals were not shown.

The lighthouse provides an example of a public good that is exclusive (so that users can be charged for the service). A similar public good is education. Entrepreneurs often show great ingenuity in making public goods exclusive. An example is the provision of in-place paying binoculars at Niagara Falls and other scenic sights. Another example is the placing of super-large TV screens in some bars. These and other similar services would not be provided if they were not, or if they could not be made, exclusive (i.e., if consumers could not be charged for them). Other examples of public goods that can be made exclusive are the findings of government-paid basic research. Although any firm can make use of basic-research findings, the specific offshoots or commercial applications of basic research developed by a particular firm can be patented and thus made exclusive.

Sources: Ronald R. Coase, "The Lighthouse in Economics," *Journal of Law and Economics*, October 1974, pp. 357–376, and "Vast Sums for New Discoveries Pose Threat to Basic Science," *New York Times*, May 27, 1990, p. 1.

▲

Provision of Public Goods

We have seen that the optimal amount of a public good is that at which the sum of the marginal benefits of all the individuals consuming the good equals its marginal cost. Graphically, this is given by the point at which the aggregate demand curve for the good (obtained from the vertical summation of the individuals' demand curves) intersects the market supply curve of the good. However, less than this optimal amount of the public good is likely to be supplied by the private sector.

There are two related reasons for this. First, when the public good is nonexclusive (i.e., when those individuals not paying for it cannot be excluded from also consuming it), there is a tendency for each consumer to be a free rider. A **free-rider problem** arises because each consumer believes that the public good will be provided anyway, whether he or she contributes to its payment or not. That is, because there are many people sharing the cost of providing the public good, each individual feels that withdrawing his or her financial support will practically go unnoticed by others and will have little or no effect on the provision of the good. The problem is that since many individuals behave this way (i.e., behave as free riders), less than the optimal amount of the public good will be provided.[8] In general, as the group size

---

[8]Note that even a private (rival) good leads to market failure if it is characterized by nonexclusion (i.e., if each individual consuming it cannot be adequately charged for it).

increases, the free-rider problem becomes more acute. This problem can be and generally is overcome by the government taxing the general public to pay for the public good. A good example of this is national defense.[9]

The second (related) problem cannot be resolved as satisfactorily by government intervention. This arises because each individual has no incentive to accurately reveal his or her preferences or demand for the public good. Therefore, it is practically impossible for the government to know exactly what is the optimal amount of the public good that it should provide or induce the private sector to provide. Then there is the problem of possible government inefficiency in providing public goods and in otherwise intervening in the market (see section 17.5).

17.4 BENEFIT-COST ANALYSIS

Governments play many roles in modern societies. These range from the provision of public goods, to the redistribution of income, the regulation of monopoly, and pollution control. In carrying out these functions, government agencies must constantly decide which projects to implement and which to reject. A useful procedure for determining which are the most worthwhile projects is **benefit-cost analysis.** This compares the present value of the benefits to the present value of the costs of a project. Government should carry out a project only if the present value of the social benefits from the project exceeds the present value of its social costs (i.e., if the benefit-cost ratio for the project exceeds 1). Often, the government does not have the resources (i.e., cannot raise taxes or borrow sufficiently) to undertake all the projects with a benefit-cost ratio exceeding 1. In such cases, government should rank all possible projects from the highest to the lowest (but exceeding 1) benefit-cost ratio, and starting at the top of the list, it should undertake all projects until its resources are fully utilized.

Although this sounds straightforward, a number of serious difficulties arise in the actual application of benefit-cost analysis, because it is often very difficult to correctly estimate the social benefits and the social costs of a project and determine the appropriate rate of interest to use to calculate the present value of benefits and costs. First, since the benefits and the costs of most public projects (such as a dam, a highway, a training program, and so on) take place over many years, it is difficult to estimate them correctly so far into the future.

Second, benefits and costs are frequently estimated on the basis of current or projected prices, even though these prices may not reflect the true scarcity value or opportunity cost of the outputs resulting from or the inputs used in the project. For example, commodity prices under imperfectly competitive

---

[9]Sometimes a free-rider problem can partially be resolved by the private sector. Examples are educational television stations, tenants' associations, and charitable associations such as the Salvation Army.

commodity markets exceed their marginal cost. Similarly, if a project results in the employment of otherwise unemployed labor, the real cost of hiring labor is zero, in spite of the positive wage paid to these workers. In other words, it is the real or opportunity value of the benefits and costs of the project that should be used in benefit-cost analysis. But it may be difficult to estimate them. Real costs may also rise as the project increases the demand for inputs.

Third, some of the benefits and costs of a project may not be quantifiable. For example, while it may be possible to estimate the rise in workers' income resulting from a training program, it is next to impossible to assign a value to their enhanced self-esteem and to their becoming more responsible citizens. Similarly, it is practically impossible to assign a value to the loss of scenery resulting from the construction of a dam. Yet, all of these social benefits and costs should be included in benefit-cost analysis for it to lead to correct public investment decisions.

Fourth, and perhaps the most serious difficulty with benefit-cost analysis, arises in the choice of the proper interest rate to be used to find the present value of the benefits and costs of the project. That is, since the benefits and costs of most projects occur over a number of years, they must be discounted to the present. For this a rate of interest must be used, as indicated in section 15.3.[10] The question is *which* is the proper interest rate to use? As indicated in section 15.4, there are a large number of rates of interest in the market (ranging from nearly zero to 40%) depending on the risk, duration, cost of administering, and the tax treatment of the loan. Since the use of resources by the government competes with their private use, the interest (discount) rate to be used to find present values should reflect the opportunity cost of funds for a project of similar riskiness, duration, and administrative costs in the private sector. However, because different people may come up with a different rate of interest to use, benefit-cost analysis is usually prepared for a range of interest rates (from a low, to a medium, and a high one) rather than for a single interest rate. The lower the interest rate (or range of interest rates) used, the higher the benefit-cost ratio usually is and the greater the likelihood of the project being undertaken. The reason for this is that the benefits of a project usually arise later or over a longer period of time than its costs.

In spite of the great difficulties inherent in benefit-cost analysis, it is nevertheless a very valuable procedure for organizing our thoughts on the social benefits and the social costs of each project. If nothing else, it forces government officials to make explicit all the assumptions underlying the analysis. Scrutiny of the assumptions has sometimes led to decision reversals. For

---

[10]In section 15.3 we showed how to find the present value of a project. For benefit-cost analysis we need to find the present value of the benefits and costs of the project *separately*. The procedure, however, is the same. Note that a positive present value for a project is equivalent to a greater-than-one benefit-cost ratio.

example, in 1971, the Federal Power Commission (now the Federal Energy Regulatory Commission) approved the construction of a hydroelectric dam on the Snake river, which flows from Oregon to Idaho and forms Hell's Canyon (the deepest in North America). The decision was based on a benefit-cost analysis that ignored some environmental costs. Because of that, the Supreme Court, on appeal from the secretary of the interior, revoked the order to build the dam pending a new benefit-cost analysis that properly included *all* benefits and costs. Finally, Congress passed a law prohibiting the construction of the dam.[11]

Although benefit-cost analysis is still more of an art than a science and is somewhat subjective, its usefulness has been proven in a wide variety of projects—water, transportation, health, education, and recreational. In fact, in 1965, the federal government formally began to introduce benefit-cost analysis for its budgetary procedures under the Planning-Programming-Budgeting System (PPBS). The practice has now spread to state and local governments as well.

Example 4
Benefit-Cost Analysis and the SST

Based on benefit-cost analysis, the development of a supersonic transport plane (SST) was abandoned by the United States in 1971. The benefits were simply not sufficient to justify the costs. However, the British and French governments jointly continued to pursue the project and build the Concorde at a huge cost. Today, there are only a handful of such planes operated exclusively by the British and French national airlines. With operating costs more than four times higher than the Boeing 747, the Concorde must be classified as a clear market failure and would not fly without heavy government subsidies. Specifically, a one-way seat from New York to London or Paris on the Concorde would have to be priced at over $4,000 (as compared with less than $1,000 on the Boeing 747) for the Concorde to break even. This means that the passenger would be paying about $1,000 for each of the three hours saved in flying on the Concorde. We may all be hurried today but not that hurried! As it is, the British and French governments subsidize about half of the operating costs of the Concorde. Still, business is not brisk for the Concorde.

It seems that in their benefit-cost analysis, the British and French greatly overestimated the benefits arising from building and operating the Concorde and grossly underestimated costs. This only points to how imprecise benefit-cost analysis can sometimes be. The question is why do the British and the

[11]J. V. Krutilla and A. C. Fisher, *The Economics of Natural Environments: Studies in the Valuation of Commodity and Amenity Resources* (Baltimore: The Johns Hopkins University Press, 1975), pp. 101–103.

French governments continue to heavily subsidize flying the Concorde now, thereby "throwing good money after bad." The answer may be national pride in being the only two nations flying a supersonic passenger plane. If that is true, it only points to how expensive national pride can be.

In fact, despite the economic failure of the Concorde, the French and the British are now talking of building the "Son of the Concorde" to fly early in the next century at a speed of 1,700 MPH, as compared with 1,350 MPH for the Concorde; with a passenger capacity of more than 200, or twice that of the Concorde; and with much more fuel-efficient engines. It will be interesting to see how the Son of the Concorde will be justified on a benefit-cost basis, if the French and the British decide to go ahead with the project, and then how the outcome of the project compares with the projected outcome. Not to be outdone in this competitive round, the United States has talked about building a space plane at a cost of more than $4 billion. The plane would carry passengers from Washington to Tokyo in 2 hours instead of the present 14 hours. Although this ambitious government project was quietly shelved—a victim of the U.S. budget deficit—Boeing is trying to organize a far-reaching international partnership to develop a 600- to 800-seat super-jumbo jet at a cost of $10 to $15 billion to be ready for delivery early next century.

Sources: "The Concorde's Destination," *New York Times*, September 28, 1979, p. 26; "Son of the Concorde Planned by the French," *New York Times*, January 22, 1986, p. D1; "Space Plane Gets a Go from Reagan," *U.S. News & World Report*, February 17, 1986, pp. 65–66; "A Partnership at Home for a Hypersonic Plane," *New York Times*, March 15, 1992, Section 3, p. 1; and "Boeing Launches a Stealth Attack on Airbus," *Business Week*, January 18, 1993, p. 32.

▲

17.5   THE THEORY OF PUBLIC CHOICE

In this section, we examine the meaning, importance, and policy implications of public-choice theory. Specifically, we explore the process by which government decisions are made and the reasons that they might not increase social welfare.

Meaning and Importance of Public-Choice Theory

The **theory of public choice** is the study of how government decisions are made and implemented. It studies how the political process and government *actually* work rather than how they should work, and it recognizes the possibility of **government failures** or situations in which government policies do not reflect the public's interests and reduce rather than increase social welfare. The fact that markets do not operate efficiently does not necessarily mean that government policies will improve the situation; it is always possible that government intervention will make a bad situation worse. The opposite situation is also invalid. That is, the fact that government policies are inefficient does not necessarily mean that private markets can do better. For example, great waste in government defense expenditures does not mean that the provision of national defense can be left to private markets.

The theory of public choice is based on the premise that individuals attempt to further their own personal interests in the political arena just as they seek to further their own economic interests in the marketplace. According to the law of the invisible hand postulated by Adam Smith over two centuries ago, an individual who pursues his or her own selfish economic interests also and at the same time promotes the welfare of society as a whole. This was the basis for favoring and stimulating competition in the marketplace. The theory of public choice seeks to answer the question of whether such an invisible hand mechanism is also at work in the political system. That is, as each individual attempts to further his or her own interests in political activities, is he or she also and at the same time promoting society's welfare?

The Public-Choice Process

The theory of public choice examines how government decisions are made and implemented by analyzing the behavior of individuals within each of four broad groups or participants in the political process. These are voters, politicians, special-interest groups, and bureaucrats. Let us examine each in turn.

Voters   The voter in the political process can be regarded as the counterpart of the consumer in the marketplace. Rather than purchasing goods and services for himself or herself in the marketplace, the voter elects government representatives who make and enforce government policies and purchase goods and services for the community as a whole. Other things being equal, voters tend to vote for candidates who favor policies that will further their own individual interests. This is, in fact, the general process by which elected officials are responsive to the electorate.

According to public-choice theorists, however, voters are much less informed about political decisions than about their individual market decisions. This is often referred to as **rational ignorance.** There are three reasons for this. First, with elected officials empowered to act as the purchasing agents for the community, there is less need for individual voters to be fully informed about public choices. Second, it is generally much more expensive for individuals to gather information about public choices than about individual market choices. For example, it is much more difficult for an individual to evaluate the full implications of a proposed national health insurance plan than to evaluate the implications of an individual insurance policy. Third, as a single individual, a voter feels—and, indeed, *is*—less influential in and less affected by public choices than by his or her own private market choices.

Politicians   Politicians are the counterpart in the political system of the entrepreneurs or managers of private firms in the market system. They both seek to maximize their personal benefit. While the entrepreneur or manager of a private firm seeks to maximize his or her interest by maximizing the firm's profits, the politician seeks to maximize chances of reelection. In doing so, politicians often respond to the desires of small, well-organized, well-informed, and well-funded special interest groups. These include associations of farmers, importers, medical doctors, and many others. Faced with rational ignorance on the part of the majority of voters, politicians often support policies that greatly benefit small, vocal interest groups (who can contribute heavily to a candidate's reelection campaign) at the expense of the mostly silent and uninformed majority.

For example, in the early 1980s, U.S. automobile manufacturers were able to greatly increase their profits by having the U.S. government restrict auto imports from Japan (see the example in section 12.7). The fact that politicians face reelection every few years also leads politicians to pay undue attention to the short run, even when this leads to more serious long-run problems. For example, public policies are often adopted to reduce the rate of unemployment at election time in November, even though this might lead to higher inflation later. This has led some to postulate the existence of a "political business cycle."

Special-Interest Groups Perhaps the most maligned of the groups participating in the political process are special-interest groups. These pressure groups or organized lobbies seek to elect politicians who support their cause, and they actively support the passage of laws and regulations that they seek. For example, the American Medical Association for decades succeeded in limiting admissions to medical schools, thereby increasing doctors' incomes; farmers' associations successfully lobbied the government to provide billions of dollars in subsidies each year; as pointed out earlier, U.S. automakers succeeded in having auto imports from Japan restricted in the early 1980s, thereby greatly increasing their profits. Even though not all lobbies are as successful as these, thousands are in operation, and this, according to many, represents the worst aspects of our political system.[12]

The reason for the great influence of some of these special-interest groups is that they are well organized and stand to benefit a great deal when their efforts are successful. Thus, they are very vocal and often can provide millions of dollars in financial support to politicians who advocate their cause. At the same time, most people are usually not aware of the losses (usually small) that they individually face from these laws and regulations. Furthermore, these laws and regulations are invariably rationalized in terms of the national interest. For example, import restrictions on shoes might only increase the price of shoes by $1 per pair while providing millions of dollars in extra profits to the few remaining shoe manufacturers in the nation. Supposedly, these

[12]In recent years, lobbying in Washington by foreign firms and nations (especially Japan) has increased sharply.

import restrictions are temporary and are essential to give time to American producers to increase efficiency and be able to meet what is regarded as unfair foreign competition.

Bureaucrats Bureaus are the government agencies that carry out the policies enacted by Congress. They do so by receiving annual lump-sum appropriations to cover the cost of providing the services that they are directed to provide. Bureaus often provide these services under conditions of monopoly (i.e., without any competition from other bureaus or private firms) and so have little incentive to promote internal efficiency. While it is difficult to compare the efficiency of government bureaus and private firms, there have been spectacular cost overruns in many defense projects. For example, the cost of the Lockheed C5A transport plane increased from an estimated $3.4 billion in 1965 to $5.3 billion in 1968.

According to public-choice theory, bureaucrats are not simply passive executors of adopted policies, but they seek to influence such policies in order to further their own personal interests. They do so by constantly seeking to increase the scope of the bureau's activities and the amount of funding, even when the raison d'etre for the bureau no longer exists. This is due to the fact that a top bureaucrat's career, income, power, prestige, and promotion are, in general, closely related to the size and growth of the bureau. In essence, the bureau often becomes a separate special-interest group within the government!

Policy Implications of Public-Choice Theory

The above characterization of the political process by public-choice theorists is, perhaps, excessively cynical. Voters elect only politicians who promote their individual interests, and are mostly ignorant and indifferent about most other public choices; politicians only seek to maximize their chances of reelection; special-interest groups only seek special advantages at the expense of the mostly silent and ignorant majority; and bureaucrats only seek to maximize their own interests by promoting the bureau's growth at the expense of efficiency.

Although there is some truth in all of this, we must also point out that many voters are well informed and often unselfish; many politicians have refused to compromise their principles simply to maximize their chances of reelection; many powerful special-interest groups have been unsuccessful in furthering their causes; and many bureaucracies have operated efficiently and sometimes even proposed their own abolition when their function was no longer required. For example, the majority of voters consistently vote for and support most social welfare policies, even though these involve a redistribution of income to poor people; President Reagan refused to back away from large defense spending in spite of strong opposition in and out of Congress and the resulting huge budget deficits; the American Medical Association is no longer able to restrict admissions to medical schools as it did over many decades; and the CAB (the Civil Aeronautics Board) proposed its own abolition and is now no longer in existence.

These examples, however, do not necessarily represent contradictions of the theory of public choice. This theory seeks only to identify the forces that must be examined to properly analyze public choices. It reaches the conclusion that while public policies can improve the functioning of the economic system in the presence of market failures, the government itself is subject to systematic forces that can lead to government failures. Public policies could then reduce, rather than increase, social welfare. More important, perhaps, the theory of public choice can be used to suggest specific institutional changes and to devise policies that can lead to improvements in public-sector performance.

One way that public-choice theory suggests for improving public-sector performance is to subject government bureaus or agencies to competition whenever feasible. One method of achieving this is by contracting out to private firms as many public services as possible. For example, market evidence suggests that garbage collection and fire protection can be provided more efficiently by private contractors than by public agencies. Another method advocated by public-choice theory to promote efficiency in public choices is to allow private firms to compete with government agencies in the provision of services that are not entirely public in nature.[13] For example, families could be provided with vouchers that they could use for public or private education. This would stimulate public schools to provide better education and increase efficiency. Still another method of increasing efficiency in government is to encourage interagency competition. While streamlining government operations is likely to eliminate some duplication and waste, it also eliminates competition and incentives for efficient operation. For example, it has been estimated that the cost-effectiveness of the Department of Defense operations declined by one-third following the consolidation of the three branches of the armed forces within the department.

Public-choice theory also suggests at least two ways of reducing the influence of special-interest groups. One would be to rely more on referenda to decide important political issues. Although the influence of special-interest groups is not entirely eliminated (since they can still spend a great deal of money on influencing the general public through advertisements), reverting from representative to direct democracy in deciding some important issues does overcome the interaction between special-interest groups and politicians. Today, referenda are much more common in European countries than in the United States. Another method of reducing the influence of special-interest groups is to specify the total amount of public funds budgeted for the year and encourage different groups to compete for government funding. Because the total amount of funds is fixed, one group can only gain at the expense of

---

[13]See, "Public Services Are Found Better if Private Agencies Compete," *New York Times*, April 28, 1988, p. 1.

others. Each group is then likely to present its best case for funding while exposing the weaknesses in competitors' funding requests. In the process, a great deal of essential information is made available to government officials, who can therefore allocate funds more effectively. Many policies (such as import restrictions), however, do not involve direct public funding, and so this is not possible.

17.6 STRATEGIC TRADE POLICY

One qualified argument in favor of an activist government policy in the international arena is **strategic trade policy.** According to this argument, a nation can create a comparative advantage (through temporary trade protection, subsidies, tax benefits, and cooperative government-industry programs) in such fields as semiconductors, computers, telecommunications, and other industries that are deemed crucial to future growth in the nation. These high-tech industries are subject to high risks, require large-scale production to achieve economies of scale, and give rise to extensive external economies when successful. Strategic trade policy suggests that by encouraging such industries, the nation can reap the large external economies that result from them and enhance its future growth prospects. Most nations do some of this. Indeed, some economists would go so far as to say that a great deal of the post-World War II industrial and technological success of Japan is due to its strategic industrial and trade policies.

Examples of strategic trade and industrial policies are in the steel industry in the 1950s and in semiconductors in the 1970s and 1980s in Japan, and in the development of the supersonic aircraft, the Concorde, in the 1970s (see Example 4) and the Airbus aircraft in the 1980s in Europe. Semiconductors in Japan are usually given as the textbook case of successful strategic trade and industrial policy. The market for semiconductors (such as computer chips that are used in many products) was dominated by the United States in the 1970s. Starting in the mid-1970s, Japan's powerful Ministry of International Trade and Industry targeted the development of this industry by financing research and development, granting tax advantages for investments in the industry, and fostering government-industry cooperation, while protecting the domestic market from foreign (especially U.S.) competition.

These policies are credited for Japan's success in wresting control of the semiconductor market from the United States in the mid-1980s and dominating world markets thereafter. Most economists remain skeptical, however, and attribute Japan's stunning performance in this field primarily to other forces, such as greater educational emphasis on science and mathematics, higher rates of investment, and a willingness to take a long-run view of investments rather than stressing quarterly profits as is done in the United States. In steel, the other targeted industry in Japan, the rate of return was lower than the average return for all Japanese industries during the postwar period. In Europe, the Concorde was a technological feat but a commercial disaster, and

Airbus Industrie would not survive without continued heavy government subsidies.

While strategic trade policy can theoretically improve the market outcome in oligopolistic markets subject to extensive external economies and increase the nation's growth and welfare, even the originators and popularizers of this theory recognize the serious difficulties in carrying it out. First, it is extremely difficult to pick winners (i.e., choose the industries that will provide large external economies in the future) and devise appropriate policies to successfully nurture them. Second, since most leading nations undertake strategic trade policies at the same time, their efforts are largely neutralized, so that the potential benefits to each may be small. Third, when a country does achieve substantial success with strategic trade policy, this comes at the expense of other countries (i.e., it is a beggar-thy-neighbor policy), and so other countries are likely to retaliate. Faced with all these practical difficulties, even supporters of strategic trade policy grudgingly acknowledge that *free trade is still the best policy, after all.*

17.7 GOVERNMENT CONTROL AND REGULATION OF ENVIRONMENTAL POLLUTION

Now let us use the tools of analysis developed in this chapter to analyze environmental pollution and the best way for government to control or regulate it.

Environmental Pollution

We have seen in section 17.2 that externalities (and inefficiencies) may be eliminated by the clear definition of property rights if the parties involved are not very numerous. Otherwise, transaction costs are too high and externalities persist. This is precisely the case with **environmental pollution**, which refers to air pollution, water pollution, thermal pollution, pollution resulting from garbage disposal, and so on. Environmental pollution has become one of the major political and economic issues in recent decades. Environmental pollution results from and is an example of negative externalities.[14]

Air pollution results mostly from automobile exhaust and smoke from factories and electrical generating plants through the combustion of fossil fuels, which release particles into the air. While it is difficult to measure precisely the harmful effects of sulfur dioxide, carbon monoxide, and other air pollutants, they are known to create damage to health (in the form of breathing illnesses and aggravating other diseases, such as circulatory problems) and

---

[14]See, "Priority One: Rescue the Environment," *Science*, February 16, 1990, p. 777, and M. L. Cropper and W. Oates, "Environmental Economics: A Survey," *Journal of Economic Literature*, June 1992, pp. 675–740.

to property (in the form of higher cleaning bills, and so on). *Water pollution* results from the dumping into streams, lakes, and seashores of raw (untreated) sewage, chemical waste products from factories and mines, and runoff of pesticides and fertilizers from farms. This reduces the supply of clean water for household uses (drinking, bathing, and so on) and recreational uses (swimming, boating, fishing, and so on). *Thermal pollution* results from the cooling off of electrical power plants and other machinery. This increases water temperature and kills fish. The disposal of garbage such as beer cans, newspapers, cigarette butts, and so on, spoils the natural scenery, as do billboards and posters. To this visual pollution must be added noise pollution and many others.

Environmental pollution results whenever the environment is used (abused) as a convenient and cheap dumping ground for all types of waste products. It is convenient and cheap from the private point of view to use the environment in this manner because no one owns property rights to it. As a result, air and water users pay less than the full social cost of using these natural resources, and by so doing they impose serious external costs on society. In short, society produces and consumes too much of products that generate environmental pollution. Since property rights are ambiguous and the parties involved are numerous (often running into the millions), it is impossible or impractical (too costly) to identify and negotiate with individual agents. The external costs of environmental pollution cannot be internalized by the assignment of clear property rights and so government intervention is required. This can take the form of regulation or taxation. However, appropriate corrective action on the part of the government requires knowledge of the exact cost of pollution.

Optimal Pollution Control

If one asked a stout environmentalist how much environmental pollution society should tolerate, his or her answer would probably be zero. This would be the wrong answer. The optimal level of pollution is the level at which the marginal social cost of pollution equals the marginal social benefit (in the form of avoiding alternative and more expensive methods of waste disposal). Zero pollution is an ideal situation, but as long as pollution is the inevitable byproduct of the production and consumption of commodities that we want, it is downright silly to advocate zero pollution. Economists advocate optimal pollution control instead. That is, we should be prepared to accept (as inevitable) that amount of pollution which, at the margin, just balances the social costs and benefits of pollution. This is shown in Figure 17–3.

In Figure 17–3, the horizontal axis measures the quantity of pollution per year, and the vertical axis measures costs and gains in dollars. The *MC* curve, for example, could measure the value of the marginal loss of fish suffered by fishermen for various amounts of water pollution generated by a firm. The marginal loss (cost) increases with rising amounts of pollution. The *MB* curve would then measure the marginal benefit or saving that the firm that pollutes the water receives by being able to freely dump its waste into the water rather

FIGURE 17–3   Optimal Pollution Control

The *MC* curve shows the rising marginal cost or loss to society from increasing amounts of pollution. The *MB* curve shows the declining marginal benefit to the polluter (and to society) by being able to freely dump increasing amounts of waste into the water rather than disposing of it by other costly alternatives. Since the firm does not pay for discharging its waste into the water, it will do so until *MB* = 0 (point *A*). From society's point of view, the optimal level of pollution for the firm is eight units per year (point *E*, at which *MC* = *MB*).

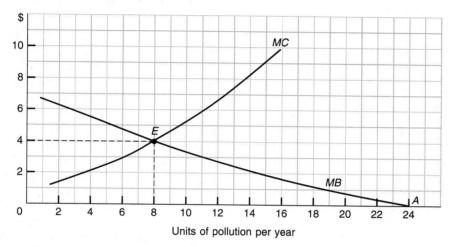

Units of pollution per year

than disposing of it by the next-best alternative method (at a positive cost). The *MB* is negatively sloped, indicating declining benefits for the firm for each additional unit of pollution that it discharges into the water.

When the firm does not incur any cost for discharging waste into the water, it will do so until the marginal benefit is zero (point *A* in the figure). That is, as long as the firm saves some cost by discharging its waste into the water, it will do so until the *MB* is zero. However, pollution does impose a cost on society as a whole. The optimal amount of pollution from society's point of view is eight units, given by the intersection of the *MC* and the *MB* curves at point *E*. Only when pollution is eight units per year is the marginal benefit to the individual and to society equal to the marginal social cost of pollution. To the left of point *E*, *MB* > *MC* and it pays for society to increase the level of pollution (see the figure). The opposite is true to the right of point *E*. As strange as it might have sounded earlier, we now know that the optimal level of pollution is not zero, but it is positive.

Direct Regulation and Effluent Fees for Optimal Pollution Control

We have just seen that the optimal level of pollution from society's point of view is not zero, but it is given by the level at which the marginal cost of pollution is equal to the private (and social) marginal benefit of disposing of waste by the cheapest method possible. Even though this prescription is theoretically precise, it is often very difficult to actually estimate the marginal social costs and benefits of pollution. Without government intervention, environmental pollution is certainly likely to be excessive (compare point *A* to point *E* in Figure 17–3).

There are generally two ways to achieve the optimal amount of pollution control: direct regulation and effluent fees. By direct regulation, government could legislate that the industry must limit pollution to the optimal level (eight units per year in Figure 17–3) or install a particular pollution-abatement device. Alternatively, government could set the **effluent fee** that brings the private cost of pollution equal to its social cost. An effluent fee is a tax that a firm must pay to the government for discharging waste or otherwise polluting. For example, an effluent fee of $4 per unit of waste or pollution per year in Figure 17–3 results in the optimal level of pollution of eight units per year. That is, an effluent fee of $4 per unit will make the marginal private (and social) cost of pollution equal to its marginal private (and social) benefit.

While direct regulation is sometimes necessary (as in the case of radioactive and other very dangerous waste materials), economists generally prefer effluent fees to achieve optimal pollution control. There are two reasons for this. First, effluent fees generally require less information on the part of the government than direct regulation. Secondly, and more importantly, effluent fees minimize the cost of optimal pollution control, whereas direct regulation does not. This is so because with effluent fees, each polluter will pollute until the marginal benefit of pollution equals the effluent fee. Thus, the optimal amount of pollution is allocated to those firms that benefit the most from polluting. As a result, the social cost of pollution is minimized.

The 1990 amendments to the Clean Air Act called for a 50% reduction in sulfur emissions from power plants (a major source of air pollution in the United States today) and the establishment of a market for pollution permits.[15] A plant that generates less emission than granted could then sell the extra permits to pollute to a plant that generates more pollution than permitted. Plants facing lower marginal costs of reducing emissions would then make greater reductions in emissions and sell the permit for the extra pollution to plants facing greater marginal costs. The process would continue until the marginal cost of reducing emissions is the same for both types of plants. The allowed level of pollution would then be achieved at the lowest cost to society.

This is to be contrasted to the traditional approach under which the Environmental Protection Agency (EPA) specifies the amount of pollution a plant can emit, and often, even the technology that must be used to attain that level.

---

[15]"Bush Signs Major Revision of the Anti-Pollution Law," *New York Times*, November 16, 1990, p. 28; "New Rules Harness Power of Free Markets to Curb Air Pollution," *Wall Street Journal*, April 4, 1992, p. A1, and "Sold: $21 Million of Air Pollution," *New York Times*, March 30, 1993, p. D22.

It has been estimated that the market system would lead to savings ranging from 50% to 90% in the cost of reducing pollution to a specified level from the cost under the present "command" system.[16] The establishment of a market for pollution permits represents a significant victory for economists (who have been advocating this for many years) and changes the direction of antipollution efforts in the United States for decades to come. Indeed, in 1992, the United Nations proposed the establishment of an international market where *nations* could purchase or sell pollution permits or credits in order to cut the cost of reducing the greenhouse effect and resulting global warming.[17]

SUMMARY

1. Externalities are harmful or beneficial side effects borne by those not directly involved in the production or consumption of a commodity. Externalities are classified into external economies or diseconomies of production or consumption, and technical externalities. With external diseconomies of production or consumption, the commodity price falls short of the full social cost of the commodity and too much of the commodity is produced or consumed. With external economies of production or consumption, the commodity price exceeds the full social cost of the commodity and too little of the commodity is produced and consumed. Technical externalities may prevent marginal cost pricing.

2. Externalities arise when property rights are not clearly defined and transaction costs are very high. The Coase theorem postulates that when property rights are clearly defined and transaction costs are zero, perfect competition results in the absence of externalities, regardless of how property rights are assigned among the parties involved.

3. Public goods are commodities that are nonrival in consumption. That is, consumption of a public good by some individual does not reduce the amount available for others (at zero marginal cost). Some public goods, such as national defense, exhibit nonexclusion. That is, once the good is produced, it is impossible to confine its use to only those paying for it. Other public goods, such as TV broadcasting, can exhibit exclusion. Because of the free-rider problem, public goods are usually underproduced and underconsumed.

4. Benefit-cost analysis is based on the government calculating the ratio of the present value of all the benefits to the present value of all the costs for each proposed public project. The projects are then ranked from the highest to the lowest in terms of benefit-cost ratios. Government should undertake those projects with the highest benefit-cost ratio (as long as that ratio exceeds 1) and until government resources are fully employed. There are many difficulties in estimating all benefits and costs of a project and in determining the interest

---

[16]"Cheapest Protection of Nature May Lie in Taxes, Not Laws," *New York Times*, November 24, 1992, p. C1 and "Road Pricing: The Solution to Highway Congestion," *The Margin*, Spring 1993, p. 30.

[17]"Global Market for Pollution Rights Proposed by the U.N.," *Wall Street Journal*, January 30, 1992, p. C1.

rate to use to find the present value of the benefits and costs.

5. According to the theory of public choice, individuals vote for politicians who promote their individual interests; politicians seek to maximize their chances of reelection; special-interest groups seek special advantages for the group; and bureaucrats seek to promote the bureau's growth. The theory postulates that it is possible for government policies to reduce rather than increase social welfare (government failures). It proposes to increase efficiency by increasing competition in public choices and relying more on referenda to decide important issues.

6. According to strategic trade policy, a nation can create a comparative advantage (through temporary trade protection, subsidies, tax benefits, etc.) in such fields as computers, that can give rise to extensive external economies, and which are deemed crucial to future growth in the nation. However, it is very difficult to determine which industry to promote, and other nations are likely to retaliate.

7. Environmental (air, water, thermal, scenic, and noise) pollution arises because of unclearly defined property rights and too-high transaction costs. The optimal level of pollution from society's point of view is not zero, but is given by the level at which the marginal cost of pollution to society is equal to the private (and social) marginal benefit of disposing of waste by the cheapest method available. Optimal pollution control can be achieved by direct regulation or effluent fees. Although direct regulation is sometimes necessary (as in the case of dangerous waste materials), economists generally prefer effluent fees and the establishment of a market for pollution permits because they are much more efficient.

KEY TERMS

Externalities
External Costs
External Benefits
External Diseconomies of Production
External Diseconomies of Consumption
External Economies of Production

External Economies of Consumption
Technical Externalities
Common Property
Coase Theorem
Internalizing External Costs
Public Goods
Nonrival Consumption
Nonexclusion

Free-Rider Problem
Benefit-Cost Analysis
Theory of Public Choice
Government Failures
Rational Ignorance
Strategic Trade Policy
Environmental Pollution
Effluent Fee

REVIEW QUESTIONS

1. How can typing a report late at night create a negative externality? How can this result in an externality that is mutually harmful?
2. Why is a public-housing project in a high-income neighborhood not likely to satisfy the Pareto optimality criterion?
3. Why does free access to a common resource usually lead to the overuse of the resource?
4. Why during the Cold War period did the knowledge that the United States would not have accepted a Soviet invasion of Europe lead to less defense expenditures in Western Europe?
5. What is the basic difference between using a subsidy to induce producers to install antipollution equipment and a tax on producers who pollute?
6. How does the market demand for a public good

differ from the market demand of a private good?

7. Why is it generally more difficult to estimate the benefits and the costs of a public than of a private project?

8. Everyone agrees that large federal budget deficits are bad. Why do budget deficits then persist?

9. What is the unifying concept by which public-choice theory analyzes individual behavior in the political process?

10. What policies does the theory of public choice prescribe (a) in order to increase efficiency in public choices and reduce government failures and (b) to reduce the influence of special-interest groups?

11. Is there a conflict between the theory of comparative advantage and strategic trade policy?

12. When would direct regulation be better than effluent fees in pollution control?

PROBLEMS

1. Explain why
   a. in a system of private education (i.e., a system in which individuals pay for their own education), there is likely to be underinvestment in education.
   b. the discussion of external economies and diseconomies is in terms of marginal rather than total social costs and benefits.

2. Start with D and S as in Figure 17–1.
   a. Draw D' with the same vertical intercept as D but with twice the absolute value of its slope. Suppose that D' portrays the marginal social benefit of the public consuming various quantities of the commodity.
   b. Does D' indicate the existence of external economies of production or consumption?
   c. What is the marginal external benefit or cost and the marginal social benefit or cost at the competitive equilibrium point?
   d. What is the socially optimal price and consumption of the commodity?

*3. a. Draw a figure showing the corrective tax or subsidy that would induce society to consume the socially optimum amount of the commodity.
   b. What is the total value of the economic gain resulting from the imposition of the corrective tax or subsidy?

4. Start with D and S as in Figure 17–1.
   a. Draw S' with the same vertical intercept as S but with half of its slope. Suppose that S' portrays the marginal *social* costs of supplying various quantities of the commodity.
   b. Does S' indicate the existence of external

economies or diseconomies of production or consumption?
   c. What is the marginal external cost or benefit and the marginal social cost at the competitive equilibrium point?
   d. What is the socially optimum price and output of the commodity?

*5. a. Draw a figure showing the corrective tax or subsidy that would induce the industry to produce the socially optimal amount of the commodity.
   b. What is the total value of the economic inefficiency eliminated by the corrective tax or subsidy?

6. Start with D and S as in Figure 17–1.
   a. Draw D' with the same vertical intercept as D but with half the absolute value of its slope. Suppose that D' portrays the marginal social benefit of the public consuming various quantities of the commodity.
   b. Does D' indicate the existence of external economies or diseconomies of production or consumption?
   c. What is the marginal external benefit or cost and the marginal social benefit or cost at the equilibrium point?
   d. What is the socially optimum price and consumption of the commodity?

7. a. Draw a figure showing the corrective tax or subsidy that would induce the society to consume the socially optimal amount of the commodity.

---

* = Answer provided at end of book.

b. What is the total value of the economic gain resulting from the imposition of the corrective tax or subsidy?

8. Explain what would be the outcome if the cost of avoiding polluting the stream (with its waste products) by the paper mill of section 17.2 was $1,200 rather than $400 per month, and property rights to the stream were assigned to the
   a. brewery.
   b. paper mill.
   c. When would the socially optimal solution be reached?

*9. Explain why in each of the following cases, externalities arise and how they would be avoided or corrected when
   a. one individual owns an oil field next to another oil field owned by another individual.
   b. a firm develops a recreational site (golf, skiing, boating, or the like).

*10. a. Draw a figure showing the market demand curve for good X for Figure 17–2 if good X were a private rather than a public good.

b. State the condition for the Pareto optimal output of commodity X when X is a private good and when it is a public good.

c. What is the relationship between public goods and externalities?

11. Three possible solutions were proposed at the time of the severe water shortage experienced by New York City in 1949–1950. These were (1) building a dam that would cost $1,000 per million gallons of water supplied, (2) sealing leaks in water mains, which would cost about $1.60 per million gallons of water gained, or (3) installing water meters that would cost $160 per million gallons of water saved. The city chose the first project. Was New York's choice correct? If not, why might New York have chosen it?

12. With reference to Figure 17–3, calculate the total social gains by
   a. increasing the level of pollution from 4 to 8 units per year.
   b. reducing pollution from 12 to 8 units per year.

18

THE ECONOMICS
OF INFORMATION

In this chapter, we study the economics of information. This field of study is becoming increasingly important—and deservingly so. The chapter begins by examining the economics of search: search costs, the process of searching for the lowest price, and the informational content of advertising. The chapter goes on to examine commodity and currency futures markets, speculation, and hedging. Subsequently, we discuss asymmetric information and the market for lemons (i.e., defective products), the insurance market and adverse selection, moral hazard, market signaling, and the principal-agent problem. The several examples and applications of the theory provided in the chapter show the real-world importance and great relevance of the economics of information.

18.1 THE ECONOMICS OF SEARCH

We begin our study by discussing search costs, outlining the process of searching for the lowest commodity price, and examining the informational content of advertising.[1]

Search Costs

One cost of purchasing a product is the time and money we spent seeking information about the product—what are the properties of the product, what are the alternatives, how good is the product, how safe, how much does the product cost in one store as opposed to another? **Search costs** include the time spent reading ads, telephoning, traveling, inspecting the product, and comparative shopping for the lowest price. Although the most important component of search costs is the time spent learning about the attributes of the product, consumers sometimes also spend money purchasing information

---

[1]The discussion draws heavily on G. J. Stigler's "The Economics of Information," *Journal of Political Economy*, June 1961, pp. 213–225.

to aid them in their search. They might purchase *Consumer Reports* magazine to check on the quality of a product, pay an impartial mechanic to evaluate a used car before deciding on purchasing it, or seek professional help from a financial advisor before making a major investment. In most cases, however, the major cost of search is the time required to learn about the product. Often the government provides a great deal of information in the form of mileage disclosures for new automobiles, safety standards for some products, and weather forecasts, which greatly reduce uncertainty in purchasing many products.

One of the most important and time-consuming aspects of purchasing a product is comparison shopping for the lowest price. Even when a product is standardized and conditions of sale are identical (i.e., locational convenience, courteousness of service, availability of credit, returns policy, etc.), there will be a dispersion of prices in the absence of perfect information on the part of buyers. Since it takes time and money to gather information, and different consumers place different valuations on their time, some price dispersion will persist in the market even if the product is perfectly standardized and sales conditions are identical.

The general rule is that a consumer should continue the search for lower prices as long as the marginal benefit from continuing the search exceeds the marginal cost, and until the marginal benefit equals the marginal cost. The marginal benefit (*MB*) is equal to the degree by which a lower price is found as a result of each additional search times the number of units of the product purchased at the lower price. The marginal cost (*MC*) of continuing the search depends on the value that consumers place on their time (assuming that consumers do not find shopping itself pleasurable). Since the value that consumers place on their time differs for different consumers, the product will be purchased at different prices by different consumers when each consumer behaves according to the *MB* = *MC* rule. Specifically, those consumers forgoing higher wages when searching for lower prices will stop the search before consumers who face lower opportunity costs for their time, and thus will purchase the product at a higher price.[2]

Searching for the Lowest Price

At any time, there will be a dispersion of prices in the market even for a homogeneous product. A consumer can accept the price quoted by the first seller of the product he or she approaches, or the consumer can continue the search for lower prices. Unless the consumer knows that the price quoted by the first seller is the lowest price in the market, he or she should continue

---

[2]The same general rule applies in searching for a better-quality product. A consumer should continue the search as long as the *MB* exceeds the *MC* and until *MB* = *MC*. The actual application of this rule, however, is usually more difficult than in searching for lower product prices because it is difficult to assign higher monetary values correctly for better-quality products.

the search for lower prices as long as the marginal benefit from continuing the search exceeds the marginal cost of additional search. In general, the marginal benefit from searching declines as the time spent searching for lower prices continues. Even if the marginal cost of additional search is constant, a point is reached where $MB = MC$. At that point, the consumer should end the search.

For example, suppose that a consumer wants to purchase a small portable TV of a given brand and knows the prices of different sellers range from $80 to $120. All sellers are identical in location, service, and so on, so that price is the only consideration. Suppose also that sellers are equally divided into five price classifications: Sellers of type I charge a price of $80 for the TV, type II sellers charge $90, type III charge $100, type IV charge $110, and type V charge $120. For a single search, the probability of each price is 1/5, and the expected price is the weighted average of all prices, or $100.[3] The consumer can now purchase the TV at the price of $100, or she can continue the search for lower prices. With each additional search the consumer will find a lower price, until the lowest price of $80 is found. The reduction in price with each search gives the marginal benefit of the search. How many searches the consumer conducts depends on the marginal cost that he faces. The consumer will end the search when the marginal benefit from the search equals the marginal cost.

We can use a simple formula to obtain the approximate lowest price expected with each additional search.[4] This is

$$\text{Expected Price} = \text{Lowest Price} + \frac{\text{Range of Prices}}{\text{Number of Searches} + 1} \qquad \textbf{[18–1]}$$

For example, the lowest TV price expected from one search is

$$\text{Expected Price} = \$80 + \frac{\$40}{1 + 1} = \$100 \text{ (as found earlier)}$$

The approximate lowest expected price from two searches is $80 + $\frac{\$40}{3}$ = $93.33.[5] Thus, the approximate marginal benefit from the second search is $100 − $93.33 = $6.67. The lowest expected price with three searches is $80 + $\frac{\$40}{4}$ = $90, so that MB = $3.33. The lowest expected price with four

---

[3] The expected price is equal to $80(1/5) + $90(1/5) + $100(1/5) + $110(1/5) + $120(1/5) = $16 + $18 + $20 + $22 + $24 = $100.

[4] The formula gives only an approximation of the lowest price found with each additional search, because prices are discrete rather than continuous variables (i.e., market prices are not infinitesimally divisible). Nevertheless, the formula provides a quick method of showing that the marginal benefit (in the form of lower prices) declines with each additional search. For the calculation of the precise lowest price for the second search, see problem 1, with answer at end of the book.

[5] The *precise* expected price with two searches is $92 and is found with a much longer calculation, as shown in the answer to problem 1 at end of the book.

searches is $80 + \dfrac{\$40}{5}$ = \$88, so that MB = \$2. The lowest expected price with five searches is $80 + \dfrac{\$40}{6}$ = \$86.67, so that MB = \$1.33.

Note how the marginal benefit from each additional search declines. MB = \$6.67 for the second search, \$3.33 for the third search, \$2 for the fourth search, \$1.33 for the fifth search, and so on. If the marginal cost of each additional search for the consumer is \$2, the consumer should, therefore, conduct four searches, because only with the fourth search is the marginal benefit equal to the marginal cost. For fewer searches, $MB > MC$, and it pays for the consumer to continue the search. For more than four searches, $MB < MC$, and it does not pay for the consumer to conduct that many searches. Furthermore, the higher is the price of the commodity, and the greater is the range of product prices, the more searches a consumer will undertake. The reason for this is that the marginal benefit of each search is then greater (see problem 3). Finally, note that because consumers face different marginal costs of search, they will end the search at different points and end up paying different prices for the product. This allows different producers to charge different prices. Producers selling the product at a higher price will sell only to those consumers who have less information because they stop searching for lower prices before others.

Search and Advertising

Even though most advertising contains an important manipulative component, it also provides a great deal of useful information to consumers on the availability of products, their use and properties, the firms selling particular products, retail outlets that carry the product, and product prices. Thus, advertising greatly reduces consumers' search costs. In most cases, it also reduces both price dispersion and average prices. For example, we saw in section 10.2 that the price of eyeglasses was much higher in New York, which prohibits advertising by optometrists, than in New Jersey, which does not prohibit such advertising. Similarly, the price of an uncontested divorce dropped from \$350 to \$150 in Phoenix, Arizona, after the Supreme Court allowed advertising for legal services. Clearly, advertising often results in increased competition among sellers and lower product prices, and it provides very useful information to consumers.

In examining the role of advertising, Philip Nelson distinguishes between search goods and experience goods.[6] **Search goods** are those goods whose quality can be evaluated by inspection at the time of purchase. Examples of search goods are fresh fruits and vegetables, apparel, and greeting cards. **Experience goods,** on the other hand, are those which cannot be judged by

---

[6]P. Nelson, "Advertising as Information," *Journal of Political Economy*, July/August 1974, pp. 729–754.

inspection at the time of purchase but only after using them. Examples of experience goods are automobiles, TV sets, computers, canned foods, and laundry detergents. Some goods, of course, are borderline. For example, the content of a book or magazine can be partially gathered by quick inspection at the bookstore before purchasing it. But its quality can only be fully evaluated after reading it more carefully after the purchase.

Nelson points out that the advertisements of search goods must by necessity contain a large informational content. Any attempt on the part of the seller to misrepresent the product in any way would be easily detected by potential buyers before the purchase and would thus be self-defeating. The situation is different for experience goods, where the buyer could not determine the true properties of the product before use. Nevertheless, the very fact that a large and established seller is willing to spend a great deal on advertising the product provides indirect support for the seller's claims. After all, a large seller that has been in business for a long time must have enjoyed repeated purchases from other satisfied customers.

In 1991, nearly $130 billion was spent on advertising in the United States, of which 25% was in newspapers, 22% in magazines, 22% on TV, 18% in direct mail, 7% on radio, and the rest in other forms of advertising.[7] Newspaper advertising was found to be the most informative, while TV advertising was found to be the least informative among major forms of advertising.[8] Another study found that industries with higher-than-average advertising expenditures relative to sales had lower rates of price increases and higher rates of output increases than the average for 150 major industries.[9] From this, it can be inferred that advertising has a large informational content.

When the cost of gathering information is very high or when use of the product can be dangerous, the government usually steps in to provide the information (as in the case of gas mileage for automobiles) or regulates the use of the product (as in the case of prescription drugs). Indeed, and as Example 1 explains, the U.S. government is now promoting the development of an "information superhighway" to increase the spread of information, thereby increasing the overall efficiency of the U.S. economy.

Example 1

An "Information Superhighway"?

In 1991, the U.S. government started to promote the idea first advanced by Vice President Albert Gore (when he was a Democratic senator from

[7]U.S. Department of Commerce, *Statistical Abstract of the United States* (Washington, D.C.: U.S. Government Printing Office, 1992), pp. 558–559.

[8]F. M. Scherer and D. Ross, *Industrial Market Structure and Economic Performance* (Boston: Houghton Mifflin, 1990), p. 572.

[9]E. W. Eckard, "Advertising, Concentration Changes, and Consumer Welfare," *Review of Economics and Statistics*, May 1988, pp. 340–343.

Tennessee) to develop a national high-speed computer network. The five-year plan received $150 million funding for fiscal year 1992. The goal is to build faster and more sophisticated computers (hardware) and programs (software) for running them and to link them throughout the nation via what Gore called an "information superhighway."

"Far-flung researchers could hook up with libraries, data bases, and vastly improved super computers. . . . Every individual will have at his command information and computational ability unknown before in the world." This information superhighway would increase the availability of information and increase the U.S. lead in computer technology, or prevent losing it to Japan. It also would, more importantly, increase the general competitiveness of the U.S. economy vis-à-vis the rest of the world. Even the previous Republican administration in Washington, which was generally against anything that resembled industrial policy, supported this program because it was generic or precompetitive technology rather than an aid to any particular industry. Of course, with the Clinton administration in Washington, it is very likely that this program will be continued and expanded. Indeed, Clinton is the first U.S. president to clearly understand that access to information is essential for economic success.

The creating of such an information superhighway is a monumental and very expensive endeavor and may take decades to fully implement. It involves devising the needed hardware and software and then hooking everyone up to the network. Given the huge federal budget deficit and the commitment of the Clinton administration to reduce it, financing the information superhighway may require cuts in other government-financed mega-science projects, such as the $8 billion supercollider and possibly even the space program. There is also the danger that only those individuals and firms that can truly afford being hooked up to the system will benefit from the system. The Clinton administration's call to "put people first" requires that all have access to the system, regardless of where they live or their ability to pay, so as to make everyone equally competitive.

Sources: "An 'Information Superhighway' "? *Business Week,* February 1991, p. 28, and "Let's Get Going on a Data Highway," *New York Times,* March 14, 1993, Section 3, p. 11.

▲

18.2 COMMODITY AND CURRENCY FUTURES MARKETS, SPECULATION, AND HEDGING

When the price of a commodity (such as wheat) or a currency (such as the British pound) differs at different locations (say, New York and Chicago or New York and London), people will purchase the commodity or currency where it is cheaper, resell it where it is more expensive, and earn a profit. In the process, the price difference in the two locations is eliminated (except for transaction costs). This is called **arbitrage.** Because payment and delivery of the commodity or currency occur at the time of the transaction, these are called **spot transactions;** the market where these transactions takes place is called the **spot market;** and the price or rate at which the transaction takes place is called the **spot price or rate.**

Spot transactions are to be contrasted with forward or futures transactions, which take place in the forward or futures markets. A **forward or futures transaction** is an agreement entered upon today to purchase or sell a specific quantity of a commodity, stock, or currency for delivery at a specific future date (usually three months from today) at a price or rate specified today. At maturity, the delivery of and payment for the commodity, stock, or currency take place at the preestablished rate, regardless of the rate prevailing at the time the contract is fulfilled. The market for these forward contracts is called the **forward or futures market,** and the price or rate at which the forward or futures transaction takes place is called the **forward or futures price or rate.**[10]

Speculators and hedgers usually operate in the forward market. A **speculator** is an individual or firm that specializes in information about future demand, supply, and prices of commodities or currencies. A speculator buys a commodity or currency forward at today's forward rate if he anticipates that the commodity or currency price will increase by the time the forward contract matures. At maturity, the speculator makes the payment and receives delivery of the commodity or currency at the price or rate specified in the forward contract. He then immediately resells the commodity or currency in the spot market at the prevailing spot rate. If the speculator is correct (i.e., if the spot price of the commodity or currency is indeed higher than the forward rate on the maturing forward contract as he anticipated), he earns a profit; otherwise he incurs a loss. If the speculator, on the other hand, believes that the future spot rate will be lower than today's forward rate, he sells the commodity or currency forward. Upon maturity of the contract, if he is correct, he will be able to purchase the commodity or currency at the lower spot price prevailing and immediately resell the commodity or currency at the higher price or rate specified in the forward contract. The speculator's profits are equal to the difference between the buying and selling price times the number of units of the commodity or currency traded.

Without speculators, hedging would not be possible. **Hedging** refers to the covering of a commodity or foreign-exchange risk. A commodity or foreign-exchange risk arises because the price of the commodity or currency that an

---

[10]While in the above elementary introduction no distinction is made between forward and futures contracts, they are not identical. Futures contracts are standardized transactions for predetermined quantities of a commodity or currency (for example, 5,000 bushels of wheat or £25,000) for delivery at selected calendar dates. On the other hand, forward contracts can be written for any amount and for any agreed on delivery date. Because of this, futures contracts are more liquid than forward contracts. But if economic agents have rational expectations and share common information, then the two types of contracts will be basically the same. We assumed that this is the case here.

individual or firm expects to deliver or receive in the future changes. For example, suppose a firm exports $2 million worth of goods to England and agrees to receive £1 million in three months. At today's exchange rate of $2/£1, the firm expects to receive $2 million in three months. But in three months the exchange rate may have fallen to $1.60/£1. In that case, the firm would receive only $1.6 million. Of course, the exchange rate could rise so that the firm would receive more dollars than it expected. However, the firm has enough to worry about its product line and cannot worry about changes in exchange rates, which could jeopardize its very existence.

Therefore, the exporter hedges his foreign-exchange risk. He does so by selling £1 million forward at today's forward rate for delivery in three months, so as to coincide with the receipt of the £1 million from his exports. Even if today's forward rate is only $1.98/£1, the exporter willingly "pays" 2 cents per pound to avoid the foreign-exchange risk. In three months, when the U.S. exporter receives £1 million, he will be able to immediately exchange it for $1.98 million by fulfilling the forward contract. An importer avoids the foreign-exchange risk by doing the opposite (see problem 7).

By hedging, an individual or firm can thus avoid or cover the risks arising from changing future commodity and currency prices. But hedging would not be possible without speculators, who willingly seek and accept market risks in the expectation of making a profit. Thus, *the existence of forward or futures markets and speculators, in general, increases the amount of information available in the market and reduces transaction costs.* This results in a larger volume of economic transactions and trade, which increase economic welfare. Futures markets exist in many commodities (corn, oats, soybeans, wheat, cotton; cattle, hogs, pork bellies; cocoa, coffee, orange juice, sugar; copper, gold, silver, platinum). There is also a forward market in many of the world's currencies and a futures market in the world's most important currencies. Most of the time, speculation in commodity and currency markets is stabilizing (i.e., it reduces price fluctuations over time). This further reduces risks, increases the level of economic transactions and trade, and results in rising economic welfare.

18.3 ASYMMETRIC INFORMATION: THE MARKET FOR LEMONS AND ADVERSE SELECTION

We now discuss asymmetric information and the market for lemons as well as the problem of adverse selection in the insurance market.

Asymmetric Information and the Market for Lemons

Often one party to a transaction (i.e., the seller or the buyer of a product or service) has more information than the other party regarding the quality of the product or service. This is a case of **asymmetric information.** An example of the problems created by asymmetric information is the market for "lemons" (i.e., a defective product, such as a used car, that will require a great deal of costly repairs and is not worth its price) discussed by Ackerlof.[11]

Specifically, sellers of used cars know exactly the quality of the cars that they are selling but prospective buyers do not. As a result, the market price for used cars will depend on the quality of the average used car available for sale. The owners of "lemons" would then tend to receive a higher price than their cars are worth, while the owners of high-quality used cars would tend to get a lower price than their cars are worth. The owners of high-quality used cars would therefore withdraw their cars from the market, thus lowering the average quality and price of the remaining cars available for sale. Sellers of the now above-average quality cars withdraw their cars from the market, further reducing the quality and price of the remaining used cars offered for sale. The process continues until only the lowest-quality cars are sold in the market at the appropriate very low price. Thus, the end result is that low-quality cars drive high-quality cars out of the market. This is known as **adverse selection.**

The problem of adverse selection that arises from asymmetric information can be overcome or reduced by the acquisition of more information by the party lacking it. For example, in the used-car market, a prospective buyer can have the car evaluated at an independent automotive service center, or the used-car dealer can provide guarantees for the cars they sell. With more information on the quality of used cars, buyers would be willing to pay a higher price for higher-quality cars, and the problem of adverse selection can be overcome. More generally, brand names (such as Bayer aspirin), chain retailers (such as Sears, McDonald's, and Hilton), and professional licensing (of doctors, lawyers, beauticians, etc.) are important methods of ensuring the quality of products and services, and they thus reduce the degree of asymmetric information and the resulting problem of adverse selection. Travelers are often willing to pay higher prices for nationally advertised products and services than for competitive local products, because they do not know the quality of local products and services. This is why tourists often pay more for products and services than residents. Sometimes, higher prices are themselves taken as an indication of higher quality.[12]

---

[11]G. A. Ackerlof, "The Market for 'Lemons': Qualitative Uncertainty and the Market Mechanism," *Quarterly Journal of Economics*, August 1970, pp. 488–500.

[12]See, J. E. Stiglitz, "The Causes and Consequences of the Dependence of Quality on Price," *Journal of Economic Literature*, March 1987, pp. 1–48.

The Insurance Market and Adverse Selection

The problem of adverse selection arises not only in the market for used cars, but in any market characterized by asymmetric information. This is certainly the case for the insurance market. Here, the individual knows much more about the state of her health than an insurance company can ever find out, even with a medical examination. As a result, when an insurance company sets the insurance premium for the average individual (i.e., an individual of average health), unhealthy people are more likely to purchase insurance than healthy people. Because of this adverse selection problem, the insurance company is forced to raise the insurance premium, thus making it even less advantageous for healthy individuals to purchase insurance. This increases even more the proportion of unhealthy people in the pool of insured people, thus requiring still higher insurance premiums. In the end, insurance premiums would have to be so high that even unhealthy people would stop buying insurance. Why buy insurance if the premium is as high as the cost of personally paying for an illness?

The problem of adverse selection arises in the market for any other type of insurance (i.e., for accidents, fire, floods, and so on). In each case, only above-average risk people buy insurance, and this forces insurance companies to raise their premiums. The worsening adverse selection problem can lead to insurance premiums being so high that in the end no one would buy insurance. The same occurs in the market for credit. Since credit-card companies and banks must charge the same interest rate to all borrowers, they attract more low- than high-quality borrowers (i.e., more borrowers who either do not repay their debts or repay their debts late). This forces up the interest rate charged, which increases even more the proportion of low-quality borrowers, until interest rates would have to be so high that it would not pay even for low-quality borrowers to borrow.

Insurance companies try to overcome the problem of adverse selection by requiring medical checkups, charging different premiums for different age groups and occupations, and offering different rates of coinsurance, amounts of deductibility, length of contracts, and so on. These limit the variation in risk within each group and reduce the problem of adverse selection. Because there will always be some variability in risk within each group, however, the problem of adverse selection cannot be entirely eliminated in this way. The only way to avoid the problem entirely is to provide compulsory insurance to all the people in the group. Individuals facing somewhat lower risks than the group average will then get a slightly worse deal, while individuals facing somewhat higher risks will get a slightly better deal (in relation to the equal premium that each group member must pay). Indeed, this is an argument in favor of *universal*, government-provided, compulsory health insurance and no-fault auto insurance. On the other hand, credit companies significantly reduce the adverse selection problem that they face by sharing "credit histories" with other credit companies. Although such sharing of credit histories is justifiably attacked as an invasion of privacy, it does allow the credit market to operate and keep interest charges to acceptably low levels.

18.4 THE PROBLEM OF MORAL HAZARD

Another problem that arises in the insurance market is that of **moral hazard.** This refers to the increase in the probability of an illness, fire, or other accident when an individual is insured than when she is not. With insurance, the loss from an illness, fire, or other accident is shifted from the individual to the insurance company. Therefore, the individual will take fewer precautions to avoid the illness, fire, or other accident, and when a loss does occur she will tend to inflate the amount of the loss. For example, with medical insurance, an individual may spend less on preventive health care (thus increasing the probability of getting ill); and if she does become ill, she will tend to spend more on treatment than would be the case if she had no insurance. With auto insurance, an individual may drive more recklessly (thus increasing the probability of a car accident) and then is likely to exaggerate the injury and inflate the property damage that he suffers if he does get into an accident. Similarly, with fire insurance, a firm may take fewer reasonable precautions (such as the installation of a fire-detector system, thereby increasing the probability of a fire) than in the absence of fire insurance; and then the firm is likely to inflate the property damage suffered if a fire does occur. Indeed, the probability of a fire is high if the property is insured for an amount greater than the real value of the property.

If the problem of moral hazard is not reduced or somehow contained, it could lead to unacceptably high insurance rates and costs and thus defeat the very purpose of insurance. The socially valid purpose of insurance is to share *given* risks of a large loss among many economic units. But if the ability to buy insurance increases total risks and claimed losses, then insurance is no longer efficient and may not even be possible. One method by which insurance companies try to overcome the problem of moral hazard is by specifying the precautions that an individual or firm must take as a condition for buying insurance. For example, the insurance company might require yearly physical checkups as a condition for continuing to provide health insurance to an individual, increase insurance premiums for drivers involved in accidents, and require the installation of a fire detector before providing fire insurance to a firm. By doing this, the insurance company tries to limit the possibility of illness, accident, or fire, and thereby reduce the number and amount of possible claims it will face.

Another way used by insurance companies to overcome or reduce the problem of moral hazard is **coinsurance.** This refers to insuring only part of the possible loss or value of the property being insured. The idea is that if the individual or firm shares a significant portion of a potential loss with the insurance company, the individual or firm will be more prudent and will take more precautions to avoid losses from illness or accidents. Although we have examined moral hazard in connection with the insurance market, the problem of moral hazard arises whenever an externality is present (i.e., any time an economic agent can shift some of its costs to others). This is clearly shown in Example 2.

Example 2

▽

Increased Disability Payments Reduce Labor-Force Participation

The Social Security program that pays disability benefits to individuals who are able to prove that they are unable to work is a socially useful program. Nevertheless, it may have resulted in a moral hazard problem by encouraging some individuals, who would otherwise be working despite their disability, to withdraw from the job market when receiving disability benefits. For example, an individual who is injured in a non-job-related accident and is unable to walk could train to be an accountant or to hold another sedentary occupation, but that individual may choose instead to remain unemployed and live on disability benefits. There are, of course, many forms of disability that would prevent an individual from doing *any* type of work, but this is not always the case.

Some indirect evidence exists that providing disability benefits since the early 1950s and raising them over time has led to a moral hazard problem. For example, the labor nonparticipation rate for men between the ages of 45 and 54 increased from nearly 4% in 1950 to more than 12% in 1990 at the same time that the Social Security disability-recipiency rate for men in the same age group increased from zero to about 4.6%. The nonparticipation rate refers to the proportion of people in a particular age group who are neither working nor seeking employment because of all causes (disability and other). On the other hand, the Social Security disability-recipiency rate refers to the proportion of people in a particular age group who are neither working nor seeking employment because of a disability.

Providing disability benefits and increasing them over time, thus, seems to have resulted in a moral hazard problem. There are, of course, other reasons besides disability that might have led to the large increase in the nonparticipation rate since the 1950s. However, the sharp and parallel increase in the two rates over time leads to the suspicion that a moral hazard problem was also at work. By providing disincentives for work, the current U.S. welfare program seems to have led to the same situation.

Sources: Donald O. Parsons, "The Decline in Labor Force Participation," *Journal of Political Economy*, February 1980, pp. 117–134; "Disability Insurance and Male Labor-Force Participation," *Journal of Political Economy*, June 1984, pp. 542–549; *U.S. Statistical Abstract* (Washington, D.C.: U.S.

Government Printing Office, 1992) p. 367; and Robert Moffitt, "Incentive Effects of the U.S. Welfare System: A Review," *Journal of Economic Literature*, March 1992, pp. 1–61.

▲

18.5 MARKET SIGNALING

The problem of adverse selection resulting from asymmetric information can be resolved or greatly reduced by **market signaling**.[13] If sellers of higher-quality products, lower-risk individuals, better-quality borrowers, or more-productive workers can somehow inform or send signals of their superior quality, lower risk, or greater productivity to potential buyers of the products, insurance companies, credit companies, and employers, then the problem of adverse selection can, for the most part, be overcome. Individuals would then be able to identify high-quality products; insurance and credit companies would be able to distinguish between low- and high-risk individuals and firms; and firms would be able to identify higher-productivity workers. As a result, sellers of higher-quality products would be able to sell their products at commensurately higher prices; lower-risk individuals could be charged lower insurance premiums; better-quality borrowers would have more access to credit; and higher-productivity workers could be paid higher wages. Such market signaling can thus overcome the problem of adverse selection.

A firm can signal the higher quality of its products to potential customers by adopting brand names, by offering guarantees and warranties, and by a policy of exchanging defective items. A similar function is performed by franchising (such as McDonald's) and the existence of national retail outlets (such as Sears) that do not produce the goods they sell themselves, but select products from other firms and on which they put their brand name as an assurance of quality. The seller, in effect, is saying "I am so confident of the quality of my products that I am willing to put my name on them and guarantee them." The high rate of product returns and need to service low-quality merchandise would make it too costly for sellers of low-quality products to offer such guarantees and warranties. The acceptance of coinsurance and deductibles by an individual or firm similarly sends a powerful message to insurance companies indicating that they are good risks. The credit history of a potential borrower (indicating that he or she has repaid past debts in full and on time) also sends a strong signal to credit companies that he or she is a good credit risk.

Education serves as a powerful signaling device regarding the productivity of potential employees. That is, higher levels of educational accomplishments (such as years of schooling, degrees awarded, grade-point average achieved,

[13]A. M. Spence, *Market Signaling* (Cambridge, Mass.: Harvard University Press, 1974), and A. M. Spence, "Job Market Signaling," *Quarterly Journal of Economics*, August 1973, pp. 355–379.

etc.) represent not only an investment in human capital (see section 15.7) but also serve as a powerful signal to an employer of the greater productivity of a potential employee. After all, the individual had the intelligence and perseverance to complete college. A less-intelligent and/or a less-motivated person is usually not able to do so, or it might cost her so much more (for example, it may take five or six years rather than four years to get a college degree) as not to pay for her to get a college education even if she could. Thus, a college degree provides a powerful signal that its holder is in general a more productive individual than a person without a degree. Even if education did not in fact increase productivity, it would still serve as an important signal to employers of the greater *innate* ability and higher productivity of a potential employee.[14]

A firm could fire an employee if it subsequently found that her productivity is too low. But this is usually difficult (the firm might have to show due cause) and expensive (the firm might have to give severance pay). In any event, it usually takes a great deal of on-the-job training before the firm can correctly evaluate the productivity of a new employee. Thus, firms are eager to determine as accurately as possible the productivity of a potential employee before he or she is hired. There is empirical evidence to suggest that education does in fact provide such an important signaling device. Liu and Wong found that while firms pay higher *initial* salaries to holders of educational certificates (such as college degrees) than to non-certificate holders, employees' salaries subsequently depend on their actual on-the-job productivity.[15] Thus, the firm relies on the market signal provided by education when it first hires an employee, for lack of a better signaling device, but then relies on actual performance after it has had adequate opportunity to determine the employee's true productivity on the job.

18.6 THE PRINCIPAL-AGENT PROBLEM

A firm's managers act as the *agents* for the owners or stockholders (legally referred to as the *principals*) of the firm. Because of this separation of ownership from control in the modern corporation, a **principal-agent problem** arises.[16] This refers to the fact that while the owners of the firm want to maximize the total profits or the present value of the firm, the managers or agents want to maximize their own personal interests, such as their salaries, tenure, influence,

---

[14]See, K. J. Arrow, "Higher Education as a Filter," *Journal of Public Economics,* July 1973, pp. 193–216.

[15]P. W. Liu and C. Wong, "Educational Screening by Certificates: An Empirical Test," *Economic Inquiry,* January 1984, pp. 72–83.

[16]See, E. F. Fama, "Agency Problems of the Theory of the Firm," *Journal of Political Economy,* April 1980, pp. 288–307.

and reputation.[17] The principal-agent problem often becomes evident in the case of takeover bids for a firm by another firm. Although the owners or stockholders of the firm may benefit from the takeover if it raises the value of the firm's stock, the managers may oppose it for fear of losing their jobs in the reorganization of the firm that may follow the takeover.

One way of overcoming the principal-agent problem and ensuring that the firm's managers act in the stockholders' interests is by providing managers with **golden parachutes.** These are large financial settlements paid out by a firm to its managers if they are forced or choose to leave as a result of the firm being taken over. With golden parachutes, the firm is in essence buying the firm managers' approval for the takeover. Even though golden parachutes may cost a firm millions of dollars, they may be more than justified by the sharp increase in the value of the firm that might result from a takeover. Note that a principal-agent problem may also arise in the acquiring firm. Specifically, the agents or managers of a firm may initiate and carry out a takeover bid more for personal gain (in the form of higher salaries, more secure tenure, and the enhanced reputation and prestige in directing the resulting larger corporation) than to further the stockholders' interest. In fact, the managers of the acquiring firm may be carried away by their egos and bid too much for the firm being acquired.

More generally (and independently of takeovers) a firm can overcome the principal-agent problem by offering big bonuses to its top managers based on the firm's long-term performance and profitability or a generous deferred-compensation package, which provides relatively low compensation at the beginning and very high compensation in the future. This would induce managers to stay with the firm and strive for its long-term success. In the case of public enterprises such as a public-transportation agency, or in a nonprofit enterprise such as a hospital, an inept manger can be voted out or removed.

As Example 3 shows, trying to overcome the principal-agent problem between owners or stockholders (principals) and managers (agents) with golden parachutes may not solve the principal-agent problem and may lead to abuses.

Example 3

 $100 Million in Golden Parachutes for Primerica's Ten Top Executives

One method used by firms to overcome their managers' objections to a takeover that might greatly increase the value of the firm is by golden

---

[17]See, W. Baumol, *Business Behavior, Value, and Growth* (New York: Harcourt-Brace, 1967), and O. Williamson, *Corporate Control and Business Behavior* (Englewood Cliffs, N.J.: Prentice-Hall, 1964).

parachutes. The proliferation and size of golden parachutes has sharply increased during the great wave of mergers that has taken place in the United States since the early 1980s. Some of the largest and most controversial golden parachutes (amounting to a total of nearly $100 million) were set up for ten of Primerica's executives for retiring as a result of its friendly merger with the Commercial Credit Corporation in 1988. These golden parachutes represented 6% of Primerica's $1.7 billion book value and cost stockholders $1.88 a share. Gerald Tsai, Jr., the chairman of Primerica, who arranged the merger, was to receive $19.2 million as severance pay, $8.6 million to defray the excise taxes resulting from the compensation agreement, and several other millions of dollars from Primerica's long-term incentive, life insurance, and retirement benefits program—for an overall total of nearly $30 million!

Even before the final approval of the merger in December 1988, some of Primerica's stockholders filed suit in New York State Supreme Court charging that Primerica's top executives had violated their fiduciary role and had acted in their own interest and against the stockholders' interests; they demanded that the termination agreements for the ten executives be canceled. The lawsuit pointed out that golden parachutes were originally set up in 1985 for six of Primerica's executives to cover only hostile takeovers; they were then extended to ten executives in 1987; and finally they were revised in 1988, three months after Primerica agreed to the merger, to also cover friendly takeovers.

It has been estimated that 15% of the nation's largest corporations offered golden parachutes to its top executives in 1981. This figure rose to 33% in 1985 and to nearly 50% in 1990. Indeed, golden parachutes are no longer confined to the corporation's top executives; they are offered farther and farther down the corporate ladder to middle-level management and sometimes even to all employees. This has resulted in a public outcry and has led the Securities and Exchange Commission to rule that a firm must hold a shareholder vote on its golden parachute plans. Until now, corporations typically did not make public their offer of golden parachutes.

Sources: "Ten of Primerica Executives' Parachutes Gilded in $98.2 Million Severance Pay," *Wall Street Journal*, November 29, 1988, p. A3; "Primerica Holders File Lawsuit to Halt 'Golden Parachutes'," *Wall Street Journal*, December 2, 1988, p. A9; and "Ruling by SEC May Threaten Parachute Plans," *Wall Street Journal*, January 1990, p. A3.

▲

18.7 THE EFFICIENCY WAGE THEORY

We have seen in section 13.5 that in a perfectly competitive labor market, all workers who are willing to work find employment and the equilibrium wage rate reflects (i.e., it is equal to) the marginal productivity of labor. In the real world, however, we often observe higher-than-equilibrium wages and a great deal of involuntary unemployment. Why don't firms then lower wages?

According to the **efficiency wage theory,** firms willingly pay higher than equilibrium wages to induce workers to avoid *shirking* or slacking off on the job.[18] The theory begins by pointing out that it is difficult or impossible for firms to accurately monitor workers' productivity (thus, firms face a principal-agent problem resulting from asymmetric information). If workers are paid the equilibrium wage, they are likely to shirk or slack off on the job because if fired, they can easily find another equally-paying job (remember, there is no involuntary unemployment at the equilibrium wage, and in any event, it is not easy for a firm to catch a working shirking). According to the efficiency wage theory, by paying a higher-than-equilibrium or *efficiency* wage the firm can induce employees to work more productively and not shirk, because the employees fear losing their high-paying jobs. Even if all firms paid efficiency wages, employees would not shirk and risk being fired, because it is not easy to find another similarly rewarding job in view of the great deal of unemployment that exists at the efficiency wage.

The efficiency wage theory can be examined graphically with Figure 18–1. In the figure, D_L is the usual negatively sloped demand curve for labor of the firm, and S_L is the supply curve of labor (assumed to be fixed for simplicity) facing the firm. The intersection of D_L and S_L at point E determines the equilibrium wage of $10 per hour and equilibrium number of 600 workers hired by the firm. There are no unemployed workers and this wage is equal to the marginal productivity of labor.

But at this equilibrium wage, workers have an incentive to shirk. To induce workers not to shirk, the firm will have to pay a higher or efficiency wage. The efficiency wage is higher the smaller is the level of unemployment, because workers can then more easily find another job at the efficiency wage (if fired from the present job because of shirking). This is shown by the no-shirking constraint (*NSC*) curve shown in the figure. The *NSC* curve shows the minimum wage that workers must be paid for each level of unemployment to avoid shirking. For example, the efficiency wage of $10 requires 300 workers (*EA*) to be unemployed. With 200 workers (*BE**) unemployed, the efficiency wage is $20, and with only 100 workers unemployed (*CF*) the efficiency wage will have to be $40. Note that the *NSC* curve is positively sloped (i.e., the efficiency wage is higher the smaller is the level of unemployment) and gets closer and closer to the fixed S_L curve but never crosses it (i.e., there will always be some unemployment at the efficiency wage).

In Figure 18–1, the intersection of the D_L and *NSC* at point E^* determines the *efficiency* wage of $20 per hour. At this wage rate, the firm employs 400 workers and 200 workers are unemployed. The reason that $20 is the equilibrium efficiency wage is that only at this wage is the level of unemployment (*BE**) just enough to avoid shirking. For $10 to be the efficiency wage, 300 workers (*EA*) would have to be unemployed. But at the wage of $10 there

FIGURE 18–1   Efficiency Wage and Unemployment in a Shirking Model

D_L and S_L are, respectively, the firm's demand and the supply curve for labor. Their intersection at point E determines the equilibrium wage of $10 per hour at which the firm employs 600 workers and there is no unemployment. Workers, however, have an incentive to shirk at this wage. The no-shirk constraint (NSC) curve is positively sloped and shows that the efficiency or minimum wage that the firm must pay to avoid shirking is higher the smaller is the level of unemployment. The no-shirking equilibrium is determined at point E^* where D_L and NSC cross. The efficiency wage is $20 per hour and 200 workers (BE^*) are unemployed.

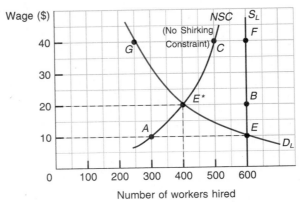

is no unemployment (point E). Thus, *the equilibrium* efficiency wage must be higher. On the other hand, for $40 to be the efficiency wage, only 100 workers (FE) need to be unemployed. But at the wage of $40, 350 workers ($FG$) are unemployed. Thus, the equilibrium efficiency wage must be lower. The efficiency wage is $20 because only at this wage is the number of unemployed workers ($200 = BE^*$) just right for workers not to shirk.

One example of the efficiency wage theory is provided by the decision by Henry Ford in January 1914 to reduce the length of the working day from nine to eight hours while increasing the minimum daily wage from $2.34 to $5. This sharply reduced labor turnover and increased labor productivity sufficiently to actually reduce the cost of producing each automobile.[19] In short, what Ford did in 1914 was to pay the efficiency wage—and it took 70 years for economists to develop the theory to fit the facts!

18.8 SOME APPLICATIONS OF THE ECONOMICS OF INFORMATION

In this section, we examine a number of important applications of the tools of analysis developed in the chapter. These include (1) showing how time as

---

[19]See, D. Raff and L. Summers, "Did Henry Ford Pay Efficiency Wages," *Journal of Labor Economics,* October 1987, pp. S57–S58.

an economic good can be incorporated into the analysis, (2) allocation over time, and (3) the effect of Medicare and Medicaid on the price of medical services. These applications and the several examples presented in the chapter highlight the importance and relevance of the economics of information.

Time as an Economic Good

So far, we have considered income as the only constraint on consumption. However, the consumption of most goods and services (such as eating a meal in a restaurant or going to a baseball game) involves spending time as well as money. Therefore, it is only appropriate to consider time as an additional constraint on consumption. Time and information are, of course, related.

Suppose an individual has a maximum income of $100 and 24 hours *per month* available to attend baseball games (good Y) or to consume restaurant meals (good X). Suppose that the admission price for a baseball game and the price of a restaurant meal are each $10. Suppose also that it takes 3 hours to watch a game and 2 hours to consume a restaurant meal. The usual income constraint is given by budget line CF in the left panel of Figure 18–2. That is, if the individual spent the entire income attending baseball games, he or she could attend 10 games per month (point C, given by $100/$10). On the other

FIGURE 18–2   Time as a Constraint

In the left panel, the binding constraint is time over segment GE and income over EF, so that GEF is the overall constraint boundary. With indifference curve U_2 in the right panel, the individual maximizes utility at point E by purchasing 6X and 4Y. At point E both income and time are binding constraints. With U_2', only the time constraint is binding, and the individual can reach a higher indifference curve by working less. With U_2'', only income would be binding and the individual can reach a higher indifference curve by working more.

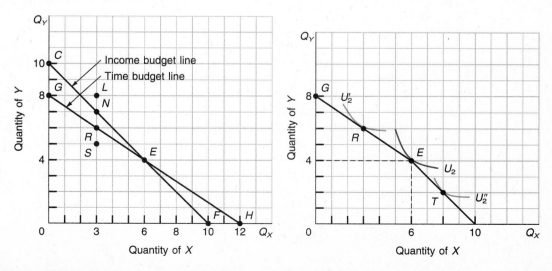

hand, if the individual spent the entire income on meals, he or she could purchase 10 meals per month (point F, given by \$100/\$10). By joining points C and F, we obtain the usual income budget line. The individual can purchase any combination of X and Y on or below *income* budget line CF. Budget line CF reflects only the individual's income constraint.

We can similarly derive the individual's **time budget line.** That is, if the individual spent the entire 24 hours per month for baseball games, he or she could attend 8 games per month (point G, given by 24 hours/3 hours). On the other hand, if the individual spent the entire 24 hours on restaurant meals, he or she could consume 12 meals per month (point H, given by 24 hours/2 hours). By joining points G and H, we get the individual's time budget constraint. The individual can achieve any combination of X and Y on or below time budget line GH in the left panel (ignoring the income constraint). That is, budget line GH reflects only the individual's time constraint.

Let us now look at both budget lines together. The combination of X and Y given by point L in the left panel is above and can be achieved neither with income budget line CF nor with time budget line GH. Point N is on CF but above GH. Thus, the individual would have the income to purchase combination N but does not have sufficient time per month to enjoy N. The individual can achieve combination R because R is on GH and below CF. The individual can also achieve combination S since S is below both CF and GH. Thus, only combinations on or below GEF satisfy both the income and time constraint simultaneously.[20] Over the range GE, time is the binding constraint, while over segment EF, income is the binding constraint. The area bounded by the axes and GEF is the feasible region (what the individual can achieve with both his or her income and time constraints). The feasible region is repeated in the right panel.

In the right panel, if the individual's indifference curve is U_2, he or she would maximize satisfaction at point E (where both constraints are binding) by purchasing $6X$ (meals) and $4Y$ (games). If the individual's indifference curve were instead U_2', only the time constraint would be binding at tangency point R. It would then pay for the individual to work less (and have less money to spend) in order to have more time for meals and games. This would shift down the income budget line and shift up the time budget line. The individual would then be able to reach an indifference curve higher than U_2' at the point where both budget lines cross so that both constraints would just be binding (not shown in the figure). Note that at equilibrium, $MRS_{XY} = P_X/P_Y$.

The opposite is true if the individual's indifference curve is U_2''. That is, with U_2'', income is the only binding constraint at tangency point T. The individual, therefore, should work more (so as to have more money to spend). As he or she does, the income budget line shifts up and the time budget line

---

[20]Note that GEF is not a straight line but bends at point E.

shifts down. This individual should continue to substitute work for free time until both constraints become binding. The individual would then reach the highest indifference curve of type U_2''' (higher than U_2'') possible (not shown in the figure).

Allocation Over Time

Prices not only ration the available supply of a commodity among potential buyers of the commodity, but also ration it over the time of the market period. For example, the price of wheat is not so low right after harvest that most of the wheat available is sold long before the next harvest. At the same time, the price of wheat is usually not so high during the year that large quantities of wheat are left unsold by the next harvest or must be sold at very low prices. In general, the price of wheat is lowest immediately after harvest and rises over the year sufficiently to just cover the opportunity cost of holding the wheat, plus the cost of insurance and the risk of unexpected price changes. In the real world, this is accomplished by speculators operating in the futures market for the commodity. In this market, wheat can be purchased and sold for future delivery at a predetermined price.

For example, suppose that the market period is one year and the demand in each of the three four-month periods of the year is given by D in Figure 18–3. Because sellers have the option of selling the total quantity of the commodity available for the year during any of the three four-month periods,

FIGURE 18–3   Allocation Over Time

Suppose the market period is one year and demand in each of the three four-month periods of the year is given by D, while the supply curves are, respectively, S_1, S_2, and S_3. S_1 is more elastic than S_2, and S_3 is vertical because all remaining wheat must be sold in the last four months. With D and S_1, $P = \$30$ and $Q = 150$; with D and S_2, $P = \$35$ and $Q = 110$; with D and S_3, $P = \$40$ and $Q = 80$.

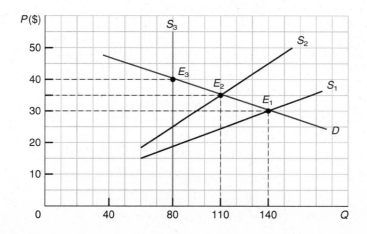

the supply curve for the first four-month period is not vertical, but is positively sloped (S_1 in the figure).[21] With D and S_1, $P = \$30$ and $Q = 150$ in the first period. The supply curve for the second four-month period is S_2. Supply curve S_2 is above S_1 because sellers require higher prices to be induced to hold over part of the commodity to the second period. Also, S_2 is less elastic than S_1 because sellers have fewer options (i.e., two periods instead of three during which) to dispose of the quantities of the commodity they hold. With D and S_2, $P = \$35$ and $Q = 110$.

In the third four-month period, the supply is S_3 and is vertical, since the remaining quantity of the commodity must be sold in this period (i.e., before the next harvest when the price will be much lower). Thus, with D and S_3, $P = \$40$ and $Q = 80$. It should be noted, however, that the process will occur exactly as described only if sellers and/or speculators correctly anticipate the market for each of the three four-month periods. If sellers hold over too much of the commodity for the last period, price may fall below that in earlier periods. When correct, speculative activity will smooth out the price of the commodity over the time of the market period. The explanation is basically the same for generally rising prices of exhaustible (i.e., nonreplenishable) natural resources, such as minerals, over time (see section 14.8).

Medicare and Medicaid and Moral Hazard

Medicare is a government program that covers most of the medical expenses of the elderly, while Medicaid covers practically all medical expenses of the poor. Both programs were enacted in 1965. The effect of Medicare and Medicaid on the price and quantity of medical services consumed by people not covered by either program is analyzed in Figure 18–4. For simplicity, we assume that all medical costs of the elderly and the poor are covered by the programs and all medical services take the form of doctors' visits.

In the figure, D_c is the demand curve of medical services of the elderly and the poor *before the subsidy* or coverage under Medicare and Medicaid, while D_n is the demand curve of the rest of the population. $D_c + D_n = D_t$. The intersection of D_t and S (point E) defines the equilibrium price of \$15 per visit (and a total of 900 million visits) for the to-be covered group and for the noncovered group. At $P = \$15$, the elderly and the poor purchase 200 million doctors' visits per year, while the rest of the population consumes 700 million per year, for a total of 900 million visits for the entire population.

When the government covers the entire cost of the doctors' visits of the elderly and the poor, their demand curve becomes D_c'. This is vertical at the quantity purchased at zero price. That is, the covered group will demand 400

FIGURE 18–4   Medicare and Medicaid and the Price of Medical Services

D_c is the demand curve of medical services of the elderly and the poor before the subsidy, while D_n is the demand curve of the rest of the population. $D_c + D_n = D_t$. With D_t and S, P = \$15 (point E). The to-be covered group purchases 200 million visits and others 700 million. When the government covers the entire cost of the doctors' visits of the elderly and the poor, their demand curve becomes D'_c. $D'_c + D_n$ = D'_t. Then P = \$20 and Q = 600 million (point E') for the noncovered group.

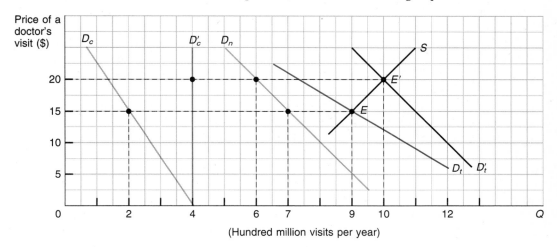

million visits per year regardless of price. $D'_c + D_n = D'_t$. The intersection of D'_t and S (point E') defines the new equilibrium price of \$20 for the noncovered group. The noncovered group now pays a higher price than before (\$20 per visit instead of \$15) and consumes a smaller quantity of medical services as read off D_n (600 million instead of the previous 700 million visits per year). The nonsubsidized group also pays the taxes to pay for the subsidy; the covered group, as well as doctors, receive the benefits. The conclusion of the foregoing analysis has been broadly borne out by the events that followed the adoption of Medicare and Medicaid.

SUMMARY

1. Search costs refer to the time and money we spend seeking information about a product. The general rule is to continue the search for lower prices, higher quality, and so on until the marginal benefit from the search equals the marginal cost. In most instances, advertising provides a great deal of information and greatly reduces consumers' search costs, especially for search goods. These are goods whose quality can be evaluated by inspection at the time of purchase (as opposed to experience goods, which can only be judged after using them).

2. Speculation refers to the seeking and accepting of the risks resulting from changing commodity and currency prices in the hope of making a profit. Hedging refers to

the covering of a market risk resulting from changing commodity and currency prices over time. The existence of forward or futures markets and speculators increases the amount of information available in the market and makes hedging possible. Hedging results in a larger volume of economic transactions and trade and increases economic welfare.

3. When one party to a transaction has more information than the other on the quality of the product (i.e., in the case of asymmetric information), the low-quality product or "lemon" will drive the high-quality product out of the market. One way to overcome such a problem of adverse selection is for the buyer to get, or the seller to provide, more information on the quality of the product or service. Such is the function of brand names, chain retailers, professional licensing, and guarantees. Insurance companies try to overcome the problem of adverse selection by requiring medical checkups, charging different premiums for different age groups and occupations, and offering different rates of coinsurance, amounts of deductibility, and length of contracts. The only way to avoid the problem entirely is with universal compulsory health insurance. Credit companies reduce the adverse selection process that they face by sharing "credit histories" with other insurance companies.

4. The insurance market also faces the problem of moral hazard, or the increase in the probability of an illness, fire, or other accident when an individual is insured above when he or she is not. If not contained, this could lead to unacceptably high insurance costs. Insurance companies try to overcome the problem of moral hazard by specifying the precautions that an individual or firm must take as a condition of insurance, and by coinsurance (i.e., insuring only part of the possible loss). The problem of moral hazard arises whenever an externality is present (i.e., any time an economic agent can shift some of its costs to others).

5. The problem of adverse selection resulting from asymmetric information can be resolved or greatly reduced by market signaling. Brand names, guarantees, and warranties are used as signals for higher-quality products, for which consumers are willing to pay higher prices. The willingness to accept coinsurance and deductibles signals low-risk individuals to whom insurance companies can charge lower premiums. Credit companies use good credit histories to make more credit available to good-quality borrowers, and firms use educational certificates to identify more-productive potential employees to receive higher salaries.

6. Because ownership is divorced from control in the modern corporation, a principal-agent problem arises. This refers to the fact that managers seek to maximize their own benefits rather than the owners' or principals' interests, which are to maximize the total profits or value of the firm. The firm may use golden parachutes (large financial payments to managers if they are forced or choose to leave if the firm is taken over by another firm) to overcome the managers' objections to a takeover bid that sharply increases the value of the firm. The firm may also set up generous deferred-compensation schemes for its managers to reconcile their long-term interests to those of the firm.

7. According to the efficiency wage theory, firms willingly pay higher than equilibrium wages to induce workers to avoid shirking or slacking off on the job. The no-shirk constraint curve is positively sloped and shows that the efficiency or minimum wage that the firm must pay to avoid shirking is higher the smaller is the level of unemployment. The equilibrium efficiency

wage is the one given by the intersection of the firm's demand curve for labor and the no-shirking constraint curve.

8. Since the consumption of most goods involves the expenditures of both time and money, time (which is closely associated to information) should be included as an additional constraint. Prices ration the available supply of a commodity among potential buyers and over the time of the market period. Medicare and Medicaid increase the price and reduce the quantity of medical services consumed by the noncovered population.

KEY TERMS

Search Costs
Search Goods
Experience Goods
Arbitrage
Spot Transactions
Spot Market
Spot Price or Rate
Forward or Futures
  Transaction

Forward or Futures Market
Forward or Futures Price or
  Rate
Speculator
Hedging
Asymmetric Information
Adverse Selection

Moral Hazard
Coinsurance
Market Signaling
Principal-Agent Problem
Golden Parachutes
Efficiency Wage Theory
Time Budget Line

REVIEW QUESTIONS

1. a. In which market structure was perfect information assumed on the part of all economic agents?
   b. If all consumers have perfect information, can a price dispersion for a given homogeneous product exist in the market if all conditions of the sale are identical? Why?
2. On which do you think consumers spend more time shopping for lower prices, sugar or coffee? Why?
3. Can you explain why the price dispersion for salt is much greater than the price dispersion for sugar?
4. Frozen vegetables are search goods because they are purchased frequently by consumers. True or false? Explain.
5. Most advertising is manipulative and provides very little information to consumers. True or false? Explain.
6. What is the relationship between speculation and the economics of information?

7. a. Adverse selection is the direct result of asymmetric information. True or false? Explain.
   b. How can the problem of adverse selection be overcome?
8. a. How do credit companies reduce the adverse selection problem that they face?
   b. What complaint does this give rise to?
9. a. What problem can arise for the Chrysler Corporation by providing a 50,000-mile guarantee for its new automobiles sold?
   b. How can Chrysler reduce this problem?
10. What is the relationship between moral hazard and externalities?
11. Should education be viewed as an investment in human capital or a market signaling device? Explain.
12. What is meant by the efficiency wage? What problem is this intended to solve?

PROBLEMS

*1. Determine the precise expected price for the TV from the second search in the problem discussed in the section on "Searching for the Lowest Price" without the use of formula [18–1].

2. Draw a figure showing the marginal benefit and the marginal cost of each additional search, and show the point of equilibrium for the TV problem using the information given in the text.

*3. a. Suppose that type I sellers charged the price of $60 for the portable TV, type II sellers charged $80, type III sellers charged $100, type IV sellers charged $120, and type V sellers charged $140. Determine the expected lowest price for the TV from one, two, three, four, and five searches.
   b. Determine the marginal benefit from each additional search.

4. Using the data of problem 3 indicate
   a. How many searches should a consumer undertake if the marginal cost of each additional search is $4?
   b. If it is $2?
   c. How many searches should a consumer undertake if the marginal cost of each additional search is $5.34 and the consumer plans to purchase two TV sets?

5. a. Suppose that type I sellers charged the price of $96 for the portable TV, type II sellers charged $98, type III sellers charged $100, type IV sellers charged $102, and type V sellers charged $104. Determine the expected lowest price for the TV from one, two, three, four, and five searches.
   b. Determine the marginal benefit from each additional search.
   c. How many searches should a consumer undertake if the marginal cost of each additional search is $1.00?

*6. Suppose that a U.S. firm imports $200,000 worth of goods from the United Kingdom and agrees to pay £100,000 in three months. The spot rate today is $2/£1.
   a. What foreign-exchange risk does the U.S. importer face?
   b. Explain how the importer can hedge her foreign-exchange risk in the spot market.

c. Why does hedging usually take place in the forward market?

7. Explain how the importer of problem 6 hedges her foreign-exchange risk in the forward market if the three-month forward rate is $2.02/£1.

*8. Suppose that there are only two types of used cars in the market: high-quality and low-quality, and all the high-quality cars are identical and all the low-quality cars are identical. With perfect information, the quantity demanded of high-quality used cars is zero at $16,000 and 100,000 at $12,000, while the quantity demanded of low-quality cars is zero at $8,000 and 100,000 at $4,000. Suppose also that the supply curve for high-quality cars is horizontal at $12,000, while the supply curve of low-quality used cars is horizontal at $4,000 in the relevant range. Draw a figure showing that with asymmetric information, no high-quality cars will be sold and 100,000 low-quality cars will be sold at the price of $4,000 each. Explain the precise sequence of events that leads to this result.

9. Draw another figure similar to the figure in the answer to problem 8 but with the supply curves of high-quality and low-quality cars positively sloped rather than horizontal. Assume further that used cars are of many different qualities rather than being simply of high-quality and low-quality. With reference to the figure, explain the precise sequence of events that leads to only cars of the lowest quality being sold.

10. An insurance company is considering providing fire insurance for $120,000, $100,000, or $80,000 to the owner of a house with a market value of $100,000.
   a. How much insurance is the company likely to sell for the house? Why?
   b. If the probability of a fire is 1 in 1,000, what would be the premium charged by the company?

11. Explain how franchising signals quality.

12. Suppose that the returns to education are 12% for an intelligent and motivated person but

---

only 8% for a less-intelligent and less-motivated person (because it takes longer for the
latter to get a college degree). Suppose also
that the return on investing in stock is 10% and
that such an investment is as risky as getting a
college education. Suppose furthermore that

getting a college education is viewed as a
strictly investment undertaking (i.e., assume
that there are no psychological benefits to getting a college education). Explain how a college
education can serve as a market signaling device in this case.

A

MATHEMATICAL APPENDIX

A.1 INDIFFERENCE CURVES

(Refers to section 3.2, p. 64)

Suppose that a consumer's purchases are limited to commodities X and Y, then

$$U = U(X,Y) \qquad \text{[1A]}$$

is a general utility function. Equation [1A] postulates that the utility or satisfaction that the consumer receives is a function of, or depends on, the quantity of commodity X and commodity Y that he or she consumes. The more of X and Y the individual consumes, the greater is the level of utility or satisfaction that he or she receives.

Using a subscript on U to specify a given level of utility or satisfaction, we can write

$$U_1 = U_1(X,Y) \qquad \text{[2A]}$$

This is the general equation for an indifference curve. Equation [2A] postulates that the individual can get U_1 of utility by various combinations of X and Y. Of course, the more of X the individual consumes, the less of Y he or she will have to consume in order to remain on the same indifference curve. Higher subscripts refer to higher indifference curves. Thus, $U_2 > U_1$.

Taking the total differential of equation [1A], we get

$$dU = \frac{\delta U}{\delta X} dX + \frac{\delta U}{\delta Y} dY \qquad \text{[3A]}$$

Since a movement along an indifference curve leaves utility unchanged, we set $dU = 0$ and get

$$\frac{\delta U}{\delta X} dX + \frac{\delta U}{\delta Y} dY = 0 \qquad \text{[4A]}$$

so that

$$\frac{\delta U}{\delta X} dX = -\frac{\delta U}{\delta Y} dY \qquad \text{[5A]}$$

and

$$-\frac{dY}{dX} = \frac{\delta U/\delta X}{\delta U/\delta Y} = \frac{MU_X}{MU_Y} = MRS_{XY} \qquad \text{[6A]}$$

Equation [6A] indicates that the negative value of the slope of an indifference curve ($-dY/dX$) is equal to the ratio of the marginal utility of X to the marginal utility of Y (MU_X/MU_Y), which, in turn, equals the marginal rate of substitution of X for Y (MRS_{XY}).

A.2 UTILITY MAXIMIZATION

(Refers to section 3.5, p. 69)

We now wish to maximize utility (i.e., equation [1A]) subject to the budget constraint. The budget constraint of the consumer is

$$P_X X + P_Y Y = I \qquad \text{[7A]}$$

where P_X and P_Y are the price of commodity X and commodity Y, respectively, X and Y refer to the quantity of commodity X and commodity Y, and I is the consumer's income, which is given and fixed at a particular point in time.

To maximize equation [1A] subject to equation [7A], we form

$$V = U(X,Y) + \lambda(I - P_XX - P_YY) \quad \text{[8A]}$$

where λ is the Lagrangian multiplier.

Taking the first partial derivative of V with respect to X and Y and setting them equal to zero gives

$$\frac{\delta V}{\delta X} = \frac{\delta U}{\delta X} - \lambda P_X = 0$$

$$\frac{\delta V}{\delta Y} = \frac{\delta U}{\delta Y} - \lambda P_Y = 0 \quad \text{[9A]}$$

It follows that

$$\frac{\delta U}{\delta X} = \lambda P_X, \frac{\delta U}{\delta Y} = \lambda P_Y \quad \text{[10A]}$$

Dividing, we get

$$\frac{\delta U/\delta X}{\delta U/\delta Y} = \frac{MU_X}{MU_Y} = MRS_{XY} = \frac{P_X}{P_Y} \quad \text{[11A]}$$

Equation [11A] indicates that the consumer maximizes utility at the point where the marginal rate of substitution of X for Y, $\frac{\delta U/\delta X}{\delta U/\delta Y}$, equals the ratio of the price of X to the price of Y. Graphically, this occurs at the point where the budget line is tangent to the highest indifference curve possible (and their slopes are equal). Equation [11A] is only the first order condition for maximization (and minimization). The second order condition for maximization is that the indifference curves be convex to the origin.

A.3 CONSUMER SURPLUS

(Refers to section 4.5, p. 104)

In section 4.5, we defined consumer surplus as the difference between what a consumer is willing to pay for a given quantity of a good and what he or she actually pays for it. Graphically, consumer surplus is given by the difference in the area under the demand curve and the area representing the total expenditures of the consumer for the given quantity of the good that he or she purchases.

Starting with $P = g(Q)$, where g is the inverse of $Q = f(P)$. For a given price (P_1) and its associated quantity (Q_1),

$$\text{consumer surplus} = \int_0^{Q_1} g(Q)dQ - P_1Q_1 \quad \text{[12A]}$$

where the integral sign ($\int$) represents the process of calculating the area under inverse demand function $P = g(Q)$ between zero quantity of the commodity and quantity Q_1, and P_1Q_1 is the total expenditure of the consumer for Q_1 of the commodity.

A.4 SUBSTITUTION AND INCOME EFFECTS

(Refers to section 4.3, p. 96)

The substitution effect of a price change can be measured by a movement along a given indifference curve (so that utility or purchasing power is constant). With a change in the price of commodity X, we have

$$\text{substitution effect} \quad \text{[13A]}$$
$$= \delta X/\delta P_X \text{ with constant utility } (U)$$

The income effect can be measured by a shift to a different indifference curve (to reflect the change in utility or purchasing power) with prices constant. This is given by the change in the demand for X per dollar increase in income, weighed by the quantity of X purchased. That is,

$$\text{income effect} \quad \text{[14A]}$$
$$= X(\delta X/\delta I) \text{ with constant prices}$$

When the price of X falls, the income effect tells us how much the consumer's income should be *reduced* in order to leave his or her purchasing power constant.

Combining the substitution and the income effects we get the Slutsky equation:

$$\delta X/\delta P_x = \underset{\text{for constant } U}{\delta X/\delta P_x} - \underset{\substack{\text{for constant} \\ \text{prices}}}{X(\delta X/\delta I)} \quad \text{[15A]}$$

The first term on the right side gives the substitution effect (shown by a movement along a given indifference curve). The second term gives the income effect (shown by a shift to a different indifference curve but with constant goods prices).

A.5 ELASTICITIES

(Refers to sections 5.2 to 5.4, pp. 122–123)

In sections 2.2 and 5.2 we defined the *price elasticity of demand*, η, as the percentage change in the quantity demanded of a commodity divided by the percentage change in its price. That is, for $Q = f(P)$,

$$\eta = -\frac{\Delta Q/Q}{\Delta P/P} = -\frac{\Delta Q}{\Delta P}\frac{P}{Q} \quad \text{[16A]}$$

We also pointed out that since quantity and price move in opposite directions, we multiply by -1 in order to make the value of η positive. Equation [16A] can be used to measure *arc elasticity*. In that case, P and Q refer to the average price and the average quantity, respectively.

As the change in price approaches zero in the limit, we can measure *point elasticity* by

$$\eta = -\frac{dQ}{dP}\frac{P}{Q} \quad \text{[17A]}$$

If the demand curve is linear and given by

$$Q \doteq a - bP \quad \text{[18A]}$$

the slope of the demand curve is constant and is given by

$$\frac{dQ}{dP} = \frac{\Delta Q}{\Delta P} = -b \quad \text{[19A]}$$

and

$$\eta = -b\frac{P}{Q} \quad \text{[20A]}$$

For example, if $b = -2$ and $P/Q = 1$, then $\eta = 2$. Since P/Q is different at every point on the negatively sloped, straight-line demand curve, η varies at every point.

For a curvilinear demand curve of the form

$$Q = aP^{-b} \quad \text{[21A]}$$

$$\frac{dQ}{dP} = -abP^{-b-1} \quad \text{[22A]}$$

and

$$\eta = -abP^{-b-1}\frac{P}{Q} = -\frac{abP^{-b}}{Q} = -b \quad \text{[23A]}$$

since $aP^{-b} = Q$. Thus, equation [21A] is a demand curve with a constant price elasticity equal to the exponent of P (i.e., $\eta = -b$). Thus, if $b = 2$, $\eta = -2$ at every point on the demand curve. As pointed out in section 5.2, demand is elastic if $|\eta| > 1$ and inelastic if $|\eta| < 1$.

The *income elasticity of demand*, η_I is defined as the ratio of the relative change in the quantity purchased (Q) to the relative change in income (I), other things remaining constant. That is, for $Q = f(I)$,

$$\eta_I = \frac{dQ}{dI}\frac{I}{Q} \quad \text{[24A]}$$

For the following linear income-demand function

$$Q = a + cI \quad \text{[25A]}$$

where $c > 0$, the derivative of Q with respect to I is

$$\frac{dQ}{dI} = c \quad \text{[26A]}$$

Therefore,

$$\eta_I = c\left(\frac{I}{Q}\right) \quad \text{[27A]}$$

For the following nonlinear income-demand function

$$Q = aI^c \quad \text{[28A]}$$

the derivative of Q with respect to I is

$$\frac{dQ}{dI} = acI^{c-1} \qquad \text{[29A]}$$

Therefore,

$$\eta_I = acI^{c-1}\frac{I}{Q} = \frac{acI^c}{Q} = c \qquad \text{[30A]}$$

As pointed out in section 5.3, a commodity is normal if $\eta_I > 0$ and inferior if $\eta_I < 0$. A normal good is a luxury if $\eta_I > 1$ and a necessity if η_I is between 0 and 1.

The *cross elasticity of demand* of commodity X for commodity Y, η_{XY}, is defined as the ratio of the relative change in the quantity purchased of commodity X (Q_X) to the relative change in the price of commodity Y (P_Y). That is,

$$\eta_{XY} = \frac{dQ_X/Q_X}{dP_Y/P_Y} = \frac{dQ_X}{dP_Y}\frac{P_Y}{Q_X} \qquad \text{[31A]}$$

Consider the following linear demand function for commodity X:

$$Q_X = a + bP_X + cP_Y \qquad \text{[32A]}$$

The above function indicates that Q_X depends on P_X and P_Y. The derivative of the function with respect to P_Y is

$$\frac{dQ_X}{dP_Y} = b\frac{dP_X}{dP_Y} + c \qquad \text{[33A]}$$

If the P_X remains unchanged when P_Y changes, then

$$\frac{dP_X}{dP_Y} = 0 \text{ while } \frac{dQ_X}{dP_Y} = c \qquad \text{[34A]}$$

Therefore,

$$\eta_{XY} = c\frac{P_Y}{Q_X} \qquad \text{[35A]}$$

As pointed out in section 5.4, commodities X and Y are substitutes if $\eta_{XY} > 0$ and complements if $\eta_{XY} < 0$.

As pointed out in section 2.2, the *price elasticity of supply*, ϵ, is defined as the ratio of the relative change in the quantity supplied of a commodity (Q_s) to the relative change in its price (P). That is, for $Q_s = f(P)$,

$$\epsilon = \frac{dQ_s/Q_s}{dP/P} = \frac{dQ_s}{dP}\frac{P}{Q_s} \qquad \text{[36A]}$$

Since the quantity supplied and price move in the same direction (i.e., supply curves are usually positively sloped), ϵ is positive.

For the following linear supply function

$$Q_s = a + bP \qquad \text{[37A]}$$

the derivative of Q_s with respect to P is

$$\frac{dQ_s}{dP} = b \qquad \text{[38A]}$$

Therefore,

$$\epsilon = b\frac{P}{Q_s} \qquad \text{[39A]}$$

Substituting equation [37A] for Q_s into equation [39A], we get

$$\epsilon = \frac{bP}{a + bP} \qquad \text{[40A]}$$

Thus, if $a = 0$ (so that the supply curve starts at the origin), $\epsilon = 1$ throughout the supply curve, regardless of the value of its slope (b). If $a > 0$ (so that the supply curve cuts the quantity axis), $\epsilon < 1$ throughout the supply curve. If $a < 0$ (so that the supply curve cuts the price axis), $\epsilon > 1$ throughout. When $a = 0$, ϵ varies with price.

A.6 RELATIONSHIP AMONG INCOME ELASTICITIES

(Extension of sections 5.2 and 5.3, pp. 122, 128)

If a consumer's income increases, say by 10%, and the consumption of some commodities increases by less than 10%, the consumption of other commodities must increase by more than 10% for the entire increase in the consumer's income to be fully spent. This leads to the proposition that the income elasticity of demand must be unity, on the average, for all commodities. Assuming, for simplicity, that the entire consumer's income is spent on commodities X and Y, we can restate the above proposition mathematically as

$$K_X\eta_{IX} + K_Y\eta_{IY} \equiv 1 \qquad \text{[41A]}$$

where K_X is the proportion of the consumer's income (I) spent on commodity X (i.e., $K_X = P_X X/I$), η_{IX} is the income elasticity of demand for commodity X, K_Y is the proportion of income spent on Y (i.e., $K_Y = P_Y Y/I$), and η_{IY} is the income elasticity of demand for Y.

Starting with the consumer's budget constraint [7A]

$$I = P_X X + P_Y Y \qquad \text{[7A]}$$

we can prove proposition [41A] by differentiating equation [7A] with respect to income, while holding prices constant. This gives

$$\frac{dI}{dI} = 1 \equiv P_X \frac{dX}{dI} + P_Y \frac{dY}{dI} \qquad \text{[42A]}$$

If we multiply the first term on the right-hand side by $(X/X)(I/I)$, which equals one, and the second term by $(Y/Y)(I/I)$, which equals one, the value of

the expression will not change, and we get

$$1 \equiv P_X \frac{dX}{dI} \frac{X}{X} \frac{I}{I} + P_Y \frac{dY}{dI} \frac{Y}{Y} \frac{I}{I} \qquad \text{[42A']}$$

Rearranging equation [42A'], we get

$$\frac{P_X X}{I} \frac{dX}{dI} \frac{I}{X} + \frac{P_Y Y}{I} \frac{dY}{dI} \frac{I}{Y} \equiv 1 \qquad \text{[43A]}$$

Since $P_X X/I = K_X$, $(dX/dI)(I/X) = \eta_{IX}$, $P_Y Y/I = K_Y$, and $(dY/dI)(I/Y) = \eta_{IY}$, we have

$$K_X \eta_{IX} + K_Y \eta_{IY} \equiv 1 \qquad \text{[41A]}$$

That is, with the K's providing the weights, the weighted average of all income elasticities equals unity. Thus, the income elasticity of demand of a commodity on which the consumer spends a great proportion of his or her income cannot be too different from unity (see problem 12 in Chapter 5).

A.7 RELATIONSHIP AMONG MARGINAL REVENUE, PRICE, AND ELASTICITY

(Refers to section 5.6, p. 135)

Let P and Q equal the price and the quantity of a commodity, respectively. Then the total revenue of the seller of the commodity (TR) is given by

$$TR = PQ \qquad \text{[44A]}$$

and the marginal revenue is

$$MR = \frac{d(TR)}{dQ} = P + Q \frac{dP}{dQ} \qquad \text{[45A]}$$

Manipulating expression [45A] mathematically, we get

$$MR = P\left(1 + \frac{Q}{P} \frac{dP}{dQ}\right) = P\left(1 - \frac{1}{\eta}\right) \qquad \text{[46A]}$$

where, η equals -1 times the coefficient of price elasticity of demand. For example, if $P = \$12$ and $\eta = 3$, $MR = \$8$. If $\eta = \infty$, $P = MR = \$12$.

A.8 ISOQUANTS

(Refers to sections 6.3 and 6.4, pp. 162, 166)

Suppose that there are two inputs, labor and capital. Then

$$Q = Q(L,K) \qquad \text{[47A]}$$

is a general production function. Equation [47A] postulates that output (Q) is a function of, or depends on, the quantity of labor (L) and capital (K) used in production. The more L and K are used, the greater is Q.

Using a subscript on Q to specify a given level of output, we can write

$$Q_1 = Q_1(L,K) \qquad \text{[48A]}$$

This is the general equation for an isoquant. Equation [48A] postulates that output Q_1 can be produced with various combinations of L and K. The more L is used, the less K will be required to remain on the same isoquant. Higher subscripts refer to higher isoquants. Thus, $Q_2 > Q_1$.

Taking the total differential of equation [47A], we get

$$dQ = \frac{\delta Q}{\delta L} dL + \frac{\delta Q}{\delta K} dK \qquad \text{[49A]}$$

Since a movement along an isoquant leaves output unchanged, we set $dQ = 0$ and get

$$\frac{\delta Q}{\delta L} dL + \frac{\delta Q}{\delta K} dK = 0 \qquad \text{[50A]}$$

so that

$$\frac{\delta Q}{\delta K} dK = -\frac{\delta Q}{\delta L} dL \qquad \text{[51A]}$$

and

$$-\frac{dK}{dL} = \frac{\delta Q/\delta L}{\delta Q/\delta K} = \frac{MP_L}{MP_K} = MRTS_{LK} \qquad \text{[52A]}$$

Equation [52A] indicates that the negative value of the slope of an isoquant ($-dK/dL$) is equal to the ratio of the marginal product of L to the marginal product of K (MP_L/MP_K), which, in turn, equals the marginal rate of technical substitution of L for K ($MRTS_{LK}$).

A.9 COST MINIMIZATION

(Refers to section 7.2, p. 191)

A firm may wish to minimize the cost of producing a given level of output. The total cost of the firm (TC) is given by

$$TC = wL + rK \qquad \text{[53A]}$$

where w is the wage rate of labor and r is the rental price (per unit) of capital. A given level of output ($\overline{Q}$) can be produced with various combinations of L and K:

$$\overline{Q} = \overline{Q}(L,K) \qquad \text{[54A]}$$

To minimize equation [53A] subject to equation [54A], we form

$$Z = wL + rK + \lambda^*[\overline{Q} - \overline{Q}(L,K)] \qquad \text{[55A]}$$

where λ^* is the Lagrangian multiplier.

Taking the first partial derivative of Z with respect to L and K and setting them equal to zero gives

$$\frac{\delta Z}{\delta L} = w - \lambda^*\frac{\delta Q}{\delta L}$$

and

$$\frac{\delta Z}{\delta K} = K - \lambda^*\frac{\delta Q}{\delta K} \qquad \text{[56A]}$$

It follows that

$$w = \lambda^*\frac{\delta Q}{\delta L} \text{ and } r = \lambda^*\frac{\delta Q}{\delta K} \qquad \text{[57A]}$$

Dividing, we get

$$\frac{w}{r} = \frac{\delta Q/\delta L}{\delta Q/\delta K} = MRTS_{LK} \qquad \text{[58A]}$$

Equation [58A] indicates that a firm minimizes the cost of producing a given level of output by hiring labor and capital up to the point where the ratio of the input prices (w/r) equals the ratio of the marginal products of labor and capital, $\frac{\delta Q/\delta L}{\delta Q/\delta K}$, which equals the marginal rate of technical substitution of labor for capital ($MRTS_{LK}$). Graphically, this occurs at the point where a given isoquant is tangent to an isocost line (and their slopes are equal). Equation [58A] is only the first order condition for minimization (and maximization). The second order condition for minimization is that the isoquant be convex to the origin.

A.10 PROFIT MAXIMIZATION

(Refers to section 8.3, p. 228)

A firm usually wants to produce the output that maximizes its total profits. Total profits (π) are equal to total revenue (TR) minus total cost (TC).

That is,

$$\pi = TR - TC \qquad \text{[59A]}$$

where π, TR, and TC are all functions of output (Q).

Taking the first derivative of π with respect to Q and setting it equal to zero gives

$$\frac{d\pi}{dQ} = \frac{d(TR)}{dQ} - \frac{d(TC)}{dQ} = 0 \qquad \text{[60A]}$$

so that

$$\frac{d(TR)}{dQ} = \frac{d(TC)}{dQ} \qquad \text{[61A]}$$

and

$$MR = MC \qquad \text{[62A]}$$

Equation [62A] indicates that in order to maximize profits, a firm must produce where marginal revenue (MR) equals marginal cost (MC).

Furthermore, since for a perfectly competitive firm P is constant and $\frac{d(TR)}{dQ} = MR = P$, the first order condition becomes

$$MR = P = MC \qquad \text{[63A]}$$

Equation [61A] is only the first order condition for maximization (and minimization). The second order condition for profit maximization requires that the second derivative of π with respect to Q be negative. That is,

$$\frac{d^2\pi}{dQ^2} = \frac{d^2(TR)}{dQ^2} - \frac{d^2(TC)}{dQ^2} < 0 \qquad \text{[64A]}$$

so that

$$\frac{d^2(TR)}{dQ^2} < \frac{d^2(TC)}{dQ^2} \qquad \text{[65A]}$$

According to equation [65A], the algebraic value of the slope of the MC function must be greater than the algebraic value of the MR function. Under perfect competition, MR is constant (i.e., the MR curve of the firm is horizontal) so that equation [65A] requires that the MC curve be rising at the point where $MR = MC$ for the firm to maximize its total profits (or minimize its total losses).

A.11 PRICE DETERMINATION

(Refers to section 8.4, p. 235)

At equilibrium, the quantity demanded of a commodity (Q_d) is equal to the quantity supplied of the commodity (Q_s). That is,

$$Q_d = Q_s \qquad \text{[66A]}$$

The demand function can be written as

$$Q_d = a - bP (a,b > 0) \qquad \text{[67A]}$$

where a is the positive quantity intercept, and $-b$ is the negative of the multiplicative inverse of the slope of the demand curve (so that when P rises, Q_d falls). The supply function can take the form of

$$Q_s = -c + dP (c,d > 0) \qquad \text{[68A]}$$

where $-c$ refers to the negative quantity intercept (so that the supply curve crosses the price axis at a positive price), and d is the positive of the multiplicative inverse of the slope of the supply curve (so that when P rises, Q_s also rises).

Setting $Q_d = Q_s$ for equilibrium, we get

$$a - bP = -c + dP \qquad \text{[69A]}$$

Solving for P, we have

$$\overline{P} = \frac{a + c}{b + d} \qquad \text{[70A]}$$

where the bar on P refers to the equilibrium price. Since parameters a, b, c, and d are all positive, $\overline{P}$ is also positive.

To find the equilibrium quantity ($\overline{Q}$) that corresponds to $\overline{P}$, we substitute equation [70A] into equation [67A] or [68A]. Substituting equation [70A] into equation [67A], we get

$$\overline{Q} = a - \frac{b(a + c)}{(b + d)}$$

$$= \frac{a(b + d) - b(a + c)}{b + d} = \frac{ad - bc}{b + d} \qquad \text{[71A]}$$

Since the denominator of equation [71A], $(b + d)$, is positive, for $\overline{Q}$ to be positive (and for the model to be economically meaningful) the numerator, $(ad - bc)$, must also be positive. That is, $ad > bc$.

A.12 PRICE DISCRIMINATION

(Refers to section 9.5, p. 285)

A monopolist selling a commodity in two separate markets must decide how much to sell in each market in order to maximize its total profits. The total profits of the monopolist (π) are equal to the sum of the total revenue that it receives from selling the commodity in the two markets (i.e., $TR_1 + TR_2$) minus the total cost of producing the total output (TC). That is,

$$\pi = TR_1 + TR_2 - TC \qquad \text{[72A]}$$

Taking the first partial derivative of π with respect to Q_1 (the quantity sold in the first market) and Q_2 (the amount sold in the second market), and setting them equal to zero, we get

$$\frac{\delta\pi}{\delta Q_1} = \frac{\delta(TR_1)}{\delta Q_1} - \frac{\delta(TC)}{\delta Q_1} = 0,$$

$$\frac{\delta\pi}{\delta Q_2} = \frac{\delta(TR_2)}{\delta Q_2} - \frac{\delta(TC)}{\delta Q_2} = 0 \qquad \text{[73A]}$$

or

$$MR_1 = MR_2 = MC \qquad \text{[74A]}$$

That is, in order to maximize its total profits, the monopolist must distribute its sales between the two markets in such a way that the marginal revenue is the same in both markets and equal to the common marginal cost. If $MR_1 > MR_2$, the monopolist could increase its total profits by redistributing sales from market 2 to market 1, until $MR_1 = MR_2$.

Equations [73A] and [74A] give the first order condition for profit maximization. The second order condition is given by

$$\frac{\delta^2\pi}{\delta Q_1^2} < 0 \text{ and } \frac{\delta^2\pi}{\delta Q_2^2} < 0 \qquad \text{[75A]}$$

Since we know from equation [46A] that

$$MR = P(1 - 1/\eta) \qquad \text{[46A]}$$

profit maximization requires that

$$P_1(1 - 1/\eta_1) = P_2(1 - 1/\eta_2) \qquad \text{[76A]}$$

where P_1 and P_2 are the prices in market 1 and market 2, respectively, and η_1 and η_2 are the coefficients of price elasticity of demand in market 1 and market 2. If $\eta_1 < \eta_2$, equation [76A] will hold only if $P_1 > P_2$. That is, in order to maximize total profits the monopolist must sell the commodity at a higher price in the market with the lower price elasticity of demand (see also Figure 9–11). For example, if $\eta_1 = 2$, $\eta_2 = 3$, and $P_2 = \$6$, then $P_1 = \$8$ (so that $MR_1 = MR_2 = \$4$).

A.13 EMPLOYMENT OF INPUTS

(Refers to section 13.5, p. 415)

A firm employs the quantity of inputs that allows it to produce the profit-maximizing level of output. As indicated by equation [59A], total profits (π) are equal to total revenue (TR) minus total cost (TC). Total revenue is given by

$$TR = PQ \qquad \text{[77A]}$$

where P is the price of the commodity that the firm produces and Q is the output, such that $Q = Q(L, K)$. The total cost of the firm was defined by equation [53A]. Thus, the firm employs labor and capital so as to maximize:

$$\pi = PQ(L,K) - (wL + rK) \qquad \text{[78A]}$$

When P, w, and r are constant, the firm is a perfect competitor in the product and input markets.

Taking the first partial derivative of π with respect to L and K and setting them equal to zero gives

$$\frac{\delta\pi}{\delta L} = P\frac{\delta Q}{\delta L} - w = 0,$$

$$\frac{\delta\pi}{\delta K} = P\frac{\delta Q}{\delta K} - r = 0 \qquad \text{[79A]}$$

It follows that

$$P\frac{\delta Q}{\delta L} = w, \, P\frac{\delta Q}{\delta K} = r \qquad \text{[80A]}$$

or

$$MRP_L = w, \, MRP_K = r \qquad \text{[81A]}$$

Equation [65A] indicates that a firm maximizes

profits by hiring labor and capital up to the point where the marginal revenue product of labor [$MRP_L = P(\delta Q/\delta L)$] equals the wage rate ($w$) and the marginal revenue product of capital [$MRP_K = P(\delta Q/\delta K)$] equals the rental price of capital (r). Geometrically, this occurs where the MRP_L curve intersects the (horizontal) supply curve of labor and the MRP_K curve intersects the (horizontal) supply curve of rental capital. Equation [65A] is only the first order condition for maximization. The second order condition is that the MRP_L and MRP_K curves be negatively sloped (i.e., that the firm be in stage II of production or produce in the area of diminishing returns).

A.14 INPUT PRICE, MARGINAL EXPENSE, AND THE PRICE ELASTICITY OF INPUT SUPPLY

(Refers to sections 14.4 and 14.5, pp. 441, 445)

The total cost (TC) of a firm hiring only labor is given by

$$TC = wL \qquad \text{[82A]}$$

where w is the wage rate and L is the number of workers hired.

If the firm is a monopsonist (i.e., the only employer of labor in the market), it will have to pay higher wages the more labor it wants to hire. That is, the wage rate is a function of or depends on the amount of labor the firm hires (and the amount of labor the firm hires depends on the wage rate).

The firm's marginal resource cost of labor (MRC_L) is then given by

$$MRC_L = \frac{dC}{dL} = w + L\frac{dw}{dL} \qquad \text{[83A]}$$

Rearranging equation [83A], we get

$$MRC_L = w\left(1 + \frac{L}{w}\frac{dw}{dL}\right) \qquad \text{[84A]}$$

Therefore,

$$MRC_L = w\left(1 + \frac{1}{\epsilon_L}\right) \qquad \text{[85A]}$$

where ϵ_L is the price (wage) elasticity of the supply curve of labor. Graphically, this means that the MRC_L curve lies above the (positively sloped) S_L curve (see also Figure 14–3). The same would be true for capital or any other input for which the firm is the only employer in the market.

If the firm were a perfect competitor in the labor market, $\epsilon_L \to \infty$ and $MRC_L = w$ (i.e., the MRC_L curve would coincide with the horizontal S_L curve faced by the firm at the given level of w).

A.15 DERIVATION OF THE FORMULA TO FIND THE PRESENT VALUE OF AN INVESTMENT

(Refers to section 15.3, p. 480)

We have seen in section 15.3 that the present discounted value (PDV) of an investment that yields a constant stream of net cash flows in each future year, is given by equation [86A]:

$$PDV = \frac{R}{r} \qquad \text{[86A]}$$

where R is the constant net cash flow received the next year and in every subsequent year (i.e., in perpetuity), and r is the rate of interest.

To derive equation [86A], we start with

$$PDV = \frac{R}{(1+r)} + \frac{R}{(1+r)^2}$$
$$+ \cdots \frac{R}{(1+r)^n} \qquad \text{[87A]}$$

which is similar to equation [15–6] in section 15.3.

If we let $1/(1 + r) = k$, then

$$PDV = R(k + k^2 + \ldots k^n) \qquad \textbf{[88A]}$$

Multiplying both sides of equation [88A] by k, we get

$$kPDV = R(k^2 + k^3 + \ldots k^{n+1}) \qquad \textbf{[89A]}$$

Subtracting equation [89A] from equation [88A] we have

$$PDV - kPDV = R(k - k^{n+1}) \qquad \textbf{[90A]}$$

From equation [90A], we get

$$PDV = \frac{R(k - k^{n+1})}{1 - k} \qquad \textbf{[91A]}$$

Since $k = 1/(1 + r)$ is smaller than 1, for n very large, k^{n+1} is very small and can be ignored. Thus, we are left with

$$PDV = R\left(\frac{k}{1 - k}\right) \qquad \textbf{[92A]}$$

Substituting $1/(1 + r)$ for k into equation [92A], we get

$$PDV = R\left(\frac{\dfrac{1}{1 + r}}{1 - \dfrac{1}{1 + r}}\right)$$

$$= R\left(\frac{\dfrac{1}{1 + r}}{\dfrac{1 + r - 1}{1 + r}}\right)$$

$$= R\left(\frac{1}{1 + r}\right)\left(\frac{1 + r}{r}\right) \qquad \textbf{[93A]}$$

$$= \frac{R}{r}$$

A.16 A MODEL OF GENERAL EQUILIBRIUM

(Refers to section 16.5, p. 528)

In this section we outline the Walras-Cassel general equilibrium model.*

Let $x_1, x_2, \ldots, x_n$ refer to the quantity of the n commodities in the economy, with prices $p_1, p_2, \ldots, p_n$. Let $r_1, r_2, \ldots r_m$ refer to the quantity of the m resources or inputs in the economy, with prices $v_1, v_2, \ldots, v_m$.

The market demand equations for the n commodities can be written as

$$
\begin{aligned}
x_1 &= f_1(p_1, p_2, \ldots, p_n; v_1, v_2, \ldots, v_m) \\
x_2 &= f_2(p_1, p_2, \ldots, p_n; v_1, v_2, \ldots, v_m) \quad \textbf{[94A]} \\
&\cdots \cdots \cdots \cdots \cdots \cdots \cdots \cdots \\
x_n &= f_n(p_1, p_2, \ldots p_n; v_1, v_2, \ldots, v_m)
\end{aligned}
$$

The market demand for each commodity is the sum of the demand for the commodity by each consumer and is a function of, or depends on, the prices of all commodities and of all inputs. Input prices affect individuals' incomes and, thus, influence the demand for commodities.

Since in long-run perfectly competitive equilibrium, commodity prices equal their production costs, we have

$$
\begin{aligned}
a_{11}v_1 + a_{21}v_2 + \ldots + a_{m1}v_m &= p_1 \\
a_{12}v_1 + a_{22}v_2 + \ldots + a_{m2}v_m &= p_2 \quad \textbf{[95A]} \\
\cdots \cdots \cdots & \cdots \cdots \cdots \cdots \\
a_{1n}v_1 + a_{2n}v_2 + \ldots + a_{mn}v_m &= p_n
\end{aligned}
$$

where a_{11} refers to the quantity of input 1 required to produce one unit of commodity 1. Since v_1 is the price of input 1, $a_{11}v_1$ is then the dollar amount spent on input 1 to produce one unit of commodity 1. On the other hand, a_{21} refers to the quantity of input 2 required to produce one unit of commodity 1, so that $a_{21}v_2$ is the dollar amount spent on input 2 to produce one unit of commodity 1. Finally, a_{m1} is the amount of input m required to produce one unit of commodity 1, and $a_{m1}v_m$ is the expenditure on input m to produce one unit of commodity 1. Therefore, the left-hand side of equation [95A] refers to the total cost of producing one unit of commodity 1. This is equal to the unit price of

---

*The presentation is adapted from R. Dorfman, P. A. Samuelson, and R. M. Solow, *Linear Programming and Economic Analysis* (New York: McGraw-Hill, 1958), pp. 351–355.

commodity 1 (p_1). The second equation gives the expenditure on each input to produce one unit of commodity 2, and this is equal to p_2. The same is true for each of the n commodities. The a_{ij}'s are called input or production coefficients, and they are assumed to be fixed in our simple model.

Setting the total demand for each resource or input (required to produce all commodities) equal to the total supply of the input, we have

$$
\begin{aligned}
a_{11}x_1 + a_{12}x_2 + \ldots + a_{1n}x_n &= r_1 \\
a_{21}x_1 + a_{22}x_2 + \ldots + a_{2n}x_n &= r_2 \quad \textbf{[96A]} \\
&\cdots \\
a_{m1}x_1 + a_{m2}x_2 + \ldots + a_{mn}x_n &= r_m
\end{aligned}
$$

where $a_{11}x_1$ is the quantity of resource or input 1 required to produce x_1 units of commodity 1, $a_{12}x_2$ is the quantity of input 1 required to produce x_2 of commodity 2, and $a_{1n}x_n$ is the quantity of input 1 required to produce x_n of commodity n. Thus, the first equation sets the total quantity demanded of input 1 (required to produce x_1, x_2, to x_n) equal to the total supply of resource or input 1 (r_1). Similarly, the second equation sets the total quantity demanded of input 2 used in all commodities to equal the quantity supplied of input 2, and so on for each of the m resources or inputs.

The last step to close the model is to specify the set of equations that relate the supply of each resource or input to prices. This is given by

$$
\begin{aligned}
r_1 &= g_1(p_1, p_2, \ldots, p_n; v_1, v_2, \ldots, v_m) \\
r_2 &= g_2(p_1, p_2, \ldots, p_n; v_1, v_2, \ldots, v_m) \quad \textbf{[97A]} \\
&\cdots \\
r_m &= g_m(p_1, p_2, \ldots, p_n; v_1, v_2, \ldots, v_m)
\end{aligned}
$$

That is, the supply of each resource or input is a function of, or depends on, the price of all inputs (the v_i's) and the price of all commodities (the p_i's). For example, the supply of steel depends on the price of steel, the price of aluminum, the wages of autoworkers, and other input prices. The price of steel also depends on the price of automobiles, washing machines, steaks, and other commodity prices. Therefore, a change in any part of the system affects every other part of the system.

Summing up, in equation [94A] to equation [97A], we have $2n + 2m$ equations and an equal number of unknowns (the x_j's, the p_j's, the v_i's, and the r_i's). However, according to Walras's law, equations [94A] and [97A] have only $n + m - 1$ independent equations, since if all but one of these $n + m$ equations are satisfied, the last one must also be satisfied. However, we can arbitrarily set any commodity price, say, $p_1 = 1$ and express all other prices in terms of p_1 (the *numéraire*). This reduces the number of unknowns in the system by 1, so as to equal the number of independent equations. The system may then have a unique solution (i.e., set of prices and quantities that simultaneously satisfies all the equations of the model).

ANSWERS TO SELECTED PROBLEMS

Chapter 1

1. We study microeconomic theory to understand the economic behavior of individual consumers, resource owners, and business firms; to examine how individual commodity and resource prices are determined; and to understand the conditions for the efficient allocation of consumption and production in a free-enterprise economy. One cannot become an expert in any other field of economics without a thorough understanding of microeconomic theory.

6. a. With a price ceiling, consumers want to purchase more of the commodity than producers are willing to produce. This results in a shortage of the commodity, which leads to rationing and a black market.

   b. With a price floor, consumers want to purchase less of a commodity than producers are willing to produce. This results in a surplus of the commodity.

8. One way to measure the interdependence of the U.S. economy with the rest of the world is to calculate the percentage that imports and exports are to GNP. The percentage that the sum of imports and exports are to GNP increased from about 8% in 1970 to almost 15% in 1993. Thus, U.S. interdependence increased sharply during the past two decades.

12. a. The positive income aspects of positive economics refer to such things as the shift in the kinds and quantities of goods and services produced, its effect on employment and incentives to work, on economic

growth, and so on. All of these can be objectively measured or estimated.

   b. The normative aspects of income redistribution refer to the value-based disagreement on how much income should be redistributed.

Chapter 2

2. a.

P($)	8	7	6	5	4	3	2	1	0
QD'	0	10	20	30	40	50	60	70	80

   b. See Figure 2a.

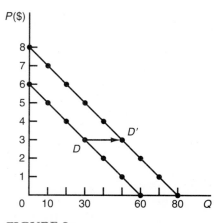

FIGURE 2a

c. D' represents an increase in demand because consumers demand more of the commodity at each and every price.

5. a.

Market Supply Schedule, Market Demand Schedule, and Equilibrium

Price	Quantity Supplied	Quantity Demanded	Surplus (+) Shortage (−)	Pressure on Price
$6	60	0	60	Down
5	50	10	40	Down
4	40	20	20	Down
3	30	30	0	Equilibrium
2	20	40	−20	Up
1	10	50	−40	Up
0	0	60	−60	Up

b. See Figure 2b.

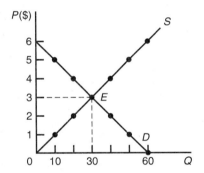

FIGURE 2b

9. a. The demand for hamburgers increases, and this results in a higher price and quantity.
   b. The supply of hamburgers declines, and this results in an increase in the equilibrium price and a reduction in the equilibrium quantity.
   c. The supply of hamburgers increases, and this lowers the equilibrium price and increases the quantity purchased.
   d. The demand for hamburgers increases, and this has the same effect as in part (a).
   e. A per-unit subsidy is the opposite of a per-unit tax. The per-unit subsidy increases the supply of hamburgers, and this has the same effect as in part (c).

12. a. See Figure 2c.

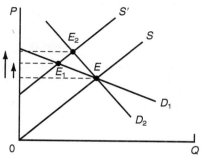

FIGURE 2c

b. See Figure 2d.

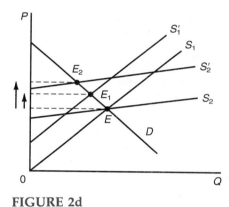

FIGURE 2d

Chapter 3

3. a. See Figure 3a.

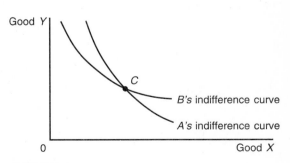

FIGURE 3a

b. Point C is the original equal endowment of

good X and good Y of individual A and individual B. Since A prefers X to Y, A's indifference curve is steeper than B's indifference curve. That is, A is willing to give up more of Y for an additional unit of X, and MRS_{XY} for A at point C is greater than for B.

7. a. See Figure 3b.

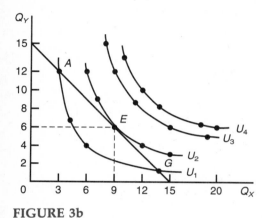

FIGURE 3b

b. The individual maximizes utility at point E, where U_2 is tangent to the budget line by purchasing $9X$ and $6Y$. To maximize utility, the individual should spend all income in such a way that MRS_{XY} (the absolute slope of the indifference curve) equals P_X/P_Y (the absolute slope of the budget line).
c. Points A and G are on U_1 even though the individual spends all income.
d. The individual does not have sufficient income to reach U_3 and U_4.

9. a. The individual would spend \$4 to purchase $4X$ and the remaining \$3 to purchase $3Y$.
b. $MU_X/P_X = MU_Y/P_Y = 6/\$1$ and ($1)($4X$) + ($1)($3Y$) = \$7.
c. The individual would receive 41 utils from consuming $4X$ (the sum of the MU_X up to $4X$) plus 27 utils from purchasing $3Y$ (the sum of the MU_Y up to $3Y$) for a total utility of 68 utils. If the individual spent all \$7 on $7X$, he or she would get 49 utils (the sum of all MU_X). If the individual spent all income on $7Y$, he or she would get 38 utils (the sum of all MU_Y).

12. See Figure 3c. The vertical intercepts in the two

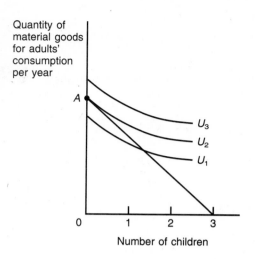

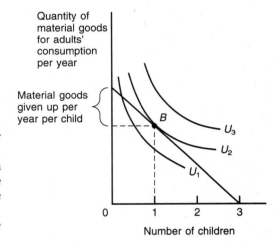

FIGURE 3c

figures measure the amount of material goods that each couple could enjoy without children. The slope of the budget lines measures the amount of material goods per year that each couple would have to give up per child. The couple portrayed in the top panel is at corner equilibrium A and chooses to have no children. The couple in the bottom panel is in equilibrium at point B by having one child. This couple is willing to give up the amount of material goods indicated on the vertical axis of the graph to have one child.

As the possibility for women to find high-paying jobs since World War II increased in the United States and in other industrial countries, birth rates declined because the opportunity costs of having children increased. High-income people also seem to have fewer children but tend to spend more on their education, health, and so on. It seems that high-income people have traded the number of children for better quality of children.

Chapter 4

3. a. See Figure 4a.

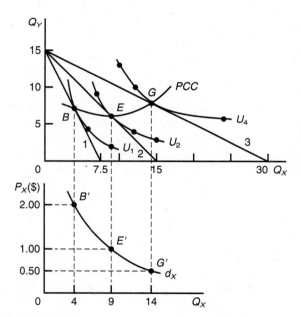

FIGURE 4a

b. At $P_X = \$0.50$, the consumer maximizes utility at point G where U_4 is tangent to budget line 3 by purchasing $14X$. This gives point G' in the bottom panel. With $P_X = \$1$, the optimum is at point E where U_2 is tangent to budget line 2 and the consumer purchases 9_X. This gives point E' in the bottom panel.

Finally, with $P_X = \$2$, the consumer is at optimum at point B where U_1 is tangent to budget line 1 by buying $4X$. This gives

point B' in the bottom panel. Joining points $G'E'B'$ in the bottom panel we derive d_X.

6. See Figure 4b. The sequence in the figure is from A to B to C.

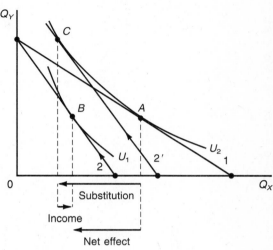

FIGURE 4b

8. In very poor Asian countries, people can purchase little else besides rice. If the price of rice falls, the substitution effect tends to lead people to substitute rice for other goods. However, if rice is an inferior good in these nations, the increase in real income resulting from the decline in the price of rice leads people to purchase less rice. People spend most of their income on rice, so a decline in the price of rice will lead to a relatively large increase in purchasing power, which will allow people to purchase so much more of other goods that they need to purchase less rice.

That is, it is conceivable that the substitution effect (which leads people to purchase more rice when its price falls) could be overwhelmed by the opposite income effect. The net effect would then be that people purchase less rice when its price falls, so that the demand curve for rice would be positively sloped in these countries. However, there is no proof that this is indeed the case.

10. See Figure 4c. The poor family is originally maximizing utility at point A where U_1 is tangent to budget line 1. With the government

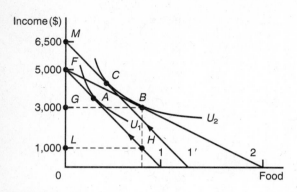

FIGURE 4c

paying half of the family's food bill, we have budget line 2. With budget line 2, the poor family maximizes utility at point B on U_2. To get to point B, the family spends $2,000 of its income ($FG$). Without the subsidy the family would have to pay $4,000 ($FL$).

Thus, the cost of the subsidy to the government is $2,000. The family, however, could reach U_2 at point C with a cash subsidy of $1,500 ($FM$). The government may still prefer to subsidize the family's food consumption (even if more expensive) if one of its aims is to improve nutrition.

Chapter 5

3. a. When two demand curves are parallel, their slopes ($-\Delta P/\Delta Q$) and their inverse ($-\Delta Q/\Delta P$) are the same at every price. However, P/Q (the other component of the price elasticity formula) is smaller (since Q is larger) for the demand curve further to the right at every price. Therefore, the price elasticity of the demand curve further to the right is smaller.

    b. When two demand curves intersect, P/Q is the same for both demand curves at the point of intersection. However, $-\Delta Q/\Delta P$ is larger for the flatter demand curve. Therefore, the flatter demand curve is more elastic at the point where the demand curves intersect.

7. a. In a two-commodity world, both commodities cannot be luxuries because that would

imply that a consumer could increase the quantity purchased of both commodities by a percentage larger than the percentage increase in his or her income. This is impossible if the consumer already spent all income on the two commodities before the increase in income (and does not borrow money).

    b. A 10% increase in income results in a 25% increase in the quantity of cars purchased if the income elasticity is 2.5. That is, since $2.5 = \%\Delta Q/10\%$, $(2.5)(10\%) = 25\%$.

9. a. Since $\eta = 0.13$ in the short run and 1.89 in the long run, the demand for electricity is inelastic in the short run and elastic in the long run. With a 10% increase in price, the quantity demanded of electricity will decline by 1.3% in the short run and by 18.9% in the long run.

    b. Since the income elasticity of demand exceeds unity, electricity is a luxury. With a 10% increase in incomes, consumers would purchase 19.4% more electricity.

    c. Since the cross elasticity of demand between electricity and natural gas is positive, natural gas is a substitute for electricity. However, a 10% increase in the price of natural gas increases electricity consumption by only 2%.

12. a. Since $K_X = 0.75$, K_Y must be 0.25. Then,

$$(0.75)(0.90) + (0.25)(\eta_{IY}) = 1$$

$$0.25\eta_{IY} = 0.325$$

$$\eta_{IY} = 1.3$$

    b. Commodity Y is a luxury, and commodity X is a necessity. For Y to be an inferior good, η_{IY} must be negative. For this to occur, $(0.75)(\eta_{IY})$ must be larger than 1, which means that η must exceed 1.33. Since most goods are normal, the income elasticity of demand of a commodity on which the consumer spends a great proportion of his or her income cannot be too much higher than 1.

Chapter 6

3. a. See Figure 6a.

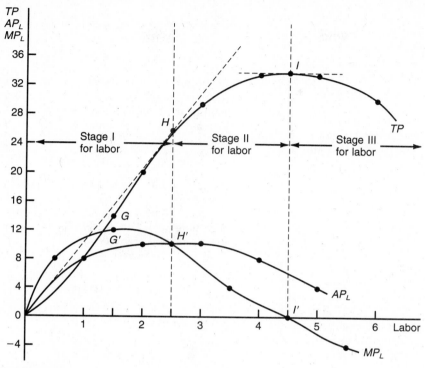

FIGURE 6a

b. The law of diminishing returns begins to operate past point G on the total product curve. This corresponds to G' on the marginal product of labor curve. As more and more units of the variable input (here labor) are used on one acre of land, eventually, "too much" labor is used and the marginal product of labor begins to fall.

8. See Figure 6b. The right angle or L-shaped

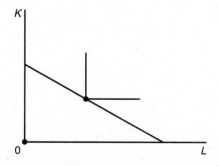

FIGURE 6b

isoquant shows no possibility of substituting one input for the other in production. The straight-line isoquant shows that inputs are perfectly substitutable for each other in production (the $MRTS_{LK}$ is constant). That is, the given level of output could be produced with only labor or only capital.

11. a. The production function $Q = 10\sqrt{LK}$ exhibits constant returns to scale throughout. For example, when $L = 1$ and $K = 1$, $Q = 10\sqrt{1} = 10$. When $L = 2$ and $K = 2$, $Q = 10\sqrt{4} = 20$. When $L = 3$ and $K = 3$, $Q = 10\sqrt{9} = 30$. With $L = 4$ and $K = 4$, $Q = 10\sqrt{16} = 40$, and so on.

b. The production function exhibits diminishing returns to capital and labor throughout. For example, holding capital constant at $K = 1$ and increasing labor from $L = 1$ to $L = 2$, increases Q from 10 to $10\sqrt{2} = 14.14$. Therefore, the marginal product of labor (MPL) is 4.14. Increasing labor to $L = 3$, results in $Q = 10\sqrt{3} = 17.32$. Thus, MPL declines to 3.18. The law of diminishing returns operates throughout, but MPL remains always positive. The same is true if labor is held constant and capital changed.

12. a. False. As long as returns are diminishing but positive, the student still benefits from additional hours of study.

b. True. If economies of scale were present, larger and more efficient firms would drive smaller and less efficient firms out of business.

Chapter 7

1. a. The explicit costs are $10,000 + $30,000 + $15,000 = $55,000.

b. The implicit costs are the foregone earnings of $15,000 in the previous occupation.

c. The total costs are equal to the $55,000 of explicit costs plus the $15,000 of implicit costs, or $70,000. Since the total earnings or revenues are only $65,000, from the economist's point of view, the woman actually lost $5,000 for the year by being in business for herself.

6. a. Since to expand output in the short run to meet peak electricity demand, electrical utility companies bring into operation older and less efficient equipment, their short-run marginal costs rise sharply.

b. New generating equipment would have to be run around the clock, or nearly so, for AFC to be sufficiently low to make ATC lower than for older equipment. To meet only peak demand, older and *fully* depreciated equipment is cheaper.

9. a. The LTC curve would be a positively sloped straight line through the origin when constant returns to scale operate at all levels of output.

b. The LAC and the LMC curves would coincide and be horizontal at the value of the constant slope of the LTC curve.

c. Horizontal LAC and LMC curves are consistent with U-shaped $SATC$ curves.

12. a. Rewriting learning curve equation $AC = 1,000\,Q^{-0.3}$ in double log form we get

$$\log(AC) = \log(1,000) - 0.3\log(Q)$$

Substituting the value of 100 for Q into the previous equation we get

$$\log(AC) = \log(1,000) - 0.3\log(100)$$

Substituting 3 for the log of 1,000 and 2 for the log of 100 (obtained by simply entering the numbers 1,000 and 100, respectively, in your calculator and pressing the "log" key), we get

$$\log(AC) = 3 - 0.3(2) = 2.4$$

Thus, AC equals the antilog of 2.4, which equals $251.19 (obtained by simply entering the log of 2.4 in your calculator and pressing the antilog key). The AC for the 100th unit of the product is $251.19.

b. For $Q = 200$, we have

$$\log(AC) = \log(1,000) - 0.3\log(200)$$
$$= 3 - 0.3(2.30103)$$
$$= 3 - 0.69039$$
$$= 2.309691$$

Thus, AC for the 200th unit of the product equals the antilog of 2.309691, which equals $204.03.

c. For $Q = 400$, we have

$$\log(AC) = \log(1,000) - 0.3\log(400)$$
$$= 3 - 0.3(2.60206)$$
$$= 3 - 0.780618$$
$$= 2.219382$$

Thus, AC for the 400th unit of the product equals the antilog of 2.219382, which equals $165.72.

d. Figure 7a shows the figure for the learning curve estimated above.

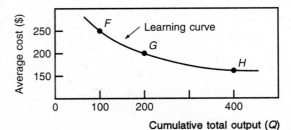

FIGURE 7a

Chapter 8

1. a.

$$QD = QS$$
$$4{,}750 - 50P = 1{,}750 + 50P$$
$$3{,}000 = 100P$$
$$P = \$30 \text{ (equilibrium price)}$$

Market Demand and Supply Schedules

P ($)	QD	QS
50	2,250	4,250
40	2,750	3,750
30	3,250	3,250
20	3,750	2,750
10	4,250	2,250

c. See Figure 8a.
d. $P = \$30$.

4. a. See Figure 8b. In Figure 8b, the slope of the TR curve refers to the constant price of $10 at which the perfectly competitive firm can sell its output. The TC curve indicates total fixed costs of $200 and a constant average variable cost of $5 (the slope of the TC curve). This is often the case for many firms for small changes in outputs. The firm breaks even at $Q = 40$ per time period (point B in the figure). The firm incurs a loss at smaller outputs and earns a profit at higher

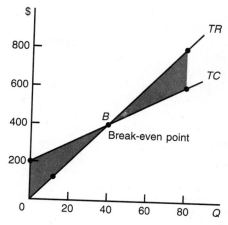

FIGURE 8b

output levels. A figure such as Figure 8b is called a *break-even chart*.

b. An increase in the price of the commodity can be shown by increasing the slope of the TR curve; an increase in the total fixed costs of the firm can be shown by an increase in the vertical intercept of the TC curve, and an increase in average variable costs by an increase in the slope of the TC curve. The chart will then show the change in the break-even point of the firm and the profits

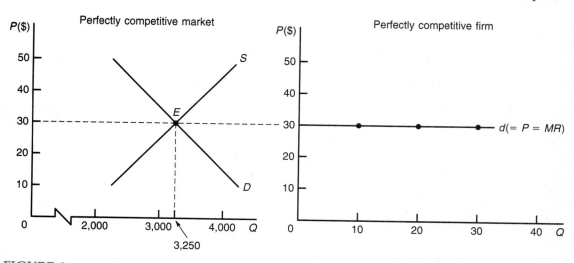

FIGURE 8a

or losses at other output levels. Thus, the break-even chart is a flexible tool to analyze quickly the effect of changing conditions on the firm.

c. An important shortcoming of break-even charts is that they imply that firms will continue to earn larger and larger profits per time period with greater output levels. From our discussion in Chapter 8, we know that, eventually, the TC curve will begin to rise faster than TR, and total profits will fall. Thus, break-even charts must be used with caution. Nevertheless, under the appropriate set of circumstances, they can be a useful tool; and they are being used extensively today by business executives, government agencies, and nonprofit organizations.

8. See Figure 8c.

10. See Figure 8d. The original long-run equilibrium point is E (where D crosses S and LS). If D shifts up to D', the equilibrium point is E' in the market period (where D' and S cross), E" in the short run (where D' and S' cross), and E* in the long run (where D' crosses S" and LS). Thus, the adjustment to an increase in demand falls entirely on price in the market period, mostly on price in the short run, and

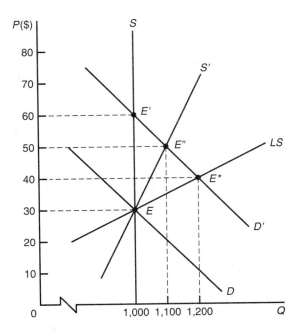

FIGURE 8d

mostly on output in the long run. With a constant cost industry, long-run adjustment would fall entirely on output.

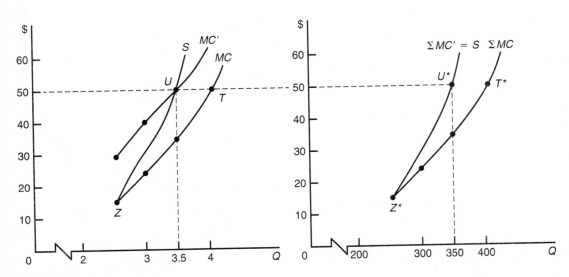

FIGURE 8c

Chapter 9

4. a. See Figure 9a. The best level of output is about $Q = 2$, where the MC curve intersects the MR' curve from below.
   b. Since at $Q = 2$, $P = \$20$ while $ATC = \$30$, the firm incurs a loss of $10 per unit and $20 in total. However, since $AVC = \$15$, the monopolist covers $10 out of its $30 of total fixed costs. Were the monopolist to go out of business, it would incur a total loss equal to its $TFC = \$30$. The shutdown point of the monopolist is at $Q = 2.5$, where $P = AVC = \$14$.

7. a. See Figure 9b.
   b. See Figure 9c.

10. With third degree price discrimination, $MR_1 = MR_2$. Also with formula [5–6], $MR_1 = P_1(1 - 1/\eta_1)$ and $MR_2 = P_2(1 - 1/\eta_2)$. Setting MR_1 equal to MR_2, we get

$$P_1(1 - 1/\eta_1) = P_2(1 - 1/\eta_2),$$

so that

$$\frac{P_1}{P_2} = \frac{1 - 1/\eta_2}{1 - 1/\eta_1}$$

and

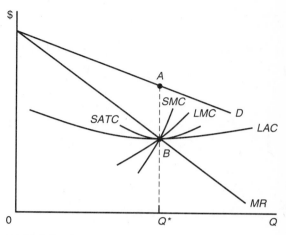

FIGURE 9b

$$P_1 = \left(\frac{1 - 1/\eta_2}{1 - 1/\eta_1}\right)4.5.$$

Since we were given that $P_2 = \$4.50$, we need only to calculate η_1 and η_2 to prove that P_1 should be $7. By extending D_1 to the horizontal axis and labeling H the intersection point at $Q = 11$ and also labeling J the point on the horizontal axis directly below point A, we get

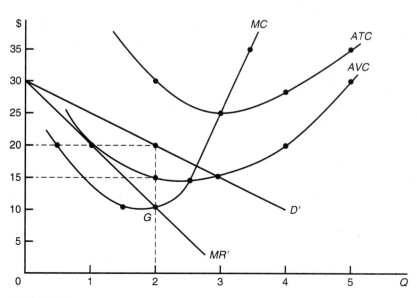

FIGURE 9a

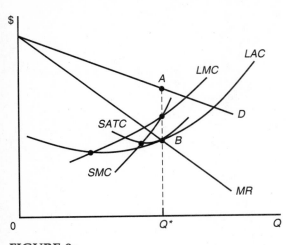

FIGURE 9c

$\eta_1 = JH/OJ = 7/4$. Doing the same for D_2, we get $\eta_2 = 3$. Substituting the η_1, η_2, and P_2 values into the formula for P_1 derived above, we get

$$P_1 = \left(\frac{1 - 1/3}{1 - \frac{1}{4/7}}\right) 4.5 = \left(\frac{2/3}{1 - 7/4}\right) 4.5$$

$$= \left(\frac{2/3}{3/7}\right) 4.5 = \left(\frac{2}{3}\right)\left(\frac{7}{3}\right) 4.5 = 7.$$

12. a. See the following table and Figure 9d where the prime indicates the effect of the lump-sum tax of $4.50.

Q	STC	MC	ATC	STC'	ATC'
0	$ 6	. . .	. . .	$10.50	. . .
1	10	$ 4	$10	14.50	$14.50
2	12	2	6	16.50	8.25
*3	13.50	1.50	4.50	18	6
4	19	4.50	4.75	23.50	5.88
5	30	11	6	34.50	6.90
6	48	18	8	52.50	8.75

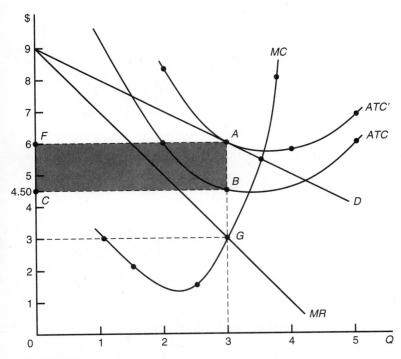

FIGURE 9d

The *STC'* values are obtained by adding $4.50 to the *STC* values. *ATC'* = *STC'*/*Q*. Since the lump-sum tax is liked a fixed cost, it does not affect *MC*. Thus, the best level of output of the monopolist remains at three units, at which *P* = $6, *ATC'* = $6 and the monopolist breaks even.

b. See the following table and Figure 9e, where the prime indicates the effect of a $2.50 per-unit tax.

Q	STC	MC	ATC	STC'	MC'	ATC'
1	$10	$ 4	$10	$12.50	. . .	$12.50
2	12	2	6	17	$ 4.50	8.50
3	13.50	1.50	4.50	21	4	7
4	19	4.50	4.75	29	8	7.25
5	30	11	6	42.50	13.50	8.50

The *STC'* values are obtained by adding $2.50 per unit of output to *STC*. *ATC'* =

STC'/*Q*. *MC'* = Δ*STC'*/Δ*Q*. Since a per-unit tax is like a variable cost both the *ATC* and the *MC* curves shift up to *ATC'* and *MC'*. The new equilibrium point is 2.5 units, given at point *G'* where the *MC'* curve intersects the *MR* curve from below. At *Q* = 2.5, *P* = $6.50, *ATC'* = $7.50, and the monopolist incurs a loss of $0.50 per unit and $1.25 in total (as opposed to a profit of $4.50 before the per-unit tax). Thus, the monopolist can shift part of the burden of the per-unit tax to consumers.

Chapter 10

2. The more price elastic is the demand curve faced by a monopolistically competitive firm when in long-run equilibrium, the closer to the lowest point on its *LAC* curve will the firm be when in long-run equilibrium. Since excess capacity is measured by the distance between

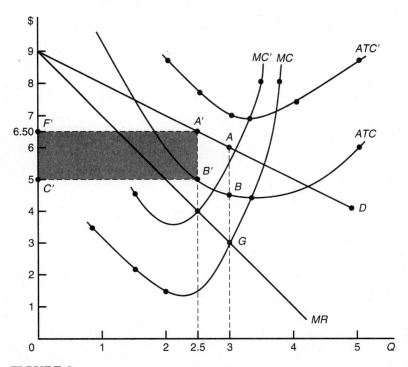

FIGURE 9e

the two points, the more elastic the demand curve is, the smaller is the amount of excessive capacity under monopolistic competition.

6. a. See Figure 10a. If the demand curve that the oligopolist faces shifts up by $0.50 but the kink remains at $P = \$8$, we get demand curve d^* or $H^*B^*C^*$. The marginal revenue curve is then mr^* or $H^*K^*F^*G^*$. Since the SMC curve intersects the mr^* curve at point K^*, $Q = 6$ and price remains at $P = \$8$.

   b. See Figure 10b. If the demand curve that the oligopolist faces shifts down by $0.50 but the kink remains at $P = \$8$, we get demand curve d^{**} or $H^{**}B^{**}C^{**}$. The marginal revenue curve is then mr^{**} or $H^{**}J^{**}J^*G^{**}$. Since the SMC' curve intersects the mr^{**} curve at point J^*, $Q = 2$ and price remains at $P = \$8$.

9. a. See Figure 10c. Duopolist 1 (the low-cost duopolist) produces 2 units of the commodity and charges $P = \$8$ (given by point E_1,

at which $SMC_1 = mr$, as in Figure 10–6). Duopolist 2 produces 1 unit of the commodity and would like to charge $P = \$10$ (given by point E_2, at which $SMC_2 = mr$). However, since the commodity is homogeneous, duopolist 2 (the high-cost duopolist) is forced to also sell at $P = \$8$ set by low-cost duopolist 1.

   b. With $P = \$8$ and $SATC_1 = \$5$ at $Q = 2$, duopolist 1 earns a profit of $3 per unit and $6 in total. With $P = \$8$ and $SATC_2 = \$8$ at $Q = 1$, duopolist 2 breaks even. At $P = \$10$ duopolist 2 would have earned a profit of $2. Thus, only duopolist 1 maximizes profits.

   If the high-cost duopolist would go out of business at the profit-maximizing price set by the low-cost duopolist, the latter would probably set a price sufficiently high to allow the high-cost duopolist to remain in the market and avoid possible prosecution

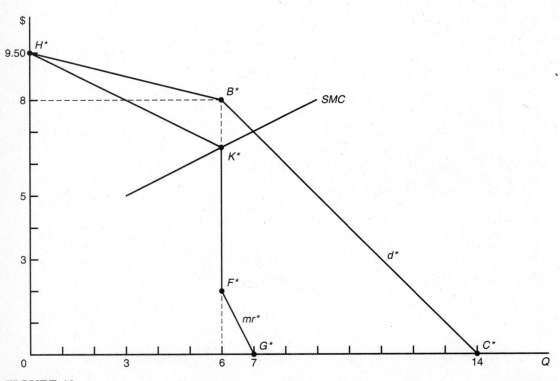

FIGURE 10a

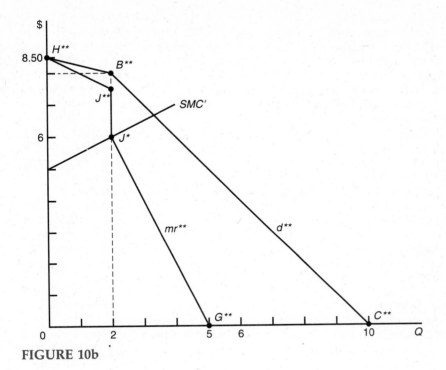

FIGURE 10b

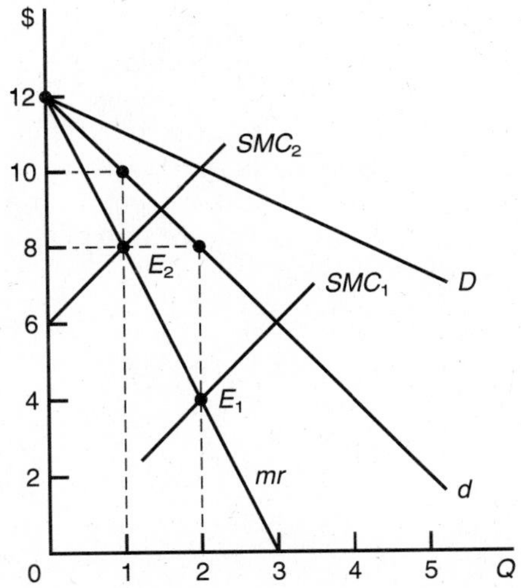

FIGURE 10c

under antitrust laws for monopolizing the market. In that case, the low-cost firm would not be maximizing profits.

12. a. The markup that the oligopolist should use in pricing its product is

$$m = 1/(\eta - 1)$$
$$= 1/(4 - 1)$$
$$= 1/3 \text{ or } 33.33\%.$$

b. Since $AVC = \$10$ and the markup (m) equals 33.33%, the oligopolist should charge

$$P = AVC(1 + m)$$
$$= 10(1 + 0.3333)$$
$$= 10(1.3333)$$
$$= \$13.33$$

Chapter 11

3. a. If firm B produces small cars, firm A will earn a profit of 4 if it produces large cars and have a payoff of -2 (i.e., incurs a loss of 2) if it produces small cars. If firm B produces large cars, firm A will incur a loss of 2 if it also produces large cars and firm A earns a

profit of 4 if it produces small cars. Therefore, firm A does not have a dominant strategy.

b. If firm A produces large cars, firm B will earn a profit of 4 if it produces small cars and have a payoff of − 2 (i.e., incurs a loss of 2) if it also produces large cars. If firm A produces small cars, firm B will incur a loss of 2 if it also produces small cars and firm B earns a profit of 4 if it produces large cars. Therefore, firm B does not have a dominant strategy.

c. The optimal strategy is for one firm to produce small cars and the other to produce large cars. In that case, each firm earns a profit of 4. If both firms produce either small cars or large cars, each incurs a loss of 2.

d. In this case we have *two* Nash equilibria: either firm A produces large cars and firm B produces small cars (the top left cell in the payoff matrix), or firm A produces small cars and firm B produces large cars (the bottom right cell in the payoff matrix).

e. A situation such as that indicated in the payoff matrix of this problem might arise if each firm does not have the resources to invest in the plant and equipment necessary to produce both large and small cars, and the demand for either small or large cars is not sufficient to justify the production of small or large cars by both firms. Specifically, if both firms produced the same type of car, the oversupply of that type of car will result in low car prices and losses for both firms.

4. The following table is a hypothetical payoff matrix for example 2 in Chapter 11.

| | | Other Computer Firms | |
		No Mail Orders	Mail Orders
Dell	No Mail Orders	0,1	0,8
Computers	Mail Orders	6,2	4,4

The payoff matrix in this table shows that when other computer companies do not sell computers through mail orders, Dell Computer earns zero profit if it also does not sell through the mail (since Dell was created specifically to sell

only through the mail) but a profit of 6 if it does. Similarly, when other computer companies do sell through the mail, Dell earns zero profits if it does not sell through the mail and 4 if it does. Thus, Dell's dominant strategy is to sell computers through the mail, regardless of what the other computer companies do.

On the other hand, when Dell does not sell through the mail (i.e., when Dell is not in the market), other computer companies earn a profit of 1 if they do not sell through the mail and 8 if they do (at least that is what they believed). But if Dell is in the market and sells through the mail, other computer companies will earn 2 if they do not accept mail orders and 4 if they do. Thus, the other computer companies do not have a dominant strategy.

With Dell in the market and following its dominant strategy of selling through the mail, however, the other computer companies are also forced to enter the mail-order business. This is the Nash equilibrium.

8. a. Each firm adopts its dominant strategy of cheating (the top left cell) but could do better by cooperating not to cheat (the bottom right cell). Thus, the firms face the prisoners' dilemma.

b. If the payoff in the bottom right cell were changed to (5,5), the firms would still face the prisoners' dilemma by cheating.

9. The tit-for-tat strategy for the first 5 of an infinite number of games for the payoff matrix of problem 1, when firm A begins by cooperating but firm B does not cooperate in the next period is given by the following table:

Period	Firm A	Firm B
1	2	2
2	−1	3
3	1	1
4	3	−1
5	2	2

The above table shows that in the first period, firm A sets a high price (i.e., cooperates) and so does firm B (so that each firm earns a profit of 2). If in the second period firm B does not cooperate and sets a low price while firm A is still cooperating and setting a high price, firm B earns a profit of 3 and firm A incurs a loss of 1. In the third period, firm A retaliates and also sets a low price. As a result, each firm earns a profit of only 1 in period 3. In period 4, firm B cooperates again by setting a high price. With firm A still setting a low price, firm A earns a profit of 3 while firm B incurs a loss of 1. In the fifth period, firm A also cooperates again and sets a high price. Since both firms are now setting a high price, each earns a profit of 2.

Chapter 12

2. In Figure 12a, $P = \$8$ at the best level of output of $Q = 4$ given by point E at which $MR = MC$

$= \$4$, so that $L = (8 - 4)/8 = 0.5$. This value of the Lerner index and the MC curve in Figure 12a is consistent with ATC_1 and ATC_2 and with profits of $3 per unit and $12 in total with ATC_1 and $2 per unit and $8 in total with ATC_2. All that is required is that both the ATC_1 and ATC_2 intersect the MC curve at the lowest points of the former. Thus, a high degree of monopoly power is consistent with high or low profits for the firm.

5. In Figure 12b, D is the market demand curve and MC is the positively sloped marginal cost curve faced by the monopolist. The demand curve shows the maximum price that consumers would be willing to pay and the marginal benefit that they would receive for various quantities of the commodity. On the other hand, the MC curve shows the opportunity

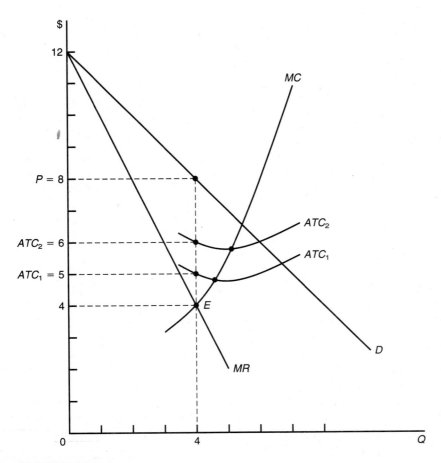

FIGURE 12a

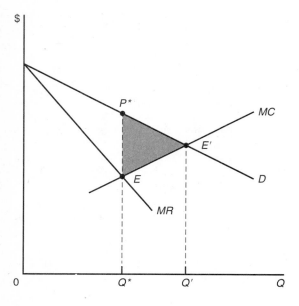

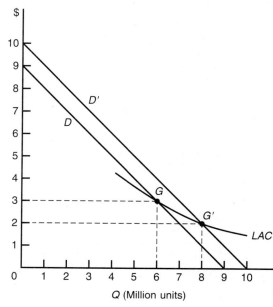

FIGURE 12c

cost (in terms of the commodities forgone that could have been produced with the same inputs) of producing various quantities of the commodity. The best level of output for the monopolist is Q^* at which $MR = MC$ (point E). The price of the commodity is then P^*. The excess of P^* over MC between outputs Q^* and Q' (shaded triangle P^*EE' in Figure 12b) measures the net social losses of monopoly. Other social losses arise from the rent-seeking activities of the monopolist.

7. In Figure 12c, D and D' are, respectively, the original and new market demand curves. With the new demand curve D' and the unchanged LAC curve, the regulatory commission would set $P' = LAC = \$2$ (point G') and the public-utility company would supply 8 million units of the service per time period (as compared with $P = LAC = \$3$ with $Q = 6$ million units per time period shown by point G on D). In either case, the public-utility company breaks even.

12. a. When substitution in consumption is taken into account with peak-load pricing, the off-peak demand will be higher and the peak demand will be lower as compared with the case where substitution in consumption is

not taken into account. This is shown by D_1' and D_2', respectively, in Figure 12d.

b. The gain in shifting from constant pricing to peak-load pricing (shown by the sum of the two shaded triangles in Figure 12d) is smaller when substitution in consumption is taken into account than when it is not. The reason is that the demand curves differ less with peak-load pricing when substitu-

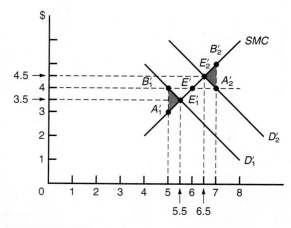

FIGURE 12d

tion in consumption is taken into account than when it is not.

Chapter 13

1. a. $MP_L/w < MP_K/r$.

   This means that the firm is above the AVC curve at the point where its MC curve intersects its MR curve.

   b. The firm is on its AVC cost curve to the right of the point of intersection of its MC and MR curves.

   c. $w/MP_L = r/MP_K = MC < MR$.

The firm is on its AVC curve to the left of the intersection of its MC and MR curves.

5. a. See Figure 13a. The left panel of Figure 13a shows that the individual maximizes satisfaction at point H (with 16 hours of leisure per day, 8 hours of work, and a daily income of $8) on U_1 with $w = \$1$; at point E (with 14 hours of leisure, 10 hours of work, and an income of $20) on U_2 with $w = \$2$; at point N (with 15 hours of leisure, 9 hours of work, and an income of $27) on U_3 with $w = \$3$; and at point R (with 17 hours of leisure, 7 hours of work, and an income of $28) on U_4 with $w = \$4$. Plotting the hours

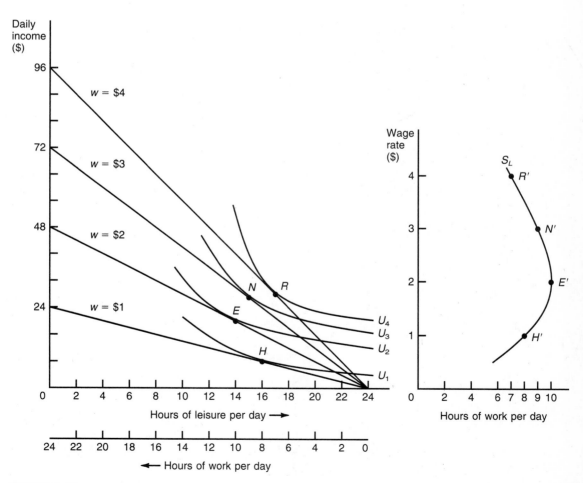

FIGURE 13a

of work per day at various wage rates, we get the individual's supply curve of labor (S_L) in the right panel. Note that S_L bends backward at the wage rate of $2 per hour.

b. An increase in the wage rate, just like an increase in the price of a commodity, leads to a substitution effect and an income effect. The substitution effect leads individuals to substitute work for leisure when the wage rate (the price of leisure) increases. On the other hand, an increase in wages increases the individual's income, and when income rises, the individual demands more of every normal good, including leisure. Thus, the income effect, by itself, leads the individual to demand more leisure and work fewer hours.

Up to $w = \$2$ (point E' on S_L in the right panel of Figure 13a), the substitution effect exceeds the opposite income effect and the individual supplies more hours of work (i.e., S_L is positively sloped). At $w = \$2$, the substitution effect and the opposite income effect are in balance and the individual supplies the same number of hours of work (S_L is vertical). Above $w = \$2$, the substitution effect is smaller than the opposite income effect and the individual works fewer hours (i.e., S_L is negatively sloped or bends backward).

9. See Figure 13b. The movement from point E to point R is the combined substitution and income effects of the wage increase from $2 to $4 (as in Figure 13a). The substitution effect

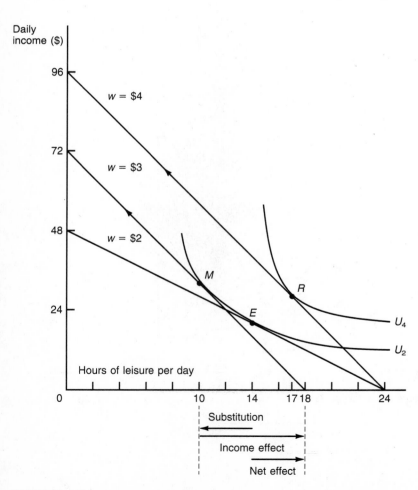

FIGURE 13b

can be isolated by drawing the budget line with slope w = $4 which is tangent to U_2 at point M. The movement along U_2 from point M to point E measures the substitution effect. By itself, it shows that the increase in w leads the individual to reduce leisure time and increase work by four hours per day.

The shift from point M on U_2 to point R on U_4 is the income effect of the wage increase. By itself, the income effect leads the individual to increase leisure and reduce work by seven hours. The net result is that the individual increases leisure (works less) by three hours per day (ER).

11. See Figure 13c. In Figure 13c, D_T is the total demand for labor and S_T is the total supply of labor in both industries or regions. D_T is obtained from the horizontal summation of D_A and D_B, while S_T is obtained from the horizontal summation of S_A and S_B.

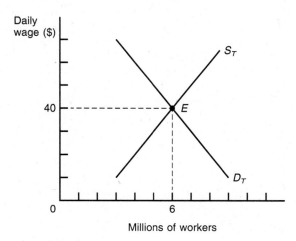

FIGURE 13c

D_T and S_T intersect at point E, defining the equilibrium daily wage of $40 per day (the same as in both panels of Figure 13–6) and the equilibrium employment of labor of 6 million workers—the sum of the workers employed in industry or region A (the left panel in Figure 13–6) and industry or region B (the right panel of Figure 13–6).

Chapter 14

3. a. See the following table.

L	Q_X	MP_L	P_X	TR_X	MR_X	MRP_L	VMP_L	w
1	12	12	$13	$156	...	...	...	$40
2	22	10	12	264	$10.80	$108	$120	40
3	30	8	11	330	8.25	66	88	40
4	37	7	10	370	5.71	40	70	40
5	43	6	9	387	2.83	17	54	40
6	48	5	8	376	−1.80	−9	40	40

MR_X is obtained by the change in TR_X per unit change in the quantity of the commodity sold. That is, $MR_X = \Delta TR_X/\Delta Q_X = \Delta TR_X/MP_L$. For example, when the firm increases the number of workers it hires from one to two, Q_X rises from 12 to 22 units (i.e., MP_L = 10) and TR_X rises from $156 to $264 or by $108. Thus, MR_X = $108/10 = $10.80. When the firm increases the number of workers it hires from two to three, TR_X increases by $66 and Q_X increases by (i.e., MP_L equal to) eight units. Thus, MR_X = $66/8 = $8.25, and so on.

$MRP_L = (MP_L)(MR_X)$. For example, when the firm increases the number of workers hired from one to two workers, MP_L = 10 and MR_X = $10.80. Thus, MRP_L = (10)($10.80) = $108. This is equal to $\Delta TR_X/\Delta L$ or $108/1 = $108 (as found in the text).

$VMP_L = (MP_L)(P_X)$. For example, when the firm increases the number of workers it hires from one to two, MP_L = 10 and P_X = $12, so that the VMP_L = (10) ($12) = $120.

b. See Figure 14a. If the firm were a perfect competitor in the product market as well as in the labor market, the firm would hire six workers (point E) because only by hiring six workers would VMP_L = w = $40.

Since the firm is a monopolist in the product market but a perfect competitor in the labor market, it hires only four workers (point B) because only by hiring four workers would the MRP_L = w = $40. The difference between the VMP_L and the MRP_L at L = 4 (BC = $30 per worker and $120 in total) is the amount of monopolistic exploitation.

9. a. See Figure 14b. The monopsonist's supply curve becomes HMB' and the ME_L curve

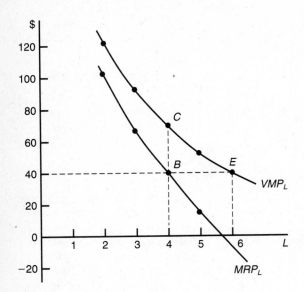

FIGURE 14a

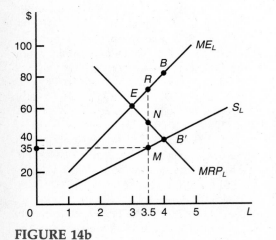

FIGURE 14b

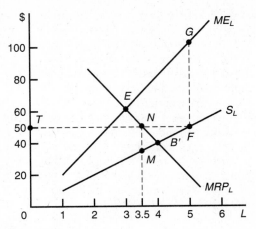

FIGURE 14c

profits by hiring three workers on a full time basis and one worker on a half-time basis (given by point N, where the MRP_L curve intersects the horizontal segment of the new ME_L curve). Now, $MRP_L = w = \$50$ at $L = 3.5$, and the monopsonistic exploitation of labor is zero.

10. See Figure 14d. The union (the monopolist seller of labor time) would like to have 40 workers employed (given by point E, where $MR = MC$) at the daily wage of $40 (point E' on D_L). The firm (the monopsonist employer of labor) would maximize profits by employing 40 work-

becomes $HMNRB$. The monopsonist maximizes profits by hiring three workers on a full time basis and one worker on a half-time basis (given by point N, where the MRP_L curve intersects the vertical segment of the new ME_L curve). Monopsonistic exploitation is NM or $15 per worker.

b. See Figure 14c. The monopsonist's supply curve becomes TNF, and the ME_L curve becomes $TNFG$. The monopsonist maximizes

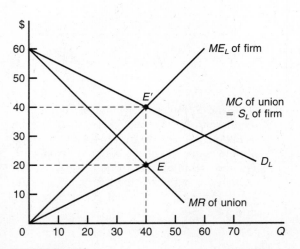

FIGURE 14d

ers (given by point E', where its D_L or MRP_L curve intersects its ME_L curve) at $w = \$20$ (point E on its S_L curve).

Thus, there is agreement between the union and the firm on the number of workers to be employed but not on the wage. The greater is the relative bargaining strength of the union, the closer the wage rate will be to $40. The greater is the relative bargaining strength of the firm, the closer the wage rate will be to $20. Note that it is not entirely certain that the union will behave entirely as a monopolist. (see section 14.8).

11. See Figure 14e. In the figure, the demand for union labor (D_U) plus the demand for non-union labor (D_N) gives the total demand for labor (D_T). The intersection of D_T and S_T (the market supply of labor) at point E determines the equilibrium daily wage of $60 for union and nonunion labor (in the absence of any effect of unions on the wages). At $w = \$60$, 4 million union workers (point E') and 8 million nonunion workers (point E'') are employed.

If unions are now successful in raising union wages from $60 to $65, the employment of union labor falls from 4 to 3 million (point A on D_U). The 1 million workers who cannot find union employment will now have to find employment in the nonunion sector. This increases employment in the nonunion sector from 8 to 9 million workers. But 9 million workers can only be employed in the nonunion sector at $w = \$55$ (point B on D_N).

Thus, when unions increase wages in the unionized sector, employment in the unionized sector falls. More workers must find employment in the nonunionized sector and nonunion wages fall. Thus, what union workers gain comes mostly at the expense of nonunion workers.

Chapter 15

4. See Figure 15a. Starting at point B ($Y_0 = 5$ and $Y_1 = 6$) in the figure, individual B moves to point E (7.5, 3) on indifference curve U_2 by borrowing 2.5 units of the commodity at $r = 20\%$. On the other hand, starting from point A ($Y_0 = 5$ and $Y_1 = 6$) in the figure, individual A moves to point E' (2.5, 9) on indifference curve U_1' by lending 2.5 units of the commodity at $r = 20\%$. Since at $r = 20\%$, desired borrowing equals desired lending, this is the equilibrium rate of interest.

On the other hand, at $r = 50\%$, individual B moves from point B to point E^* on U_1 by borrowing only 2 units of the commodity this year and repaying 3 units next year, while indi-

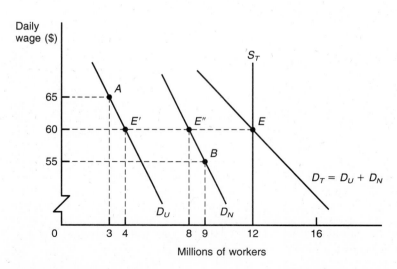

FIGURE 14e

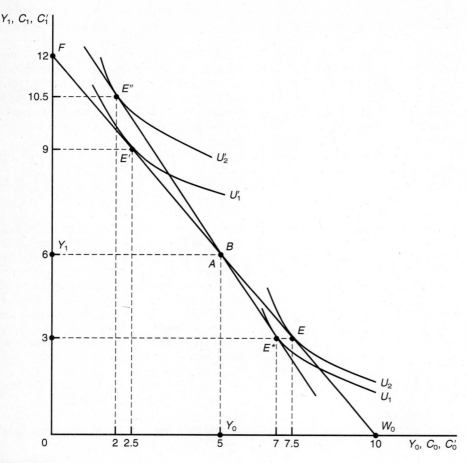

FIGURE 15a

vidual A moves from point A to point E'' on U_2' by lending 3 units this year for 4.5 units next year (so that $r = 50\%$). Since at $r = 50\%$ desired lending exceeds desired borrowing, $r = 50\%$ is higher than the equilibrium rate of interest and r will fall toward 20%.

5. a. The supply curve of loans (lending) is usually positively sloped, indicating that lenders will lend more at higher rates of interest. However, when the interest rate rises, the lender will face a substitution effect and an income or wealth effect (just as a worker does when the wage rate rises). The substitution effect induces the lender to substitute future for present consumption and lend more since the reward for lending has increased.

On the other hand, when the interest rate rises, the lender's wealth rises and he or she will want to consume more both in the present (and lend less) and in the future. Thus, the substitution effect tends to lead the lender to lend more while the wealth effect leads the lender to lend less.

Up to a point, the substitution effect overwhelms the wealth effect and the lender will lend more at higher rates of interest. After a point, however, higher rates of interest will cause the wealth effect to exceed the opposite substitution effect so that the lender will lend less. Thus, at a sufficiently high rate of interest, the lender's supply curve will bend backward (as at r^* in Figure 15b).

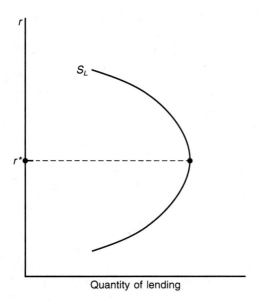

Quantity of lending

FIGURE 15b

b. For borrowers, both the substitution effect and the wealth effect operate to reduce the amount of desired borrowing when the rate of interest rises, so that the demand curve for borrowing is negatively sloped throughout. The substitution effect reduces the amount of borrowing as the rate of interest rises, because future consumption becomes more expensive in terms of the present consumption to be given up. The wealth effect

also tends to reduce the amount of borrowing, because an increase in the rate of interest reduces the borrower's wealth.

9. See the accompanying table. Note that the net present value of the project is higher with $r = 5\%$ than with $r = 10\%$.

10. The cost of equity capital for this firm (k_e) can be calculated with the dividend valuation model, as follows

$$k_e = \frac{D}{P} + g$$

where D is the amount of the yearly dividend paid per share of the common stock of the firm, P is the price of a share of the common stock of the firm, and g is the expected annual growth rate of dividend payments.

Since the company pays half of its expected $200 million in net after-tax earnings in dividends and there are 100 million shares of common stock of the firm, the dividend per share is $1. With a share of the common stock of the firm selling for eight times current earnings, the price of a share of the common stock of the firm is $8.

With the expected annual growth of earnings and dividends of the firm of 7.5%, the cost of equity capital for this firm is

$$k_e = \frac{\$1}{\$8} + 0.075 = 0.125 + 0.075 = 0.20$$

or 20%

Benefit-Cost Analysis of an Investment Project

End of Year	Investment (year 0) and Cost	Revenue	Net Revenue	Present Value Coefficient $1/(1 + 0.05)^n$	Present Value of Net Revenue
0	$1,000	. . .	−$1,000	. . .	−$1,000
1	200	$600	400	0.952	381
2	300	800	500	0.907	454
3	300	800	500	0.864	432
4	400	800	400	0.823	329
4	. . .	200*	200	0.823	165
					$761

*Salvage value

Chapter 16

2. See Figure 16a. The Edgeworth box diagram of Figure 16a was obtained by rotating individual B's indifference curve diagram by 180 degrees (so that O_B appears in the top right-hand corner) and superimposing it on individual A's indifference curve diagram (with origin O_A), in such a way that the size of the box is 14X and 9Y (the combined amount of X and Y owned by individuals A and B). The contract curve for exchange is $O_A DEFO_B$ and is given by the tangency points of the indifference curves (at which MRS_{XY} are equal) for the two individuals.

4. See Figure 16b. The Edgeworth box diagram of Figure 16b was obtained by rotating the isoquant diagram for commodity Y by 180 degrees (so that O_Y appears in the top right-hand corner) and superimposing it on the isoquant diagram for commodity X (with origin O_X) in such a way that the size of the box is 14L and 9K (the total amount of L and K available). The

production contract curve is $O_X JMNO_Y$ and is given by the tangency points of the isoquants (at which $MRTS_{LK}$ are equal) for commodities X and Y.

8. See Figure 16c. The simple economy portrayed in Figure 16c would be simultaneously in general equilibrium of production and exchange at point E, where

$$MRT_{XY} = MRS_{XY}^A = MRS_{XY}^B = 1$$

12. a. See Figure 16d. Point D' in Figure 16d corresponds to point D (on A_1 and B_3) in Figure 16a, point E' corresponds to point E (on A_2 and B_2), and point F' to point F (on A_3 and B_1). Other points can be similarly obtained. By joining these points, we get utility-possibilities frontier $U_M U_{M'}$. This shows the various combinations of utilities received by individuals A and B at which this economy (composed of individuals A and B) is in general equilibrium and Pareto optimum in exchange. A point outside $U_M U_{M'}$ cannot

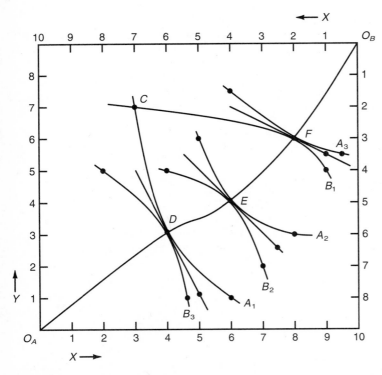

FIGURE 16a

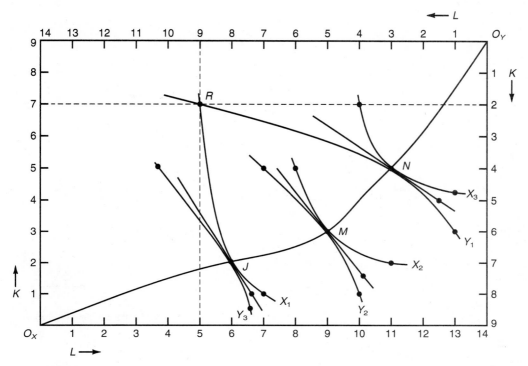

FIGURE 16b

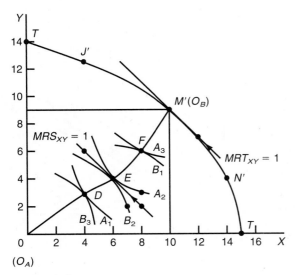

FIGURE 16c

be reached with the available amount of commodities X and Y.

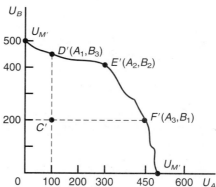

FIGURE 16d

b. See Figure 16e. Utility-possibilities frontier $U_{M'}U_{M'}$ is that of part (a). Utility-possibilities frontier $U_{N'}U_{N'}$ is derived from the contract curve for exchange in the Edgeworth box diagram drawn from point N' on the production possibilities frontier in Figure 16b (not shown in that figure). By joining E',

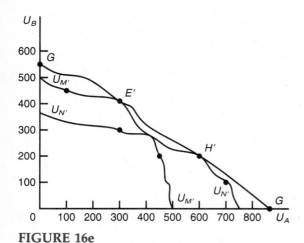

FIGURE 16e

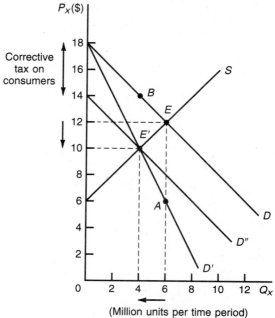

FIGURE 17a

H', and other Pareto optimum points of production and exchange, we get grand utility-possibilities frontier GE'H'G in Figure 16e.

Chapter 17

3. a. See Figure 17a. A corrective tax of $4 per unit imposed on the consumers of commodity X will make D'' the new industry demand curve. With D'', $P_X = \$10$ and $Q_X = 4$ million units per time period (given by the intersection of D'' and S at point E'). This is the socially optimum price and output. Consumers would now pay $P_X = \$10$ plus the $4 tax per unit ($E'B$) or a net $P_X = \$14$ (as compared with $P_X = \$12$ under the previous competitive equilibrium at point E).

   b. The total value of the economic gain resulting from the imposition of the corrective tax is equal to $6 million (given by area $EE'A$ in the figure). This is the excess of the MSC (shown by supply curve S) over MSB (shown by demand curve D') between $Q_X = 4$ and $Q_X = 6$ million units.

5. a. See Figure 17b. A corrective subsidy of $4 per unit given to producers of commodity X will make S'' the new industry supply curve. With S'', $P_X = \$10$ and $Q_X = 8$ million units per time period (given by the intersection of D and S'' at point E'). This is the socially optimal price and output. Produc-

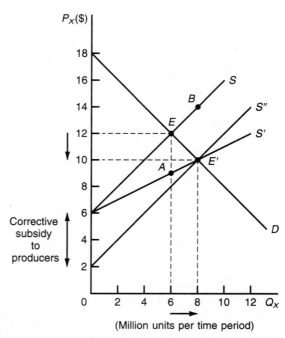

FIGURE 17b

ers would now receive P_X = $10 plus the $4 subsidy per unit (*BE'*) for a total of $14 per unit.

b. The total value of the economic inefficiency eliminated by the corrective subsidy is equal to $3 million (given by area *EE'A* in the figure). This is the excess of the marginal social value (shown by demand curve *D*) over the *MSC* (shown by supply curve *S'*) between Q_X = 6 and Q_X = 8 million units.

9. a. Each individual will drill more wells and pump oil faster than he or she would if no other oil field was located adjacent to his or hers, in order to prevent some of the oil under his or her field to flow to the neighbor's field. The external diseconomies arise because oil is pumped faster than is socially desirable. The external diseconomies can be avoided by merging the two adjacent oil fields under joint ownership, by government regulation, or by taxation.

b. The development of a recreational site confers external benefits to shops, gasoline stations, and motels in the area. In order to internalize the external benefits, the recreational site developer may also set up and operate establishments that provide these other services near the recreational site.

10. a. See Figure 17c. Market demand curve *D* (*CFEG*) is obtained by the *horizontal* summation of demand curves D_A and D_B. D_X and S_X intersect at point *E* and define equilibrium price of P_X = $5.50 and the equilibrium quantity of Q_X = 7.5, if the market for commodity *X* is perfectly competitive. Individual A consumes 1X, and individual B consumes 6.5X.

b. When *X* is a private good, the condition for Pareto optimal output is MRT_{XY} = MRS_{XY}^A = MRS_{XY}^B. That is, at the optimal output level, the marginal benefit that each consumer receives from an additional unit of commodity *X* equals its marginal cost. That is, *HJ* = *FR* = *EV* in Figure 17c.

On the other hand, when *X* is a public good, the condition for the Pareto optimal output is MRT_{XY} = MRS_{XY}^A = MRS_{XY}^B. That is, since each consumer can consume the *same* quantity of commodity *X* when *X* is a public good, it is the sum of the marginal benefits that each consumer receives from the additional unit of commodity *X* that must equal its marginal cost (i.e., *AB* + *AC* = *AE* in Figure 17b).

c. Public goods that exhibit nonexclusion convey external economies of consumption on free riders (i.e., on the consumers not paying for the public goods).

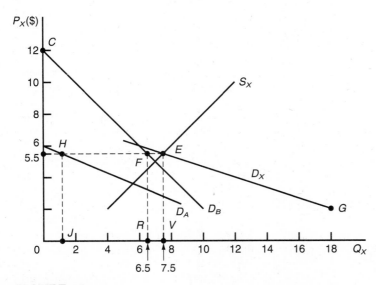

FIGURE 17c

Chapter 18

1. Because there is an equal number of five types of sellers, each price will be encountered one-fifth of the time on the first search.

   If search one yields the price of $120, four-fifths of the time search two will yield a lower price, averaging $95, and so the expected minimum price for search two is $120(1/5) + $95(4/5) = $24 + $86 = $100.

   If search one yields the price of $110, two-fifths of the time search two will yield a price of $120 or $110 (but in that case the price of $120 on search two would be disregarded), and three-fifths of the time search two will yield a lower price, averaging $90. Thus, the expected minimum price for search two in this case is $110(2/5) + $90(3/5) = $44 + $54 = $98.

   If search one yields the price of $100, three-fifths of the time search two will yield a price of $100 or higher (but in that case any price higher than $100 on search two would be disregarded), and two-fifths of the time search two will yield a lower price, averaging $85. Thus, the expected minimum price for search two in this case is $100(3/5) + $85(2/5) = $94.

   If search one yields the price of $90, four-fifths of the time search two will yield a price of $90 or higher (but in that case any price higher than $90 on search two would be disregarded), and one-fifth of the time search two will yield a price of $80. Thus, the expected minimum price for search two in this case is $90(4/5) + $80(1/5) = $88.

   If search one yields the price of $80, the consumer will end the search because $80 is already the lowest price possible.

   The expected minimum price for the second search is then the average of the above expected minimum prices for the second search. That is, the *precise* minimum price on the second search is ($100 + $98 + $94 + $88 + $80)/5 = $92 (as compared with $93.33 found with the use of formula [18–1] in the text).

3. a. The formula for the lowest expected price for each search is

$$\text{Expected Price} = \text{Lowest Price} + \frac{\text{Range of Prices}}{\text{Number of Searches} + 1}$$

   The lowest expected price with one search is $60 + \dfrac{\$80}{1+1} = \$100.00$.

   With two searches, the lowest expected price is $60 + \dfrac{\$80}{3} = \$86.67$.

   With three searches, the lowest expected price is $60 + \dfrac{\$80}{4} = \$80.00$.

   With four searches, the lowest expected price is $60 + \dfrac{\$80}{5} = \$76.00$.

   With five searches, the lowest expected price is $60 + \dfrac{\$80}{6} = \$73.33$.

   b. The marginal benefit from each search is measured by the reduction in the expected price resulting from the search. Thus, for the second search the marginal benefit (MB) is $100 − $86.67 = $13.37. For the third search, $MB = \$86.67 − \$80.00 = \$6.67$. For the fourth search, $MB = \$80.00 − \$76.00 = \$4.00$. For the fifth search, $MB = \$76.00 − \$73.33 = \$2.67$.

   Note that the marginal benefits of each additional search are now twice as large as those found in the text where the range of prices was half what they are in this problem.

6. a. The foreign-exchange risk that the U.S. importer faces is that the exchange rate could be higher three months from now and that as a result she will have to pay more dollars to obtain the £100,000 that she needs to make the payment.

   b. The U.S. importer can hedge the foreign-exchange risk in the spot market by purchasing £100,000 in the spot market today at today's spot rate of $2/£1 and hold them on deposit in a bank (and thus earn interest) until the payment is due in three months. By doing this, the U.S. importer avoids possibly having to pay more than $200,000 to obtain the £100,000 in three months if the dollar exchange rate rises in the meantime.

   c. Hedging usually takes place in the forward market, because in that case the firm does not have to tie down its own capital until it needs to make the payment.

8. See Figure 18a. In the figure, the subscripts H,

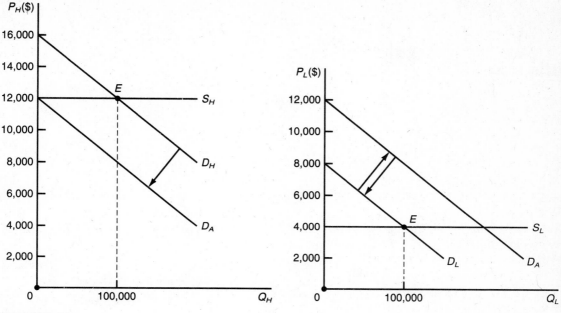

FIGURE 18a

L, and A refer, respectively, to high quality, low quality, and average quality. In the absence of perfect information (i.e., with asymmetric information), the demand for used cars will be the average of the demand curves for the high-quality and the low-quality used cars that would prevail in the market if all potential buyers had perfect information. As a result, the left panel

of Figure 18a shows that no high-quality cars will be offered for sale at the price of $12,000.

But with all the high-quality cars withdrawn from the market, only the low-quality cars will be offered for sale. Thus, D_A will fall to D_L in the right panel and only the 100,000 low-quality cars will be sold in the market at $P_L = \$4,000$.

C

Glossary

Adverse selection   The situation where low-quality products drive high-quality products out of the market as a result of the existence of asymmetric information between buyers and sellers.

Alternative or opportunity cost doctrine   The doctrine that postulates that the cost to a firm in using any input (whether owned or hired) is what the input could earn in its best alternative use.

Appreciation   A decrease in the domestic-currency price of the foreign currency.

Arbitrage   The purchase of a commodity or currency where it is cheaper and its sale where it is more expensive.

Arc elasticity of demand   The price elasticity of demand between two points on the demand curve; it uses the average price and the average quantity in calculating the percentage change in price and quantity.

Arc elasticity of supply   The price elasticity of supply between two points on the supply curve; it uses the average price and the average quantity in calculating the percentage change in price and quantity.

Arrow's impossibility theorem   The theorem that postulates that a social welfare function cannot be derived by democratic vote to reflect the preferences of all the individuals in society.

Asymmetric information   The situation where one party to a transaction has more information on the quality of the product or service offered for sale than the other party.

Average fixed cost (*AFC*)   Total fixed costs divided by output.

Average product (*AP*)   The total product divided by the quantity of the variable input used.

Average revenue (*AR*)   Total revenue divided by the quantity sold.

Average total cost (*ATC*)   Total costs divided by output. Also equals *AFC* + *AVC*.

Average variable cost (*AVC*)   Total variable costs divided by output.

Averch-Johnson (A-J) effect   The overinvestments and underinvestments in plant and equipment resulting when public utility rates are set too high or too low, respectively.

Bad   An item of which less is preferred to more.

Bandwagon effect   The situation where some people demand a commodity because other people purchase it (i.e., in order to "keep up with the Joneses").

Barometric firm   An oligopolistic firm that is recognized as a true interpreter or barometer of changes in demand and cost conditions warranting a price change in the industry.

Benefit-cost analysis   A procedure for determining the most worthwhile public projects for the government to undertake. It prescribes that government should undertake those projects with the highest benefit-cost ratio, as long as that ratio exceeds 1, and until government resources are fully employed.

Bergson social welfare function A social welfare function based on the explicit value judgments of society.

Beta coefficient (β) The ratio of the variability of the return on the common stock of the firm to the variability of the average return on all stocks.

Bilateral monopoly The case where the monopsonist buyer of a product or input faces the monopolist seller of the product or input.

Brain drain The migration of highly skilled people from one nation to another. This benefits the receiving nation and harms the nations of emigration.

Break-even point The point where total revenues equal total costs and profits are zero.

Budget constraint The limitation on the amount of goods that a consumer can purchase imposed by his or her limited income and the prices of the goods.

Budget line A line showing the various combinations of two goods that a consumer can purchase by spending all income at the given prices of the two goods.

Bundling A common form of tying in which the monopolist requires customers buying or leasing one of its products or services to also buy or lease another product or service when customers have different tastes but the monopolist cannot price discriminate.

Capital asset pricing model (CAPM) The method of measuring the equity cost of capital as the risk-free rate plus the beta coefficient (β) times the risk premium on the average stock.

Capital budgeting The ranking of all investment projects from the highest present value to the lowest.

Cardinal utility The ability to actually provide an index of utility from consuming various amounts of a good or baskets of goods.

Cartel An organization of suppliers of a commod-

ity aimed at restricting competition and increasing profits.

Centralized cartel A formal agreement of the suppliers of a commodity that sets the price and allocates output and profits among its members so as to increase joint profits. It can result in the monopoly solution.

Circular flow of economic activity The flow of resources from households to business firms and the opposite flow of money incomes from business firms to households. Also, the flow of goods and services from business firms to households and the opposite flow of consumption expenditures from households to business firms.

Clayton Act It prohibits mergers that "substantially lessen competition" or tend to lead to monopoly.

Coase's theorem It postulates that when property rights are clearly defined and transaction costs are zero, perfect competition results in the absence of externalities, regardless of how property rights are assigned among the parties involved.

Cobb-Douglas production function The relationship between inputs and output expressed by $Q = AL^\alpha K^\beta$, where Q is output, L is labor, K is capital, and A, α, and β are positive parameters estimated from the data.

Coinsurance Insurance that covers only a portion of a possible loss.

Collusion A formal or informal agreement among the suppliers of a commodity to restrict competition.

Common property Property, such as air, owned by no one.

Comparative static analysis The analysis of the effect of a change in demand and/or supply on the equilibrium price and output of a commodity.

Compensation principle The amount that those who gain from a change could pay to the losers to fully compensate for their losses.

Complementary inputs Inputs related to one another in such a way that an increase in the employment of one input raises the marginal product of the other input.

Complements   Two commodities are complements if an increase in the price of one of them leads to less of the other being purchased.

Composite cost of capital   The weighted average of the cost of debt and equity capital to the firm.

Concentration ratio   The percentage of total industry sales of the 4, 8, and 20 largest firms in the industry.

Concept of the margin   The central unifying theme in all of microeconomics, according to which the total net benefit is maximized when the marginal benefit is equal to the marginal cost.

Conscious parallelism   The adoption of similar policies by oligopolists in view of their recognized interdependence.

Constant cost industry   An industry with a horizontal long-run supply curve (a minimum LAC). It results if input prices remain constant as industry output expands.

Constant returns to scale   Output changes in the same proportion as inputs.

Constrained utility maximization   The process by which the consumer reaches the highest level of satisfaction given his or her income and the prices of goods. This occurs at the tangency of an indifference curve with the budget line.

Consumer equilibrium   Constrained utility maximization.

Consumer optimization   Constrained utility maximization.

Consumer surplus   The difference between what the consumer is willing to pay for a given quantity of a good and what he or she actually pays for it.

Contract curve for exchange   The locus of tangency points of the indifference curves (at which the MRS_{XY} are equal) for the two individuals when the economy is in general equilibrium of exchange.

Contract curve for production   The locus of tangency points of the isoquants (at which the $MRTS_{LK}$ are equal) for the two commodities when the economy is in general equilibrium of production.

Corner solution   Constrained utility maximization with the consumer spending all of his or her income on only one or some goods.

Cost of debt   The net (after-tax) interest rate paid by a firm to borrow funds.

Cost-plus pricing   The setting of a price equal to average cost plus a markup.

Cournot model   The oligopoly model in which each firm assures that the other keeps output constant. With two firms, each will sell one-third of the perfectly competitive output.

Cross elasticity of demand (η_{XY})   The percentage change in the quantity purchased of a commodity divided by the percentage change in the price of another commodity.

Deadweight loss   The excess of the combined loss of consumers' and producers' surplus from a tax.

Decreasing cost industry   An industry with a negatively sloped long-run supply curve. It results if input prices fall as industry output expands.

Decreasing returns to scale   Output changes by a smaller proportion than inputs.

Default risk   The possibility that a loan will not be repaid.

Depreciation   An increase in the domestic-currency price of the foreign currency.

Deregulation movement   The reduction or elimination of many government regulations since the mid-1970s in order to increase competition and efficiency.

Derived demand   The demand for an input that arises from the demand for the final commodities that the input is used in producing.

Differentiated oligopoly   An oligopoly where the product is differentiated.

Differentiated products   Products that are similar, but not identical, and satisfy the same basic need.

Discrimination in employment   The (illegal) unwillingness on the part of employers to hire some group of equally productive workers based on sex, color, religion, or national origin under any circumstances or at the same wage rate.

Disemployment effect   The reduction in the number of workers employed as a result of an increase in the wage rate (as with the imposition of an effective minimum wage).

Dividend valuation model   The method of measuring the equity cost of capital to the firm with the ratio of the dividend per share of the stock to the price of the stock, plus the expected growth rate of dividend payments.

Dominant strategy   The optimal strategy for a player no matter what the other player does.

Dumping   International price discrimination or the sale of the commodity at a lower price abroad than at home.

Duopoly   An oligopoly of two firms.

Economic efficiency   The situation in which the marginal rate of transformation in production equals the marginal rate of substitution in consumption for every pair of commodities and for every pair of individuals consuming both commodities.

Economic growth   The increase in resources, commodities, and incomes, and the improvements in technology over time.

Economic rent   That portion of a payment made to the supplier of an input that is in excess of what is necessary to retain the input in its present employment in the long run.

Economic resources   Resources that are limited in supply or scarce and thus command a price.

Economics   A field of study that deals with the allocation of scarce resources among alternative uses to satisfy human wants.

Economies of scope   The lowering of costs that a firm often experiences when it produces two or more products together rather than producing each product separately.

Edgeworth box diagram   A diagram constructed from the indifference map diagrams of two individuals, which can be used to analyze voluntary exchange.

Edgeworth box diagram for exchange   A diagram constructed from the indifference curves diagram of two individuals, which can be used to analyze voluntary exchange.

Edgeworth box diagram for production   A diagram constructed from the isoquants diagram of the two commodities, which can be used to analyze general equilibrium of production.

Efficiency   The situation where the price of a commodity (which measures the marginal benefit to consumers) equals the marginal cost of producing the commodity.

Efficiency wage theory   It postulates that firms willingly pay higher than equilibrium wages to induce workers to avoid *shirking* or slacking off on the job.

Effluent fee   A tax that a firm must pay for discharging waste or polluting.

Endowment position   The quantity of a commodity that the consumer receives in each year.

Engel curve   It shows the amount of a good that a consumer would purchase at various income levels.

Engel's law   The proportion of total expenditures on food declines as family incomes rise.

Entrepreneurship   The introduction of new technologies and products to exploit perceived profit opportunities.

Environmental pollution   The lowering of air, water, scenic, and noise qualities of the world around us that results from the dumping of waste products. It arises because of unclearly defined property rights and too-high transaction costs.

Equalizing wage differentials   Wage differences that compensate workers for the nonmonetary differences among jobs.

Equilibrium   The condition that, once achieved, tends to persist. It occurs when the quantity demanded of a commodity equals the quantity supplied and the market clears.

Equilibrium price   The price at which the quan-

that compensate workers for the nonmonetary differences among jobs.

Excess capacity   The difference between the output indicated by the lowest point on the *LAC* curve and that actually produced by a monopolistically competitive firm when in long-run equilibrium.

Excess demand   The amount by which the quantity demanded of a commodity is larger than the quantity supplied of the commodity at below-equilibrium prices; with a tradable commodity, it gives the quantity demanded of imports of the commodity.

Excess supply   The amount by which the quantity supplied of a commodity is larger than the quantity demanded of the commodity at above-equilibrium prices; for a tradable commodity, it gives the quantity supplied of exports of the commodity.

Exchange rate   The price of a unit of the foreign currency in terms of the domestic currency.

Excise tax   A tax on each unit of the commodity.

Exhaustible resources   Nonrenewable resources, such as petroleum and other minerals, which are available in fixed quantities and are nonreplenishable.

Expansion path   The line joining the origin with the points of tangency of isoquants and isocost lines with input prices held constant. It shows the least-cost input combination to produce various output levels.

Expected income ($\bar{I}$)   The probability of one level of income (p) times that income level plus the probability of an alternative income ($1 - p$) times that alternative income level.

Experience goods   Goods whose quality can only be judged after using them.

Experimental economies   The newly developing field of economics that seeks to determine how real markets operate by examining how paid volunteers behave within a simple experimental institutional framework.

Explicit costs   The actual expenditures of the firm to purchase or hire inputs.

External benefits   Beneficial side effects received by those not directly involved in the production or consumption of a commodity.

External costs   Harmful side effects borne by those not directly involved in the production or consumption of a commodity.

External diseconomies of consumption   Uncompensated costs borne by those not directly involved in the consumption of a commodity.

External diseconomies of production   Uncompensated costs borne by those not directly involved in the production of a commodity.

External diseconomy   An upward shift in all firms' per-unit cost curves, resulting from an increase in input prices as the industry expands.

External economies of consumption   Uncompensated benefits received by those not directly involved in the consumption of a commodity.

External economies of production   Uncompensated benefits received by those not directly involved in the production of a commodity.

External economy   A downward shift in all firms' per-unit cost curves resulting from a decline in input prices as the industry expands.

Externalities   Harmful or beneficial side effects borne by those not directly involved in the production or consumption of a commodity.

Firm   An organization that combines and organizes resources for the purpose of producing goods and services for sale at a profit.

First degree price discrimination   The charging of the highest price for each unit of a commodity that each consumer is willing to pay rather than go without it.

First theorem of welfare economics   It postulates that equilibrium in competitive markets is Pareto optimal.

Fixed inputs   The resources that cannot be varied or can be varied only with excessive cost during the time period under consideration.

Food stamp program   A federal program under which eligible poor families receive free food stamps to purchase food.

For whom to produce   The way that output is distributed among the members of society.

Foreign exchange market   The market where national currencies are bought and sold.

Foreign exchange rate   The price of a unit of a foreign currency in terms of the domestic currency.

Forward or futures contract   The purchase and sale of a commodity or currency for future delivery at a price agreed upon today.

Forward or futures market   The market where forward transactions take place.

Forward or futures price or rate   The price or rate at which a commodity or currency is bought and sold in the forward market.

Free-enterprise system   The form of market organization where economic decisions are made by individuals and firms.

Free-rider problem   The problem that arises when an individual does not contribute to the payment of a public good in the belief that it will be provided anyway.

Fringe benefits   Goods and services provided to employees and paid by employers.

Game theory   The theory that examines the choice of optimal strategies in conflict situations.

General equilibrium analysis   It studies the interdependence that exists among all markets in the economy.

Giffen good   An inferior good for which the positive substitution effect is smaller than the negative income effect, so that less of the good is purchased when its price falls.

Globalization of economic activity   The increasing proportion of consumer goods, and parts and components of manufactured goods imported from abroad; the increasing share of domestic production exported; and the rising repercussions of domestic policies on other nations.

Golden parachute   A large financial settlement paid out by a firm to its managers if they are forced or choose to leave as a result of a takeover that greatly increases the value of the firm.

Good   A commodity of which more is preferred to less.

Government failures   Situations where government policies do not reflect the public's interests and reduce rather than increase social welfare.

Grand utility-possibilities frontier   The envelope to utility-possibilities frontiers at Pareto optimum points of production and exchange.

Hedging   The covering of risks arising from changes in future commodity and currency prices.

Herfindahl index   A measure of the degree of monopoly power in an industry, which is given by the sum of the squared values of the market sales shares of all the firms in the industry.

Homogeneous of degree 1   In production, it refers to constant returns to scale.

Hotelling paradox   The observation that competition often results in products that are too similar to maximize society's satisfaction.

How to produce   The way resources or inputs are combined to produce the goods and services that consumers want.

Human wants   All the goods, services, and the conditions of life that individuals desire, and which provide the driving force for economic activity.

Identification problem   The difficulty sometimes encountered in estimating the market demand or supply curve of a commodity from quantity-price observations.

Implicit costs   The value of the inputs owned and used by the firm; value is imputed from the best alternative use of the inputs.

Import tariff   A per-unit tax on the imported commodity.

Incidence of tax   The relative burden of the tax on buyers and sellers.

Income-consumption curve   The locus of consumer optimum points resulting when only the consumer's income varies.

Income effect   The increase in the quantity purchased of a good resulting only from the increase in real income that accompanies a price decline.

Income elasticity of demand (η_I)   The percentage change in the quantity purchased of a commodity over a specific period of time divided by the percentage change in consumers' income.

Income or expenditure index (E)   The ratio of period 1 to base period money income or expenditures.

Increasing cost industry   An industry with a positively sloped long-run supply curve. It results if input prices rise as industry output expands.

Increasing returns to scale   Output changes by a larger proportion than inputs.

Indifference curve   The curve showing the various combinations of two commodities that give the consumer equal satisfaction and among which the consumer is indifferent.

Indifference map   The entire set of indifference curves reflecting the consumer's tastes and preferences.

Individual's demand curve   It shows the quantity that the individual would purchase of the good per unit of time at various alternative prices of the good, while keeping everything else constant.

Inferior good   A good of which a consumer purchases less with an increase in income.

Inputs   The resources or factors of production used to produce goods and services.

Interdependence   The relationship among all markets in the economy, such that a change in any of them affects all the others.

Intermediate good   The output of a firm or industry that is the input of another firm or industry producing final commodities.

Internalizing external costs   The process whereby an external cost becomes part of the regular business expense of the firm.

Internationalization of economic activity   The trend toward producing and distributing goods throughout the world.

Intraindustry trade   The international trade in the differentiated products of the same industry or broad product group.

Investment   The formation of new capital assets.

Investment in human capital   Any activity, such as education and training, that increases an individual's productivity.

Isocost line   It shows the various combinations of two inputs that the firm can hire with a given total cost outlay.

Isoquant   A curve showing the various combinations of two inputs that can be used to produce a specific level of output.

Kaldor-Hicks criterion   It postulates that a change is an improvement if those who gain from the change can fully compensate the losers and still retain some of the gain.

Kinked-demand curve model   The model that seeks to explain price rigidity by postulating a demand curve with a kink at the prevailing price.

Labor union   An organization of workers devoted to increasing the wages and welfare of its members through bargaining with employers.

Laspeyres price index (L)   The ratio of the cost of purchasing base period quantities at period 1 prices relative to base period prices.

Law of demand   The inverse price-quantity relationship illustrated by the negative slope of the demand curve.

Law of diminishing marginal utility   Each additional unit of a good eventually gives less and less extra utility.

Law of diminishing returns   After a point, the marginal product of the variable input declines.

Law of the invisible hand   The law stated by Adam Smith over 200 years ago that postulates that in a free market economy, each individual by pursuing his or her own selfish interests is led, as if by an invisible hand, to promote the welfare of society more so than he or she intends or even understands.

Learning curve   The curve showing the decline in average costs with rising cumulative total outputs over time.

Least-cost input combination The condition where the marginal product per dollar spent on each input is equal. Graphically, it is the point where an isoquant is tangent to an isocost line.

Lerner index A measure of the degree of a firm's monopoly power which is given by the ratio of the difference between price and marginal cost to price.

Limit pricing The charging of a sufficiently low price by existing firms to discourage entry into the industry.

Long run The time period when all inputs can be varied.

Long-run average cost (*LAC*) The minimum per-unit cost of producing any level of output when the firm can build any desired scale of plant. It equals long-run total cost divided by output.

Long-run marginal cost (*LMC*) The change in long-run total costs per-unit change in output; the slope of the *LTC* curve.

Long-run total cost (*LTC*) The minimum total costs of producing various levels of output when the firm can build any desired scale of plant.

Lorenz curve A curve showing income inequality by measuring cumulative percentages of total income along the vertical axis, for various cumulative percentages of the population (from the lowest to the highest income) measured along the horizontal axis.

Luxury A commodity with income elasticity of demand greater than 1.

Macroeconomic theory The study of the total or *aggregate* level of output, national income, national employment, consumption, investment, and prices for the economy *viewed as a whole*.

Marginal analysis The analysis based on the application of the marginal concept according to which net benefits increase as long as the marginal benefit exceeds the marginal cost and until they are equal.

Marginal benefit The change in the total benefit, or extra benefit, resulting from an economic action.

Marginal cost The change in the total cost, or extra cost, resulting from an economic action.

Marginal product (*MP*) The change in total product per-unit change in the variable input used.

Marginal productivity theory The theory according to which each input is paid a price equal to its marginal productivity.

Marginal rate of substitution (*MRS*) The amount of a good that a consumer is willing to give up for an additional unit of the other good while remaining on the same indifference curve.

Marginal rate of technical substitution (*MRTS*) The absolute value of the slope of the isoquant. It also equals the ratio of the marginal product of the two inputs.

Marginal rate of transformation of *X* for *Y* (MRT_{XY}) The amount of *Y* that must be given up to release just enough labor and capital to produce one additional unit of *X*. It is equal to the absolute value of the slope of the production-possibilities frontier and to the ratio of the marginal cost of *X* to the marginal cost of *Y*.

Marginal resource cost (*MRC*) The extra cost of hiring an additional unit of the input.

Marginal resource cost of capital (MRC_k) The extra cost of hiring an additional unit of capital.

Marginal resource cost of labor (MRC_L) The extra cost of hiring an additional unit of labor.

Marginal revenue (*MR*) The change in total revenue per-unit change in the quantity sold.

Marginal revenue product (*MRP*) The marginal physical product of the input (*MP*) multiplied by the marginal revenue of the commodity (*MR*).

Marginal utility (*MU*) The extra utility received from consuming one additional unit of the good.

Market The network of communication between individuals and firms for the purpose of buying and selling goods, services, and resources.

Market demand curve It shows the quantity demanded of a commodity in the market per time period at various alternative prices of the commodity, while holding everything else constant.

Market demand schedule A table showing the quantity of a commodity that consumers are willing and able to purchase during a given period of time at each price of the commodity, while holding constant all other relevant economic variables on which demand depends.

Market failures   The existence of monopoly, monopsony, price controls, externalities, and public goods that prevent the attainment of economic efficiency or Pareto optimum.

Market line   A line from any point on the production-possibilities curve showing the various amounts of a commodity that the individual can consume in each period by borrowing or lending.

Market period   The time period during which the market supply of a commodity is fixed. Also called the very short run.

Market-sharing cartel   An organization of suppliers of a commodity that overtly or tacitly divides the market among its members.

Market signaling   Signals that convey product quality, good insurance or credit risks, and high productivity.

Market supply curve   The graphic representation of the market supply schedule showing the quantity supplied of a commodity per time period at each commodity price, while holding constant all other relevant economic variables on which supply depends.

Market supply schedule   A table showing the quantity supplied of a commodity during a given period of time at each price of the commodity, while holding constant all other relevant economic variables on which supply depends.

Markup   The percentage over average cost in cost-plus pricing.

Maximum social welfare   The point at which a social indifference curve is tangent to the grand utility-possibilities frontier; also called constrained bliss.

Methodology of economics   The proposition that a model is tested by its predictive ability, the consistency of its assumptions, and the logic with which the predictions follow from the assumptions.

Microeconomic theory   The study of the economic behavior of *individual* decision-making units such as individual consumers, resource owners, and business firms, and the operation of individual markets, in a free-enterprise economy.

Minimal income maintenance   The transfer or subsidy going to families that have no other income under a negative income-tax program.

Mixed economy   An economy, such as our own, characterized by private enterprise and government actions and regulations.

Mixed strategy   The best strategy for each player in a non-strictly determined game.

Model   Another name for theory, or the set of assumptions from which the result of an event is deduced or predicted.

Monopolistic competition   The form of market organization in which there are many sellers of a differentiated product, and entry into or exit from the market is rather easy in the long run.

Monopolistic exploitation   The excess of an input's value of marginal product over its marginal revenue product at the level of utilization of the input.

Monopsonistic competition   One of many firms hiring a differentiated input.

Monopsonistic exploitation   The excess of the marginal revenue product of an input over the price of the input at the level of utilization of the input.

Monopsony   The single buyer of an input.

Moral hazard   The increased probability of a loss when an economic agent can shift some of its costs to others.

Multiple regression   A statistical technique that allows the economist to disentangle the independent effect of the various determinants of demand, so as to identify from the data the average market demand curve for the commodity.

Nash equilibrium   The situation when each player has chosen his or her optimal strategy, *given the strategy chosen by the other player.*

Natural monopoly   The case of declining long-run average costs over a sufficiently large range of outputs so as to leave a single firm supplying the entire market.

Necessity   A commodity with income elasticity of demand between 0 and 1.

Negative income tax (NIT)   A type of welfare program involving declining cash transfers to low-income families as the family's earned income rises.

Net present value (*NPV*)   The value today from the stream of net cash flows (positive and negative) from an investment project.

Neuter   A commodity of which an individual is indifferent between having more or less.

Nominal rate of interest (*r'*)   The real rate of interest plus the anticipated rate of price inflation.

Noncompeting groups   Occupations requiring different capacities, skills, education and training, and, therefore, receiving different wages.

Nonexclusion   The situation in which it is impossible or prohibitively expensive to confine the benefit or the consumption of a good (once produced) to selected people (such as only to those paying for it).

Nonexhaustible resources   Renewable resources, such as fertile land, forests, rivers, and fish, which need never be depleted if they are properly managed.

Nonprice competition   Competition based on advertising and product differentiation rather than on price.

Nonrival consumption   The distinguishing characteristic of a public good whereby its consumption by some individuals does not reduce the amount available to others.

Normal good   A good of which the consumer purchases more with an increase in income.

Normative economics   The study of what *ought* to be or how the basic economic functions *should* be performed. It is based both on positive economics and value judgments.

Oligopoly   The form of market organization in which there are few firms selling either a homogeneous or a differentiated product.

Oligopsony   One of a few firms hiring either a homogeneous or a differentiated input.

Ordinal utility   The rankings of the utility received by an individual from consuming various amounts of a good or various baskets of goods.

Output elasticity of capital   The percentage increase in output resulting from a 1% increase in the quantity of capital used. For the Cobb-Douglas production function, this is given by the exponent of K.

Output elasticity of labor   The percentage increase in output resulting from a 1% increase in the quantity of labor used. For the Cobb-Douglas production function, this is given by the component of L.

Overtime pay   The higher hourly wage of many workers for working additional hours after the regular workday.

Paasche price index (*P*)   The ratio of the cost of purchasing period 1 quantities at period 1 prices relative to base period prices.

Pareto criterion   It postulates that a change increases social welfare if it benefits some members of society (in their own judgment) without harming anyone.

Pareto optimality   The situation in which no reorganization of production and consumption is possible by which some individuals are made better off without making someone else worse off.

Pareto optimum   The situation in which no reorganization of production or consumption can lead to an increase in the welfare of some without, at the same time, reducing the welfare of others.

Partial equilibrium analysis   It studies the behavior of individual decision-making units and individual markets, *viewed in isolation*.

Payoff   The outcome or consequence of each combination of strategies by the players in game theory.

Payoff matrix   The table of all the outcomes of the players' strategies.

Peak-load pricing   It refers to the charging of a price equal to short-run marginal cost, both in the peak period when demand and marginal cost are higher and in the off-peak period when both are lower.

Perfectly competitive market A market where no buyer or seller can affect the price of the product, all units of the product are homogeneous, resources are mobile, and knowledge is perfect.

Planning horizon The time period when the firm can build any desired scale of plant; the long run.

Players The decision-makers in the theory of games (here the oligopolistic firms or its managers) whose behavior we are trying to explain and predict.

Point elasticity of demand The price elasticity of demand at a specific point on the demand curve.

Point elasticity of supply The price elasticity of supply at a specific point on the supply curve.

Positive economics The study of what *is* or how the economic system performs the basic economic functions. It is entirely statistical in nature and devoid of ethical or value judgments.

Price ceiling The maximum price allowed for a commodity. If it is below the equilibrium price, it leads to a shortage of the commodity.

Price-consumption curve The locus of consumer optimum points resulting when only the price of a good varies.

Price discrimination The charging of different prices (for different quantities of a commodity or in different markets) that are not justified by cost differences.

Price elasticity of demand (η) The percentage change in the quantity demanded of a commodity during a specific period of time divided by the percentage change in its price.

Price elasticity of demand for imports The percentage change in the quantity purchased of imports by a nation divided by the percentage change in their prices.

Price elasticity of supply (ϵ) The percentage change in the quantity supplied of a commodity during a specific period of time divided by the percentage change in its price.

Price floor A minimum price for a commodity. If it is above the equilibrium price, it leads to a surplus of the commodity.

Price leadership The form of market collusion in oligopolistic markets whereby the firm that serves as the price leader initiates a price change and the other firms in the industry soon match it.

Price system The system whereby the organization and coordination of economic activity is determined by commodity and resource prices.

Price theory Another name for microeconomic theory that stresses the importance of prices in the determination of what goods are produced and in what quantities, the organization of production, and the distribution of output or income.

Principal-agent problem The fact that the agents (managers and workers) of a firm seek to maximize their own benefits (such as salaries) rather than the total profits or value of the firm, which is the owners' or principals' interest.

Prisoners' dilemma The situation where each player adopts his or her dominant strategy but could do better by cooperating.

Private costs The costs incurred by individuals and firms.

Producer surplus The excess of the market price of the commodity over the marginal cost of production.

Product group The sellers of a differentiated product.

Product cycle model The introduction of new products by firms in an advanced nation, which are then copied and produced by firms in lower-wage countries.

Product innovation The introduction of new or improved products.

Process innovation The introduction of new or improved production processes.

Production The transformation of resources or inputs into outputs of goods and services.

Production function The unique relationship between inputs and outputs represented by a table, graph, or equation showing the maximum output of a commodity that can be produced per period of time with each set of inputs.

Production-possibilities frontier or transformation curve It shows the alternative combinations of commodities that a nation can produce by fully utilizing all of its resources with the best technology available to it.

Product variation   Differences in some of the characteristics of differentiated products.

Public goods   Commodities for which consumption by some individuals does not reduce the amount available for others. That is, once the good is provided for someone, others can consume it at no additional cost.

Pure monopoly   The form of market organization in which there is a single seller of a commodity for which there are no close substitutes.

Pure oligopoly   An oligopoly in which the product of the firms in the industry is homogeneous.

Quasi-rent   The return or payment to inputs that are fixed in the short run (i.e., $TR - TVC$).

Rate of interest (r)   The premium received in one year for lending one dollar this year.

Rational consumer   An individual who seeks to maximize utility or satisfaction in spending his or her income.

Rational ignorance   The condition whereby voters are much less informed about political decisions than about their individual market decisions because of the higher costs of obtaining information and the smaller direct benefits that they obtain from the former than from the latter.

Rationing   Quantitative restrictions imposed by the government on the amount of a good that an individual can purchase per unit of time.

Rationing over time   The allocation of a given amount of a commodity over time.

Real rate of interest (r)   The premium on a unit of a commodity or real consumption income today compared to a unit of the commodity or real consumption income in the future.

Repeated games   Prisoners' dilemma games of more than one move.

Ridge lines   The lines that separate the relevant (i.e., the negatively sloped) from the irrelevant (or the positively sloped) portions of the isoquants.

Saddle point   The solution or outcome of a strictly determined game.

Saving   The refraining from present consumption.

Scitovsky criterion   It postulates that a change is an improvement if it satisfies the Kaldor-Hicks criterion and, if, after the change, a movement back to the original position does not satisfy the Kaldor-Hicks criterion.

Search costs   The time and money spent seeking information about a product.

Search goods   Goods whose quality can be evaluated by inspection at the time of purchase.

Second degree price discrimination   The charging of a lower price for each additional batch or block of the commodity.

Second theorem of welfare economics   It postulates that equity in distribution is logically separable from efficiency in allocation.

Selling expenses   Expenditures (such as advertising) that the firm incurs to induce consumers to purchase more of its product.

Separation theorem   The independence of the optimum investment decision from the individual's preferences.

Sherman Antitrust Act   It prohibits all contracts and combinations in restraint of trade and all attempts to monopolize the market.

Shortage   The excess quantity demanded of a commodity at lower than equilibrium prices.

Short run   The time period when at least one input is fixed.

Shutdown point   The output level at which price equals average variable cost and losses equal total fixed costs, whether the firm produces or not. Also, the lowest point on the AVC curve at which $MC = AVC$.

Snob effect   The situation where some people demand a smaller quantity of a commodity as more people consume it in order to be different and exclusive.

Social costs   The costs incurred by society as a whole.

Speculator   An individual or firm that buys a commodity or currency when it expects the price to rise, and sells it if it expects the price to fall.

Spot market   The market where spot transactions take place.

Spot price or rate   The price or rate of a commodity or currency in the spot market.

Spot transaction   The purchase and sale of a commodity or currency for immediate delivery and payment.

Stackelberg model   The extension of the Cournot model in which one duopolist knows how the other behaves and, by using this information, earns higher profits than in the Cournot solution at the expense of the other duopolist.

Stage I of production   The range of increasing average product.

Stage II of production   The range from maximum average product to zero marginal product.

Stage III of production   The range over which marginal product is negative.

Strategies   The potential choices that can be made by the players (firms) in the theory of games.

Strategic move   A player's strategy of constraining his or her own behavior to make a threat credible so as to gain a competitive advantage.

Substitutes   Two commodities are substitutes if an increase in the price of one of them leads to more of the other being purchased.

Substitution effect   The increase in the quantity demanded of a good when its price falls, resulting only from the relative price decline and independent of the change in real income.

Surplus   The excess quantity supplied of a commodity at higher than equilibrium prices.

Technical coefficients   Coefficients in input-output analysis that indicate the dollar value of each input required to produce one dollar's worth of output in each industry or sector; also called production or input coefficients.

Technical externalities   Economies of scale.

Technological progress   It refers to the develop-

ment of new and better production techniques to make a given, improved, or an entirely new product.

Theory of contestable markets   The theory that postulates that even if an industry has only one or a few firms, it would still operate as if it were perfectly competitive if entry is absolutely free and if exit is entirely costless.

Theory of public choice   The study of how government decisions are made and implemented.

Third degree price discrimination   The charging of a higher price for a commodity in the market with the less elastic demand in such a way as to equalize the *MR* of the last unit of the commodity sold in the two markets.

Tit-for-tat   The best strategy in repeated prisoners' dilemma games which postulates "do to your opponent what he or she has just done to you".

Time budget line   A line showing the various combinations of two goods that an individual can obtain with his or her available time.

Total costs (*TC*)   TFC plus TVC.

Total fixed costs (*TFC*)   The total obligations of the firm per time period for all fixed inputs.

Total product (*TP*)   Total output.

Total revenue (*TR*)   The price of the commodity times the quantity sold of the commodity.

Total utility (*TU*)   The aggregate amount of satisfaction received from consuming various amounts of a good or baskets of goods.

Total variable costs (*TVC*)   The total obligations of the firm per time period for all the variable inputs the firm uses.

Transfer pricing   The determination of the price of intermediate products sold by one semiautonomous division of the firm to another semiautonomous division of the same enterprise.

Two-part tariff   The pricing practice whereby a monopolist maximizes its total profits by charging a usage fee or price equal to its marginal cost and an initial or membership fee equal to the entire consumer surplus.

Tying   The requirement that a consumer who

buys or leases a monopolist's product also purchase another product needed in the use of the first.

Unemployment gap   The excess in the quantity supplied over the quantity demanded of labor at above equilibrium wages.

Util   The arbitrary unit of measure of utility.

Utility   The ability of a good to satisfy a want.

Utility-possibilities frontier   It shows the various combinations of utilities received by two individuals at which the economy (composed of the two individuals) is in general equilibrium or Pareto optimum in exchange.

Value of the marginal product (*VMP*)   The marginal (physical) product of the input (*MP*) multiplied by the commodity price (*P*).

Variability risk   The possibility that the return on an investment, such as on a stock, may vary considerably above or below the average.

Variable inputs   The resources that can be varied easily and on short notice during the time period under consideration.

Veblen effect   The situation in which some people purchase more of certain commodities the more expensive they are; also called conspicuous consumption.

Voluntary export restraints (*VER*)   The situation in which an importing country induces another nation to reduce its exports of a commodity "voluntarily," under the threat of higher all-around trade restrictions.

Water-diamond paradox   The question of why water, which is essential to life, is so cheap while diamonds, which are not essential, are so expensive.

Wealth   The individual's income this year plus the present value of future income.

Welfare economics   It examines the conditions for economic efficiency in the production of output and in the exchange of commodities, and for equity in the distribution of income.

What to produce   Which goods and services to produce and in what quantities.

NAME INDEX

SUBJECT INDEX